OUR COUNTRY

AUTHORS

Dr. Herbert J. Bass
Professor of History
Temple University
Philadelphia, PA

SERIES CONSULTANTS

Dr. James F. Baumann
Professor of Reading Education
Associate Director, National Reading Research Center
The University of Georgia
Athens, GA

Dr. Theodore Kaltsounis
Professor of Social Studies Education
University of Washington
Seattle, WA

LITERATURE CONSULTANTS

Dr. Ben A. Smith
Assistant Professor of Social Studies Education
Kansas State University
Manhattan, KS

Dr. John C. Davis
Professor of Elementary Education
University of Southern Mississippi
Hattiesburg, MS

Dr. Jesse Palmer
Assistant Professor, Department of Curriculum and Instruction
University of Southern Mississippi
Hattiesburg, MS

COVER PHOTOGRAPH
The stern-wheeler *Delta Queen*, a national historic landmark, on the Mississippi River

SILVER BURDETT GINN

MORRISTOWN, NJ • NEEDHAM, MA
Atlanta, GA • Deerfield, IL • Irving, TX • San Jose, CA

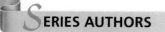

SERIES AUTHORS

Dr. W. Frank Ainsley, Professor of Geography, University of North Carolina, Wilmington, NC

Dr. Herbert J. Bass, Professor of History, Temple University, Philadelphia, PA

Dr. Kenneth S. Cooper, Professor of History, Emeritus, George Peabody College for Teachers, Vanderbilt University, Nashville, TN

Dr. Claudia Crump, Professor of Elementary Social Studies Education, Indiana University Southeast, New Albany, IN

Dr. Gary S. Elbow, Professor of Geography, Texas Tech University, Lubbock, TX

Roy Erickson, Program Specialist, K–12 Social Studies and Multicultural Education San Juan Unified School District, Carmichael, CA

Dr. Daniel B. Fleming, Professor of Social Studies Education, Virginia Polytechnic Institute and State University, Blacksburg, VA

Dr. Gerald Michael Greenfield, Professor and Director, Center for International Studies, University of Wisconsin — Parkside, Kenosha, WI

Dr. Linda Greenow, Associate Professor of Geography, SUNY — The College at New Paltz, New Paltz, NY

Dr. William W. Joyce, Professor of Education, Michigan State University, East Lansing, MI

Dr. Gail S. Ludwig, Former Geographer-in-Residence, National Geographic Society, Geography Education Program, Washington, D.C.

Dr. Michael B. Petrovich, Professor Emeritus of History, University of Wisconsin, Madison, WI

Dr. Norman J. G. Pounds, Former University Professor of History and Geography, Indiana University, Bloomington, IN

Dr. Arthur D. Roberts, Professor of Education, University of Connecticut, Storrs, CT

Dr. Christine L. Roberts, Professor of Education, University of Connecticut, Storrs, CT

Parke Rouse, Jr., Virginia Historian and Retired Executive Director of the Jamestown-Yorktown Foundation, Williamsburg, VA

Dr. Paul C. Slayton, Jr., Distinguished Professor of Education, Mary Washington College, Fredericksburg, VA

Dr. Edgar A. Toppin, Professor of History and Dean of the Graduate School, Virginia State University, Petersburg, VA

GRADE LEVEL WRITERS/CONSULTANTS

Joan Garland Atkinson, Head Teacher, Harold B. Emery, Jr. Elementary School, Limington, ME

Dr. Marianne Geiger, Teacher, John Philip Sousa Elementary School, Port Washington, NY

Mary Jo Paniello, Teacher, John G. Anderson Elementary School, Tampa, FL

Mary Shy Taylor, Teacher, Atwater Avenue School, Los Angeles, CA

ACKNOWLEDGMENTS

Pages 88–89: From SOCIAL EDUCATION November/December 1989. Used by permission of World Eagle, Inc., 64 Washburn Ave., Wellesley, MA 02181.

Page 108: By Victor W. von Hagen.

Page 161: Copyright © 1986 by Marcia Sewall. Reprinted with permission of Atheneum Publishers, an imprint of Macmillan Publishing Company.

Page 201: From AMOS FORTUNE, FREE MAN by Elizabeth Yates. Copyright 1950 by Elizabeth Yates McGreal, renewed 1978 by Elizabeth Yates McGreal. Reprinted by permission of the publisher, Dutton Children's Books, a division of Penguin Books USA Inc.

Page 535: "One-Way Ticket" © 1949 SELECTED POEMS by Langston Hughes. Used by permission of Alfred A. Knopf Inc. "Harlem" from THE PANTHER AND THE LASH by Langston Hughes. Copyright 1951 by Langston Hughes. Used by permission of Alfred A. Knopf Inc.

Page 531: From THE GLORY AND THE DREAM by William Manchester © 1973–1974. Used by permission of Little, Brown and Company.

Page 572: From ONCE UPON A TIME WHEN WE WERE COLORED by Clifton L. Taulbert. Copyright © 1989 by Clifton L. Taulbert. Used by permission of Council Oak Publishing.

CONTENTS

Unit 2 A NEW WORLD

Unit 3
FORMING A NEW NATION

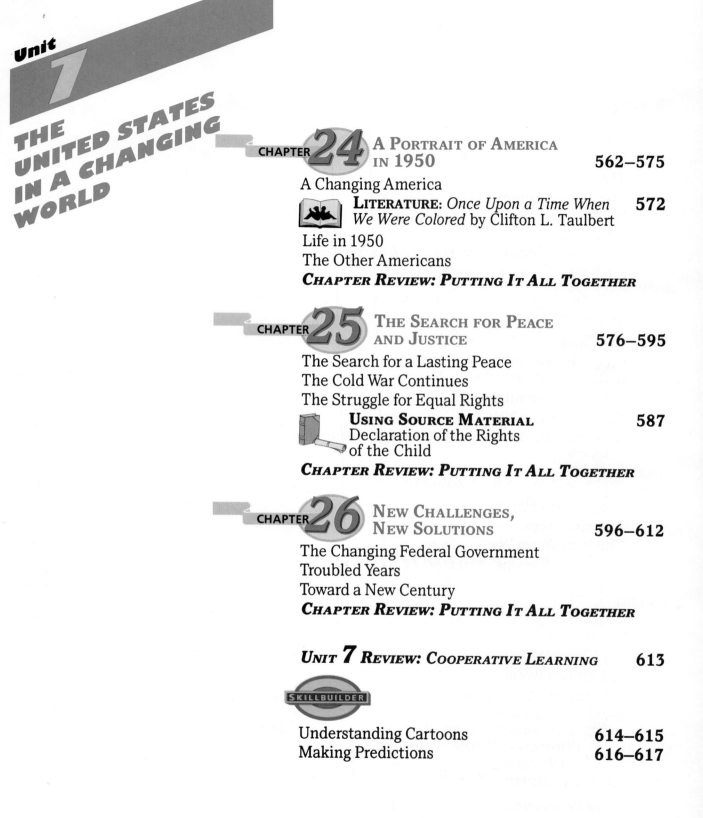

RESOURCE SECTION

MAPS

ATLAS

TIME LINES

GRAPHS

TABLES

CHARTS

DIAGRAMS

SPECIAL FEATURES

USING SOURCE MATERIAL

LITERATURE

CITIZENSHIP AND AMERICAN VALUES

SKILLBUILDER

SOCIAL STUDIES

LANGUAGE ARTS

MAP SKILLS HANDBOOK

Knowing how to work with maps is a social studies skill that everyone must have. You can't learn history and geography without being able to read maps. Maps, however, have uses that go beyond what you are learning in school.

Watch the nightly news. How many times are maps used? The next time you are in the library, take a copy of a weekly newsmagazine and count the number of maps that accompany the articles. Are maps used in any of the advertisements in the magazine? Keep a record over a week of all the times you see or use a map.

As you study United States history this year, you will be using map skills that you already have. You will also be learning some new map skills. All the map skills you will need appear in this Map Skills Handbook. Study the lesson titles on these two pages to see what you will learn.

LESSON *1*
Maps, Geography, and You page 4

LESSON *2*
Finding Places on a Map
page 8

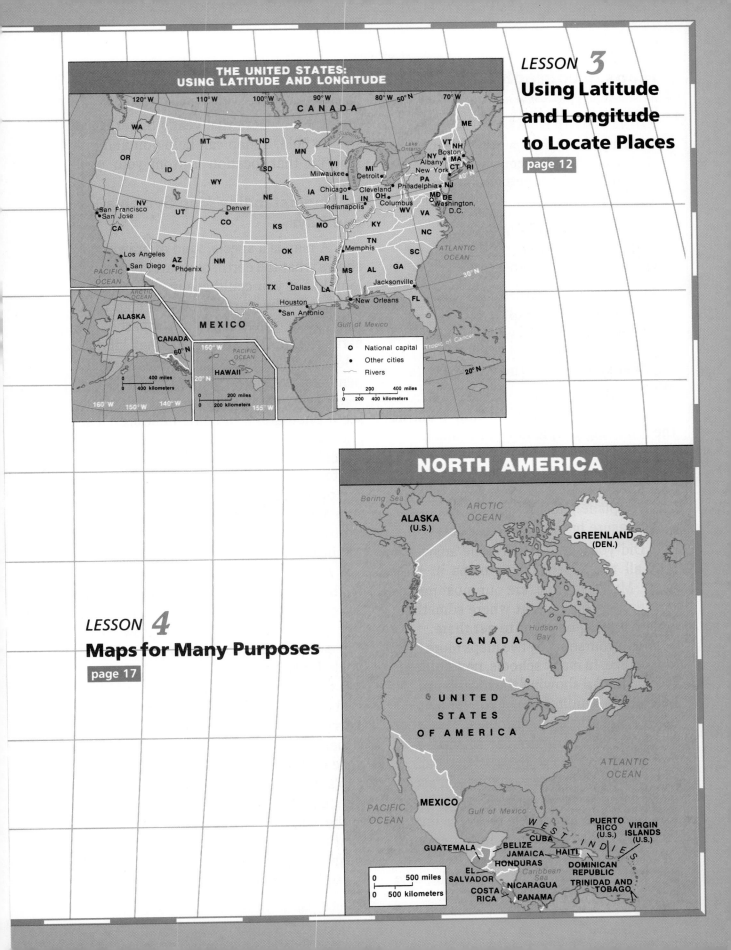

THE UNITED STATES: USING LATITUDE AND LONGITUDE

CANADA

WA
OR
ID
MT
ND
MN
WI
MI
SD
WY
NE
IA
Chicago
Milwaukee
Detroit
Cleveland
NV
UT
CO
KS
MO
IL
IN
OH
Columbus
Indianapolis
San Francisco
San Jose
CA
Denver
Los Angeles
San Diego
AZ
Phoenix
NM
OK
AR
TN
Memphis
KY
WV
VA
NC
PACIFIC
OCEAN
ARCTIC
OCEAN
TX
Dallas
Houston
San Antonio
LA
MS
AL
GA
SC
Jacksonville
ATLANTIC
OCEAN
New Orleans
FL
Rio Grande
Gulf of Mexico

Lake Superior
Lake Michigan
Lake Ontario
Missouri River
Mississippi River
Ohio River

ME
VT NH
NY Boston
Albany MA
New York CT RI
PA
Philadelphia NJ
MD DE
Washington, D.C.

120° W 110° W 100° W 90° W 80° W 50° N 70° W
40° N
30° N
20° N

ALASKA
CANADA
60° N
160° W

HAWAII
20° N
PACIFIC
OCEAN
160° W 150° W 140° W
155° W

MEXICO

0   400 miles
0   400 kilometers

0   200 miles
0   200 kilometers

Tropic of Cancer

◉ National capital
● Other cities
〜 Rivers

0   200   400 miles
0   200   400 kilometers

NORTH AMERICA

Bering Sea
ARCTIC OCEAN
ALASKA (U.S.)
GREENLAND (DEN.)
CANADA
Hudson Bay
UNITED STATES OF AMERICA
ATLANTIC OCEAN
PACIFIC OCEAN
MEXICO
Gulf of Mexico
W E S T   I N D I E S
PUERTO RICO (U.S.)
VIRGIN ISLANDS (U.S.)
CUBA
GUATEMALA
BELIZE
JAMAICA
HAITI
HONDURAS
DOMINICAN REPUBLIC
EL SALVADOR
NICARAGUA
COSTA RICA
PANAMA
TRINIDAD AND TOBAGO
Caribbean Sea

0   500 miles
0   500 kilometers

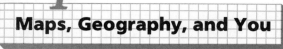

Maps, Geography, and You

THINK ABOUT WHAT YOU KNOW

With a partner, draw a one-page map that would help someone find his or her way from the front entrance of the school to your classroom.

STUDY THE VOCABULARY

cartographer   key
symbol   scale

FOCUS YOUR READING

How do we read a map?

A. Maps Help Us Understand the World

Here's a little quiz for fun. What do the following people have in common?

A truck driver
A TV weather forecaster
An explorer
An airplane pilot
A treasure hunter

Did you figure it out? The answer is that all these people use maps in their work. Maps, you see, are our most important tool for finding out where something is and figuring out how to get there.

You yourself may use maps more than you realize. In many schools, new students receive a map showing the location of the lunchroom, auditorium, gym, principal's office, and other schoolrooms. Has your family taken a trip by car to visit your grandparents or to go to a national park or the seashore? Chances are that you used a map to find your way there.

Maps are important tools for understanding what is going on in our country and in the world. Suppose you heard on the television news that an earthquake had occurred in Pakistan. A map of the world could help you learn where that country is located. And when the newspaper reports where this year's Super Bowl will be held, a map can help you find out how far that location is from your own town.

B. Understanding Map Symbols and Keys

A map is a special kind of drawing. It shows what the earth, or a part of it, would look like if you could see it from straight overhead. The purpose of any map is to give you information about the part of the earth the map is showing. What kind of information does a map show? That depends on the map you are using.

For example, on the next page you see a photograph of some buildings. The photograph was taken from an airplane flying high above the buildings. Below the photograph is a map of the same area. A **cartographer**, or map maker, drew the map to show the important features of the photograph. The cartographer has used **symbols**, or signs, to show these features.

Almost any color, shape, or drawing can be used as a map symbol. A heavy red line could stand for a main highway. A thin blue line could stand for a narrow road. The cartographer could also use a heavy black dot to stand for a city.

Of course, the map would be of little use to you if you didn't know what each of the symbols stood for. So the cartographer gathers all these symbols together in one place on the map. This place is called the map's **key**. The key tells you the meaning of each symbol on the map. Look at the key on the map on page 5. Find the symbol for a parking lot. Now find the parking lot on the map. What is the symbol for the pond? Try to find the pond on the map.

FROM PHOTOGRAPH TO MAP

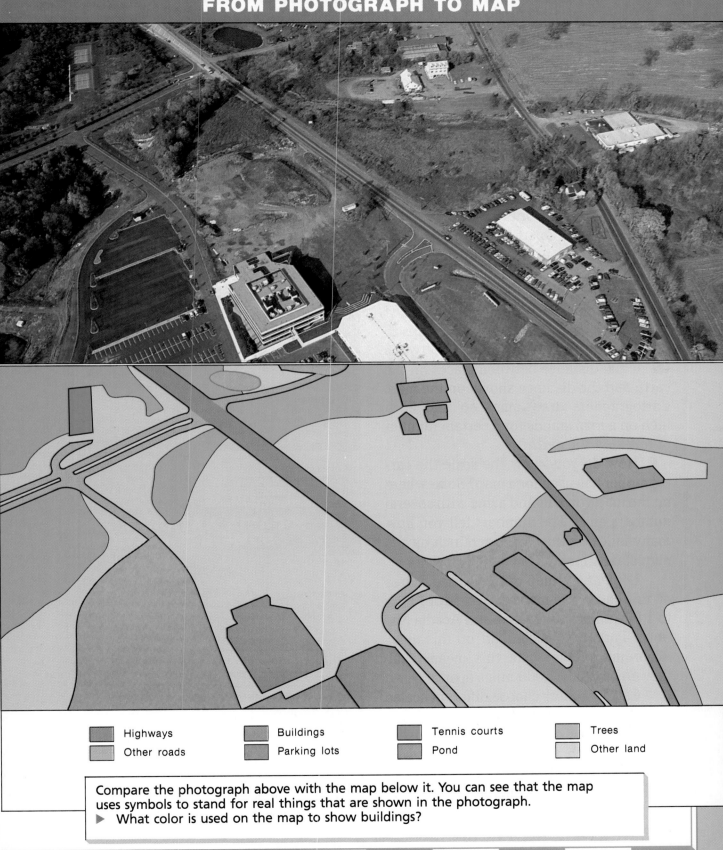

Highways Buildings Tennis courts Trees

Other roads Parking lots Pond Other land

Compare the photograph above with the map below it. You can see that the map uses symbols to stand for real things that are shown in the photograph.

▶ What color is used on the map to show buildings?

C. Using Scale to Measure Distance

Maps are never the same size as the places they show. They are always smaller —sometimes much smaller. A map of the United States must fit on a page or two of your book, but it shows an area that is really thousands of miles wide.

That creates a problem for you, the map reader. Suppose two cities are 3 inches apart on the map. How far apart are they on the earth: 1 mile? 5 miles? 100 miles? 1,000 miles? Until you can find their actual distance apart, you won't know whether you can best get from one city to the other by bicycling, riding in a car, or taking a plane.

Cartographers show how far apart places really are by drawing their maps to **scale**. Scale is the relationship between the actual distance between places on the earth and the distance shown on the map. Cartographers draw maps so that each inch on a map stands for a certain number of miles on the earth.

How do you know the scale the cartographer has used for a map? Somewhere on the map you will find a line with several numbers on it. The numbers tell you how many miles on the earth each inch on the map stands for.

Look at the map of the United States on this page. This map has a scale of 1 inch to 1,000 miles. Milwaukee and Acadia National Park are 1 inch apart on this map. According to the scale this means that they are actually 1,000 miles apart.

Cartographers choose different scales for different maps. If they are showing a very large area of land, they might use a scale of 1 inch to 500 miles. If the area shown on the map is very small, the scale of the map could be 1 inch to 1 mile.

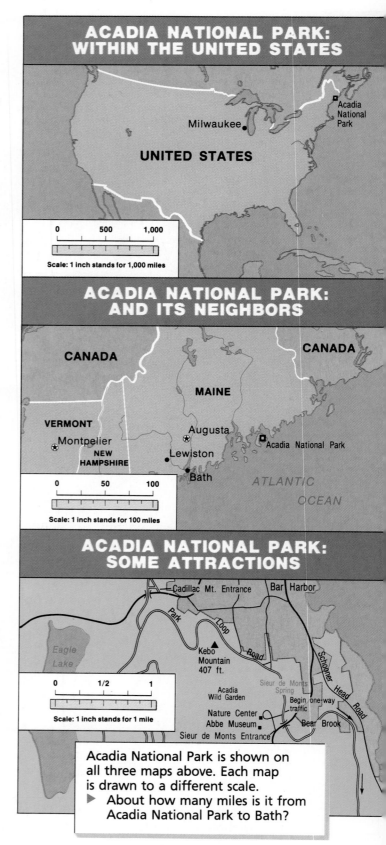

ACADIA NATIONAL PARK: WITHIN THE UNITED STATES

Milwaukee

UNITED STATES

Acadia National Park

0   500   1,000

Scale: 1 inch stands for 1,000 miles

ACADIA NATIONAL PARK: AND ITS NEIGHBORS

CANADA

CANADA

MAINE

VERMONT

Augusta

Montpelier

NEW HAMPSHIRE

Acadia National Park

Lewiston

Bath

ATLANTIC OCEAN

0   50   100

Scale: 1 inch stands for 100 miles

ACADIA NATIONAL PARK: SOME ATTRACTIONS

Cadillac Mt. Entrance

Bar Harbor

Park Loop Road

Eagle Lake

Kebo Mountain 407 ft.

Sieur de Monts Spring

Schooner Head Road

Acadia Wild Garden

Begin one-way traffic

0   1/2   1

Nature Center

Abbe Museum

Bear Brook

Scale: 1 inch stands for 1 mile

Sieur de Monts Entrance

Acadia National Park is shown on all three maps above. Each map is drawn to a different scale.
▶ About how many miles is it from Acadia National Park to Bath?

In 1916, Acadia was the first national park in the United States to be established east of the Mississippi River.

▶ Have you ever visited one of our country's national parks?

For example, look at the map of the United States on page 6. This map shows Acadia National Park within the United States. The park is only a dot on the map. The next map shows the location of Acadia National Park within Maine. This map uses a scale of 1 inch to 100 miles, so we can see a bit more detail about the park and its surrounding areas. The third map uses a scale of 1 inch to 1 mile. Now we can see two park entrances, the Nature Center, and Eagle Lake. By using a scale of 1 inch for 1 mile, you have enough information to find your way around the park.

LESSON *1* REVIEW

THINK AND WRITE

A. In what ways are maps useful?
B. How does a map key help you understand map symbols?
C. Why are maps drawn to scale?

SKILLS CHECK

MAP SKILL

Turn to the Atlas map of the United States. Use the scale to find the distances between the following capital cities: Richmond, Virginia, and Raleigh, North Carolina; Baton Rouge, Louisiana, and Nashville, Tennessee; Denver, Colorado, and Sacramento, California.

Finding Places on a Map

THINK ABOUT WHAT YOU KNOW

Tell how you might find a city on a map of the United States if you do not know in what part of the country the city is located.

STUDY THE VOCABULARY

cardinal   South Pole
  direction   compass rose
North Pole   grid system

FOCUS YOUR READING

How do we use directions to locate places on a map?

A. Using the Cardinal Directions to Locate Places

Maps are useful because they show us where places are. But how do we find those places on a map? One way is to know what direction to look in. Let's briefly review what you know about direction.

You'll remember that there are four **cardinal directions**: north (N), south (S), east (E), and west (W). North is the direction toward the **North Pole**. This is the most northern point on the earth. South is the direction of the **South Pole**. The South Pole is at the opposite end of the earth from the North Pole. It is the most southern point on the earth.

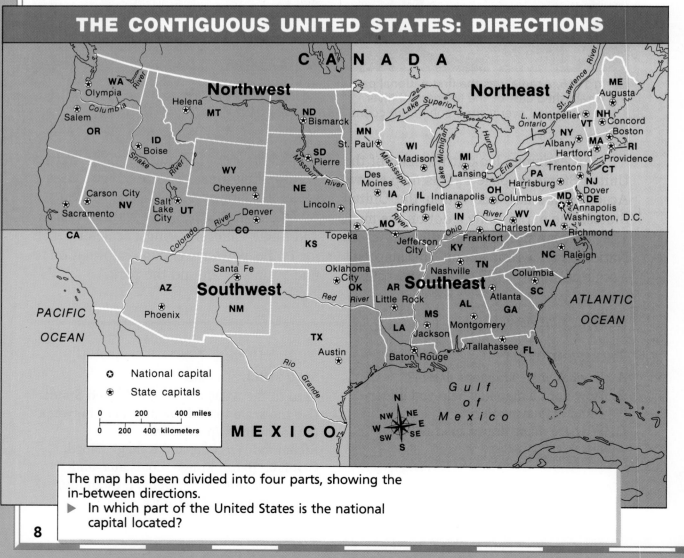

THE CONTIGUOUS UNITED STATES: DIRECTIONS

The map has been divided into four parts, showing the in-between directions.
▶ In which part of the United States is the national capital located?

Once you know where north is, you can find the other two cardinal directions, east and west. When you face north, east is the direction to your right. West is the direction to your left. Like north and south, east and west are also opposite each other.

B. Using the Compass Rose to Locate Places

On some maps you will find a small drawing called a **compass rose.** A compass rose is a direction finder that shows the cardinal directions. Sometimes a compass rose gives even more help by showing the directions that are in between the cardinal directions.

Look for the compass rose on the map on page 8. The direction that is in between north and west is labeled NW. That stands for northwest. The direction between north and east is labeled NE, which stands for northeast. Look at the direction in between south and east on the compass rose. What letters are used for that direction? What do you think those letters stand for? What do you think the direction between south and west is called?

Now let's try using directions to locate places on a map. Look again at the map on page 8. Find Little Rock, Arkansas, in the part of the United States that is marked *Southeast.* What capital city is directly north of Little Rock? Name a city that is southeast of Little Rock. Name a city that is northwest of Little Rock.

C. Using a Grid to Locate Places

When a map shows few cities or towns, you can find the place you are looking for quite easily. For example, the map on this page shows the state of Indiana. If you are looking for the capital of Indiana, you can quickly pick it out from the other

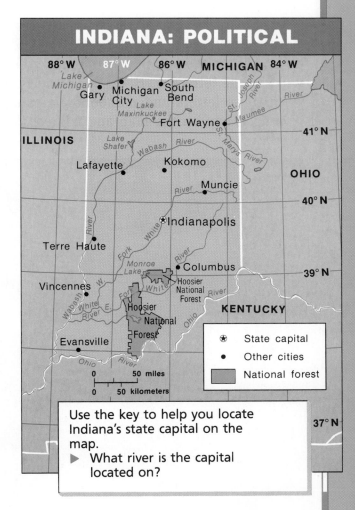

Use the key to help you locate Indiana's state capital on the map.
▶ What river is the capital located on?

cities on the map. Now look at the map on page 10. This is a map of the entire United States. Finding the capital of Indiana is not as easy. In fact, just finding Indiana is hard enough!

A map's **grid system** will help us find places on detailed maps such as the one on page 10. A grid system is a network of lines that crisscross. Look again at the map on page 10. There are some lines running from side to side and other lines running up and down the map. These crisscrossing lines are the map's grid system. Where four of these lines cross, a box is formed. In fact, we can think of the map as being divided into a series of boxes.

Across the top of the map on this page you will see the numbers *1, 2, 3, 4, 5* and *6*. Along the left-side of the map you will see the letters *A, B, C, D, E,* and *F*. With these letters and numbers, we can give each box on the map an "address."

The address is made up of a letter and a number. For example, here's how to find the box whose address is B-4: Put a finger on the letter *B*. Next put a finger of your other hand on the number 4. Now move your fingers, one across and the other

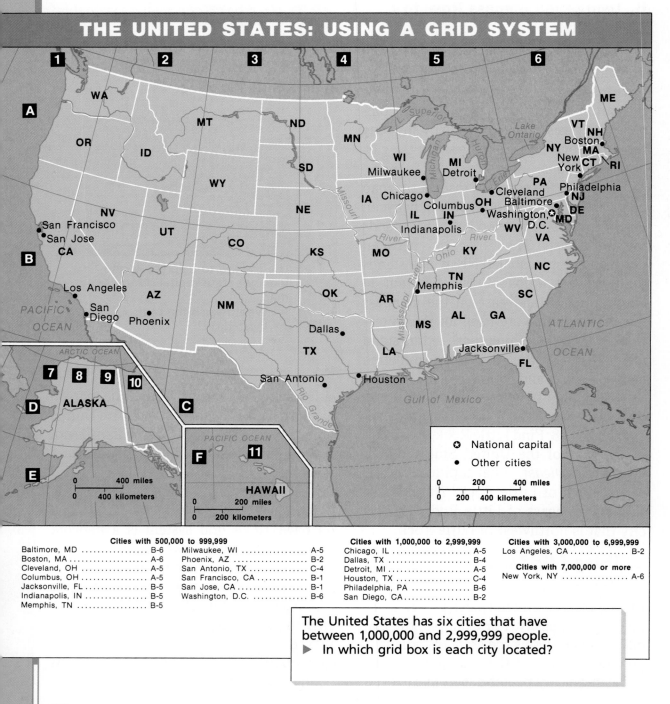

THE UNITED STATES: USING A GRID SYSTEM

| ◎ | National capital |
| ● | Other cities |

Cities with 500,000 to 999,999		Cities with 1,000,000 to 2,999,999	Cities with 3,000,000 to 6,999,999
Baltimore, MD B-6	Milwaukee, WI A-5	Chicago, IL A-5	Los Angeles, CA B-2
Boston, MA A-6	Phoenix, AZ B-2	Dallas, TX B-4	**Cities with 7,000,000 or more**
Cleveland, OH A-5	San Antonio, TX C-4	Detroit, MI A-5	New York, NY A-6
Columbus, OH A-5	San Francisco, CA B-1	Houston, TX C-4	
Jacksonville, FL B-5	San Jose, CA B-1	Philadelphia, PA B-6	
Indianapolis, IN B-5	Washington, D.C. B-6	San Diego, CA................. B-2	
Memphis, TN B-5			

The United States has six cities that have between 1,000,000 and 2,999,999 people.
► In which grid box is each city located?

The girl in this photograph is preparing for a class trip to Washington, D.C. Note that she is using the map grid to locate places she wants to visit.

▶ Have you ever used a map like the one shown in this picture?

down, until they meet. At this point you will find the box whose address is B-4. What is the name of the city that is located at this address?

Look at the listing of cities under the map. This *city index* lists all the cities on the map. The name of each city is followed by the letter and the number of the box in which the city is located. For example, the city index for this map tells us that Phoenix, Arizona, is in box B–2. Find box B–2 on the map. You can look in the box to quickly locate Phoenix. The city index and the grid system enable you to find any place on the map easily. For example, what cities are found in box B-6?

LESSON 2 REVIEW

THINK AND WRITE

A. What are the four cardinal directions?
B. What are the four in-between directions found on the compass rose?
C. How do you use the grid system to find the location of a place on a map?

SKILLS CHECK

MAP SKILL

Look at the map on page 10. Name the cities that are found in the following grid boxes: B–2, C–4, and A–5.

Using Latitude and Longitude to Locate Places

THINK ABOUT WHAT YOU KNOW

Imagine that you are on a ship that has run out of fuel. How could you give your location to a rescue ship?

STUDY THE VOCABULARY

latitude   **hemisphere**
longitude   **Prime Meridian**
Equator

FOCUS YOUR READING

How can we find places on maps by using latitude and longitude?

A. Lines of Latitude Run East and West

A grid system is a useful tool, but it does not allow us to find the exact location of any city, town, or village in the world. To do that, cartographers have created a special kind of grid system for the entire earth. This system also uses two sets of lines that crisscross. These grid lines are called lines of **latitude** and lines of **longitude.**

Lines of latitude extend east and west around the earth. Find the lines of latitude for 10°S and 20°S on the map below. These two lines are always the same distance from each other. Any two lines of latitude that you might choose are

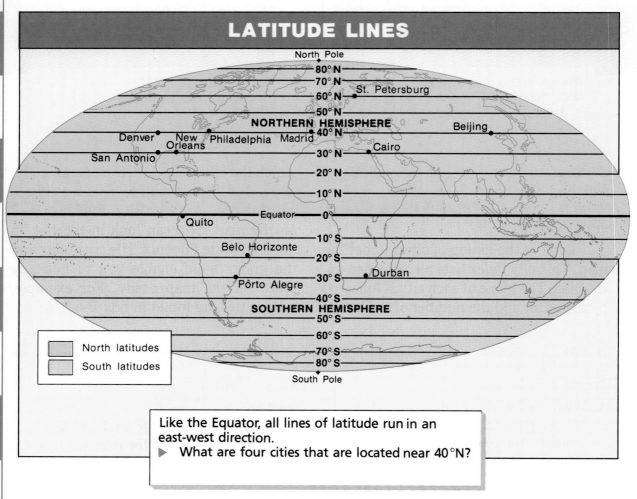

LATITUDE LINES

North Pole
80° N
70° N
60° N — St. Petersburg
50° N
NORTHERN HEMISPHERE
40° N — Beijing
Denver New Philadelphia Madrid
Orleans
30° N — Cairo
San Antonio
20° N
10° N
Equator — 0°
Quito
10° S
Belo Horizonte
20° S
30° S — Durban
Pôrto Alegre
40° S
SOUTHERN HEMISPHERE
50° S
60° S
70° S
80° S
South Pole

North latitudes
South latitudes

Like the Equator, all lines of latitude run in an east-west direction.
▶ What are four cities that are located near 40°N?

always the same distance from each other. The main line of latitude is called the **Equator** (ee KWAYT ur). The map on page 12 shows that the Equator lies exactly halfway between the North Pole and the South Pole. The Equator divides the earth into two equal halves that are called **hemispheres** (HEM ih sfihrz). The northern half is called the Northern Hemisphere. The southern half is called the Southern Hemisphere.

Because it is the main line of latitude, the Equator is marked 0°. This is read "zero degrees." All other lines of latitude measure the distance from the Equator in degrees. Lines of latitude in the Northern Hemisphere, or north of the Equator, are called lines of north latitude. On the globe or map, they are shown as 20°N, 30°N, and so on. The latitude for the North Pole is 90° north latitude.

Lines of latitude in the Southern Hemisphere, or south of the Equator, are called lines of south latitude. On the map they are shown as 20°S, 30°S, and so on. The South Pole is 90° south latitude.

B. Lines of Longitude Run North to South

Lines of longitude are the second part of the grid system that is used to locate places on the earth. If you look at the map on this page, you can see that lines of longitude are different from lines of latitude

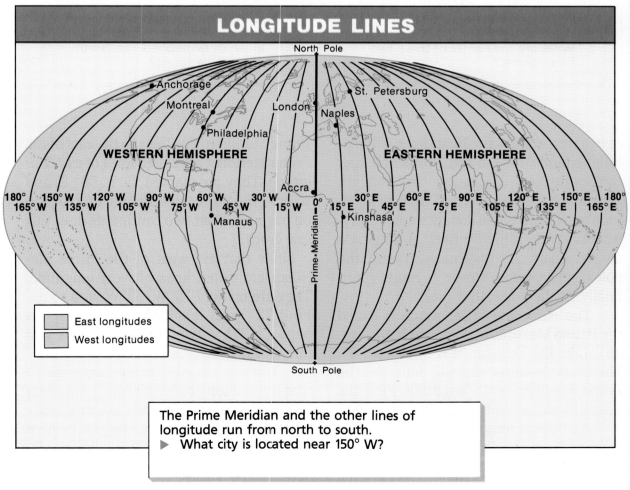

LONGITUDE LINES

The Prime Meridian and the other lines of longitude run from north to south.
▶ What city is located near 150° W?

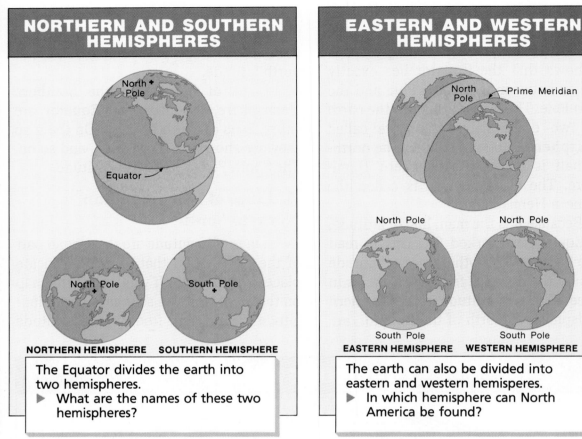

North Pole

Equator

North Pole

South Pole

NORTHERN HEMISPHERE   SOUTHERN HEMISPHERE

The Equator divides the earth into two hemispheres.
▶ What are the names of these two hemispheres?

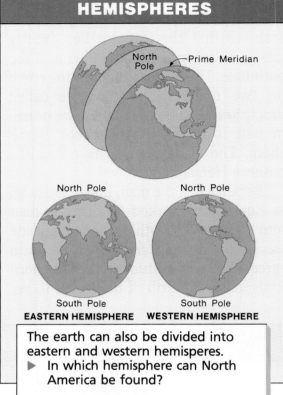

North Pole — Prime Meridian

North Pole

North Pole

South Pole   South Pole

EASTERN HEMISPHERE   WESTERN HEMISPHERE

The earth can also be divided into eastern and western hemisperes.
▶ In which hemisphere can North America be found?

in two important ways. First, lines of longitude extend between the North Pole and the South Pole. This means that they run from north to south. Second, lines of longitude are not the same distance apart everywhere. At the Equator, lines of longitude are far apart. As they move toward the poles, they come closer together until finally, at the poles, they meet.

The main line of longitude is called the **Prime Meridian** (prym muh RIHD ee-un). Like the Equator, it is numbered 0°. The Equator, however, is 0° *latitude*. The Prime Meridian is 0° *longitude*. Find the Prime Meridian on the map on page 13.

All lines of longitude are measured in degrees from the Prime Meridian. These lines measure distance east and west of the

Prime Meridian. The lines to the east of the Prime Meridian are called lines of east longitude. They are marked 15°E, 30° E, and so on. Find 60° east longitude on the map on page 13. What two continents does this line cross?

Lines that are west of the Prime Meridian are called lines of west longitude. They are marked 15°W, 30°W, and so on. Find 75° west longitude on the map on page 13. What two continents does this line cross?

You can see on the map on page 13 that lines of longitude continue to the east and to the west until they reach exactly halfway around the earth. The point where they meet is numbered 180° longitude. The Prime Meridian and the 180° longitude line form a full circle that divides the earth into the Eastern Hemisphere and the Western Hemisphere. The continent of Australia and almost all of the continent of Asia are located in the Eastern Hemisphere. The continents of North America and South America are in the Western Hemisphere. Parts of Europe, Africa, and Antarctica lie in both hemispheres.

C. Using Latitude and Longitude

Lines of latitude and longitude form a grid system that covers the entire earth. When we know the latitude and longitude of a place, we can use that information to find the place quickly on a map.

Try it. Look at the map of the United States on this page. The latitude of New Orleans, Louisiana, is 30° north latitude.

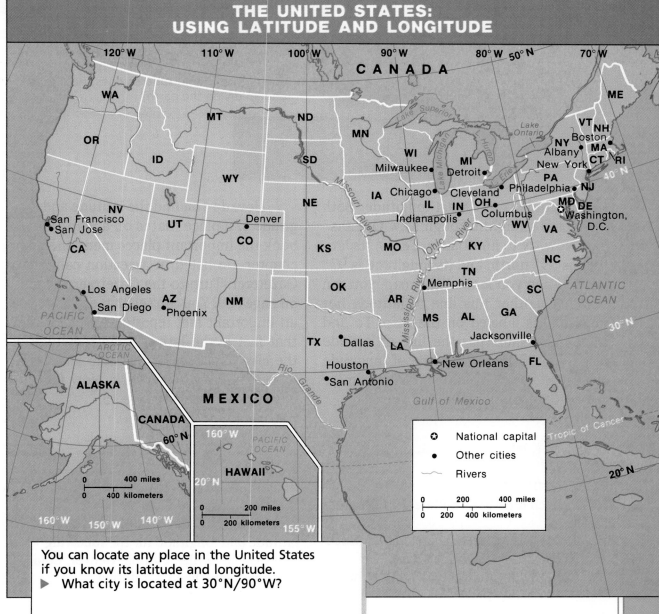

THE UNITED STATES:
USING LATITUDE AND LONGITUDE

You can locate any place in the United States if you know its latitude and longitude.
▶ What city is located at 30°N/90°W?

15

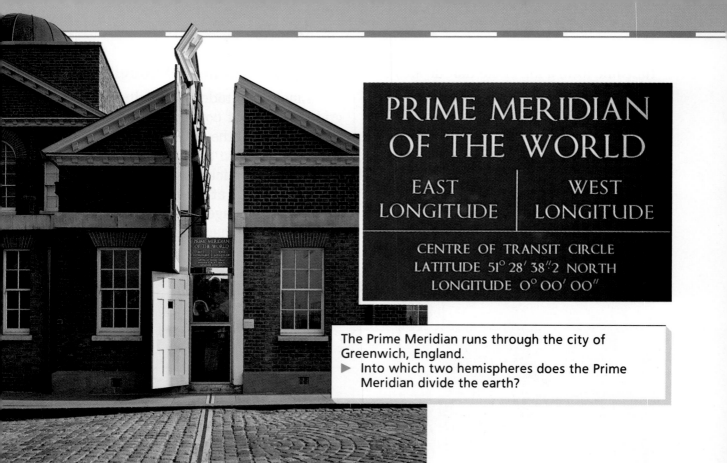

PRIME MERIDIAN
OF THE WORLD

| EAST LONGITUDE | WEST LONGITUDE |

CENTRE OF TRANSIT CIRCLE
LATITUDE 51° 28' 38"2 NORTH
LONGITUDE 0° 00' 00"

The Prime Meridian runs through the city of Greenwich, England.
▶ Into which two hemispheres does the Prime Meridian divide the earth?

Its longitude is 90° west longitude. Both lines pass straight through New Orleans.

Now try to find Dallas, Texas. Its latitude is 33° north, and its longitude is 97° west. When you look at the map, you can see that neither this line of latitude nor longitude is labeled on the map. To find Dallas, you must use the line of latitude closest to 33°N and the line of longitude closest to 97°W. You must then estimate the latitude and longitude of Dallas.

How do you find the latitude and longitude of a place that is on a map? In this book the important places mentioned in a chapter are listed in a section called the Gazetteer. Turn to the Gazetteer, starting on page 628. You can see that each city has an important fact reported about it. After that fact is the latitude and longitude of the city. Look up the latitude and longitude of Albany, New York. Now find Albany on the map on page 15.

LESSON 3 REVIEW

THINK AND WRITE

A. In which directions do lines of latitude run?

B. In which directions do lines of longitude run?

C. How are lines of latitude and longitude used to locate places?

SKILLS CHECK

MAP SKILL

Turn to the map on page 15. Find the latitude and longitude for the following cities: Jacksonville, Florida; Denver, Colorado; and San Diego, California.

16

Maps for Many Purposes

THINK ABOUT WHAT YOU KNOW

You already know that maps can show countries, states, and cities. What are some other features of the earth that maps can show?

STUDY THE VOCABULARY

political map	contour line
landform	climate
plain	precipitation
physical map	natural resource
elevation	

FOCUS YOUR READING

What are the different kinds of maps we can use to study the earth?

A. Political Maps Show Countries and Their Boundaries

Maps can tell us more things about a place than just its location. The most familiar type of map is a **political map**. A political map uses a variety of colors to show different countries or states and their *boundaries*. A boundary is the line that separates one state or country from other states or countries.

The map on this page is a political map. Look for the boundary between the United States and Canada. You will notice that the United States has two boundaries with Canada. Now find the boundary between the United States and Mexico. What are the other two countries that have a boundary with Mexico?

Political maps can also show the location of the capitals and major cities of a state or country. The capital cities of many of our 50 states are shown on the Atlas map on page 620. Find the capital of your state on this map.

B. Physical Maps Show Landforms

The surface of the earth has a great variety of **landforms**. Landforms are features of the earth's surface that are made by nature. They include mountains, hills, and plains. A **plain** is an area of flat land. Rivers, lakes, and oceans are also considered landforms.

A **physical map** of Canada will help you become more familiar with the earth's many landforms. A physical map shows landforms mainly by showing differences

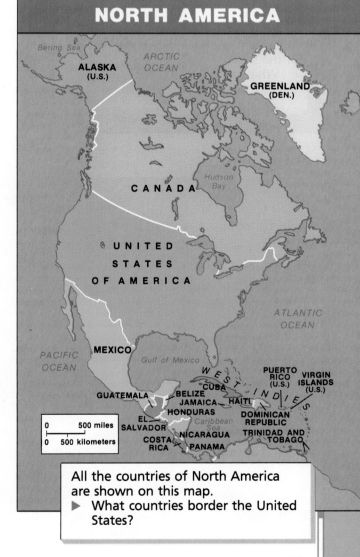

NORTH AMERICA

All the countries of North America are shown on this map.
▶ What countries border the United States?

17

in the earth's **elevation**. Elevation measures the height of the land above or below sea level, or the level of the world's oceans. If an area of land is exactly as high as the sea, its elevation is 0 feet. If we say a mountain is 12,000 feet (3,658 m) high, we mean that it is 12,000 feet (3,658 m) above sea level.

Let's practice reading a physical map. The map on page 19 is a physical map of the country of Canada. Find the St. Lawrence River on the map. What is the elevation of the land it passes through? What is the elevation of the land around Lake Winnepeg?

A physical map shows elevation by using **contour lines**. Contour lines come in all shapes. On a map they may look round like a circle or long like a hot dog or even squiggly. However, all points along each contour line are at exactly the same height above sea level.

It is clear that the base of the mountains shown above is the level of the sea.
► What kind of map shows the earth's elevation?

THE METRIC SYSTEM OF MEASUREMENT

In this handbook you have learned how to measure distances and read elevations on a map by using the mile as the unit of measurement. Another way of expressing distances or elevations is by using the kilometer. One kilometer and a little more than half a mile are about the same distance. A kilometer is a unit of measure in the metric system. The system is called metric because it uses the meter in measuring length.

The metric system is used for measuring distance. It is also used for measuring such things as weight, volume, and temperature. The metric system is in use or is being introduced in all the major countries of the world except the United States.

To introduce you to the metric system, in this book we use both the customary measurements that are in use in the United States and the metric measurements. When a customary measurement appears, its followed in parentheses ( ) by the metric measurement that is about equal to it. Inches are changed to centimeters (cm), feet and yards to meters (m), miles to kilometers (km), and acres to hectares (ha). Pounds are changed to kilograms (kg), and quarts, to liters (L). Degrees Fahrenheit (°F) are changed to degrees Celsius (°C).

CANADA: PHYSICAL

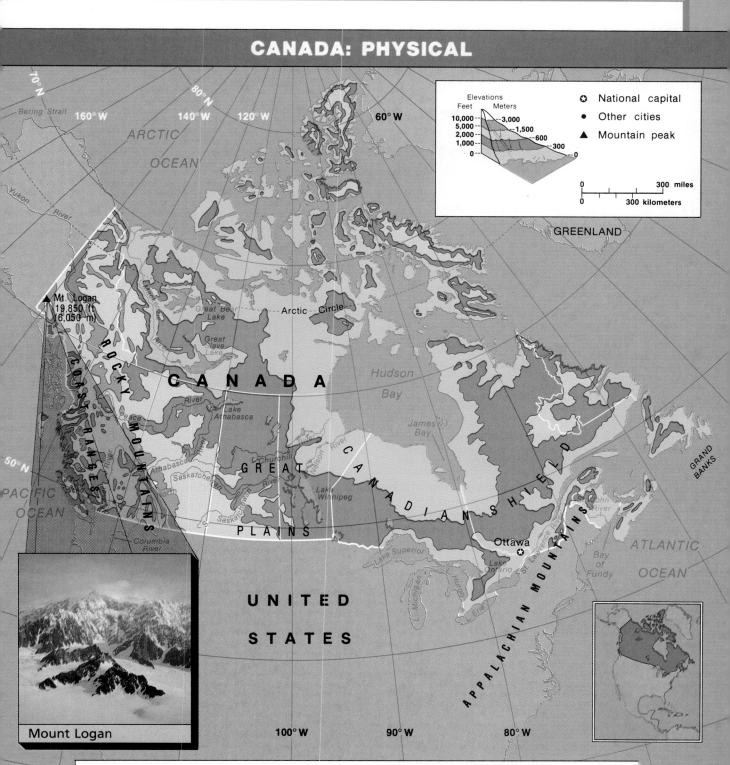

Elevations

Feet	Meters
10,000	3,000
5,000	1,500
2,000	600
1,000	300
0	0

✧ National capital
● Other cities
▲ Mountain peak

300 miles
300 kilometers

70° N
160° W
140° W
120° W
80° N
60° W

Bering Strait
ARCTIC OCEAN
GREENLAND

Yukon River

▲ Mt. Logan
19,850 ft
(6,050 m)

Great Bear Lake
Arctic Circle

Great Slave Lake

C A N A D A

ROCKY MOUNTAINS
COAST RANGES

Peace River

Lake Athabasca

River

Hudson Bay

James Bay

50° N

Athabasca

Saskatchewan

North

South Saskatchewan River

Churchill River

Nelson River

Lake Winnipeg

G R E A T

C A N A D I A N   S H I E L D

GRAND BANKS

PACIFIC OCEAN

Columbia River

P L A I N S

Lake Superior

Ottawa ✧

St. John River

APPALACHIAN MOUNTAINS

ATLANTIC OCEAN

Bay of Fundy

L. Michigan

Lake Huron

Lake Ontario

St. Lawrence River

Lake Erie

U N I T E D

S T A T E S

Mount Logan

100° W
90° W
80° W

Canada, like the United States, extends from the Atlantic Ocean to the
Pacific Ocean. Mount Logan, the highest point in Canada, is located in
the western part of the country.
► What is the elevation of Mount Logan?

UNDERSTANDING CONTOUR LINES

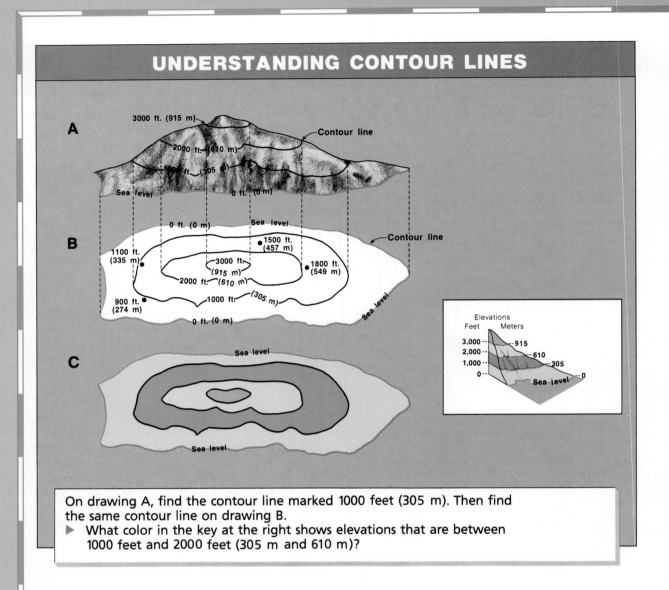

On drawing A, find the contour line marked 1000 feet (305 m). Then find the same contour line on drawing B.

▶ What color in the key at the right shows elevations that are between 1000 feet and 2000 feet (305 m and 610 m)?

Let's see how contour lines work. Look at the drawing of a hill on this page. To show that this land is hilly on a map, a cartographer would draw contour lines like these. Trace the contour line marked 1000 feet with your finger. Every point on this line is 1000 feet above sea level.

The closer the contour lines are to each other, the more steeply the land rises. The farther apart the lines are, the flatter the land is. With the help of these contour lines, you can figure out what the hill looks like — where it rises gradually, where it rises sharply, and how high it is.

Often a cartographer adds different colors between the contour lines to help you see the changes in elevation more clearly. Each color represents a different height of elevation. Use the key on the map above to find the different elevations of the hill.

C. Maps That Show the Climate of a Region

Besides political and physical maps, there are many other kinds of *special-purpose maps*. For example, certain maps tell us about the **climate** of an area. Climate is the pattern of weather a place has over a long period of time.

The two most important parts of the climate of a place are its temperature and **precipitation** (pree sihp uh TAY shun). Temperature is a measure of the amount of heat in the air. The more heat in the air, the higher the temperature. The less heat in the air, the lower the temperature. Precipitation is the amount of moisture, mainly rain or snow, that falls in a region.

The maps on this page and page 22 show the yearly precipitation in the United States and the average January temperatures in the United States. Together these two maps give a clear view of the climate of the United States. Yearly precipitation across the United States is different. The eastern states receive more precipitation than most western and central states. As you can see on the map on page 22, the climate of our country also varies greatly.

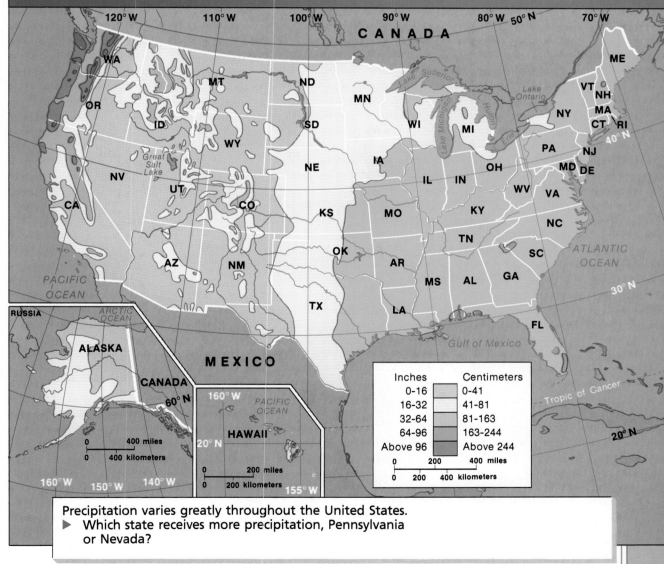

THE UNITED STATES: YEARLY PRECIPITATION

Inches	Centimeters
0-16	0-41
16-32	41-81
32-64	81-163
64-96	163-244
Above 96	Above 244

Precipitation varies greatly throughout the United States.
▶ Which state receives more precipitation, Pennsylvania or Nevada?

January temperatures in the northern parts of the United States are generally lower, while temperatures in the southern parts are generally higher.

Compare the precipitation map with the average January temperatures map. Which states do you think receive snowfall during the winter months? Which states would probably receive rainfall?

D. Maps That Show Natural Resources

A special-purpose map that tells us about the **natural resources** of an area is called a resource map. Natural resources are those things found in nature that are useful to people. For example, water and soil are natural resources. And trees from which we make lumber and paper are, too.

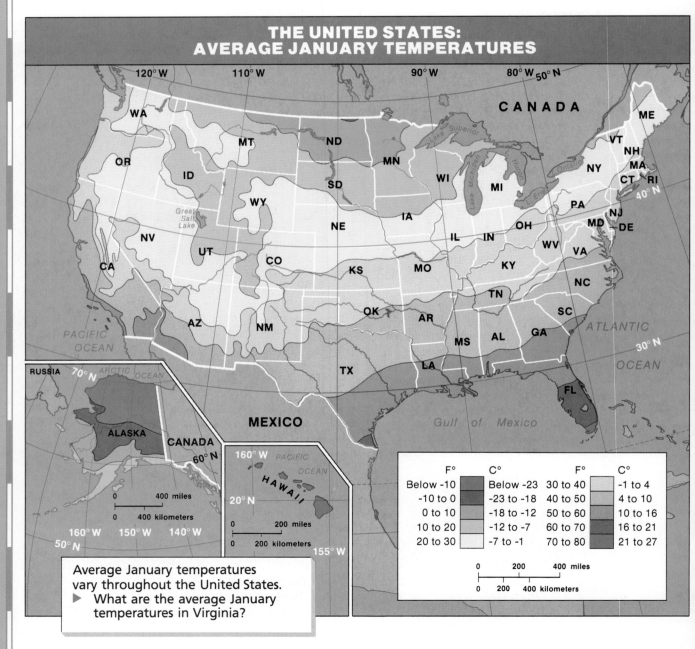

THE UNITED STATES: AVERAGE JANUARY TEMPERATURES

F°	C°	F°	C°
Below -10	Below -23	30 to 40	-1 to 4
-10 to 0	-23 to -18	40 to 50	4 to 10
0 to 10	-18 to -12	50 to 60	10 to 16
10 to 20	-12 to -7	60 to 70	16 to 21
20 to 30	-7 to -1	70 to 80	21 to 27

Average January temperatures vary throughout the United States.
▶ What are the average January temperatures in Virginia?

Sometimes, oil must be mined from beneath the ocean floor.
► Why is oil an important natural resource?

Many of the most important natural resources are minerals found underneath the ground. The two resource maps on this page show the location of coal, uranium, iron ore, and zinc deposits in the United States. Resource maps help us understand why some industries develop in certain parts of the country.

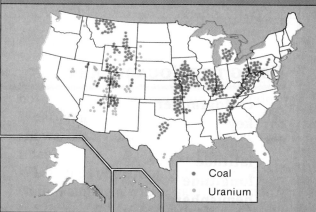

THE UNITED STATES: COAL AND URANIUM

- Coal
- Uranium

THE UNITED STATES: IRON ORE AND ZINC

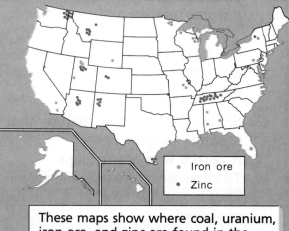

- Iron ore
- Zinc

These maps show where coal, uranium, iron ore, and zinc are found in the United States.
► Which of these resources does your state have?

LESSON 4 REVIEW

THINK AND WRITE

A. What does a political map show?
B. How does a physical map show elevation?
C. What determines the climate of a place?
D. What can we learn from a resource map?

SKILLS CHECK

MAP SKILL

Turn to the physical map on page 621. Find the elevation of the land surrounding the following cities: Washington, D.C.; Detroit, Michigan; Denver, Colorado; and Phoenix, Arizona. List these cities in order of their elevation, starting with the city closest to sea level.

23

Savannah   **RANK** 11

Brown thrasher   Cherokee rose   Live oak

STATE CHARTS

	SOURCE OF NAME	NICKNAMES	FLAG	STATE ECONOMY	LAND AREA
HAWAII Honolulu	May be for traditional discoverer, Hawaii Loa; or Polynesian home, Hawaiki	Aloha State			6,425 sq mi 16,641 sq km **RANK** 47
IDAHO Boise	Means "gem of the mountains"	Gem State Spud State Panhandle State			82,412 sq mi 213,447 sq km **RANK** 11
ILLINOIS Springfield	From Illiniwek Indians; means "superior men"	Prairie State			55,645 sq mi 144,120 sq km **RANK** 24
INDIANA Indianapolis	Means "land of Indians"	Hoosier State			35,932 sq mi 93,064 sq km **RANK** 38
IOWA Des Moines	From an Indian word; means "this is the place," or "Beautiful Land"	Hawkeye State			55,965 sq mi 144,950 sq km **RANK** 23
KANSAS Topeka	From Sioux Indians; means "people of the south wind"	Sunflower State Jayhawk State			81,778 sq mi 211,805 sq km **RANK** 13
KENTUCKY Frankfort	From Iroquoian word *Ken-tah-ten*, meaning "land of tomorrow"	Bluegrass State			39,669 sq mi 102,743 sq km **RANK** 37
LOUISIANA Baton Rouge	For Louis XIV of France	Pelican State Sportsman's Paradise Creole State Sugar State			44,521 sq mi 115,310 sq km **RANK** 33
MAINE Augusta	From "mainland" or "Mayne," a French province	Pine Tree State			30,995 sq mi 80,277 sq km **RANK** 39
MARYLAND Annapolis	For Henrietta Maria, queen of Charles I of England	Free State Old Line State			9,837 sq mi 25,477 sq km **RANK** 42

■ Agriculture □ Industry ■ Services

LARGEST CITIES	POPULATION	URBAN POPULATION	BIRD	FLOWER	TREE
Honolulu Hilo Kailua	1,108,229 RANK 41		Nene (Hawaiian goose)	Hibiscus	Kukui
Boise Pocatello Idaho Falls	1,006,749 RANK 42		Mountain bluebird	Syringa	White pine
Chicago Rockford Peoria	11,430,602 RANK 6		Cardinal	Violet	White oak
Indianapolis Fort Wayne Evansville	5,544,159 RANK 14		Cardinal	Peony	Tulip
Des Moines Cedar Rapids Davenport	2,776,755 RANK 30		Eastern goldfinch	Wild rose	Oak
Wichita Kansas City Topeka	2,477,574 RANK 32		Western meadowlark	Sunflower	Cottonwood
Louisville Lexington-Fayette Owensboro	3,685,296 RANK 23		Kentucky cardinal	Goldenrod	Coffee tree
New Orleans Baton Rouge Shreveport	4,219,973 RANK 21		Brown pelican	Magnolia	Bald cypress
Portland Lewiston Bangor	1,227,928 RANK 38		Chickadee	White pine cone & tassel	White pine
Baltimore Rockville Frederick	4,781,468 RANK 19		Baltimore oriole	Black-eyed Susan	White oak

■ Urban ☐ Rural

	SOURCE OF NAME	NICKNAMES	FLAG	STATE ECONOMY	LAND AREA
MASSACHUSETTS — Boston	From Algonquian words meaning "great mountain place"	Bay State Old Colony State			7,824 sq mi 20,265 sq km **RANK** 45
MICHIGAN — Lansing	From Chippewa Indians; *Michigama* means "great lake"	Wolverine State			56,954 sq mi 147,511 sq km **RANK** 22
MINNESOTA — St. Paul	From Dakota Indian word meaning "sky-tinted water"	North Star State Gopher State Land of 10,000 Lakes			79,548 sq mi 206,030 sq km **RANK** 14
MISSISSIPPI — Jackson	From Indian word meaning "Father of Waters"	Magnolia State			47,233 sq mi 122,333 sq km **RANK** 31
MISSOURI — Jefferson City	From Missouri Indians; means "town of the large canoes"	Show Me State			68,945 sq mi 178,568 sq km **RANK** 18
MONTANA — Helena	Latinized Spanish word meaning "mountainous region"	Treasure State			145,388 sq mi 376,555 sq km **RANK** 4
NEBRASKA — Lincoln	From Oto Indians; *Nebrathka* means "flat water"	Cornhusker State Beef State Tree Planters State			76,644 sq mi 198,508 sq km **RANK** 15
NEVADA — Carson City	Spanish word meaning "snowcapped"	Sagebrush State Silver State Battle-born State			109,894 sq mi 284,624 sq km **RANK** 7
NEW HAMPSHIRE — Concord	From English county, Hampshire	Granite State			8,993 sq mi 23,292 sq km **RANK** 44
NEW JERSEY — Trenton	From Channel Isle of Jersey	Garden State			7,468 sq mi 19,342 sq km **RANK** 46

■ Agriculture □ Industry ■ Services

LARGEST CITIES	POPULATION	URBAN POPULATION	BIRD	FLOWER	TREE
Boston Worcester Springfield	6,016,425 RANK 13		Chickadee	Mayflower	American elm
Detroit Grand Rapids Warren	9,295,297 RANK: 8		Robin	Apple blossom	White pine
Minneapolis St. Paul Bloomington	4,375,099 RANK 20		Common loon	Showy lady slipper	Norway pine
Jackson Biloxi Greenville	2,573,216 RANK 31		Mockingbird	Magnolia	Magnolia
Kansas City St. Louis Springfield	5,117,073 RANK 15		Bluebird	Hawthorn	Flowering dogwood
Billings Great Falls Missoula	799,065 RANK 44		Western meadowlark	Bitterroot	Ponderosa pine
Omaha Lincoln Grand Island	1,578,385 RANK 36		Western meadowlark	Goldenrod	Cottonwood
Las Vegas Reno Henderson	1,201,833 RANK 39		Mountain bluebird	Sagebrush	Single-leaf piñon
Manchester Nashua Concord	1,109,252 RANK 40		Purple finch	Purple lilac	White birch
Newark Jersey City Paterson	7,730,188 RANK 9		Eastern goldfinch	Purple violet	Red oak

■ Urban □ Rural

STATE CHARTS

	SOURCE OF NAME	NICKNAMES	FLAG	STATE ECONOMY	LAND AREA
NEW MEXICO Santa Fe	From country of Mexico	Land of Enchantment Sunshine State			121,335 sq mi 314,258 sq km **RANK** 5
NEW YORK Albany	For English Duke of York, later King James II of England	Empire State			47,377 sq mi 122,707 sq km **RANK** 30
NORTH CAROLINA Raleigh	For Charles I of England	Tar Heel State			48,843 sq mi 126,504 sq km **RANK** 29
NORTH DAKOTA Bismarck	From Dakotah Indians; means "allies"	Sioux State Flickertail State			69,300 sq mi 179,486 sq km **RANK** 17
OHIO Columbus	From Iroquois Indians; means "great river"	Buckeye State			41,004 sq mi 106,201 sq km **RANK** 35
OKLAHOMA Oklahoma City	From Chocktaw Indian words meaning "red people"	Sooner State			68,655 sq mi 117,817 sq km **RANK** 19
OREGON Salem	From French name for a river, Ouragon, meaning "hurricane"	Beaver State			96,184 sq mi 249,117 sq km **RANK** 10
PENNSYLVANIA Harrisburg	For Admiral Penn, father of William Penn; means "Penn's Woods"	Keystone State			44,888 sq mi 116,260 sq km **RANK** 32
RHODE ISLAND Providence	From Greek island of Rhodes	Ocean State			1,055 sq mi 2,732 sq km **RANK** 50
SOUTH CAROLINA Columbia	For Charles I of England	Palmetto State			30,203 sq mi 78,227 sq km **RANK** 40

■ Agriculture □ Industry ■ Services

LARGEST CITIES	POPULATION	URBAN POPULATION	BIRD	FLOWER	TREE
Albuquerque Las Cruces Santa Fe	1,515,069 RANK 37		Roadrunner	Yucca	Piñon
New York Buffalo Rochester	17,990,455 RANK 2		Bluebird	Rose	Sugar maple
Charlotte Raleigh Greensboro	6,628,637 RANK 10		Cardinal	American dogwood	Pine
Fargo Grand Forks Bismarck	638,800 RANK 47		Western meadowlark	Wild prairie rose	American elm
Columbus Cleveland Cincinnati	10,847,115 RANK 7		Cardinal	Scarlet carnation	Buckeye
Oklahoma City Tulsa Lawton	3,145,585 RANK 28		Scissortailed flycatcher	Mistletoe	Redbud
Portland Eugene Salem	2,842,321 RANK 29		Western meadowlark	Oregon grape	Douglas fir
Philadelphia Pittsburgh Erie	11,881,643 RANK 5		Ruffed grouse	Mountain laurel	Hemlock
Providence Warwick Pawtucket	1,003,464 RANK 43		Rhode Island red	Violet (unofficial)	Red maple
Columbia Charleston North Charleston	3,486,703 RANK 25		Carolina wren	Carolina yellow jessamine	Palmetto

■ Urban ☐ Rural

STATE CHARTS

	SOURCE OF NAME	NICKNAMES	FLAG	STATE ECONOMY	LAND AREA
SOUTH DAKOTA ★ Pierre	From Dakotah Indians; means "allies"	The Mount Rushmore State			75,952 sq mi 196,715 sq km **RANK** 16
TENNESSEE ★ Nashville	From Tanasia, a Cherokee Indian village	Volunteer State			41,155 sq mi 106,591 sq km **RANK** 34
TEXAS Austin ★	From Indian word *Tejas*, meaning "friends"	Lone Star State			262,017 sq mi 678,623 sq km **RANK** 2
UTAH ★ Salt Lake City	From name of Ute Indian group, meaning "people of the mountains"	Beehive State			82,073 sq mi 212,569 sq km **RANK** 12
VERMONT ★ Montpelier	From French *vert mont*, meaning "green mountain"	Green Mountain State			9,273 sq mi 24,017 sq km **RANK** 43
VIRGINIA Richmond ★	For Queen Elizabeth I of England	The Old Dominion Mother of Presidents			39,704 sq mi 102,832 sq km **RANK** 36
WASHINGTON ★ Olympia	For George Washington	Evergreen State Chinook State			66,511 sq mi 172,264 sq km **RANK** 20
WEST VIRGINIA ★ Charleston	For Queen Elizabeth I of England	Mountain State			24,119 sq mi 62,468 sq km **RANK** 41
WISCONSIN Madison ★	Miskonsing Indian name for river; means "gathering of the waters"	Badger State			54,426 sq mi 140,964 sq km **RANK** 25
WYOMING Cheyenne ★	From Delaware Indian word meaning "upon a great plain"	Equality State			96,989 sq mi 251,202 sq km **RANK** 9

■ Agriculture □ Industry ▨ Services

LARGEST CITIES	POPULATION	URBAN POPULATION	BIRD	FLOWER	TREE
Sioux Falls Rapid City Aberdeen	696,004 RANK 45		Ring-necked pheasant	American pasqueflower	Black Hills spruce
Memphis Nashville Knoxville	4,877,185 RANK 17		Mockingbird	Iris	Tulip poplar
Houston Dallas San Antonio	16,986,510 RANK 3		Mockingbird	Bluebonnet	Pecan
Salt Lake City West Valley Provo	1,722,850 RANK 35		Sea gull	Sego lily	Blue spruce
Burlington Rutland Bennington	562,758 RANK 48		Hermit thrush	Red clover	Sugar maple
Virgina Beach Norfolk Richmond	6,187,358 RANK 12		Cardinal	American dogwood	Flowering dogwood
Seattle Spokane Tacoma	4,866,692 RANK 18		Willow goldfinch	Rhododendron	Western hemlock
Charleston Huntington Wheeling	1,793,477 RANK 34		Cardinal	Rhododendron	Sugar maple
Milwaukee Madison Green Bay	4,891,769 RANK 16		Robin	Wood violet	Sugar maple
Cheyenne Casper Laramie	453,588 RANK 50		Meadowlark	Indian paintbrush	Cottonwood

■ Urban □ Rural

AMERICA'S GEOGRAPHY

The geographical regions of the
United States take many forms. The
way people live determines how they will use
the land.

▶ *Waves crash against the rocky shore at Coos Bay, Oregon.*

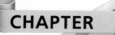

CHAPTER **1** PHYSICAL REGIONS OF THE UNITED STATES

★ ★ ★

The United States is a land of mountains and flat land, rivers and lakes, and streams and oceans. The land influenced the way people lived in the past and the way we live today.

The Coastal Plain

THINK ABOUT WHAT YOU KNOW

THINK ABOUT WHAT YOU KNOW

What do you know about the geography of the place where you live? Is it flat or hilly? Are there bodies of water nearby? How do people use the land and water where you live?

STUDY THE VOCABULARY

region   petroleum
coastal plain   textile
harbor

FOCUS YOUR READING

What are the main physical features of the Coastal Plain?

A. Studying the United States by Regions

America the Beautiful This book is about the history of the United States. It tells the story of the American people from early times to the present day. As you read it, you will learn how our country grew from a few tiny settlements to become the great nation it is today.

This book is also about America's geography—its towering mountains, its rivers and forests and other natural resources, and its farms and cities. Most important, throughout this book you will be reading about how people have used the American land.

The United States of America is surely one of the most beautiful lands in all the world. Its beauty has inspired many songs and poems. You probably know some of them by heart. One of the best-known of the songs is "America, the Beautiful." Do you know the words to this song?

History and Geography Why is this book about both history *and* geography? And why do we begin our story of the American people with a review of American geography? The reasons are that in order to understand *how* people lived, you must first learn about the places *where* they lived. To understand *how* people used the land, you must first know *what* the land was like. History and geography, you see, go hand in hand.

Different Features To help us learn about a country as large as the United States, geographers often divide the land into **regions**. A region is a part of the earth's surface that has one or more features that make it special. These features make a region different from other parts of the earth.

For example, we might divide the country into regions according to climate. One region might be hot and have a large amount of rainfall all year. Another region might be hot and very dry. Still another might be hot and wet for part of the year and cold and dry for another part of the year. Or we might divide the country into regions according to their crops. Then we would have a wheat-growing region, a cotton-growing region, and so on.

Geographers sometimes use landforms as the basis for dividing our country into regions. In this chapter we will divide our country into five regions according to five major landforms. These five landform regions of the United States are the Coastal Plain, the Appalachian (ap uh-LAY chun) region, the Central Plains, the Mountain West, and the Pacific region.

Most early settlers in North America arrived on the east, or Atlantic, coast. Settlement moved westward over the years, eventually reaching all five landform

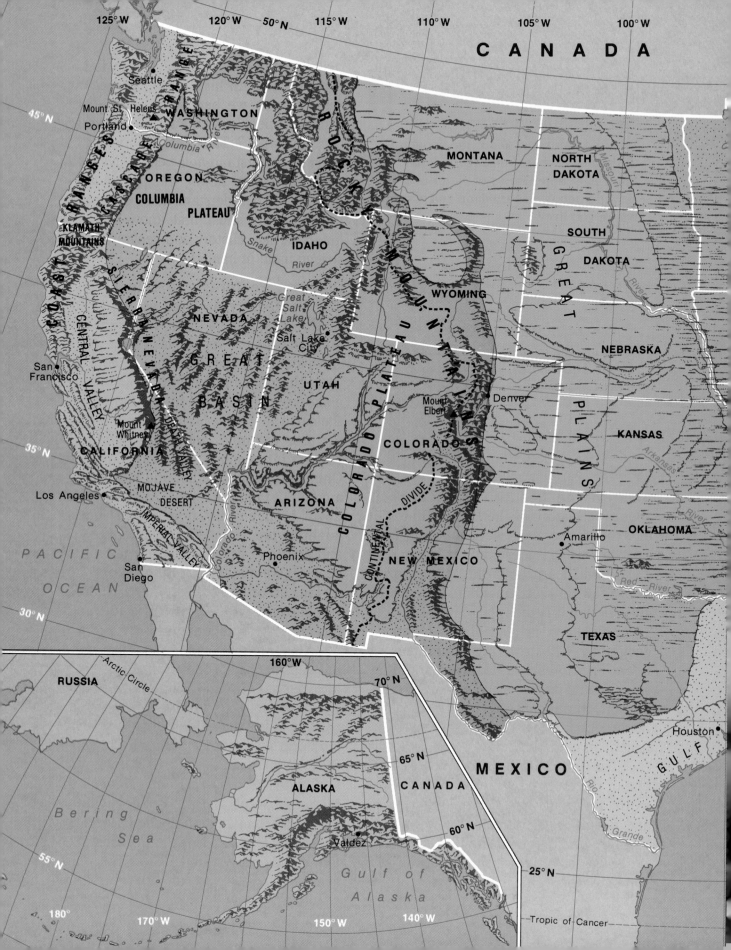

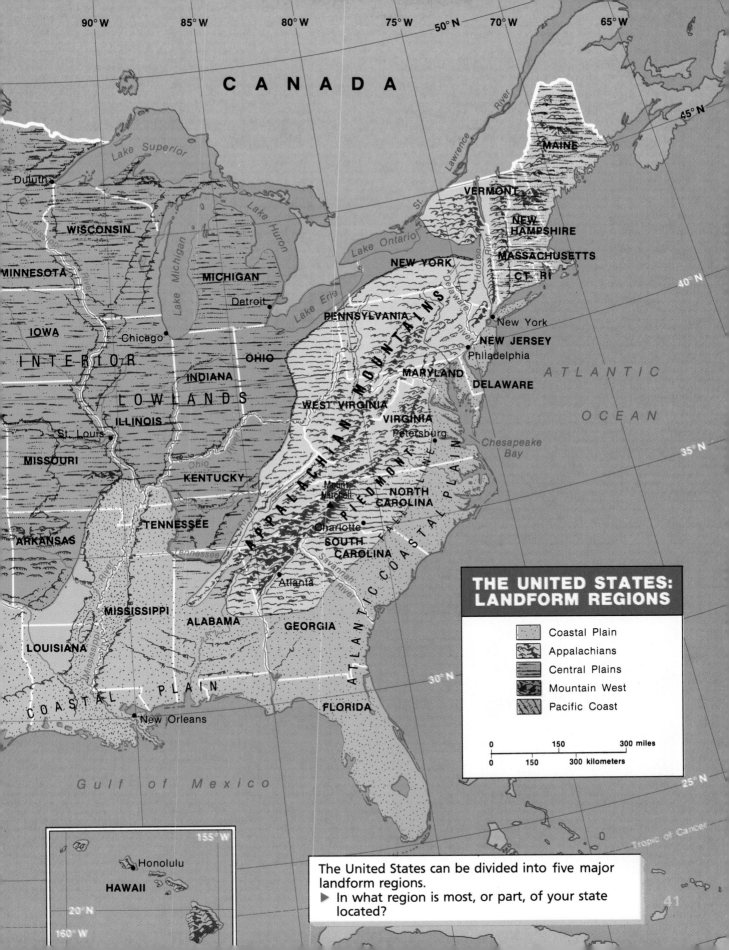

THE UNITED STATES:
LANDFORM REGIONS

Coastal Plain
Appalachians
Central Plains
Mountain West
Pacific Coast

0   150   300 miles
0   150   300 kilometers

The United States can be divided into five major
landform regions.
► In what region is most, or part, of your state
located?

41

regions of the United States. So, like the early settlers, we will start in the East and move westward, studying these regions in the same order in which the settlers crossed them.

B. The Coastal Plain, from Maine to Texas

Two Parts As you can see on the physical map on pages 40–41, most of the land along the Atlantic Ocean and the Gulf of Mexico is a plain, or an area of flat land. A plain that borders a coast is known as a coastal plain. The region that we call the Coastal Plain extends from Maine all the way to Texas.

Part of the Coastal Plain that runs along the Atlantic Ocean is called the *Atlantic Coastal Plain*. A second part runs along the Gulf of Mexico. It is called the *Gulf Coastal Plain*. Even though the two parts have separate names, together they make up one large coastal plain.

At its northern end the Atlantic Coastal Plain is very narrow. In some places it is only 20 to 30 miles (32 to 48 km) wide. The coastline here dips in and out, forming many fine natural harbors. A harbor is a protected body of water where ships and boats can safely anchor. The Gulf Coastal Plain is even broader. It stretches several hundred miles inland from the coast.

Early Land Use When Europeans first arrived in North America, nearly the entire Coastal Plain was thick with trees. Trees were so plentiful that they often blocked the sunlight from the forest floor. Sailors said that when the wind blew in the right direction, they could smell the pine trees even before they saw land.

The Coastal Plain did not remain a forest for long, however. Settlers found that the soil and climate along most of the plain were good for farming. Along both the Atlantic and Gulf coasts, they cut down trees and turned the land into farms.

Those who lived at the edge of the Coastal Plain also made a living from the sea. They found to their delight that coastal waters were full of fish, shrimps, crabs, and lobsters. The many harbors along the coast made possible the growth of shipping and trade. America's earliest cities grew up on the sites of these harbors.

C. The Coastal Plain Today

Forests and Farms Although some of the forests of the Coastal Plain were cut long ago, many of the forests remain. Large pine-tree forests are still found in most of the states of the Coastal Plain. This is especially true in Georgia and Alabama.

Along the northern Atlantic Coastal Plain, there are many small natural harbors.
▶ What is a harbor?

The wood from pine trees is known as soft-wood. Softwood forests provide us with lumber for homebuilding and wood pulp for making paper. Most paper made in the United States comes from these pine forests of the Coastal Plain.

There are also still many farms in this region. In states like New Jersey, Pennsylvania, Delaware, and New York, farmers grow vegetables and fruits to be sold in nearby cities. In addition, the states of Louisiana, Arkansas, and Mississippi produce much of the rice and sugar that Americans eat. And Florida provides us with many of the oranges and grapefruit that are on our breakfast tables.

Important Fuels Two of our country's most important natural resources are found in the Gulf Coastal Plain. These are natural gas and **petroleum** (puh TROH-lee um), or oil. In fact, gas and oil are also found underneath the coastal waters.

THE UNITED STATES: DISTRIBUTION OF PETROLEUM

Millions of barrels
- Less than 5
- 5-100
- 100-400
- 400-800
- 800 or more
- Landform region boundaries

Texas is our nation's leading producer of petroleum.
▶ What three states produce the next largest amount?

Natural gas and oil are fuels. They make it possible for us to cook our meals, heat our homes, and run our cars and machines. The production of petroleum and natural gas is an important industry in Louisiana and Texas.

Petroleum has also made possible the growth of a large petrochemical industry. The petrochemical industry produces goods made from oil. Hundreds of products that we use every day are made from oil. These products include paints, fertilizers, plastics, detergents, medicines, and even lipstick.

Using the Sea People of the Coastal Plain still make a living from the sea, too. More than half of our nation's catch of fish comes from the waters off the Coastal Plain. Long Island, New York, is famous for its oysters and clams. To many people, Chesapeake Bay crabs are a special treat. Louisiana and other Gulf Coast states sell shrimps to buyers all over the nation.

A Region of Cities More than anything else, though, the Coastal Plain is noted for its great cities. Many of these cities are important trade centers. The three busiest ports in our country—New Orleans, New York, and Houston—are all on the Coastal Plain. In fact, seven of our ten busiest ports are on the Coastal Plain.

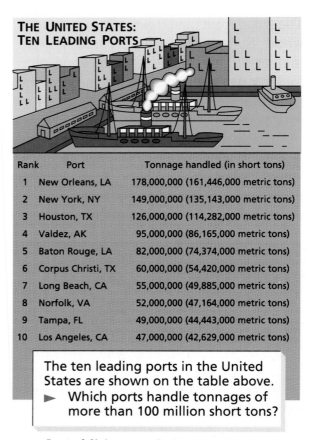

THE UNITED STATES: TEN LEADING PORTS

Rank	Port	Tonnage handled (in short tons)
1	New Orleans, LA	178,000,000 (161,446,000 metric tons)
2	New York, NY	149,000,000 (135,143,000 metric tons)
3	Houston, TX	126,000,000 (114,282,000 metric tons)
4	Valdez, AK	95,000,000 (86,165,000 metric tons)
5	Baton Rouge, LA	82,000,000 (74,374,000 metric tons)
6	Corpus Christi, TX	60,000,000 (54,420,000 metric tons)
7	Long Beach, CA	55,000,000 (49,885,000 metric tons)
8	Norfolk, VA	52,000,000 (47,164,000 metric tons)
9	Tampa, FL	49,000,000 (44,443,000 metric tons)
10	Los Angeles, CA	47,000,000 (42,629,000 metric tons)

The ten leading ports in the United States are shown on the table above.
► Which ports handle tonnages of more than 100 million short tons?

In addition to being trade centers, many cities on the Coastal Plain are important manufacturing centers. Submarines and other naval ships are built in Connecticut and Virginia. Airplanes are made in New York. Cities in South Carolina and North Carolina are the leading **textile**, or cloth, manufacturing centers of our country. Cities in Delaware lead the nation in the production of chemicals.

LESSON **1** *REVIEW*

THINK AND WRITE
A. What is a region?
B. Describe the two parts of the Coastal Plain.
C. Compare the way early settlers used the Coastal Plain with the way it is used today.

SKILLS CHECK
MAP SKILL
Look at the map on pages 40–41. Make a list of the states that are at least partly on the Coastal Plain.

44

The Appalachian Region

THINK ABOUT WHAT YOU KNOW

Have you ever driven through or camped out in a mountainous area? If so, tell the class about your experiences.

STUDY THE VOCABULARY

Piedmont   **Fall Line**

FOCUS YOUR READING

What are the main differences between the Appalachian region and the Coastal Plain?

A. The Piedmont

To the west of the Atlantic Coastal Plain is the Appalachian region. Along the western edge of the Coastal Plain, the land begins to rise gently. This stretch of high, hilly land is called the **Piedmont** (PEED-mahnt). *Piedmont* means "foot of the mountain," and that is just where this hilly land lies. The hills of the Piedmont are often called foothills.

No state border marks the place where the Coastal Plain ends and the Piedmont begins. However, you can find the dividing line wherever there is a river. As rivers cross the higher Piedmont and flow toward the lower Coastal Plain, they come to a place where the land drops sharply. There the water tumbles down, forming rapids or small waterfalls. The place where the river falls is called the **Fall Line**. That fall line is the boundary between the Coastal Plain and the Piedmont.

The Fall Line is an important feature of the geography of the Appalachian region. Before gasoline engines and electric motors were invented, machines were run by water power. Early factories were often built at the Fall Line to take advantage of fast-falling water. Towns then grew up around these factories. That is why today you will find a trail of cities along the Fall Line. Trenton, New Jersey; Petersburg, Virginia; and Columbia, South Carolina, are three Fall-Line cities.

B. The Appalachian Mountains

The mountains that lie just to the west of the Piedmont are the Appalachian Mountains. These mountains stretch from southern Canada all the way to Georgia and Alabama.

The Appalachian Mountains have different names in different states. In New

Many small farms are found in the low, rolling hills at the base of the Appalachian Mountains.
► What is this region called?

York they are called the Adirondacks. In Virginia and North Carolina, they are called the Blue Ridge Mountains. And in Tennessee they are called the Great Smoky Mountains. The highest point in the Appalachian Mountains is Mount Mitchell, which is in North Carolina. It has an elevation of 6,684 feet (2,037 m).

A number of important rivers start in the Appalachian Mountains. Some of them — such as the Hudson, Delaware, and Savannah rivers — flow southeast and empty into the Atlantic Ocean. Others — such as the Ohio and Tennessee rivers — flow toward the west, where they join with the Mississippi River.

C. The Appalachian Region Today

Natural Resources Like the Coastal Plain, the Appalachian region was covered with trees when settlers first arrived. Unlike the forests of the Coastal Plain, however, few Appalachian forests have been completely cut down.

The trees in the Appalachian region are hardwoods — oak, ash, maple, hickory, and so on. You'll remember that softwood forests provide us with lumber for home-building and wood pulp for papermaking. Hardwood forests are important in the making of pieces of furniture and even baseball bats.

The Appalachian Trail is a 2,000-mile (3,218-km) hiking trail that runs from the state of Georgia to the state of Maine. Many people enjoy hiking along the trail every year.
▶ How have these hikers prepared for their trip along the trail?

The city of Atlanta, Georgia, with a population of about 400,000 people, is the largest city in the Appalachian region.
▶ What large cities have you visited?

The Appalachian region produces two important fuels. One of these is natural gas. There are large deposits of this gas throughout the region. Tapping those deposits is an important industry today in the Appalachian region.

The second fuel is coal. The Appalachian region is the largest coal-producing region in the country. In fact, three of the leading coal-producing states in the United States — Kentucky, West Virginia, and Pennsylvania — are in this region.

Population The Appalachian region is not nearly as heavily populated as the Coastal Plain. Nor does it have as many large cities. However, there are several large cities in this region. The largest is Atlanta, Georgia. Atlanta is one of the most important transportation centers in our country. Its airport is one of the largest in the United States. Other large cities in the Appalachian region include Charlotte, North Carolina; Charleston, West Virginia; and Knoxville, Tennessee.

LESSON **2** *REVIEW*

THINK AND WRITE

A. What is the Fall Line?
B. What are the major rivers of the Appalachian region?
C. Compare the natural resources of the Appalachian region with those of the Coastal Plain.

SKILLS CHECK

THINKING SKILL

What do the photographs in this lesson tell you about the geography of the Appalachian region?

The Central Plains

THINK ABOUT WHAT YOU KNOW

Describe the differences between a place that is flat and a place that is hilly or mountainous.

STUDY THE VOCABULARY

landlocked   river mouth
canal   tributary
river source   drought

FOCUS YOUR READING

What is the main difference between the two parts of the Central Plains?

A. Miles of Plains

A Flat Land Moving westward across the Appalachian Mountains, we reach the Central Plains region. This region has two major parts. The first part lies just west of the Appalachian Mountains. It is called the Interior Lowlands. Chicago, Illinois, is the largest and most important city in the Interior Lowlands.

The second part of the Central Plains lies to the west of the Interior Lowlands. This area is called the Great Plains. The largest city on the Great Plains is Denver, Colorado. That city lies at the western edge of the Great Plains. Together the Interior Lowlands and the Great Plains stretch about 1,500 miles (2,414 km) across the United States.

Here and there on these vast plains are some hilly areas. There are even a few small mountains. But mostly the Central Plains region is flat. Standing on these plains, one can see straight out to the horizon, where sky and land seem to meet, without a single rise in the land to interrupt the view.

Rainfall The main difference between the Interior Lowlands and the Great Plains is the amount of precipitation each gets. The Interior Lowlands receives 30 to 40 inches (76 to 102 cm) of precipitation a year. That is more than enough precipitation to support the growth of tall grasses, which are often as tall as a person.

To settlers first seeing the Interior Lowlands, the tall grasses were a welcome sign. They knew that if there was enough rainfall for tall grass to grow, there would be enough for farming.

In contrast, many parts of the Great Plains receive only 20 to 25 inches (51 to 64 cm) of precipitation a year. Also, precipitation is not the same each year. While the average yearly precipitation for an area might be 20 inches (51 cm), that same place might get more precipitation in some years and less in others. For example, it

Farming is an important business in the Central Plains.
▶ What does this picture say about the geography of this region?

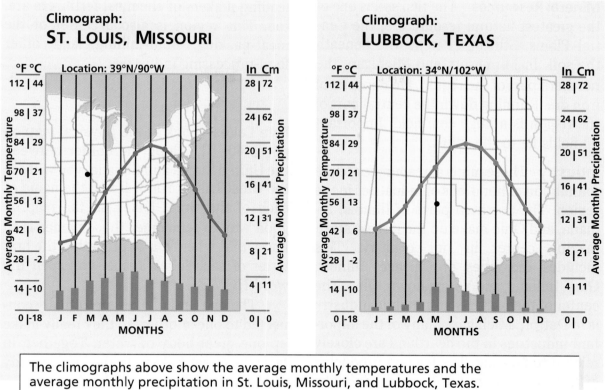

Climograph:
ST. LOUIS, MISSOURI
Location: 39°N/90°W

Climograph:
LUBBOCK, TEXAS
Location: 34°N/102°W

The climographs above show the average monthly temperatures and the average monthly precipitation in St. Louis, Missouri, and Lubbock, Texas.
► Which city, St. Louis or Lubbock, receives more precipitation in a year?

might get 5 inches (13 cm) of precipitation one year, 20 inches (51 cm) each of the next two years, then 30 inches (76 cm), and finally 25 inches (64 cm). The five-year average would be 20 inches (51 cm), but precipitation the first year would have been too low to support grasses and trees.

As a result there are almost no trees on the Great Plains. There is hardly enough rain from year to year for short grass to grow. When settlers first arrived on the Great Plains, they took one look at the short grass turning brown in the summer sun and decided that this was no place for them.

In time, Americans did settle on the Great Plains. As you will read later, they learned how to farm with little rainfall. They also found the short grasses of the plains ideal for grazing cattle and sheep.

B. Heartland of America

The World's Breadbasket Many people call the Central Plains the Heartland of America. They call it the heartland for two reasons. The first reason is location. The Central Plains is located between the two coasts, in the center or heart of our nation.

The second reason the Central Plains region is called the heartland is that it is our country's greatest farming region. Like the heart that pumps life-giving blood through the human body, the Central Plains sends out its life-giving products to the entire country.

The products of the heartland go to other parts of the world as well. Farmers of the Central Plains sell so much food to other countries that this region is also known by another name, the World's Breadbasket.

Mineral Resources   The rich soil is one of the greatest natural resources of the Central Plains. Still other riches lie beneath the soil. In Minnesota and Michigan, the northern part of the region, are deposits of iron ore. Running down the central part of the region is a huge coal field. Important oil fields lie to the south.

Industry   These mineral resources are the foundation of hundreds of industries in the region. The northern parts of Illinois, Indiana, and Ohio make up the largest steel-making center in our country. This includes the cities of Chicago, Illinois; Gary, Indiana; and Youngstown, Ohio. The center of the nation's automobile industry is in Detroit, Michigan. Many of the important industries in the heartland are closely related to farming. The leading producers of farm machinery are located here. The

The making of farm machinery is an important industry in the Central Plains.
▶ Why is this an important industry?

leading makers of chemical fertilizers are, too. This region is also a center of the meat-packing, flour-milling, and other food-processing industries.

C. The Great Lakes

Five Lakes   Look at the physical map on pages 40–41. Along the border between the United States and Canada, you will see the Great Lakes. You will find the name of each of the Great Lakes on the map. A good way to remember those names is to know that when you put together the first letter of each lake's name, you spell the word HOMES.

The five Great Lakes are actually connected to one another, so they really make up one great body of water. Together, in fact, the Great Lakes are the largest body of fresh water in the world.

As you see them on the map, the Great Lakes appear to be **landlocked**. *Landlocked* means that they are surrounded by land, with no way to get from them to the ocean by water. In very early times the Great Lakes really were cut off from the oceans. But waterways have been built by people to connect the lakes with rivers that lead to the ocean.

Waterways to the Sea   In 1825, the Erie Canal was opened. A **canal** is a waterway that has been built across land to connect two bodies of water. The Erie Canal connected Lake Erie to the Hudson River in New York. The Hudson leads out to the Atlantic Ocean. Today this canal is part of the New York State Barge Canal.

An even more important link between the Great Lakes and the Atlantic Ocean was opened in 1959. This is the St. Lawrence Seaway. The St. Lawrence Seaway is a series of canals connecting the

THE ST. LAWRENCE SEAWAY

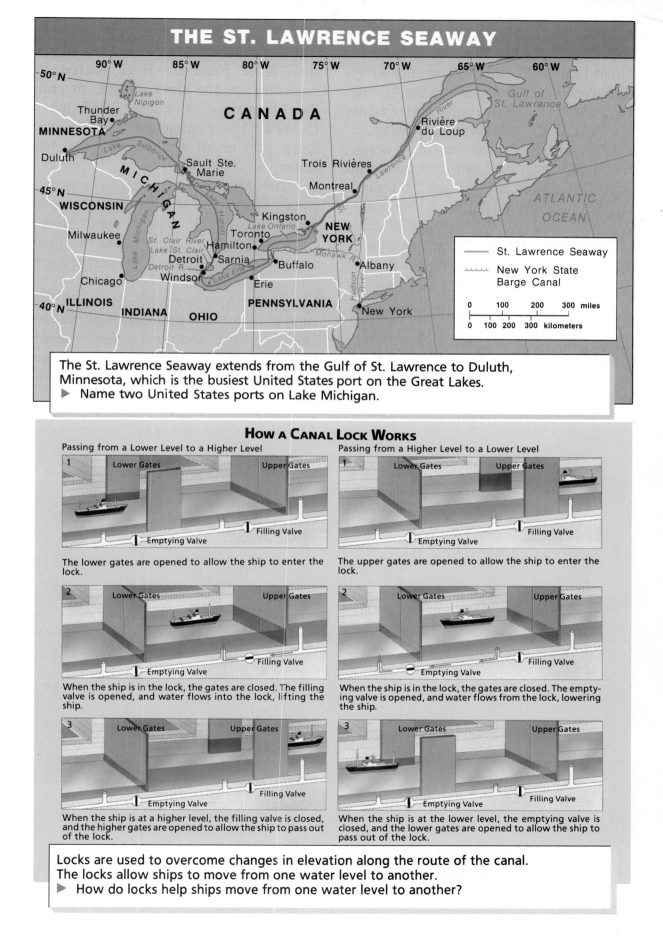

The St. Lawrence Seaway extends from the Gulf of St. Lawrence to Duluth, Minnesota, which is the busiest United States port on the Great Lakes.

▶ Name two United States ports on Lake Michigan.

HOW A CANAL LOCK WORKS

Passing from a Lower Level to a Higher Level

1. The lower gates are opened to allow the ship to enter the lock.

2. When the ship is in the lock, the gates are closed. The filling valve is opened, and water flows into the lock, lifting the ship.

3. When the ship is at a higher level, the filling valve is closed, and the higher gates are opened to allow the ship to pass out of the lock.

Passing from a Higher Level to a Lower Level

1. The upper gates are opened to allow the ship to enter the lock.

2. When the ship is in the lock, the gates are closed. The emptying valve is opened, and water flows from the lock, lowering the ship.

3. When the ship is at the lower level, the emptying valve is closed, and the lower gates are opened to allow the ship to pass out of the lock.

Locks are used to overcome changes in elevation along the route of the canal. The locks allow ships to move from one water level to another.

▶ How do locks help ships move from one water level to another?

Great Lakes with the St. Lawrence River. The river in turn empties into the Atlantic Ocean. The United States and Canada jointly built the St. Lawrence Seaway.

As a result of the seaway, huge ocean-going ships can now sail directly to and from such Great Lakes ports as Duluth, Minnesota; Chicago, Illinois; Toledo, Ohio; and Detroit, Michigan. These and other cities along the Great Lakes can now trade directly with countries on other continents as well as with cities in other states.

D. The Mississippi River

A Mighty River Running through the middle of the Central Plains is the greatest river in the United States and one of the greatest in the world. This is the Missis-sippi River. From the **river source**, or beginning, to the **river mouth**, or end, the Mississippi is nearly 2,350 miles (3,781 km) long. Along its way this river forms part or all of a boundary of ten states.

The Mississippi starts as a small stream in northern Minnesota. On its path southward, other streams and rivers empty into it. Rivers and streams that flow into a larger river and become part of it are called **tributaries**.

The map on pages 40–41 shows the main tributaries of the Mississippi River. The Ohio River and the Tennessee River flow into the Mississippi from the east. The Missouri, Arkansas, and Red rivers flow into it from the west.

The St. Lawrence Seaway enables large oceangoing ships to travel from the Great Lakes to the Atlantic Ocean.
► Who built the seaway?

In 1988 a drought lowered the level of the Mississippi River.
▶ What effect did the drought have on river transportation?

The waters from these tributaries swell the Mississippi into an ever-widening river. By the time it reaches the Gulf of Mexico, the Mississippi River is nearly a mile (1.6 km) wide.

Highways of Water The Mississippi and its many tributaries have been important water highways throughout our country's history. Even in today's world of trucks, trains, and planes, they remain important. Every year, ships carry thousands of tons of coal, steel, iron ore, grain, and other goods along these waterways.

Just how important these river highways are to our nation was shown in the spring and summer of 1988. A serious **drought**, or shortage of precipitation, caused the level of the rivers to drop. The Mississippi and Ohio rivers became too shallow for boats to travel on them.

Television programs and newspaper photographs showed long lines of boats unable to move, waiting for the waters to rise. Businesses waiting for the goods on these boats had to slow down. Several months went by before rains caused the waters to rise, allowing the ships to travel again.

Many of our large cities today got their start as river ports on the Mississippi. Five of our largest cities, in fact, are located on this great river.

LESSON **3** REVIEW

THINK AND WRITE

A. Compare the two parts of the Central Plains.

B. How are the industries and the natural resources of the Central Plains connected?

C. How does the St. Lawrence Seaway help cities along the Great Lakes?

D. How is the Mississippi River important to our country today?

SKILLS CHECK

THINKING SKILL
Using the diagram on page 51, write an explanation of how canal locks work.

The Mountain West

THINK ABOUT WHAT YOU KNOW

What do you think it would be like to take a hiking trip up a mountain?

STUDY THE VOCABULARY

canyon   intermontane
Continental   plateau
   Divide

FOCUS YOUR READING

What are the main physical features of the Mountain West?

A. The Rocky Mountains

High, Rugged Mountains As you reach the western end of the Great Plains, the land rises quite sharply. You'll recall that Denver, Colorado, is a city at the western edge of the Great Plains. Its elevation is 5,280 feet (1,609 m) — exactly one mile above sea level. But just about 100 miles (161 km) west of Denver is a peak of land called Mount Elbert. The elevation of Mount Elbert is 14,433 feet (4,399 m) — nearly 3 miles above sea level!

Mount Elbert is the highest point in the broadest chain of mountains in our country. These are the Rocky Mountains.

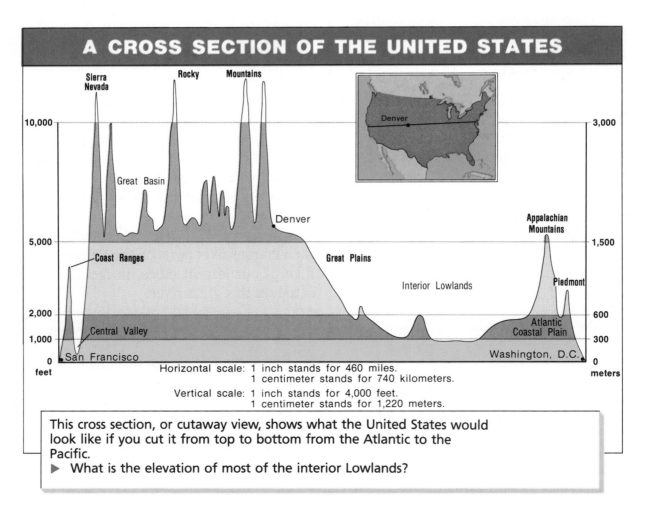

A CROSS SECTION OF THE UNITED STATES

Horizontal scale: 1 inch stands for 460 miles.
1 centimeter stands for 740 kilometers.
Vertical scale: 1 inch stands for 4,000 feet.
1 centimeter stands for 1,220 meters.

This cross section, or cutaway view, shows what the United States would look like if you cut it from top to bottom from the Atlantic to the Pacific.
▶ What is the elevation of most of the interior Lowlands?

The Rocky Mountains are about 3,000 miles (4,827 km) long. This mountain range runs like a giant spine, or backbone, down the North American continent from Alaska to New Mexico.

Some peaks in the Rockies are so high that their tops are often hidden in the clouds. The snow never melts on some of these peaks. That is because as a general rule, the higher a place is, the cooler it is. In fact, a mountain peak as high as Mount Elbert is about 45° colder than another place at the same latitude but at sea level.

Powerful Rivers Water from rain and melted snow runs down the sides of the Rocky Mountains in countless tiny streams. Some of these streams are the sources of mighty rivers. These include the Snake River in the north and the Colorado River in the south.

Over millions of years the Colorado River has carved out a **canyon**, or deep and narrow cut through the land, on its path southward. This is the famous Grand Canyon, one of the most beautiful natural sights in the world.

The highest ridges in the Rocky Mountains form the **Continental Divide**. Rivers that begin on the western side of the Continental Divide flow westward. The Colorado is one such river. Rivers that start on the eastern side of the Continental Divide flow toward the southeast. Most of these rivers eventually empty into the Gulf of Mexico.

B. The Intermontane Lands

The Driest and the Lowest Between the Rocky Mountains and the mountain ranges of the Pacific Coast is an area called the **intermontane**. *Intermontane* means "between mountains."

The intermontane area contains a number of **plateaus**. A plateau is an area of flat or gently rolling land that stands high above sea level. To be called a plateau, such land must rise steeply from the land around it on at least one of its sides. Find the names of the intermontane plateaus shown on the map on pages 40–41.

The intermontane area also includes the Mojave (moh HAH vee) Desert, which is the driest place in the United States, and Death Valley, which is the country's lowest spot. Both of these places are in the state of California.

Settling the Mountain West For many years, people showed almost no interest in the Mountain West. Most of the settlers who first entered the region wanted to make their living by farming. They could see right away that this mountain region

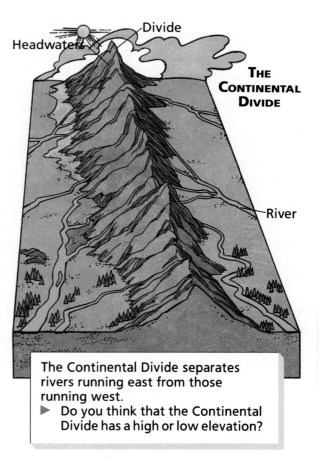

Headwaters — Divide

THE CONTINENTAL DIVIDE

River

The Continental Divide separates rivers running east from those running west.
▶ Do you think that the Continental Divide has a high or low elevation?

was not the place for them. Some of them went back to the East. Others traveled farther west in search of more inviting land.

In later years other people would discover that they could make a living in the Mountain West. Most did so by mining. These mountainous lands were rich in gold, silver, lead, zinc, and other important metals. Still others found that the land was good for grazing cattle and sheep.

C. The Mountain West Today

Population Compared with other regions, the land of the Mountain West has changed little since the first settlers reached it. Fewer people live here than in any other region of our country.

You can see that when you fly over the United States in an airplane. Most other areas of the country are either patchworks of farmers' fields or networks of cities and suburbs. But the Rocky Mountains and most of the surrounding land still look as they did in the days when they were known only to the Indians.

Mining Parts of this region, however, are booming. Mining is a major industry here. There are copper deposits in Utah that are among the largest in the world. And large deposits of coal and oil shale have been found in the region. Colorado is one of our leading coal-producing states. Colorado, Utah, and Wyoming have huge

undeveloped sites of oil shale. Shale is a kind of rock. Oil shale contains oil. Someday, people may start removing the oil from the oil shale in large quantities.

Cities Cities in the Mountain West are among the fastest growing in our country. These include Phoenix, Arizona; Albuquerque, New Mexico; and Salt Lake City, Utah. These cities offer many activities and employment opportunities to their residents. Recently, many people have moved to cities in the Mountain West.

The city of Salt Lake City, Utah, is surrounded by the Rocky Mountains.
► What, do you think, is that domed building in the picture?

LESSON 4 REVIEW

THINK AND WRITE

A. Compare the Rockies and the Appalachians.
B. What is the land of the intermontane area like?
C. How do people in the Mountain West use the land today?

SKILLS CHECK

THINKING SKILL

Make a list of questions you would ask someone from the Mountain West if you wanted to find out about living in that region.

The Pacific Region

THINK ABOUT WHAT YOU KNOW

Make a list of the kinds of activities you think people who live near the ocean might take part in.

STUDY THE VOCABULARY

earthquake   **fertile**
Ring of Fire   **irrigate**
valley

FOCUS YOUR READING

What are the main physical features of the Pacific Region?

A. The Ring of Fire

On October 17, 1989, over 62,000 baseball fans filled Candlestick Park in San Francisco, California. They were ready to enjoy Game 3 of the World Series. Millions of Americans had just turned on their televisions. Moments before game time, a powerful shock was felt. This shock was an **earthquake**, which is a violent shaking and splitting of the earth's surface.

The shock lasted only about 15 seconds. But in those few seconds, the earthquake had done more than make it impossible to play the baseball game. It had destroyed roads, bridges, and buildings in San Francisco, Oakland, and surrounding

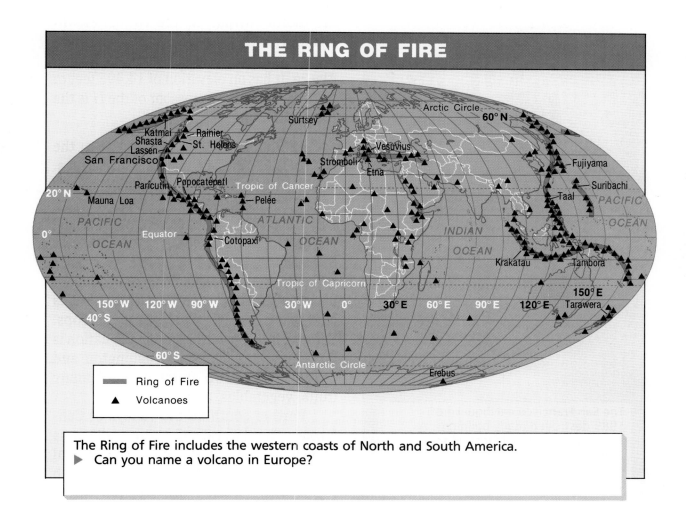

THE RING OF FIRE

The Ring of Fire includes the western coasts of North and South America.
▶ Can you name a volcano in Europe?

areas. When it was all over, many people had been killed. The area of destruction reached from north of San Francisco to south of San Jose. People in places as far away as Los Angeles and Reno, Nevada, felt the earthquake.

The western coasts of North and South America are part of an unusual belt called the **Ring of Fire**. It is called the Ring of Fire because of the dangers of earthquakes and volcanic eruptions.

Although such violent acts of nature are not frequent, they are not unusual in this area. In 1906 a stronger earthquake devastated San Francisco. In 1980 and again in 1984, Mount St. Helens in Washington erupted. Even though there was plenty of warning, many people were killed by this eruption. Vegetation and wildlife for miles around Mount St. Helens suffered serious damage.

B. High Mountains and Fertile Valleys

High Mountains San Francisco and Mount St. Helens are both in the Pacific region. You can think of the shape of this region as a tall letter *H*. The mountains are the vertical lines that make up the *H*. The entire left side of the *H* is the Coast Ranges. These mountains hug the Pacific Coast all the way from Alaska to southern California. The right side of the *H* is made up of the Cascade Range in the north and the Sierra Nevada in the south. Mount Whitney, in the Sierra Nevada, is the highest point in the United States, excluding Alaska. It has an elevation of 14,495 feet or 4,418 m. The small crossbar of the *H* is the Klamath Mountains.

Fertile Valleys The spaces between the lines of the *H* include many broad **valleys**. A valley is a long, low area of land usually between mountains or hills. Often, streams that begin in the mountains bring water to valleys, feeding rivers that run through them.

The soil in many of the valleys of the Pacific region is very **fertile**. Fertile land is land that can grow an abundance of crops. Some of the finest farmland in the nation is found in the valleys of Washington and Oregon. These two states produce many fruits, vegetables, and grains.

Farther south lie the valleys of California. The largest of these valleys is known as the Central Valley. The Central Valley runs 500 miles (805 km) from north to south and is 100 miles (161 km) wide. Here the land is fertile, the temperature is

The San Francisco earthquake of 1989 destroyed many buildings. As a result, many people lost all that they owned.
▶ What evidence of the earthquake is shown in this photograph?

In 1989 an oil tanker traveling through Alaska's Prince William Sound accidentally spilled millions of gallons of oil into the bay.
► What are the people in this photograph doing?

warm, and the growing season is long. However, the climate is too dry to support many crops.

At first there was little farming in the Central Valley. Then people found ways to **irrigate** the land, that is, to bring water to it from rivers and streams. Irrigation gave new life to the rich soil in this valley. Today the Central Valley is one of the richest farming areas in the United States.

Farther to the south, irrigation has also made the Imperial Valley of California come to life. The production from the Imperial, the Central, and several other valleys help make California the largest farming state in the country.

C. Alaska and Hawaii

Alaska Two parts of the Pacific region are unusual because they do not share a border with any other state. These two parts are Alaska and Hawaii.

Alaska is a vast mountainous state that lies far to the north. Parts of Alaska lie so close to the North Pole that during the summer months it remains light even at midnight. This has earned Alaska the nickname of Land of the Midnight Sun. However, during the winter months a large part of Alaska is dark most of the day.

Alaska's climate is very cold, with long, bitter winters. In the summer, temperatures rise well above freezing, but only in a few places does it stay warm long enough to make farming possible.

Hawaii Hawaii is made up of a series of islands in the Pacific Ocean, about 2,500 miles (4,023 km) southwest of the Pacific coast of North America. These islands are really the tops of volcanic mountains that rise from the floor of the Pacific Ocean. Hawaii is part of the Ring of Fire, and many of these mountaintops are active volcanoes.

For many years, Hawaii's sugar and pineapple crops were an important source of income. Today much of the state's income comes from tourism. Visitors from all over the world come to Hawaii to enjoy its climate and beautiful beaches.

D. Natural Resources

Fishing and Mining The Pacific region has many natural resources in addition to its rich farmland. There is an abundance of fish in the waters along the coastlines. Alaska is our leading fishing state.

Petroleum is another important natural resource. California has large deposits of oil. Alaska's deposits are even larger. Alaska's main oil-producing area is Prudhoe Bay. Many ships are required to

Pineapples, which grow well in a mild climate, were a leading crop in Hawaii for many years.
▶ What do you think the machine in this picture is used for?

carry Alaska's oil to other parts of the United States and the world. As a result the city of Valdez, Alaska, has become the nation's fourth-largest port. To get the oil from Prudhoe Bay to Valdez a long pipeline, called the Trans-Alaska Pipeline, was built. You can trace the route of this pipeline on the map on page 61.

Forests One of the greatest natural resources of the Pacific region is its forests. From Alaska in the north to California in the south, thick forests cover this region. Lumbering has become an important industry in this area. The Pacific region produces more lumber than any other region in the country.

Some of the trees in these forests grow to an astonishing size. The giant sequoia (sih KWOI uh) trees that grow in northern California are the largest trees in the entire world. A giant sequoia grows to an average height of 175 feet (53 m), which is about the height of a 15-story building. Some have been known to grow as high as 400 feet (122 m)!

The trunk of one giant sequoia measures more than 100 feet (30 m) around. To get an idea of how large that is, measure the distance around the four walls of your classroom and compare that distance with the size of this tree.

The forests in this region have a value that goes beyond their use as lumber. People use the forests for recreation. These forests are among the natural wonders of our country, and Americans of today and tomorrow should have a chance to see and enjoy them. That is why we all have a responsibility to preserve them.

E. Cities of the Pacific Region

Many people have moved to the Pacific region because of the abundance of

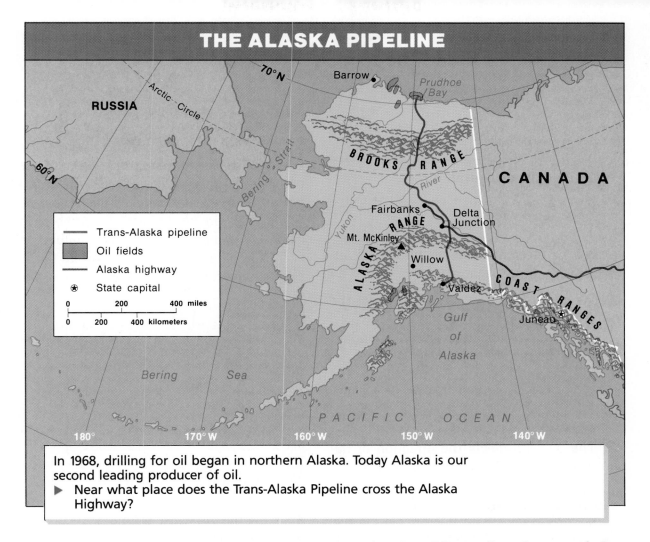

THE ALASKA PIPELINE

Legend:
- Trans-Alaska pipeline
- Oil fields
- Alaska highway
- ⊛ State capital

0   200   400 miles
0 200 400 kilometers

RUSSIA

Arctic Circle

70°N

Barrow

Prudhoe Bay

BROOKS RANGE

CANADA

River

Fairbanks

Delta Junction

ALASKA RANGE

Mt. McKinley

Willow

Yukon

Valdez

COAST RANGES

Juneau ⊛

Gulf of Alaska

Bering Strait

60°N

Bering Sea

PACIFIC OCEAN

180°   170° W   160° W   150° W   140° W

In 1968, drilling for oil began in northern Alaska. Today Alaska is our second leading producer of oil.
► Near what place does the Trans-Alaska Pipeline cross the Alaska Highway?

natural resources found there. This is especially true of California, which is now our most populated state. Four of California's cities are among the 15 most populated cities in the United States. Los Angeles is the second most populated city in the country. Only New York has more people. San Diego, San Jose, and San Francisco are also in the top 15.

Seattle, Washington, and Portland, Oregon, are major cities in the Northwest. The beautiful city of Honolulu is the largest city in Hawaii. With the exception of San Jose, all of these cities are port cities.

LESSON 5 REVIEW

THINK AND WRITE

A. What is the Ring of Fire?
B. What are the major physical features of the Pacific region?
C. Compare the climates of Alaska and Hawaii.
D. Name three natural resources of the Pacific region.

E. Which state has the largest population?

SKILLS CHECK

WRITING SKILL

Use the headings in this lesson to help you outline the major sections of the lesson. Add subheads to your outline to show additional detail.

USING THE VOCABULARY

Fall Line	Continental
canal	Divide
drought	fertile

On a separate sheet of paper, write your answers in complete sentences.

1. People built the _____ to connect the two waterways.
2. The _____ land had grown abundant crops for many years.
3. Early factories were built along the _____ .
4. Because of the _____ , crops cannot grow well.
5. The _____ affects the direction of the water flow in the Rocky Mountains.

REMEMBERING WHAT YOU READ

On a separate sheet of paper, write your answers in complete sentences.
1. Why is it important to study history and geography together?
2. How might geographers go about dividing a country into regions?
3. What are the five landform regions of the United States studied in this book?
4. Why is the region of the Central Plains called the Heartland of America?
5. What is the St. Lawrence Seaway?

TYING MATH TO SOCIAL STUDIES

On a separate sheet of paper copy the magic square shown here. You will use the words and definitions given here to make the magic square work. In each box of the square there is a letter that is the same as the letter of one of the definitions. In the box, write the **number** of the word that matches the definition. If your answers are correct, the numbers in each row going across and the numbers in each column going down will add up to the same number. Box **A** has been done for you.

A 12	B	C
D	E	F
G	H	I

The magic number is _____ .

1. textile
2. canyon
3. Piedmont
4. petroleum
5. harbor
6. earthquake
7. valley
8. landlocked
9. irrigate
10. river mouth
11. intermontane
12. Ring of Fire

A. An area of earthquakes and volcanos
B. A place where ships can anchor
C. Another word for cloth
D. Another word for oil
E. An area of high, hilly land
F. Between mountains
G. A deep, narrow cut through land
H. The end of a river
I. A violent shaking of the earth's surface
J. A long, low area of land, often between mountains or hills
K. An area without an outlet to an ocean
L. To bring water to farmland

THINKING CRITICALLY

On a separate sheet of paper, write your answers in complete sentences.

1. Is it easier to study geography if an area is divided into regions? Explain your answer.
2. Which region, do you think, has been changed the most by the people living there? Explain your answer.
3. Which region has been changed the least by people living there? Explain your answer.
4. What might people who live in the Ring of Fire belt do to protect themselves from danger?
5. In which region would you like to live? Tell why in a short paragraph or in a poem.

SUMMARIZING THE CHAPTER

On a separate sheet of paper, draw a graphic organizer like the one shown here. Copy the information from this graphic organizer to the one you have drawn. Under each heading, list five important features. The first one has been done for you.

CHAPTER THEME

The many and varied landforms of the United States make it easy for geographers to divide the land into physical regions.

LESSON 1

The Coastal Plain

1. Two parts
2. Pine forests and farmland
3. Half the nation's fish catch
4. Natural gas and petroleum
5. Busy ports

LESSON 2

The Appalachian Region

1. _____
2. _____
3. _____
4. _____
5. _____

LESSON 3

The Central Plains

1. _____
2. _____
3. _____
4. _____
5. _____

LESSON 4

The Mountain West

1. _____
2. _____
3. _____
4. _____
5. _____

LESSON 5

The Pacific Region

1. _____
2. _____
3. _____
4. _____
5. _____

2

THE UNITED STATES TODAY

The United States is a great industrial and agricultural power. Most Americans today live and work in or near large cities. Yet American farmers still produce enough to feed our country and many other parts of the world.

Where Americans Live

THINK ABOUT WHAT YOU KNOW

What is the place where you live like? Is it city or country? Do people live close to one another, or are homes spread out?

STUDY THE VOCABULARY

rural
urban
suburb
metropolitan
  area
megalopolis

population
  density
cartogram
Sunbelt
census

FOCUS YOUR READING

Where do people live in the United States?

A. Studying Geography by Topics

Today the population of the United States is about 254 million. Our country has the third largest population in the world. Only China and India have larger populations. And only Russia, Canada, and China have larger land areas.

Where do all these Americans live? How do they use the land? How do they make a living? You began to learn the answers to these important geography questions in Chapter 1, when you studied our country's landform regions. In this chapter you will study geography in another way —by *topics*. Studying geography by regions *and* topics will give you a more complete understanding of how the people of our nation have been affected by geography and how they have used the land.

B. Most Americans Live in Cities and Suburbs

From Farm to City Later in this book you will read about our country's early years,

when George Washington became our country's first President. That was more than 200 years ago. At that time nearly all Americans lived on the Atlantic Coastal Plain and in the Piedmont. Nearly all of them lived in **rural** areas — that is, on farms or in small villages.

How times have changed! And how America has grown! Today, Americans are spread all across our vast land, from the Atlantic to the Pacific Ocean and from Alaska in the north to Hawaii in the south. The table on page 66 shows the population of each of the states in the United States. Today nearly eight of every ten Americans live in **urban** areas. That is, they live in or near cities. The table on page 72 shows the 50 largest cities in the United States.

Large Populations This table showing our biggest cities doesn't show how much of America is urban today. That is because each of America's large cities is surrounded by many smaller towns called

Many Americans still live in rural communities like this one.
► How is this photo different from the one on page 64?

POPULATION BY STATE

State	Population in 1980	Population in 1990	Population in 2000 (Estimate)	Population in 2010 (Estimate)	Population Density per sq mi (per sq km)		Population Growth Rate Since 1980
Alabama	3,893,888	4,040,587	4,358,000	4,469,000	80	(31)	3.8
Alaska	401,851	550,403	599,000	669,000	1	(.4)	36.9
Arizona	2,718,215	3,665,228	4,633,000	5,537,000	32	(12)	34.8
Arkansas	2,286,435	2,350,725	2,509,000	2,559,000	45	(17)	2.8
California	23,667,902	29,760,021	33,963,000	38,096,000	190	(74)	25.7
Colorado	2,889,964	3,294,394	3,424,000	3,385,000	32	(12)	14.0
Connecticut	3,107,576	3,287,116	3,422,000	3,514,000	675	(261)	5.8
Delaware	594,338	666,168	802,000	933,000	345	(133)	12.1
Florida	9,746,324	12,937,926	16,315,000	19,702,000	239	(92)	32.7
Georgia	5,463,105	6,478,216	8,005,000	9,378,000	110	(43)	18.6
Hawaii	964,691	1,108,229	1,362,000	1,590,000	173	(67)	14.9
Idaho	943,935	1,006,749	1,008,000	985,000	12	(5)	6.7
Illinois	11,426,518	11,430,602	11,722,000	11,571,000	205	(79)	0.0
Indiana	5,490,224	5,544,159	5,696,000	5,655,000	154	(60)	1.0
Iowa	2,913,808	2,776,755	2,549,000	2,251,000	50	(19)	-4.7
Kansas	2,363,679	2,477,574	2,534,000	2,488,000	30	(12)	4.8
Kentucky	3,660,777	3,685,296	3,689,000	3,562,000	93	(36)	0.7
Louisiana	4,205,900	4,219,973	4,141,000	3,876,000	95	(37)	0.3
Maine	1,124,660	1,227,928	1,344,000	1,430,000	40	(15)	9.2
Maryland	4,216,975	4,781,468	5,608,000	6,446,000	486	(188)	13.4
Massachusetts	5,737,037	6,016,425	6,159,000	6,431,000	769	(297)	4.9
Michigan	9,262,078	9,295,297	9,365,000	9,301,000	163	(63)	0.4
Minnesota	4,075,970	4,375,099	4,566,000	4,632,000	55	(21)	7.3
Mississippi	2,520,638	2,573,216	2,772,000	2,858,000	55	(21)	2.1
Missouri	4,916,686	5,117,073	5,473,000	5,665,000	74	(29)	4.1
Montana	786,690	799,065	744,000	692,000	6	(2)	1.6
Nebraska	1,569,825	1,578,385	1,539,000	1,443,000	21	(8)	0.5
Nevada	800,493	1,201,833	1,409,000	1,618,000	11	(4)	50.1
New Hampshire	920,610	1,109,252	1,410,000	1,650,000	123	(48)	20.5
New Jersey	7,364,823	7,730,188	8,382,000	8,846,000	1,035	(400)	5.0
New Mexico	1,302,894	1,515,069	1,735,000	1,922,000	13	(5)	16.3
New York	17,558,072	17,990,455	17,966,000	18,129,000	380	(147)	2.5
North Carolina	5,881,766	6,628,637	7,717,000	8,735,000	136	(52)	12.7
North Dakota	652,717	638,800	596,000	531,000	9	(4)	-2.1
Ohio	10,797,630	10,847,115	10,930,000	10,803,000	265	(102)	0.5
Oklahoma	3,025,290	3,145,585	2,924,000	2,660,000	46	(27)	4.0
Oregon	2,633,105	2,842,321	2,903,000	2,922,000	30	(11)	7.9
Pennsylvania	11,863,895	11,881,643	12,069,000	12,038,000	265	(102)	0.1
Rhode Island	947,154	1,003,464	1,048,000	1,105,000	951	(367)	5.9
South Carolina	3,121,820	3,486,703	3,962,000	4,304,000	115	(44)	11.7
South Dakota	690,768	696,004	715,000	704,000	9	(4)	0.8
Tennessee	4,591,120	4,877,185	5,424,000	5,727,000	119	(46)	6.2
Texas	14,229,191	16,986,510	17,828,000	17,990,000	65	(25)	19.4
Utah	1,461,037	1,722,850	1,845,000	1,879,000	21	(8)	17.9
Vermont	511,456	562,758	619,000	658,000	61	(23)	10.0
Virginia	5,346,818	6,187,358	7,275,000	8,222,000	156	(60)	15.7
Washington	4,132,156	4,866,692	5,191,000	5,369,000	73	(28)	17.8
West Virginia	1,949,644	1,793,477	1,651,000	1,482,000	74	(29)	-8.0
Wisconsin	4,705,767	4,891,769	4,844,000	4,652,000	90	(35)	4.0
Wyoming	469,557	453,588	409,000	366,000	5	(2)	-3.4

This table shows the population of each state in 1980 and in 1990. It also estimates the population of each state in the years 2000 and 2010.

▶ Which state will have the largest population by the year 2010?

suburbs. The large city and its suburbs together form a **metropolitan** (me troh-PAHL ih tun) **area**.

The population of a metropolitan area may be several times greater than the population of its main city. For example, the city of Boston, Massachusetts, has a population of 574,283. But the population of the whole Boston metropolitan area is 4,171,643. The population of New York City is 7,322,564. But the population of the New York metropolitan area is 18,087,251.

In some parts of our nation, there is so little countryside remaining between cities that it is hard to tell where one city ends and another begins. This kind of urban area is called a **megalopolis** (meg uh-LAHP uh lihs). *Megalopolis* means "one very large city."

C. United States Population

Although the American people live in every part of the United States, some parts of the country are more heavily populated

THE UNITED STATES: MAJOR METROPOLITAN AREAS

Each of the metropolitan areas on this map has a population of at least 1,000,000. New York, with a population of 18,000,000 is the largest.
▶ What three metropolitan areas in Texas are shown?

than others. **Population density** is the measure of the number of people living in a square mile, or a square area whose sides are 1 mile (1.6 km) long. The more people per square mile, the higher the population density. The squares to the right will help you understand the idea of population density. Which has the higher density of dots, square *A* or *B*? Which has the higher density of dots, square *C* or *D*?

Look at the population density map below. You will see three large areas where the population is extremely dense. One

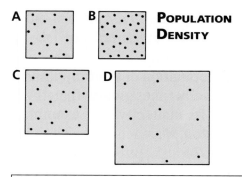

POPULATION DENSITY

Comparing these squares will help you understand population density.
▶ Does square A or square B have a lower density of dots?

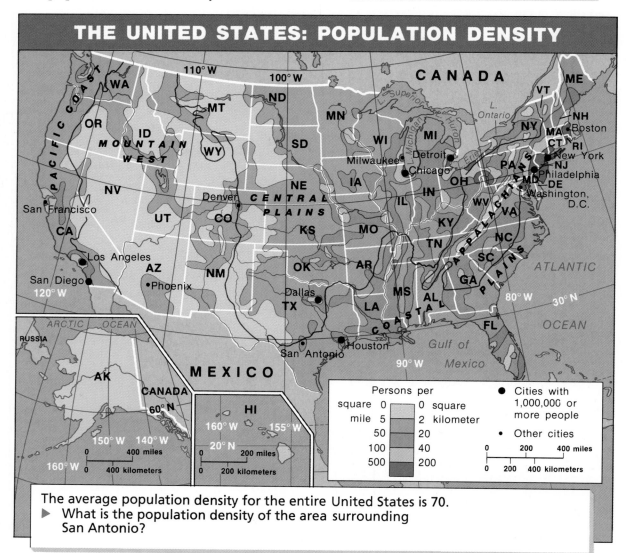

THE UNITED STATES: POPULATION DENSITY

Persons per		
square	0	0 square
mile	5	2 kilometer
	50	20
	100	40
	500	200

● Cities with 1,000,000 or more people

• Other cities

The average population density for the entire United States is 70.
▶ What is the population density of the area surrounding San Antonio?

area runs from a little north of Boston, Massachusetts, to a little south of Washington, D.C. A second area of very dense population is along the southern shores of the Great Lakes. A third densely populated area is in the West, stretching from San Diego to San Francisco in California. Each of these three areas is a megalopolis.

The table on page 66 shows the population density of each of our 50 states. Look up the population density of New Jersey. New Jersey has the highest population density of the 50 states. Next, look up the population density of Alaska. Alaska has the lowest population density. Now look for the population density of your state.

Most United States maps that you have studied show comparative sizes, or areas, of the states. The population density map on page 68 is one such map. Let's now see what the United States would look

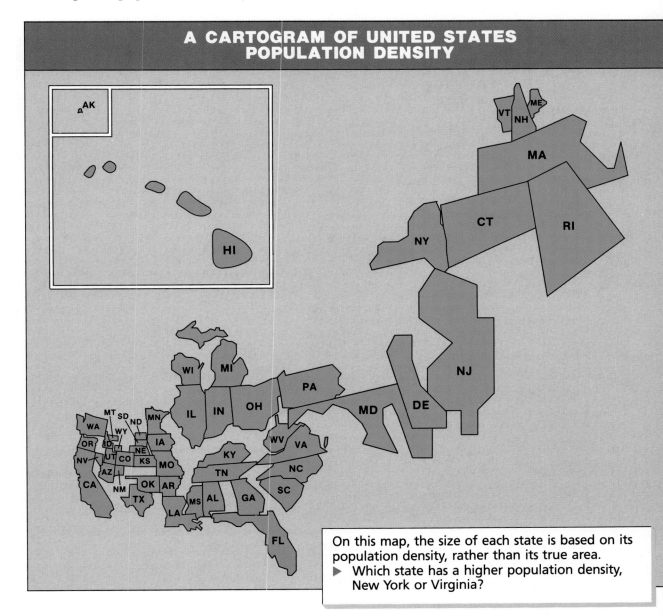

A CARTOGRAM OF UNITED STATES POPULATION DENSITY

On this map, the size of each state is based on its population density, rather than its true area.
▶ Which state has a higher population density, New York or Virginia?

like on a map that shows the states according to their population density rather than the actual size of their areas. To do this, a map maker must distort, or change, the size of each state so that the states with the greatest population density become the largest in area. The states with the lowest population density become the smallest in area.

On this kind of map, states such as Rhode Island, which has a high population density, are shown as very large states. States such as huge Alaska, which has a low population density, are shown as very small states. Maps that change the size of states or countries to have them represent something other than the true land areas are called **cartograms**.

D. A Belt of Fast Growth

Fast-Growing States In a country as large as ours, it is only natural that the

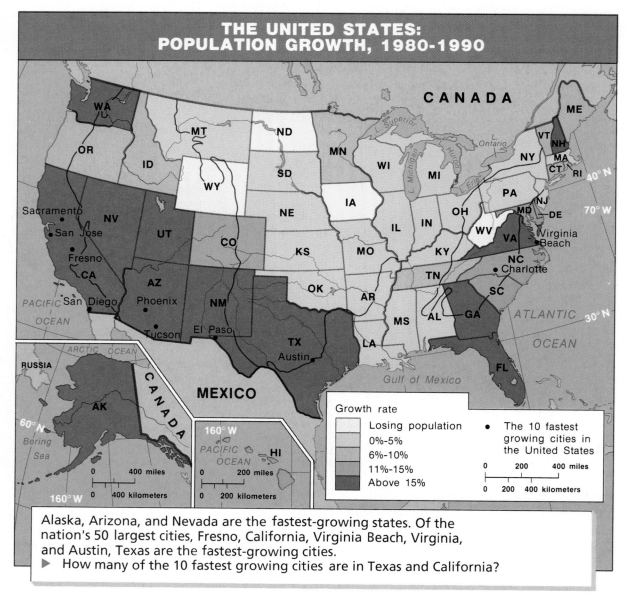

Alaska, Arizona, and Nevada are the fastest-growing states. Of the nation's 50 largest cities, Fresno, California, Virginia Beach, Virginia, and Austin, Texas are the fastest-growing cities.
▶ How many of the 10 fastest growing cities are in Texas and California?

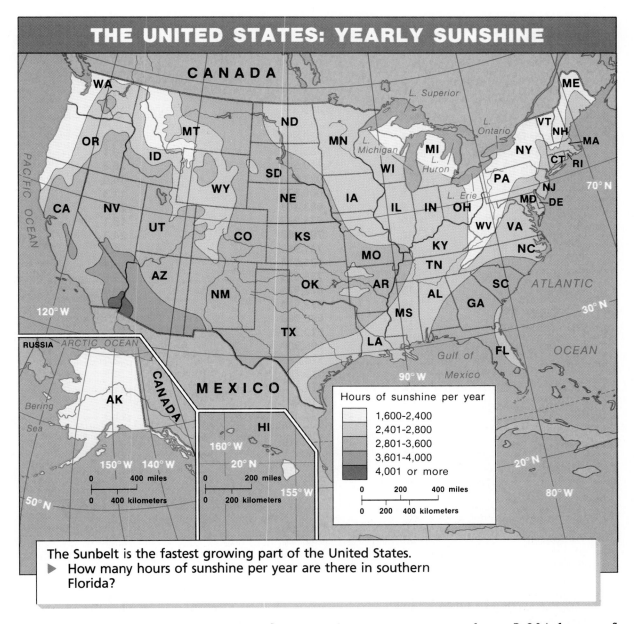

THE UNITED STATES: YEARLY SUNSHINE

Hours of sunshine per year

- 1,600–2,400
- 2,401–2,800
- 2,801–3,600
- 3,601–4,000
- 4,001 or more

The Sunbelt is the fastest growing part of the United States.
▶ How many hours of sunshine per year are there in southern Florida?

population of some areas will grow faster than that of others. On page 70 you will find a map that shows how much the population of each state in the United States has grown in recent years.

There are 14 states that have a growth rate of at least 11 percent. Now look at the map above. It shows the hours of sunshine the states get each year. You will find that most of the 14 fastest-growing states are also among the states that have a great deal of sunshine. These states, or parts of these states, get at least 2,801 hours of sunshine a year.

These states are located in an area that is known as the **Sunbelt.** The Sunbelt stretches across the lower third of the United States. The states in this region receive a lot of sunshine and are warm much of the year.

Pleasant climate is one reason for the rapid growth of the states in the Sunbelt. Jobs are another. Many of the new industries that have grown up in America, such

THE UNITED STATES: 50 LARGEST CITIES

City	Rank	Population	Population Growth Rate: 1980–1990
New York, NY	1	7,322,564	3.5
Los Angeles, CA	2	3,485,398	17.4
Chicago, IL	3	2,783,726	-7.4
Houston, TX	4	1,630,553	2.2
Philadelphia, PA	5	1,585,577	-6.1
San Diego, CA	6	1,110,549	26.8
Detroit, MI	7	1,027,974	-14.6
Dallas, TX	8	1,006,877	11.3
Phoenix, AZ	9	983,403	24.5
San Antonio, TX	10	935,933	19.1
San Jose, CA	11	782,248	24.3
Indianapolis, IN	12	741,952	4.3
Baltimore, MD	13	736,014	-6.4
San Francisco, CA	14	723,959	6.6
Jacksonville, FL	15	672,971	17.9
Columbus, OH	16	632,910	12.0
Milwaukee, WI	17	628,088	-1.3
Memphis, TN	18	610,337	-5.5
Washington, DC	19	606,900	-4.9
Boston, MA	20	574,283	2.0
Seattle, WA	21	516,259	4.5
El Paso, TX	22	515,342	21.2
Nashville, TN	23	510,784	6.9
Cleveland, OH	24	505,616	-11.9
New Orleans, LA	25	496,938	-10.9
Denver, CO	26	467,610	-5.1
Austin, TX	27	465,622	34.6
Fort Worth, TX	28	447,619	16.2
Oklahoma City, OK	29	444,719	10.1
Portland, OR	30	437,319	18.8
Kansas City, MO	31	435,146	-2.9
Long Beach, CA	32	429,433	18.8
Tucson, AZ	33	405,390	22.6
St. Louis, MO	34	396,685	-12.4
Charlotte, NC	35	395,934	25.5
Atlanta, GA	36	394,017	-7.3
Virginia Beach, VA	37	393,069	49.9
Albuquerque, NM	38	384,736	15.6
Oakland, CA	39	372,242	9.7
Pittsburgh, PA	40	369,879	-12.8
Sacramento, CA	41	369,365	34.0
Minneapolis, MN	42	368,383	-0.7
Tulsa, OK	43	367,302	1.8
Honolulu, HI	44	365,272	0.1
Cincinnati, OH	45	364,040	-5.5
Miami, FL	46	358,548	3.4
Fresno, CA	47	354,202	62.9
Omaha, NE	48	335,795	7.0
Toledo, OH	49	332,943	-6.1
Buffalo, NY	50	328,123	-8.3

This table shows the rate at which the populations of some cities in the United States changed between 1980 and 1990.

► What is the population growth rate of San Diego?

In many of the Sunbelt states, making computers and computer parts is an important industry.
► Have you ever used a computer?

as the aerospace industry and the computer industry, are located in the Sunbelt.

Checking Our Population Of course, no one knows exactly what changes will take place between now and the year 2010. However, the United States Bureau of the Census offers us an estimate, or a reasonable guess. The word **census** (SEN sus) means "count," and that is what the Bureau of the Census does. Every ten years it makes a count of the American people. It also gathers a great deal of other useful information about where and how Americans live.

The table on page 66 shows the Bureau of the Census estimate for the population of each state in the year 2010. Which state is the second in population now? Which will be the second in 2010? Where will your state rank in 2010?

LESSON *1* REVIEW

THINK AND WRITE

A. What are two ways of studying geography?

B. What is a megalopolis?

C. Which state is most densely populated? Which is least densely populated?

D. Give two reasons for the growth of the Sunbelt.

SKILLS CHECK

WRITING SKILL

Look at the table on page 66. Using complete sentences, describe five changes in population that the Bureau of the Census expects will take place between now and 2010.

CITIZENSHIP AND AMERICAN VALUES

YOU DECIDE:
WHAT WILL HAPPEN TO THE FOREST?

Most countries in the world have problems with land use. Progress and growth often mean turning forests and farms into housing and industrial projects. Conflict arises between developers and the people who say it is important to keep land as it is. The following story is an example of this conflict.

Not far from a middle-sized city is a large forest. Map *A* shows the boundaries of the city and the location of the forest. The forest is home to much wildlife, some of it quite rare. The people who live in the city enjoy walking and picnicking in the forest. The city even built a campground there. People love to camp out overnight and get away from the city for a short while.

Last year things began to happen to the forest. First, the city leaders voted to add the forest to the city. Map *B* shows the new boundaries of the city. Then, a few months later, something else happened. The city leaders were thinking seriously of letting a large company build some big apartment houses in a portion of the forest. The company was going to pay the city a large amount of money to be able to use the land. The city leaders felt they could use the money to provide better services for the people in the city. But the city leaders had to call a meeting before they could decide to let the company use the forest land. They had to find out how the people felt about it.

The people of the city were divided at the meeting. Some wanted the apartment houses to be built. Others did not want the forest disturbed. Here is a list of some of the arguments the city leaders heard at the meeting.

1. Our city is growing. We need more houses.
2. There will not be enough land left for nature study if part of the forest is used for apartment buildings.
3. The apartments will bring new people to the city. This will be good for the stores in the city.
4. Not everyone uses the forest. The land will be more useful for more people if the apartment houses are built.
5. There will be no place nearby for people to get away from the city if the forest is used for apartment houses.

6. The money the city gets can be used to build parks and playgrounds in other parts of the city.
7. This forest was here for our parents and our grandparents. What will we leave for our children?
8. What will happen to the rare birds and animals that live in the forest?
9. We have to be willing to accept changes in the way we live if we want our city to grow.

Thinking for Yourself

On a separate sheet of paper, write your answers using complete sentences.

1. Group the people's arguments in two categories — those for and those against the building of the apartments.
2. What would you do if you were a city leader? Should the forest be kept as it is or should the apartments be built? Be prepared to defend your choice.
3. Are there any problems in your community similar to this one? What are the arguments on each side of the issue? Which side do you favor?

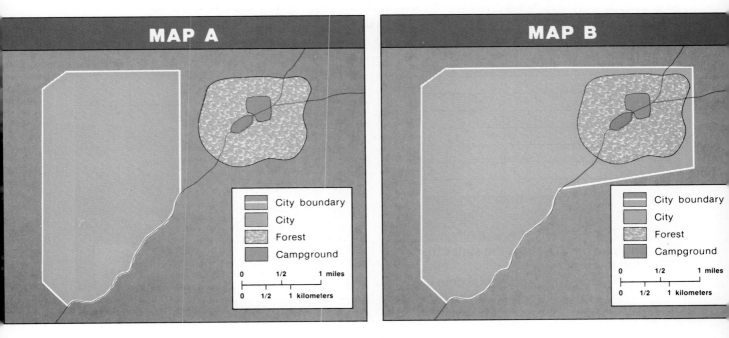

| MAP A | MAP B |

Map A legend:
- City boundary
- City
- Forest
- Campground

0   1/2   1 miles
0   1/2   1 kilometers

Map B legend:
- City boundary
- City
- Forest
- Campground

0   1/2   1 miles
0   1/2   1 kilometers

Producing Food for Our Nation and the World

THINK ABOUT WHAT YOU KNOW

Read the labels on a variety of containers or packages of food that you have at home. Make a list of all the states where the food was grown or packaged.

STUDY THE VOCABULARY

gasahol   **conserve**
renewable resource

FOCUS YOUR READING

How have America's farms become so productive in modern times?

A. America's Farms

World's Most Productive Another great change since our country's early years is in the way Americans make their living. Two hundred years ago, about 90 of every 100 Americans made their living by farming. Today fewer than 3 of every 100 Americans farm for a living.

You might think that with so few people farming, the United States is not an important farming country. But just the opposite is true. The United States is the most important farming country in the world. Our farms produce more than half the world's supply of soybeans and nearly half its supply of corn. In addition the United States produces about 15 percent of all the wheat, cotton, and tobacco grown in the entire world.

American farmers also raise a large amount of fruits and vegetables and produce a great deal of hog, beef, and dairy products. Much of what we grow is sold to other countries.

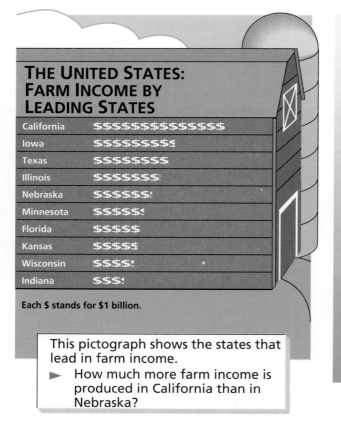

THE UNITED STATES: FARM INCOME BY LEADING STATES

California	$$$$$$$$$$$$$
Iowa	$$$$$$$$$
Texas	$$$$$$$$
Illinois	$$$$$$$
Nebraska	$$$$$$
Minnesota	$$$$$
Florida	$$$$$
Kansas	$$$$$
Wisconsin	$$$$
Indiana	$$$

Each $ stands for $1 billion.

This pictograph shows the states that lead in farm income.
► How much more farm income is produced in California than in Nebraska?

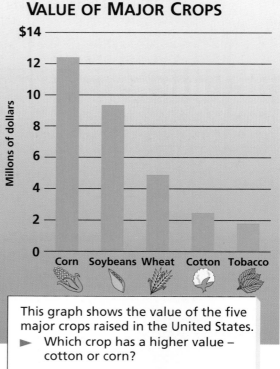

THE UNITED STATES: VALUE OF MAJOR CROPS

Millions of dollars

Corn   Soybeans   Wheat   Cotton   Tobacco

This graph shows the value of the five major crops raised in the United States.
► Which crop has a higher value – cotton or corn?

76

Today, with the use of new machinery and methods, farms in the United States are the most productive in the world.
▶ What crop is being harvested?

New Farming Methods How is it possible for so few farmers to raise so much food? The answer is that American farmers have learned methods that are amazingly efficient. By using fertilizers and improved seed, a few farmers can grow large crops. By using modern machinery, today's farmers can plant, cultivate, and harvest as much land in a few minutes as farmers once did in a whole day. On the average, one American farmer produces enough food for 80 people.

B. Crops Are Grown in All Parts of Our Country

All States Contribute Every state in our country makes a contribution to this great agricultural production. Some states produce an especially large amount.

On pages 78 and 79 you will see four maps that show how much corn, wheat, cotton, and soybeans are produced in each state. Also, on page 80 you will see a table listing each state's rank in agricultural production. These maps and table will give you a clearer picture of our country's agricultural production.

Corn As you can see from the table, corn earns more income for American farmers than any other crop. There are two kinds of corn—sweet corn and field corn. Sweet corn is the kind people eat—straight from the cob, frozen, canned, or even popped. Most corn, however, is field corn, which is raised mainly to be fed to animals.

Scientists have developed other uses for corn, too. Corn is sometimes used in making certain plastics and fiberboard as well as in paint products, such as varnish and shellac. An important and surprising new use for corn is as a fuel for cars.

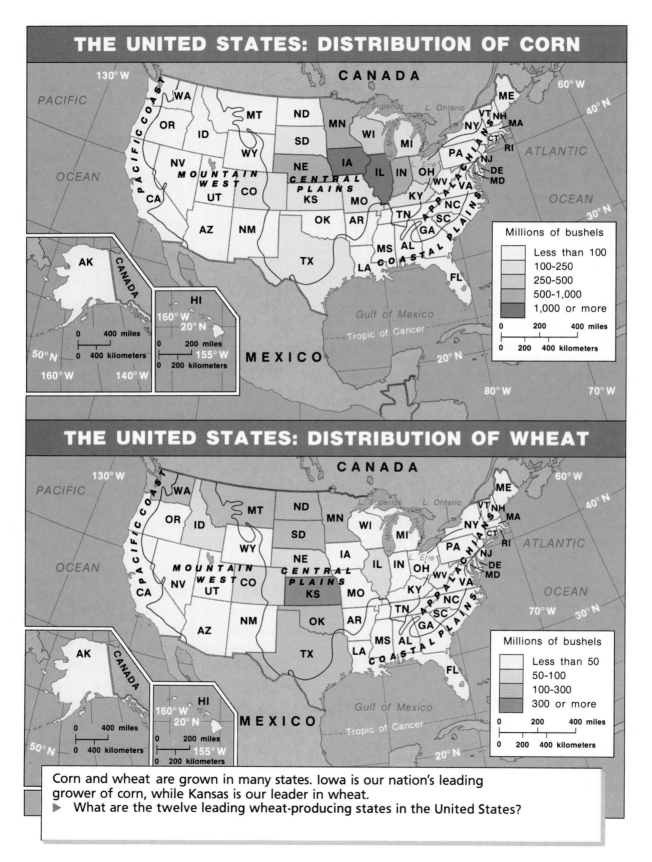

THE UNITED STATES: DISTRIBUTION OF CORN

Millions of bushels
- Less than 100
- 100-250
- 250-500
- 500-1,000
- 1,000 or more

THE UNITED STATES: DISTRIBUTION OF WHEAT

Millions of bushels
- Less than 50
- 50-100
- 100-300
- 300 or more

Corn and wheat are grown in many states. Iowa is our nation's leading grower of corn, while Kansas is our leader in wheat.

▶ What are the twelve leading wheat-producing states in the United States?

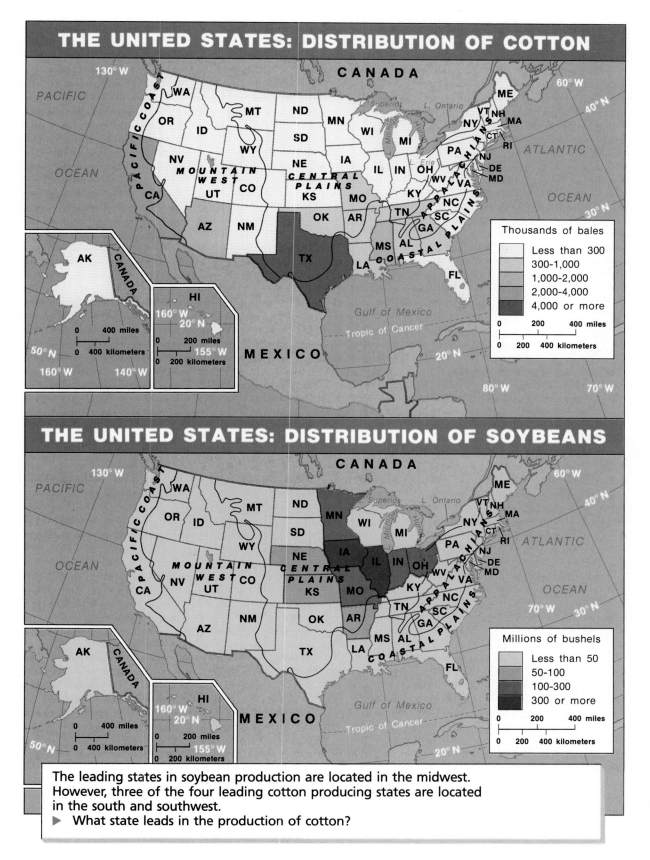

THE UNITED STATES: DISTRIBUTION OF COTTON

Thousands of bales

- Less than 300
- 300–1,000
- 1,000–2,000
- 2,000–4,000
- 4,000 or more

THE UNITED STATES: DISTRIBUTION OF SOYBEANS

Millions of bushels

- Less than 50
- 50–100
- 100–300
- 300 or more

The leading states in soybean production are located in the midwest.
However, three of the four leading cotton producing states are located
in the south and southwest.

▶ What state leads in the production of cotton?

RANKING OF UNITED STATES AGRICULTURAL PRODUCTION BY STATE

State	Cattle	Corn	Cotton	Oranges	Soybeans	Tobacco	Vegetables	Wheat
Alabama	23	26	8				28	32
Alaska	49							
Arizona	34	40	6	3			7	30
Arkansas	18	33	5		8		30	17
California	6	23	2	2			1	14
Colorado	11	14				13	13	9
Connecticut	45						31	
Delaware	48	29					22	36
Florida	16	32	15	1		9	2	37
Georgia	25	19	10		17	6	29	23
Hawaii	42						32	
Idaho	24	34					12	11
Illinois	15	2			2		14	12
Indiana	27	5			4	10	15	16
Iowa	5	1			1		26	41
Kansas	2	11	17					1
Kentucky	12	13			15	2		21
Louisiana	33	24	4		12		33	33
Maine	43							21
Maryland	40	21				8	20	29
Massachusetts	46					15	27	
Michigan	32	10			11		9	19
Minnesota	10	4			3		5	7
Mississippi	28	27	3		9			24
Missouri	7	8	11		5	12		15
Montana	13	41						3
Nebraska	3	3			7			10
Nevada	38							38
New Hampshire	47							
New Jersey	44	30					16	40
New Mexico	29	31	13				17	25
New York	21	17					8	35
North Carolina	35	16	14		13	1	19	20
North Dakota	20	20			18			2
Ohio	19	6			6		10	13
Oklahoma	4	35	9					4
Oregon	26	37					4	18
Pennsylvania	17	15				7	18	31
Rhode Island	50							
South Carolina	37	22	12		16	3	21	26
South Dakota	9	9			10			6
Tennessee	14	18	7		14	4	23	22
Texas	1	12	1	4			11	8
Utah	36	39					24	27
Vermont	41							
Virginia	22	25	16		20	5	25	39
Washington	30	28					6	5
West Virginia	39	38				14		42
Wisconsin	8	7			19	11	3	34
Wyoming	31	36						28

The table above shows how the states rank in the production of some major crops and cattle.

► What state is the leading producer of both cattle and cotton?

80

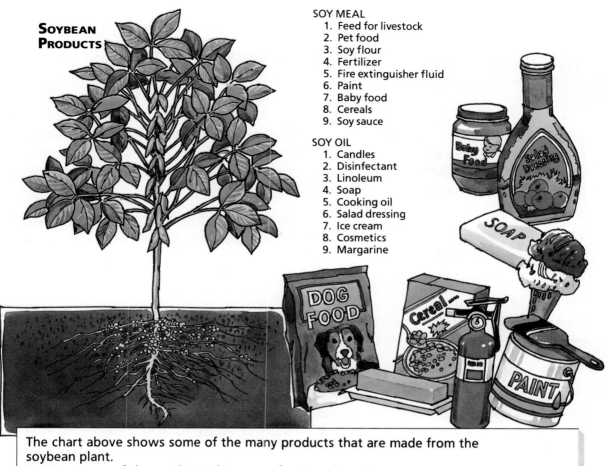

SOYBEAN PRODUCTS

SOY MEAL
1. Feed for livestock
2. Pet food
3. Soy flour
4. Fertilizer
5. Fire extinguisher fluid
6. Paint
7. Baby food
8. Cereals
9. Soy sauce

SOY OIL
1. Candles
2. Disinfectant
3. Linoleum
4. Soap
5. Cooking oil
6. Salad dressing
7. Ice cream
8. Cosmetics
9. Margarine

The chart above shows some of the many products that are made from the soybean plant.
▶ How many of the products shown are food products?

The corn is turned into alcohol, which is mixed with gasoline to make **gasohol**. Gasohol is cheaper than gasoline, and it does not pollute the air as much.

Corn is a **renewable resource**. A renewable resource is one that people or nature can replace in a reasonable period of time. Petroleum, which gasoline is made from, is not a renewable resource. Therefore, using gasohol can help us **conserve**, or use wisely, our natural resources. Gasohol is now sold in a number of states.

Soybeans Soybeans, like corn, are grown mainly for animal feed. Because soybeans provide the same kind of nutrition as meat, eggs, and cheese, they are also a favorite food of vegetarians, or people who do not eat meat or meat products. In addition, cooking oil is often made from soybeans.

LESSON **2** REVIEW

THINK AND WRITE

A. Name two things that American farmers have done to make their farms more productive.
B. Describe the uses of two major crops grown in the United States.

SKILLS CHECK

MAP SKILL

Use the maps on pages 78 and 79 to make a list of the leading states in the production of cotton, wheat, corn, and soybeans.

Producing Goods and Services

THINK ABOUT WHAT YOU KNOW

List as many different kinds of workers as you can think of. Then add your list to those of your classmates to see how many your class can come up with.

STUDY THE VOCABULARY

occupation   services
goods

FOCUS YOUR READING

How do people in our country earn a living?

A. New Kinds of Jobs Are Created Every Year

Many Kinds of Jobs If most Americans no longer farm, what kinds of work do they do for a living? For the answer to this question, we can turn to a book published by the United States government. The book is called *Dictionary of Occupational Titles*. An **occupation** is a job, or kind of work. You will be amazed to find that the *Dictionary of Occupational Titles* lists more than 20,000 different kinds of jobs that Americans do!

And new kinds of jobs are created every year. One hundred years ago no one had even heard of a computer. Today more than a million Americans make their living in hundreds of different jobs connected with computers.

Goods Workers Usually we group these many different kinds of workers into two large categories. One category is made up of people who produce **goods**. Goods are things that can be sold. People who work in farming, manufacturing, mining, and construction all produce goods.

Service Workers The second category is made up of people who provide **services**. A service is an activity performed for the benefit of other people. Bus drivers provide a service. Teachers, nurses, salespeople, computer operators, plumbers, baseball players, and firefighters provide services, too.

Manufacturing A large number of Americans work in manufacturing jobs. Just as in agriculture, every state contributes to our nation's production of manufactured goods. Some states have become especially important centers of manufacturing. The bar graph on the next page shows the ten leading manufacturing states in the United States.

B. Providing Services

Service Workers Everywhere In America's early days, most people worked to produce goods. Those who did not farm made cloth or shoes, built furniture, or made other needed goods by hand.

Today more and more computers are being used in service industries.
► What are some ways that computers make service jobs easier?

82

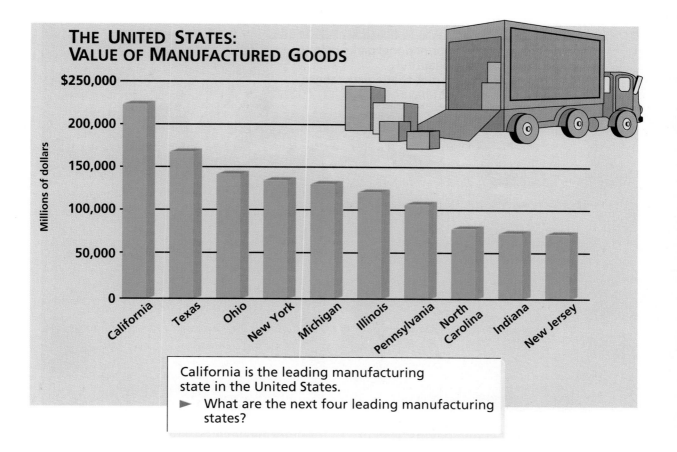

THE UNITED STATES: VALUE OF MANUFACTURED GOODS

Millions of dollars

$250,000
200,000
150,000
100,000
50,000
0

California · Texas · Ohio · New York · Michigan · Illinois · Pennsylvania · North Carolina · Indiana · New Jersey

California is the leading manufacturing state in the United States.
► What are the next four leading manufacturing states?

Over time, machines have been invented that produce mountains of goods. As a result, people are freed to do other kinds of service work. In fact, today far more Americans earn a living by providing services than by producing goods.

When we looked at agriculture and manufacturing, we could note the individual states that were the leading producers of certain crops or goods. But every town and city needs police, doctors, firefighters, teachers, and mail carriers. So those who work in services are spread pretty evenly across our country.

Special Cities A few places in the United States specialize in providing one or more services. For example, the cities of New York and Los Angeles are the major centers of the entertainment industry.

The cities of Chicago, Atlanta, New York, Newark, Denver, and San Francisco are important transportation centers. All these cities have major airports. Hartford, Newark, San Francisco, and New York are important insurance centers, and New York is the leading financial, or banking, center in the world.

The Tourist Industry One of our largest service industries is the tourist industry. Tourist attractions can be found in every one of our 50 states. Certain places, however, specialize in tourism. Big cities like New York, Chicago, Los Angeles, and New Orleans draw millions of tourists every year. People flock to Cape Canaveral, Florida, to see the Kennedy Space Center. Disneyland in California and Disney World in Florida are favorite attractions for young

Government workers in our national parks help to keep the parks safe and beautiful.
▶ Can you name some duties that a park ranger at a national park might have?

and old. When the snow begins to fall, thousands of skiers head for the mountains of Utah, Colorado, and Vermont. That same winter weather makes many others head for the sunny beaches of southern Florida, southern California, and Hawaii. America's wonderful national parks are other tourist attractions.

Government Workers The largest employers of service workers in our country are the federal, state, and local governments. More than 18 million people work for various levels of government. These people provide services to us every day of the year. There are police officers and firefighters. There are librarians, teachers, and county farm agents. Judges, mail carriers, and park rangers are all service workers.

One of the largest groups of people who work for the United States government is the military. About 2 million men and women work in the military forces. They serve on military bases in our country and in many other countries around the world.

LESSON 3 REVIEW

THINK AND WRITE

A. What are the two major categories of jobs?
B. Name three kinds of service jobs in the United States.

SKILLS CHECK

THINKING SKILL
Look at the graph of the ten leading manufacturing states on page 83. Are most of these states found east or west of the Mississippi River?

USING THE VOCABULARY

rural   census
urban   renewable resource
megalopolis   conserve
population   occupations
  density services
Sunbelt

From the list choose the term that means nearly the same as the underlined words in the sentence. Write your answers on a separate sheet of paper.

1. It is important to <u>save</u> our resources.
2. Many people want to live in the <u>places where the climate is warm and sunny for most of the year</u>.
3. There is so little countryside remaining between New York and Boston that the area could be called a <u>single very large city</u>.
4. Jobs today are divided into jobs that produce goods and jobs that are <u>performed for the benefit of others</u>.
5. The <u>number of people living in smaller states</u> of the Northwest is great.
6. Most Americans lived in <u>countryside</u> areas in the early years of our country's history.
7. Inventions can create many new <u>kinds of work</u>.
8. A <u>count of the population</u> is taken every ten years.
9. Petroleum is not a <u>replaceable material</u> once it has been taken from the ground.
10. Today more people live near <u>city</u> areas than in the countryside.

REMEMBERING WHAT YOU READ

On a separate sheet of paper, write your answers in complete sentences.

1. What are suburbs?
2. Which state in the United States has the lowest population density?
3. Why is the Sunbelt the fastest-growing area in the United States?
4. Which is the most important farming country in the world?
5. What are the most important farm crops grown in the United States?
6. List five uses for corn.
7. Into what two categories can workers be divided?
8. What are the two major centers of the entertainment industry?
9. What are three important transportation centers in the United States?
10. What is the world's leading banking center?

TYING SCIENCE TO SOCIAL STUDIES

You have learned that scientists have discovered many uses for corn and soybeans. Look in science books or other books in the library to find information about other plants for which many uses have been found. Choose a plant and make a chart like the one on page 81 to show how the plant can be used.

THINKING CRITICALLY

On a separate sheet of paper, write your answers in complete sentences.

1. Why will Rhode Island probably always appear greater in size than most Sunbelt states on a cartogram showing population density?
2. Do you think it possible that one day the eastern coast of the United States will be one huge megalopolis? Be prepared to explain your answer.
3. Why is agriculture still important in the United States even though the number of farmers is decreasing?
4. Make a list of at least five renewable resources.
5. What occupations do you think will be important by the time you are ready to work?

SUMMARIZING THE CHAPTER

On a separate sheet of paper, draw a graphic organizer like the one shown here. Copy the information from this graphic organizer to the one you have drawn. Under the main idea for each lesson, write three statements that support the main idea. The first one has been done for you.

CHAPTER THEME

Today most Americans live in urban areas or in the surrounding suburbs and work in service industries. Agriculture is still an important part of the economy, however.

LESSON 1

There have been many changes in where the American people live.

1. Rural areas
2. Metropolitan areas
3. Sunbelt

LESSON 2

Farming is very important in the United States.

1.
2.
3.

LESSON 3

There are many ways to earn a living in the United States.

1.
2.
3.

COOPERATIVE LEARNING

In this unit you learned about the geography of the United States. There are many landforms and climates. The country is rich in natural resources. You also learned how people used the land in the past and how they are using it today.

PROJECT

Your teacher will assign one of the regions you studied in Chapter 1 to your group. Your group project is to create a bulletin-board display that tells about the region. The bulletin board will show information about the physical features, the climate, the natural resources, the largest cities, and the recreation and tourist areas in the region. In addition it will show how many people live in the region and how they earn their living.

Hold a group meeting to plan the bulletin board. Study Chapters 1 and 2 to find the information you will need. Decide how best to present this information. At this point, be sure that everyone in your group is encouraged to share his or her ideas and that everyone listens carefully as others speak. Choose someone to record the group's suggestions.

Divide tasks among group members. Your group might decide to assign the following tasks.

● Draw a map of the region, locating important physical features and major cities.

● Make signs and labels.

● Look through old magazines for pictures of natural resources, recreation areas, and tourist attractions.

● Make charts and graphs to show climate, population, and ways that people earn their living.

● Coordinate the project and help the other group members.

Hold another group meeting when each person has finished his or her part of the project. Under the leadership of the coordinator, discuss the way the bulletin board will look. What colors should be used? How should the material be arranged?

PRESENTATION AND REVIEW

● Display your group's work for the class.

● Allow time for the class to study the bulletin board.

● Answer any questions.

● Ask your classmates to evaluate how well the group has presented the information about the region.

The group should meet for a final time to evaluate its own work.

● How did people react to the bulletin board?

● What things would you do differently the next time you had to do a bulletin board?

● How well did you work together?

REMEMBER TO:
- Give your ideas.
- Listen to others' ideas.
- Plan your work with the group.
- Present your project.
- Discuss how your group worked.

Understanding SKILLBUILDER Graphs

A. WHY DO I NEED THIS SKILL?

Graphs present information in a visual way. They show facts in ways that are clear and easy to read. When facts are organized in a graph, it is easier to understand the facts and to see the relationships between them.

B. Learning the Skill

There are different kinds of graphs. The most common are pie graphs, bar graphs, line graphs, and pictographs. The graphs shown here are all about the population of the United States. The numbers used in each graph are based on population figures that were compiled by the Bureau of the Census after the 1990 census was taken.

A **pie graph** is used to show and compare percentages, or parts of a whole. Each part represents a certain percentage—a part of the whole pie. The pie graph on the next page shows the distribution of population in the United States by census regions. The whole circle stands for 100 percent—the total population—of the United States. Each slice stands for a region and the percentage of the total population that lives in that region. You can also compare the regions with each other.

A **bar graph** can also be used to compare information. The bar graph shows the population of each state and also ranks the states by size of population. The top of the graph is labeled *Millions of Persons*. The graph is divided into segments that each measure 2 million persons. The names of the states, using the post office abbreviations,

are shown at the left side of the graph. Each bar that extends from the left side shows the 1990 population for that state. By studying the length of the bars, you can compare the sizes of populations of various states.

A **line graph** is used to show change over time. The line graph shows how the median age of the people of the United States has changed from 1800 to 1990. The median age is the middle number that results from comparing the ages of all the people. The median age is lower when the greater part of the population is made up of young people.

A **pictograph** is a graph that uses pictures or symbols to show amounts. To see an example of a pictograph, turn to page 569 in Chapter 24. That graph shows the number of households in the United States that have television sets.

C. PRACTICING THE SKILL

Answer the following questions to see if you are able to read the graphs. Write your answers on a separate sheet of paper.

1. Which region has the largest percentage of the national population?
2. About how many people does the Census Bureau think lived in the state of California in 1990?
3. How many states have populations of fewer than two million?
4. Until what year did the median age in the United States continue to go up?
5. What was the median age of the United States population in 1990?

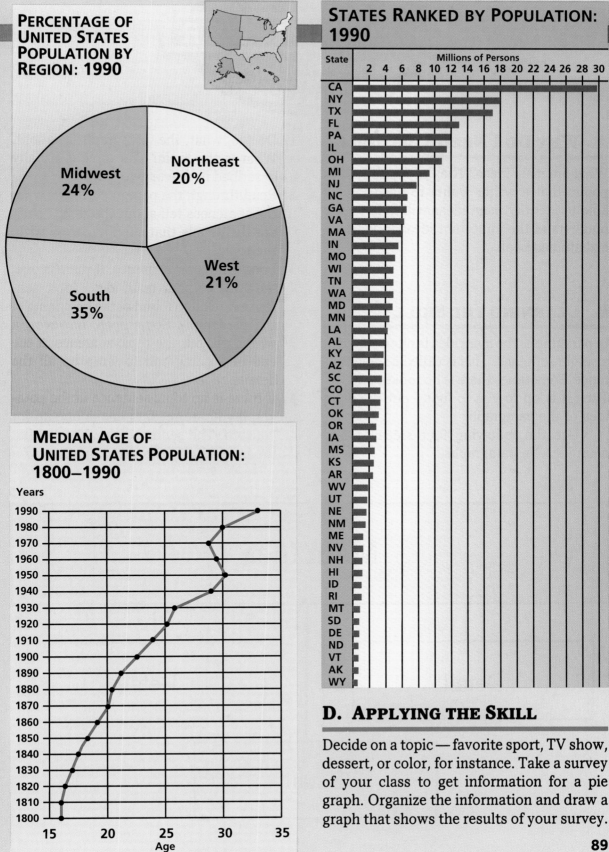

PERCENTAGE OF UNITED STATES POPULATION BY REGION: 1990

- Northeast 20%
- Midwest 24%
- West 21%
- South 35%

MEDIAN AGE OF UNITED STATES POPULATION: 1800–1990

Years

1990, 1980, 1970, 1960, 1950, 1940, 1930, 1920, 1910, 1900, 1890, 1880, 1870, 1860, 1850, 1840, 1830, 1820, 1810, 1800

Age: 15, 20, 25, 30, 35

STATES RANKED BY POPULATION: 1990

State	Millions of Persons

Millions of Persons: 2 4 6 8 10 12 14 16 18 20 22 24 26 28 30

States: CA, NY, TX, FL, PA, IL, OH, MI, NJ, NC, GA, VA, MA, IN, MO, WI, TN, WA, MD, MN, LA, AL, KY, AZ, SC, CO, CT, OK, OR, IA, MS, KS, AR, WV, UT, NE, NM, ME, NV, NH, HI, ID, RI, MT, SD, DE, ND, VT, AK, WY

D. APPLYING THE SKILL

Decide on a topic — favorite sport, TV show, dessert, or color, for instance. Take a survey of your class to get information for a pie graph. Organize the information and draw a graph that shows the results of your survey.

89

Recognizing SKILLBUILDER Main Ideas

A. WHY DO I NEED THIS SKILL?

What are main ideas? They're the important points that a writer wants to make. Being able to identify main ideas will help you to understand the important ideas in your social studies book.

B. LEARNING THE SKILL

In paragraphs the main idea is often stated in a single sentence. This is called a topic sentence. Sometimes there is no topic sentence. Then it is up to you to figure out the main idea of the paragraph.

   Use the following four steps to find main ideas in paragraphs.

1. Decide what the paragraph is about. What is the topic? The topic is usually described in one or two words.
2. Read through the paragraph to see what the sentences tell about the topic. What are the details that support, or go with, the topic.
3. Look for a topic sentence. If there is one, that will be your main idea. Topic sentences are often found at the beginning of the paragraph. Sometimes, however, a writer will put the topic sentence at the end of a paragraph to wrap up all the details.
4. If there is no topic sentence in the paragraph you are reading, make one up for yourself. The sentence should tell what the main idea of the paragraph is.

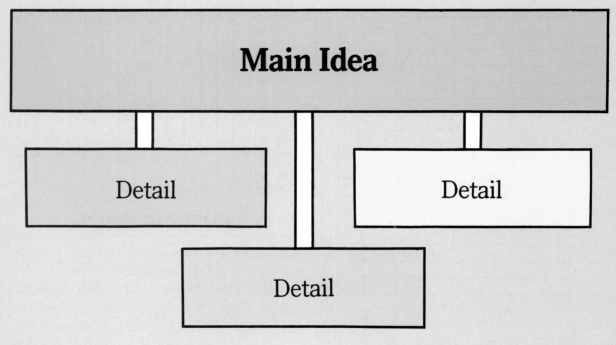

C. PRACTICING THE SKILL

Try to figure out the main idea for the paragraphs in the boxes on this page, using the four steps. Notice that the details in the paragraph support the main idea.

On a separate sheet of paper, draw and fill in a graphic organizer like the one on page 90 for each paragraph. Only one of the paragraphs has a topic sentence. You will have to write a topic sentence for the paragraph that does not have one.

The rich soil is one of the greatest natural resources of the Central Plains. Still other riches lie beneath the soil. In Minnesota and Michigan, the northern part of the region, are deposits of iron ore. Running down the central part of the region is a huge field of coal. Important oil fields lie to the south.

Why is this book about both history and geography? Why do we begin our story of the American people with a review of American geography? The reasons are that in order to understand how people lived, you must first learn about the places where they lived. To understand how people used the land, you must first know what the land was like. History and geography, you see, go hand in hand.

D. APPLYING THE SKILL

Turn back to Chapter 2, "The United States Today." Read the paragraphs under the section "A. America's Farms," which begins on page 76. On a separate sheet of paper, write the main idea or topic sentence for each paragraph. You will have to make up a topic sentence of your own if you think a paragraph does not have one.

Unit **2**

A NEW WORLD

The New World was settled by many groups of people. The first people to come to the Americas arrived many thousands of years ago.

▶ *The silver alpaca (left) and the llama (right) are examples of the fine artwork that came from the Inca Empire.*

3 THE FIRST AMERICANS

★ ★ ★ ★

The first Americans probably came from Asia thousands of years ago. As time passed, the people spread throughout North America and South America, dividing into separate groups. They developed cultures suited to the areas they lived in and, in three places, also developed great civilizations.

Learning About the First Americans

Suppose someone who knew very little about your community visited your home. What could the visitor learn about how you live by studying the things in your home?

prehistoric	mammoth
strait	artifact
migration	archaeologist

What have archaeologists learned about America's past?

A. Native Americans Arrive from Asia

As you learned in Unit 1, the land of North America is large and varied, with great beauty and many resources. No one knows for sure exactly when people first lived on this vast land. Scientists, looking for clues about **prehistoric** times, believe that for many thousands of years, North and South America were without people. *Prehistoric* means "before written accounts of the past."

Many thousands of years ago the continents of North and South America were without people. Animals large and small roamed the land freely, but no human had ever set foot on it. No humans had paddled down the rivers or gazed upon the mountains or left footprints on the sandy beaches of these continents.

It was not until about 30,000 years ago that the first people arrived on the continents of North and South America.

Scientists believe that these people came from the continent of Asia. Scientists also believe that these early people got here by walking.

A look at the map on this page shows that today it is not possible to walk from Asia to North America. Find Asia on the map. You can see that even in the far north, where Asia and North America are closest to each other, they are separated by a body of water called the *Bering Strait.* Find the Bering Strait on the map. A **strait** is a narrow body of water that joins two larger bodies of water. The Bering Strait is 56 miles (90 km) wide.

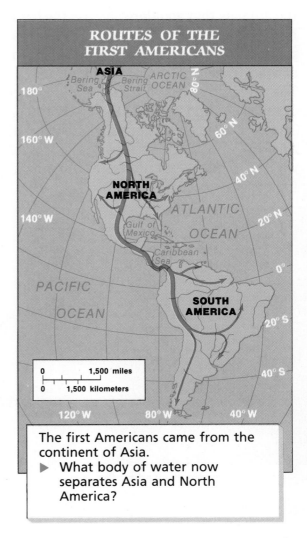

ROUTES OF THE FIRST AMERICANS

The first Americans came from the continent of Asia.
▶ What body of water now separates Asia and North America?

But 30,000 years ago the level of the oceans was lower than it is today. The land that now lies underneath the Bering Strait—in fact, the land that lies underneath the Bering Sea—was above water. So at that time, Asia and North America were connected by a bridge of land more than 1,000 miles (1,609 km) wide. It was across this land bridge that the first people came from Asia to North America.

The men and women who crossed over that land bridge were hunters. They depended on animals for their food, clothing, and shelter. We don't know for certain why these people came to North America. Chances are they were simply following the animals that wandered across the land bridge from Asia. This was the start of a **migration**, or movement from one place to another, that lasted for about 20,000 years. The migration did not end until after the oceans rose and covered the land bridge. Those people who migrated to North America were the first Americans, whom we call Native Americans, or American Indians.

The mammoths hunted by the early Americans probably looked like this.
▶ Why did mammoths need such thick, woolly hair?

B. Farming Begins in the Americas

Hunters and Gatherers Many of the animals these early Americans hunted were huge. Some animals were many times the size of the hunters. There was the giant bison, an animal much like the buffalo, only larger. There was also a giant hairy elephant called a **mammoth**, an animal nearly as tall as a two-story house.

As these animals searched for food, they gradually moved south. And where the animals went, the hunting people followed. Over time, the people migrated throughout the continents of North America and South America. You can see the routes the first Americans followed on the map on page 95.

In time, the huge animals disappeared. Scientists think the reason is that the climate became warmer, and the large animals were not able to adjust. Hunters had to change their ways. Some began to hunt smaller animals. Those who lived near the ocean learned to catch fish and gather shellfish. Some of these people began to gather the roots and seeds of plants for food.

Farming Then about 7,000 or 8,000 years ago, some gatherers of roots and seeds made a discovery that changed their lives and the lives of all who came after them. Somehow—maybe by trial and error, maybe in a sudden flash of understanding—they learned that by planting seeds they could grow their own food. These gatherers no longer had to wander from place to place in search of food. Now they could settle down in one place and farm. Over the years these farmers developed such plant foods as corn, beans, squash, and pumpkins.

A scientist puts together an early Native American jar from broken pieces. A whole jar is also shown.
► Why must this scientist have a great deal of patience?

In time, some farming groups were able to grow more food than they needed. Then it was no longer necessary for all people in the group to grow crops. Some of them were free to develop other skills. They learned to weave material, make pottery, and create works of art. Eventually some groups went on to build great buildings and cities.

C. Archaeologists Discover Clues to the Past

The earliest Native Americans had no written language. They left no books, no letters, and no newspapers that tell about themselves. How, then, do we know anything about the way they lived?

The answer is that these people left behind tools, weapons, and other objects that they used in their daily lives. A few of these **artifacts** (AHRT uh fakts) have survived. An artifact is an object made by people who lived long ago.

Scientists who study these artifacts are called **archaeologists** (ahr kee AHL-uh jihsts). Archaeologists treat each artifact as a clue to the past. Nothing is too small or too ordinary for the attention of these scientific detectives.

Where do archaeologists find their clues? Usually they must dig in the earth for them. Over thousands of years, most artifacts of early peoples have been covered over by layers of dirt and dust. So archaeologists dig where they believe groups of people once lived. For weeks or months they may find nothing. Then suddenly comes a discovery—a spearhead lying among the bones of an animal, a stone ax, or perhaps just a piece of broken pottery. The clue provides the archaeologists with a key that helps them to unlock the doors of the past.

D. The Mound Builders Left Many Clues

How archaeologists "read" clues can be seen in the story of Native Americans who once lived in the middle and eastern parts of the United States until 500 or 1,000 years ago. We do not know who these Indians were, or what they called themselves. We know them only by what they left behind: mounds, or piles of earth. They built small mounds and huge mounds; square mounds; round mounds; mounds that looked like cones; and mounds in the shapes of animals, birds, or snakes — thousands and thousands of them. So we call these groups of Native Americans the Mound Builders.

Many of these mounds can still be seen today. The most famous are in Cahokia, Illinois. There, Mound Builders built a city of 30,000 people. The main mound in Cahokia is as tall as a ten-story building. On the mound's flat top once stood a large temple and the houses of the great chiefs.

Mound Builders buried their leaders in the mounds. Along with the bodies, they buried a number of objects. These are some of the items that have been found:

- Stone axes, arrowheads, knives, and scrapers
- Needles made from animal bones
- Flat, thin stones
- Sea turtle shells and shark teeth
- Teeth of a grizzly bear
- Copper earrings
- Carved animals of stone
- Beautiful pottery
- Tobacco pipes shaped like small birds and animals
- Bits of cloth

This picture shows how archaeologists believe one Mound Builders' city looked about 1,000 years ago.
▶ Can you find one way in which the Mound Builders traveled?

This bird cut from copper and the stone beaver perched on a pipe are the work of the Mound Builders.
► What do you think the stone beaver's eye is made of?

The grizzly bear teeth are an interesting clue. The closest place they could have come from is the Rocky Mountains, which are more than a thousand miles away. So we know the Mound Builders traded with people from far away. The copper earrings and the shells are more evidence of the same thing. Copper came from the Great Lakes region. The shells and shark teeth came from the shores of the Gulf of Mexico and from the Atlantic coast. The carved stone animals, beautiful pottery, and pipes shaped like birds and animals tell us that the Mound Builders were fine craftworkers.

Of course there is much about the Mound Builders we cannot learn from these artifacts. We do not know anything about their religion. We do not know how they raised their children, or what their family life was like, or what beliefs they held. These things will probably remain a mystery forever.

E. Archaeologists Tell Us What the Clues Mean

What can archaeologists tell us from these artifacts? Well, we know from the stone axes that Mound Builders were able to cut down trees and make things from wood. The stone arrowheads and knives tell us they killed animals. Native Americans everywhere in the Americas used stone scrapers to remove meat from animal skins and bone needles to sew the skins into clothing. So we know that Mound Builders made at least some of their clothing from animal skins. The flat, thin stones were parts of hoes, so we know they also farmed for a living.

LESSON 1 REVIEW

THINK AND WRITE

A. How was it possible for animals and people to migrate from Asia to North America thousands of years ago?

B. In what ways did the early people of North America get food?

C. How do archaeologists find clues about early peoples?

D. Who were the Mound Builders?

E. Explain what archaeologists have learned from four of the artifacts left by Mound Builders.

SKILLS CHECK

THINKING SKILL

Look on page 98 at the list of items left behind by the Mound Builders. Like an archaeologist, tell which items might be used to make guesses about Mound Builders' beliefs. Give reasons for your choice.

The Indians of North America

THINK ABOUT WHAT YOU KNOW

Pretend that you get all of your food by hunting, fishing, or farming. Describe the physical characteristics of a place that would best meet your needs. List reasons for your choices.

STUDY THE VOCABULARY

environment	tepee
wigwam	desert
long house	totem
slash and burn	

FOCUS YOUR READING

How did the different environments of the North American Indians affect the way they lived?

A. The Eastern Woodland Indians Depend on the Forests

Indian Groups Many groups of Native Americans lived in North America before the Europeans arrived. These Indian groups developed their own ways to meet their need for food, clothing, and shelter. They also developed their own languages and their own rules for living together.

You are going to study four main Native American groups. They are the Eastern Woodland Indians, the Plains Indians, the Indians of the Southwest, and the Indians of the Pacific Northwest.

Five hundred years ago the eastern part of the United States was thick with forests. These forests were home to many animals, including deer, bears, turkeys, squirrels, and rabbits.

This was the natural **environment** in which the Eastern Woodland Indians lived. When we speak of an environment, we mean the land, air, water, plants, animals — everything that affects the way people live. The forest environment provided these Indians with everything they needed. They got food by hunting, fishing, gathering, and farming. Animals provided skins for clothing. Forests supplied the materials for their homes.

In building their homes, the Woodland Indians first made a frame with poles cut from young trees. They tied these poles together with vines. Then they covered the frame with bark, branches, and leaves.

The Eastern Woodland Indians built two kinds of homes. One group of Woodland Indians, the Algonquins (al GAHNG-kihns), made small single-family houses that were called **wigwams**. Another group, the Iroquois (IHR uh kwoi), made houses in which eight or ten families lived. These were called **long houses**.

Dividing the Work Eastern Woodland Indians divided the work between men and women. Men hunted, fished, built houses, and scraped the animal skins. Women grew gardens of corn, squash, beans, and pumpkins. They also made clothing. Children helped both men and women gather fruits, nuts, and berries.

To clear a field for farming, Eastern Woodland Indians used a method known as **slash and burn**. First they cut deep rings all the way around the tree trunks. This caused the trees to die after several months. Then they set fire to the dead trees. Once the clearing was made, they planted seeds among the tree stumps.

All the Indians of a village farmed together. They all shared equally in the harvest. They also shared the hunting grounds and favorite fishing places.

Eastern Woodland Indians are building a new long house in their village. The Indian women are busy with other important work.
▶ Describe the kinds of work going on in this picture.

A village might last for about ten years. After that, the soil that the Indians had farmed would be worn out. Then the Indians moved on, made another clearing, and built new houses.

B. The Plains Indians Depend on the Buffalo

The Great Plains West of the Mississippi River, between about 90° and 100° west longitude, the environment of North America changes dramatically. The air becomes dry, and there is less rainfall. The land is a plain—a nearly level area that stretches as far as the eye can see. The wind sweeps across this plain. Winters are bitterly cold. Summer temperatures can reach over 100°F (38°C).

This area is the Great Plains, a region that stretches westward to the Rocky Mountains. You will find the Great Plains on the map on pages 40–41. The many Native Americans who lived in this region are known as the Plains Indians.

In some parts of the Great Plains, there is enough rainfall for tall grasses to grow. There are also a few rivers and streams. Some Indians, such as the Lakotah (luh KOH tuh) and the Pawnee (paw-NEE), were able to farm this land.

But most of the land that makes up the Great Plains is dry and hard. There are almost no trees. The land is covered by short grass with tough roots, making it almost impossible to dig up the soil without metal tools.

Hunting the Buffalo At first it would seem that this environment would offer neither food nor clothing nor shelter to people. However, the Indians who lived on the plains were hunters. The Great Plains had one resource that made life possible for hunters. That resource was the bison, commonly called the buffalo. Great herds of buffaloes roamed the grassy plains.

The buffalo has been called a "walking department store" for the Plains Indians. It provided them with everything they needed. Indians ate buffalo meat. They made tools from buffalo bones. They made buffalo hides into blankets and robes for warmth, and into shoes and clothing as well. The stomachs of buffaloes were used to make containers for carrying water and for cooking. Other parts of the buffalo were used to make strings for the Indians' hunting bows.

The buffalo also provided material for the houses of the Plains Indians. As hunters these Indians had to be ready to move whenever and wherever the buffalo herds moved. Plains Indians therefore

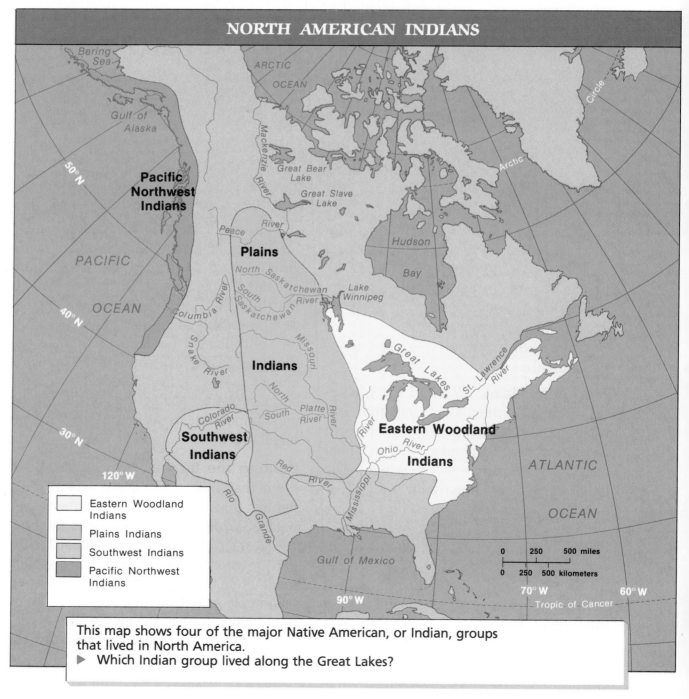

NORTH AMERICAN INDIANS

This map shows four of the major Native American, or Indian, groups that lived in North America.
▶ Which Indian group lived along the Great Lakes?

A famous artist made this picture of a Plains Indian village. Several women are busy scraping and stretching buffalo hides.
▶ In the picture, find an important use for these buffalo hides.

needed homes that could be taken apart quickly, carried easily, and set up again at their new camp. So they invented a home called a **tepee**.

To make a tepee, Indians started with the limbs of young willow trees. They stood about 12 limbs in a circle and tied them together at the top. Then the Indians wrapped buffalo hides around this frame.

C. The Indians of the Southwest Develop an Advanced Society

Desert Life If Indians found it difficult to farm on the Great Plains, you would hardly expect them to be able to farm in the Southwest. That area is even drier than the Great Plains. Much of the land in the Southwest is made up of **deserts**. A desert is a very dry place with little rainfall and few plants. The Southwest is also a land of mountains and high plateaus. A plateau is a large, high, rather level area that is raised above the surrounding land.

Even though they lived in a very hot, dry area, many Indians of the Southwest did farm. In fact, they were among the most successful of all Native American farmers. They grew corn, beans, and squash for food. These Native Americans also grew cotton, which they wove into cloth for blankets and clothing.

These were the Pueblo (PWEB loh) Indians. *Pueblo* is the Spanish word for "town." The first Spaniards who came to the Southwest gave them this name because they lived in communities. The Pueblo Indians included the Zuni (ZOO-nee) and the Hopi (HOH pee).

Everyday chores made the ancient pueblos of the Southwest busy places.
▶ How might the pueblo's ladders help the people defend themselves?

thousand families. The painting on this page shows what a pueblo looked like. Find the ladders in the picture. The Indians used ladders to go from one level of the pueblo to another.

Dividing the Work   Like other North American Indians, the Indians of the Southwest divided work between men and women. But the Pueblo Indians divided the work differently than the Eastern Woodland Indians.

Among the Eastern Woodland Indians, the men hunted and fished, and the women farmed. Among the Pueblos, however, farming was done by the men. Men also made cloth from the cotton that had been grown in the village. Often the men wove beautiful designs into the cloth. Older men who could no longer farm might spend all of their time weaving. Women ground the grain and cooked it. They also made pottery and baskets. Today, the Pueblos are still making beautiful pottery.

D. The Pacific Northwest Indians Have Many Resources

The Northwest Coast   In the northwest part of North America, between a chain of mountains and the Pacific Ocean, runs a narrow strip of coastal land. This strip stretches from southern Alaska to northern California. The climate there is usually mild. Strong, wet winds blowing in from the Pacific Ocean bring plenty of rain. In this region's fertile soil grow the tallest trees in all of North America.

Using Resources   The Pacific Northwest Indians lived in this region. Nature was generous to these people. From the giant trees, Pacific Northwest Indians made planks for building large, solid houses. Food was plentiful. Every summer,

How were the Pueblos able to farm the dry lands? They irrigated, or brought water to their crops, by digging ditches to nearby rivers, streams, and ponds.

Adobe Houses   Like other North American Indians, the Pueblos built their houses from materials in the environment. In the dry Southwest those materials were mainly stone and clay. The Pueblos built their houses out of a clay mixture called *adobe* (uh DOH bee). The adobe walls were a foot thick. They kept the homes cool in summer and warm in winter.

Often one adobe house was attached to others, making a long row of houses. Sometimes one house was built on the roof of another. A number of the Pueblo buildings rose four or five stories high, like an apartment building. One of the largest pueblos in the Southwest was home to a salmon swam from the ocean into the many rivers of the region to lay their eggs upstream. By building traps across the rivers, Indians caught enough salmon in just a few months to last them the whole year. In addition, some of the Pacific Northwest Indians went out into the ocean to hunt whales.

Since they could get all their food in a few months, the Pacific Northwest Indians had enough free time to enjoy other activities. They became very skilled woodworkers. They made furniture, pots, bowls, and beautiful masks out of wood. The Pacific Northwest Indians also knew how to make items from copper, and they made pottery and fine woven baskets, too.

Legends Indians of the Pacific Northwest believed that animals had played an important role in their early history. The Indians' legends told how a bear, a salmon, a beaver, a whale, or some other animal had helped their people in the past. So some Indian families took on a particular animal as a symbol, or **totem**. They made masks that looked like the animal for use in religious ceremonies. And they carved the likeness of the animal on the large corner posts of their houses. Sometimes they

This beautiful carved and painted totem pole is topped with the giant form of a bird.
▶ What would you like as your totem?

carved these likenesses on separate poles, called *totem poles,* and placed the poles in front of their houses. The photograph above shows part of a totem pole.

LESSON *2* REVIEW

THINK AND WRITE

A. How did Eastern Woodland Indians use their environment to meet their needs for food, clothing, and shelter?

B. Why did the Plains Indians follow the buffalo herds instead of living in villages like the Eastern Woodlands Indians?

C. How were Pueblo Indians able to grow crops on their dry land?

D. Why could the Indians of the Pacific Northwest become skilled craftspeople?

SKILLS CHECK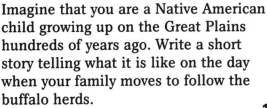

WRITING SKILL

Imagine that you are a Native American child growing up on the Great Plains hundreds of years ago. Write a short story telling what it is like on the day when your family moves to follow the buffalo herds.

105

The Indians of Middle and South America

and other buildings still stand in the jungle as reminders of that society's greatness.

THINK ABOUT WHAT YOU KNOW
What achievements, in your opinion, make a community or country great?

STUDY THE VOCABULARY
empire   tax
causeway   terrace

FOCUS YOUR READING
How were the Maya, Aztecs, and Incas alike?

A. The Maya Develop an Advanced Society

More than 1,500 years ago, the Maya (MAH yuh) Indians began to create a society in the jungles of Central America and southern Mexico. Find where the Maya lived, on the map on this page. The Maya built beautiful, carefully planned cities, with huge temples and public buildings made of stone and earth. Some of these structures were as tall as a 20-story building. Even more important, the Maya created a government and a system of laws. The Maya also developed a system of writing. It was not a written language of letters and words as is our language. Instead, Maya writing used pictures and symbols.

The Maya also developed mathematics. They studied the heavens, noting the locations of the moon, the stars, and the sun as they changed day by day. With this information they created a calendar far more accurate than anything known in Europe at the time.

Maya society declined about 900 years ago. Today, we still do not know why. However, the ruins of Maya temples

B. The Aztecs Build an Advanced Society in Mexico

A second important society in Central America was built by the Aztecs. These Indians lived in Mexico and gained fame as warriors. About 700 years ago they began to conquer neighboring Indian peoples. Altogether the Aztecs ruled an **empire** of more than 10 million people. An empire is an area in which a people spreads its rule over other lands and peoples.

The Aztec capital, Tenochtitlán (te-nawch tee TLAHN), was one of the largest cities in the world at the time. You can see what Tenochtitlán looked like from the

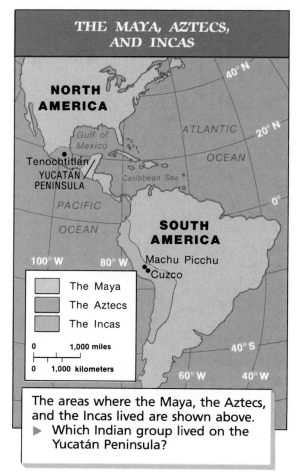

THE MAYA, AZTECS, AND INCAS

The areas where the Maya, the Aztecs, and the Incas lived are shown above.
▶ Which Indian group lived on the Yucatán Peninsula?

A Mexican artist made this picture of a busy marketplace overlooking the great city of Tenochtitlán.
▶ How are people carrying loads in this marketplace?

painting on this page. Tenochtitlán was built on an island in a lake so that the Aztecs could defend it against attack. **Causeways,** which are roadways raised above the water, connected the city to the rest of the land. Canals and roads made it possible to move throughout the city.

In the center of the city were the great temples of the Aztec gods as well as grand government buildings. The city had a busy marketplace. People brought goods from hundreds of miles away to sell or trade.

Like the Maya, the Aztecs developed a written language. With writing, the Aztecs could record important events in their history. Priests could write down the prayers and rules of their religion, and government officials could keep track of **taxes**. A tax is money that must be paid to a government. The money is used to support that government. Taxes were used to build roads and canals, as well as temples and other public buildings in Tenochtitlán. Some of these temples and buildings in the

city are shown in the painting on this page. Like the Maya before them, the Aztecs also developed an accurate calendar.

C. The Incas Build a Great Society in South America

A Great Empire Farther to the south, along the western coast of South America, lived another remarkable Native American group known as the Incas. Incas worshiped the sun, and they believed their leader, the Inca, was descended from it. They obeyed his orders without question. Everyone was expected to work, and laziness was considered a crime. So the Incas worked hard, and they prospered. They created an empire that stretched for 2,500 miles (4,023 km) along the coast of South America. You can read a story of how the Incas built their empire in the literature selection on page 108.

Today the visitor to Peru, home of the Incas, stands in wonder before their achievements. These people had no iron.

107

The Incas: People of the Sun

By: Victor W. von Hagen
Setting: Peru, 1466

The Inca ruled a great empire. It included three regions. There was the region of the great Andes Mountains, the region of rain forests, and the region of desert that lay between the mountains and the ocean. In this last region lived the Chimús, who were enemies of the Incas. This is the story of how the Incas were able to conquer the Kingdom of Chimor.

The Inca sent his ambassadors up to the wall and demanded that the Great Chimú yield. They came back with their eyes torn out. Angry, the Topa Inca ordered his troops to scale the walls. No sooner were the ladders against them than the Chimús knocked them down. The Inca himself was struck by a stone. Many men were lost. . . .

He [the Topa Inca] was thinking of water.

Without it, Chan-Chan [the capital city] must wither and die. And where did the water come from? Why, from the Andes. And who controlled the Andes? Why, he, the Topa Inca, controlled it. Now if the water . . .

The next day he sent a thousand of his soldiers far up the valleys to where the Chimús had diverted [turned] the flow of a river into the aqueducts. The Incas changed the flow. . . .

The Inca then went up to the walls of Chan-Chan. His men blew a long blast from their conch shells. He asked to be heard. The Great Chimú appeared on the high walls, adorned by a golden crown with tall tapers of gold. . . .

"I am Topa Inca," said the son of the Sun. "I have domination over the air and the waters. I have taken your water from you, and I will keep it until you surrender the Kingdom of Chimor."

It is said that the Great Chimú laughed.

Yet not for long. The water had been diverted. . . . So the Great Chimú came out from behind his walls and surrendered his whole kingdom to the Inca.

This picture of terraced farmland was taken at the ruins of an Inca city in Peru.
▶ Would it be possible to use large machinery on this kind of a farm?

Yet they were able to carve huge blocks of stone for their buildings. They had no wheel and no horse to help them carry heavy loads. Yet they were able to move these blocks long distances and even get them up steep mountains. They had no cement to hold the stones together. Yet they fit these blocks so tightly that you could not squeeze a blade of grass between them. They had no writing. Yet they knew enough about mathematics and engineering to put up buildings that could stand up against powerful earthquakes.

Using Resources Their achievements in farming were just as amazing. Peru is about one-third desert and dry land, one-third mountains, and one-third jungle. In the desert there was not enough water to grow crops. In the mountains, heavy rains washed the soil down the hillsides, leaving only rocks behind.

The Incas solved these problems. They dug irrigation canals to bring water from the mountain streams to the dry lands. Some of these canals were 500 miles (805 km) long. The Incas cut **terraces** into the sides of the mountains. These terraces were rows of flat steps bordered by stone walls that kept the soil in place. Instead of the rainwater rushing down the hills, it dropped gently from terrace to terrace, leaving the soil and plants as they were.

The land of the Incas was also rich in gold and silver. You might think that this made them a fortunate people. In fact, it was their gold and silver that led to their doom. That is a story for Chapter 5.

LESSON **3** REVIEW

THINK AND WRITE

A. What were some of the achievements of the Maya Indians?
B. How did the Aztecs create an empire?
C. How did the Incas farm land in the mountains and deserts?

SKILLS CHECK

MAP SKILL
Use the Gazetteer to find out what modern city is built on the site of Tenochtitlán. Then find that city on the Atlas map found on page 622.

USING THE VOCABULARY

prehistoric   environment
strait   slash and burn
migration   empire
artifact   causeway
archaeologist   terrace

On a separate sheet of paper, complete each sentence correctly by using the words listed above.

1. The way people live is affected by their _____.
2. The islands were connected by a _____.
3. The movement of groups of people from one place to another is called _____.
4. An _____ studies objects from long ago to learn how people in the past lived.
5. The ruler of an _____ controls many different groups of people.
6. The time before people kept written records is called _____.
7. An _____ is something left by people who lived in the past.
8. Early farmers cleared their fields using the _____ method.
9. A _____ makes it possible to raise crops on the side of a mountain.
10. The _____ connects two bodies of water.

REMEMBERING WHAT YOU READ

On a separate sheet of paper, write your answers in complete sentences.

1. By what route might the first Americans have come to North America?
2. What were some of the animals the first Americans hunted?
3. What kinds of clues help scientists learn about the past?
4. Who were the Mound Builders?
5. Why were the forests important to the Eastern Woodland Indians?
6. What were three ways that the Plains Indians used the buffalo?
7. How were the dwellings of the Pueblos different from Native American dwellings in other areas?
8. How did Native Americans in the Northwest record legends that were part of the story of their ancestors?
9. What are three ways in which the Aztecs and the Maya were similar?
10. What are two ways in which the Incas solved their farming problems?

TYING ART TO SOCIAL STUDIES

The Maya had a written language. They used hieroglyphics, or picture writing. Some of the pictures stood for words and ideas. Other pictures stood for sounds. Create a picture alphabet by matching each letter of the alphabet to a different symbol or simple picture. Then write the following statements using the alphabet you have created.

The Indians of North America developed many different cultures. The hunters of the Great Plains followed the buffalo.

THINKING CRITICALLY

On a separate sheet of paper, write your answers in complete sentences.

1. How did the discovery of farming affect the way people lived?
2. Why is knowing about how people lived in the past important to people today?
3. Which Indian group, do you think, made the best use of its environment?
4. In what ways were the Maya, Aztecs, and Incas great civilizations?
5. The last paragraph in this chapter has the words ". . . gold and silver led to their doom." Without reading ahead, tell what you think happened to the Incas.

SUMMARIZING THE CHAPTER

On a separate sheet of paper, draw a graphic organizer like the one shown here. Copy the information from this graphic organizer to the one you have drawn. Under the main idea for each lesson, write three statements that support it. The first one has been done for you.

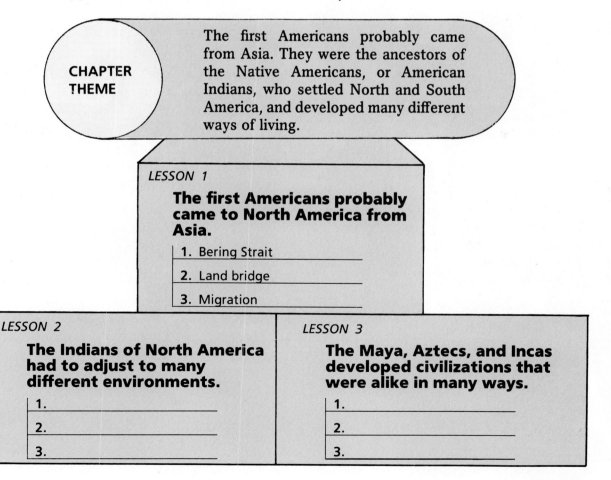

CHAPTER THEME

The first Americans probably came from Asia. They were the ancestors of the Native Americans, or American Indians, who settled North and South America, and developed many different ways of living.

LESSON 1

The first Americans probably came to North America from Asia.

1. Bering Strait
2. Land bridge
3. Migration

LESSON 2

The Indians of North America had to adjust to many different environments.

1. _____
2. _____
3. _____

LESSON 3

The Maya, Aztecs, and Incas developed civilizations that were alike in many ways.

1. _____
2. _____
3. _____

CHAPTER 4

EUROPEANS COME TO AMERICA

Christopher Columbus was one of many brave sailors looking to find new ways to reach Asia. Though he did not realize it, he reached a world unknown to Europeans of his time. Explorers from many countries followed Columbus to the New World.

Viking Explorers

The Granger Collection, New York

THINK ABOUT WHAT YOU KNOW

Imagine that you were given the opportunity to be a great explorer in the past, present, or future. Where or what would you choose to explore?

STUDY THE VOCABULARY

explore   **saga**
Vikings

FOCUS YOUR READING

What is the proof that the Vikings landed in America?

A. The Thrill of Exploration

Have you ever gone exploring? Perhaps your family moved to another home and you went for a walk around your new neighborhood. You might have found streets and buildings you had never seen before and people you had never met. Or perhaps you have hiked deep into the woods near your home, deeper than you have ever been before. You might have discovered trees or flowers there that were new to you. You probably brought back a leaf or a plant to show your parents.

If you have done anything like these things, you were exploring. To **explore** means to search for new things or places. There was a time in history when there were a great many explorers. They were daring people who voyaged to lands that were unknown to them. They made strange and wonderful discoveries. They brought back plants and treasures from the places they explored. They even brought back people that no one at home had ever seen before. Some of these daring adventurers found their way to America. You will be learning about them in this chapter.

We know that people came to America from Asia thousands and thousands of years ago. These were the Native Americans. Many centuries later people from other places also came to America. Who were the first brave explorers to reach America after the Native Americans? Many claims have been made that different groups from Africa, Asia, or Europe were the first to arrive in America after the Native Americans. But no real proof has been found for any — except one. Here is the story of that one.

B. Leif Ericson Plans a Voyage of Discovery

Far into the night, father and son talked about the son's exciting plan for a voyage of exploration. The son, Leif, and the father, Eric the Red, were **Vikings**, a people who came mainly from Norway. The Vikings were the best and boldest sailors in Europe. In the 800s they had sailed to

These small, open Viking ships were able to cover great distances.
► What might it be like to be in one of these ships during a storm?

Iceland and built settlements there. In 982, Eric the Red arrived in Greenland, an island in the North Atlantic Ocean. He started the first settlements there a few years later.

Eric and Leif were now living in Greenland. The year was 1002. Leif had just returned from a visit to a nearby settlement. There he learned that some years earlier, other Vikings had sailed to a body of land farther to the west. However, they had returned home without exploring it.

This tale fired Leif Ericson's imagination. He wanted to be the one to find and explore the new land. On his return home, Leif tried to persuade Eric the Red to go with him. He reminded his father how much their settlement needed wood. Trees did not grow on Greenland, and the sailors who had seen the new land had reported that it had plenty of trees. Shouldn't they sail to that land and bring back wood for

the settlement, urged Leif? After much persuasion, Eric the Red finally agreed to join his son on the new voyage.

C. Leif Ericson Reaches Vinland

But the plan did not work out. Some days later, as the men were getting ready to board ship, Eric the Red's horse stumbled. Eric fell off and injured his foot. He could not go after all.

So it was that 23-year-old Leif Ericson led the crew of 30 sailors as they took their small boat to the open sea. Some weeks later Ericson and his crew arrived at the island we know as Newfoundland. Leif called the land *Vinland*, or "land of vines," because of the many wild grapes he found there. After spending a winter in Vinland, the Vikings loaded their boat with wood and returned to Greenland.

Twenty years later another group of Vikings made the voyage to Vinland. These people built a small settlement and stayed for two years before leaving. But then the Vikings stopped coming.

At the Vikings' Newfoundland settlement, men are erecting a large building for the winter.
▶ In the picture, find some sources of food for the Vikings.

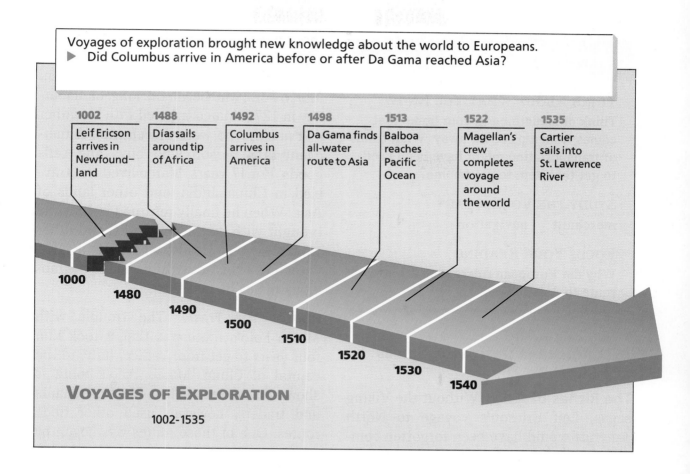

Voyages of exploration brought new knowledge about the world to Europeans.
▶ Did Columbus arrive in America before or after Da Gama reached Asia?

1002 Leif Ericson arrives in Newfoundland

1488 Días sails around tip of Africa

1492 Columbus arrives in America

1498 Da Gama finds all-water route to Asia

1513 Balboa reaches Pacific Ocean

1522 Magellan's crew completes voyage around the world

1535 Cartier sails into St. Lawrence River

1000 · 1480 · 1490 · 1500 · 1510 · 1520 · 1530 · 1540

VOYAGES OF EXPLORATION

1002-1535

How do we know about the Vikings and Vinland? For many years our only source of information was Viking stories, called **sagas**. Sagas are folk tales telling of battles, customs, and legends. These sagas tell about the history and adventures of the Norse people, and they include the stories of Eric the Red and Leif Ericson. But no one knew for sure that these stories were true.

Then in 1961, archaeologists found new evidence about the Vikings and Vinland in a meadow on the coast of Newfoundland. There they dug up the foundations of houses and a few stone artifacts that are about 1,000 years old. As a result of the discoveries made by these archaeologists, we know that the Vikings really were in Vinland—the first Europeans to land in North America.

LESSON *1* REVIEW

THINK AND WRITE

A. What is the importance of explorers and exploration?
B. What was the plan that Leif Ericson discussed with his father, Eric the Red?
C. How do we know the Vikings actually were in Vinland?

SKILLS CHECK

MAP SKILL

Locate the islands of Greenland and Newfoundland on the Atlas map of North America on page 622.

The Lure of Asia

THINK ABOUT WHAT YOU KNOW
Think of something in your home that comes from a place far away. What forms of transportation might have been used to get that item to your home?

STUDY THE VOCABULARY
merchant   navigation

FOCUS YOUR READING
Why did European rulers seek a water route to Asia?

A. Europeans Desire the Spices and Silks of Asia

The Riches of Asia   Without the Viking sagas, Leif Ericson's voyage to North America would have been forgotten completely, for other Europeans were hardly aware of Ericson. At that time, most Europeans were turning their attention to a continent to their east — Asia. From Asia came the valuable spices, perfumes, silks, cottons, and jewels that Europeans of that time desired.

Europeans especially valued spices from the Indies, or the Spice Islands, as they were sometimes called. In those days before the refrigerator, meat went bad quickly. Spices helped to keep meat from spoiling, but mostly they just made spoiled meat taste better. As for perfumes, Europeans of that day did not often bathe or use much soap. They would often use perfumes to cover up bad odors.

Marco Polo's Journey   There already existed a number of trade routes for getting these desired goods from Asia to Europe. One route went over land for thousands of miles, across deserts and through mountain passes. This was the route followed by a 17-year-old Italian, Marco Polo, who began the long, hard journey in 1271. Marco traveled with his father and uncle, who were **merchants**. A merchant is a person who buys and sells goods. For 17 years, Marco lived and traveled in China, India, and other lands of Asia. When he finally returned to Italy, he brought with him jewels, silks, and other valuable goods. He also wrote a book filled with tales of his adventures and of the fabulous riches he had seen.

Routes for Trade   The trouble with Marco Polo's route was that it took him four years to get from Venice, Italy, to the capital of China. Marco Polo's route is shown on the map below. Most merchants and traders, however, used other trade routes. One of those routes was begun by

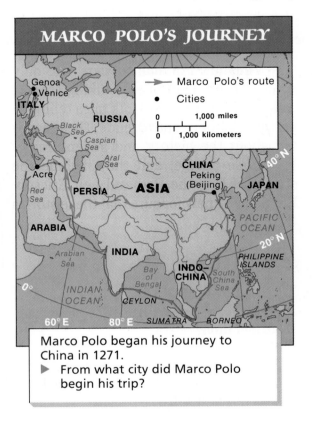

MARCO POLO'S JOURNEY

Marco Polo's route
Cities
0   1,000 miles
0   1,000 kilometers

Genoa, Venice, ITALY, Black Sea, RUSSIA, Caspian Sea, Aral Sea, Acre, Red Sea, PERSIA, ASIA, CHINA, Peking (Beijing), JAPAN, 40°N, PACIFIC OCEAN, ARABIA, Arabian Sea, INDIA, Bay of Bengal, INDO-CHINA, South China Sea, PHILIPPINE ISLANDS, 20°N, 0°, INDIAN OCEAN, CEYLON, 60°E, 80°E, SUMATRA, BORNEO

Marco Polo began his journey to China in 1271.
▶ From what city did Marco Polo begin his trip?

This colorful picture shows Venice at the time that Marco Polo began his travels.

▶ What is strange about the picture?

Arab traders who carried goods by ship from Asia to the Middle East. From there, other Arab traders took the goods over land on horses, donkeys, and camels to the Mediterranean Sea. There, Italian merchants bought the goods and sailed them across the Mediterranean Sea to Genoa and Venice, in Italy. They then sold the goods throughout Europe.

Arab and Italian merchants had this trade to themselves, so they were able to charge very high prices. They charged so much for pepper that people called it "black gold." A merchant who could bring a single shipload of spices to a European port could become rich.

Rulers and merchants of other countries looked at the merchants of Genoa and Venice with envy. If they could find some other way to reach Asia, especially an all-water route, they also would be able to make a lot of money.

B. Portugal Searches for an All-Water Route to Asia

Prince Henry of Portugal How could such a route be found? Some thought it might be possible to reach Asia by sailing south around Africa. No one knew if that really could be done, for no one knew the shape of that continent or how far south it went.

In the search for a new route to Asia, one man led the way. He was Prince Henry, son of the king of Portugal. Prince Henry started a school for sea captains. These captains were taught the science of **navigation**. That is, they were taught how to figure out a ship's location and the direction and distance that it traveled. They learned to keep careful records of their voyages, noting the direction of the winds and sketching maps of coastlines.

Knowledge of Geography Year by year, Portuguese sea captains sailed farther south along the African coast. They also sailed west into the Atlantic Ocean. On their return, Prince Henry would talk to each captain about his voyage. He turned over their records and sketches of coastlines to mapmakers who fit the information into their maps. Bit by bit, Prince Henry helped to increase knowledge about the oceans.

These voyages into the unknown oceans took great courage. Many in that day believed that sea monsters lay in the deep oceans, waiting to swallow up ships that came near. The sun in the south was so hot, said some, that it boiled the ocean. No wonder that sailors did not like to be out of sight of land for very long.

C. Días and Da Gama Sail Around the Tip of Africa

Sails Around Africa Prince Henry died in 1460, but others carried on his work. In 1488 came the great breakthrough. While sailing far south along the African coast with three ships under his command, Bartholomew Días (bahr THAHL uh myoo DEE us) was caught in a fierce storm. For 13 days the storm carried Días's ships toward the south and east before blowing itself out. Feeling lucky to be alive, Días turned back north to return to Portugal. Soon his lookouts saw land once more.

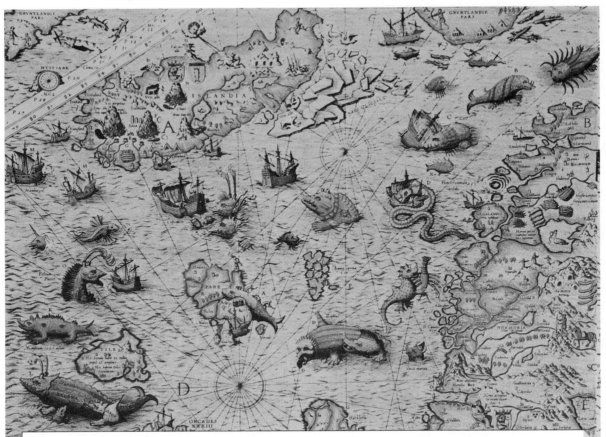

This map, made at the beginning of the sixteenth century, shows that some mapmakers may still have believed in sea monsters.
► If you were a sailor at the time this map was made, would you have wanted to sail into these waters?

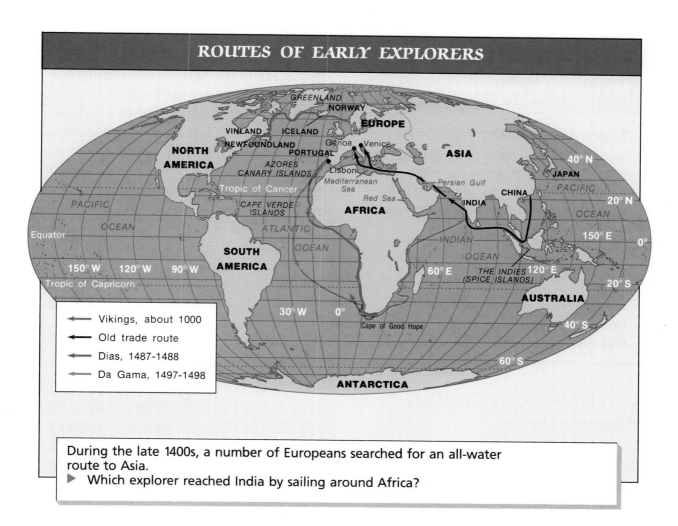

ROUTES OF EARLY EXPLORERS

Legend:
- ← Vikings, about 1000
- ← Old trade route
- ← Dias, 1487-1488
- ← Da Gama, 1497-1498

During the late 1400s, a number of Europeans searched for an all-water route to Asia.

▶ Which explorer reached India by sailing around Africa?

But something was wrong. Since the ships were now going north, the land should have been on their *right*. Instead, it was on the *left* side of the ships. That was impossible, unless — unless the storm had blown them right around the tip of Africa and they were now going up the *other side* of Africa! That was it, of course!

All-water Route Found   Días returned to Portugal with the exciting news. Ten years later, Vasco da Gama (VAHS koh duh GAM uh) picked up where Días left off. With a fleet of four ships, Da Gama rounded the tip of Africa and went on to reach India. An all-water route to Asia had been found.

LESSON *2* REVIEW

THINK AND WRITE

A. Why did the people of Europe want the spices of Asia?
B. How did Portugal become a leader in exploring the oceans?
C. How did a storm help Días make an important discovery?

SKILLS CHECK

MAP SKILL

Use the map above to find out which oceans Vasco da Gama sailed to find an all-water route to Asia.

119

Christopher Columbus Makes a Great Voyage

THINK ABOUT WHAT YOU KNOW

Imagine that you want to be the captain of a ship when you grow up. What are some things you could do now to help you learn more about oceans, ships, and being a ship captain?

STUDY THE VOCABULARY

port

FOCUS YOUR READING

How did Columbus's new idea lead to his first voyage to America?

A. Columbus Shows an Early Interest in the Sea

Christopher Columbus was born in Genoa, one of the great trading centers and **ports** of Italy. A port is a place where ships can load and unload cargo. His father was a weaver, and his mother was the daughter of a weaver. Columbus's father expected his son to follow in his footsteps. Christopher did learn to be a weaver, but he had other dreams — dreams of traveling to far-away places, dreams of living a life of adventure. In his spare hours he could be found at the city docks, listening to sailors' tales about their travels across the Mediterranean Sea. Christopher Columbus got his first job on a ship at 14. From then on, the sea was his life.

When Columbus was 24 years old, he almost lost his life at sea. Sailing off the coast of Portugal, Columbus's merchant ship was mistaken for an enemy warship by the Portuguese navy and was sunk. Columbus was wounded, but he managed to get to shore.

After recovering from his wound, Columbus made his way to the Portuguese city of Lisbon, where his brother, Bartholomew, was a mapmaker. The two men became partners in a mapmaking business. Columbus had never learned to read or write, but he did so now. He read about shipbuilding, learned about sailing by the stars, and studied mathematics.

Columbus was never really happy when away from the sea for long, so he also took jobs as a captain on merchant ships. By the age of 30, Christopher Columbus was known as one of the most skilled sea captains in Portugal.

B. Columbus Has a New Idea for Reaching Asia

Columbus's Plan Sometime during his early 30s, Columbus began to consider a bold new plan for reaching the Indies. Like most Portuguese captains of his time,

As a boy, Columbus loved to watch the activity in the harbor.
► Can you guess what Columbus was dreaming about as he watched?

Columbus tried to study as much about the geography of the world as he could.
▶ What helped him in his studies?

that Columbus's figures were wrong. The distance to Asia was not 4,500 miles (7,240 km) as Columbus thought. It was more than 11,000 miles (17,699 km). There was not a ship in Europe that could make such a voyage. No, said the geographers, the plan was impossible. So the king of Portugal turned Columbus down.

Things do sometimes work out strangely. The king's geographers were actually correct about the distance to Asia. Columbus was wrong, so he set out on the ocean and reached a world that was entirely new to Europeans. Today no one remembers who the geographers were. But everyone certainly knows the name of Christopher Columbus.

C. Columbus Seeks Help from Spain

Columbus next tried King Ferdinand and Queen Isabella of Spain. They were interested in his ideas. However, Spain was in the middle of a war, and the queen told Columbus he must wait for an answer. Columbus waited—for six years. When the answer came, it was "no." The queen's advisors told her that Columbus's plan would not work.

Disappointed and angry, Columbus set out for France, hoping for support from the French king. Meanwhile, Queen Isabella thought the matter over. It was true, she thought, that the cost of such a voyage would be high. But if it succeeded, the trade with the Indies would make Spain rich. Also, Spain could carry the Christian religion to Asia.

Isabella sent a messenger to catch up to Columbus and tell him to come back. She would help him after all! So it was that when Columbus set sail in 1492 on a voyage that would make history, he sailed under the flag of Spain.

Columbus knew that the world was round. Therefore, a ship starting from Europe should be able to reach the other side of the world by sailing in *any* direction. Well, then, thought Columbus, why not sail *west*, across the Atlantic Ocean?

The more Columbus thought about it, the more he felt it could be done. Soon he could think of nothing else. He studied many maps. He read geography books. He talked with sailors about the winds and the weather in the Atlantic Ocean. Yes, it could be done—Christopher Columbus was certain of it!

The King's Geographers In 1484, Columbus set his plan before the king of Portugal and asked for ships and supplies. This was before Días had sailed around the tip of Africa. The king turned to his geographers for advice. Would Columbus's plan work, he asked? The geographers replied

D. Columbus Arrives in America

Columbus's First Voyage In August of 1492, Columbus set sail on his voyage of exploration with three small Spanish ships, the *Niña,* the *Pinta,* and the *Santa Maria.* He had under his command a crew of only 90 sailors.

Columbus's men were in high spirits as their ships sailed out of their home harbor in Spain on that warm August morning. But as day followed day with no sign of land, their spirits sank. After two months a number of frightened sailors had had enough. They threatened to remove Columbus from command unless he turned back. But Columbus remained firm. The three ships sailed on.

Then in the early hours of the morning of October 12, the quiet of the moonlit sea was broken by the excited cry of Rodrigo de Triana, the lookout of the *Pinta:* "Land! Land!" The Indies at last, thought Columbus. Soon he and his men rowed to shore in small boats.

When Columbus and his men went ashore, they fell to their knees and gave thanks to God for delivering them safely to this land. Columbus named the land San Salvador, which is Spanish for "Holy Savior."

Look at the map below. Use the key to help you find the route of Columbus's first voyage. You can see that Columbus landed on one of a group of islands. These islands are now called the Bahamas. You can also see from the map that Columbus explored a number of other islands in the area. In fact he left some of his men to start a settlement on one of these islands. These men named their island Hispaniola. Find Hispaniola on the map.

Meeting Native Americans Columbus and his men were greeted by the Arawaks, the inhabitants of the islands. Columbus called them Indians because he thought he was in the East Indies. Of course, Columbus was mistaken. He had not reached the Far East at all. Unknown to him, or to any other Europeans, two large continents stood in the way—North America and South America. Columbus had actually come upon an island not far from present-day Florida.

The two peoples exchanged gifts. The Spaniards gave the Indians blue glass beads, red cloth caps, and little copper and brass bells. In return, the Indians gave them gifts of food, cotton yarn, spears for

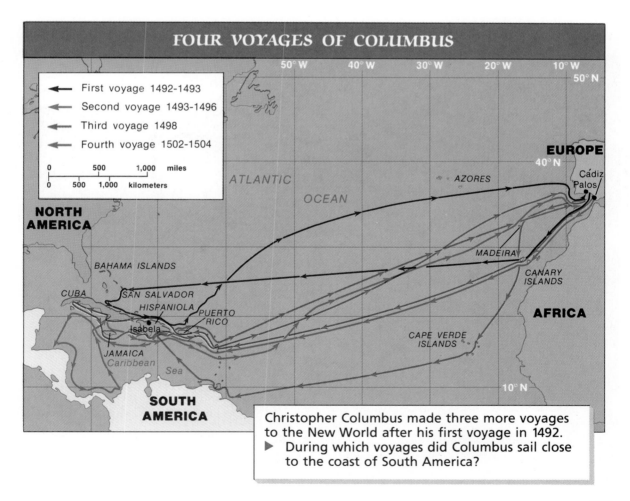

FOUR VOYAGES OF COLUMBUS

First voyage 1492-1493
Second voyage 1493-1496
Third voyage 1498
Fourth voyage 1502-1504

Christopher Columbus made three more voyages to the New World after his first voyage in 1492.
▶ During which voyages did Columbus sail close to the coast of South America?

fishing in the shallow waters, and even parrots. But these friendly Native Americans offered no silks or spices or gold, for they had none of these to give.

Columbus was disappointed that he had found no gold and had not yet found China or Japan. But he was sure he had reached Asia. To prove it, he brought six Indians with him when he returned to Spain. He also brought back cinnamon, tobacco, coconuts, a few ornaments, and several parrots.

E. Three More Voyages

Exploring New Lands When the *Niña* and the *Pinta* sailed into the harbor at Palos, Spain, in March 1493, Columbus was greeted as a hero. Queen Isabella ordered that preparations be started for a second voyage. This time the queen provided a fleet fitting for the great Admiral of the Ocean Seas — 17 ships and 1,500 men.

Columbus set out on his second voyage in September 1493. He returned to Hispaniola, where he left a number of his men to start a settlement. Then he sailed from island to island, looking for the fabulous cities of Japan and China. Finally, he returned to Spain empty-handed.

This time his welcome was not so grand. The king and queen were losing patience. Still, they put up the money to pay for two more trips to try to reach Asia. Each trip was a failure.

After that, the king and queen were no longer willing to support Columbus's trips. He was ignored by all. Columbus

Columbus is being greeted by the king and queen of Spain on his return from his first voyage.
► Which group, do you think, was more astonished by the other, the Europeans or the Indians?

died in 1506, a bitter man. Slowly, however, it began to dawn on others that Columbus had stumbled onto a land that Europeans had not known existed. He had reached what was to them a whole new world full of wonderful and amazing people and things.

Naming the Americas   One of the first persons to realize this was an Italian merchant and sailor named Amerigo Vespucci (ah me REE goh ves POOT chee). After Columbus's third voyage, other sailors also sailed to the west. Vespucci went along on several of these voyages. He later wrote many letters, saying this land was really a new continent and calling it a New World. When a German mapmaker made a new map of the world, he included this new continent and named it America in Vespucci's honor.

Meanwhile another brave European explorer had stumbled upon still another part of the New World. Pedro Cabral (PAY-droh kuh BRAHL) had set out from Portugal to sail down the coast of Africa. A huge storm blew his ship far off course, and he landed on the coast of South America in the present-day country of Brazil. Cabral claimed this land for Portugal.

This fine statue of the Portuguese explorer Pedro Cabral stands in the city of Lisbon, in Portugal.
▶ What country's flag, do you think, is Cabral carrying?

LESSON *3* *REVIEW*

THINK AND WRITE

A. What were some things that Columbus did that helped him become a skilled sea captain?
B. Why did Columbus believe that he could reach Asia by sailing west?
C. Why did the king and queen of Spain refuse to help Columbus and then later change their minds?
D. Why did Columbus believe that he had reached Asia?

E. After his fourth voyage, why did people think Columbus was a failure?

SKILLS CHECK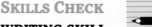

WRITING SKILL
Imagine that Queen Isabella asked Columbus to put the reasons she should aid him in a letter. Pretending you are Columbus, write a letter persuading the Queen to support your plan.

CITIZENSHIP AND AMERICAN VALUES

WHAT MAKES A GOOD LEADER?

As you learned in this chapter, the years from about 1450 to 1550 were a period when Europeans explored what were to them unknown areas of the world. Christopher Columbus reached and claimed a new world for Spain. Portugal, England, France, and Holland also sponsored the voyages of many explorers.

What kind of people were the explorers? It is possible to describe them as leaders. But what makes a leader? Since in a democracy we elect our leaders, it is important to know what makes a good leader.

Here is a list of some qualities that people have. Some of these can be used to describe a good leader. Which ten, do you think, are the most important qualities for a good leader to have?

- Courage
- Honesty
- Ability to work well with others
- Patience
- Ability to make decisions
- Reliability
- Sense of humor

The Granger Collection, New York

- Ability to create new ideas
- Generosity
- Loyalty
- Intelligence
- Good health
- Determination
- Modesty
- Common sense

Suppose you are Queen Isabella of Spain. One of your ministers has come to you with a request from a man who wants your support for a voyage of exploration. The minister describes the man in the following way.

> Once X is convinced that an idea or theory is correct, he will do anything he can to prove it. He has a strong belief in himself and his ideas. Sometimes X is impatient with the people who don't agree with him. X learned as an adult most of what he needs to know for his life's work. He has been described as a man of great intelligence with very little book learning. The stars and their movement in the sky fascinate him. He has a great deal of imagination and is artistic and creative. He is a religious person. X can get people to do more than they think they can do. He has a sense of adventure and a good deal of courage.

Thinking for Yourself

On a separate sheet of paper, answer the following questions in complete sentences.

1. Do you think the person in the minister's description is a good leader?
2. How many of the ten qualities you picked does X have?
3. Does he have any qualities that are not on your list?
4. Do you think the person described might be Christopher Columbus?

Europe Follows Columbus's Lead

THINK ABOUT WHAT YOU KNOW

Imagine that you are the king or queen of a country in Europe. You realize that Columbus has reached a New World that you did not know existed. Would you send explorers to the New World? What would be the advantages and disadvantages of doing this?

STUDY THE VOCABULARY

isthmus	gulf
northwest passage	rapid

FOCUS YOUR READING

What other European explorers tried to reach Asia by sailing west, as Columbus did?

A. England Joins the Search for a Route to Asia

News that Christopher Columbus had found a new route to Asia for Spain spread through Europe quickly. Other countries rushed to follow his lead. John Cabot, an Italian sailor living in England, believed there was an even shorter way to Asia. Cabot planned to sail west, as Columbus had. But he would take a route much farther to the north.

Cabot and a crew of 18 men set out on the ship *Matthew* in the spring of 1497. A month later he arrived at Newfoundland, the same island that Leif Ericson had found nearly 500 years before. Like Columbus, Cabot believed he had reached some part of Asia. He hurried back to England with his news. The next year, Cabot set out with a fleet of four ships, but no one ever saw or heard of him again.

With the disappearance of Cabot, England's effort to find a short route to Asia ended in failure: no spices, no gold, no Asia. People in England lost interest in the New World for the next hundred years.

But Cabot's voyage had not been wasted. He had found one of the world's richest fishing areas, the *Grand Banks*. After Europeans learned about the Grand Banks, fishing crews from England, Portugal, and France crossed the Atlantic Ocean each year to fish in these waters.

B. Spanish Sailors Explore the Pacific Ocean

Balboa   By the early 1500s all of Europe realized that Columbus had not really reached Asia. They now knew that a large body of land stood in the way of a direct route to Asia. But just how large was it? How far south did it stretch? And how far north? Was there a way around it? Or perhaps a way through it?

In 1513 a Spanish explorer named Vasco Nuñez de Balboa sailed from the island of Hispaniola to the Isthmus (IHS-mus) of Panama. An **isthmus** is a narrow strip of land between two bodies of water. Slashing his way through thick jungles and climbing over mountains, Balboa managed to cross this isthmus. On the other side he saw a great ocean. Balboa called this ocean the South Sea.

Magellan   A few years later a Portuguese sailor named Ferdinand Magellan believed he could find a way to get to the South Sea by sailing around South America. The king of Spain hired Magellan to try. In the year 1519, Magellan set out for South America with a fleet of five ships.

Magellan landed first in the northern part of South America, in what is now the

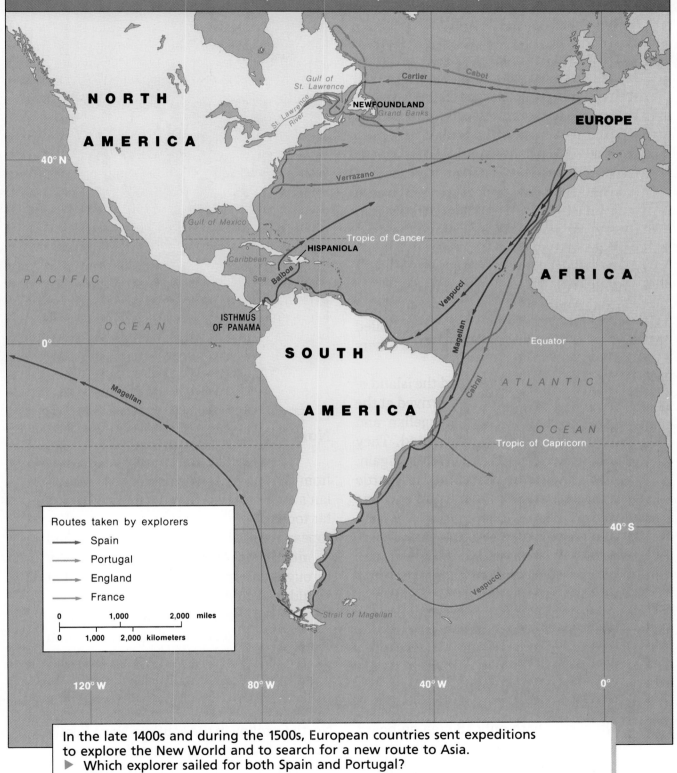

EXPLORERS FOR SPAIN, PORTUGAL, ENGLAND, AND FRANCE

NORTH AMERICA

SOUTH AMERICA

EUROPE

AFRICA

PACIFIC OCEAN

ATLANTIC OCEAN

Gulf of St. Lawrence

St. Lawrence River

NEWFOUNDLAND
Grand Banks

Gulf of Mexico

Caribbean Sea

HISPANIOLA

Balboa

ISTHMUS OF PANAMA

Strait of Magellan

40° N

0°

40° S

Tropic of Cancer

Equator

Tropic of Capricorn

120° W

80° W

40° W

0°

Cartier

Cabot

Verrazano

Vespucci

Magellan

Cabral

Magellan

Routes taken by explorers

→ Spain
→ Portugal
→ England
→ France

| 0 | 1,000 | 2,000 miles |

| 0 | 1,000 | 2,000 kilometers |

In the late 1400s and during the 1500s, European countries sent expeditions to explore the New World and to search for a new route to Asia.
▶ Which explorer sailed for both Spain and Portugal?

country of Brazil. Then he followed the coast south. More than a year after leaving Spain, Magellan found the waterway he was looking for. It was a stormy, dangerous strait that we call today the Strait of Magellan. It took more than a month to sail through this short passage. Finally Magellan and his crew entered calm waters. This was the ocean Balboa had called the South Sea, but Magellan named it the Pacific Ocean, because *pacific* means "peaceful."

Magellan now set a course that would take him to Asia. He did not know that there were several islands along the way, and he had the bad luck to miss all of them. As a result, his ships sailed for three months without seeing land and with no fresh supplies. The men were so hungry that they ate sawdust, rats, and boiled leather. Many died, and most of the others became ill and weak.

Finally the ships reached the island of Guam, and a week later they arrived at the Philippine Islands. There, Magellan and his crew got plenty of fresh food. They began to feel strong and healthy again. However, Magellan got involved in a battle over religion with a native group and was killed.

Magellan's crew — what was left of it — continued on to the Indies, where they traded for spices. From there, they followed the route that Vasco da Gama had discovered 25 years earlier. They went around the southern tip of Africa and then turned north to Spain. They arrived back in Spain in the year 1522, three years after Magellan had left. Five ships and 240 sailors had started out on this journey. One lone ship with only 18 men on board made it home. But those 18 had achieved what no others had ever done — they had sailed around the world!

C. French Explorers Search for a Northwest Passage

Of course, no one who wanted to go from Europe to Asia would choose Magellan's route around South America. It was far too long and too dangerous. Some European rulers, however, still hoped to find a **northwest passage**, a waterway through or around North America that would lead to Asia.

One of them was the king of France. In 1524 he hired an Italian sailor, Giovanni da Verrazano (joh VAHN ee dah ver uh-ZAH noh), to look for a northwest passage. Verrazano explored the coast of North America from what is now the state of North Carolina in the south to Nova Scotia and Newfoundland in Canada in the north. But to his great disappointment, he found no sign of a waterway to Asia.

In July of 1534, Cartier first sets foot in what was to become part of Canada, on the Gulf of St. Lawrence.
▶ Do the Indians seem to be afraid of the Europeans?

The French king, however, was not ready to give up. When a French sailor named Jacques Cartier (zhahk kahr tee-AY) asked for help to search for a northwest passage, the king gave him ships and money. In 1534, Cartier crossed the Atlantic Ocean with two small ships. Sailing past Newfoundland, he arrived at a large **gulf**, or a part of an ocean or a sea that pushes inland. He named this body of water the Gulf of St. Lawrence. Cartier thought that this opening might be the beginning of a northwest passage. He returned to France to report his discovery.

The next year, the king sent Cartier back to the Gulf of St. Lawrence with more ships and men. Sailing farther into the gulf, Cartier found the mouth of a large river, which he named the St. Lawrence River. He sailed up this river until he came to a **rapid**. A rapid is a place where shallow water races rapidly across a rocky river bottom. Ships cannot pass across a rapid. Disappointed, Cartier had to turn back. Cartier claimed the land for the king of France and called it New France. But he had not found the Northwest Passage.

Cartier went back to North America once more, in 1541. This time it was to look not for a northwest passage but for gold. American Indians had told him tall tales about the riches to be found, but he found nothing of value. Cartier's voyages marked the end of France's exploring in North America for the rest of the 1500s.

With neither England nor France showing any interest in the New World, Spain had a clear field for itself for nearly a hundred years. As you will see, Spain took advantage of this opportunity to become the richest country in Europe.

LESSON  REVIEW

THINK AND WRITE

A. Why was John Cabot's voyage important even though he failed to find a northwest passage?

B. Why can it be said that Ferdinand Magellan succeeded in doing what Columbus had tried to do?

C. What parts of North America were explored by Verrazano and Cartier?

SKILLS CHECK

THINKING SKILL

Use the map on page 129 to make a chart of each explorer named in this lesson and the country or countries that he sailed for.

USING THE VOCABULARY

explore	port
Vikings	isthmus
saga	Gulf
merchant	Northwest Passage
navigation	rapids

On a separate sheet of paper, complete the sentences by using the words listed above.

1. Prince Henry thought it was important for sea captains to have the skill of _____.
2. Ships arrived at the busy _____ and unloaded their cargoes.
3. Adventurous people set out to _____ the New World.
4. The _____ sailed to North America from Norway in the 900s.
5. Many people explored new lands as they searched for the _____.
6. Cartier sailed across the Atlantic Ocean and entered the _____ of St. Lawrence.
7. A Viking folk tale, which is often about events that really happened, is called a _____.
8. The _____ stopped Cartier from sailing farther west.
9. Balboa crossed the narrow _____ and saw a great ocean.
10. Marco Polo was a _____ from Venice who spent many years in China.

REMEMBERING WHAT YOU READ

On a separate sheet of paper, write your answers in complete sentences.

1. Who were the Vikings?
2. What proof is there that the Vikings settled in North America?
3. What goods did the Europeans want from Asia?
4. Why were Europeans searching for an all-water route to Asia?
5. What did Bartholomew Días and Vasco da Gama accomplish?
6. What was Columbus's bold plan for reaching the Indies?
7. How many voyages did Columbus make across the Atlantic?
8. How did Portugal establish a claim to land in the New World?
9. What attracted European explorers after Columbus to the New World?
10. What did Magellan's crew finally accomplish that had not been done before?

TYING SCIENCE TO SOCIAL STUDIES

Use the library or a science textbook to find information on how the sun and the stars can be used for navigation. Write a paragraph, telling how the early explorers depended on the sun and the stars to help them find their way when they were out of sight of land. You could also make a diagram to illustrate this information.

THINKING CRITICALLY

On a separate sheet of paper, write your answers in complete sentences.

1. Why, do you think, did the Vikings' explorations of the New World go unnoticed by other Europeans?
2. How might events have differed if the overland trade routes to Asia had been safe and easy to travel?
3. Why did Columbus's voyages lead to exploration by other Europeans?
4. Even though Prince Henry did not sail on any voyage of exploration, he is considered one of the most important people in the age of exploration. Why, do you think, is this so?
5. What are some qualities that you think many explorers over the centuries might have had in common?

SUMMARIZING THE CHAPTER

On a separate sheet of paper, draw a graphic organizer like the one shown here. Copy the information from this graphic organizer to the one you have drawn. Under the main idea for each lesson, write three statements that support the main idea. The first one has been done for you.

CHAPTER THEME
Europeans came to the Americas and explored what was to them a new world.

LESSON 1

The Vikings were the first Europeans to explore North America.

1. Vinland
2. Sagas
3. Foundations, artifacts

LESSON 2

Europeans searched for an all–water route to Asia.

1.
2.
3.

LESSON 3

Columbus's voyages made Europeans aware of lands that were new to them.

1.
2.
3.

LESSON 4

The search for a northwest passage led to further exploration in the Americas.

1.
2.
3.

5 SPANISH EXPLORATION AND CONQUEST

Spain established colonies on islands in the Caribbean Sea and then went on to explore the mainland of North America and South America. The Spanish settled vast areas on the two continents.

Spain Takes the Lead

Explorers are people who search for new places and new things. List some reasons why people, like the astronauts in our space program, want to explore new places.

STUDY THE VOCABULARY

conquistador   peninsula

FOCUS YOUR READING

Why was Cortés able to conquer the Aztecs?

A. Ponce de León Discovers Florida

Columbus, Cabot, Magellan, Verrazano, Cartier — if there were a Hall of Fame for the history of early America, these fearless explorers would surely be in it. As you know, an explorer is a person who searches for new things and places. Yet none of these men actually had much interest in America. Their aim was to find a route to the Indies in Asia. To all of them, America was just something in the way — something to find a way around.

In time it dawned on the Spanish that America might have even greater riches than the Indies. Led by a small group of bold, daring, and sometimes cruel men, Spain set out to take control of the new territory in America. These men were called **conquistadores** (kahn kwihs tuh-DOR eez), which is the Spanish word for "conquerors." And conquerors they were — some of the best known in history.

One such conquistador was Juan Ponce de León (wahn PAHN say day lay OHN). Ponce de León had sailed with Columbus on his second voyage and was a soldier on Hispaniola. Early in the 1500s, he went to Puerto Rico to look for gold. He found some, and he also conquered the Native American population there and started Spanish rule.

In the year 1513, Ponce de León sailed off again in search of gold. Some say he was also looking for a fountain whose magical waters could keep a person from growing old. He did not find gold, and he did not find a fountain of youth. He did, however, find a beautiful **peninsula** filled with flowers. A peninsula is a narrow strip of

Ponce de León and his men enjoy a beautiful new land.
▶ What shows you that this area probably got plenty of rain?

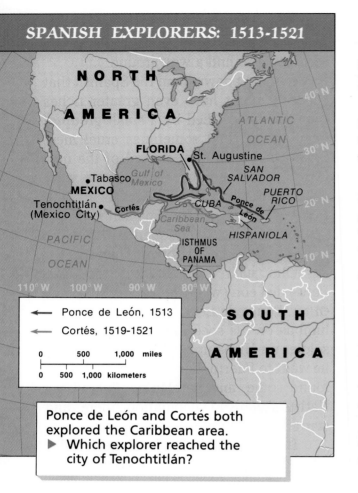

NORTH AMERICA

ATLANTIC OCEAN

FLORIDA
● St. Augustine

● Tabasco *Gulf of Mexico*

MEXICO

SAN SALVADOR

Tenochtitlán ● *Cortés* PUERTO RICO

(Mexico City) CUBA Ponce de León

Caribbean Sea

HISPANIOLA

PACIFIC OCEAN

ISTHMUS OF PANAMA

SOUTH AMERICA

← Ponce de León, 1513
← Cortés, 1519–1521

0   500   1,000 miles
0   500 1,000 kilometers

Ponce de León and Cortés both explored the Caribbean area.
▶ Which explorer reached the city of Tenochtitlán?

In the year 1519, Cortés won permission from the Spanish governor of the island of Cuba to explore Mexico. Gathering 11 ships, 100 sailors, and 500 soldiers, he set off for Mexico. Along with the men, Cortés took 10 cannons and 16 horses. It was lucky for him that he did.

Soon after landing in Mexico, the Spaniards fought a fierce battle with some Indians near a village called Tabasco. The Tabascan Indians greatly outnumbered Cortés's army. They attacked with arrows and spears. For a time it appeared the Tabascans might defeat the Spaniards and drive them away.

But this is where the cannons and horses came in. The Indians had never seen either before. They were startled by the thunder and lightning that came from the mouths of the cannons. They were terrified when they saw a horse and rider, for they thought the two were all one animal. They agreed to make peace.

C. A Case of Mistaken Identity Helps Cortés

Not long afterward, a messenger arrived with gifts. He was a servant of Moctezuma (mohk tay SOO mah), ruler of the Aztecs. The messenger asked where the bearded, white-skinned stranger was from and why he had come to Mexico.

Moctezuma had a special reason for asking these questions. The Aztecs believed that hundreds of years earlier, one of their gods, Quetzalcoatl (ket sahl koh-AHT ul), had lived among them as their king. Quetzalcoatl had light skin and a beard. One day, went the story, Quetzalcoatl left the Aztecs. As he sailed away to the east, he promised to return someday to be their king again. The Aztecs counted time in 52-year periods. This would be very

---

land surrounded on three sides by water. Ponce de León named this peninsula Florida. Many years later, in 1565, Spain founded the first European colony in present-day United States at St. Augustine, near the spot where Ponce de León had landed.

B. Cortés Seeks Gold, Adventure, and Conquest

Hernando Cortés (hur NAN doh kor-TEZ) was an even greater conquistador than Ponce de León. While working in Cuba, Cortés often heard the Indian natives speak of a great city of gold in Mexico. He began to think of conquering this city. Gold, adventure, conquest—wasn't this why he had come to America?

similar to the way that we count 100-year periods of time as centuries. Quetzalcoatl had said he would return at the beginning of one of those 52-year periods.

For hundreds of years, the Aztecs had looked eastward to the sea, waiting for Quetzalcoatl's promised return. Now, this light-skinned, bearded man had arrived from the east. It was also the start of a 52-year period on the Aztec calendar. Could this man, then, be Quetzalcoatl? Was he returning to replace Moctezuma as the ruler of the Aztecs?

Some weeks later, Moctezuma sent a second messenger with gifts of gold and silver. In today's money, the gold alone would be worth more than a million dollars. Moctezuma hoped that the gifts would satisfy the strangers and that they would go away. But the great Aztec ruler was badly mistaken. Instead, the gifts made Cortés more determined to take Moctezuma's city.

But how could he do this? Cortés had only several hundred soldiers, while Moctezuma had many thousands. The answer

(Left) Cortés and his soldiers approach the capital city of the great Aztec Empire. (Right) Moctezuma and his chiefs come to welcome Cortés.

▶ What shows you that Moctezuma was important?

137

came from several Native Americans who walked into Cortés's camp. Their people had been conquered by the Aztecs and treated cruelly. They told Cortés that their people would gladly help fight the Aztecs. Cortés also learned that some other Native Americans felt the same way.

D. Cortés Conquers the Aztecs

Cortés now set out for Tenochtitlán. His men marched through the jungle and across mountains. After 45 days, they arrived at Tenochtitlán. Moctezuma was still not sure whether Cortés was Quetzalcoatl, but he was taking no chances. He welcomed Cortés to Tenochtitlán. He even turned over his own palace to Cortés.

These acts of friendship toward his strange visitors did not help Moctezuma.

Several days later, Cortés ordered him seized and held prisoner. Cortés had decided to rule the Aztecs by telling Moctezuma what orders to give the people.

For a while, Cortés's plan worked. During this time the Spaniards took all the gold they could. To keep the Aztecs in fear of them, they fired off their cannons every so often.

After several months, however, the Aztecs had had enough of the Spanish. Fighting broke out between the two groups. When Moctezuma stepped outdoors to calm his people, he was struck by a stone and killed. Heavy fighting followed, and many Spaniards were killed. The Spanish were forced to retreat from the city, leaving behind much of the treasure they had taken.

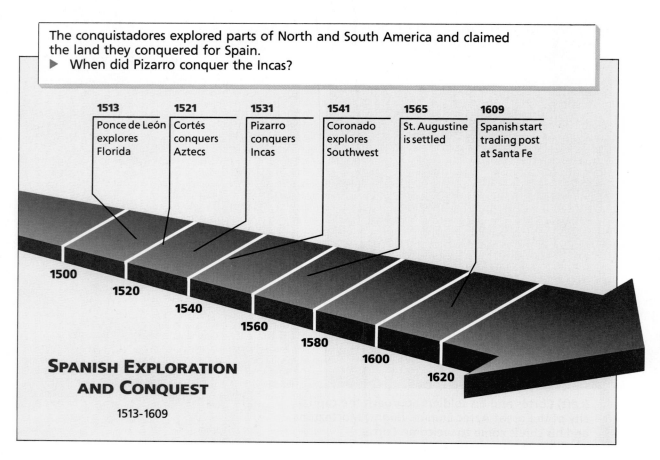

The conquistadores explored parts of North and South America and claimed the land they conquered for Spain.
▶ When did Pizarro conquer the Incas?

1513	1521	1531	1541	1565	1609
Ponce de León explores Florida	Cortés conquers Aztecs	Pizarro conquers Incas	Coronado explores Southwest	St. Augustine is settled	Spanish start trading post at Santa Fe

1500
1520
1540
1560
1580
1600
1620

SPANISH EXPLORATION AND CONQUEST
1513-1609

Cortés and his men are shown here storming Tenochtitlán and setting fire to an Aztec temple.
▶ Where was the temple built?

Finally, in the year 1521, more Spanish soldiers arrived with guns, horses, and cannons to help Cortés. Thousands of Native American enemies of the Aztecs also joined the Spaniards. That summer they attacked Tenochtitlán.

Cortés conquered the city. The Spaniards destroyed the Aztec temples and palaces, and on their ruins they built a city of their own. This was the beginning of Mexico city. With its capital city destroyed, the Aztec nation was beaten. Cortés went on to conquer the rest of Mexico for the king of Spain.

LESSON *1* REVIEW

THINK AND WRITE

A. Why can Ponce de León be called both an explorer and a conqueror?
B. Why was Cortés able to conquer the Tabascans even though the Indians outnumbered the Spaniards?
C. Why didn't Moctezuma order Aztec soldiers to stop Cortés?
D. How did Cortés succeed in conquering the Aztecs?

SKILLS CHECK

WRITING SKILL

Imagine that you are an Aztec living in Tenochtitlán at the time of Cortés's arrival. Express your feelings in writing.

Pizarro and the Incas

THINK ABOUT WHAT YOU KNOW

What do you think when you hear about a country that conquers other countries?

STUDY THE VOCABULARY

ancestor   epidemic

FOCUS YOUR READING

How did Pizarro conquer the Inca Empire?

A. Pizarro's Trick Leads to Victory

Francisco Pizarro's (fran SIHS koh pih ZAHR ohz) conquest of the Incas was even more incredible than Cortés's conquest of the Aztecs. Pizarro was living in Panama when he learned of the rich Inca Empire farther to the south. In 1531 he led a group of 167 men to Peru. Pizarro was nearly 60 years old and unable to read or write. Most of his men were not even soldiers. But they were well armed with guns and steel swords, and they had horses. They set up a small settlement near the coast of Peru.

The ruler of the Incas was Atahualpa (ah tah WAHL pah). It is not likely that Atahualpa was worried by the news that a small band of strangers had arrived in his land. After all, Atahualpa's armies numbered in the thousands, and he had great stone forts for protection. What reason could he possibly have had to be afraid? So when Hernando de Soto, one of the Spanish commanders, rode into his camp to invite the great Inca ruler to meet Pizarro, Atahualpa agreed.

The invitation was a trick. The meeting place was the square of a nearby town. The Spaniards hid in the buildings around the square. Atahualpa entered the square with about 3,000 followers, nearly all of them unarmed. Pizarro rode out to meet the Inca. Through an interpreter, he demanded that Atahualpa accept the Christian religion. Atahualpa refused.

Suddenly the roar of a cannon split the air. This was the signal for the Spaniards to charge forward on horseback. With guns firing and swords slashing, they

Atahualpa, the Inca ruler, is being carried to meet Francisco Pizarro.
▶ Find an armed Inca. How can you tell that he does not plan to use his weapon?

killed thousands of Incas and took Atahualpa prisoner. Impossible as it may seem, 168 men destroyed the power of the great Inca Empire—not in months or weeks or even days but in half an hour of merciless killing.

B. Pizarro Breaks a Promise

The land of the Incas was rich in gold and silver. Hoping to win his freedom, Atahualpa offered to fill the room he was held in with gold, and another room with silver. For the next eight months, Incas brought beautiful gold and silver statues, plates, and ornaments to Atahualpa's rooms. Finally the rooms were filled. Atahualpa had kept his part of the bargain.

But Pizarro did not keep his. He ordered that Atahualpa be strangled. As for the gold and silver works of art, Pizarro ordered them melted down and formed into bars. With that command, much of the finest art of the great Inca Empire was lost to the flames forever. Pizarro and his men next marched on the Inca capital city of Cuzco. Without their leader, the Incas were helpless. The capital city fell without

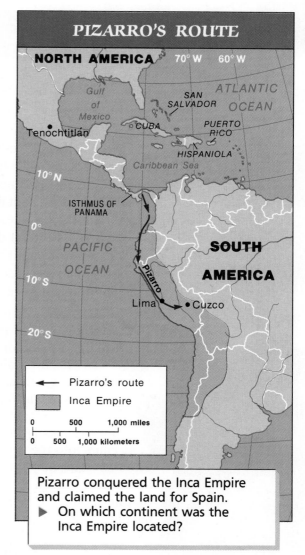

PIZARRO'S ROUTE

Pizarro conquered the Inca Empire and claimed the land for Spain.
▶ On which continent was the Inca Empire located?

a struggle. The Spaniards soon took over the whole Inca Empire and all its wealth.

Today, in Lima, the capital city of Peru, there stands a statue of Francisco Pizarro. Many Peruvians see the statue as a fitting monument to the man they consider the founder of the modern nation of Peru. However, there are countless others who feel differently about the statue. To many proud descendants of the Incas, the statue is a painful reminder of the destruction of the once-mighty empire of their **ancestors**. An ancestor is a family member who lived long ago.

This gold ceremonial vessel is from the Inca Empire in Peru.
▶ What kind of bird does this vessel represent?

141

THE DEATH OF ATAHUALPA

How do people today know what happened in Peru long ago? One way is to read what people who were there wrote about what happened. Francisco Pizarro could not read or write. So he asked one of his captains to act as his secretary and to write a history of the conquest of Peru. Among the events Francisco de Xeres (day HE res.) described was the death of the Inca Atahualpa.

The account written by de Xeres states that Pizarro claimed that Atahualpa was secretly readying an army to attack the Spaniards. He accused Atahualpa of treason.

Then the Governor [Pizarro], with the concurrence [agreement] of the officers of his Majesty [Charles V of Spain], and of the captains and persons of experience, sentenced [Atahualpa] to death. . . . he should die by burning, unless he became a Christian; and this execution was for the security of the Christians, the good of the whole land, and to secure its conquest. . . . They brought [Atahualpa] to execution; and, when he came into the square, he said would become a Christian. The Governor was informed, and ordered him to be baptized. . . . The Governor then ordered that he should not be burnt, but that he should be fastened to a pole in the open space and strangled. This was done, and the body was left until the morning of the next day, when the Monks and the Governor with other Spaniards, conveyed it into the church, where it was interred [buried] with much solemnity, and with all honours that could be shown it. Such was the end of this man, who had been so cruel. He died with great fortitude [courage], and without shrewing [showing] any feeling, saying that he entrusted his children to the Governor.

Understanding Source Material

1. Who charged Atahualpa with treason and who found him guilty?
2. Why was Atahualpa strangled and not burned to death?
3. Do you think the followers of the Inca would have described these events differently? Explain your answer.

C. European Diseases Destroy the Native Americans

The coming of the Spaniards was a disaster to the Native Americans of Middle and South America. The invaders destroyed cities, tore down temples, and stole everything of value. They killed thousands of inhabitants, and they made slaves of thousands more.

Far more terrible than Spanish guns and swords was the **epidemic** of diseases that the Spaniards had brought from Europe. An epidemic is the spread of disease to a large number of people in a short period of time. Diseases such as smallpox and measles had been unknown among the American Indians. Their bodies had developed no defense against them.

European diseases led to the greatest decline of population in history. Millions of Native Americans died. Disease killed off more than half of the Inca population and most of the Aztec population. The conquering of the Aztec and Inca empires destroyed two powerful Native American civilizations.

Here, Indian slave labor is being used by the Spaniards to build what is probably a church.
► Why, do you think, are there Spaniards present at this site?

LESSON 2 REVIEW

THINK AND WRITE

A. What was the main reason that Pizarro's small band of soldiers was able to conquer Atahualpa's 3,000 followers?

B. Why do the people of Peru today have two different attitudes toward Pizarro?

C. Why did the coming of the Europeans have such bad effects on the Native Americans of Middle and South America?

SKILLS CHECK

MAP SKILL

Use the Gazetteer to find two important facts about Lima, Peru, and Tenochtitlán. Use the scale on the map on page 141 to find out the distance between the two places.

In Search of Gold

THINK ABOUT WHAT YOU KNOW

Why, do you think, did the Spanish want gold so badly? Why is gold still so valuable today?

STUDY THE VOCABULARY

slave   mission
colony   missionary
trading post

FOCUS YOUR READING

What did the Spaniards find when they explored lands north of Mexico?

A. Spaniards Search for the Seven Cities of Gold

Desire for Treasure After conquering Mexico the Spaniards turned their attention to lands to the north. As always, it was the search for treasure that drove them.

One group explored the west coast of Florida in the year 1527. From there they sailed west across the Gulf of Mexico, only to be shipwrecked on the coast of Texas. For the next six years, the survivors of this shipwreck wandered through Texas, New Mexico, and Arizona. By the time the group made its way back to Mexico, there were only four survivors. One was a Spaniard named Núñez Cabeza de Vaca. Another was an African **slave** named Estevanico (es tay vah NEE koh). A slave is a person who is owned by another person and must work for that owner for nothing.

Tales of Riches In Mexico, Cabeza de Vaca amazed his listeners with his stories about the land to the north. He had seen great herds of strange humpbacked cows with curly, shaggy hair, he said. (These were buffaloes, of course!) And he reported that some Indians had told him of great rich cities that lay farther on.

Cabeza de Vaca's story seemed to fit with an old Spanish legend. According to this legend, bishops of the church had left Spain and founded Seven Cities of Gold somewhere across the ocean. The Seven Cities were called Cíbola. Many of those who heard Cabeza de Vaca believed that his story must be about Cíbola.

Seven Cities of Gold In 1539 a priest, Friar Marcos, was sent northward from Mexico with a small group to scout the area. Estevanico served as his guide. Estevanico had traveled these paths before, and he knew several Indian languages. He decided to go on ahead, leaving markers

along the way for Marcos's group to follow. For a time, all went well. But in a small Zuñi town, the inhabitants killed Estevanico. On learning this, Friar Marcos returned to Mexico.

Friar Marcos had seen the town where Estevanico was killed from a distance. But when he got back to Mexico, he used plenty of imagination in describing it. The city he saw was larger than Mexico City, he said. The doorways of its stone houses were trimmed with emeralds and turquoise—two precious stones. And, he added for good measure, even richer cities lay just beyond. Surely here were the Seven Cities of Gold!

B. Exploring the American Southwest

The Spanish could hardly wait to get going. Early in 1540, Francisco Coronado (fran SIHS koh kor uh NAH doh) set out northward with an army of 300. After four months he arrived at the place that Friar Marcos described. What he found was not a great city, but several simple little Indian villages. To Coronado's great disappointment, the Seven Cities of Gold were nothing but seven little villages of clay.

You would think that after falling for Friar Marcos's story, Coronado had learned his lesson. He hadn't. The Spanish troops had taken prisoner an Indian they

Coronado leads his Spanish expedition to what are now the states of Arizona and New Mexico. A Native American is showing the way. The picture on the left shows the kind of armor and helmet that some of the Spaniards are wearing.
▶ Of what material are the Spaniards' armor and helmets made?

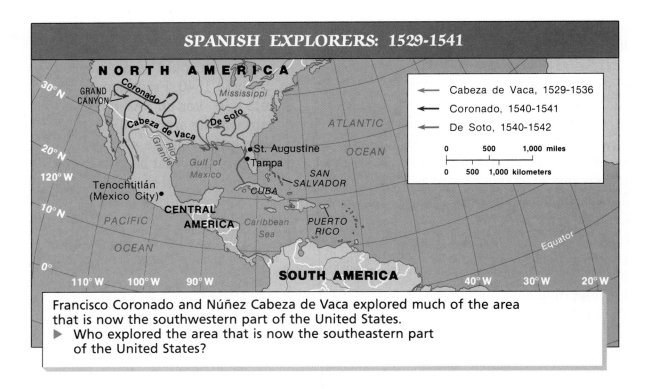

SPANISH EXPLORERS: 1529-1541

Cabeza de Vaca, 1529-1536
Coronado, 1540-1541
De Soto, 1540-1542

Francisco Coronado and Núñez Cabeza de Vaca explored much of the area that is now the southwestern part of the United States.
▶ Who explored the area that is now the southeastern part of the United States?

called the Turk. The Turk wanted to win favor with his Spanish captors.

He began to tell stories of a fantastic country to the east. He told of a river 6 miles (10 km) wide, full of fish bigger than horses. There were great rulers in this land, with plenty of gold. Gold, asked Coronado? How much gold? So much, answered the Turk, that even the rulers' canoes had gold oarlocks. The name of this country was Quivira (kih VIHR uh).

In 1541, Coronado set out to find Quivira. All spring, summer, and fall, his army marched through what is now New Mexico, Texas, Oklahoma, and Kansas. Of course, they did not find what they were seeking. There was no river 6 miles (10 km) wide, no great rulers, no canoes —and no gold.

Coronado believed his trip was a failure. In a way, it was. But though he had found no treasure, his journey was still important to his country and king. It gave Spain a claim to the huge region that forms the American Southwest today.

C. Hernando de Soto Explores the American Southeast

While Coronado was hunting for the Seven Cities of Gold in America's Southwest, another Spanish explorer was looking for them in America's Southeast. His name was Hernando de Soto. De Soto's exploration of the New World took him from Florida across the southeastern part of North America.

De Soto had been one of Pizarro's men in Peru. In 1539, he and several hundred Spaniards landed near what is today Tampa, Florida. Like Coronado, De Soto was ready to believe the stories that Indians told him about golden cities. The Native Americans were glad to tell the Spaniards whatever they wanted to hear. *"Poco mas allá,"* they told the Spanish — "just a little farther on."

So, for the next three years, De Soto zigzagged through parts of Georgia, South Carolina, Tennessee, Alabama, Mississippi, Arkansas, and Louisiana. In 1541 he and his men came upon the Mississippi River. They were the first Europeans to see North America's greatest river.

In 1542, De Soto fell ill and died. Like Coronado, he had found no gold. But, like Coronado, De Soto had performed a great service to his country and king. Just as Coronado's journey gave Spain a claim to the Southwest, De Soto's explorations gave Spain a claim to much of the southeastern part of today's United States.

Below is an artist's idea of how Hernando de Soto and his men looked when they first saw the mighty Mississippi River. Behind De Soto you can see a banner bearing his name.

▶ Which person, do you think, is Hernando de Soto?

147

D. The Spaniards Build Farms and Missions in the Americas

New World Farms While Coronado and De Soto were chasing after gold without success, other Spaniards were discovering that the New World offered other ways to wealth. They got the king of Spain to give them large pieces of land in South America, Middle America, and the islands in the Caribbean Sea. On this land the Spaniards developed huge sugar and wheat farms. They also raised cattle and sheep. The landowners made money by selling their farm products to Spain.

Native Americans provided the back-breaking work on these farms. The landowners made the Indians slaves. The Spanish treated these slaves cruelly. As a result of this miserable treatment, terrible working conditions, and European diseases, many Indian slaves died. To replace them, in the mid-1500s the Spanish began to buy slaves from Africa. By the end of the 1500s, most of the slaves were African.

All of the Spaniards' farms and ranches were in South America, Middle America, and the islands of the Caribbean Sea. Except for St. Augustine, the Spanish did not start any **colonies** north of Mexico in the 1500s. A colony is a place that is settled at a distance from the country that governs it.

Forts and Missions In 1609 the Spanish built a small fort and **trading post** at Santa Fe, in present-day New Mexico. A trading post is a place where people trade goods with the people who live in the area. They

This 1584 drawing shows a Spanish silver mine in what is now the country of Bolivia, in South America.
▶ Find Bolivia on the map on page 618.

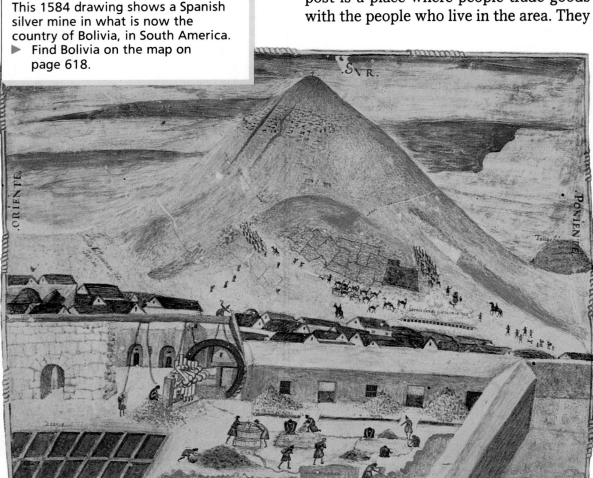

The ruins of a 1620s Spanish church still stand at San Gregorio de Abó Mission, in present-day New Mexico. A Pueblo town lies buried here.

▶ Why, do you think, did the Spanish build a mission in an Indian village?

also built a **mission** there. A mission is a settlement of religious teachers. It has a church and several other buildings. The teachers, who are called **missionaries**, try to convert other people to their religion and also try to provide these people with help they might need. Catholic priests were sent from Spain to teach the Indians Christianity at the Santa Fe mission. They also taught the Native Americans European methods of farming and cattle raising and introduced Spanish crops and fruit trees, such as orange and lemon trees. By the 1630s there was a sprinkling of Spanish missions along the Rio Grande. *Rio* is the Spanish word for "river."

LESSON 3 REVIEW

THINK AND WRITE

A. Why, do you think, did the Spaniards believe Friar Marcos's story that he had found the Seven Cities of Gold?

B. How did Spain come to claim a large area of land that is the American Southwest today?

C. What were some ways in which De Soto's exploration of the Southeast was similar to Coronado's exploration of the Southwest?

D. How did some Spaniards become wealthy in the New World, even though they did not find gold?

SKILLS CHECK

THINKING SKILL

Pretend that you are a missionary at a Spanish mission in the Southwest who has just met an Indian slave. Make a list of ways in which the Indian's life has changed since the Spaniards came to the New World.

USING THE VOCABULARY

conquistadores	colony
peninsula	trading post
ancestor	mission
epidemic	missionary
slave	

On a separate sheet of paper, complete these sentences, using some of the words listed above.

1. Spanish explorers, who were also soldiers, were called _____.
2. A place set up in the wilderness where goods were exchanged with the people who lived there was a _____.
3. Land surrounded on three sides by water is a _____.
4. A family member who lived long ago is an _____.
5. A _____ is a settlement of religious teachers.

REMEMBERING WHAT YOU READ

On a separate sheet of paper, write your answers in complete sentences.

1. What were the Spanish conquistadores looking for?
2. Who conquered Puerto Rico and began Spanish rule there?
3. Why did some Native Americans help Cortés fight the Aztecs?
4. What is the Aztec city of Tenochtitlán now called?
5. Why did Atahualpa agree to meet with Pizarro and his men?
6. What was the bargain Atahualpa made with Pizarro?
7. Why did diseases such as smallpox and measles have such a terrible effect on the Native Americans?
8. What was the legend about the Seven Cities of Gold?
9. Why were Coronado's and De Soto's journeys successful even though the explorers found no gold?
10. Why did the Spaniards begin to import people from Africa to work as slaves on their farms?

TYING LANGUAGE ARTS TO SOCIAL STUDIES

School children for generations have remembered the year Christopher Columbus made his first voyage by reciting this jingle:

> In fourteen hundred ninety-two,
> Columbus sailed the ocean blue.

Choose one of the explorers you studied in this chapter and write some jingles or rhymes that will help you remember important facts about him.

Here is another example:

> "I came to conquer," said Pizarro,
> Carefully ducking an Inca arrow.

Now you go ahead and write a few.

THINKING CRITICALLY

On a separate sheet of paper, write your answers in complete sentences.

1. You have read that the conquistadores were "bold, daring, sometimes cruel men." Do you think this is an accurate description? Explain your answer.
2. Why, do you think, did the Spaniards destroy Moctezuma's city?
3. The people of Peru have two opinions about Pizarro. He was great because he founded their nation, and he was bad because he destroyed the Inca Empire. Which opinion do you agree with? Do you have still another opinion about Pizarro? Explain your answer.
4. Why did the Native Americans tell the Spaniards about great cities and golden treasure that were always just a little farther away, and why did the Spaniards keep believing them?
5. What were some of the long-term effects of the Spanish conquest of Central and South America?

SUMMARIZING THE CHAPTER

Copy this chart on a separate sheet of paper. Complete the chart by filling in the missing information.

CHAPTER THEME > Through exploration and conquest, Spain claimed territory in both North America and South America.

EXPLORER	REGION	RESULTS
	Puerto Rico and Florida	
		Conquered and destroyed Aztec Empire Claimed land and treasure for Spain
Pizarro		
	Southwestern United States	
De Soto		

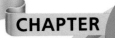

CHAPTER 6

EUROPEAN SETTLEMENTS IN NORTH AMERICA

France, England, and the Netherlands explored and settled in the New World. The French and English claimed large portions of North America. After a poor start, the English colonies grew quickly.

England Turns to the New World

Imagine that you are going to move to a colony in the New World. Make a list of some of the things you want to know about the colony before you go there.

STUDY THE VOCABULARY

pirate
joint-stock
  company
bay

represent
assembly
House of Burgesses

FOCUS YOUR READING

What happened to the first colonies England tried to start in the Americas?

A. A Different Idea

As the New World's gold and silver poured into Spain's treasury, other countries were filled with envy. Several of them sent explorers to claim land in the Americas, hoping to find riches for themselves.

Francis Drake, an English sea captain, had a different idea about sharing in the riches. Drake's idea was simple. Let the Spaniards take the gold from the New World; then he would take the gold from the Spaniards.

Drake was not the only English sea captain with this idea, but he was the most daring. His boldest move against the Spanish came in 1577. The queen of England sent him to sail through the Strait of Magellan to explore the western coast of South America. Drake decided to make this a profitable trip. He attacked several Spanish towns on the coast, taking supplies and gold. Then he attacked two Spanish ships and took over $9 million worth of gold, silver, and jewels.

Drake figured that Spanish warships would wait for him to return the way he had come. Instead of returning by the same route, he sailed across the Pacific Ocean, rounded the southern tip of Africa, and headed home to England. The voyage took three years. The English queen and English people greeted Drake as a hero. The Spanish, of course, were outraged. To them Drake was nothing but a **pirate**—a person who stole riches from their ships.

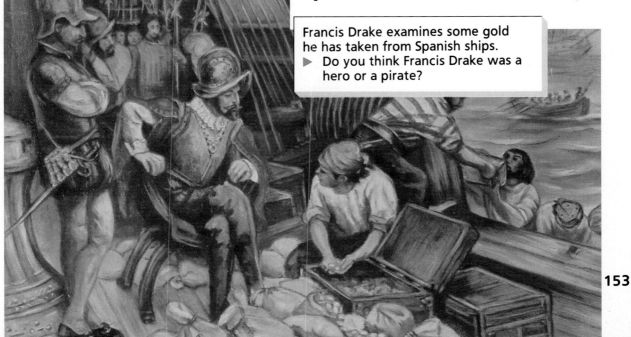

Francis Drake examines some gold he has taken from Spanish ships.
▶ Do you think Francis Drake was a hero or a pirate?

153

English colonies were founded at Roanoke, Jamestown, and Plymouth.
▶ Which colony was founded first, Plymouth or Jamestown?

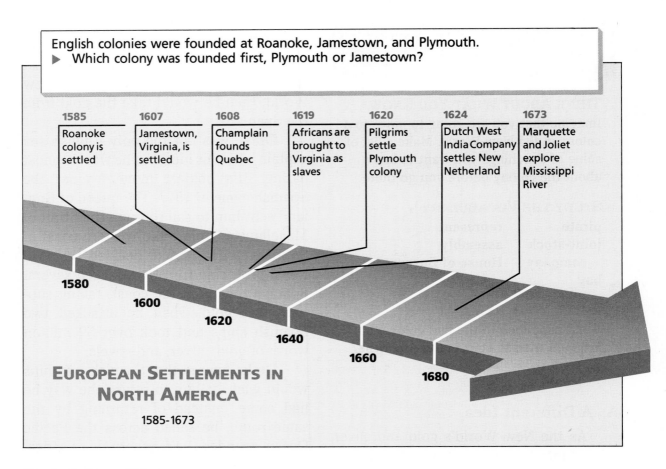

1585 Roanoke colony is settled

1607 Jamestown, Virginia, is settled

1608 Champlain founds Quebec

1619 Africans are brought to Virginia as slaves

1620 Pilgrims settle Plymouth colony

1624 Dutch West India Company settles New Netherland

1673 Marquette and Joliet explore Mississippi River

1580 1600 1620 1640 1660 1680

EUROPEAN SETTLEMENTS IN NORTH AMERICA

1585-1673

B. A Colony Disappears

Roanoke While Drake was stealing Spanish gold, other English people were planning colonies in the New World. One of these people was Sir Walter Raleigh, a wealthy friend of the queen. The queen gave Raleigh permission to start a colony in North America.

In 1585, Raleigh sent 100 colonists with food and supplies to Roanoke Island, off the coast of present-day North Carolina. Things went badly from the beginning. Thinking they could depend on the friendly Native Americans to give them food, the settlers did not plant their own crops. Indians did help the English for a while, but they soon tired of that.

Before the end of the year, the settlers were starving. Fortunately, Francis Drake stopped at Roanoke Island on one of his voyages. He brought the settlers back to England.

Raleigh did not give up. In 1587 he sent more colonists to Roanoke. This time the settlers went right to work. The colonists built a fort and planted crops. The Roanoke colony was off to a good start. Some months later the number of colonists was increased by one with the birth of Virginia Dare. She was the first English child born in the New World.

The Lost Colony Soon after, however, England became involved in a war. For over three years, Raleigh was out of touch with the colony. Finally, in 1591, an English ship returned to Roanoke Island. There was no sign of life anywhere. All that was found were a few empty trunks, several rotted maps, some rusty armor, and the word CROATOAN (kroh uh toh AN) carved on the doorpost of the fort—nothing else.

Croatoan was an island about 100 miles (161 km) to the south. Why was CROATOAN carved into the doorpost? Were the settlers attacked by the Croatoan Indians? Did the settlers decide to live on this island? If so, why? The English ship had to return to England before anyone could find out, and no one has found out since. The fate of the Lost Colony of Roanoke remains one of the great mysteries of American history.

C. The English Raise Money for a Colony

Sir Walter Raleigh had lost a fortune trying to start a colony on Roanoke Island. His experience showed that trying to plant a colony was too risky for one person. So in 1606 a group of English merchants decided to share the costs of starting a colony by forming a **joint-stock company**. In a joint-stock company, instead of one person's putting up *all* the money, a number of people each put up *part* of the money and share ownership. Each owner receives a certificate called a *stock,* or *share.* If the company makes money, all the *stockholders* share in the gains. If the company loses money, all share in the losses. But no one risks everything.

The merchants called their joint-stock company the Virginia Company of London. Stockholders planned to send settlers to America. The settlers were to send back furs, lumber, and other products to England for sale. The stockholders also hoped that settlers would find gold and silver.

Stockholders in a joint-stock company shared the cost and the risks of starting a colony in the New World.
▶ Who gave permission for the stock company to start a new colony?

4. Company sends ships to explore and to trade, and sends people to start a colony.

1. Stockholders put up the money to form a stock company.

3. The stock company buys ships and supplies to start a colony.

5. The company receives profits from trade in lumber, fish, and furs.

Charter
This stock company shall have land along the Atlantic coast from....
It shall have the power to make laws for the colony.
George

2. The king grants the stock company a charter that tells what land the company will receive to start a colony.

HOW A JOINT-STOCK COMPANY WORKS

155

Looking forward to adventure and a chance to get rich quickly, 120 men and boys signed up to be settlers in the new colony. On a cold, gray day in December, 1606, they sailed from London aboard three ships — the *Susan Constant*, the *Discovery*, and the *Godspeed*.

D. English Settlers Arrive in Jamestown

Coming To Jamestown The journey to America took more than four months, and 15 passengers died at sea. Finally, in April 1607, the three ships reached the Virginia coast and sailed into Chesapeake Bay. A

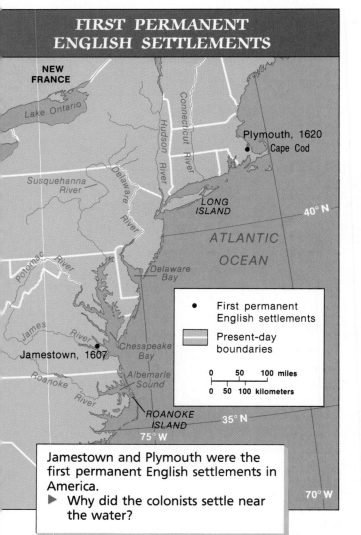

FIRST PERMANENT ENGLISH SETTLEMENTS

NEW FRANCE

Lake Ontario

Susquehanna River

Hudson River

Connecticut River

Delaware River

Plymouth, 1620
Cape Cod

LONG ISLAND

40° N

ATLANTIC OCEAN

Potomac River

Delaware Bay

• First permanent English settlements

Present-day boundaries

0   50   100 miles

0   50 100 kilometers

James River

Chesapeake Bay

Jamestown, 1607

Roanoke River

Albemarle Sound

ROANOKE ISLAND

35° N

75° W

70° W

Jamestown and Plymouth were the first permanent English settlements in America.
▶ Why did the colonists settle near the water?

bay is a part of the ocean that cuts deep into the land. The settlers chose a place on the bank of a river. They believed this place would be easy to defend. The settlers built a fort, several houses, and a storehouse for food and supplies. They named the settlement Jamestown in honor of their king.

The settlers of Jamestown could hardly have picked a worse spot to live. The land was low and swampy. This was a perfect place for disease-carrying mosquitoes to breed. The air, which was pleasant and warm in the spring, became hot and humid in summer. Thick woods had to be cleared before planting could begin.

Troubles in Jamestown It would have been hard to find a group of people less suited to starting a colony. Half of the men in Jamestown were from the "gentleman" class. They had never worked with their hands in England, and they did not plan to start now. Most of the other colonists had never farmed before. The Virginia Company made matters worse by ordering the colonists to share the food they grew. Since people knew that they would eat whether they worked or not, nobody worked very hard.

Also, instead of trying to get along with the Indians, the colonists stole their corn and fought with them. Instead of clearing trees and planting, the colonists spent their time searching for gold.

By winter the food brought from England was almost gone. Week after week, settlers died from disease and starvation. Of the 105 who had landed in Jamestown, only 38 were still alive by Christmas. Two things kept the colony going. First, a ship with fresh supplies and more settlers arrived early in 1608. Second, John Smith became the new leader of the colony.

The first Jamestown settlers built homes inside the walls of a fort.
▶ Why, do you think, did later settlers build outside the walls?

E. John Smith Becomes the Leader of Jamestown

Smith Takes Charge John Smith was a remarkable man. He had already had a life of adventure before he arrived in Jamestown. He had been a soldier for several kings in Europe and had fought in many battles. Once he was captured and was sent to the country of Turkey as a slave. He escaped and made his way back to England.

Smith's adventures continued in the New World when he was captured by the Powhatan Indians. He was to be killed, but Pocahontas (poh kuh HAHNT us), the 11-year-old daughter of the chief, pleaded for Smith's life.

Once John Smith was made the leader of Jamestown, he quickly took charge of the colony. He put an end to the settlers'

laziness with a simple order. "He that will not work, shall not eat," said Smith. The settlers set to work. They repaired houses. They cleared land and planted crops. They hunted for food. They learned to get along better with the Native Americans and traded with them. Although more food and supplies were still needed, things were getting better. More settlers arrived. By early 1609 the colony had 500 people.

Jamestown Nearly Fails Early in 1609, Smith was injured when his gunpowder accidentally blew up. He had to return to England for medical help. Still worse, the Virginia Company of London did not send enough supplies that year. As a result, the winter of 1609–1610 was known as the "starving time." To keep alive, the colonists ate roots, dogs, cats, snakes, and rats. Of the 500 who started out that winter, only 60 were still alive the next spring.

By the summer of 1610, the handful of survivors decided to return to England. As they sailed down the James River toward the ocean, they met ships with food, supplies, and 300 colonists coming toward them. The settlers returned to Jamestown to try again. If the ship had arrived only a few hours later, Jamestown would have been just another English colony that failed. Instead, it became the first English colony in America to succeed.

F. Jamestown Prospers and Grows

Tobacco Saves the Colony For several more years the colony struggled. Then one colonist, John Rolfe, tried planting tobacco he had brought from the West Indies. By 1613, Rolfe had developed a mild-tasting tobacco. He sent some to England, and the English liked it. Soon, settlers were shipping tobacco to England and getting high prices for it. They began to plant tobacco everywhere — even in the streets and graveyards of Jamestown!

Meanwhile, the Virginia Company of London made two important decisions that helped the colony grow. First, the company gave land to settlers who had already lived in the colony for seven years. Up until then, the company had owned all the land. Once the colonists owned their own land, they worked much harder and raised more crops. Second, the company offered 50 acres (20 ha) of free land to anyone who paid his own way to get to the settlement. It gave another 50 acres (20 ha) of land to anyone who paid to bring over a worker.

Fifty acres for becoming a colonist! That was more land than most English people dreamed of owning in a lifetime. This offer brought many settlers to America. Settlements appeared up and down

This picture shows a Jamestown home some time after women arrived.
▶ How might it differ from an earlier Jamestown home?

the James River, and farther inland, too. These settlements, together, formed the colony of Virginia. In the year 1622 a third of the settlers living in the colony were killed in a terrible war with Native Americans. Even this did not stop the Jamestown colony's rapid growth.

Women Come to Virginia The year 1619 saw three events of great importance to the future of Virginia. One was the arrival of a ship with 90 women from England. Until then, Virginia's population was made up mostly of men who planned to get rich quickly and return to England. The Virginia Company wanted settlers to make Virginia their home. So it advertised for single women to go to Virginia, promising that they would find husbands there.

African Americans The second important event of 1619 was the arrival of a Dutch ship with 20 Africans on board. The ship was headed for the West Indies, where the Africans would be sold as slaves, but high winds blew it off course. Jamestown colonists bought these Africans from the Dutch to work as servants for a number of years and then be set free. In later years, more Africans were brought to Virginia. But as you will read in Chapter 8, those Africans were forced to become slaves.

Making Laws The third major event of 1619 came when the Virginia Company gave colonists the right to have a say in making laws for the colony. Colonists could elect people to **represent**, or act for them, in an **assembly**, or a lawmaking body. This assembly was called the **House of Burgesses** (BUR jihs ez).

Virginia's House of Burgesses met for the first time in this Jamestown church on July 10, 1619. This was one of the most important events in America's history.
► Why, do you think, was this meeting so important?

LESSON **1** *REVIEW*

THINK AND WRITE

A. Why did the Spanish and the English have different attitudes toward Francis Drake?

B. How did the first group of settlers in the Roanoke colony differ from the second group?

C. Why was it less of a risk for a joint-stock company to start a colony than for just one person to do it?

D. Why was the Jamestown settlement unsuccessful at first?

E. How did John Smith help the Jamestown colony survive?

F. List four reasons why the Jamestown colony grew and prospered between the years 1613 and 1619.

SKILLS CHECK

MAP SKILL

Locate the Strait of Magellan on the Atlas map on page 623. Which two bodies of water are connected by this strait?

The Pilgrims in Plymouth Colony

THINK ABOUT WHAT YOU KNOW

Why, do you think, is it important to respect the rights and beliefs of others?

STUDY THE VOCABULARY

Separatist   **Mayflower Compact**
Pilgrim

FOCUS YOUR READING

How was Plymouth colony established, and how did it survive?

A. The Pilgrims Are Driven Out of England

In 1620 a second group of English settlers started a colony farther north, at a place called Plymouth. Unlike the Jamestown settlers, however, these people did not seek riches or adventure. They wanted only to be left alone to worship God in their own way.

Their story begins in England, about 20 years before their journey to America. In those days everyone in England was supposed to belong to the Church of England. However, some English people had different religious beliefs. A number of them chose to separate from the church, and so they were known as **Separatists**.

King James vowed to make life miserable for the Separatists. He even had some of them thrown into prison. Fearing for their safety, a group of Separatists left England in 1608 to live in a different country in Europe, the Netherlands.

In the Netherlands the Separatists worshiped as they pleased. The Dutch, as the people of the Netherlands are called, were friendly to them. The Separatists wanted their families to remain English. But year by year the Separatists watched their children become more Dutch in their ways. The children were also becoming less religious.

A number of Separatists decided to look for a new home. They got permission from the Virginia Company to start a colony on its land in North America. The Separatists could not afford to pay for a ship and supplies, so they got a group of English merchants to put up the money. The Separatists were to pay back the merchants by sending them furs, fish, and lumber from America.

B. The Pilgrims Write the Mayflower Compact

In September 1620 there were 102 men, women, and children who crowded onto the *Mayflower* and left for America.

The Pilgrims on the *Mayflower* had a very rough journey to the New World.
► Why did the Pilgrims have a harder journey than Columbus had?

160

FROM:

The Pilgrims of Plimoth

By: Marcia Sewall
Setting: Plymouth Colony, 1620s

To learn more about life in the Plymouth colony, you might like to read about how the Pilgrims themselves saw their lives. Here is a selection from a book written as though the children of the Pilgrims were describing their daily lives.

N ay, we have neither school nor schoolmaster here, but our elders hope for a schoolmaster soon to come from England. We learn obedience from our parents and if we are naughty we are told to "go mend our manners or we will get a proper thump on the britch!". . .

At dawn we take buckets and run to fetch water from the village spring. The grass is damp and the cobwebs sparkle in the early morning light of summer. The air smells of salt from the ocean. And we must also fetch wood for the hearth fire. After breaking fast . . . we begin to work. We will feed scratch to the hens, milk the cows and goats and take them to the meadow to graze, and on the way home we will stop to pick

sky-blue whortleberries [blueberries]. In the fall we will drive our swine to oak woods to feed on acorn and other ground nuts. And there are days when we must muck [clean] out the animal pens.

In early spring we will help poke seeds into the freshly worked earth and then spend hours stoning crows away from those seeds. And as the seeds sprout, we must pull unwanted tares [weeds] from the garden. At harvest time, in late summer, we pick Indian corn and peas and beans. We gather in wheat and rye and barley and crabapples. . . .

We play "hide and seek" and sometimes hide under a pile of sweet hay in the cowshed. We play "blindman's bluff" and "stoolball." We play "pitch the bar" and "tug o'war." And we love to footrace down the broad street of our village.

Most of the people on board the ship were Separatists. The Separatists were now calling themselves by the name we all know — **Pilgrims.** A pilgrim is a person who makes a journey for religious reasons. After two stormy months at sea, the *Mayflower* arrived at the coast of North America. The Pilgrims were 200 miles (322 km) north of the place they were aiming for. But it was already autumn, and they tried to make the best of the situation.

Since the Pilgrims had landed outside the land of the Virginia Company, they would not be living under the company's rules and laws. Either the Pilgrims must make their own rules and laws, or there would be none. So before leaving the ship the Pilgrim leaders drew up an agreement, called the **Mayflower Compact**.

In the Mayflower Compact, the signers agreed to form a government that would make "just and equal laws . . . for the general good of the colony." All 41 men on board signed the agreement. It established the idea of self-government in America — that is, that people should govern themselves.

C. Native Americans Help the Plymouth Colony Survive

Hardship in Plymouth   In December 1620 the Pilgrims went ashore to start their new life. They called their new settlement Plymouth Plantation. The Pilgrims were not prepared for the hardship that lay ahead of them that first winter. The crude shelters they hurriedly built could not keep out the cold. They had barely enough food to last until spring. Many settlers fell sick. Few days passed without the death of at least one of the tiny group. By March 1621, half of the 102 settlers who started out were dead.

Help From Indians   One day that March, colonists were surprised to see an Indian walk into Plymouth Plantation. They were even more startled when they heard him speak. "Much welcome, Englishmen," said the Native American in plain English! His name was Samoset, and he was a Wampanoag Indian. Samoset had learned a few English words from English fishing people who had stopped along the coast.

A few days later, Samoset brought Massasoit, who was chief of the Wampanoags, to see the Pilgrims. Massasoit told the Pilgrims that his people wished to be friends.

Samoset also brought to Plymouth Plantation an Indian named Squanto. Squanto helped the Pilgrims to survive. He showed them how to fertilize corn by mixing small fish into the soil. He also showed them the best fishing and hunting places.

Some of the Pilgrims are shown signing the Mayflower Compact while still on board ship.
► How is the signing of the Mayflower Compact like the formation of the House of Burgesses?

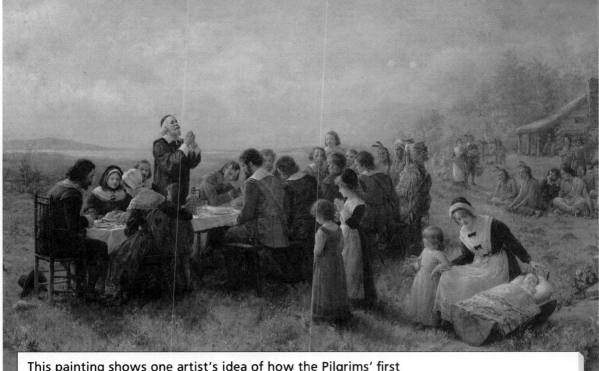

This painting shows one artist's idea of how the Pilgrims' first Thanksgiving looked.
▶ How can you tell that religion was important to these Pilgrims?

So the Pilgrims could hunt and fish for food until their crops were grown. Squanto remained with the settlers in Plymouth for the rest of his life.

First Thanksgiving With this help from their Indian friends, the English settlers survived their first year. Pilgrim leaders decided to have a special celebration of Thanksgiving. They invited Massasoit and the Wampanoag to help them celebrate. For three days the Pilgrims and their guests feasted and entertained each other with games and dancing. This was America's first Thanksgiving. The literature selection on page 161 describes some games the children of the colony played.

The Plymouth colony never became rich. But it did survive. Spanish conquerors like Cortés and Pizzaro had won a continent with their courage in battle. The Pilgrims gained their success with courage of a different kind. It was the courage to stand by their religious beliefs in the face of hardship. In doing this they left their mark on America's history.

LESSON *2* REVIEW

THINK AND WRITE

A. How was the reason for the founding of the Plymouth colony different from the reason for the founding of Jamestown?
B. Why was the Mayflower Compact important?
C. How did Indians help the Pilgrims?

SKILLS CHECK

THINKING SKILL

Make a chart comparing Jamestown and Plymouth. Include information on the following topics: year of settlement, goals of settlers, early problems, reasons for success.

163

France and the Netherlands

THINK ABOUT WHAT YOU KNOW

Imagine that you are the founder of a New World colony. What would its name be? Explain your answer.

STUDY THE VOCABULARY

culture

FOCUS YOUR READING

Which areas of North America were claimed by France and the Netherlands?

A. France Renews Its Interest in the New World

While the English struggled to start their first colonies in America, other European countries were also trying to plant colonies there. One of these countries was France. After Jacques Cartier had failed to find a northwest passage, France lost interest in New France. Then around 1600, a new French king turned his attention to the New World. He gave merchants permission to build trading posts in New France. One of these merchants hired the king's mapmaker, Samuel de Champlain, (sham PLAYN) to go to North America.

Champlain made his first trip to New France in 1603. Over the next 30 years, he returned nearly a dozen times. In a birchbark canoe, he paddled along rivers and streams never before seen by Europeans. He even reached one of our Great Lakes, Lake Huron. Everywhere Champlain went, French fur traders and trappers followed. Champlain also started the first permanent settlement in New France at Quebec in 1608. He richly deserved the title Father of New France.

Here, Samuel de Champlain and his men are building a wall at what would later become the great Canadian city of Montreal.
► What is this wall being built of?

The French got along very well with most of the Indians of Canada. Unlike the Spanish, the French did not try to conquer the Indians. They showed respect for Indian **culture**. Culture is the way of life of a people. French fur traders lived among the Indians. The traders learned the Indian languages and ways of life. Many French priests went to New France to introduce Christianity to the Native Americans.

B. French Exploration

One of these French missionaries also became a great explorer. His name was Father Jacques Marquette (mahr KET). Father Marquette was interested in geography and was a fine mapmaker. He teamed up with a fur trapper named Louis Joliet (joh lee ET). Both men knew several

164

Painting by S. A. Scott, National Archives of Canada, Ottawa (C-33195)

France now claimed an enormous amount of land in North America. It included most of present-day Canada and the United States. The map on page 166 shows how large this area was. Over the years, France set up trading posts, villages, and forts along the Mississippi River and elsewhere in this territory. The French also founded cities such as New Orleans.

C. The Netherlands Starts a Colony in North America

Hudson's Exploration The Netherlands was another European country that was interested in North America. In the 1600s the Dutch were the greatest merchants in the world. Like other countries, the Netherlands hoped to increase their trading even more by finding an all-water route to Asia through North America. Some Dutch

Indian languages. They had also heard Indians speak of a great river farther south. This might be the long-sought Northwest Passage, thought Joliet and Marquette.

In 1673, Marquette, Joliet, and five other men set out in two canoes to look for the river. After many weeks they found a river that flowed into the great Mississippi River. They paddled down the Mississippi to the place where the Arkansas River flows into it. But the Mississippi continued to flow south, not west. They knew they hadn't found a northwest passage.

Nine years later another French explorer continued down the Mississippi River to the Gulf of Mexico. He was Robert de La Salle. La Salle claimed a huge area of land along the Mississippi River for France. He called the area *Louisiana*, in honor of King Louis XIV of France.

Marquette is shown discovering the Mississippi River.
▶ Why is there an Indian with him in the first canoe?

detail, Lithograph by J. N. Marchand, National Archives of Canada, Ottawa (C-8486)

165

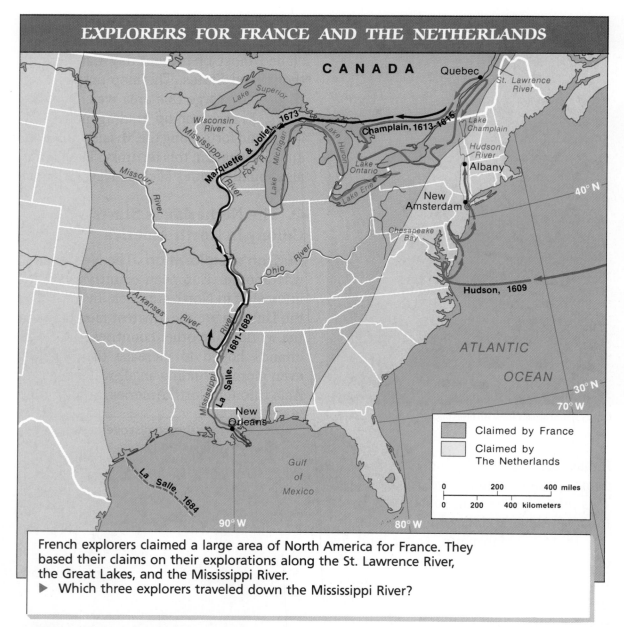

EXPLORERS FOR FRANCE AND THE NETHERLANDS

French explorers claimed a large area of North America for France. They based their claims on their explorations along the St. Lawrence River, the Great Lakes, and the Mississippi River.

▶ Which three explorers traveled down the Mississippi River?

merchants hired an English sailor named Henry Hudson to find one. Earlier, Hudson had been hired by the king of England. He had made two voyages in search of a northwest passage.

In 1609, Henry Hudson sailed to North America in his small ship, the *Half Moon*. After exploring the Chesapeake Bay, he sailed north and found the mouth of a wide, deep river. This was the river we know today as the Hudson River. Hudson

sailed up the river. However, after some distance the river became narrow and shallow. Hudson knew that he had failed to find a northwest passage. He returned to the Netherlands.

Hudson's voyage gave the Netherlands a claim to the land along the Hudson River. The Dutch called this area New Netherland. Soon, Dutch traders were coming to this area to trade with the Indians for fur.

Above is a view of seventeenth-century New Amsterdam, which would one day become the huge city of New York.

▶ What geographical feature is as important to New York as it was to New Amsterdam?

Dutch Settlements In 1624 the Dutch West India Company brought over a number of families to start settlements and trading posts along the Hudson River. They spread as far north as the present-day city of Albany, New York. In 1626 the company bought the entire island of Manhattan from the Indians for a handful of trinkets, beads, and knives. At the very tip of that island, facing the great harbor where the Hudson River meets the Atlantic Ocean, the company started the town of New Amsterdam. An early view of the town is shown in the painting on this page. You can see that the settlers built their homes close to the harbor.

Throughout the 1600s, the Netherlands was the most tolerant country in Europe. That means the government accepted the beliefs and practices of others. New Netherland was the first European colony in the New World to allow freedom of religion. As a result, Catholics, Jews, and Protestants of all kinds came to live there. So did people from many different countries.

By the end of the 1620s, England, France, and the Netherlands each had footholds in North America. No one knew which of the three countries would finally be able to win the race for colonies in North America.

LESSON **3** *REVIEW*

THINK AND WRITE

A. Why, do you think, is Samuel de Champlain called the Father of New France?

B. How did France use the explorations of Marquette, Joliet, and La Salle to claim a large area of land in North America?

C. Why were Henry Hudson's explorations important to the Netherlands?

SKILLS CHECK

WRITING SKILL

Write a paragraph or two explaining why you think it is important to show respect for cultures different from your own.

6 PUTTING IT ALL TOGETHER

USING THE VOCABULARY

> pirate
> joint-stock company
> bay
> represent
> assembly
> House of Burgesses
> Separatist
> Pilgrim
> Mayflower Compact
> culture

Match these words with their definitions. On a separate sheet of paper, write the correct word next to the number of the definition.

1. A group of people sharing profit and losses
2. To act for
3. A person who steals, especially one who steals from ships
4. The way of life of a people
5. A part of an ocean that cuts deeply into the land
6. A person who chose to break his or her ties with the Church of England
7. An agreement that set up a government in Massachusetts
8. The legislature in the Virginia colony
9. A person who makes a journey for religious reasons
10. A lawmaking body

REMEMBERING WHAT YOU READ

On a separate sheet of paper, write your answers in complete sentences.

1. Why was Sir Francis Drake considered to be a pirate by the Spaniards?
2. Why were the first group of settlers ready to leave Roanoke?
3. Why was the Virginia Company of London started?
4. Who became the leader of the Jamestown colony?
5. How did tobacco help save the Jamestown colony?
6. Why did the Separatists leave England?
7. Why did the Pilgrims draw up and sign the Mayflower Compact?
8. Why did the Pilgrims set aside a time to give thanks?
9. How did French settlement in the New World differ from that of the English and the Spaniards?
10. What land did the Dutch claim in North America?

TYING LANGUAGE ARTS TO SOCIAL STUDIES

Imagine that you are a Pilgrim boy or girl who has just arrived on the *Mayflower*. Write an essay of several paragraphs, describing your feelings about the land that will be your new home. You might want to write about meeting a Native American, or you might describe the house in which you soon will be living.

THINKING CRITICALLY

On a separate sheet of paper, write your answers in complete sentences.

1. What, do you think, happened to the people of the Roanoke colony?
2. Summarize the things that went wrong with the founding of Jamestown.
3. Who, in your opinion, really saved Jamestown colony—John Smith or John Rolfe?
4. Why didn't the Pilgrims have the same difficulties establishing their colony that the settlers of Jamestown had?
5. How was France able to claim so much land in North America?

SUMMARIZING THE CHAPTER

On a separate sheet of paper, draw a graphic organizer like the one shown here. Copy the information from this graphic organizer to the one you have drawn. List several items about each of the colonies shown in the organizer. The first has been done for you.

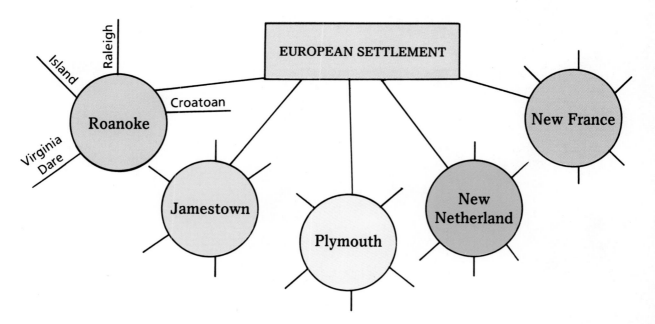

CHAPTER THEME → Many European countries wanted a share of the New World. England, France, and the Netherlands started settlements in North America.

EUROPEAN SETTLEMENT

Roanoke — Island — Raleigh — Croatoan — Virginia Dare

Jamestown

Plymouth

New Netherland

New France

CHAPTER 7

THE NEW ENGLAND COLONIES

*T*here were many reasons why people were willing to leave their homes to settle in a wilderness. Most of the New England colonies were settled by people looking for religious freedom.

The Puritans of Massachusetts Bay Colony

THINK ABOUT WHAT YOU KNOW

Suppose you had a chance to talk to some Pilgrims living in a colony in America. What questions might you ask them?

STUDY THE VOCABULARY

Puritan   **Fundamental Orders of Connecticut**

FOCUS YOUR READING

What goals did the Puritans have for the colony they founded in America?

A. The Puritans Leave England for America

For about a thousand men and women in England, 1629 was a year of preparation for the great event. Next spring they would leave for America. Before leaving, they had to sell their houses and land and use the money to buy supplies. Their leaders told them it would take time to plant fields and harvest crops. Therefore, they should take along enough food for 18 months. Also, they should take leather, nails, glass, iron, guns, gunpowder, farming tools, and farm animals. Their leaders knew that it was important to take tools and other supplies. The settlers would not be able to buy these things in their new homes.

One more thing, added the leaders: If anyone was going to America to get rich, he or she should just stay home in England. This group was going to America for a different reason. They were going to build a community based on the Bible, and to show the world how people could live according to the word of God.

These people were called **Puritans**. Like the Pilgrims, Puritans were unhappy with the Church of England. But unlike the Pilgrims, Puritans did not separate from the church. Instead, they wished to "purify" the church by doing away with many of its ceremonies and practices. For example, Puritans wanted to get rid of religious statues, colorful church windows, and music during church services. They believed that these things took people's attention away from the real reason they were in church.

The English king treated the Puritans badly. Many Puritans remained in England to struggle against the king. But a small group of them decided to go to America.

These Puritans formed their own joint-stock company, which they called the Massachusetts Bay Company. In the spring of 1630, more than a thousand men, women, and children boarded 11 ships for the long journey to the Massachusetts Bay Colony in New England.

B. The Puritans Build Their First Communities in America

Massachusetts Bay Colony The Puritans built their main settlement in Boston in what is now the state of Massachusetts. They also started several smaller settlements nearby. Unlike earlier English colonies at Jamestown and Plymouth, the Massachusetts Bay Colony was successful from the start. The settlers had arrived early enough in the spring to plant crops and build homes. Some turned to the ocean to make a living. As a result, the Puritans were far better prepared for their first winter than the Pilgrims had been. Very few of them died.

Encouraged by the success of the colony, more English people came to live in

Massachusetts Bay. Many left England because of hard times. Going to America meant a chance to improve their lives. Between 1630 and 1643, thousands of people came to live in Massachusetts Bay. These settlers farmed, fished, cut lumber, built ships, and traded for beaver and other animal furs with the Indians.

Puritan Beliefs The leaders of the Massachusetts Bay Colony set up an assembly to make laws for the colony. Only church members could vote in the elections for this assembly. As you know, the Puritans did not travel 3,000 miles (4,827 km) across the Atlantic Ocean just for a better life. Remember that their main goal was to build a community where everyone lived by the Bible and Puritan beliefs.

People who disobeyed a commandment of the Bible or a rule of the church were also breaking a law of the colony. The government could punish them for this. If people failed to go to church, the government fined them. If they refused to accept Puritan beliefs, the government could force them to leave the colony or even put them to death.

Massachusetts was the first New England colony to be settled. The other New England colonies were Connecticut, Rhode Island, and New Hampshire. Find these colonies on the map on page 174.

C. Roger Williams Is Forced to Leave Massachusetts

Rhode Island It didn't take long for two members of the colony to question the Puritans' practices. One was a minister named Roger Williams. Williams believed that people should be free to choose their own religious beliefs. He believed that the church and government should be separate, and that neither should mix in the other's proper business. This angered the Puritan leaders.

POPULATION OF THE NEW ENGLAND COLONIES: 1650-1700

Colony	1650	1660	1670	1680	1690	1700
Massachusetts (includes Plymouth)	15,603	22,062	35,333	46,152	56,928	55,941
Connecticut	4,139	7,980	12,603	17,246	21,645	25,970
Rhode Island	785	1,539	2,155	3,017	4,224	5,894
New Hampshire	1,305	1,555	1,805	2,047	4,164	4,958

The population of the New England colonies is shown for the years from 1650 to 1700.

► What was the population of Massachusetts in 1650?

This old picture shows how Roger Williams might have looked as he escaped from the Massachusetts Bay Colony.

▶ How, do you think, did the people who watched Roger Williams feel?

These leaders were also angered by Williams's views about the Indians. Williams believed the land belonged to the Indians, not to the king of England. He said the Indians should be paid for the land. Puritan leaders warned Williams to stop spreading "dangerous ideas." When he refused, they sent officers to his home to put him on a ship bound for England. Williams escaped before they arrived.

Williams and several followers headed south through the woods in the snow and bitter cold. Narragansett (nar-uh GAN siht) Indians gave them food and sheltered them during the winter. The chief of the Narragansett Indians gave Williams land to start a settlement in what later became the colony of Rhode Island. Williams called his settlement Providence.

Anne Hutchinson Anne Hutchinson was also forced to leave Massachusetts Bay. Each Sunday, Hutchinson held meetings at her home to discuss the minister's sermon. In time, she began to express ideas about religion that differed from those of the Puritan leaders. The leaders warned her to stop. As Hutchinson's following grew, Puritan leaders decided that she must be forced to leave the colony. So in 1637, Puritan leaders put Anne Hutchinson on trial. They found her guilty, and declared that she was "a woman not fit for our society." She was ordered to leave the

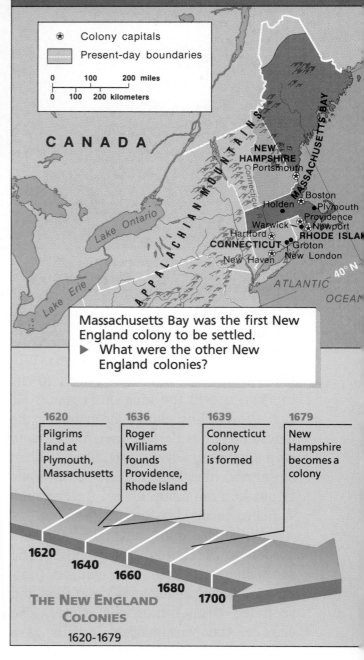

Because of her religious ideas, Anne Hutchinson was put on trial.
► Do you think Hutchinson was brave or cowardly at her trial?

colony. Mrs. Hutchinson, her husband, her children, and a number of her followers went south. They started a settlement not far from Providence. Like Providence, this settlement eventually became part of the colony of Rhode Island.

D. Connecticut and New Hampshire Are Founded

Founding Connecticut The colony of Connecticut owes its birth to another group of colonists who left Massachusetts Bay. This group was led by a Puritan minister named Thomas Hooker. Hooker did not agree with Puritan leaders that only church members should be allowed to vote in the government of the colony. Hooker also had his eye on the rich soil of the Connecticut River valley. There Hooker and his group began a settlement that they named Hartford.

Over the next few years, several other groups left Massachusetts Bay to start settlements along the Connecticut River. In 1639, these settlements came together in a new colony called Connecticut. The colonists drew up a set of rules to govern

THE NEW ENGLAND COLONIES

* Colony capitals
☐ Present-day boundaries

0   100   200 miles
0   100   200 kilometers

CANADA

Lake Ontario

Lake Erie

APPALACHIAN MOUNTAINS

NEW HAMPSHIRE
Portsmouth

MASSACHUSETTS BAY

Holden   Boston
Plymouth
Warwick   Providence
Hartford   Newport
CONNECTICUT   RHODE ISLAND
New Haven   Groton
New London

ATLANTIC OCEAN

40°N

Massachusetts Bay was the first New England colony to be settled.
► What were the other New England colonies?

1620	1636	1639	1679
Pilgrims land at Plymouth, Massachusetts	Roger Williams founds Providence, Rhode Island	Connecticut colony is formed	New Hampshire becomes a colony

1620
1640
1660
1680   1700

THE NEW ENGLAND COLONIES
1620-1679

This painting shows some of Thomas Hooker's followers nearing the camp that was to become the city of Hartford, Connecticut.

▶ Why was the Connecticut River valley a good place to start a settlement?

themselves as one united colony. These rules became known as the **Fundamental Orders of Connecticut**.

Connecticut was the first English colony to have a written plan of government. Under this plan, Connecticut had an assembly in which the people made their own laws. People in Connecticut did not have to belong to the Puritan church to have the right to vote.

New Hampshire Some settlers moved farther to the north. They settled in what is today New Hampshire, Maine, and part of Vermont. Some of these people moved because they disagreed with the strict rule of the Puritans in Massachusetts. Most, however, were simply looking for good farmland or fishing grounds. In 1679, the king of England finally made New Hampshire a separate colony.

LESSON **1** *REVIEW*

THINK AND WRITE

A. Why did some English Puritans go to America?

B. Why was the Massachusetts Bay Colony successful?

C. Why were Roger Williams and Anne Hutchinson forced to leave Massachusetts Bay?

D. For what reasons were the colonies of Connecticut and New Hampshire founded?

SKILLS CHECK

THINKING SKILL

Look at the time line on the map on page 174. Which became a colony first, New Hampshire or Connecticut?

The Geography of the New England Colonies

THINK ABOUT WHAT YOU KNOW

Make a list of some of the physical features or landforms in the area where you live.

STUDY THE VOCABULARY

mountain range

FOCUS YOUR READING

What is the geography of New England like?

A. Climate in New England

The first settlers in Massachusetts Bay arrived in April and May. The air was pleasantly warm, and leaves were starting to appear on the trees. Springtime in New England, it seemed, was not very different from the spring back home in England.

The new settlers soon discovered that the climate of New England was different from that of England. For one thing, New England summers were hotter than English summers. Although New England summers were hot, they were short. By mid-September, brilliant red and gold leaves announced the arrival of fall, and the end of the growing season. The winters that followed were colder and more snowy than any the settlers had known in England. Forty inches (102 cm) of snow a year was normal in Boston. In areas farther west and north, 60 to 70 inches (152 cm to 178 cm) was quite common.

These are the beautiful White Mountains in the New England state of New Hampshire.
▶ What might it be like to farm in this area?

B. New England Has Varied Landforms

A Region of Mountains Many settlers came from a part of England where one could see the horizon—the point in the distance where the sky and the land seem to meet. The land was flat and easy to farm. In New England, however, one often can see only as far as the next hill or mountain. One of the main landforms of New England is a **mountain range**. A mountain range—a series of mountains—runs along the western part of the region. In Vermont these mountains are the Green Mountains, in New Hampshire they are the White Mountains, and in Massachusetts they are the Berkshires. They are all part of the Appalachian Mountain range. Find this range on the map on page 177.

NEW ENGLAND COLONIES: PHYSICAL

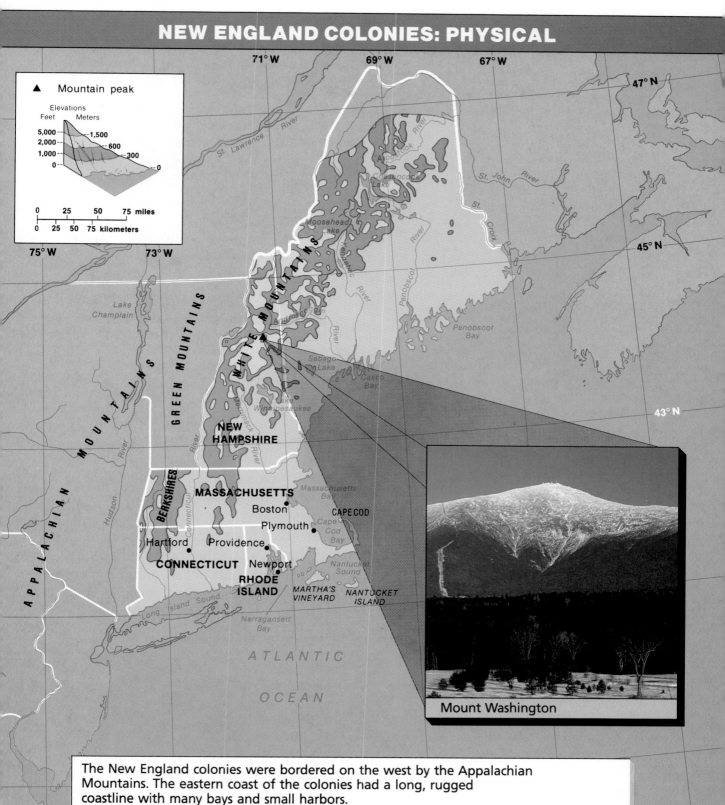

▲ Mountain peak

Elevations
Feet   Meters
5,000 -- -- 1,500
2,000 -- -- 600
1,000 -- -- 300
0 -- -- 0

0   25   50   75 miles
0   25 50 75 kilometers

St. Lawrence River

Aroostook River

Chesuncook Lake

St. John River

Moosehead Lake

St. Croix River

Lake Champlain

Kennebec River

Penobscot River

Penobscot Bay

GREEN MOUNTAINS

WHITE MOUNTAINS

Androscoggin River

Sebago Lake

Casco Bay

APPALACHIAN MOUNTAINS

Merrimack River

Lake Winnipesaukee

NEW HAMPSHIRE

BERKSHIRES

Hudson River

Connecticut River

MASSACHUSETTS

Massachusetts Bay

Boston

Plymouth

CAPE COD

Cape Cod Bay

Hartford

Providence

CONNECTICUT

Newport

Nantucket Sound

RHODE ISLAND

MARTHA'S VINEYARD

NANTUCKET ISLAND

Long Island Sound

Narragansett Bay

ATLANTIC OCEAN

Mount Washington

The New England colonies were bordered on the west by the Appalachian Mountains. The eastern coast of the colonies had a long, rugged coastline with many bays and small harbors.

▶ In what mountain range is Mount Washington located?

177

Today, people from all over visit the rocky coast of Maine.
▶ Why would people come from many miles away to visit here?

Between the mountains and the ocean, most of the land of New England is hilly. The soil is rocky and not well suited for farming.

New England has many streams and rivers that begin inland high up in the mountains and run swiftly down to the ocean. Most of these rivers, however, are not wide or deep enough to allow ships to go very far upstream.

The Atlantic Coast Another important feature of New England's geography is its coastline. Looking at the map on page 177, you will notice that instead of running straight, New England's coastline dips in and out, creating many small harbors. A harbor is an area of deep water where ships are protected from winds and storms. The ocean waters along the coast are rich with many different kinds of fish, and the many harbors of New England were perfect places for small boats to bring their catches of fish.

LESSON *2* REVIEW

THINK AND WRITE

A. In what ways is New England's climate different from that of England?
B. Why was New England better suited for fishing than for farming?

SKILLS CHECK

MAP SKILL

Look up the Berkshires, the Green Mountains, and the White Mountains in the Gazetteer. What is the name and the elevation of the highest peak in each of these mountains?

The Economy of the New England Colonies

THINK ABOUT WHAT YOU KNOW

List some facts you know about New England's geography. How might these facts affect the way people make a living?

STUDY THE VOCABULARY

blubber   **naval stores**
shipwright   **triangular trade**

FOCUS YOUR READING

How did people in New England earn a living?

A. New England Settlers Farm the Land

Raising Crops and Animals Many New England settlers struggled to make their living by farming. There were many forests with few open spaces to farm in New England. Settlers first had to chop down trees. The tree stumps and roots remained in the ground, so farmers were not able to use plows. Instead, they poked holes in the soil around the tree stumps and planted seeds in the holes. Native Americans had taught them this way of farming. New England farmers planted mainly corn and rye. They also planted vegetables such as squash, beans, and turnips.

Early settlers who raised sheep and cows ran into a problem. Wild forest animals often ate the sheep and cows before the settlers could. Colonists soon learned that pigs could protect themselves from most wild animals. People near villages and towns still raised cows and sheep, but those who lived close to the forests began raising pigs. Pork became the main meat eaten by New England settlers.

Farms were small in New England. On the poor, rocky soil, families managed to produce enough to live on, but not much more. Even producing that much took the help of everyone in the family. Men worked in the fields. They also spent many evenings in front of the fireplace, scraping animal hides to prepare them to be turned into leather for coats, hats, and shoes. They also made simple, usable furniture, like tables and chairs.

The farm women took care of all the household chores. They cooked and prepared food. They took care of the vegetable garden. They salted and smoked meats, pickled cabbages, and dried fruits and nuts in order to preserve these foods. They made soap and candles from animal fats. They spun wool into yarn, wove it into

On this farm, in Connecticut, even the children had to work so that their family could have enough to eat.
▶ How does the tool the woman is using help her care for her crops?

179

Many workers made a living building ships along the New England coast.
▶ Find two ways that the workers might have been able to reach the deck of this ship.

cloth, and made clothing for the family. At harvest time, they often helped with the work in the fields.

Farm children also worked. Girls learned the work their mothers did. They helped with the cooking and the spinning. Older boys worked in the fields with their fathers. The younger children took care of the farm animals and gathered berries in the woods.

B. Settlers Used Resources from the Ocean and the Forests

Fishing and Whaling Few of the early settlers in New England knew much about fishing when they arrived there. But they quickly learned to make use of the ocean. Many New Englanders made their living fishing for cod. Most of their catch was dried and salted, packed into barrels, and sold in the West Indies or Europe.

Other New Englanders hunted whales. People ate whale meat. The **blubber**, or whale fat, was boiled to make candles and later oil to burn in lamps. The blubber from a single whale could provide enough oil to light the lamps of an entire village for many months.

Using Forest Resources New England's forests were also an important natural resource. The tall pine, spruce, oak, and maple trees were turned into lumber. Much of the lumber was sold to England.

Some of the lumber was used to start a shipbuilding industry. There were several **shipwrights** among the early settlers of New England. A shipwright is a carpenter who is skilled in shipbuilding. With lumber both plentiful and cheap, these shipwrights built ships for half what they cost in England. English merchants began to order ships from New England builders. By 1700, Massachusetts alone was producing 150 new ships a year.

New England's pine trees also provided products, called **naval stores**, which were needed for building ships. These products were pitch, tar, and turpentine.

The wooden planks used in making a ship never fit together exactly. Pitch and tar were used to seal the spaces between them and make the ship watertight. Turpentine was used in making paint that helped to protect the ships against water and weather.

C. Trade Helps New England Grow

Three-Cornered Trade Trade was important to the growth of New England. Merchants sent their ships to ports in the West Indies, England, and cities of Europe, loaded with lumber, fur, and salted fish. These ships returned with furniture, dishes, clothes, glass, and other manufactured goods from England.

By 1700, New England merchants were also taking part in trade between New England, Africa, and the West Indies.

This three-cornered trade is known as a **triangular trade.** In New England port cities like Newport, Rhode Island, merchants turned molasses into rum. Molasses is a thick syrup made from sugar. The sugar came from the West Indies. The merchants shipped the rum, along with other New England products, like candles and guns, from New England to Africa. In Africa, ship captains traded the rum and other products for slaves and gold. Then the captains took the slaves to the West Indies and sold them to West Indian sugar farmers. These farmers paid for the slaves with money and with sugar or molasses. From the West Indies, the ships sailed back to New England, where the sugar and molasses would be made into still more rum. Find these trade routes on the map on page 182.

PRODUCTS OF THE PINE TREE

	In Colonial Times	Today
	RESIN	RESIN
	Tar	Tar products
	Pitch	Turpentine
	Turpentine	Paint
		Soap
	LUMBER	LUMBER
	Small boats	Furniture
	Logs for fuel	Wood pulp for paper-making
	Furniture	Building materials
	Building materials	

This chart shows some of the products of pine tree forests in colonial times and today.
▶ Was wood pulp a product that was used in colonial times?

COLONIAL TRADE

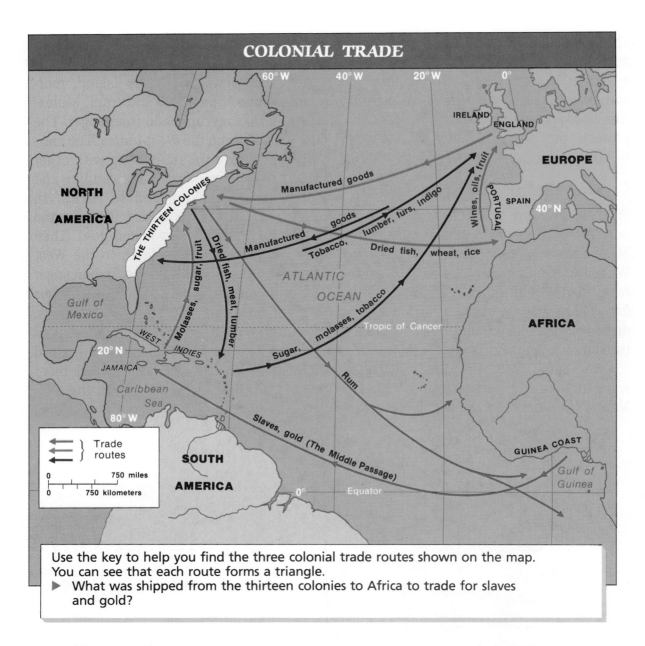

Use the key to help you find the three colonial trade routes shown on the map.
You can see that each route forms a triangle.
▶ What was shipped from the thirteen colonies to Africa to trade for slaves
and gold?

Port Cities Trade made some shipowners and merchants rich. Trade also created jobs and caused the population of New England port cities, such as Boston and Newport, to grow. Workers built ships and repaired them. They loaded and unloaded ships at the docks.

Many workers who lived in port cities were skilled craftspersons. They made shoes, clothes, candlesticks, iron pots, furniture, and many other items. They also made barrels, sails, and ropes for ships. Some craftspersons set up workshops in their homes and sold the goods to customers who came there. Other craftsworkers made and sold goods in small shops that lined the towns' main streets.

All this activity made the New England port cities lively places. In addition to the shops where people could buy local goods and goods from England, there were inns, taverns, and coffee shops. Here, visi-

The village center and the docks are busy places in this eighteenth-century New England village.
▶ Describe the different buildings and activities you see in this picture.

tors to town could eat, sleep, and do business. Here also, friends could spend time together. Sometimes they would gather to discuss the news that they had read in the town's newspaper.

Most of the businesses were run by men, but a few were run by women. Women sometimes took over a family business when a husband or father died. Women ran taverns and inns and small shops. They operated ferries. In Boston, a number of women ran printing shops and put out newspapers. There were also a few women in the colonies who were merchants who owned ships. They sent their ships around the world to trade.

LESSON 3 REVIEW

THINK AND WRITE

A. What were some problems that the settlers faced when they tried to farm in New England?

B. What were some ways in which New Englanders made a living from the ocean and forests?

C. How did trade help New England towns to grow?

SKILLS CHECK

MAP SKILL

Look in the Gazetteer to find out which bodies of water Boston and Newport are located on.

Life in a New England Village

THINK ABOUT WHAT YOU KNOW

Where do people get together in your community? How do families spend their time?

STUDY THE VOCABULARY

common	town meeting
meetinghouse	grammar school

FOCUS YOUR READING

What was life in a New England village like?

A. The Village Was the Center of Life in New England

Most New Englanders lived in villages and small towns. At the center of the village was the **common**. This was a large, grassy area that was owned by the town. It was often used as a place for animals to graze. The common was also called the *village green*.

On one side of the common was the most important building in the village, the **meetinghouse**, or place of worship. Meetinghouses were also used for public meetings. The other sides of the common were lined by houses. In time, a school might appear along the village common, and perhaps a few shops and an inn. The fields that the village people farmed were just outside of town.

Farming villages might have as many as 50 or 100 families. When a village became crowded, some families moved on and started another one. By the 1700s these small settlements were all through New England.

The village was the center of New England life. Everyone knew everyone else. The people of a village helped each other in time of need. They celebrated each other's joys, and they comforted each other in times of sorrow.

They also met together—or at least the men did—in **town meetings** to make important decisions about the village. Here they decided whether to build a road or hire a new school teacher or open up more fields for farming. They elected the village officers. They voted on the taxes that had to be paid to the government. In other words, they governed themselves.

Old Ship Church, built in 1681, in Hingham, Massachusetts, is the oldest wooden church in our country.
► Why is there a wheel under the spire of this church?

This picture shows what the inside of an early New England church looked like on a cold Sunday. Look for the little coal-filled metal boxes that helped keep the colonists' feet warm during the long hours of service.
▶ What is unusual about the way the seats in this church are arranged?

B. New England Colonists Were a Religious People

Religion played a large part in New Englanders' daily lives. They gave thanks to God at every meal, and said prayers every morning and evening. The *Sabbath*, or day of rest and worship, began on Saturday night and ended on Sunday night, and it was strictly observed. No work, travel, recreation, or even unnecessary walking in the streets and fields was permitted.

On Sundays the people of New England spent the whole day at meeting, or church services. Meetinghouses had no fireplaces, and on cold winter days they were very uncomfortable. Some people brought along small metal boxes filled with hot coals to warm their chilly feet during the Sunday service.

Services were long. The minister's sermon usually lasted several hours. Families would then take a break for their noon meal. After that, church services continued into the afternoon. Often the services were followed by a discussion about the minister's sermon in a neighbor's home.

C. Going to School in New England

The Puritans' religious beliefs had a lot to do with their ideas on education. They believed that everyone should be able to read the Bible. Therefore the government ordered that every town with 50 families must have an elementary, or common, school. These schools were one-room buildings. It was at these common schools that New England children learned how to read.

Students' first reading lessons were taken from a hornbook. This was a piece of wood, shaped like a paddle, with a piece of paper attached to it. Printed on the paper were the alphabet, a few simple words, and some common prayers. The entire board was covered with a flat piece of clear animal horn. The horn was made clear by scraping and boiling. After finishing the hornbook, students moved on to a short book called a primer, which contained prayers and religious rhymes.

After common school a few boys went on to a secondary school that was called a **grammar school.** Grammar schools were like high schools today. School started at 6:00 A.M. and lasted until 5:00 P.M. Everyone paid taxes to support the schools. People who could afford it were also expected to supply wood to keep the schools warm in winter.

D. New England Houses Were Simple and Practical

New Englanders built houses like those they had in England. Walls, ceilings, and floors were made of wooden planks. The roof was steep and covered with shingles or thatch. Thatch is made of long grasses and other plant materials bundled tightly together. It is very good for keeping out rain.

The furniture in a New England home was homemade and simple. There were no rugs on the floor. Chairs were made of wood, and there was no soft chair in which to take it easy after a hard day's work. Each house had a table, several plain benches, and a few chests of drawers. New Englanders slept on straw mattresses or perhaps just a few piles of straw in a corner of the room.

The center of every New England home was the fireplace. On cold, windy days even getting close to the fireplace didn't keep one completely warm. One New Englander who was writing a letter next to the fireplace told how the ink on his quill pen froze before he could write.

This drawing gives us an idea of how the inside of an early New England school looked.
► How were the pupils' desks made?

In the cold New England winter, everyone in the family gathered around the huge fireplace to do the chores.
► What chores are the people in this picture doing?

In the fireplace in most New England homes hung a number of iron pots. Women cooked meals in these pots, for the homes had no stoves. The fireplace, along with a few candles, also provided light in the evening. In the late 1700s, whale oil lamps provided better lighting.

Although most New England houses during the 1600s and 1700s were not very comfortable, New Englanders were satisfied with their lives. They had learned to make a living in their new environment. They could worship according to their Puritan beliefs. These colonists had been able to build a good and productive life for themselves in America. At last, they felt they could look to the future with confidence.

LESSON 4 REVIEW

THINK AND WRITE

A. What did the common of a New England village look like?
B. How did religious beliefs affect life in New England?
C. Summarize the importance of education in New England.
D. Describe an early New England house.

SKILLS CHECK

WRITING SKILL

Pretend that you are a child growing up in a New England colony. Write a letter to your grandparents in England, telling them what your home is like on a cold winter day.

USING THE VOCABULARY

On a separate sheet of paper, write the word or words that best complete each statement.

1. A person wishing to purify the church was
   (a) a Reformer   (b) a Puritan
   (c) a Protester.
2. A person skilled in shipbuilding is
   (a) a cartwright   (b) a playwright
   (c) a shipwright.
3. A place of worship in New England was called
   (a) a meeting house
   (b) a town meeting
   (c) a grammar school.
4. A large grassy area, usually in the center of a town or village, was
   (a) a meadow   (b) a common
   (c) a cemetery.
5. Tar, pitch, and turpentine are
   (a) used to make horseshoes
   (b) farm products
   (c) naval stores.

REMEMBERING WHAT YOU READ

On a separate sheet of paper, write your answers in complete sentences.

1. What did the Puritans hope that their colony in America would represent to other people?
2. How did the early settlers in Massachusetts Bay Colony make a living?
3. Why were Anne Hutchinson and Roger Williams driven from Massachusetts Bay Colony by the Puritans?
4. Why are the Fundamental Orders of Connecticut important?
5. What colonies were started by people who left Massachusetts Bay Colony?
6. How was the climate in New England different from the climate in England?
7. What is one of the major landforms in New England?
8. Why were the forests an important part of New England's economy?
9. What happened at New England town meetings?
10. Why was education important to the Puritans?

TYING READING TO SOCIAL STUDIES

Volunteer to read *The Witch of Blackbird Pond* by Elizabeth George Speare. It is the story of Kit Taylor, a young girl who arrives in Connecticut from the English colony of Barbados in the West Indies.

Kit is a misfit in the Puritan settlement. Make a list that shows how Kit's beliefs differ from those of the Puritans. Discuss with your classmates the conflict that arises among the settlers.

Elizabeth George Speare. *The Witch of Blackbird Pond*. Boston: Houghton Mifflin, 1958.

THINKING CRITICALLY

On a separate sheet of paper, write your answers in complete sentences.

1. The Puritans left England because they wanted freedom of religion. Compare freedom of religion in Massachusetts Bay Colony and freedom of religion in the United States today.

2. Choose one of the geographic features mentioned in the chapter and describe its value to the settlers in New England.

3. How did the slave trade help some New England merchants get very rich?

4. Why was whaling an important New England industry?

5. Describe the kind of work you would have liked to do if you had lived in New England around 1700.

SUMMARIZING THE CHAPTER

On a separate sheet of paper, draw a graphic organizer like the one shown here. Copy the information from this graphic organizer to the one you have drawn. Under the main idea for each lesson, write at least three items that support the main idea. The first one has been done for you.

CHAPTER THEME
The New England colonies were founded on a strong religious base. Poor soil made farming difficult, so the economy quickly grew to include fishing, trading, and lumbering.

LESSON 1

The Puritans wanted to build a community to show the world that people could live according to the word of God.

1. Based on the Bible

2. Only Puritan beliefs

3. Laws of church and laws of colony the same

LESSON 2

The geography of New England was different from that which the Puritans had known.

1.

2.

3.

LESSON 3

The settlers of New England earned their living in many different ways.

1.

2.

3.

LESSON 4

New England villages varied in size but were alike in many ways.

1.

2.

3.

CHAPTER 8

THE SOUTHERN COLONIES

★ ★

The climate and soil of many of the southern colonies made farming profitable. People were brought as slaves from Africa to work on these farms. A different style of living developed in the south.

England Founds the Southern Colonies

THINK ABOUT WHAT YOU KNOW

Imagine that you want to start a colony in the New World. However, you don't want to risk putting all of your money into a colony. What could you do to lessen the risk of starting the colony by yourself?

STUDY THE VOCABULARY

proprietor   debtor
Huguenot

FOCUS YOUR READING

What goals did the founders of each Southern colony have?

A. The Calvert Family Founds Maryland

A New Kind of Colony England's first three colonies — Virginia, Plymouth, and Massachusetts — were started by joint-stock companies. Most of England's later colonies, though, were started by friends of the king. The king gave these friends land in America as gifts. And what gifts they were! The smallest of these gifts was 10 million acres (4,050,000 ha). That is the size of a number of states in the United States today. Some gifts were many times that large.

The first **proprietor**, or owner, of a colony in America was a friend of the king named George Calvert. In 1632, King Charles I of England gave Calvert a large piece of land around Chesapeake Bay. Calvert named the land Maryland, in honor of Henrietta Maria, the king's wife.

Calvert had two reasons for wanting a colony of his own. First, he thought it would make him wealthy. Second, Calvert was a Roman Catholic. In England at that time, Catholics were treated even worse than Puritans. Calvert wanted to start a colony where English Catholics would be free to practice their religion.

Maryland George Calvert died before he could realize his dream. But his son, Cecilius Calvert, carried through the plan. In 1634 the first 200 settlers arrived in Maryland. They settled in a small village they named St. Marys.

The Maryland colony was successful from the start. Calvert told settlers not to waste time searching for gold. He ordered them to plant food crops before they did anything else. Settlers also traded for food with friendly Indians. In addition, they

St. Marys has been rebuilt. Visitors come to see how people lived and worked there long ago.
▶ How did crops help Maryland?

bought food and supplies from several nearby Virginia settlements. The Virginians also taught the settlers in Maryland how to grow tobacco.

Calvert was disappointed in one thing, however. Not as many Catholics went to his colony as he had expected. Therefore, to build up the population, Calvert also encouraged Protestants to go to Maryland. Before long there were more Protestants than Catholics living in the new English colony.

Calvert allowed Maryland colonists to set up an assembly and have a part in making laws. And in 1649 the assembly passed the Toleration Act. This act said that all Christians, whether Catholic or Protestant, could worship as they pleased.

B. Eight Proprietors Start a Colony in Carolina

In 1663, King Charles II gave a large piece of land in America to eight of his friends. The eight proprietors named their colony Carolina, in honor of the king. The men had great plans for making money from their new colony. They thought they would give land to settlers free of charge and then tax them. They also planned to have the settlers raise olives for oil, grapes for wine, and silkworms for silk. The proprietors would then buy these products from their settlers cheaply and sell them at high prices in England. Meanwhile, the proprietors would rule the colony by themselves.

It was quite a plan, but it didn't work. Settlers wouldn't go to Carolina if they had to pay a big tax. So the proprietors gave up that idea. Neither would settlers go to Carolina unless they could have a say in their own government. So the proprietors had to give in on that, too. When some settlers

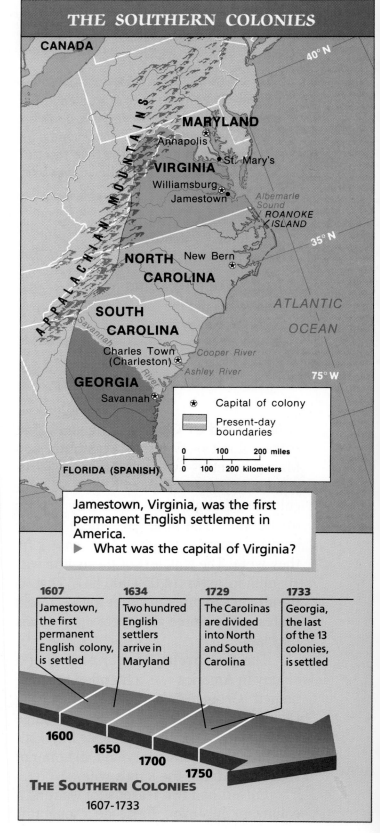

THE SOUTHERN COLONIES

Jamestown, Virginia, was the first permanent English settlement in America.
▶ What was the capital of Virginia?

1607	1634	1729	1733
Jamestown, the first permanent English colony, is settled	Two hundred English settlers arrive in Maryland	The Carolinas are divided into North and South Carolina	Georgia, the last of the 13 colonies, is settled

1600
1650
1700
1750

THE SOUTHERN COLONIES
1607-1733

finally did move to Carolina, they would not raise olives, grapes, and silkworms.

In 1670 the settlers built the town of Charles Town. Years later the name of Charles Town was changed to Charleston. Charleston had a fine harbor. The town attracted people from England, Scotland, and from British colonies in the West Indies. **Huguenots**, who were French Protestants, also came to settle in Charleston. They fled from France because they were being persecuted. Carolina offered freedom of religion to all its settlers.

C. Carolina Splits into North and South Carolina

By the early 1700s most of the people in Carolina were living near either Albemarle Sound in the north or Charleston in the south. As you can see on the map on page 192, these two places are very far apart. So the proprietors decided to divide Carolina into two parts, North Carolina and South Carolina. They gave each part its own government.

The colony of North Carolina grew very slowly. But South Carolina became prosperous. However, the proprietors never made money from either colony. Meanwhile, the colonists felt that the proprietors were not doing enough for them. They wanted the king to take over the colonies. The proprietors sold their colonies back to the king.

D. Oglethorpe Founds Georgia

By the early 1700s the English had many settlements around Charleston. Meanwhile, the Spanish built settlements in northern Florida. England and Spain quarreled over the land between their colonies. The English government wanted to

This old picture shows the British ship *Carolina* in 1670. It is anchored for the first time in the harbor at the site that was to become Charleston. However, it was to be ten years before settlers actually built a town here.
▶ What country's flag, do you think, is the ship flying?

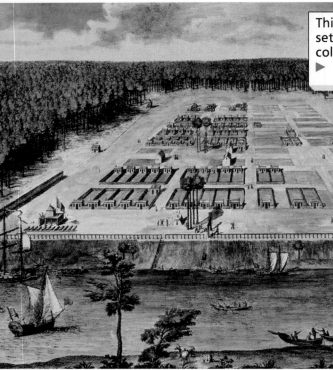

This 1734 picture shows Savannah, the first settlement that James Olgethorpe founded in the colony of Georgia.
▶ What, do you think, are these buildings made of?

find a way to block the Spanish from moving north. The English did not want Spanish colonies too close to their own.

At about the same time, James Oglethorpe and a number of other people in England were thinking about ways to help poor English **debtors**. A debtor is a person who owes money. In the England of those days, people who couldn't pay their debts went to prison. Many stayed there the rest of their lives.

Oglethorpe got the idea of starting a colony between South Carolina and Spanish Florida where debtors could get a new start. Others would also be welcome. The settlers would be able to serve as part-time soldiers who could block attacks from Florida by the Spanish. King George II liked this idea, and so the colony of Georgia was established. Oglethorpe and the first group of colonists settled near the mouth of the Savannah River in 1733.

Georgia did block the Spanish from moving north. But the colony grew very slowly. Few debtors came to live in Georgia, and not many other settlers came either. This was partly because Georgia had stricter rules than other English colonies. Settlers were allowed to own only a small amount of land. They had to grow grapes and raise silkworms to help the colony pay for itself. No slavery was allowed in Georgia. And settlers were not allowed to have liquor. Most of these rules were changed by the early 1750s. After that, settlement slowly increased.

LESSON 1 REVIEW

THINK AND WRITE

A. Why didn't Maryland become a colony for English Catholics, as George Calvert had planned?

B. How were settlers able to change the plans the proprietors had for running the Carolina colony?

C. What are two reasons North Carolina and South Carolina were sold back to the king?

D. Were the two goals for starting the Georgia colony achieved?

SKILLS CHECK

MAP SKILL

Look at the map on page 192. List the names of the southern colonies and the capital of each colony.

Geography of the Southern Colonies

THINK ABOUT WHAT YOU KNOW
What are some benefits of living in a place with a mild climate?

STUDY THE VOCABULARY
Tidewater

FOCUS YOUR READING
What were the main geographical features of the southern colonies?

A. The Southern Colonies Have Good Bays and Harbors

The environment, land, and climate of the southern colonies were very different from those of the New England colonies. So the southern colonists had to develop different ways of making a living and different ways of life.

In the southern colonies was one of the finest bays on the Atlantic coast—Chesapeake Bay. The bay borders Virginia and Maryland. It is rich in fish, especially shellfish. It also has many good harbors.

Farther south the shoreline is very different from New England's rocky and jagged coast. Here the coast curves gently and has long stretches of sandy beach. It also has a number of good harbors, such as the one at Charleston. There are several rivers that flow into the Atlantic Ocean. The widths and depths of most of these rivers allowed ocean ships of colonial days to sail far upstream.

B. The Southern Colonies Are Divided into Three Regions

The Atlantic Coastal Plain The land of the southern colonies is divided into three regions. The three regions are the Atlantic Coastal Plain, the Piedmont, and the Appalachian Mountains.

The wide, flat land of the Chesapeake Bay area is broken up in many places by large and small inlets pushing their way into the low-lying plain.
▶ Why might the early settlers have wanted to live here?

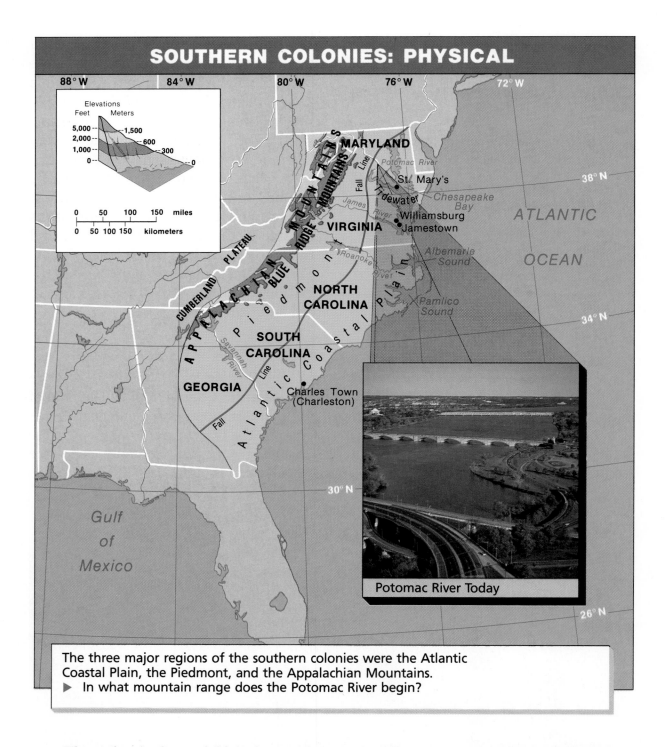

SOUTHERN COLONIES: PHYSICAL

Elevations
Feet   Meters
5,000 — —1,500
2,000 — —600
1,000 — —300
0 — —0

0   50   100   150   miles
0 50 100 150   kilometers

MARYLAND

Potomac River

St. Mary's

Tidewater

Chesapeake Bay

Williamsburg
Jamestown

VIRGINIA

James River

ATLANTIC OCEAN

APPALACHIAN MOUNTAINS

BLUE RIDGE MOUNTAINS

CUMBERLAND PLATEAU

Piedmont

Fall Line

Roanoke River

Albemarle Sound

NORTH CAROLINA

Pamlico Sound

Atlantic Coastal Plain

SOUTH CAROLINA

Savannah River

GEORGIA

Charles Town (Charleston)

Fall Line

Gulf of Mexico

Potomac River Today

The three major regions of the southern colonies were the Atlantic Coastal Plain, the Piedmont, and the Appalachian Mountains.
▶ In what mountain range does the Potomac River begin?

The Atlantic Coastal Plain is a wide area of low, flat land. It begins at the Atlantic shoreline and runs about 200 miles (322 km) inland. The lowest, flattest part of the Atlantic Coastal Plain is the land around Chesapeake Bay. Many rivers flow across this low plain and into the ocean.

This is the area where the early settlements in Virginia were founded. It is called the **Tidewater**. The Tidewater gets its name from the fact that salty ocean water pushes back the fresh waters of the rivers for many miles when the tide comes in. Settlers found good farmland here.

The Piedmont In the west the Atlantic Coastal Plain rises gently and then levels out, meeting the Piedmont. The land is more hilly in the Piedmont. But here, too, the soil is rich in many places.

The place where the Atlantic Coastal Plain meets the Piedmont is called the Fall Line. This is the point where rivers tumble from the higher land of the Piedmont down to the low-lying coastal plain. This drop creates waterfalls, or sometimes rapids. The Fall Line marks the farthest point that ships can travel upstream, for even a small waterfall keeps them from going farther. On the map on page 196, you can follow the Fall Line from Maryland and Virginia all the way down to Georgia.

The Appalachians West of the Piedmont a high ridge runs down the western part of the southern colonies. In Virginia and North Carolina, this ridge is called the Blue Ridge. These mountains get their name from the fact that the forests on their slopes have a bluish appearance when seen from a distance. Running between the mountains are a number of beautiful valleys with rich soil.

The Blue Ridge is part of the Appalachian Mountains. This is the mountain range that starts in Canada in the north and stretches as far south as Georgia. The Appalachian Mountains make up the third land region of the southern colonies.

C. The Climate of the Southern Colonies Is Mild

The climate of the southern colonies is far different from the climate of New England. In the coastal areas of the South, the temperature remains above freezing

These are some of the waterfalls and rapids that form the rough, swiftly flowing waters of the Fall Line.
► How did settlers get to the land west of the Fall Line?

Today, cotton grows well in the warm climate of North Carolina's Coastal Plain. The flat, well-watered land produces fine crops. A large cotton-picking machine is at work in this wide field.

▶ In what part of the machine is the cotton stored?

most of the year. There is plenty of rainfall, and the growing season is long. Plants such as tobacco, rice, and cotton can be grown here. Farther west, in the Piedmont and the Appalachian Mountains, the temperature is cooler.

Winter comes much later in the South than it does in New England. It is also much milder. There are few bitterly cold days, and very little snow falls except in the mountains. Even in Virginia and Maryland, which are the northernmost colonies of the South, there is less snow in a whole season than New England might get in a single storm. The farther south you go, the less cold and snow there are.

LESSON *2* REVIEW

THINK AND WRITE

A. Describe the coastline of the southern colonies.
B. Describe the landforms found in the three regions of the southern colonies.
C. How did the climate of the southern colonies differ from that of the New England colonies?

SKILLS CHECK

MAP SKILL

Look at the map on page 196. What river forms the boundary between Georgia and South Carolina?

The Economy of the Southern Colonies

THINK ABOUT WHAT YOU KNOW

How do you depend on farming? Think of goods that you use every day that come from farms or are made from farm goods.

STUDY THE VOCABULARY

cash crop   indigo
plantation   indentured servant

FOCUS YOUR READING

How did people in the southern colonies make a living?

A. Southern Colonies Have Small Farms and Large Plantations

Farms and Plantations In all the southern colonies, most people farmed for a living. Before 1700 most of these farms were small and located on the Atlantic Coastal Plain. With the South's long growing season, farmers produced all the food they needed to live. In addition, they usually raised a **cash crop**, which is a crop they could sell for money.

In time, a few people came to own very large farms. These large farms were called **plantations**. The plantation owners were called planters. By 1700 some plantations were bigger than 100 small farms put together. The painting on page 204 shows what a plantation looked like.

Cash Crops The main business of a plantation was to grow a single cash crop to sell. In Maryland and Virginia, this crop was tobacco. In South Carolina and Georgia, it was rice. In the 1740s a young woman named Eliza Lucas introduced another cash crop to South Carolina. Eliza

Lucas ran her father's plantation near Charleston. She began to experiment with **indigo** (IHN dih goh), a plant from which a blue dye was made. This dye was highly valued in Europe. After Eliza Lucas developed a successful crop, she gave indigo seed to other South Carolina planters. Soon, South Carolina was shipping great amounts of the dye to England.

B. Indentured Servants Provide the Labor at First

Many workers were needed to raise and harvest a cash crop. Even the owner of a small farm usually had the help of one or two workers. Large plantations might need 50 or 100 workers, or even more.

Nearly all workers in the South in colonial times were *unfree*. That is, they could not leave their jobs and take others if

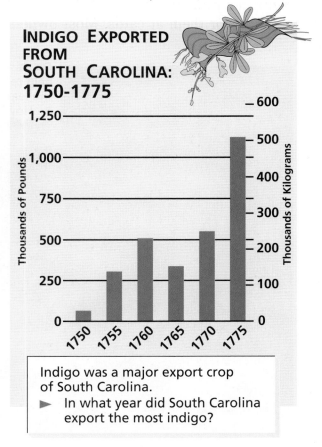

INDIGO EXPORTED FROM SOUTH CAROLINA: 1750-1775

Indigo was a major export crop of South Carolina.

▶ In what year did South Carolina export the most indigo?

199

they wished. There were two main groups of unfree labor. They were **indentured servants** and slaves. Indentured servants were people who agreed to work for five or seven years for whoever paid for their passage to America. In England the word *servant* was just another word for "worker." Indentured servants received food, shelter, and clothing, but they got no wages for their work. At the end of their term, they would sometimes receive some land and a chance to start out on their own.

The life of indentured servants was hard. They had few rights. For example, they could not marry without their master's permission. They had to do whatever work their master gave them and had to obey their master's wishes. Some masters treated their servants fairly. But there were masters who bought and sold servants like property, and others who even gambled for them at cards. Most owners just wanted to get all the work they could out of their servants. Many indentured servants died from overwork or sickness before serving out their time.

Why were men and women willing to become indentured servants? The reason was that they hoped to get land of their own when their service was over. For a poor person, becoming an indentured servant was a grand opportunity for a new start in life.

C. Slaves Replace Indentured Servants

Slavery In the late 1600s, plantation owners began to replace indentured servants with the second group of unfree workers. These were slaves from Africa. You'll remember that the first Africans arrived in Jamestown in the year 1619. Those Africans were treated like indentured servants. However, later arrivals

On this small tobacco farm, indentured servants help to plant the seeds and harvest, dry, and pack the leaves for shipment.
▶ How will the tobacco be taken away?

Amos Fortune, Free Man

By: Elizabeth Yates
Setting: Africa, 1725

In this story, a group of African and European slave catchers have raided a village of the peaceful At-mun-shi tribe. They have kidnaped many At-mun-shi and taken them to the seacoast to be sold. This is what happens next.

Some of the captors waved whips, others brandished guns as they drove the At-mun-shi to the pits. These were a series of holes ten feet deep in the ground and into them the people freed of their shackles [chains] were herded. Cocoanuts were split open and tossed into the pits and the people, now almost crazed with hunger, grabbed at them. . . . Once a day . . . food was tossed into the pits. And for three weeks the At-mun-shi waited. . . . .

[Finally the master of a slave ship in the harbor came ashore.]

He would soon exchange his cargo of molasses and rum, tobacco and gunpowder for a black cargo of slaves. But only the healthiest and largest, the youngest and ablest of all those gathered in the pits would interest him.

Before the trade was made, the captives were brought up from the pits and fastened together by twos, at ankles and wrists. They were washed and fed well, then their hair was shaved and their bodies oiled. They stood in a long patient row, like animals trained at last to obey commands. The traders were pleased at what the time and treatment in the pits had done. For the African tribesmen and women now were what they wanted them to be—merchandise that could be exchanged for merchandise. . . .

Often, buyers of slaves like the ship's master in this story branded their new property with a hot iron, just like cattle. Then they packed the slaves into the ships for the voyage across the ocean.

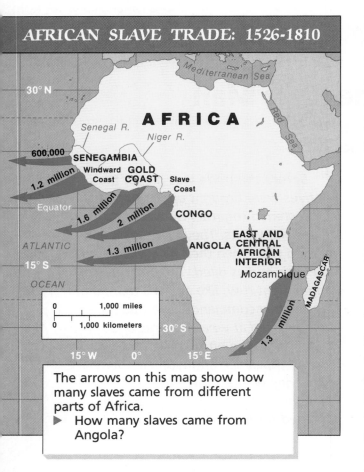

AFRICAN SLAVE TRADE: 1526–1810

AFRICA

Mediterranean Sea

Senegal R.
Niger R.
Red Sea

600,000
SENEGAMBIA
Windward GOLD
Coast COAST
Slave
Coast

1.2 million
1.6 million
2 million
CONGO

EAST AND
CENTRAL
AFRICAN
INTERIOR

1.3 million
ANGOLA

Mozambique

MADAGASCAR

1.3 million

Equator

ATLANTIC

OCEAN

30° N
15° S
15° W
0°
15° E
30° S

0   1,000 miles
0   1,000 kilometers

The arrows on this map show how
many slaves came from different
parts of Africa.
▶ How many slaves came from
   Angola?

have had indentured servants. Most servants came from England, and it was easier to deal with workers who spoke the
colonists' language and shared their ways.
It cost more to buy a slave than to pay the
passage of an indentured servant.

The Slave Trade   In the late 1600s, the
cost of buying a slave came down. At the
same time, English servants decided to go
to other colonies rather than to work for
tobacco planters. So planters began to buy
more slaves. By the 1700s most workers in
the South were slaves.

It is impossible today to capture in
words the horrors of the slave trade.
Young Africans were torn away from their
families and villages and marched to the
coast many miles away. There they were
sold to waiting slave traders. The buyers
branded their new property like cattle,
with a hot iron. Then they packed the
slaves onto ships for the voyage across the
ocean. The literature selection on page 201
will tell you more about how young Africans were forced into slavery.

Most slaves were sold to the sugar
planters in the West Indies. Some of the
slaves from Africa wound up in the southern colonies. There, the slaves were mainly
put to work in the tobacco and rice fields of
the large plantations.

from Africa were not. In the 1660s, Maryland and Virginia passed laws that made
them and their children slaves.

Slavery Spreads   Slavery spread slowly
at first. Plantation owners would rather

LESSON **3** *REVIEW*

THINK AND WRITE

A. How did Eliza Lucas help improve the
   economy of South Carolina?
B. Describe the life of an indentured servant.
C. Why did slaves replace indentured
   servants in the southern colonies?

SKILLS CHECK

WRITING SKILL

Pretend that you are an indentured servant.
Write a letter to a friend in England who is
thinking about coming to the colonies as an
indentured servant. Tell your friend what
your life is like. Include some advice about
whether your friend should become an
indentured servant.

Life in the Southern Colonies

THINK ABOUT WHAT YOU KNOW

How do you think you would feel if you were never allowed to go where you wanted to go or do the things you wanted to do?

STUDY THE VOCABULARY

county seat   back country
slave quarter

FOCUS YOUR READING

What was life like in the southern colonies?

A. The South Had Few Towns

In colonial times, cities and towns grew up around harbors where traders brought goods for sale. Most southern plantations, however, were built along rivers and had their own docks. A captain could sail his ship right up to the front door of a plantation. There he could pick up a load of tobacco and drop off the goods the plantation owner had ordered from England. Therefore, few towns and cities grew in the colonial South.

Since there were so few towns, the South had few of the things that people can have when they live close together. There were few schools, few newspapers, and few stores. There were no town meetings. To deal with local problems, southerners developed county government. A county usually covered hundreds of square miles. At the **county seat,** or main town of a county, was a courthouse. That was where residents of the county gathered to make laws and vote on taxes.

A ship docks at a tobacco plantation in Virginia.
▶ To what country do you think the ship might carry the tobacco grown on this plantation?

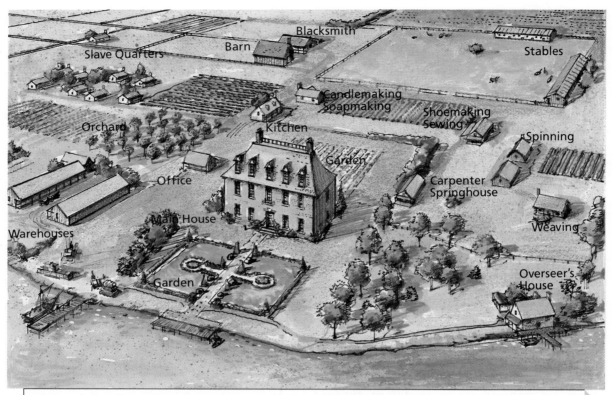

Many of the plantations in the South were very large. Some of the largest plantations were like small towns.
▶ Can you find the warehouses in the diagram above? Why, do you think, were the warehouses close to the waterfront?

B. A Plantation Is like a Village

Each plantation grew the food and made the goods its inhabitants needed. The plantation even looked something like a small village. Its main building was the Great House. This is where the planter's family lived. The Great House was usually built near the plantation dock and had a fine view of the river.

Behind the Great House were vegetable gardens. A bit to the side of the gardens, or perhaps just behind them, was the building where the family's carriages were kept. Farther away were a number of work buildings. These included the barns, a tool shop, stables for the horses, and sheds for drying tobacco. At the very back of the plantation was the **slave quarter**. Here were the one-room cabins where the slaves lived.

C. Planters Lived a Comfortable Life

Planters in the South lived a comfortable life. They had to spend a good deal of time managing their plantations to make them successful businesses. But they also had time for such entertainments as horseback riding and hunting.

Planters also had a busy social life. Much of this social life involved visits to other plantations. Planters lived far from each other, so when guests came from another plantation, they usually stayed for days at a time. During their visit they would be entertained with dancing, fox hunts, card games, and especially horse races, for that was the favorite sport of the southern planters.

To educate their children, planters hired private tutors, or teachers. A tutor usually lived in the Great House with the family and taught all the children. In the South, as elsewhere in the colonies, girls received just enough education to learn to read and write. Boys continued to study until they were 11 or 12. Then they might be sent to school in England to complete their education.

D. Slaves Provide the Labor for the Southern Colonies

Slaves and white owners of small farms were the two largest groups in the South's population. By the 1700s most white families in the Tidewater and the Piedmont in Virginia owned slaves. In other southern colonies, slaves were owned mainly by plantation owners.

On small farms, slaves usually worked in the fields alongside their owner. They also did many other tasks, for on a small farm everyone did a little bit of everything. Some slaves became very skilled craftspersons.

On a large plantation a small number of slaves became skilled carpenters, blacksmiths, brick makers, and barrel makers. Another small number worked and lived in the Great House with the master's family. These house servants cooked, cleaned, and did other housework. They also helped to raise the children in the master's family. By far, however, most slaves on a large plantation worked in the fields.

Slavery was a terrible wrong. It was not just that slaves were made to work

Below, slaves on a large plantation are packing tobacco for shipment.
▶ Find the ships that will be used to transport the tobacco.

POPULATION OF THE SOUTHERN COLONIES: 1630-1750

Colony	1630	1670	1710	1750
Virginia	2,500	35,309	78,281	231,033
Maryland		13,226	42,741	141,073
North Carolina		3,850	15,120	72,984
South Carolina		200	10,883	64,000
Georgia				5,200

The population of the southern colonies is shown for the years from 1630 to 1750.

► By 1750, which colony had the largest population?

hard that made it wrong. After all, most people in colonial America worked hard. It was that slaves were not free. They were owned by another person. They could be treated like any other piece of property. Their owner could sell them, separating wives from their husbands and parents from their children.

Slaves could not leave the plantation without their owner's permission. They were given no chance for education. They could be whipped for the smallest things. Although many owners were decent people, others treated their slaves cruelly.

Working in the fields from sunup to sundown was not the whole life of slaves, however. After work, they returned to the slave quarter. Here slave families could be by themselves.

Slaves created their own community in the slave quarter. They told and retold stories and folk tales handed down from the earliest slaves. They kept alive African music and dancing. As they blended their old culture with the culture of the New World, they created something new and different—the beginnings of an African-American culture. You will learn much more about the life and culture of slaves when you read Chapter 18.

E. Life in the Back Country Is Different

As the population of the South grew, more settlers pushed farther inland. They began to settle above the Fall Line, in the Piedmont. This area was often called the **back country**. Here settlers carved farms out of the wilderness. They chopped down trees and planted their corn, beans, and wheat between the tree stumps. They raised animals, mostly pigs and cattle.

On the small back-country farms, women not only did household tasks but also worked in the fields. Without the hard work of the women, farm families could not have made a living.

The life of the farmer in the Piedmont was different from that of the New England farmer. There was no village life in the southern back country. Families lived far from each other. There were few neighbors to turn to for help or company. There were no schools. If one of the parents could

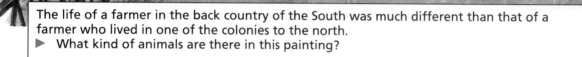

The life of a farmer in the back country of the South was much different than that of a farmer who lived in one of the colonies to the north.

▶ What kind of animals are there in this painting?

read, he or she could teach the children. If not, the children did not learn to read.

Neither were there any churches. Every now and then a minister might arrive on horseback. He would lead the family in prayer, have a meal with them, and then be off to visit another farm. The family might not see another minister, or any visitor, for many weeks. Farm families in the Piedmont lived a hard and lonely life.

Other settlers in the southern back country made their living from the forests. They hunted and trapped animals for their fur. They also turned the fine, tall pine trees of the Piedmont into lumber, masts for sailing ships, and naval stores.

LESSON **4** REVIEW

THINK AND WRITE

A. Why were there few towns in the southern colonies?
B. Describe a southern plantation.
C. What was the life of a southern planter like?
D. Describe the life of a slave on a southern plantation.
E. What was life like for a family in the back country?

SKILLS CHECK

THINKING SKILL

Look at the diagram of a plantation on page 204. Make a list of all the buildings shown and of the different kinds of work that might be done on this plantation.

USING THE VOCABULARY

proprietor	indigo
Huguenots	indentured servants
debtors	county seat
Tidewater	slave quarters
cash crops	backcountry

From the list choose the term that means nearly the same as the underlined term in the sentence. Write your answers on a separate sheet of paper.

1. Most plantation workers lived in <u>special area.</u>
2. The first <u>owner</u> of a colony was George Calvert.
3. James Oglethorpe founded the colony of Georgia for <u>persons who owed money.</u>
4. Many of the early settlements in Virginia were in the <u>places near rivers that were affected by the ocean.</u>
5. <u>French Protestants</u> also came to Charleston.
6. Many southern farmers produced <u>crops they could sell for money.</u>
7. Eliza Lucas experimented with <u>a plant from which a blue dye was made.</u>
8. A courthouse was located in the <u>main town of a county.</u>
9. Many small farms were located in the <u>frontier area.</u>
10. Much of the hard labor on southern farms was done by <u>people who worked for five or seven years to pay off the cost of their passage to America.</u>

REMEMBERING WHAT YOU READ

On a separate sheet of paper, write your answers in complete sentences.

1. Why did George Calvert want to start a colony in America?
2. What plans did the eight proprietors have for their Carolina colony?
3. What happened to the Carolina colony?
4. For what two reasons was the Georgia colony founded?
5. How does the Tidewater region differ from the Piedmont region?
6. What were three cash crops produced by the southern colonies?
7. Why did slavery spread slowly at first in the South?
8. Who made up the two largest groups in the South's population?
9. What kind of education was available for children in the South?
10. How did people in the backcountry make a living?

TYING MATH TO SOCIAL STUDIES

You are a plantation owner and have raised 300 bales of tobacco. It will sell in England for £5 a bale. (£ is the symbol for the pound, the English money of the time.) You have ordered the following goods from English merchants: a dining table and eight chairs for £100; 25 yards of silk material at £1 a yard; schoolbooks and a globe for your children for £5; three fine wigs at £20 each; and various other items that will cost about £100. How much money will you have left from the sale of the tobacco after you have paid for these goods?

THINKING CRITICALLY

On a separate sheet of paper, write your answers in complete sentences.

1. Why, do you think, did the plans the proprietors made for their colonies sometimes fail to work out?
2. Why was it easier and more profitable to farm in the southern colonies than in New England?
3. What was the major difference between indentured servants and slaves?
4. Why were there so few towns and villages in the southern colonies?
5. Compare and contrast life on a southern backcountry farm and life on a large plantation.

SUMMARIZING THE CHAPTER

On a separate sheet of paper, draw a graphic organizer like the one shown here. Copy the information from this graphic organizer to the one you have drawn. Fill in the blank spaces with information from the chapter.

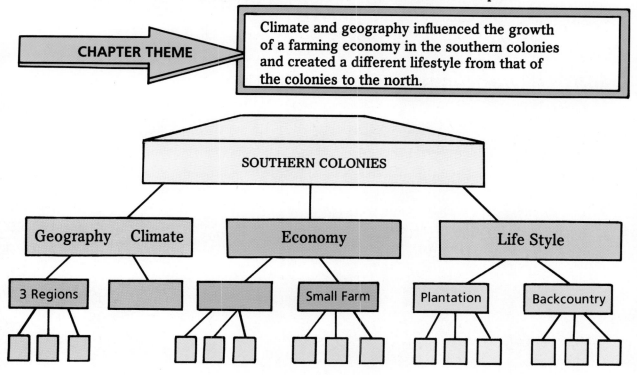

CHAPTER THEME

Climate and geography influenced the growth of a farming economy in the southern colonies and created a different lifestyle from that of the colonies to the north.

SOUTHERN COLONIES

Geography   Climate   Economy   Life Style

3 Regions   Small Farm   Plantation   Backcountry

CHAPTER 9

THE MIDDLE COLONIES

★ ★ ★ ★ ★

*S*ome of the English colonies, known as the Middle Colonies, were started by Swedish and Dutch settlers. The geography of the area encouraged farming. Farmers often had enough to sell in the growing towns and cities.

Founding the Middle Colonies

THINK ABOUT WHAT YOU KNOW

Imagine that you are the leader of a group of colonists living in North America. What rules would you write to be sure that the group gets along with the neighboring Indians?

STUDY THE VOCABULARY

Quakers

FOCUS YOUR READING

How was each of the middle colonies started?

A. New Netherland Becomes New York

The middle colonies were called this because they lay in the middle of England's North American colonies. That is, they were between New England and the southern colonies. However, one of the first middle colonies to be founded did not start as an English colony. It began as the Dutch colony of New Netherland.

Everyone who knew Peter Stuyvesant (STYE vuh sunt), the governor of New Netherland, agreed that he was an able leader. They agreed about something else, too: Peter Stuyvesant was a very stubborn man. That stubborness proved to be his downfall. It also resulted in the Netherlands losing its only colony in North America in a single day.

The Dutch West India Company sent Peter Stuyvesant to be the new governor of New Netherland in 1647. Stuyvesant did a very good job at first. Under his rule the people of New Netherland became prosperous. Some years later, Stuyvesant even took over a small Swedish colony on the Delaware River called New Sweden and made it part of New Netherland.

To Stuyvesant, however, there was only one way to run a colony — his way. When the people of New Netherland asked for a say in their government, Stuyvesant simply refused to listen. That was a big mistake. The citizens began to dislike Stuyvesant greatly. After a while they could hardly wait to be rid of him.

Stuyvesant held on until 1664. In that year England went to war against the Netherlands. Four English warships sailed

In New Amsterdam, Peter Stuyvesant angrily destroys a written message from the English enemies of the Netherlands.
► How, do you think, do the other men feel?

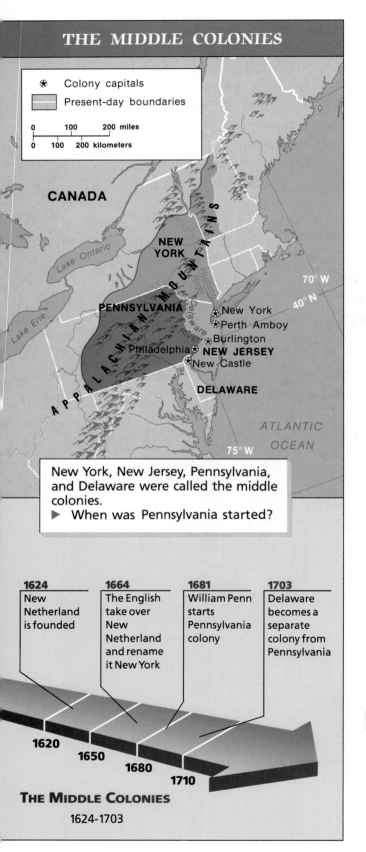

THE MIDDLE COLONIES

Colony capitals
Present-day boundaries

0   100   200 miles
0   100   200 kilometers

CANADA

Lake Ontario

NEW YORK

APPALACHIAN MOUNTAINS

PENNSYLVANIA

Lake Erie

New York
Perth Amboy
Burlington
Philadelphia   NEW JERSEY
New Castle

DELAWARE

ATLANTIC OCEAN

70° W
40° N
75° W

New York, New Jersey, Pennsylvania, and Delaware were called the middle colonies.
▶ When was Pennsylvania started?

1624 New Netherland is founded

1664 The English take over New Netherland and rename it New York

1681 William Penn starts Pennsylvania colony

1703 Delaware becomes a separate colony from Pennsylvania

1620
1650
1680
1710

THE MIDDLE COLONIES
1624-1703

into the harbor of New Amsterdam, the main city of the colony. The English demanded that the colony surrender. Stuyvesant tried to get the people to fight. If they had liked him better, maybe they would have. They refused, however, and the English took New Netherland without firing a shot. The English king gave the colony to his brother, the Duke of York, and the colony was renamed New York.

B. New Jersey Becomes a Colony

Soon after becoming the owner of New York, the Duke of York gave a large slice of it to two friends, Lord John Berkeley and Sir George Carteret. This land lay between the Hudson River and the Delaware River. The new owners called their colony New Jersey. There were already a number of Swedish, Dutch, and Finnish settlers living there when Berkeley and Carteret took it over.

Berkeley and Carteret wisely learned from the experience of others. They realized they would have to do three things to attract settlers to their colony. They must sell land cheaply, guarantee freedom of religion, and promise a say in the government. Berkeley and Carteret did all these things, and soon many people came to live in New Jersey.

C. Penn Given Land for a "Holy Experiment"

William Penn belonged to a religious group called the Society of Friends, or **Quakers** as they were commonly known. Quakers said that everyone, even kings, should quake, or tremble, before God. Quakers worshipped in a simple way. They had no priests or ministers. They met in a meetinghouse. Believing that all people are equal in the eyes of God, they treated

This quiet scene painted by an unknown artist shows a group of English Quakers in a meeting house.

▶ How would you describe the clothes that most of the Quakers are wearing?

all as equals. Quakers refused to take part in fights or wars and believed that all problems should be solved peacefully.

Quakers in England were treated badly for their beliefs. Many, including William Penn, were sent to prison. Quakers were also unwelcome in most American colonies. Quakers who tried to settle in Massachusetts were told to leave. Penn longed for a place where Quakers could follow their beliefs in peace.

As it happened, the king of England owed a large amount of money to William Penn's father. When his father died,

William Penn asked the king to settle the debt by giving him land in America. King Charles agreed. Penn named the new colony Pennsylvania after his father. *Pennsylvania* means "Penn's Woods."

Penn said his colony would be a "holy experiment." He invited people of all religions and from all countries to live there. To advertise his colony, Penn had pamphlets written in several languages and given out in many parts of Europe. The pamphlets told of the rich land and good climate for farming in Pennsylvania. Penn offered free land to all who paid their own way there. Those people who wanted even more land could buy it. Penn would even rent them land for a penny an acre! Indentured servants would get 50 acres (20 ha) at the end of their service.

D. The Colony of Pennsylvania Begins

William Penn himself went along with the first settlers to his colony in 1682. He chose a place along the Delaware River for the colony's first settlement and named it Philadelphia. *Philadelphia* means "city of brotherly love." In just a few years, thousands of people arrived in Penn's colony. Many were German. Others came from Scotland and northern Ireland. While some of these people stayed in Philadelphia, most spread out to start farm communities farther north and west.

Soon after starting Pennsylvania, Penn asked the king of England to add another piece of land to his colony. This area was also along the Delaware River, but farther south. It was the area that had earlier been known as New Sweden. The king granted Penn's request. This area later became the colony of Delaware.

Penn believed that the Native Americans, too, were the children of God and must be treated as equals. He believed that

Penn and the Indians of Pennsylvania signed treaties with one another.
► What promises, do you think, were in the treaties?

although the King of England gave him the land, he must still buy it from its rightful owners—the Indians. And he did.

While William Penn was alive and for many years afterward, Europeans and Indians in the colony of Pennsylvania lived in peace. Later, settlers who did not share Penn's beliefs came to Pennsylvania. They caused problems with the Indians by moving onto their land without permission.

LESSON *1* REVIEW

THINK AND WRITE
A. How did New Netherland become New York?
B. What did the proprietors of New Jersey do to attract settlers?
C. What was William Penn's purpose in founding a colony?
D. What were William Penn's beliefs about the American Indians?

SKILLS CHECK
THINKING SKILL
Look at the time line on the map on page 212. Which became a colony first, New York or Pennsylvania?

The Geography of the Middle Colonies

A. The Coastal Plain Has Wide Rivers and Rich Farmland

Coastal Lowlands The Atlantic Coastal Plain, you will remember from Chapter 1, is an important landform in the region that was called the middle colonies. Nearly all of Delaware lies on this plain. So does much of New Jersey. But the plain takes up only a small corner of Pennsylvania and hardly any of New York.

Harbors and Rivers Along the coast of this area are a number of fine harbors and bays. Two of the widest and deepest rivers of these colonies empty into these bays. One, the Hudson River, flows through New York. As this river empties into New York Bay, it forms one of the finest harbors in America.

Another large river is the Delaware River. This river runs along the eastern edge of Pennsylvania and forms its border with New York, New Jersey, and Delaware. It empties into Delaware Bay. Each of these rivers served as a water highway for carrying goods to the Atlantic Ocean.

Rolling Lowlands To the west, the flat land nearest the coast soon changes to gently rolling lowlands. This is still part of the coastal plain. Most of the land in the middle colonies was very good for farming. It was far richer than the land of New England and much less rocky.

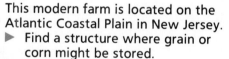

This modern farm is located on the Atlantic Coastal Plain in New Jersey.
▶ Find a structure where grain or corn might be stored.

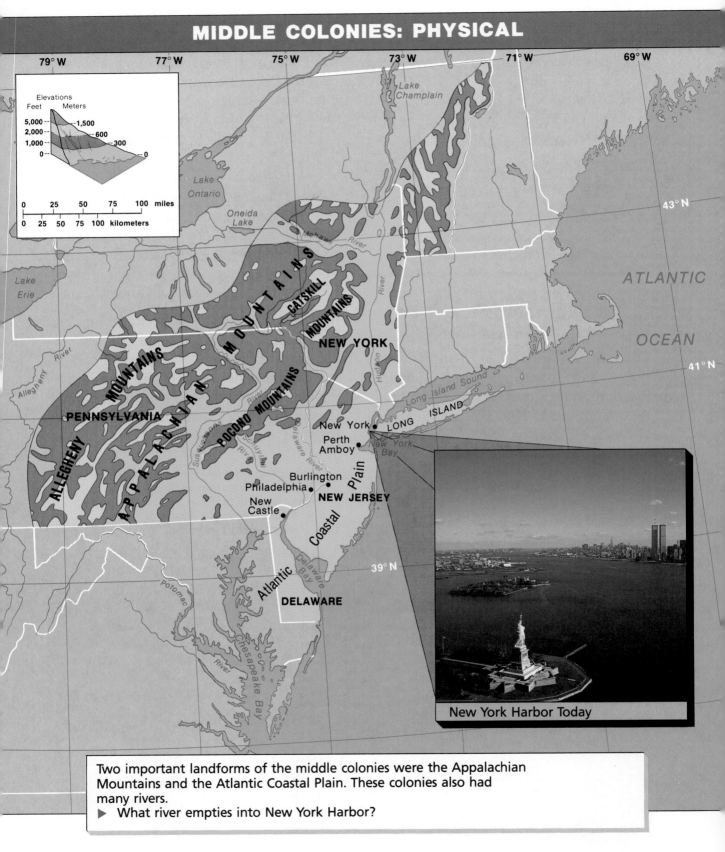

MIDDLE COLONIES: PHYSICAL

79° W   77° W   75° W   73° W   71° W   69° W

Elevations
Feet   Meters
5,000 -- -- 1,500
2,000 -- -- 600
1,000 -- -- 300
0 -- -- 0

0   25   50   75   100 miles
0   25 50   75   100 kilometers

Lake Champlain

43° N

ATLANTIC

Lake Ontario

Oneida Lake

Mohawk River

Lake Erie

APPALACHIAN MOUNTAINS

CATSKILL MOUNTAINS

NEW YORK

OCEAN

41° N

Allegheny River

ALLEGHENY MOUNTAINS

PENNSYLVANIA

POCONO MOUNTAINS

Hudson River

Long Island Sound

LONG ISLAND

New York

Perth Amboy

Susquehanna River

Schuylkill River

Delaware River

New York Bay

Burlington

Philadelphia

NEW JERSEY

New Castle

Coastal Plain

Atlantic

39° N

DELAWARE

Delaware Bay

Potomac River

Chesapeake Bay

River

New York Harbor Today

Two important landforms of the middle colonies were the Appalachian Mountains and the Atlantic Coastal Plain. These colonies also had many rivers.

▶ What river empties into New York Harbor?

B. Foothills and Mountains Lie Farther West

Foothills Farther to the west the land rises to the Fall Line. Beyond that line, the land is rougher and rockier. This area is the next important landform of the middle colonies. It is the foothills of the mountains, a belt of low ridges with valleys between. These foothills were rich in forests and animal life.

The Appalachians Even farther west lie the Appalachian Mountains. These mountains run like a spine down the back of New York and Pennsylvania and the northern corner of New Jersey. Just as in New England, the Appalachian Mountains are known by different names in different areas. In New York they are the Catskill Mountains, and in Pennsylvania they are the Allegheny Mountains. Among the mountains are a number of deep valleys where soil is good for farming.

C. Middle Colonies Have A "Middle" Climate

In the northern parts of the middle colonies the climate is often much like New England's. But the climate of most of the middle colonies is "middle" or moderate—not as cold as that of New England, and not as warm as that of the southern

Fog hides a valley between mountains in western Pennsylvania.
▶ What might there be at the bottom of the valley?

colonies. This kind of climate gives the middle colonies a good **growing season**. A growing season is the time of year when crops can be grown.

There is plenty of precipitation in the middle colonies. As you remember, precipitation is the moisture that falls to the ground in the form of rain, snow, mist, sleet, or hail. Even though the total precipitation is fairly high in the middle colonies region, the amount of snowfall varies greatly. The warmer, southern part of the region gets much less snowfall than the northern parts of the middle colonies.

LESSON *2* REVIEW

THINK AND WRITE
A. Where are the two major rivers in the middle colonies?
B. How does the land in the middle colonies change as you move west?
C. Compare the climate of the middle colonies to that of the New England colonies and the southern colonies.

SKILLS CHECK
MAP SKILL
Look at the map on page 216. Which two colonies were more mountainous—New York and Pennsylvania, or New Jersey and Delaware?

217

The Economy of the Middle Colonies

THINK ABOUT WHAT YOU KNOW

In the 1700s most colonists were trained for their jobs either by their families or by their employers. How do people today learn the skills they need for work?

STUDY THE VOCABULARY

mill

FOCUS YOUR READING

How did the people of the middle colonies make their living?

A. People Make a Living by Farming

Good Soil The table below shows the number of people who lived in the middle colonies. The majority of these people made their living by farming. Most farms were 50 or 100 acres (20 or 41 ha). Many families had the help of one or two indentured servants. These servants came to the middle colonies because they were treated better there than on the tobacco plantations of the South.

Farms in the middle colonies had some things in common with farms in New England. They produced nearly everything that the farm family needed. There was one big difference between the farms of the middle colonies and the small farms of both New England and the southern colonies. In the good soil and mild climate of the middle colonies, farmers produced not only all they needed but also a great deal more. They had crops left over to sell.

Farm Crops The biggest crops in the middle colonies were wheat and rye. Since

POPULATION OF THE MIDDLE COLONIES: 1670-1750

Colony	1670	1690	1710	1730	1750
Pennsylvania		11,450	24,450	51,707	119,666
New York	5,754	13,909	21,625	48,594	76,696
New Jersey	1,000	8,000	19,872	35,510	71,393
Delaware	700	1,482	3,645	9,170	28,704

By 1750, Pennsylvania had the largest population of the middle colonies.

► Which of the middle colonies had the smallest population in 1750?

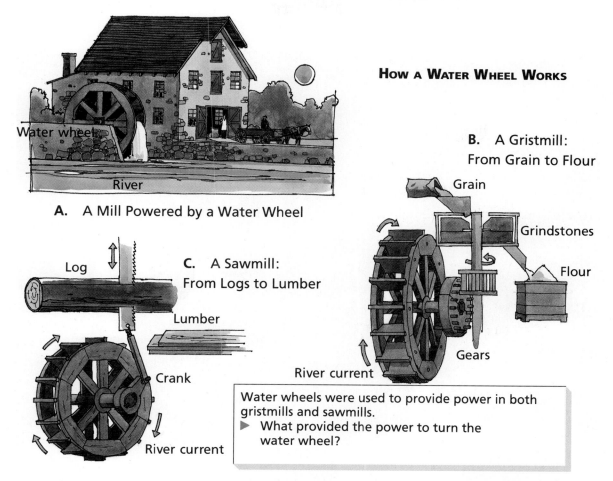

HOW A WATER WHEEL WORKS

A. A Mill Powered by a Water Wheel

B. A Gristmill: From Grain to Flour

C. A Sawmill: From Logs to Lumber

Water wheels were used to provide power in both gristmills and sawmills.
► What provided the power to turn the water wheel?

most bread was made from these two grains, the middle colonies came to be called the bread colonies. Most of the wheat grown on middle colony farms was ground into flour at local **mills**. A mill is a building with machinery for manufacturing something. Flour from the middle colonies was shipped to markets throughout the colonies and to Europe.

Farmers of the middle colonies raised other things for sale as well. They sold fruits, like apples and peaches. They also raised animals — such as cattle, pigs, sheep, and horses — for sale.

B. People Make a Living From Industry

Mills A number of settlers in the middle colonies made their living in small industries. In dozens of small mills throughout the region, colonists turned the harvests of the forests and the farms into usable products. They sawed logs into boards and ground wheat into flour.

These mills were located along fast-flowing streams that provided the power to do the work. On the outside of the mill was a large water wheel. This wheel was connected to a saw or to a grinding stone inside the mill. As the rushing water of the stream turned the wheel, the wheel turned the saw or grinding stone. The diagram above shows how a water wheel works.

The Iron Industry Another colonial industry was iron making. Once again, there were iron furnaces through all 13 colonies, but the middle colonies had most of them. These iron furnaces were small. Most of them would fit in a family's backyard, and each one produced only a few pounds of

This is a colonial blacksmith shop. The blacksmith is softening iron in order to hammer it into the shape of a horseshoe.
▶ How is the iron being softened?

iron a day. But the small production from each furnace added up to quite a lot of iron. Much of this iron was sold to England, where it was manufactured into many different products. Some was sold to colonial blacksmiths who made such products as axes and nails. The drawing above shows a blacksmith at work.

LESSON *3* REVIEW

THINK AND WRITE

A. How did farms in the middle colonies differ from those in the New England and southern colonies?

B. Why did the middle colonies have many small industries?

SKILLS CHECK

MAP SKILL

Many mills were built along the rivers and streams in the middle colonies. Look at the map on page 216. Make a list of the rivers in the middle colonies.

Life in Ben Franklin's Philadelphia

THINK ABOUT WHAT YOU KNOW

Imagine that you are given a chance to plan a city. What are some things that your city would have?

STUDY THE VOCABULARY

apprentice   volunteer
proverbs

FOCUS YOUR READING

How did Ben Franklin help to improve life in Philadelphia?

A. William Penn Plans a City

The largest city in the middle colonies—in fact, the largest city in all of North America—was Philadelphia. William Penn had designed this city before the first settlers arrived in his colony. Penn had seen the crowded, dirty cities of England. He wanted Philadelphia to be a pleasant place to live, with plenty of space for its inhabitants.

Penn planned a city of straight, tree-lined streets that crisscrossed like lines on a checkerboard. Each house would sit in the middle of a large lot. There would be room on each side of the house for gardens, fruit trees, or grass. Scattered around the town would be five large, open squares. These would allow space for churches, public buildings, and parks.

Philadelphia grew rapidly. By the mid-1700s its waterfront was the busiest in North America. On any day one could see ships from England, the West Indies, and Philadelphia itself, carrying goods to and from faraway places. As this city's population grew, houses were crowded more closely together. On many of the streets, the open spaces that William Penn had planned between homes were fast disappearing.

Along the wide main streets of the city, hundreds of skilled workers had set up their shops. Market Street, the main street of the city, was a beehive of activity, especially on Wednesdays and Saturdays. Those days were market days, when

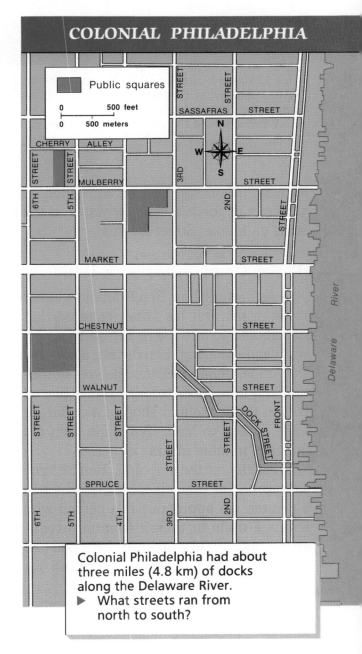

COLONIAL PHILADELPHIA

Colonial Philadelphia had about three miles (4.8 km) of docks along the Delaware River.
▶ What streets ran from north to south?

This 1750 view of colonial Philadelphia, Pennsylvania, shows a built-up city with a somewhat crowded central area. Its harbor seems to be very busy, with ships of all sizes coming and going.
► What supplied the power for the ships in the harbor?

farmers, fishers, fur traders, and sellers of all kinds of goods took their wares to the stalls on Market Street for sale.

B. Ben Franklin Learns a Trade

As a young boy, Ben Franklin wanted to go to sea. But his father believed that Ben should go into the family trade, which was candle making. Ben did not do well at this trade, mainly because he was not interested in it. Therefore his father placed him in the home and shop of a cutler, or knife maker, to learn that trade. Ben did not take to knife making either.

Finally, at the age of 12, Ben became an **apprentice** to an older brother who was a printer. An apprentice is a person who learns a trade or a craft from an experienced, successful worker. At last, Ben had found a trade that he enjoyed and for which he showed ability.

Both the master and the apprentice signed a contract. The master had to agree to house, feed, clothe, and train the apprentice. The apprentice agreed to work hard, to be honest, to not waste the master's goods or give away any secrets of the master's trade, and to not drink, gamble, or get married.

Most contracts lasted for seven years. When his time was completed, the apprentice was a young man ready and able to make his way in the world.

C. Ben Franklin Arrives in Philadelphia

After Ben's apprenticeship with his brother was completed, he decided to go to the city of Philadelphia and work on his own. As a growing and prosperous city, Philadelphia was a good place for ambitious, hard-working people to get ahead. It turned out to be just right for 17-year-old Ben Franklin.

Arriving in Philadelphia, Franklin went to work for a printer and began saving his money. At the age of 22, he borrowed more money and started his own printing business. His new business did well. The next year he bought a newspaper business that was doing poorly. Ben Franklin made it a success through talent and hard work. After printing the newspapers, Franklin often carried them through the streets himself and sold them. Franklin also printed other materials such as pamphlets and books.

One of the books Franklin printed brought him fame and fortune. This book was *Poor Richard's Almanac. Poor Richard's Almanac* contained weather predictions for every day of the year, useful bits of information on many subjects, jokes, recipes, riddles, and **proverbs,** or wise old sayings. Franklin called the proverbs "the sayings of Poor Richard."

People had heard many of the ideas in these proverbs before, but Ben Franklin made them popular by rewriting them in a catchy style. You probably know some of them: "A penny saved is a penny earned"; "Early to bed and early to rise makes a man healthy, wealthy, and wise"; "God helps those who help themselves"; and "Little strokes fell great oaks."

D. Franklin Improves Life for the People of Philadelphia

A Public Library Franklin wanted to do things that would improve life for the people of Philadelphia. He and several friends started a lending library for the city. This made it possible for people in Philadelphia to read many books without having to buy all of them. The idea spread to the other English colonies. It was the beginning of our modern public library system.

Paved Streets Franklin also took the lead in getting Philadelphia to do something about its muddy streets. Why not pave some of these roads with stone? he asked. He began to write about this idea in his newspaper. He got people talking about it. Philadelphia became the first city in the colonies with paved streets. The stone paving was a mixed blessing. The stones did keep down the dust and the mud. But the noise of wagon wheels rolling over them made Philadelphia the noisiest place in America!

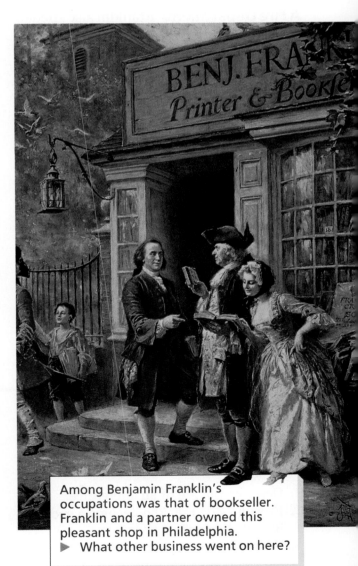

Among Benjamin Franklin's occupations was that of bookseller. Franklin and a partner owned this pleasant shop in Philadelphia.
▶ What other business went on here?

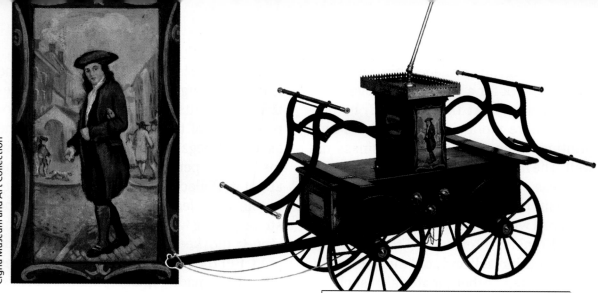

Cigna Museum and Art Collection

This is a replica of a fire wagon used in Philadelphia in the 1800s.
▶ Why is there a picture of Benjamin Franklin on the fire wagon?

A Fire Department Franklin also tried to do something about a problem that every city in the eighteenth century faced — fire. With wooden houses crowded together, a shifting wind could easily spread fire from one building to another until the whole city burned down. In fact, that had happened to a big part of Boston when Ben Franklin was a child there.

Franklin helped organize Philadelphia's first **volunteer** fire company in 1736. A volunteer is a person who offers to do something of his or her own free will. Soon there were volunteer fire companies in many neighborhoods of Philadelphia.

Other Improvements Franklin also got the people of Philadelphia to hire and train people to patrol the city at night. They were not a real police force, but they were a great improvement on night watchmen, who lit the street lights and did little else. In addition, Franklin helped to start a hospital. He also served as postmaster of Philadelphia. Mail service in the city was greatly improved under his leadership.

At age 42, Franklin retired from business so that he could devote himself to his other interests. Franklin was interested in science and inventions and also in serving the people of his city and colony. When he retired, he wrote to his mother that when he died, he wanted people to say, "He lived usefully," not "He died rich."

LESSON **4** *REVIEW*

THINK AND WRITE

A. How was William Penn's plan for Philadelphia changed by the city's rapid growth?

B. Describe the life of an apprentice.

C. How did Ben Franklin become a success in Philadelphia?

D. What were three things that Franklin did to improve life in Philadelphia?

SKILLS CHECK

WRITING SKILL

Pretend that you are Ben Franklin. Write a newspaper article telling people why Philadelphia should have a volunteer fire company.

USING THE VOCABULARY

On a separate sheet of paper, write the word beside the number of its definition.

Quaker   apprentice
growing season   proverb
mill

1. A wise saying
2. A member of the Society of Friends
3. The period of time in a year when crops can be grown
4. Someone who learns a trade from an experienced worker
5. A building with machinery that provides the power to grind grain, to saw logs, or do similar work.

REMEMBERING WHAT YOU READ

On a separate sheet of paper, write your answers in complete sentences.

1. How did Peter Stuyvesant's stubbornness lead to the Netherlands losing its only North American colony in a single day?
2. Why did King Charles II of England give a large tract of land to William Penn?
3. What did William Penn do to attract settlers to his new colony?
4. Describe two important landforms in the middle colonies.
5. How did the climate in the middle colonies affect farming?
6. How did most people in the middle colonies make their living?
7. Why were the middle colonies also called the bread colonies?
8. Why were mills located along fast-flowing streams?
9. Why was Market Street in Philadelphia given that name?
10. What kind of information did Benjamin Franklin think it was necessary to put into *Poor Richard's Almanac?*

TYING SCIENCE TO SOCIAL STUDIES

Benjamin Franklin wrote weather forecasts for his *Almanac.* How was Franklin able to predict the weather? What causes weather to change? Why is it important for people to know about weather? Think about these questions, and then do one of the activities listed below. Be prepared to share what you learn with your classmates.

1. Look in science books to learn about weather and how it is forecast today.
2. Do some research to learn how people living in Ben Franklin's time made weather predictions.
3. Some almanacs still make weather predictions. Find a copy of the current *Farmer's Almanac* and make a chart that shows the weather forecasts for the area in which you live for the remaining months of the year.

THINKING CRITICALLY

On a separate sheet of paper, write your answers in complete sentences.

1. Why, do you think, was the English king eager to have Quakers leave England?
2. What did the proprietors of the New Jersey and Pennsylvania colonies do to encourage settlement?
3. Why were farming, trade, and industry able to develop successfully in the middle colonies?
4. What made Philadelphia a pleasant city in which to live?
5. What, do you think, was Benjamin Franklin's most important contribution to improving life in Philadelphia? Explain your answer.

SUMMARIZING THE CHAPTER

On a separate sheet of paper, draw a graphic organizer like the one shown here. Copy the information from this graphic organizer to the one you have drawn. Under the main idea for each lesson, write three items that support that idea. The first has been done for you.

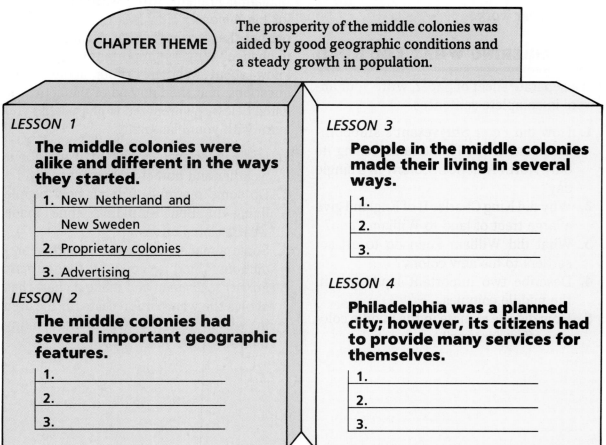

CHAPTER THEME

The prosperity of the middle colonies was aided by good geographic conditions and a steady growth in population.

LESSON 1

The middle colonies were alike and different in the ways they started.

1. New Netherland and New Sweden
2. Proprietary colonies
3. Advertising

LESSON 2

The middle colonies had several important geographic features.

1. _____
2. _____
3. _____

LESSON 3

People in the middle colonies made their living in several ways.

1. _____
2. _____
3. _____

LESSON 4

Philadelphia was a planned city; however, its citizens had to provide many services for themselves.

1. _____
2. _____
3. _____

COOPERATIVE LEARNING

Much of this unit has been about the exploration and settlement of the two continents that Europeans called the New World.

PROJECT

Your group will create a board game about the New World. You may decide that your game will deal only with exploration. Perhaps it will be a game about settlements in the New World. Or the group can make up a game that combines exploration and settlement.

Meet with your group and choose one person to be the recording secretary. Discuss what kinds of board games each of you has played. Decide which ideas from the group discussion can be used to design a new game. Make a temporary list of rules for the game. The following tasks to create a practice model of the game should then be divided among group members.

● Design the board (two people)
● Design the pieces that will move around the board
● Cut and label paper for bonus and penalty cards

Everyone in the group should be responsible for writing three bonus cards and three penalty cards based on information from the unit. Bonus cards could have messages such as *The lookout has just sighted land. Move*

ahead two spaces. Penalty cards could have messages such as *There are rapids in the St. Lawrence River. Lose a turn.*

The group should play the game with the practice model to test it.
● Fix any problems that come up.
● Decide on the final rules.

PRESENTATION AND REVIEW

Make a final version of the game for a class collection. Divide the following tasks among the group members.
● Draw the design for the board on a heavy piece of cardboard, using felt-tipped pens.
● Make the pieces that will move around the board.
● Print the bonus and penalty cards on heavy paper.
● Write a final list of the rules.
● Pack everything carefully in a box.

Trade games with another group. Ask them to tell you how they liked your game. Ask if they have any suggestions that would improve the game.

Your group should meet again to discuss how well you worked together.

● Did everyone have a chance to speak?

● Did everyone take part in making the game?

● Did everyone do his or her best to make the project a success?

REMEMBER TO:
● Give your ideas.
● Listen to others' ideas.
● Plan your work with the group.
● Present your project.
● Discuss how your group worked.

A. WHY DO I NEED THIS SKILL?

You have learned in this unit that people may have come to North America from Asia about 30,000 years ago. How long ago is that compared to the time that Christopher Columbus came to North America? What do B.C. and A.D. mean? Time lines can help you answer questions like these.

B. LEARNING THE SKILL

A time line is one way to organize historical information. It helps put events in the order in which they happened. A time line is like a scale. It measures time.

Time lines can organize events that occurred over many thousands of years. Look carefully at the time line on the next page. Events that took place long ago are far to the left on the time line. Events that happened closer to the present are more to the right.

The time line is divided into two parts —B.C. and A.D. The letters B.C. stand for the words *before Christ*. The letters A.D. stand for the Latin words *anno Domini*, which mean "in the year of our Lord." This way of measuring time was invented by a Christian monk who lived nearly 1,500 years ago.

The year 5000 B.C. is marked on the time line. That is about the time when people living on this continent discovered farming. To count the B.C. years, you go from right to left. How many years before the birth of Jesus was farming discovered?

A.D. 1492 means 1,492 years after the birth of Jesus. That date, as you know, is the year of Columbus's first voyage. To count the A.D. years, you go from left to right.

There are two rules to follow when you want to find the number of years between events.

- To find the number of years between two B.C. or two A.D. events, **subtract**.

- To find the number of years between a B.C. event and an A.D. event, **add**.

C. PRACTICING THE SKILL

Use the time line on the next page to answer the following questions. Write your answers on a separate sheet of paper.

1. On which side of the time line would you put the present year?
2. Which covers more time, A.D. or B.C.?
3. Are the events that happened longest ago on the left side or the right side of the time line?
4. How many years are there between A.D. 1000 and A.D. 1492?
5. What is the number of years between 30,000 B.C. and A.D. 1492?

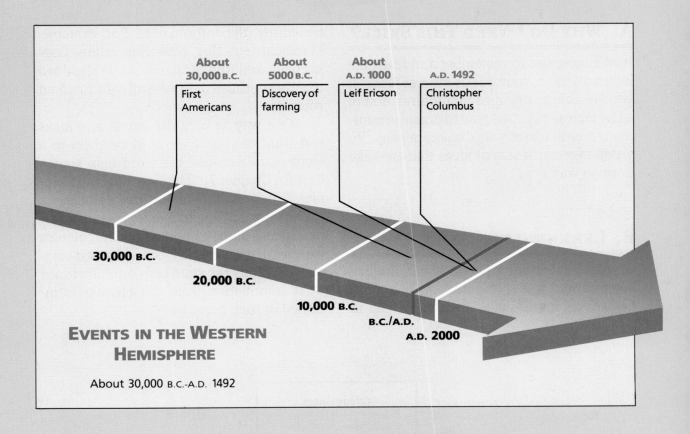

About
30,000 B.C.

About
5000 B.C.

About
A.D. 1000

A.D. 1492

First
Americans

Discovery of
farming

Leif Ericson

Christopher
Columbus

30,000 B.C.

20,000 B.C.

10,000 B.C.

B.C./A.D.

A.D. 2000

EVENTS IN THE WESTERN
HEMISPHERE

About 30,000 B.C.-A.D. 1492

D. APPLYING THE SKILL

Leif Ericson sailed for North America around A.D. 1000. Find Ericson's voyage on the time line and answer the following questions in complete sentences.

1. Who came to North America first—Leif Ericson or Christopher Columbus?
2. How many years after the discovery of farming did Ericson come to North America?
3. More than 1,500 years ago, the Maya began to create their civilization in the jungles of Central America and southern Mexico. Would you place this event on the time line before or after Ericson's voyage? Be prepared to explain your answer.

A. WHY DO I NEED THIS SKILL?

It will be easier to remember and learn the information in your social studies book if you are able to organize that information in some logical way. One way to organize information is to classify it. Classify means "to group together words or ideas that are alike in some way."

B. LEARNING THE SKILL

A great deal of information about English colonization was presented in this unit. Classifying it will make it easier for you to remember the information. For example, Massachusetts Bay, New Hampshire, Connecticut, and Rhode Island can be classified together because they were all New England colonies.

One way to organize words and ideas you want to classify is to place them in a word map. Examine the word map shown here for Chapter 7, "The New England Colonies." Information about the colonies is classified according to five topics or categories: names of the colonies, how the colonies were settled, geography, economy, and colonial life. Study the word map carefully to see what information from the chapter is included in each category.

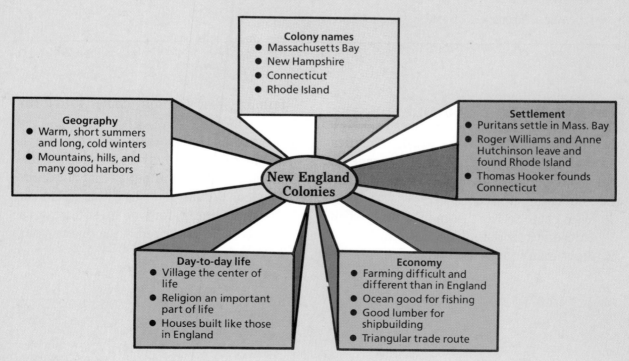

Colony names
- Massachusetts Bay
- New Hampshire
- Connecticut
- Rhode Island

Geography
- Warm, short summers and long, cold winters
- Mountains, hills, and many good harbors

New England Colonies

Settlement
- Puritans settle in Mass. Bay
- Roger Williams and Anne Hutchinson leave and found Rhode Island
- Thomas Hooker founds Connecticut

Day-to-day life
- Village the center of life
- Religion an important part of life
- Houses built like those in England

Economy
- Farming difficult and different than in England
- Ocean good for fishing
- Good lumber for shipbuilding
- Triangular trade route

C. Practicing the Skill

Prepare a word map for Chapter 8, "The Southern Colonies." On a sheet of paper, copy the form of the word map used for the New England colonies.

Part of the word map about the southern colonies has been done for you here. Copy that information on the word map you have drawn. Skim or reread Chapter 8 in order to find and classify the missing information. Complete the word map. Try to select important ideas. Compare the southern colonies word map with the New England word map. How were the two groups of colonies alike? How did they differ?

D. Applying the Skill

Make a similar word map for Chapter 9, "The Middle Colonies." Compare it to the word maps for the other two chapters.

The next unit is about the new nation that was formed as a result of the American Revolution. Think about how you might classify important events and ideas. You could make a word map to show how the Revolutionary War was fought in the North, South, and West. Or you might include topics on your map, such as important battles and famous generals. Look for other opportunities to classify ideas and make word maps in other chapters.

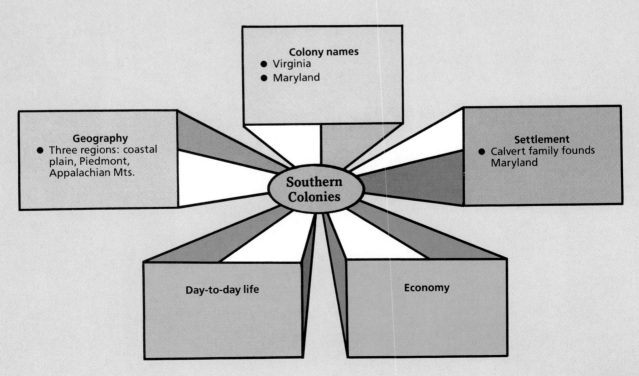

Colony names
- Virginia
- Maryland

Geography
- Three regions: coastal plain, Piedmont, Appalachian Mts.

Settlement
- Calvert family founds Maryland

Southern Colonies

Day-to-day life

Economy

Unit 3

FORMING A NEW NATION

In the 1700's, American colonists fought a war to gain their independence from Great Britain. After their victory, they created a new kind of government for their young country.

▶ *Angry colonists protest the tax on tea by dumping tea into Boston Harbor at the Boston Tea Party.*

By the 1750s the English colonies had grown strong and prosperous. The ties to Great Britain were still strong, but the colonies had developed a very American look and feeling.

The New Americans

THINK ABOUT WHAT YOU KNOW

From what parts of the world are people coming to the United States today? What things attract people to this country?

STUDY THE VOCABULARY

immigrant   **frontier**

FOCUS YOUR READING

Who were the Americans of 1750?

A. The American Spirit Forms

Newcomers   In the summer of 1750, a ship carrying 400 German **immigrants** arrived at the dock in Philadelphia. Immigrants are people who come into one country from another. If this had been a hundred years earlier, the arrival of these 400 immigrants would have been big news. But in 1750 the coming of another shipful of new Americans was an ordinary event. For, by then, thousands of immigrants arrived in the colony each year.

The immigrants of 1750 entered an America that had changed greatly since the days when the colonies of Jamestown and Plymouth were founded. In those early days, colonists had to struggle to keep their tiny settlements going. But by 1750, as you see on the map on page 236, much of the Atlantic Coastal Plain and the Piedmont was settled. America was a land of prosperous farms and busy towns. Its population had already passed 1 million, and it was growing fast.

Immigrants from Many Places   Who were these million Americans? Most had come from the country of England or were the children and grandchildren of the English settlers who had come earlier. But there were also many immigrants who came from other lands.

One large group of new Americans were the Scots-Irish. They moved to the back country, building rough homes on the **frontier**—that is, the area closest to the wild, unsettled land farther west. There, in the forests, these settlers carved out small farms.

This farmer pounds corn into cornmeal flour for cooking.
► How can you tell that this farm is on the frontier?

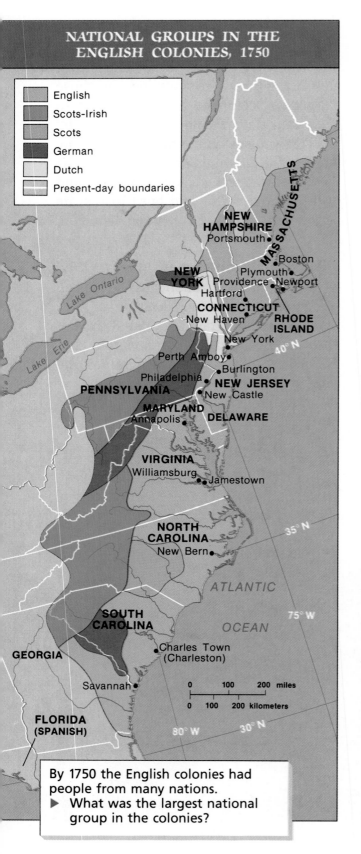

NATIONAL GROUPS IN THE ENGLISH COLONIES, 1750

English
Scots-Irish
Scots
German
Dutch
Present-day boundaries

Lake Ontario
Lake Erie

NEW HAMPSHIRE
Portsmouth
MASSACHUSETTS
Boston
NEW YORK
Plymouth
Providence Newport
Hartford
CONNECTICUT
New Haven RHODE ISLAND
New York
Perth Amboy
Burlington
Philadelphia NEW JERSEY
PENNSYLVANIA New Castle
MARYLAND
Annapolis DELAWARE
VIRGINIA
Williamsburg Jamestown
NORTH CAROLINA
New Bern
ATLANTIC
SOUTH CAROLINA OCEAN
GEORGIA Charles Town (Charleston)
Savannah
FLORIDA (SPANISH)

0   100   200 miles
0   100   200 kilometers

40° N
35° N
75° W
80° W   30° N

By 1750 the English colonies had people from many nations.
▶ What was the largest national group in the colonies?

Another large group of settlers were the Germans. Many people from Germany came to America to seek religious freedom. They were also looking for good farmland. They found both in the colony of Pennsylvania, and many settled there. Many Germans also settled in the back country of other colonies.

Other groups of immigrants came from Europe too. There were Scots, Welsh, Swedes, Finns, Dutch, Swiss, French, Irish, and religious groups such as Jews and Mennonites. To see where some of these national groups settled, look at the map on this page.

The largest group of all in 1750, next to the English, were Africans and their children and grandchildren. About one in every five Americans in the year 1750 was an African American. Nearly all African Americans were slaves in the South. But there were slaves in northern colonies as well. In the North, slaves lived mainly in the cities, where they were house servants for wealthy families. In addition, there were a few free African Americans in northern cities.

B. Immigrants Find a Land of Opportunity

Indentured Servants Why were immigrants still coming to America in 1750? Why did they continue to come year after year? The answer lies in one word: opportunity—opportunity to own a piece of land, opportunity for work, opportunity to worship as they wished, and opportunity to start a new life.

About half of all the Europeans who came to America were indentured servants. They dreamed of having land of their own someday. For many, that dream came true. In some colonies, indentured servants were given a small piece of land after finishing their years of service. Even those who did not receive land at the end of their service still had the chance to work and save to buy land. Land in America was amazingly cheap, and there was plenty of it. For instance, in the colony of Pennsylvania one could buy good farm land for just a few cents an acre!

Farmers and Workers Most immigrants who paid their own way to America became farmers. But some went to live and work in America's growing towns and cities. And no matter how many arrived here, there always seemed to be enough work for more.

POPULATION OF THE ENGLISH COLONIES: 1700-1750

The population of the English colonies increased greatly between 1700 and 1750.
► About how many people were living in the colonies in the year 1720?

Beyond this New York farm of the 1700s rise the Catskill Mountains.
► Name the different animals that were probably raised on this old farm.

America also needed shopkeepers. This elegant shop is in the rebuilt colonial city of Williamsburg, Virginia.
► What kinds of goods does this shop sell?

America needed skilled workers who could make iron goods, build ships, make barrels, print newspapers, and bake bread. There was plenty of work for unskilled workers, too. They found work loading and unloading ships at the docks, driving wagons, carting away trash and sewage, and building dirt roads in the towns. Some immigrants opened stores and shops. The photograph above shows what a colonial store might have looked like.

Americans of 1750 were a busy, hard-working people. They believed that, in this land, hard work would pay off in a better life. And, except for the slaves, it did. Most Americans owned their own land and made a good living. In the cities, workers made two or three times as much money as they could have made if they lived in Europe. Compared with the rest of the world, the America of 1750 had very few poor people.

LESSON 1 REVIEW

THINK AND WRITE

A. What were some of the groups of people who had come to America by 1750?
B. What kinds of opportunities did immigrants find in America?

SKILLS CHECK

MAP SKILL

Look at the map on page 236. Then make a list of the 13 colonies. Use the map to help you list the national groups in each colony.

Getting Around and Keeping in Touch

THINK ABOUT WHAT YOU KNOW

The colonists in 1750 did not have all the ways to travel and to communicate with one another that we have today. List some ways to travel and to exchange information and messages that you think the colonists may not have had.

STUDY THE VOCABULARY

transportation   **communication**

FOCUS YOUR READING

How were the American colonies linked to one another in 1750?

A. Americans Travel Rough Roads

Getting from one place to another in colonial America was not easy. In 1750 many roads in the back country were nothing more than old Indian trails or paths. Hardly any of them were more than 8 feet (2 m) wide. None of these roads were paved, so of course they were dusty in summer and muddy in winter. Travelers also had to dodge tree stumps in the roads.

Crossing rivers and streams was tricky. There were few bridges. The main way across rivers was by ferryboat, which was little more than a raft made of logs. If streams were shallow enough, travelers simply waded across them.

Although back country roads were poor, the roads that connected the growing cities and towns near the coast had been greatly improved by the mid-1700s. These roads were filled with traffic.

B. Improved Roads Tie the Colonies Together

Moving People and Goods In 1750 there were not many kinds of **transportation**. Transportation is the moving of people and goods from place to place. Although most Americans in 1750 traveled mainly by foot, many used horses. Wealthier people, in fact, traveled in coaches pulled by teams of horses. In the South, where horse racing was a favorite sport, planters often raced each other in their coaches, making the roads dangerous for everyone else. As a result, local governments passed the first speeding laws in America.

By 1750, Americans could travel between the main cities and towns by stagecoach. The stagecoach got its name from the fact that a journey on this coach was

Guided by a rope stretched from one bank of a river to the other, this ferry is being slowly poled across the water.
▶ Why, do you think, was a rope needed to guide the ferry?

made "in stages." Every 15 or 20 miles (24 or 32 km), the driver of the coach had to stop and change the team of horses.

If you traveled by stagecoach in 1750, you would find the journey very uncomfortable. Your trip usually started at 2:00 or 3:00 A.M., and you traveled until nightfall. In the summer you might be on the road for 18 hours straight. You felt every bump and hole in the road, because your "seat" was nothing but a wood board and the coach did not have springs.

At night your coach stopped at an inn, where you got a poor meal and a terrible night's sleep. You slept four in a bed, with men in one bedroom and women in another. You didn't sleep for long, for you were up again at 2:00 or 3:00 A.M. for the next leg of the journey.

A stagecoach traveled between 25 and 40 miles (40 and 64 km) a day, depending on how muddy the road was. Today you can drive from New York to Philadelphia by car in about 2 hours. In 1750 that same trip took three *days* by stagecoach—and that was thought to be very speedy!

Other Changes Improved roads brought about a very dramatic change in **communication**, or the exchanging of information or messages. They brought the colonies closer together. Earlier the colonies had had little to do with each other. In fact, each colony had had more to do with England, which was 3,000 miles (4,827 km) away, than it did with the colony next door. But with improved roads, Americans traveled more. They did more business

This stagecoach is shown preparing to leave an inn and continue on its journey.
▶ Why did stagecoach passengers prefer to travel in the daytime?

Franklin regularly inspected the mail routes. Here he is shown on the Boston Post Road.
▶ Why is *Post Road* a good name for this route?

with people in the other colonies. They visited each other more. They came to have more things in common.

C. Mail Service Improves in the 1750s

The main way for colonists to keep in touch with family and friends in other towns and villages was by letter. That was not as easy as it sounds. In the early years of colonial life, there was no mail service. You would just ask someone who was going to the right town — or even *near* the right town — to take your letter along, and you hoped it would get to the right place. To send a letter to Europe, you paid a ship captain to take it.

In 1750, however, things were much better. By that time there was regular mail service between the main colonial cities. Once a week, riders carried mail in their saddlebags between these cities. Wagons were also beginning to be used for carrying mail. Even with the improved roads, though, mail delivery was not very fast. In 1750 it took a week and a half for a letter to get from Philadelphia to Boston.

The next year, 1751, Benjamin Franklin was put in charge of the postal service, or colonial mails. He made many improvements in mail delivery. Franklin cut the delivery time between Philadelphia and Boston to just three days by using riders who traveled day and night.

How much did it cost to *send* a letter in 1750? Not a cent. That didn't mean mail delivery was free. The person who *received* the letter paid for the mail. How much you paid depended on how far the letter had traveled. And you paid in cash, for there were no postage stamps then.

D. News Spreads by Newspaper

Today we live in an age of radios, televisions, and newspapers. We hear about events everywhere in the world almost as soon as they happen. How did Americans of 1750 keep in touch with the world outside their own small communities?

The main source of news for Americans of 1750 was the weekly colonial newspaper. There were about 30 weekly newspapers in 1750. Most of these newspapers were printed in the larger cities and towns. Usually a printer hired someone to walk through the streets and sell the newspapers. Smaller towns received newspapers by mail about a week after they were printed.

A newspaper of 1750 did not look much like a modern newspaper. It was usually a large single sheet of paper printed on both sides and folded in half. This made a four-page newspaper. The newspaper carried the news of the town, some local gossip, and announcements about ship arrivals. It printed speeches made by the governor, and it reported any new laws or actions by the governments in the colony and in England.

At the town taverns the weekly newspaper was one of the main subjects of discussion. Taverns were the favorite gathering places of colonial men. The tavern was a hotel, a community center, an eating place, a drinking place, and a meeting place all rolled into one.

Colonial Americans depended on weekly newspapers for much of their information about important events. Colonial newspapers of the 1750s were printed on wooden printing presses like the one above.
► Why, do you think, are the printers wearing aprons?

Wooden Press from *Colonial Craftsmen and the Beginnings of American Industry,* by Edwin Tunis. (Thomas Y. Crowell). Copyright 1965 by Edwin Tunis. Reprinted by permission of Harper & Row, Publishers, Inc.

LESSON 2 REVIEW

THINK AND WRITE
A. Why was it difficult to travel from one place to another in colonial times?
B. Describe a journey on a stagecoach.
C. What improvements in mail service had been made by 1750?
D. How did people in the colonies get news?

SKILLS CHECK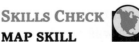
MAP SKILL
Look at the map on page 236. Use the scale of miles to measure the distance between these cities: Boston and Philadelphia, New York and Charles Town, Williamsburg and Savannah.

Growth of American Culture and Government

THINK ABOUT WHAT YOU KNOW

How do newcomers contribute to life in your community? What foods, words, or styles reflect the many cultural groups in the United States?

STUDY THE VOCABULARY

custom	smuggle
self-government	jury
Parliament	

FOCUS YOUR READING

How did the American colonies develop their own culture and ideas of self-government?

A. Americans Borrow from Each Other

The Log Cabin In 1750 the American colonies were home to peoples from many different lands and cultures. These old cultures did not disappear. But as a result of all this borrowing and mixing of ideas, of language, and of peoples, a new culture grew up alongside the old cultures—an American culture.

Most people who came to the American colonies settled near others from the same homeland. They wanted to keep their own way of life. They wanted to speak their own language and follow their own **customs**. A custom is a special way of doing things that is common to a lot of people. At first they even wore clothes and built buildings like those they had known in their European homeland.

But, in time, the settlers began to borrow the "best" from each other. For example, the Swedes brought the log cabin to America. It took only a couple of weeks for two strong men with axes to build a log cabin. This made the log cabin the perfect frontier home. Soon other settlers were building log cabins for themselves.

The Conestoga Wagon Another example of something borrowed was the Conestoga wagon. German settlers invented this wagon for carrying heavy loads over the

This large Conestoga wagon is being pulled over rough roads by six powerful horses.
▶ Why, do you think, is there an open box attached to the back of the wagon?

unpaved roads and paths in farming country. Its huge wheels were set wide apart to keep the wagon from sinking into mud. The bottom part of the Conestoga wagon was higher at each end than in the middle to keep the load from spilling out on bumpy roads. A canvas top protected the loaded-down wagon from foul weather. When other groups saw that the Conestoga wagon was best for conditions in America, they started using it.

There were dozens of other ways in which the different peoples of America borrowed from each other. Gradually, the groups dropped some of their own ways and they became more alike.

B. Settlers Develop an American English Language

People were less willing to give up their own language. But, in time, even that changed. Even though English was the main language of the American colonies, in 1750 one still heard a lot of German, French, Dutch, and Swedish being spoken.

But the longer people were in America, the more they—and their children and grandchildren—spoke English.

However, the English that Americans spoke in 1750 was a changing language. Americans borrowed words from each other, just as they borrowed the style of cabins and wagons. German words such as *cookbook, delicatessen, rifle, sauerkraut,* and *hoodlum* found their way into everyday English in America. Today if you eat a *waffle* for breakfast, *coleslaw* for lunch, and a *cookie* for dessert, you are eating foods that got their names from the Dutch. You are also using Dutch words if you refer to putting a baby in a *crib*, riding in a *wagon* or *sleigh* across the snow-covered *landscape*, or finding someone *snooping* around the front *stoop* of your house. From Native Americans come such words as *hickory, pecan, chipmunk, moccasin, skunk,* and *squash.* If you say you *tote*, or carry, a *banjo* or like to eat *yams* and *goobers*, or peanuts, you are using words from African languages. The result of all this borrowing was a new kind of English —American English.

German food is being served at a festival in an American town. The town was settled by Germans.
▶ What German food can you see?

Since 1689, no English king has been allowed to rule without the agreement of Parliament, pictured above.
▶ Why, do you think, are there no women in this picture?

C. The Colonists Plant the Idea of Self-government in America

An English Idea American colonists of 1750 had **self-government**. That is, colonists had a say in making their own laws and choosing their own leaders. Few other peoples had this right.

The right to self-government had begun in England. Owners of large areas of land and certain other important persons in England had elected people to represent them in the English **Parliament** (PAHR-luh ment). Parliament is a law-making body something like our Congress. The people of England had insisted that Parliament, not the king, should decide matters of taxes and spending. Parliament had a big say in making all other laws, too.

When English people began to settle in America, they brought their English ideas of self-government with them. They believed that they should have a say in making the laws under which they lived, just as people in England did.

Colonial Assemblies As you have already learned, joint-stock companies and proprietors quickly found that they would have to give settlers a say in government. Each colony soon had its own assembly.

The people of each colony elected representatives to the assembly. The assembly made laws for the colony, especially laws about taxes and spending. American colonists believed that they could be taxed only by an assembly in which they were represented.

Although colonists insisted on the right to elect their representatives to the assemblies, not everyone in the colonies had the right to vote. Women did not. Neither did African Americans or Indians. And neither did white men who did not own land or other property. But in 1750 most white men did own land, so most of them were able to vote.

D. Colonists Do Not Have the Final Say About Laws

Governors However, colonists did not have the final say about the laws they would live under. For one thing, each colony had a governor who was chosen either by the king or the proprietor, not by the colonists. The governor could refuse to approve any law that the colonial assembly passed. If the governor disapproved a law, that was the end of the law. The king could also kill a law by disapproving it.

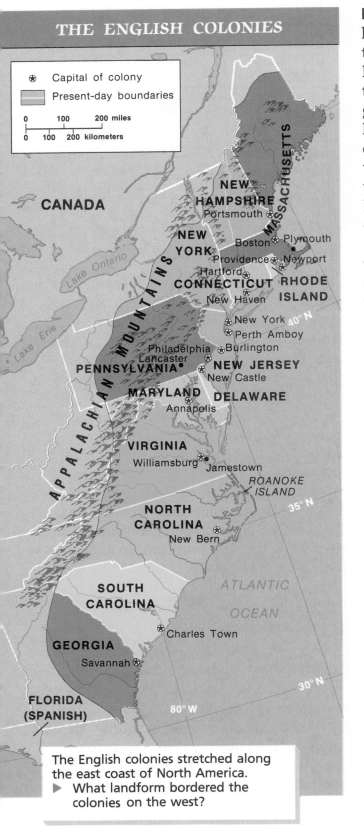

THE ENGLISH COLONIES

Capital of colony

Present-day boundaries

0   100   200 miles
0   100   200 kilometers

CANADA

Lake Ontario

Lake Erie

NEW HAMPSHIRE
Portsmouth

MASSACHUSETTS

NEW YORK
Boston
Plymouth
Providence
Newport
Hartford
CONNECTICUT
RHODE ISLAND
New Haven

APPALACHIAN MOUNTAINS

New York
Perth Amboy
Philadelphia
Burlington
Lancaster
NEW JERSEY
New Castle
PENNSYLVANIA
MARYLAND
DELAWARE
Annapolis

40° N

VIRGINIA
Williamsburg
Jamestown
ROANOKE ISLAND

35° N

NORTH CAROLINA
New Bern

ATLANTIC OCEAN

SOUTH CAROLINA
Charles Town

30° N

GEORGIA
Savannah

FLORIDA (SPANISH)

80° W

The English colonies stretched along the east coast of North America.
▶ What landform bordered the colonies on the west?

Parliament In addition, Parliament made laws about trade and certain other matters that the colonists were supposed to obey. Parliament told the colonies which countries they could trade with and which goods they could and could not buy. Parliament also passed a law that said the colonies could not make certain manufactured goods, such as hats and iron products. Parliament passed this law so that English manufacturers could sell their own hats and iron products in the colonies.

Colonists often disobeyed the laws they did not like. For example, Parliament said that the colonists must pay a tax on the sugar and molasses they imported. But the colonists **smuggled** these goods, or brought them into the colonies illegally. Ships carrying molasses and sugar would use harbors where there were no officials to see them.

E. American Colonists Have Other Rights and Liberties

The people of England enjoyed other rights and liberties in addition to the right of self-government. As members of England's large empire, the American colonists felt that they had these same rights and liberties.

Most of these rights and liberties were meant to protect the people against unfair actions by their government. For example, the government could not just take away peoples' houses, land, ships, or other property. And government officers could not just enter and search homes whenever they felt like it. The officers would first have to explain to a judge why they believed people were hiding something illegal. In addition, English people could not be put in jail unless they were accused of breaking a law. And then they had the

Not all British had a right to a trial. Many prisoners in the 1700s were jailed without trial because they did not pay their debts.
▶ Who is the person on the left?

right to be tried by a **jury** of fellow citizens. A jury is a group of people who decide whether a person is guilty or innocent after they have heard the facts of the case.

These rights might not seem so special to us today. But in 1750 few other people in the world enjoyed them. English people proudly called them the "rights of Englishmen." American colonists, too, boasted of their "rights as Englishmen."

The Americans of 1750 felt that they were among the most fortunate people on earth. They not only lived in a land blessed by nature but also enjoyed opportunity and freedom. They were proud and happy to be part of the empire of England, or Great Britain as it was now called. In that year of 1750, the idea of separating from Great Britain and the British Empire probably never entered a colonist's mind.

Just a few years later, however, that idea of independence was entering the minds of a great many colonists. And not long after that, the 13 American colonies declared their independence from Great Britain. That amazing turnabout is a story for our next chapter.

LESSON **3** *REVIEW*

THINK AND WRITE

A. How did borrowing from each other make American colonists more alike?

B. How did the English language in America change as more immigrants came to the colonies?

C. If early settlers had not come from England, do you think self-government would have developed in America? Why or why not?

D. Give some examples that show that the colonists did not have total self-government.

E. What were some rights and liberties that the colonists believed they had?

SKILLS CHECK

WRITING SKILL

Read section E on pages 246–247. Choose the right or liberty that you think is the most important one mentioned. Write a paragraph telling why you chose that right or liberty.

USING THE VOCABULARY

self-government   custom
immigrant   communication
jury

On a separate sheet of paper write the letter of the group of words that correctly complete each statement.

1. Self-government is government by
   (a) good manners.
   (b) leaders chosen by citizens.
   (c) an international organization of political leaders.

2. An immigrant is
   (a) someone who comes from one country to another country to live.
   (b) any stranger.
   (c) someone who starts a new colony.

3. A jury
   (a) is a group of people with the same interests.
   (b) makes rules and laws.
   (c) decides the guilt or innocence of a person in a court case.

4. A custom is
   (a) an invention.
   (b) a special way a group of people have of doing something.
   (c) a law.

5. Communication is
   (a) the exchange of information and messages.
   (b) the movement of goods from one place to another.
   (c) the movement of people to another country.

REMEMBERING WHAT YOU READ

On a separate sheet of paper, write your answers in complete sentences.

1. Where did most of the new settlers in Great Britain's North American colonies in the 1750s come from?
2. Why were people willing to come to America as indentured servants?
3. What kinds of work did people who lacked special skills do in 1750?
4. How did the stagecoach get its name?
5. What effect did improved roads have on colonial life?
6. Why was the log cabin an ideal dwelling for the frontier?
7. What made the Conestoga wagon particularly useful for transporting goods on colonial roads?
8. What kinds of laws did colonial assemblies make?
9. Why didn't the colonists have the final say about laws passed by their colonial assemblies?
10. Who in the colonies did not have the right to vote in 1750?

TYING LANGUAGE ARTS TO SOCIAL STUDIES

You have learned in this chapter about foreign words that are now part of American English. Here are ten more such words. Look in a dictionary to find where they came from. On a separate sheet of paper, write the word and the language it came from.

1. banana   5. indigo   9. tomato
2. clapboard   6. ketchup   10. tulip
3. dandelion   7. napkin
4. freckle   8. petunia

THINKING CRITICALLY

On a separate sheet of paper, write your answers in complete sentences.

1. Why, since the earliest years of the American colonies, have people wanted to come here?
2. What are some reasons why immigrants hold on to the old ways of the countries from which they came?
3. Why were newspapers and a good mail service important to the development of the colonies?
4. Do you think the colonists were correct in turning to smuggling because they did not approve of the tax laws passed by Parliament? Explain your answer.
5. Why did the colonists of 1750 believe they were fortunate to have the same rights as people in England?

SUMMARIZING THE CHAPTER

On a separate sheet of paper, draw a graphic organizer like the one shown here. Copy the information from this graphic organizer to the one you have drawn. Under each heading, write three facts from the chapter. The first one has been done for you.

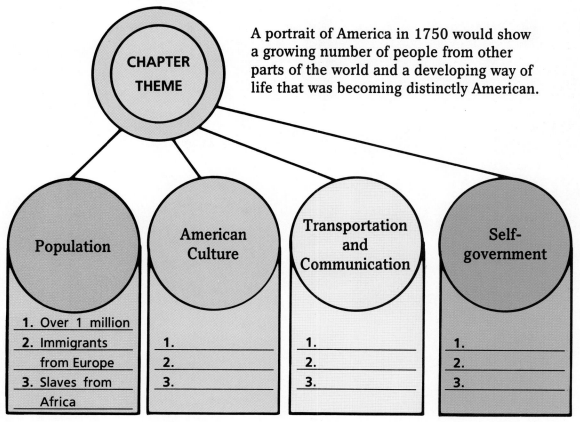

CHAPTER THEME

A portrait of America in 1750 would show a growing number of people from other parts of the world and a developing way of life that was becoming distinctly American.

Population
1. Over 1 million
2. Immigrants from Europe
3. Slaves from Africa

American Culture
1. _____
2. _____
3. _____

Transportation and Communication
1. _____
2. _____
3. _____

Self-government
1. _____
2. _____
3. _____

11

THE ROAD TO WAR

★ ★ ★ ★ ★

*T*he peace that followed the French and Indian War became a turning point in the relations between the 13 colonies and Great Britain. The colonists were upset by changes in British policy. Peaceful colonial protests gave way to battles. Talk of independence was in the air.

The French and Indian War

THINK ABOUT WHAT YOU KNOW

Imagine that there is a new playground near where you live. You and your friends want to play there. But children from another neighborhood say that it is their playground. They won't leave the play-ground and they won't let you play there. How would you feel?

STUDY THE VOCABULARY

ally   **treaty**

FOCUS YOUR READING

What were the results of the French and Indian War?

A. A Young Officer Carries an Important Message

Five hundred miles (805 km) is a long way to travel to hear someone tell you "no." But that is what a 21-year-old mili-tary officer from Virginia did in 1753. Trav-eling eight days by horseback and canoe, the young officer led his party of six to what is now western Pennsylvania. There he met with the French general in charge of the forts that France had built along the Ohio River. The young officer had brought a message from the governor of Virginia. This was the message: Your forts are on Virginia's land. Get out!

The French general was polite but he was also firm. "No," he said, "French troops will not get out. This land belongs to France. French fur trappers have lived on this land for a hundred years. French colonists have even founded several small settlements here. The forts will stay right where they are."

The disappointed young officer set out on the return journey. He and the men with him walked much of the way home. Along the way an Indian fired a rifle at the officer, barely missing him. Then, while crossing an ice-filled river on a raft, the officer nearly drowned when he was acci-dentally knocked overboard.

The young officer's unsuccessful jour-ney would soon lead to a war, as you will sée. The end of the war led to a number of events that would later result in the British colonies later becoming the United States of America.

What about the 21-year-old officer who carried the message? He would also have a lot to do with the colonies becoming the United States of America. His name was George Washington.

A young George Washington and his men pause on their way to take a message to a French general.
► Why do the men carry guns?

B. Great Britain and France Fight a War

French and Indian War The French general's refusal to leave the land around the Ohio River angered the governor of Virginia. In 1754 he sent George Washington with a force of 150 soldiers to chase out the French. By this time the French had captured a small British fort at present-day Pittsburgh and renamed it Fort Duquesne (doo KAYN). Washington was determined to win back this fort. However, as Washington and his troops neared Fort Duquesne, they were met by a much larger force of French troops and Indian warriors.

Washington's brave but outnumbered troops fought nine hours in a driving rain storm. Finally, Washington had to surrender.

This battle marked the start of the war between France and England, or Great Britain as it was now called. Colonists called it the French and Indian war, because Indians were **allies**, or partners, of the French.

Treaty of 1763 After nine years of fighting, Great Britain won the war. In the peace **treaty**, or agreement, of 1763, France gave all its land east of the Mississippi River, plus all of New France, to

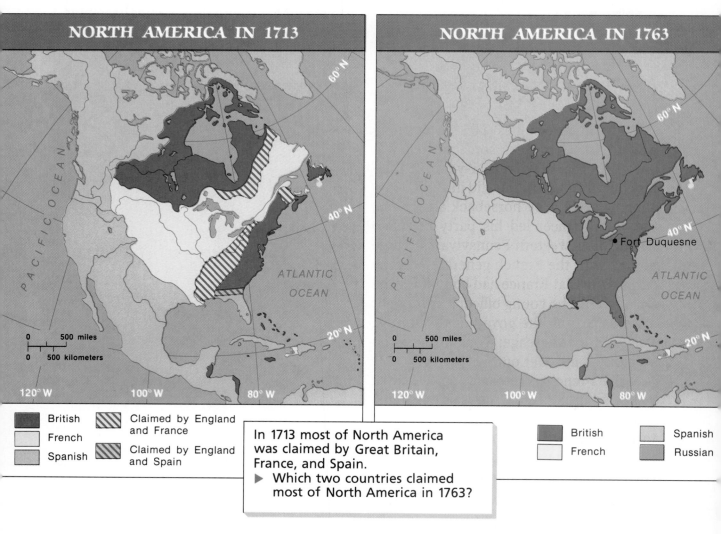

NORTH AMERICA IN 1713

- British
- French
- Spanish
- Claimed by England and France
- Claimed by England and Spain

NORTH AMERICA IN 1763

- Fort Duquesne

- British
- French
- Spanish
- Russian

In 1713 most of North America was claimed by Great Britain, France, and Spain.
▶ Which two countries claimed most of North America in 1763?

Pictured above is the 1755 defeat of the English and colonial forces by the French and Indians near Duquesne.
▶ How, do you think, did the soldiers get the cannon up the hill?

Great Britain. France had already given its land west of the Mississippi River to Spain as a reward for Spain's help in the war. As a result, France held only a small piece of land in all of North America. Look at the map of North America in 1763, on page 252. You can see that only the countries of Spain and Great Britain still held large portions of North America. Great Britain would now rule Canada and other lands that had belonged to France.

American colonists were overjoyed. Few people would have guessed that this great victory for Great Britain and the American colonists would lead to bitter quarrels between them.

LESSON 1 REVIEW

THINK AND WRITE

A. Why was George Washington disappointed after his meeting with the French general?

B. What caused war to break out between Great Britain and France in 1754?

SKILLS CHECK

MAP SKILL

Look at the maps on page 252. Between 1713 and 1763 how had the size of the land areas claimed by the British and by the French changed?

A Quarrel with Britain

THINK ABOUT WHAT YOU KNOW

If you thought that your government made a law that was unfair, what are some things you could do to let the government know how you feel?

STUDY THE VOCABULARY

proclamation	Patriot
boycott	delegate
repeal	Stamp Act Congress

FOCUS YOUR READING

Why did quarrels develop between the colonies and Great Britain?

A. Great Britain Tries to Stop Westward Settlement

Moving West Having defeated the French, many colonists wanted to move west into the Indian land between the Appalachian Mountains and the Mississippi River. Some colonists had already settled on this land before the French and Indian War. Now that the fighting was over, many more colonists looked forward to taking it all for themselves.

But this area was the homeland of many groups of Indians, including the Senecas, Delawares, Shawnees, Hurons, Ottawas, and Miamis. During the French and Indian War, these Indians had united behind an Ottawa chief named Pontiac to drive out the white settlers. In the months after the war was over, up and down the frontier, Indian warriors captured British forts, killed hundreds of settlers, and drove out many others.

Proclamation of 1763 British troops finally ended the uprising. But now that they had finished one war with France, the British did not want a new one with the Indians. So the British government decided to keep settlers out of this area, at least for the time being. The British king, George III, gave this order in his official announcement or proclamation. The king drew a line on a map along the top of the Appalachian Mountains, from New York to Georgia. No colonists were to settle west of that line.

The Proclamation of 1763 angered the colonists. They had fought the French to get this land for themselves. Now the king said they could not move there.

This picture shows a group of Pontiac's warriors attacking an American frontier fort.
▶ How might the Indians have set fire to the fort?

After the French and Indian War, bitter quarrels between the colonists and the British government brought the American colonies closer to a war with Great Britain.

▶ Which was passed first, the Stamp Act or the Intolerable Acts?

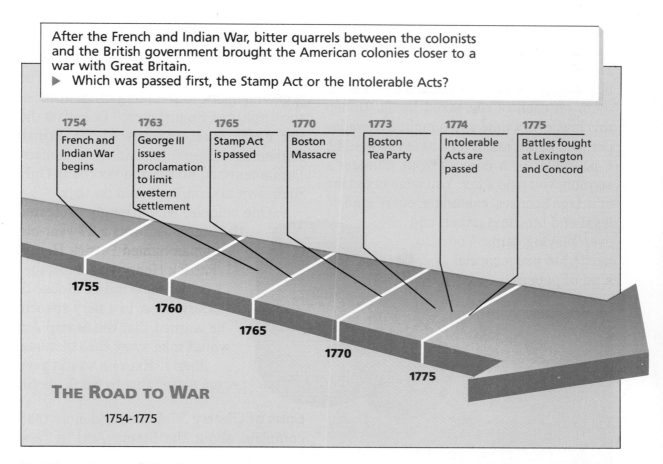

1754	1763	1765	1770	1773	1774	1775
French and Indian War begins	George III issues proclamation to limit western settlement	Stamp Act is passed	Boston Massacre	Boston Tea Party	Intolerable Acts are passed	Battles fought at Lexington and Concord

1755
1760
1765
1770
1775

THE ROAD TO WAR

1754-1775

B. New Acts of Parliament Anger the Colonists

New Taxes Great Britain and the colonies soon had an even bigger quarrel. This quarrel was over taxes. To pay for the war against France, the British government had borrowed a great deal of money. Now it was necessary to pay this money back. Great Britain also wanted to station troops along the frontier to keep peace between the colonists and the Indians. The British government would need money to pay for these troops.

Where was all this money to come from? To Parliament, the answer was clear. The colonists must help pay for all these things.

Enforcing Tax Laws In the past, the colonists had often smuggled goods into the colonies, or brought them in secretly to avoid paying taxes. The British government now decided to force the colonists to obey the tax laws. To do this, the government sent many officials to America to make sure that the colonists paid taxes on imported sugar and molasses. These officials would be allowed to enter and search colonists' homes and businesses without the permission of the owners and could search for smuggled goods or any other evidence to show that colonists had broken the law.

Colonists hated this new law. They still thought of themselves as "Englishmen." One of the important "rights of Englishmen" was that a person's home was safe from such searches by the government. Now the British government was taking this right away from them.

255

Stamp Act   Then in 1765, Parliament passed the Stamp Act. This act put a tax on about 50 different items. Colonists had to buy stamps from a tax collector and stick them on each of the taxed items. Under this law, every time you bought a newspaper, you paid a tax. Every time you bought a pamphlet or a copy of your minister's sermon, you paid a tax. You were taxed for marriage licenses, calendars, every kind of legal and business paper, and even playing cards. You also needed to use a special kind of paper.

Angry colonists sometimes burned the hated tax stamps in public. Two of these stamps are shown above.
▶ Why was the Stamp Act called "taxation without representation"?

C. Colonists Protest the Stamp Act

Patrick Henry   American colonists exploded in anger over the Stamp Act. The government was trampling on another of the "rights of Englishmen." Colonists did not elect representatives to the British Parliament. Therefore, said the colonists, Parliament had no right to tax them. Only their own assemblies could do that.

One colonist who strongly protested the Stamp Act was a 29-year-old Virginian named Patrick Henry. Patrick Henry was a member of the Virginia House of Burgesses. In a fiery speech, he warned that the Stamp Act would take away the colonists' liberty. Henry's words gave people something to think about.

Sons of Liberty   Colonists did more than complain about the Stamp Act. In New York, Boston, Newport, and other places throughout America, they formed groups called the Sons of Liberty. These groups threatened and even beat up some stamp tax collectors.

A **boycott** of British goods was organized by the Sons of Liberty. That is, they got people to refuse to buy goods from Great Britain. They said that when Parliament **repealed**, or did away with, the Stamp Act, colonists would buy British goods again. The Daughters of Liberty helped by making homemade cloth instead of buying British-made cloth. Those who supported the colonists' cause called themselves **Patriots.**

Britain Backs Down   In addition, nine colonies sent **delegates**, or representatives, to a meeting in New York that was called to protest the Stamp Act. This

To avoid buying cloth from Great Britain, colonial women spun their own thread from sheep's wool and a plant called *flax*. They wove the thread into cloth and used the cloth to make clothes.
▶ Can you think of some clothes that would not be made of cloth?

Stamp Act Congress agreed on a number of statements about the rights of colonists. It also asked Parliament to repeal the hated law.

These actions shocked leaders of the British government. These leaders in Great Britain were especially worried by the meeting of the Stamp Act Congress. The American colonies had never before acted together against the British government. British leaders did not want this to become a habit. Also, the boycott was causing merchants in Great Britain to lose a lot of money.

In 1766, Parliament did repeal the Stamp Act. When the news was heard in America, colonists lit great bonfires to celebrate the event.

LESSON *2* REVIEW

THINK AND WRITE

A. Why did King George III issue the Proclamation of 1763?
B. What two new laws or acts of Parliament angered the colonists?
C. What did the colonists do to force Parliament to repeal the Stamp Act?

SKILLS CHECK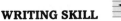

WRITING SKILL

Pretend that you are a delegate to the Stamp Act Congress. Write a letter to Parliament demanding that the Stamp Act be repealed. Include your reasons for thinking the law is unfair to the colonists.

Punishment for Boston

THINK ABOUT WHAT YOUR KNOW

If the government tried to make everybody in the country buy a certain product, how do you think people would react?

STUDY THE VOCABULARY

Boston Massacre
Committee of
  Correspondence
Boston Tea
  Party
Intolerable Acts

FOCUS YOUR READING

What happened to make the quarrel between Great Britain and the colonies get worse?

A. Parliament Tries Again to Tax the Colonists

More Taxes The British government was still determined to raise money by taxing the colonies. So the next year, in 1767, Parliament tried again. It placed taxes on paper, lead, paint, and tea.

The new taxes imposed by the British government angered the colonists. Led by the Sons of Liberty, colonists boycotted British goods again. Americans began to make their own paint, lead, glass, and paper instead of buying British goods.

Another victory Once again, the boycott was successful. Again, British merchants and manufacturers lost so much money that they demanded that Parliament end the new taxes. In 1770, Parliament did repeal the taxes — all except the tax on tea. In reply, colonists ended their boycott on British goods — all except the boycott on tea. Colonists didn't really do without tea. They simply bought their tea from Dutch merchants.

B. Tempers Flare in Boston

British Troops After the French and Indian War, the British government had sent thousands of troops to the colonies. They said that the soldiers were needed to defend the colonists against Indian attack. However, instead of going to the frontier where the Indians were, most of the soldiers remained in the cities near the coast.

The colonists were angered by the sight of soldiers on their streets day and night. They jeered at the soldiers, made fun of them, and made their lives miserable. In several cities, fights broke out between colonists and soldiers.

On the evening of March 5, 1770, a crowd of men and boys in Boston gathered around a lone British soldier on guard duty. They shouted insults and threw snowballs at him. Some of the snowballs had rocks inside them. The frightened soldier called for help.

Then more British soldiers arrived. The crowd grew larger. And the shouts, dares, and insults grew louder and angrier.

Boston Massacre Suddenly someone— no one knows who—called out "Fire!" The soldiers turned their guns on the crowd and shot. When the smoke cleared, five colonists lay dead, their blood staining the snow-covered street. One of them was Crispus Attucks, a runaway slave who worked as a sailor. Attucks was the first African American to die for the cause of American liberty, but not the last.

A few days later, more than half the population of Boston turned out for a funeral march for the dead men. Shops were closed. Church bells rang. Angry Bostonians called the killings of the colonists a *massacre*—a needless killing of defenseless people. The event became known as the **Boston Massacre.**

C. A New Act of Parliament Leads to the Boston Tea Party

Protest Continues The next three years were a time of calm between Great Britain and the colonies. During this time, Bostonians at a town meeting set up a **Committee of Correspondence.** In case of more trouble with Great Britain, the committee would send letters quickly to other towns in Massachusetts with the news. The idea quickly spread to other colonies. Meanwhile, for the first time, a number of people were saying openly that maybe the colonies should become independent from Great Britain. This was an important first step toward freedom.

This painting of the Boston Massacre is on a wall of our national Capitol in Washington, D.C. It shows the artist's idea of what happened during this terrible event.
▶ Why, do you think, is this painting located in our Capitol?

Colonists are shown throwing tea from an English ship into Boston harbor.
▶ Why might these colonists have dressed up as Indians?

Tea Act The period of quiet came to an end in 1773. In that year, Parliament passed the Tea Act. This act was a clever plan to get colonists to buy tea again from British merchants and also pay the tea tax. The Tea Act greatly *lowered* the price of British tea. Even with the tea tax added, this was the cheapest tea colonists could buy. But when colonists bought the tea, they would also be accepting Parliament's right to tax them! Soon 2,000 chests of tea were loaded aboard English ships bound for America.

The Tea Act of 1773 showed how poorly Parliament understood the colonists. Americans were not going to pay that tea tax, no matter how low the price of British tea was. As British tea ships began to arrive in the colonies, the Committees of Correspondence sent the news all over the colonies. In several ports, including New York and Philadelphia, the Sons of Liberty prevented the British ships from docking.

Boston Tea Party Early in December, three tea ships entered the harbor in Boston. At a town meeting, colonists demanded that the governor of the colony order the ships to leave. When the governor refused, the colonists took matters into their own hands. On the night of December 16, 1773, a group of men dressed as Indians boarded the tea ships and threw 342 chests of tea into the water as people along the shore watched and cheered. This famous event has became known as the **Boston Tea Party.**

D. The British Punish Boston for the Tea Party

When news of the Boston Tea Party reached Great Britain in the spring, the king and Parliament were outraged. In 1774 Parliament passed several laws to punish the people of Boston and the whole Massachusetts colony. One law closed the port of Boston until the tea that had been dumped in the harbor was paid for. Another punishing law of the British Parliament took away most of the colony's rights of self-government.

The British also appointed an army general to be the governor of Massachusetts. The British sent several thousand more troops to Boston. They also ordered the Massachusetts colonists to

One of the despised Intolerable Acts was a law forcing the American colonists to house and feed British troops in their own homes. This law was called a Quartering Act.

▶ How does this family feel about having British soldiers in their homes?

put up these troops in their homes and even to feed them. The colonists felt that all of these acts or laws trampled on the "rights of Englishmen." The angry American colonists called these detested acts the **Intolerable Acts.**

Naturally, the Intolerable Acts caused more colonists to want complete independence from Great Britain. At the same time, however, most of the colonists were not yet demanding a total separation from Great Britain.

LESSON **3** *REVIEW*

THINK AND WRITE

A. How did the colonists react to the new taxes that Parliament passed in 1767?
B. Why did the Boston Massacre occur?
C. What events led to the Boston Tea Party?
D. How did Parliament punish the colonists for the Boston Tea party?

SKILLS CHECK

THINKING SKILL

Make a time line to show the major events that were discussed in this lesson and the year that each event occurred.

The Colonists Take Action

THINK ABOUT WHAT YOU KNOW

Have you ever felt that you were punished unfairly? How did you feel? How do you think the American colonists might have felt when the British punished them for actions the colonists believed were justified?

STUDY THE VOCABULARY

**First Continental   militia
Congress   Minutemen**

FOCUS YOUR READING

Why did fighting break out between the colonists and Great Britain?

A. Other American Colonies Support Massachusetts

Because the British government had closed the port of Boston, ships carrying food and other goods were not allowed to dock in the city. As Committees of Correspondence spread the news of what had happened, other colonies came to the aid of Boston and the rest of Massachusetts. Pennsylvania sent the people of Massachusetts barrels of flour; South Carolina sent them sacks of rice. Other colonies sent food and money.

In Virginia, colonial leaders declared that the Intolerable Acts were a threat to liberty in all the colonies. If the king and Parliament could do these things to Massachusetts, what would stop them from doing the same to other colonies? Virginians called for a meeting of delegates from all the colonies to discuss what to do.

In September 1774, delegates from 12 colonies gathered at Philadelphia for the **First Continental Congress.** They drew up

a list of complaints against Parliament. In addition, they asked the king to respect their rights as British citizens. Finally, they voted to stop all trade with Great Britain until Parliament repealed the Intolerable Acts.

Most delegates did not want a war. They stated that they were still loyal to the king. At the end of the meeting, the delegates agreed to meet again in May 1775.

B. The Colonies Prepare to Fight

While all these events were taking place, something else was happening. This "something" had no exact name or date. It was hard to put a finger on. But it was very important just the same. Great

Delegates to the First Continental Congress are shown after a meeting in Carpenters' Hall, Philadelphia.
► Which delegate do you think is George Washington?

Preparing for war with Great Britain, the Massachusetts Assembly passed a new Militia Act. Soon men between the ages of 15 and 50 were gathering in towns across the colony to begin training for war.
► What, do you think, was happening in other colonies at this time?

Britain's actions were backfiring and were actually helping to bring the colonies together as never before. The colonists began to think of themselves as part of one country rather than as people living in thirteen different colonies. Patrick Henry spoke for a growing number of colonists when he said these words to the First Continental Congress: "The distinctions [differences] between Virginians, Pennsylvanians, New Yorkers, and New Englanders, are no more. I am not a Virginian, but an American."

As the months passed, more colonists expected the quarrels to end in fighting. By spring of 1775 the **militia** in many colonies were preparing for war. The militia was made up of citizens who volunteered to be part-time soldiers.

In March 1775, members of the Virginia House of Burgesses debated whether their colony should prepare for war. Some opposed the idea. But Patrick Henry believed the time had come for action. In one of the most famous speeches in American history, Henry spoke these words:

Patrick Henry delivers his stirring "Give me liberty or give me death" speech to the Virginia House of Burgesses.
► How, do you think, were his listeners feeling?

> *Shall we try argument? Sir, we have been trying that for the last ten years. . . . We must fight!*
>
> *Gentlemen may cry peace, peace—but there is no peace. The war is actually begun! The next gale that sweeps from the north will bring to our ears the clash of resounding arms! Our brethren are already in the field. Why stand we here idle? What is it the gentlemen wish? What would they have: Is life so dear, or peace so sweet, as to be purchased at the price of chains and slavery? Forbid it, almighty God! I know not what course others may take; but as for me, give me liberty, or give me death!*

C. The Fighting Begins at Lexington and Concord

Minutemen Patrick Henry was wrong when he said the war had actually begun. But three weeks after his stirring speech, the fighting did begin.

Farmers and townspeople throughout Massachusetts had been training to fight for several months. These people were called **Minutemen,** because they were expected to be ready to fight at a minute's notice. All through the early spring of 1775, Minutemen collected guns, gunpowder, and other supplies and hid them in the village of Concord. Concord was located about 15 miles (24 km) northwest of the city of Boston.

British Plan The new governor of Massachusetts, General Thomas Gage, learned about the supplies the Patriots had collected. He decided to have British troops leave Boston in the quiet of night. First they would march to Lexington, a village near Concord. At Lexington, they would capture the major troublemakers — Sam Adams and John Hancock, two leaders of the Sons of Liberty who were hiding out there. Then the troops would march to Concord and destroy the Minutemen's supplies.

The Sons of Liberty learned of General Gage's secret plan. When 700 British soldiers set out for Lexington on the night of April 18, 1775, two Sons of Liberty, Paul Revere and William Dawes, galloped on horseback ahead of them. Revere took one road, Dawes another. All through the dark night, the men rode, stopping at every village and farm, pounding on doors and sounding the alarm: "The British are coming!" In Lexington, Revere warned Adams and Hancock, and the two men got away. Read more about Paul Revere's ride in the literature selection on page 266.

First Battle When the British arrived in Lexington at dawn, they were surprised to see 70 Minutemen facing them on the village green. The leader of the Minutemen, Captain John Parker, told his men, "Don't fire unless fired upon." Then he added, "But if they mean to have war, let it begin here." The British soldiers outnumbered the Minutemen by 10 to 1. So when the British officer in charge ordered the Minutemen to leave, Captain Parker gave the order to retreat. Suddenly, however, someone opened fire. Both sides began shooting. Minutes later, eight Minutemen were dead and another ten lay wounded.

The British troops next pushed on to Concord. They found and destroyed some of the hidden supplies. Meanwhile, 300 more Minutemen gathered at North Bridge, near the Concord village green. Soldiers at the bridge opened fire. After five minutes of fighting, the British retreated and began their return to Boston.

Well-drilled British troops unexpectedly face a group of Minutemen on the green in Lexington. The group, made up of farmers and other citizens, were outnumbered, but fought bravely until the British withdrew.
► How can you tell the British soldiers from the Minutemen?

FROM:

"Paul Revere's Ride"

By: Henry Wadsworth Longfellow
Setting: Massachusetts, 1775

"Listen, my children, and you shall hear Of the midnight ride of Paul Revere. . . ."

That is how, 84 years after the event, Henry Wadsworth Longfellow began his poem about that famous ride. Longfellow describes how Revere waited "booted and spurred" for the signal. He sees two lights in the church belfry and "springs to the saddle." And then . . .

A hurry of hoofs in a village street,
A shape in the moonlight, a bulk in the dark,
And beneath, from the pebbles, in passing, a spark
Struck out by a steed flying fearless and fleet;
That was all! And yet, through the gloom and the light,
The fate of a nation was riding that night;

And the spark struck out by that steed, in his flight,
Kindled the land with its heat.

. . . .

So through the night rode Paul Revere;
And so through the night went his cry of alarm
To every Middlesex village and farm, —
A cry of defiance and not of fear,
A voice in the darkness, a knock at the door,
And a word that shall echo forevermore!
For, borne on the night-wind of the Past,
Through all our history, to the last,
In the hour of darkness and peril and need,
The people will waken and listen to hear
The hurrying hoof-beats of that steed,
And the midnight message of Paul Revere.

You can read about what happened the next day at Lexington and Concord in this poem, too. The rest is history!

LEXINGTON AND CONCORD

British troops advancing on Concord are met by the musket fire of Minutemen waiting at North Bridge.
▶ Was wearing red a good idea?

Paul Revere and William Dawes rode through the night to warn Americans that British troops were marching to Lexington.
▶ Where were battles fought?

March to Boston The long march to Boston became a nightmare for the British soldiers. All along the way, Minutemen fired on them from the woods and from behind stone fences. With their bright red uniforms, the British were easy targets for the Minutemen. Seventy-three British soldiers were killed, and another 200 were wounded. Only when they returned to Boston, where the guns of British warships protected them, were the soldiers finally safe.

The fighting had now begun. Blood had been spilled on both sides. Where would all of this end? No one in 1775 could say for sure.

LESSON 4 REVIEW

THINK AND WRITE

A. What did the other colonies do to show their support for Massachusetts?

B. What effect did Great Britain's actions against Massachusetts have on the 13 colonies?

C. What events led to the fighting at Lexington and Concord?

SKILLS CHECK

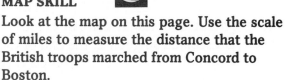

MAP SKILL

Look at the map on this page. Use the scale of miles to measure the distance that the British troops marched from Concord to Boston.

267

CHAPTER 11 *PUTTING IT ALL TOGETHER*

USING THE VOCABULARY

treaty
boycott
repeal
Patriot
delegates
Boston Massacre

Committee of
  Correspondence
Boston Tea Party
Intolerable Acts
First Continental
  Congress

On a separate sheet of paper, number from **1** to **10** and write the words from the list that would correctly complete the sentences in the paragraphs below.

When Great Britain and France signed the peace (1) _____ that ended the French and Indian War, the colonists thought all their troubles were over. The British Parliament decided, however, that the American colonists should help pay the enormous war debt and placed taxes on certain goods. The colonists, believing that Parliament did not have the right to tax them, organized a (2) _____ of the goods, hoping Parliament would (3) _____ the taxes.

A (4) _____ in each colony helped the (5) _____ leaders keep in touch with one another. Then two important events that disturbed the British government took place in Massachusetts; one was the (6) _____, and the other was the (7) _____. An angry Parliament passed the (8) _____ to punish Massachusetts. Afraid that Britain might take the same sort of action against other colonies, Virginia asked that (9) _____ be sent to the (10) _____. Relations between Great Britain and the American colonies, which had seemed so good at the end of the French and Indian War, were reaching a very low point. This would have an important effect on future relations with Parliament and the king.

REMEMBERING WHAT YOU READ

On a separate sheet of paper, write your answers in complete sentences.

1. Why did the governor of Virginia send George Washington to the backcountry of western Pennsylvania?
2. Why was the battle between the French troops and the Virginia militia near Fort Duquesne important?
3. How was Chief Pontiac able to get several Indian tribes to unite after the French and Indian War was over?
4. What did the British government hope to accomplish with the Proclamation of 1763?
5. Why did the American colonists say that the British Parliament had no right to tax them?
6. What were some of the actions taken by the Sons of Liberty and Daughters of Liberty?
7. What happened after Parliament passed the Tea Act of 1773?
8. What actions were taken by the colonists against the Intolerable Acts?
9. How did the colonies begin to prepare for war?
10. Why did General Gage want to send troops to Lexington and Concord?

TYING ART TO SOCIAL STUDIES

Posters can tell a story at a glance. Choose an event or an idea that you have read about in this chapter and make a poster supporting either the British view of it or the Patriot view of it.

268

THINKING CRITICALLY

On a separate sheet of paper, write your answers in complete sentences.

1. Was the British government wrong to expect the colonists to pay for part of the war debt and for the protection of frontier settlements? Explain your answer.
2. Why was the meeting of the Stamp Act Congress important?
3. Do you think the Boston Massacre was really a massacre? Explain your answer.
4. Why did the First Continental Congress blame Parliament and not the king for the poor relationship between Great Britain and the colonies?
5. What did Patrick Henry mean when he said in his famous speech, "Give me liberty, or give me death!"?

SUMMARIZING THE CHAPTER

On a separate sheet of paper, draw the graphic organizer shown here. Copy the information from this graphic organizer to the one you have drawn. Fill in the blank boxes with important events from the chapter that support the chapter theme. Put the events in the correct sequence. The first box has been filled in for you. Be prepared to explain why you chose the events you did.

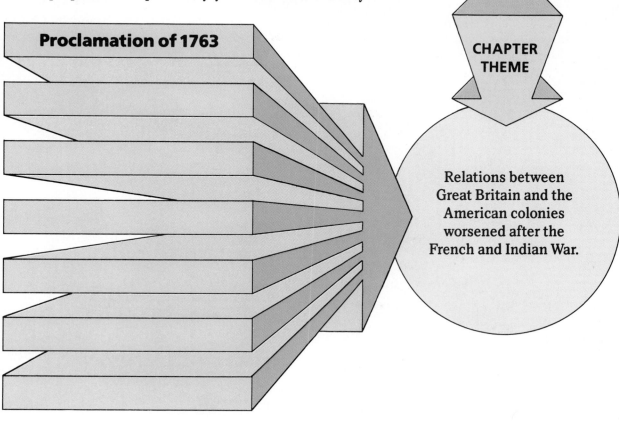

Proclamation of 1763

CHAPTER THEME

Relations between Great Britain and the American colonies worsened after the French and Indian War.

CHAPTER 12

INDEPENDENCE!
★ ★ ★ ★ ★

*T*he time for compromise had passed. On July 4, 1776, colonial representatives issued their Declaration of Independence from Great Britain. The war for independence had begun!

Preparing for War

THINK ABOUT WHAT YOU KNOW

Have you ever felt that you had to take action you were afraid of taking? Write two sentences describing how you felt before you acted and two sentences about how you felt afterwards.

STUDY THE VOCABULARY

Second
  Continental
  Congress
traitor

republic
Declaration of
  Independence
revolution

FOCUS YOUR READING

What steps did the colonists take to prepare for war?

A. George Washington Leads the Continental Army

News of the fighting at Lexington and Concord had already reached the city of Philadelphia when delegates gathered for the **Second Continental Congress** in May 1775. Soon after the meeting began, John Adams urged other delegates to quickly create an American army. He said that the members of the Massachusetts militia camped outside of Boston were ready to be the first soldiers in that army.

To lead the new American army, Adams said, Congress was fortunate to have the right man for the job in that very room. He was a man of "great talents and excellent character," an experienced military leader from Virginia.

As Adams continued to speak, eyes began to turn toward George Washington. George Washington, was indeed, the perfect man to lead the Continental army, as it was called. He had gained military experience in the French and Indian War. After

that, he had returned to Mount Vernon, Virginia, to run his plantation. As a member of the House of Burgesses, he strongly supported the Patriot cause. Colonists admired his devotion to duty, his cool head, his strong will, and his determination.

B. The Americans and British Fight at Bunker Hill

Before Washington arrived in Massachusetts to take charge, the militia around Boston fought an important battle. On the night of June 16, 1775, the militia suddenly took control of two hills that overlooked Boston. The hills were known as Bunker Hill and Breed's Hill. From these hills an army with cannons could fire down on the British troops in Boston. So British General Gage decided he must drive the militia off these hills. What Gage didn't know was that the militiamen didn't have cannons!

General George Washington takes command of American troops near Boston, Massachusetts.
▶ Why, do you think, were the officers on horseback?

271

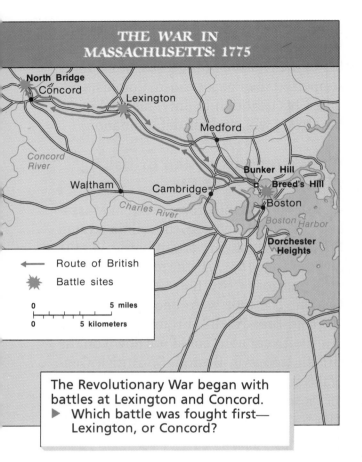

THE WAR IN MASSACHUSETTS: 1775

← Route of British

✹ Battle sites

0   5 miles

0   5 kilometers

The Revolutionary War began with battles at Lexington and Concord.
▶ Which battle was fought first— Lexington, or Concord?

The next day, British soldiers marched up Breed's Hill. The commander of the American militia sent out the order, "Don't fire until you see the whites of their eyes." When the British got close, the colonial militiamen opened fire. Hundreds of red-coated British soldiers fell. The rest retreated down the hill.

The British tried to take the hill a second time. Once again they were driven back in a hail of bullets. But the militia was running out of ammunition. When the British marched up the hill a third time, the militia retreated.

The British won the hill, but more than 1,000 British soldiers were killed or wounded. Although the fighting took place on Breed's Hill, the battle became known as the battle of Bunker Hill.

The battle of Bunker Hill was important to the colonists. It gave them confidence that they could hold their own against one of the world's greatest armies —the British army.

C. The Colonists Move Toward Independence

Peace Efforts Even after the fighting at Lexington, Concord, and Bunker Hill, most colonists still did not want to make a final break with Great Britain. Most remained loyal to their king.

The Second Continental Congress tried to patch up the differences with Great Britain. The members asked King George III to give back the rights that had been taken away from the colonists. But the king refused. King George called the colonists **traitors** and said that he would send another 20,000 troops to crush them. A traitor is a person who tries to overthrow the government of his or her country.

Battle of Bunker Hill Chicago Historical Society

Desperate hand-to-hand fighting took place at Bunker Hill.
▶ What kinds of weapons do you see in the painting?

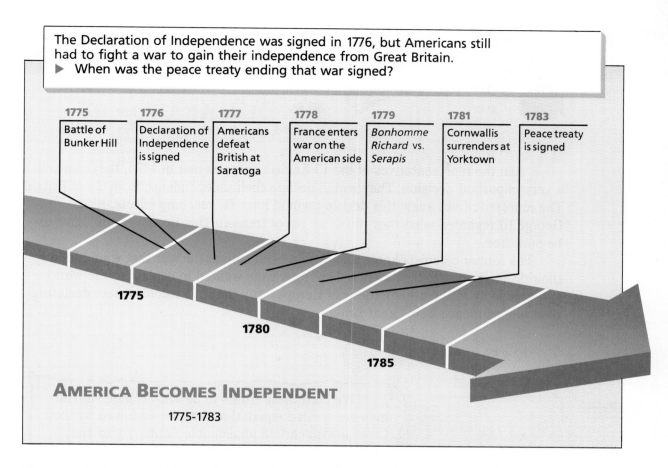

The Declaration of Independence was signed in 1776, but Americans still had to fight a war to gain their independence from Great Britain.

▶ When was the peace treaty ending that war signed?

1775	1776	1777	1778	1779	1781	1783
Battle of Bunker Hill	Declaration of Independence is signed	Americans defeat British at Saratoga	France enters war on the American side	*Bonhomme Richard* vs. *Serapis*	Cornwallis surrenders at Yorktown	Peace treaty is signed

1775

1780

1785

AMERICA BECOMES INDEPENDENT
1775-1783

Thomas Paine The man who convinced many colonists to finally break away from Great Britain was Thomas Paine. Paine, a 29-year-old immigrant from England, did this by writing a pamphlet called *Common Sense*. Paine wrote in the everyday language of the farmer, the skilled worker, and the townsperson. As the title of his pamphlet suggests, Paine appealed to the colonists' common sense. Did it make any sense, he asked, for a huge continent like America to be ruled by a small island like Great Britain? Did it make any sense for a people to be ruled by one man, just because he was born into a certain family? Thomas Paine said that Americans should cut off all ties to Great Britain and create a **republic** of their own. In a republic, the power to govern comes from the people and not from a king.

Probably half of all colonists read *Common Sense*. People talked about it on street corners, in their homes, and in taverns and inns. And many colonists agreed with it.

D. The American Colonies Declare Independence

In June 1776, Congress chose a small committee to write a declaration, or statement, of independence. The purpose of this declaration was to explain to the world why the colonies had decided to break away from Great Britain. The main task of writing this statement was given to a young lawyer from Virginia, Thomas Jefferson.

Jefferson wrote that God had given all people certain rights. These rights included the rights of life and liberty and the

THE DECLARATION OF INDEPENDENCE

When the representatives of the 13 English colonies met in 1776, they reached a very important decision. They would declare their independence from Great Britain. The representatives knew this decision would have far-reaching effects. King George III regarded what they did as an act of treason. This treason would have to be punished.

The former colonists knew they would need help in the war that would follow their declaration of independence. The Americans wanted to explain to the world, and especially to the other nations of Europe, why these 13 colonies were declaring their independence from Great Britain.

IN CONGRESS. JULY 4, 1776.

The unanimous Declaration of the thirteen united States of America

. . . We hold these truths to be self-evident, that all men are created equal, that they are endowed by their Creator with certain unalienable rights [rights that cannot be taken away], that among these are life, liberty, and the pursuit of happiness.

That to secure these rights, governments are instituted among men, deriving their just powers from the consent of the governed.

That whenever any form of government becomes destructive of these ends, it is the right of the people to alter or abolish it, and to institute new government, laying its foundation on such principles and organizing its powers in such form, as to them shall seem most likely to effect their safety and happiness.

Understanding Source Material

1. What, according to the Declaration, are the basic rights of all people?
2. Why do people "institute," or create, governments?
3. What should people do if they feel that their government is not acting in the best interests of the people?
4. On what principles, does the Declaration say, will the new American government be founded?

right of people to seek happiness. Governments were supposed to protect these rights. If a government took these rights away, the people had a right to create a new government for themselves. That was what Americans were now doing.

On July 4, 1776, Congress adopted this **Declaration of Independence**. On that day the American colonies became independent states. Together they made up the United States of America. On July 8, outside the Pennsylvania State House, the declaration was first read to the public. During the next month in towns and cities across the land, crowds gathered to hear the Declaration of Independence read aloud. Everywhere in the new United States, church bells rang out. Soldiers fired cannons and shot off guns, and citizens lit bonfires. You can read more about the Declaration of Independence on page 274.

There was still a war to be won, however. The 56 men who signed the Declaration knew that if the **revolution** failed, the king would probably put them to death. A revolution is a sudden, complete change. Benjamin Franklin summed up the need for all the states to work together. "Gentlemen," he said, "we must all hang together, [or] else we shall all hang separately."

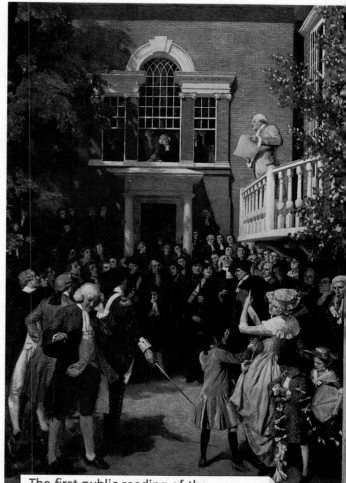

The first public reading of the Declaration of Independence took place in Philadelphia, Pennsylvania.
▶ How, do you think, did the people who were listening feel?

LESSON *1* REVIEW

THINK AND WRITE

A. Why was George Washington chosen to lead the Continental Army?
B. Describe the events of the battle of Bunker Hill.
C. How did *Common Sense* help Americans to decide in favor of independence?
D. What were the main ideas in the Declaration of Independence?

SKILLS CHECK

THINKING SKILL

Imagine that you are going to interview Thomas Paine. Write a list of questions that you would ask him about why he wrote *Common Sense*.

THINK ABOUT WHAT YOU KNOW

Imagine that your country is at war. You have to decide whether you will fight in the war. Would you be more likely to fight if the war was being fought in your country or in another country thousands of miles away?

STUDY THE VOCABULARY

Loyalist   mercenary

FOCUS YOUR READING

What advantages and disadvantages did each side have in the Revolutionary War?

A. The British Have Some Military Advantages

Many Remained Loyal   As Ben Franklin said, to win their independence the people of the new states would have to be truly united. But in fact, many colonists remained loyal to the king and to Great Britain. Most of these **Loyalists** returned to Great Britain or moved to Canada. But many stayed. About 50,000 of them fought in the war on the side of Great Britain. This was a great advantage for Great Britain.

British Forces   Great Britain also had the advantage of having a well-trained army. In addition, the British hired thousands of soldiers from other countries. Such hired soldiers are called **mercenaries**. With the mercenaries, Great Britain had an army that was five times larger than the American army. The British also had the advantage of knowing how many soldiers it had in its army. British soldiers agreed to serve in the army for a certain period of time.

On the American side, General George Washington could never count on having many soldiers at one time. Although some joined the Continental army for a three-year term, most volunteered to serve for less than a year. In fact, some served for only three months. Soldiers would often return to their farms at planting and harvesting time. Some would join the Continental army when the fighting was near their village or farm. But just as soon as the British troops moved on, these soldiers would leave the army again. With these farmer-soldiers coming and going all the time, it was almost impossible for General Washington to train them.

British Wealth   Another British advantage was that Great Britain was far wealthier and had a larger population than the

United States. It could supply its army with whatever was needed. The American army was often short of cannons, gunpowder, food, and other supplies. All through the war, most American soldiers fought in their regular clothes, for there were not enough uniforms to go around.

As for the navies, there was no comparison. The British navy was the greatest in the world. Britain's navy had 100 times as many warships as the American navy.

B. Americans Also Have Some Advantages

Fighting at Home The United States had certain advantages, too. Americans were fighting on their own land. This meant they could get fresh troops and supplies nearby. The British had to ship everything and everybody from 3,000 miles (4,827 km) away. Also, American soldiers knew the land because they lived there. In addition, Americans were defending their own homes, families, and freedoms. That made them willing to fight harder.

Washington in Charge The greatest advantage the Americans had was the leadership of George Washington. At the beginning of the war, Washington was a *good* general. By the end of the war, he was a *great* one. More important than George Washington's battlefield skills were his

The name of this old picture is *Revolutionary War Scene: Soldier Calling A Farmer From His Plow*.
▶ Find something that would help the soldier get the farmer's attention.

personality and character. Whether he won or lost a battle, he kept calm. He remained the same steady person throughout the war. Soldiers admired him, and were willing to follow him into battle.

Patriot Women The Patriot side also had important support from American women. Women worked in army camps, washing, cooking, nursing the wounded, and making gunpowder. At times, women actually went onto the battlefields, taking water and food to the fighting men. At the battle of Monmouth, New Jersey, in 1778, Mary Ludwig Hays carried pitchers of water to the men who were fighting under a blazing summer sun. This earned her the nickname Molly Pitcher. Legend has it that when Molly's husband became ill during battle, she took his place in the gun crew.

Several other women took part in the fighting. The most famous was Deborah Sampson, who dressed in men's clothing and joined the army. She served for 18 months before she was wounded and the doctors found out that she was a woman. A number of women also served as messengers and spies.

Women did not have to carry guns or be near a battlefield to do their part for the Patriot cause. They made their greatest contribution at home. In addition to doing the work they had always done, they did the work of the men who had gone to fight. Many women kept the family farms or businesses running.

C. African Americans Are Divided Over the Revolution

African Americans were divided over the Revolution, just as white Americans were. Altogether about 5,000 African Americans fought on the Patriot side during the Revolutionary War. Most were free blacks from northern states.

Nancy Hart was a hero of the Revolutionary War. When British soldiers broke into her home, she held them at gunpoint until help arrived.
► Why, do you think, might these soldiers have broken into Hart's home?

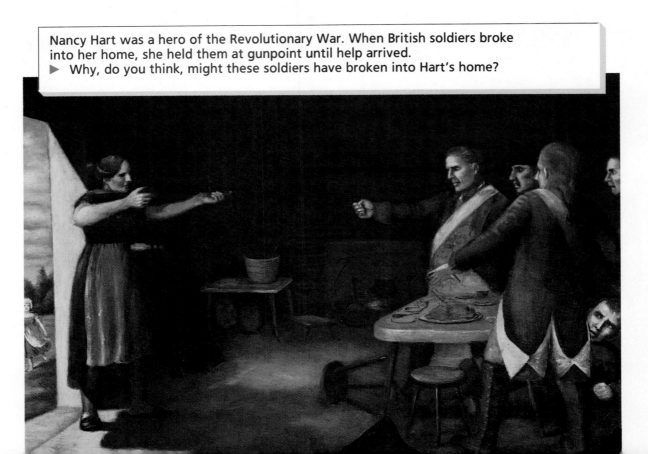

Most of the soldiers in this Rhode Island regiment were African American. Only about one third were white settlers.
► If you were a slave in 1776, would you join the Americans or the British?

African Americans also fought on the side of the British. Although some African Americans were free, most were slaves. Even if the United States was successful in winning its freedom from Great Britain, these African Americans would not be free. They would still be slaves.

The British used this knowledge to encourage slaves to fight for Britain. Soon after the fighting started, the British offered freedom to any slave or indentured servant who would fight on Great Britain's side. During the American Revolution, several thousand slaves ran away from their owners and joined the British army. The British navy carried several thousand escaped slaves to Canada, where they started free settlements.

LESSON 2 REVIEW

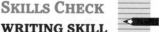

THINK AND WRITE

A. What military advantages did the British have?
B. What advantages did the Americans have in the Revolutionary War?
C. Explain why African Americans were divided during the American Revolution.

SKILLS CHECK

WRITING SKILL

Pretend that you are a soldier in the Continental army. Write a letter to your family telling them why you think George Washington is the right person to lead the Continental army.

The War in the Middle Colonies

THINK ABOUT WHAT YOU KNOW

Why does hardship sometimes draw people together?

STUDY THE VOCABULARY

Hessian

FOCUS YOUR READING

What victories and defeats did the Americans have in 1776 and 1777?

A. Defeat Turns to Victory

Retreat For the first year of the war, most of the fighting took place in New England. For the next two years, from 1776 to 1777, the fighting shifted to the middle colonies. The very same summer that the Declaration of Independence was signed, a large British army defeated the Continental army in a battle for New York City. If British General William Howe had acted quickly, he could have trapped the entire Continental army. The Americans might have lost the war right then. But Howe didn't move quickly, and Washington's army slipped away.

The Americans retreated across New Jersey into Pennsylvania. British troops followed. However, winter was coming, and the British were satisfied to take control of New York and New Jersey and stop there.

Washington's Plan By this time, Washington had developed a plan for fighting the war. You may remember that the British had the advantage of having well-trained, experienced soldiers. Washington knew his untrained troops were no match for the experienced British armies in big

head-on battles. His plan was to keep the Continental army on the move, fighting the British now and then, but avoiding any major battle. This plan meant the Americans would not win many battles. But they would not lose many, either. Meanwhile,

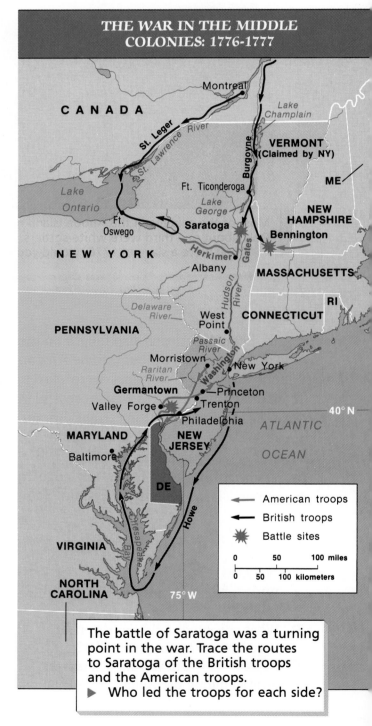

THE WAR IN THE MIDDLE COLONIES: 1776-1777

The battle of Saratoga was a turning point in the war. Trace the routes to Saratoga of the British troops and the American troops.
► Who led the troops for each side?

In order to surprise the enemy at Trenton, Washington and his troops had to cross the Delaware River under cover of darkness.
▶ What made crossing the Delaware particularly difficult at this time?

Washington would gain more time to train his armies. Also, if the war dragged on too long, the British people might tire of it and stop supporting it.

Crossing the Delaware Washington's plan required patience. After the defeats in New York and New Jersey, Washington needed a quick victory to raise the spirits of his soldiers and of the new nation. He planned a surprise attack on British mercenaries who were camped in Trenton, New Jersey. These mercenaries were called **Hessians** because they came from the German state of Hesse.

On Christmas night, 1776, shivering American soldiers stepped into the long rowboats that would carry them across the ice-filled Delaware River. By four o'clock in the morning, all 2,400 of Washington's soldiers were on the New Jersey side of the river. They marched the 9 miles (14 km) to Trenton. At daybreak they attacked the sleeping Hessians. Surprised and confused, 900 Hessians surrendered after a short fight. Only four Americans were wounded in the battle. The Continental army captured weapons and supplies. Eight days later, Washington gave the Americans another victory by defeating surprised British soldiers at Princeton, New Jersey. These two victories helped to raise the spirits of the Americans.

B. The Battle of Saratoga Is a Major Victory

The British, of course, had their own plan for quickly winning the war. Their plan was to win control of the Hudson River area in New York State. As you can see on the map on page 280, this would cut off New England from the rest of the United States. Once the United States was cut in two, the British could defeat each part, one at a time.

General William Howe was to lead soldiers north from New York City. However, Howe decided to capture Philadelphia, and his troops never set out toward the north. The other British troops marched south from Canada as planned. American soldiers defeated them in the battle of Saratoga in October 1777. The Americans captured nearly 6,000 British soldiers.

The victory at Saratoga was one of the most important victories of the war. Here is why. The French had been glad to see the American colonies rebel. France had secretly helped the Patriot side with

On January 2, 1777, Washington's troops made a surprise attack on the British rear guard at Princeton, New Jersey. The American victory at Princeton helped prevent the British from taking over most of New Jersey.
► What weapons can you see in this picture?

The winter at Valley Forge represents one of America's lowest points in the War for Independence. Washington and his men had to fight terrible cold, hunger, and disease.
▶ What condition, do you think, were the troops in by Spring?

money and supplies. But France would not openly join in the war unless the Americans showed they had a real chance of winning. The American victory at Saratoga showed that the United States could win. A few months later, in 1778, France came into the war on the side of the United States. France sent money, equipment, and soldiers to help the Americans. France also sent its large naval fleet to help the American cause. All these things boosted the United States's chances of winning.

Spain, another old enemy of Great Britain, jumped into the war the next year. The year after that, the Netherlands joined the fight against Great Britain. Britain now had its hands full. It had to fight not only in North America but also in Europe and other parts of the world.

C. A Hard Winter Is Spent at Valley Forge

The winter of 1777–1778 was the worst time of the war for the Continental army. The British had taken Philadelphia. They had defeated Washington's troops in several battles near that city. While British troops spent the winter warm and comfortable in Philadelphia, the Continental army camped in tents and drafty huts at Valley Forge, 20 miles (32 km) away.

It was a terrible winter. Supplies did not arrive. Soldiers had no boots and had to wrap their feet in rags. Most soldiers had no blankets. Food was in short supply. Hundreds of soldiers fell ill. Hundreds of others deserted the army. Only Washington's strong leadership kept together what was left of his army.

Pictured above is Baron von Steuben at Valley Forge teaching American troops to use their muskets properly.
▶ Why did Americans need this help?

Some Europeans came to help the American cause. One was a German military officer named Baron Friedrich von Steuben. Von Steuben was skilled at training men to be good soldiers. Another was a young Frenchman, the Marquis de Lafayette (MAHR kwis duh lah fee ET), who became one of Washington's most trusted aides. From Poland came Thaddeus Kosciusko (THAD ee us kahs ee US-koh) and Casimir Pulaski (KAS ih mir poo-LAHS kee). Later in the war, Pulaski was wounded in battle and died. Kosciusko eventually returned to Poland and led the fight for liberty there. Many others also came to fight for American liberty.

LESSON *3* REVIEW

THINK AND WRITE

A. What was George Washington's plan for winning the war?

B. Why was the battle of Saratoga called the turning point in the war?

C. Compare how the British soldiers and the Continental army spent the winter of 1777–1778.

SKILLS CHECK

MAP SKILL

Battles were fought at Trenton, Princeton, and Saratoga. Use the Gazetteer to find the latitude and longitude of each of these places.

The War Shifts to the West

THINK ABOUT WHAT YOU KNOW

Who are your heroes? What do they have in common? Are heroes important to a country?

STUDY THE VOCABULARY

guerrilla   privateer
   warfare

FOCUS YOUR READING

How did the Americans finally win the war?

A. George Rogers Clark Defeats the British in the West

While Washington's soldiers shivered at Valley Forge, a young Virginian named George Rogers Clark was preparing to attack British forts in the West. The British were using these forts to stir up Indians to attack American settlers. In the spring of 1778, Clark, with 200 troops, surprised the British in the fort at Kaskaskia, in the present-day state of Illinois. The Americans took the fort without firing a shot.

Later in the spring, Clark also captured the British fort at Vincennes, in present-day Indiana. Clark's victories gave the United States control of much of the land between the Appalachian Mountains and the Mississippi River.

B. The British Win Victories in the South

In 1778, fighting shifted to the South. For the next two years, American forces suffered their worst defeats of the war. The British captured Savannah, Georgia, and Charleston, South Carolina. They won control over a large part of the South.

But American forces would not give up. Led by men like Francis Marion, bands of Patriots gathered in the swamps of South Carolina. From these secret bases, they would suddenly attack small groups of British soldiers and destroy British supplies. Then, as suddenly as they had come, they would be gone—back to the safety of the swamps. This kind of hit-and-run fighting is called **guerrilla warfare**. You can see how the advantage of fighting on their own land made this kind of warfare

Francis Marion and his fighters are camped for the night in a swamp.
▶ Why weren't the British likely to find this group?

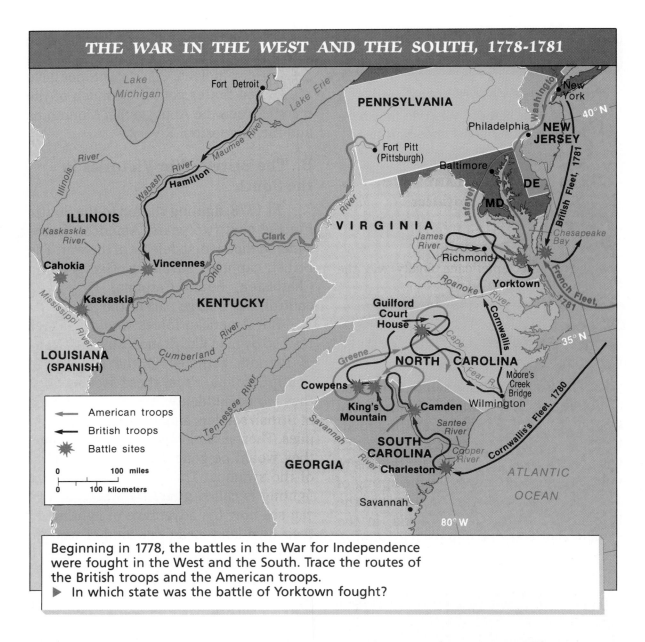

THE WAR IN THE WEST AND THE SOUTH, 1778-1781

American troops
British troops
Battle sites

0   100 miles
0   100 kilometers

Beginning in 1778, the battles in the War for Independence were fought in the West and the South. Trace the routes of the British troops and the American troops.
► In which state was the battle of Yorktown fought?

possible for the Americans. Francis Marion's successful use of guerrilla warfare in the swamps has earned him the name "Swamp Fox."

Meanwhile, Washington sent his best general, Nathanael Greene, to take charge of American forces in the South. Greene also trained his soldiers in guerrilla warfare. Although the British won many small battles, they could never catch up to the American troops and destroy them.

C. The American Navy Wins an Important Battle

The Patriots had only a small navy. To help it, Congress gave permission to private owners of ships to arm their own vessels with cannons. Such ships were called **privateers**. A privateer was no match for a British warship, but it could do great damage to enemy merchant ships. By the end of the war, American privateers had sunk or captured more than 600 British ships.

Although there were very few American warships, they could put up a good fight against one British ship at a time. One such naval battle took place in 1779. John Paul Jones was the commander of the American ship *Bonhomme Richard* when he met up with the British warship *Serapis* off the coast of Great Britain. After a few minutes of firing, the deck of the American ship burst into flames. When the British commander demanded that Jones surrender, Jones replied, "I have not yet begun to fight." And fight he did! After several more hours of battle, it was the American commander, Jones, who won the victory. His stunning victory over the *Serapis* is one of the most famous naval battles ever fought in United States history.

D. American Victory at Yorktown Wins the War

A Plan To End the War In 1781, Great Britain put General Charles Cornwallis in charge of all British troops in America. He had spent a year chasing Nathanael Greene's troops in the South. Cornwallis at last moved to Virginia and set up a base at Yorktown for his 7,000 troops.

Yorktown was located on a small peninsula on Chesapeake Bay. Cornwallis chose Yorktown because he expected the British navy to land fresh troops and supplies there. It turned out to be a costly mistake for Cornwallis.

The French and Americans made a plan to trap Cornwallis's army. The plan

John Paul Jones stands on the deck of the captured British *Serapis* and watches his ship *Bonhomme Richard* sink.
▶ Why did the victorious ship sink?

In this picture called *The Surrender of Lord Cornwallis*, General Cornwallis himself does not appear.
▶ Can you guess why Cornwallis did not come to this occasion?

was to have French troops join Washington's army in New York and then have the two forces move on to Virginia together. Meanwhile, a fleet of 20 French ships would sail into Chesapeake Bay to keep more British soldiers from landing.

Cornwallis Is Trapped Arriving in Virginia, French and American troops surrounded Cornwallis's army on land. This time, American forces outnumbered the British. Day after day, Washington moved his soldiers closer and closer, tightening the ring a little more. Cornwallis was trapped. Cannons roared on each side for days. The British general saw that it was useless to continue the fight any longer. On October 17, 1781, Cornwallis surrendered.

Yorktown was the last great battle of the war. Peace talks began one year later. In the peace treaty signed in 1783, Great Britain agreed that its colonies were now "free and independent states." It also agreed that the new nation would have all the land as far west as the Mississippi River. The war for American independence had been won.

E. How Did the Americans Win the War?

The Revolutionary War produced many heroes. Some of them became famous — Washington, Nathanael Greene, John Paul Jones, the Swamp Fox. But most of the heroes were ordinary people.

They are unknown to history. They were the Minutemen on Lexington green. They were the soldiers who shivered at Valley Forge. They were the men who dashed out of their swamp hideouts to strike at the British. They were the women who carried food and water to the men in battle, took care of the wounded and the sick, and kept farms and shops running. They were the farm families who shared their food with the soldiers and the townspeople who gave the soldiers housing and made weapons and gunpowder for them. They were the boys and girls who helped produce the food and the clothing that the American soldiers needed.

When the war was over, people everywhere asked, "How could the American colonies have won a war against one of the great military powers in the world?" The answer to this question was really not difficult to find. The main reason that the Revolutionary War was won is that ordinary Americans refused to lose it.

This fine bronze statue stands in Concord, Massachusetts. It honors all those who fought for their country's freedom.
▶ Why is a plow part of this statue?

LESSON **4** REVIEW

THINK AND WRITE

A. What did George Rogers Clark do that helped the American cause?
B. Describe the way the American soldiers fought the British in the South.
C. Why is John Paul Jones one of the heroes of the Revolutionary War?
D. What was General Washington's plan for a victory at Yorktown?

E. How did the Americans win the Revolutionary War?

SKILLS CHECK

MAP SKILL

Look at the map on page 286. Use the key to find the places where major battles were fought. List each battle and the state that it was fought in.

USING THE VOCABULARY

Second Continental
  Congress
traitors
republic
Declaration of
  Independence
revolution

Loyalists
mercenary
Hessians
guerrilla
  warfare
privateers

On a separate sheet of paper, complete the sentences by correctly using the terms listed above.

1. Many _____ returned to Great Britain because they supported the king.
2. The _____ were sleeping when the American troops marched into Trenton.
3. John Adams spoke to the delegates of the _____.
4. A _____ is a foreign soldier hired by a country to fight for it.
5. The Patriots' use of _____ confused the British army.
6. According to King George III, the colonists who fought him were _____.
7. The _____ explained why the colonists broke away from Great Britain.
8. Thomas Paine urged the Americans to form a _____.
9. Most of the American ships in naval battles were _____.
10. When the colonists declared their independence, they started a _____.

REMEMBERING WHAT YOU READ

On a separate sheet of paper, write your answers in complete sentences.

1. Why was George Washington the right man to lead the Continental army?
2. How did Thomas Paine help the cause of American independence?
3. What promises did the British make to African Americans?
4. Why was the battle of Saratoga important?
5. What did George Rogers Clark's victories gain for the United States?

TYING MUSIC TO SOCIAL STUDIES

Music was important in the American Revolution. The Americans sang such songs as "Yankee Doodle," "Chester," and "Revolutionary Tea," which is also known as "The Rich Lady over the Sea." When they surrendered at Yorktown, the British troops marched onto the field while their band played "The World Turned Upside Down." These are the words to that song.

If buttercups buzzed after the bee,
If boats were on land, churches on sea
If ponies rode men, and if grass ate the
    corn
And cats should be chased into holes by
    the mouse,
If the mammas sold their babies for half
    a crown,
If summer were spring, and the other
    way 'round,
Then all the world would be upside
    down.

On a separate sheet of paper, tell why you think the British chose this song to play at their surrender.

THINKING CRITICALLY

On a separate sheet of paper, write your answers in complete sentences.

1. Why, do you think, were the colonists influenced by Thomas Paine?
2. Which one of the people mentioned in this chapter interests you the most? Explain why you chose this person.
3. Do you think the Americans could have won the war without the aid of European countries and individual European citizens? Explain your answer.
4. John Paul Jones did not give up when the battle seemed hopeless. Why, do you think, did he continue to fight?
5. Which battle of the war, do you think, was the most important? Explain.

SUMMARIZING THE CHAPTER

On a separate sheet of paper, draw a graphic organizer like the one shown here. Copy the information from this graphic organizer to the one you have drawn. Under the main idea for each lesson, write three statements that support it. The first one has been done for you.

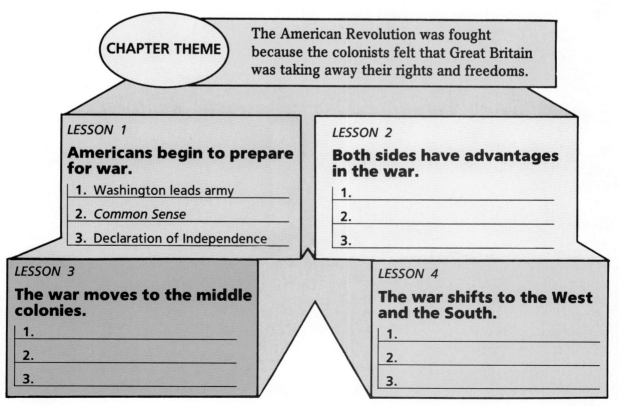

CHAPTER THEME

The American Revolution was fought because the colonists felt that Great Britain was taking away their rights and freedoms.

LESSON 1

Americans begin to prepare for war.

1. Washington leads army
2. *Common Sense*
3. Declaration of Independence

LESSON 2

Both sides have advantages in the war.

1.
2.
3.

LESSON 3

The war moves to the middle colonies.

1.
2.
3.

LESSON 4

The war shifts to the West and the South.

1.
2.
3.

★ ★ ★ ★ ★

*T*hirteen independent states had to learn to work together as one nation. In a daring act, a document was written that has been the basis of our government for over 200 years.

The Articles of Confederation

THINK ABOUT WHAT YOU KNOW
Make a list of three or four freedoms that are most important in your life.

STUDY THE VOCABULARY
constitution   territory
legislature   Northwest
Congress   Ordinance

FOCUS YOUR READING
What were some weaknesses of the government under the Articles of Confederation?

A. Americans Create Their Own Governments

In the Declaration of Independence, Thomas Jefferson wrote that governments get "their just powers from the consent of the governed." In other words, Jefferson stated that it is up to the people to decide what powers their government should and should not have.

Even today, there are few governments that live up to the ideal that governments get their powers from the people they govern. In 1776, such an idea was almost unheard of. After all, kings, conquerors, and tyrants of all kinds had been creating governments for hundreds of years. None of them had ever asked ordinary people what they thought. Ordinary people simply didn't count.

Yet Thomas Jefferson's words expressed exactly what Americans believed. Now that the American Revolution had swept away British rule, Americans began to design their own governments. In every state, Americans discussed and debated ideas for their new state governments. How much power should they give to these governments? What was the best way to protect the rights of the people? How long should their representatives serve? Should the states have governors? Back and forth went the discussions — in newspapers, in the taverns, and in special meetings of the old colonial assemblies. The world had never seen anything like it.

For hundreds of years people believed that kings received their right to rule from God.
▶ Do you think people still hold this belief?

The Granger Collection, New York

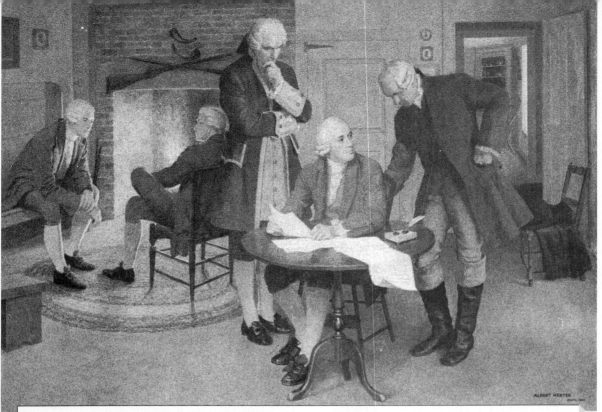

These Massachusetts leaders are talking about what should be included in the Massachusetts state constitution.
▶ Why, do you think, did they want to have a written constitution?

B. New State Governments Are Set Up

Most of the new state governments had written **constitutions**. A constitution is a plan of government. A *written* constitution is also a contract, or agreement, between the people and the government. It says, "We the people are creating this government. These are the things we agree that the government *may do*, and these are the things it *may not* do."

Each state constitution had a list of rights that protected the freedom of the people living in the state. These were rights that the government could never take away from the people. Some of these rights were freedom of speech, freedom of religion, the right to a trial by jury, and the right not to have your home searched without good reason.

The power to make laws was given to the assemblies, which were now called **legislatures** (LEJ ihs lay churz). Members of the legislatures were usually elected every year. That way, if people thought that their representative had not done a good job, they could elect a different person. All the states decided to have governors, but most states didn't give them very much power.

In addition to raising money and soldiers to help fight the American Revolution, the new state governments passed some important laws. Almost all the states passed laws protecting religious freedom. Five northern states took steps to end slavery. Southern states did not go that far, but several made it easier for slave owners to free their slaves, if they wished to do so.

C. Congress Writes the Articles of Confederation

A New National Government While the states were writing new constitutions for themselves, the Second Continental Congress wrote a constitution for a new government of the United States. After months of discussion, the delegates agreed on the Articles of Confederation. It went into effect in 1781.

You'll remember that, as colonists, Americans did not like the way Great Britain's strong central government—that is, the king and Parliament—treated them. So under the Articles of Confederation, most of the government powers were left to the states. As a result, the new central, or national, government was weak.

Weaknesses For example, **Congress**, the law-making body of the new government, had no power to tax the people. All Congress could do was ask each state to contribute its fair share to pay the government's debts. Some states paid up, but others didn't. So the national government was always short of money. Also, under the Articles of Confederation, Congress was not given the power to raise an army.

Congress had no say over United States trade with other countries. Neither did it have a say over trade among the states. So Congress could do nothing when several states began to tax each other's goods. A few states even taxed goods that were just being carried across their borders on the way to another state. These

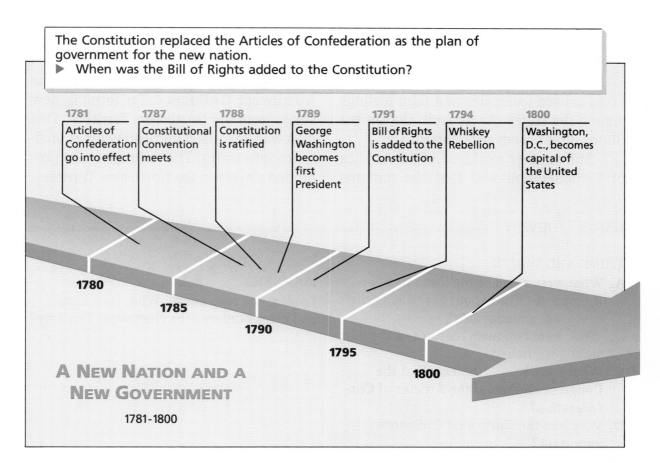

The Constitution replaced the Articles of Confederation as the plan of government for the new nation.

▶ When was the Bill of Rights added to the Constitution?

1781	1787	1788	1789	1791	1794	1800
Articles of Confederation go into effect	Constitutional Convention meets	Constitution is ratified	George Washington becomes first President	Bill of Rights is added to the Constitution	Whiskey Rebellion	Washington, D.C., becomes capital of the United States

1780   1785   1790   1795   1800

A NEW NATION AND A NEW GOVERNMENT

1781-1800

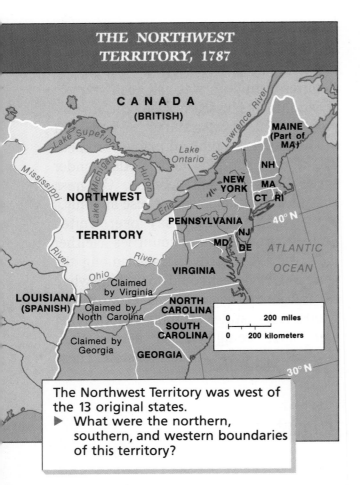

THE NORTHWEST TERRITORY, 1787

The Northwest Territory was west of the 13 original states.
▶ What were the northern, southern, and western boundaries of this territory?

government had no leader, such as a king or president. The national government also did not have its own judges and courts. It had to depend on the state courts to judge Congress's laws.

D. Some Important Laws Are Made

The most important accomplishments under the Articles of Confederation dealt with a region called the Northwest Territory. A **territory** is an area of land that has not yet become a state. The national government still controls such land.

As you can see on the map, the Northwest Territory was the large area north of the Ohio River and east of the Mississippi River. Settlers had been forbidden to move there by the Proclamation of 1763. After the United States became independent, settlers poured into this territory. Congress set up a plan for dividing and selling the land to the settlers.

Congress also set up a plan, called the **Northwest Ordinance**, for forming new states from the Northwest Territory. This plan was later used for turning other territories into states. The ordinance also prohibited slavery in the Northwest Territory.

taxes caused jealousies and hard feelings among the states. As a result, the United States didn't seem very united.

Still another weakness of the Articles of Confederation was that the national

---

LESSON **1** *REVIEW*

THINK AND WRITE

A. What were some of the ideas that Americans talked about in planning their new state governments?
B. What were two main features of the new state governments?
C. What were some problems that the Congress had under the Articles of Confederation?
D. Why was the Northwest Ordinance important?

SKILLS CHECK

MAP SKILL

Look at the map above. What land areas and lakes bordered the Northwest Territory?

296

The Constitution of the United States of America

THINK ABOUT WHAT YOU KNOW

Make a list of some rules that you have in your family or at school. Why do we need to have rules or laws?

STUDY THE VOCABULARY

rebellion	executive branch
convention	judicial branch
federal system	veto
commerce	compromise
separation of	amendment
powers	ratify
legislative branch	

FOCUS YOUR READING

What were the main features of the Constitution?

A. Shays's Rebellion Shows Weakness in the Articles

Many Americans were satisfied with the Articles of Confederation. Other Americans felt that the new government was too weak. They believed that the government must be strengthened. Only then would the United States win the respect of other nations and of its own citizens.

George Washington was one person who felt this way. Many people came to agree with him after an important event in 1786. Times were hard for farmers that year. In Massachusetts many farmers could not pay their taxes. Judges told farmers they would have to sell their land to get the money to pay their taxes.

This made farmers angry. One of them, Daniel Shays, had been an army captain during the Revolutionary War. All through the fall, angry farmers, led by Shays, gathered around courthouses in western Massachusetts to stop the judges from meeting. That way, judges could not give any more orders to farmers to sell their land. Later Shays led a march of farmers to a town where guns were stored. The national government was unable to stop them, for it had no army. The governor of Massachusetts had to send in the state militia to stop the **rebellion**, which came to be known as Shays's Rebellion. A rebellion is an act of opposition to one's government.

No blood had been shed in the rebellion. However, many Americans were troubled that their national government was too weak to deal with a small group of angry farmers.

A government supporter and one of Shays's rebels come to blows over certain tax laws.
► Do the onlookers seem ready to take part in a real fight?

297

B. The Constitutional Convention Meets in Philadelphia

Congress agreed that the national government had to be strengthened. In 1787 it called for all the states to send delegates to a **convention**, or meeting, in Philadelphia, Pennsylvania. This convention was supposed to recommend changes in the Articles of Confederation. Twelve states sent delegates. Only Rhode Island refused to send anyone. On May 25, 1787, the Constitutional Convention opened in Independence Hall in Philadelphia.

Fifty-five men attended the convention. Nearly all of them were well-known leaders in their states. George Washington and Benjamin Franklin were the most famous delegates. New York sent Alexander Hamilton. From Virginia came James Madison, a future President of the United States. Many of the delegates had studied history and law. They were very well prepared for the great task that lay ahead of them.

Everyone agreed that George Washington should be the president of the convention. Everyone also agreed that the discussions should be secret so that the delegates could talk freely. Doors and windows were closed tightly to keep anyone on the outside from hearing what was said. As a result, the meeting room was always stuffy. During the hot days of that summer the room became almost unbearable. Yet the delegates kept at their task, creating a new vision for their country.

C. The Convention Writes a New Constitution

A Bold Step Early in the convention, the delegates made a bold decision. The convention had been called to recommend changes in the Articles of Confederation. Instead, the delegates agreed to discard the Articles of Confederation and write a brand new constitution.

James Madison, Benjamin Franklin, Alexander Hamilton, and George Washington were important delegates to the Constitutional Convention.
▶ Where was the convention held?

TWO TYPES OF GOVERNMENT

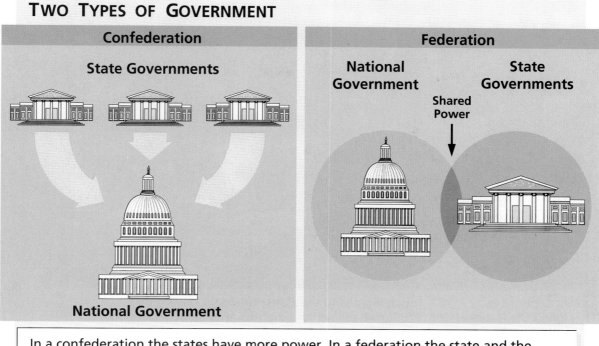

Confederation	Federation
State Governments	National Government · Shared Power · State Governments
National Government	

In a confederation the states have more power. In a federation the state and the national government have equal power and some shared powers.

▶ Which kind of government do you think would be more successful for most countries today?

The convention delegates also decided that the new constitution should create a **federal system** of government. In a federal system, the powers of government are divided between a national government and the state governments.

The national government would be given the power to raise and collect taxes and the power to raise an army. It would also control **commerce**, or trade, among the states and with foreign countries.

Three Branches At the same time, members of the Constitutional Convention did not want to give the new national government too much power. Therefore, they separated the national government into three independent branches. Each branch of government was to have its own separate duties and powers. This idea is known as the **separation of powers**.

Here is how the separation of powers works. The **legislative branch**, or Congress, makes the laws for the country. The **executive branch**, headed by the President of the United States, sees that the laws are executed, or carried out. The President also deals with other countries and serves as commander-in-chief of the armed forces. The **judicial branch** is made up of the Supreme Court and other federal courts. These courts decide on cases involving the Constitution and the laws governing the whole country.

Checks and Balances With the powers of government separated in this way, no branch of government can do whatever it wishes independently. Congress can pass a law, but the President has the right to **veto**, or disapprove, it. The President can make a treaty with another country, but

On September 17, 1787, the delegates to the Constitutional Convention signed the National Constitution. This was two months after the Convention agreed to the Great Compromise.
▶ Find the instruments with which the delegates signed the Constitution.

the Senate, which is part of Congress, has to approve it. Federal judges may decide that an act of Congress is *unconstitutional*. That is, they may say that the Constitution does not give Congress the power to pass that certain law. The President chooses who will serve as judges, and the Senate has to approve them. So you see, each branch of government *checks* and *balances* the other two branches.

D. The Constitution Is Made Up of Compromises

The Great Compromise The delegates to the Constitutional Convention, however, did not agree on everything. So they **compromised**. Compromise involves each side giving up part of what it wants in order to reach an agreement.

The biggest compromise was on the number of representatives each state would have in Congress. States with large populations, like Virginia, wanted representation to be based on the number of people in each state. States with more people would then have more representatives. Small states, like New Jersey and Delaware, said this plan would give the large states too many votes in Congress. They wanted each state to have the same number of representatives.

In the end, it was agreed that Congress would have two houses, or parts. In one house, called the House of Representatives, the number of representatives for each state would be based on population. In the other house, called the Senate, each state would have two senators. This came to be called the Great Compromise.

Planning for Change Members of the convention knew that some day changes might be needed in the new constitution.

Commissioned by the Pennsylvania, Delaware, and New Jersey State Societies, Daughters of the American Revolution. Independence National Historical Park Collection. Copyright Louis Glanzman

So they provided a way to *amend*, or change, it. The Constitution can be amended whenever two thirds of the Congress and three fourths of the states agree on an **amendment**.

In September 1787, the delegates to the Constitutional Convention completed their work. As a result of their work, ideas about government and governing were changed in many places throughout the world. Many other countries have used our Constitution as a model. The Constitution created at the Constitutional Convention continues to serve this country, more than 200 years later. It is the oldest written constitution in use in the world today.

E. The States Ratify the New Constitution

Before the new Constitution could go into effect, nine states had to **ratify**, or approve it. In each state, voters elected representatives to a special convention to decide whether or not to ratify the Constitution. Many states quickly approved it. In several states there were heated debates. Mainly, people complained because the new Constitution had no bill of rights, as state constitutions did. These people were won over when supporters of the Constitution promised to add a bill of rights after the Constitution was ratified. By July 1788, 11 states had ratified the Constitution—2 more than were needed.

Soon afterward, elections were held to choose a President and Congress. As everyone expected, George Washington was elected the first President of the United States of America.

 *LESSON* **2** *REVIEW*

THINK AND WRITE

A. What was Shays's Rebellion?

B. What was the purpose of the Constitutional Convention?

C. How does the Constitution guard against giving too much power to the national government?

D. What was the Great Compromise?

E. What was the major complaint that people had about the Constitution?

SKILLS CHECK

WRITING SKILL

Imagine that you are living in the year 1787. Write a letter to a newspaper telling why you think your state should, or should not, ratify the new constitution.

UNDERSTANDING OUR DEMOCRACY

National Anthem
The Star-Spangled Banner

Oh, say, can you see, by the dawn's early light,
What so proudly we hailed at the twilight's last gleaming,
Whose broad stripes and bright stars, through the perilous fight,
O'er the ramparts we watched were so gallantly streaming?
And the rockets' red glare, the bombs bursting in air,
Gave proof through the night that our flag was still there.
Oh, say, does that star-spangled banner yet wave
O'er the land of the free and the home of the brave?

The American system of government has been at work for over 200 years. Hopes were high when it began. No one knew, however, how it would work or how long it would last. By adopting a written plan for a democratic government, Americans were taking a step no other country had ever taken.

Why did the American experiment turn out to be such a great success? In this special lesson you will learn about the principles, or beliefs, that guide our government and make it so successful. You will also learn about how our system of government under the Constitution works.

When you have finished with this brief study of our democracy, you will understand the five principles of American government. You will also see why the Constitution is important to you.

The Pledge of Allegiance to the Flag of the United States

I pledge allegiance to the Flag of the United States of America, and to the Republic for which it stands, one Nation under God, indivisible, with liberty and justice for all.

THE PRINCIPLES OF OUR GOVERNMENT

1 The People Rule

The first principle, or belief, is that the American government gets its powers from the people. The purpose of the government is to serve the people. The writers of the Constitution stated this principle in the Preamble, or opening section, of the Constitution. "We the People of the United States," they wrote, are setting up a new government. The founders then listed the specific duties of the government they were creating. Find the Preamble on page 656, read it, and think about the reasons the government was established.

As you have learned, countries in which the people rule are called democracies. Under our form of democracy,

the people do not rule directly. Instead, we choose our leaders by voting in elections. This type of democracy is called a republic.

Read the words to the Pledge of Allegiance on this page. Notice that when you pledge loyalty to the flag, you are also expressing loyalty to our republican form of government. The United States is the oldest republic in the world today.

Notice how each of the principles you will learn about helps make sure that the people rule. Notice also how the American system of democracy is designed to keep safe the freedoms given the people by the Constitution.

2 Limited Government

Rule of Law The second principle of our democracy is that the powers of the government are limited. As you have learned, these powers are written down in the Constitution. It tells what the government may and may not do.

Basic Rights In Chapter 11 you read about the roots of the American idea of a limited government. Because of the actions of the British government before the Revolution, Americans came to fear governments that were too strong. Our government has enough power to rule but not so much power that it might threaten people's freedom.

The basic freedoms of the American people are listed in the Bill of Rights, the first ten amendments of the Constitution. Some of these freedoms are shown in the table on this page. These freedoms are protected because of the principle of limited government.

3 Separation of Powers

One way to make sure that the government does not become too powerful is to divide power among parts of the government. In this way, no single person can gain enough power to ignore the people. This way of limiting the government's power is the third principle of our government, separation of powers.

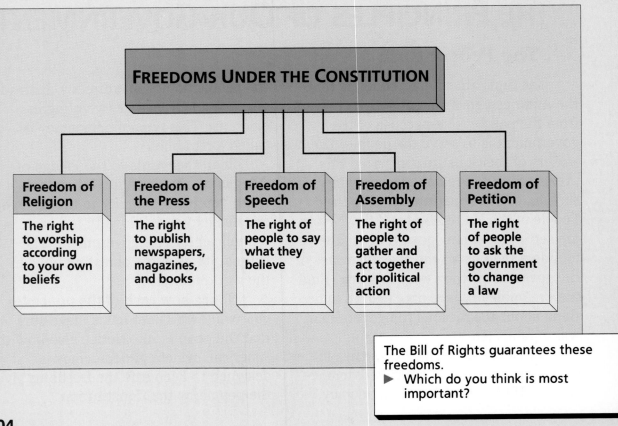

FREEDOMS UNDER THE CONSTITUTION

Freedom of Religion	Freedom of the Press	Freedom of Speech	Freedom of Assembly	Freedom of Petition
The right to worship according to your own beliefs	The right to publish newspapers, magazines, and books	The right of people to say what they believe	The right of people to gather and act together for political action	The right of people to ask the government to change a law

The Bill of Rights guarantees these freedoms.
► Which do you think is most important?

THE THREE BRANCHES OF GOVERNMENT

Executive

The power of the national government is divided among the three branches. Each of these buildings is a symbol of a branch.
▶ Can you identify the buildings?

Legislative

Judicial

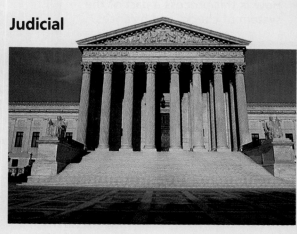

In our government, responsibility for government is split up among the three branches of the government. The legislative branch, or Congress, makes the laws. As you have learned, Congress itself has two parts, the House of Representatives and the Senate.

The executive branch, led by the President, sees that the laws are carried out. The President is helped by departments, each of which handles a special job.

The judicial branch of the national government is the federal court system. The head of this system is the Supreme Court. The courts handle cases involving federal laws. They also listen to and decide cases between the states.

The three branches check and balance one another's actions. No single branch of the government can gain too much power. This system makes it possible for each part of the government to limit the powers of the others.

Look at the diagram on the next page for some examples of how the system of checks and balances works. Notice ways the President checks the work of Congress and the courts and ways in which Congress checks the other two branches.

HOW A BILL BECOMES A LAW

A bill must be passed by Congress before it goes to the President.
▶ How is this process a part of the system of checks and balances?

BILL

HOUSE

SENATE

BILL VETO

OR

BILL Signed

2/3

2/3

LAW

306

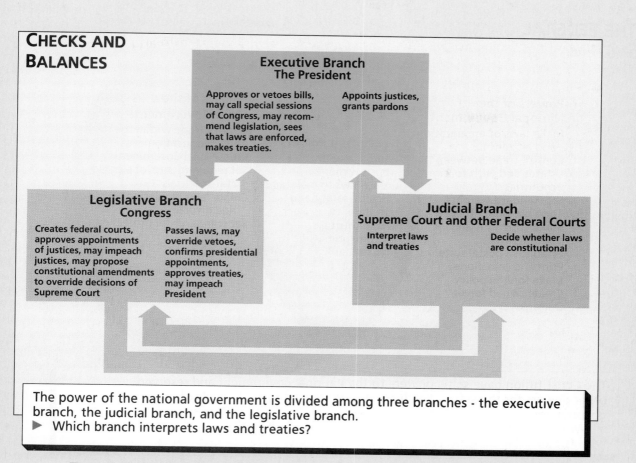

CHECKS AND BALANCES

**Executive Branch
The President**

Approves or vetoes bills, may call special sessions of Congress, may recommend legislation, sees that laws are enforced, makes treaties.

Appoints justices, grants pardons

**Legislative Branch
Congress**

Creates federal courts, approves appointments of justices, may impeach justices, may propose constitutional amendments to override decisions of Supreme Court

Passes laws, may override vetoes, confirms presidential appointments, approves treaties, may impeach President

**Judicial Branch
Supreme Court and other Federal Courts**

Interpret laws and treaties

Decide whether laws are constitutional

The power of the national government is divided among three branches - the executive branch, the judicial branch, and the legislative branch.
▶ Which branch interprets laws and treaties?

Especially important is the power of judicial review. The Supreme Court has the power to decide whether a law passed by Congress and signed by the President is permitted by the Constitution. The power of judicial review makes the Supreme Court, which has just nine members, a very important part of our government.

4 Federalism

Remember that the writers of the Constitution had a problem. They had to decide how much power to give the national government and how much power to give to the state governments. They decided on the system of federalism. Under this system, powers are divided between the national government and the states in three ways.

First, some powers are given just to the national government. These include the power to declare war, to coin money, and to regulate business among the states.

In order to help the national government deal with new conditions, the Constitution has a special clause. It gives Congress the power to make "all laws which shall be necessary and proper" to carry out its duties. Because this clause can be stretched to cover many kinds of laws, it is called the elastic clause.

Second, some powers are given to the states. In addition to responsibilities listed in the Constitution, states have other, unlisted, powers that have not been assigned to the national government.

Powers of the National Government
Make laws of immigration and citizenship
Control trade between states and with foreign countries
Set standard weights and measures
Make copyright and patent laws
Establish a postal system
Print and coin money
Make foreign policy
Create armed forces
Declare war

Concurrent Powers
Collect taxes and borrow money
Create laws to maintain health, safety, and welfare
Set up court systems
Set minimum wage
Charter banks

Powers of the State Governments
Control trade within the state
Control education
Create local governments
Set requirements for elected state officials
Create laws regulating marriage and divorce
Set standards for professional licenses

The Constitution gave some powers to the national government and reserved other powers for the states. Some powers are shared by both levels of government.
▶ Which level of government has the power to declare war?

States are responsible for public schools, local government, marriage laws, setting rules for drivers, and running elections. Because states may make such laws, there are many differences among states. For example, in most states you must be at least 18 years old in order to get a driver's license. There are some states, however, where the minimum age for a regular driver's license is only 15 years.

5 A Written Constitution

The Constitution is the written description of how our government should work. It is a plan of government. Like any other plan, it is up to the people to fill in the details. As you read the rest of America's story, you will find out just how well the plan has worked.

With their many powers, states have important responsibilities. However, under federalism, the national government is the highest government. No state law may go against a national law.

Third, some powers—called concurrent powers—belong to both levels of government. Concurrent means "at the same time." See the chart on this page for examples of some of these powers.

Our Constitution has been able to grow with our country. It has changed as the nation has changed. Our country has been tested and has grown stronger in the 200 years since that long, hot summer in Philadelphia when the Constitution was written.

Celebrations were held all over the nation in honor of the 200th anniversary of the Constitution.
▶ Why, do you think, was this such an important event?

The New Government

THINK ABOUT WHAT YOU KNOW

Who is the President of the United States? What are some problems that the President is trying to solve today?

STUDY THE VOCABULARY

inauguration   **Cabinet**
Bill of Rights   **political party**

FOCUS YOUR READING

How did the new government begin its work?

A. The Great Experiment Begins

On receiving the news of his election to the Presidency, George Washington climbed into his coach and left for New York City, the temporary capital of the United States, where his **inauguration** would be held. An inauguration is a ceremony to put someone into a government office. With him rode the hopes of the American people. As Washington's coach moved from one town to the next, crowds cheered their new President.

Finally on April 30, 1789, George Washington stood before thousands of fellow citizens in New York City. Placing his hand on a Bible, he promised to "preserve, protect, and defend the Constitution of the United States."

Soon after, Congress met and quickly acted to keep a promise. James Madison of Virginia wrote a number of amendments to the Constitution to protect the rights of the people. In 1791, ten of these amendments were ratified and added to the Constitution. They are known as the **Bill of Rights**. These rights were much the same as those listed in the different state constitutions.

George Washington is being rowed across New York Bay to prepare for his inauguration in New York City. Ships welcome him with a roar of cannons.
► What are the sailors on the left doing?

National Gallery of Art, Washington, D.C. Gift of Edgar William and Bernice Chrysler Garbisch

WASHINGTON'S FIRST CABINET

Office	Official	Duties
Secretary of State	Thomas Jefferson	To conduct the relations of the United States with other nations
Secretary of the Treasury	Alexander Hamilton	To handle the government's finances
Secretary of War	Henry Knox	To take charge of all military matters
Attorney General	Edmund Randolph	To act as chief legal adviser to the executive branch
Postmaster General	Samuel Osgood	To run the post office and mail service

The office of Postmaster General did not become a Cabinet department until 1829.

► Which cabinet position do you think is the most important one?

The Bill of Rights protects such important personal freedoms as freedom of speech, freedom of worship, and freedom of the press.

Congress also created several departments to help the President. The State Department deals with foreign countries. The Treasury Department collects taxes, pays bills, and takes care of the government's money. The War Department was in charge of the country's defense.

The head of each department was called a *secretary*. President Washington often called upon these secretaries for advice. When the President met with his advisers, the group was called the **Cabinet**.

B. Disagreements Lead to Political Parties

President Washington chose Thomas Jefferson to head the State Department. He chose Alexander Hamilton to be the first secretary of the treasury. Jefferson and Hamilton were two of the ablest people ever to serve in government. But they disagreed on almost everything. At times, President Washington felt as though he were driving a coach with horses pulling in opposite directions.

Hamilton wanted to encourage manufacturing to grow. He hoped the United States would soon have many large cities. He also favored an even stronger central government than the one that the new Constitution created.

Jefferson agreed that the country needed some manufacturing and trade. However, Jefferson did not want to see large cities grow. He wanted the United States to remain a nation of small farmers. As for the government itself, Jefferson wanted to keep it as small as possible.

The many disagreements between Hamilton and Jefferson led to the birth of **political parties**. A political party is a group of people who hold certain beliefs about how the government should be run and what it should do. These people join together to elect people who share their beliefs. In the 1790s, those Americans who favored Hamilton and his ideas were called *Federalists*. Supporters of Thomas Jefferson called themselves *Democratic-Republicans*.

C. The New Government Faces Problems

Debts One of the biggest problems the new government faced was how to pay back the money that Congress and the states had borrowed during the Revolutionary War. Alexander Hamilton proposed a plan for doing this, and Congress accepted it. Part of the plan was to raise money by putting a tax on several goods, including whiskey.

The whiskey tax angered many western farmers. Many of these farmers made whiskey out of their corn. This was done because it cost much less to ship whiskey than to ship corn. Also, the corn might rot before it got to market. For these farmers, paying a tax on whiskey was just like having to pay a tax on the corn they raised.

Whiskey Rebellion In 1794, farmers in western Pennsylvania banded together and refused to pay the tax. They threatened tax collectors. President Washington felt that the government must show that it could make people obey its laws. He led 13,000 troops to western Pennsylvania to put down this Whiskey Rebellion. When farmers heard that troops were coming, they dropped their guns and fled. That ended the rebellion. Washington had shown the new government's strength.

Trouble with Britain Another problem that President Washington faced came from outside the United States. During the 1790s, Great Britain and France were at war again. Britain's navy seized American ships that were carrying goods to French ports. Many Americans were ready to go to war over this. Because President Washington knew the young nation needed time to grow and become stronger, he kept the country out of war.

D. John Adams Becomes the Second President

George Washington was elected President twice. He could have been elected as many times as he wished, for he was the

These farmers have refused to pay the whiskey tax and are capturing the tax collectors themselves.
► Which men are the farmers and which the tax collectors?

Here L'Enfant shows Washington his plans for the future capital. On the right is Banneker, who finished carrying out these plans.
▶ For whom is our national capital named?

most popular man in the United States. Washington decided that two terms of office, or eight years, was enough, and he returned to private life at Mount Vernon.

John Adams was elected the second President. Adams had served as Washington's Vice President. He was a Federalist. While Adams was President, the United States was again almost dragged into the continuing war between Great Britain and France. This time it was mainly France that violated America's rights and insulted the United States. Again, many Americans hotly demanded war.

President Adams knew that going to war would make him popular. He also knew it would not be wise for the country. Like President Washington before him, President Adams was able to avoid a war.

E. Washington, D.C., Becomes the Capital of the United States

The Capital City Back in 1790, Congress moved the nation's capital from New York to Philadelphia. At the same time, it decided to build a new capital city for the nation. Maryland and Virginia each gave up some land for the capital, which was to be called the District of Columbia. Later it became known as Washington, D.C., in honor of our first president.

The job of designing the new capital city was given to a French engineer named Pierre L'Enfant (pee AIR lahn FAHN). L'Enfant laid out a plan for the city. However, he soon quit and returned to France, taking the written plans with him. Benjamin Banneker, an African American, had helped L'Enfant. Banneker was now put in charge of carrying out L'Enfant's plan. Banneker was able to produce this plan from memory, and he completed the work. In 1800 the government moved from Philadelphia to its new home, Washington, D.C.

Washington, D.C., in 1800 hardly looked like the beautiful city it is today. There were just a few government buildings, surrounded by tree stumps and connected by dirt roads. When the rains came and for days afterward, there was mud throughout the city.

YOU DECIDE: IS IT CONSTITUTIONAL?

As citizens of a free and democratic society, we have many rights and freedoms. As you learned in this chapter, the Constitution of the United States protects many of our most important rights and freedoms. It keeps the federal and state governments from passing laws that would take away these rights. If such laws were passed, the Supreme Court would say they were unconstitutional. As a result the laws would not be carried out. It is important, therefore, to ask every time a new law is proposed, "Is it constitutional?"

Here, in simplified language, are three parts of the Constitution. Each is an amendment, and each protects certain rights.

First Amendment—No one may interfere with freedom of religion, freedom of speech, freedom of the press, or the right of people to meet together peaceably or to send petitions to the government.

Fifth Amendment—Persons accused of serious crimes have the right to a trial by jury. They cannot be forced to give evidence against themselves. A person's life, freedom, and property may not be taken from her or him unfairly. If the government must take a person's property for public use, it must pay the owner a fair price for it.

Nineteenth Amendment—No citizen may be denied the right to vote because of his or her sex.

Thinking for Yourself

On page 315 there is a list of laws that might be passed or actions that might be taken by the government. On a separate sheet of paper, write the numbers 1–10. If you think the law would be constitutional, write **C** next to the number. Also write the number of the amendment that makes it constitutional.

314

Write **U** if you think the law or action would be unconstitutional and give the number of the appropriate amendment. For example, number 1 is unconstitutional because the nineteenth amendment says that a citizen may not be denied the right to vote because of his or her sex. Therefore, on your sheet of paper, you would write 1. U nineteen.

1. A state passes a law that allows males to vote, but not females.
2. The government does not like a certain person's ideas, so it does not allow him to make a speech in public.
3. A woman accused of a serious crime wants a jury trial, but the government says it doesn't have enough money for such a trial.
4. A town does not like the religious beliefs of a certain group, so it forbids it from building a place in which to worship.
5. A state passes a law that allows women to vote at age 18 but says men must wait until they are 21 before they can vote.
6. A person's house is in the way of a proposed public highway. The government offers the owner a fair price for the house.
7. A person accused of a serious crime refuses to give evidence against himself.
8. A group of people are arrested because they wrote to Congress saying they did not like a certain law.
9. The government orders a newspaper to stop printing editorials that are criticizing the government too much.
10. A woman receives a parking ticket. She insists on a jury trial. The government says she doesn't need a jury because her offense is not serious.

James Hoban won $500 in a design contest for a plan for the President's house. His plan was used in building the White House.
► Name some new-house problems Mrs. Adams had.

Abigail Adams

National Gallery of Art, Washington, D.C. Gift of Mrs. Robert Homans

The White House The President's Palace, later called the White House, was the first building ready for use. President Adams and his family were the first to live in it. When the Adamses arrived, not a single room had been completely finished. The plaster walls were still damp. There were fireplaces in each room to take the chill off the house, but no arrangement had been made to supply the house with firewood. The main stairway to the second floor was not finished. The President's wife, Abigail Adams, even used one of the unfinished rooms for hanging the family wash to dry. Servants carried water from a distance of five city blocks.

Still, Abigail Adams had a sense of history. She knew how far the young republic had already come. Like the new nation itself, the President's Palace was unfinished. Its rough edges would need smoothing out. In time the new house, like the new nation, would become great. "This House is built for ages to come," Abigail Adams wrote to her sister. And so it was.

LESSON 3 REVIEW

THINK AND WRITE
A. What is the Bill of Rights?
B. How did political parties begin in the United States?
C. What were some problems that the new government faced?
D. What was one major decision that John Adams made as President?
E. How was the District of Columbia created?

SKILLS CHECK

WRITING SKILL
Read the section on the Bill of Rights on pages 310–311. Select one of the rights listed. Write a paragraph telling why you think that right is important.

USING THE VOCABULARY

constitution	compromise
legislature	amendment
convention	ratify
commerce	inauguration
veto	political party

On a separate sheet of paper, write the terms you have chosen from the list that could take the place of the underlined words in the statements below.

1. The members made an <u>addition</u> to the document after they signed it.
2. The President said he would <u>not approve</u> the plan.
3. He won the support of a <u>group of people who felt the same way he did about important issues.</u>
4. In order for the plan to pass, each state had to <u>agree to</u> it.
5. It was decided to have a written <u>plan of government.</u>
6. As part of the <u>ceremony</u>, the President took the oath of office.
7. The <u>law-making assembly</u> was made up of delegates from all the states.
8. The plan was passed when each side agreed to <u>give up part of what it wanted.</u>
9. Each state had its own rules to control <u>trade.</u>
10. The <u>meeting</u> of the delegates was planned for the summer.

REMEMBERING WHAT YOU READ

On a separate sheet of paper, write your answers in complete sentences.

1. Describe three weaknesses of the new United States government under the Articles of Confederation.
2. Why was the Northwest Ordinance an important law?
3. What is a federal system?
4. How does the system of checks and balances work?
5. What was the Great Compromise?
6. How can the Constitution be changed?
7. What departments were formed to help the President?
8. Why was the Whiskey Rebellion important to the growth of the new government?
9. Why did Washington and Adams keep the United States out of war?
10. How was Benjamin Banneker important in the creation of the new capital?

TYING ART TO SOCIAL STUDIES

If you do not know what *calligraphy* means, find its definition in the dictionary. Practice the alphabet, using calligraphy. Make a copy of the Bill of Rights, using calligraphic lettering. Your work would look best on an unlined sheet of paper that could be rolled up like a scroll.

The Bill of Rights appears on pages 670–672 in your textbook.

THINKING CRITICALLY

On a separate sheet of paper, write your answers in complete sentences.

1. How did the state constitutions influence the writers of the federal Constitution?
2. Describe how Shays's Rebellion showed a weakness of the national government under the Articles of Confederation and how the Constitution had solved this weakness by the time the Whiskey Rebellion took place.
3. How does the fact that it can be amended make the Constitution a much stronger document?
4. In what ways does the Cabinet help the President?
5. Why, do you think, did Congress decide to build a completely new city to be the capital of the United States?

SUMMARIZING THE CHAPTER

On a separate sheet of paper, draw a graphic organizer like the one shown here. Copy the information from this graphic organizer to the one you have drawn. Under each main idea for a lesson, write three statements that support it. The first one has been done for you.

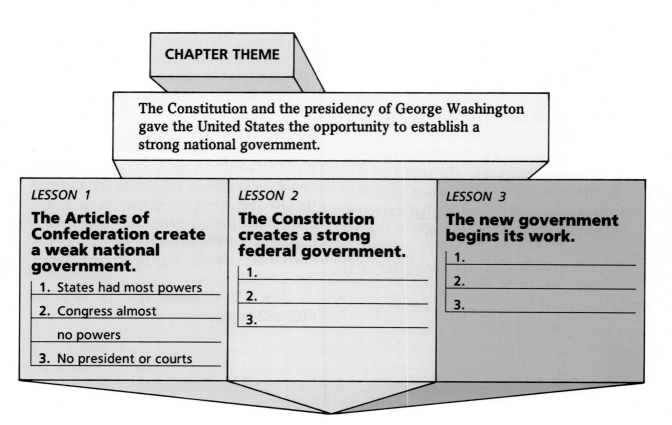

CHAPTER THEME

The Constitution and the presidency of George Washington gave the United States the opportunity to establish a strong national government.

LESSON 1
The Articles of Confederation create a weak national government.
1. States had most powers
2. Congress almost no powers
3. No president or courts

LESSON 2
The Constitution creates a strong federal government.
1. _____
2. _____
3. _____

LESSON 3
The new government begins its work.
1. _____
2. _____
3. _____

COOPERATIVE LEARNING

By the middle of the 1700s, the English colonies had developed an identity of their own. The authorities in Great Britain had difficulty in recognizing this and trouble grew between the colonies and the king and Parliament.

PROJECT

Meet with your group and talk about some of the people who were important during the time of the Revolution. The group will choose four or five of them and plan a television talk show.

- One group member will be the talk show host. The other members of the group will each take the role of one of the people the group chose for this activity.
- Use the information in this unit to make a list of questions for the host to ask the personalities.
- The host will be responsible for seeing that each guest has an opportunity to present his or her views.
- The guests should also be ready to talk to each other about their participation in the struggle for independence.
- Decide if the program is going to be presented with props or costumes.
- Rehearse the show.

PRESENTATION AND REVIEW

- Present the show for your classmates.
- Answer any questions that the audience may have.
- Try to stay in character when answering the questions.

   Hold a final meeting with your group to evaluate this activity. Everyone should answer the following questions.

- Did everyone in the group have a chance to give his or her opinion?
- Did we listen to each other?
- Did we stick to the topic?
- Did everyone complete his or her assignment?
- What advice would we give to a group that was going to prepare a similar project?

REMEMBER TO:
- Give your ideas.
- Listen to others' ideas.
- Plan your work with the group.
- Present your project.
- Discuss how your group worked.

Analyzing SKILLBUILDER Historical Maps

A. WHY DO I NEED THIS SKILL?

Turn to the table of contents of your book. Look at the list of maps. Notice how many kinds of maps there are. There are political maps, which show the boundaries between states or nations. There are physical maps, which show the geographical features of an area. There are distribution maps. Their purpose is to give information about a specific item or items.

Historical maps are another kind of special map. They help the reader understand things as they were or as they happened in the past. A historical map is one way of organizing historical information.

B. LEARNING THE SKILL

Cartographers, the people who make maps, use many tools in drawing maps. Among the most helpful tools to modern cartographers are the space satellites. They take very detailed pictures of the earth's surface. These pictures help the cartographers draw very accurate maps.

Look at the world map on pages 618–619 in the Atlas of your book. Now turn to the map on page 118. What part of the world is shown on this map? The map was drawn in

the sixteenth century by a Swedish monk. It shows the cartographer's knowledge of the world at that time.

Compare the old map with the map on pages 618–619 in the Atlas. What other differences do you see? What similarities are there? Which specific places appear to be about the same? Which are different? Are there lines of latitude and longitude?

Iceland on the old map is shaped very much like Iceland on the modern map. The coastline, however, is more accurate on the modern map. And the modern map does not have any of the drawings of ships and animals that appear on the old map.

If you were shown the old map and not told when it was made, you might be able to make a good guess. You could at least say that it was probably drawn after A.D. 1000, when the Vikings had settled this area. The ships on the map would be a clue. They do not look like Viking ships. They look more like the ships on which Columbus sailed.

C. PRACTICING THE SKILL

One purpose of historical maps is to help the reader to understand the results of events. The maps on page 252 show how control of territory changed after the French and Indian War. Comparing the maps shows that France lost the most territory after the war. What country gained most of that territory?

Maps that show battles are also useful. Some maps show the major battles that took place during a war. Study the map on page 280. How can you tell which troops were American and which were British? How many battles are shown on the map? Where did the battles shown on this map take place? Are there other maps in this section of the book that show Revolutionary War battles in other parts of the country?

D. APPLYING THE SKILL

According to the peace treaty that ended the Revolutionary War, the United States would control all the territory between the Atlantic Ocean and the Mississippi River. Some of the states claimed that land based on their colonial charters. The map on this page shows those land claims.

Study the map and tell whether the following statements are true or false. Write your answers on a separate sheet of paper.
1. All 13 states made western land claims.
2. Virginia claimed more land than any other state.
3. Some states claimed the same land.
4. An area to the east of New York was claimed at this time by New York, New Hampshire, and Massachusetts.
5. Great Britain claimed the land west of the Mississippi River.

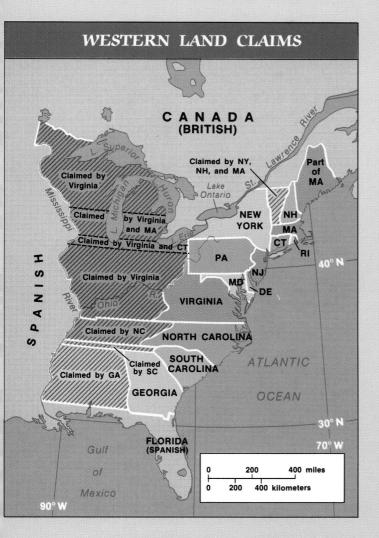

WESTERN LAND CLAIMS

Reading SKILLBUILDER to Learn

A. WHY DO I NEED THIS SKILL?

A social studies book such as this one contains information about people, places, and events. There is much to learn, understand, and remember. Using a study-reading strategy like **SQR** will help you identify and remember main ideas and important people, places, and events.

B. LEARNING THE SKILL

SQR stands for **Survey, Question,** and **Read**.

Survey — Surveying, or skimming over, the lesson helps you get a general idea of what the lesson will be about. Before you actually begin to read, skim any questions, headings, and vocabulary words; look at pictures, maps, and other illustrations in the lesson. Doing this will give you a good idea of the topic of the lesson. Think about what you already know about this topic. Also try to make some predictions, or guesses, about what will be in the lesson.

Question — Preparing a list of questions about the lesson before you actually begin to read the lesson is the next step. In this book each lesson begins with a "Focus Your Reading" question to help you focus on the main idea of the lesson. Use the vocabulary words and the headings found within the lesson for help in preparing questions about important details. You should be able to answer your questions as you read. Write your questions on a sheet of paper or make a mental list of them.

Read — Reading the lesson to find the answers to your questions is the last step. Write out the answers or say them to yourself as you read. You may find yourself asking more questions as you read. Be sure to find the answers to these questions, too.

C. PRACTICING THE SKILL

Turn to page 251. You can practice **SQR** on Lesson 1 in Chapter 11, "The French and Indian War."

First, survey the lesson, following the directions given above. Think about what you might already know about the French and Indian War. Can you make any predictions about what will be in this lesson?

Second, prepare a list of questions about the lesson and write them on a sheet of paper. Leave space after each question so that you can write in an answer later on. The question to help you focus your reading at the beginning of the lesson is an important one. Write it down. Ask a question about the vocabulary word **treaty**—"What is a treaty?" for instance. Turn each heading into one or more questions. You might ask, "Who was the young officer? What was the important message?" Make up a question or questions for the other heading in the lesson and write them down, too.

Finally, read to find the answers to your questions. Write the answers on your paper. Were there any other questions you thought of as you read the lesson? If so, write them on your paper and look for the answers.

- Use vocabulary words and headings to prepare other questions.
- Write your questions or make a mental note of them.
- Read to answer your questions.
- Write out answers or say them to yourself.
- Ask and answer other questions that come to mind as you read.

SQR will be particularly helpful when you study for a test. If you save your **SQR** questions and answers, they can be used to review the chapter.

Practice using **SQR** as you read lessons in the next chapter, which is about the American Revolution. See if using **SQR** helps you better understand and remember the information in that chapter. See if it helps on your next test!

Using **SQR**, you will have learned the main ideas and the important details of the lesson. Now it should be easy to answer the review questions at the end of the lesson.

D. APPLYING THE SKILL

The **SQR** study-reading strategy will help you learn and understand information in your social studies book. You can also use **SQR** when reading textbooks on other subjects. The **USING SQR** chart will help you remember the steps.

USING SQR	
Survey	Look at questions, vocabulary words, and visuals.
	Think about what you already know about the topic.
	Make predictions about the lesson content.
Question	Note questions already in the lesson.
	Use vocabulary words and headings to prepare other questions.
	Write your questions or make a mental note of them.
Read	Read to answer your questions.
	Write out answers or say them to yourself.
	Ask and answer other questions that come to mind as you read.

Unit 4

GROWTH OF THE NEW NATION

The United States grew in size during the first half of the 1800s. With the growth came many changes in where and how people lived.

▶ *This mural, which depicts Americans moving west, hangs in the United States Capitol in Washington, D.C.*

14

MOVING WEST

*I*n the early 1800s the new nation doubled its size. The Industrial Revolution spread from Europe to America and helped to create new ways of working in the United States.

Americans Settle New Lands

THINK ABOUT WHAT YOU KNOW

Why might people today decide to move from one part of the country to another?

STUDY THE VOCABULARY

pass   **flatboat**
pioneer

FOCUS YOUR READING

What challenges did Americans face as they began to move west?

A. Hunters and Trappers Lead the Way into the Wilderness

From the earliest days of settlement, the story of America has been the story of people moving westward. Leading the way into the wilderness were hunters and trappers. To most people the wilderness was a place of danger. To hunters and trappers it was a place of adventure as well as a place to make their living.

The most famous hunter of the 1700s was Daniel Boone. Daniel Boone was born and raised on the frontier of Pennsylvania. By the age of 12, he was already skilled with a rifle. From Indians who lived nearby, he learned to hunt and trap forest animals. When Daniel was 16, his family moved to the North Carolina frontier. At that time the Carolina frontier was only lightly settled. But Daniel Boone was one of those restless people who felt crowded whenever they saw the smoke from a neighbor's cabin. Soon Daniel was spending several months each year alone in the woods. Carrying only a rifle and a few supplies, he hunted for his food and slept under the stars. He earned money by selling the furs of animals.

Later, Daniel Boone married and cleared land for a farm so that he could provide for his family. But always he was drawn back to the wilderness. Every autumn after the crops were harvested, Boone returned to the forest. Every spring he came home to his family to plant crops for the next autumn's harvest.

B. Boone Blazes a Path to Kentucky

Cumberland Gap   For many years Boone heard stories from other hunters and traders about a rich land on the other side of the Appalachian Mountains. These hunters told of an old Indian trail called the Warriors' Path, which crossed the mountains. Several times Boone searched for this trail, but he was unable to find it.

Daniel Boone and his friends see Kentucky for the first time, after a 38-day trip from North Carolina.
► In what direction did they travel?

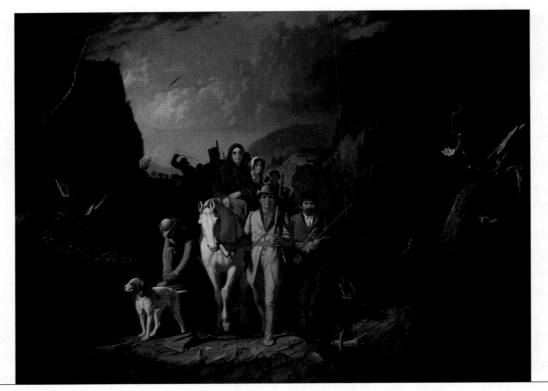

This is part of a larger picture painted by a famous American artist. It shows Daniel Boone leading a group of settlers through the Cumberland Pass.
▶ Why, do you think, were these settlers glad to have Boone guide them?

In 1769, Boone and a group of five men set out once again to find the Warriors' Path. This time they succeeded. They followed the path through a **pass**, or narrow valley between the mountains. We know this pass today as the Cumberland Gap. Reaching the western side of the mountains, Boone and his companions gazed down upon the beautiful green meadows of present-day Kentucky.

Boonesboro Over the next few years, Boone explored and hunted in Kentucky many times. In the spring of 1775, Boone was hired to turn the Warrior's Path into a trail wide enough to be used by settlers traveling with wagons and animals.

Boone and a crew of 40 men chopped down trees and cleared away the underbrush to widen the trail. In a few months the road, renamed the Wilderness Trail, was ready for use.

Boone conducted a group of relatives and friends across the fresh trail to live in Kentucky. On the journey the group was attacked by Indians, and Boone's son was killed. When they settled the town Boone's party built, it was called Boonesboro. It was one of the first permanent settlements west of the Appalachian Mountains.

Pioneers Soon many **pioneers** were traveling across the Appalachians in search of fertile land. Pioneers are the first settlers in a new area. The pioneers came over the Wilderness Trail by the hundreds, and then by the thousands. They spread out south of the Ohio River, across Kentucky and into neighboring Tennessee.

Thousands of other pioneers reached these lands by floating down the Ohio River on **flatboats**, which had flat bottoms. These boats could travel through shallow places in the river. Many flatboats were little more than rafts. By 1792, Kentucky had enough people to become a state. Tennessee became a state in 1796.

During those same years, pioneers also moved into the land north of the Ohio River, the Northwest Territory. They settled mainly along the Ohio River or near streams that emptied into it. The Ohio River and the Mississippi River became the West's water highways for getting farm goods to markets.

C. Indians Defend Their Lands

Fallen Timbers As more and more pioneers pushed westward into Indian lands, the Indians tried to drive them back. Indian warriors attacked the settlers in their forest cabins. They fired arrows at the settlers' flatboats on the Ohio River. In turn, settlers and the United States Army attacked the Indians. The warfare was bloody and cruel.

In the early 1790s, Indian nations united and scored several victories against the United States Army in Ohio. But in 1794 the army crushed the Indians at the battle of Fallen Timbers. As a result the Indians were forced to give up nearly all of Ohio and move farther west, into what is now Indiana. This opened the way for a flood of settlers into Ohio. In 1803, Ohio became a state.

Meanwhile, pioneers began to push westward into the Indiana Territory. The governor of the Indiana Territory was William Henry Harrison. Harrison would later be President of the United States. As gov-

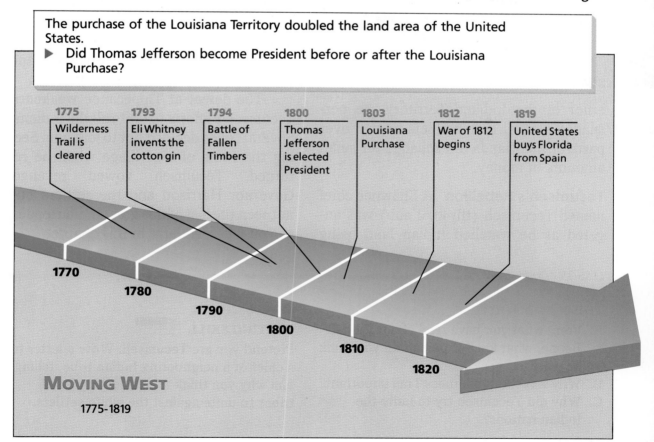

The purchase of the Louisiana Territory doubled the land area of the United States.
▶ Did Thomas Jefferson become President before or after the Louisiana Purchase?

1775	1793	1794	1800	1803	1812	1819
Wilderness Trail is cleared	Eli Whitney invents the cotton gin	Battle of Fallen Timbers	Thomas Jefferson is elected President	Louisiana Purchase	War of 1812 begins	United States buys Florida from Spain

1770
1780
1790
1800
1810
1820

MOVING WEST

1775-1819

The great Shawnee chief Tecumseh was a brave and intelligent enemy of the settlers.
▶ What might have happened if Tecumseh had succeeded in uniting all the Indian nations?

ernor of the Indiana Territory, he persuaded several Indian chiefs to sign over parts of their lands in exchange for small amounts of money.

Tecumseh's Rebellion A Shawnee chief named Tecumseh (tih KUM suh) was angered as he watched Indian land being handed over piece by piece to white settlers. Tecumseh had fought against the loss of Indian lands since he was a boy. He had fought at Fallen Timbers and knew the bitterness of being forced to leave his tribe's lands.

Tecumseh realized that the Indians could not stop the advance of the settlers unless they united. For several years he traveled up and down the frontier, urging the Indian nations to join together. A number did join.

In 1811, however, while Tecumseh was in the South trying to persuade more chiefs to join him, Harrison struck. He led an army to the main Shawnee village, which stood on the shore of Tippecanoe Creek. In the battle of Tippecanoe, Harrison's forces defeated the Shawnee and burned their village to the ground.

The defeat at Tippecanoe weakened Tecumseh's efforts to unite all the Indians. Several tribes decided not to join him. Seeing the ruins of his village when he returned, Tecumseh vowed revenge. Governor Harrison and the settlers had not seen the last of this great Indian leader, as you will read later in this chapter.

LESSON *1* REVIEW

THINK AND WRITE

A. From what you have read about Daniel Boone, what kind of person do you think he was?

B. Why was the Wilderness Trail important?

C. Why did Tecumseh try to unite the Indian nations?

SKILLS CHECK

WRITING SKILL

Pretend you are Tecumseh. Write a letter to a chief of a neighboring Indian tribe, telling him why you think it is necessary for all tribes to unite against the white settlers.

The Country Doubles Its Size

THINK ABOUT WHAT YOU KNOW

Imagine that you are getting ready to lead a long journey to explore unknown territory. What kinds of people would you want to take with you?

STUDY THE VOCABULARY

expedition

FOCUS YOUR READING

How did the region between the Mississippi River and the Rocky Mountains become part of the United States?

A. New Orleans Is an Important Port for the Western Farmers

President Jefferson In 1800, Thomas Jefferson was elected President of the United States. Jefferson and the members of his Democratic-Republican party in Congress soon changed many of the laws the Federalists had made. They got rid of the hated whiskey tax. They cut government spending. They reduced the size of the army and the navy.

President Jefferson's greatest achievement, however, had nothing to do with any of these changes. In fact it came about through an incredible stroke of good luck. Acting quickly, and wisely taking advantage of a lucky situation, President Jefferson doubled the size of the United States.

Importance of New Orleans Up until the mid-1700s, France claimed all the land between the Mississippi River and the Rocky Mountains. France called this area Louisiana. In 1763, France gave Louisiana to Spain. France also gave Spain the most important place in this huge area, the port city of New Orleans, near the mouth of the Mississippi River.

Look at the map on page 332. You can see why the port of New Orleans was vital to farmers who lived in the West. These farmers sent their crops to market down the Mississippi River to New Orleans. At the port in New Orleans the crops were loaded onto oceangoing ships and sent to Europe and the West Indies. American farmers could prosper as long as the country that owned New Orleans let them use the port. But what if they were suddenly not allowed to use it? Many American

Below is a picture of New Orleans' port in 1803.
▶ Find something in the picture that shows you what country owned New Orleans by the time the artist made this picture.

farmers, with no other way to sell their crops, would go broke.

In 1802 it looked like that was exactly what might happen. Spain announced that western farmers could no longer use New Orleans. Even worse, President Jefferson learned that Spain had secretly given back all of Louisiana, including New Orleans, to France. He knew that the French emperor, Napoleon, wanted to build a new empire in the Americas.

B. The United States Purchases the Louisiana Territory

Jefferson decided to try to buy the port city of New Orleans from the French. He sent two representatives to France to make an offer of $10 million for the port.

Here is where the luck came in. At that time France was having a short period of peace in its long war with Great Britain. But the French government knew that war would soon start again. The French needed money for that war. Also, although Jefferson did not know it, Napoleon had given up his ideas about starting a new French empire in North America. Napoleon knew he could not defend Louisiana against the British navy once the war started again.

So when the American representatives offered to pay the French $10 million for New Orleans, they were amazed by France's reply. No, said the French, we are not interested in selling New Orleans by itself. But if you would like to buy all of

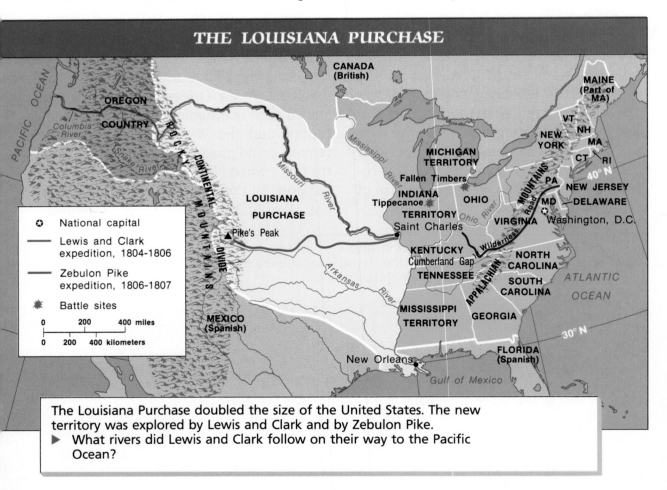

THE LOUISIANA PURCHASE

The Louisiana Purchase doubled the size of the United States. The new territory was explored by Lewis and Clark and by Zebulon Pike.
▶ What rivers did Lewis and Clark follow on their way to the Pacific Ocean?

C. Lewis and Clark Prepare to Explore Louisiana

Just what had the United States bought? What was the land of the Louisiana Territory like? Was it good for farming? What kinds of plants and animals did the land have? Were the Indians in those lands peaceful or warlike? How high were the Rocky Mountains? Was there a way to cross them? Could a way be found to reach the Pacific Coast entirely by water? President Jefferson had a hundred questions like these.

To get the answers, Jefferson asked Meriwether Lewis to lead an **expedition**, or exploring party, into the Louisiana Territory. Lewis was Jefferson's private secretary. Earlier he had served in the army on the frontier. Lewis asked a friend from his army days, William Clark, to lead the expedition with him. Clark, the younger brother of the Revolutionary War general George Rogers Clark, was an experienced Indian fighter.

During the winter and early spring of 1804, Lewis and Clark made preparations for their great journey of discovery. Fifty men were hired, many who knew Indian languages. Lewis and Clark gathered large amounts of ammunition, clothing, tools, and medical supplies. They also collected food and supplies such as several tons of salt pork, flour, cornmeal, and salt. However, the explorers knew they would have to hunt for most of their food.

Lewis and Clark also bought goods to trade and to give the Indians as gifts. These included 2,800 fish hooks, over 4,600 needles, and large quantities of beads, silk ribbons, looking glasses, and whiskey. All these goods were loaded onto one large boat and two small ones on the Missouri River near the town of St. Louis.

An American flag is raised over New Orleans to mark the transfer of Louisiana to our nation.
▶ In what year did this happen?

Louisiana, including New Orleans, for $15 million, perhaps we can make a deal.

The Americans quickly accepted the offer, and in 1803 the United States bought the large piece of land. This land was called the Louisiana Purchase. The whole territory cost the United States a few pennies an acre. It was the biggest bargain in American history.

D. Lewis and Clark Set Out

On a clear morning in May 1804, the explorers climbed into their boats and began their journey. Up the Missouri River they paddled, some days traveling 15 miles and others, only 3 or 4 miles. By autumn the group reached what is now North Dakota. There they stopped and spent the winter in a Mandan Indian village.

That winter, Lewis and Clark hired a French fur trapper who knew several Indian languages. The trapper had a 16-year-old Indian wife named Sacajawea (sak uh-juh WEE uh). She was originally from the Shoshone tribe, which lived in what is now Montana. Sacajawea had been kidnapped by other Indians when she was 11 years old. Her husband begged Lewis and Clark to let Sacajawea and their newborn baby come along.

At first Lewis and Clark said no. They did not want to worry about a young mother and her infant. But the Mandan Indians told them they would need horses to cross the Rocky Mountains. Lewis and Clark knew that the Shoshones had excellent horses. They hoped that because Sacajawea was a Shoshone, she could talk to the Shoshones and get horses. So Lewis and Clark decided to let her join the group. They would find out later how important Sacajawea was to the expedition.

In the spring of 1805, the group started up the Missouri River once more. This time they traveled in six canoes that they had made during the winter. By June they were near the *source* of the Missouri River, which is in present-day Montana. The source is the starting point of a stream or river. Here the river became a shallow,

THE LEWIS AND CLARK EXPEDITION TO THE PACIFIC OCEAN

May 1804 to October 1804	• The explorers start up the Missouri River. • They meet a hunting party of Sioux Indians. • They arrive at a Mandan Indian village.	**William Clark** **1770 - 1838**
November 1804 to March 1805	• They build Fort Mandan and spend the winter with the Mandan Indians.	
April 1805 to August 1805	• They continue up the Missouri River and find its source. • They travel across the Great Plains into the Rocky Mountains. • They meet some Shoshoni Indians and buy horses from them.	
September 1805	• They cross the Rocky Mountains on horseback and then ride down to the Columbia River.	
October 1805 to November 1805	• They travel down the Columbia River to the Pacific Ocean.	
December 1805 to March 1806	• They build a fort near the Pacific Ocean and spend the winter there.	**Meriwether Lewis** **1774 - 1809**
March 1806 to September 1806	• They leave the fort and travel back to St. Louis.	

Meriwether Lewis and William Clark led an expedition to explore the Louisiana Purchase.

► Which did Lewis and Clark do first - travel down the Columbia River or find the source of the Missouri River?

rocky, and swift-flowing stream. The group could go no further by boat. They would need horses if their expedition was to succeed. But where could they get horses, and how?

One day the group saw some Indians approaching them. As the Indians drew near, Sacajawea's eyes widened in joy and disbelief. The Indians were Shoshone, her own people, and the chief of the group was her own brother! After a tearful reunion Sacajawea arranged for the horses the explorers needed. The group was ready to move on into the Rocky Mountains.

E. The Expedition Succeeds

By early autumn Lewis and Clark had led the party to the Continental Divide, the ridge from which rivers flow to the east on one side and to the west on the other. They still had to cross dangerous rocky trails. In October the explorers lowered their canoes into the waters of the Snake River. They followed the Snake River into the Columbia River. Finally, on November 7, 1805, William Clark wrote these words in his journal: *"Ocean in view! O! the joy . . ."* The Lewis and Clark expedition had reached the Pacific Ocean.

The following spring Lewis and Clark started back to the nation's capital with

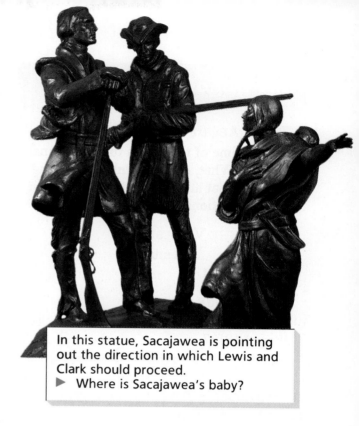

In this statue, Sacajawea is pointing out the direction in which Lewis and Clark should proceed.
▶ Where is Sacajawea's baby?

answers to many of President Jefferson's questions. They had traveled a total of 7,000 miles (11,263 km) in 28 months. For the first time, people had crossed the continent from one side to the other.

In 1806, the same year that Lewis and Clark returned home, an army officer named Zebulon Pike explored another part of the Louisiana Territory. Lieutenant Pike followed the Arkansas River to the Rocky Mountains, where he discovered Pikes Peak, in present-day Colorado.

LESSON 2 REVIEW

THINK AND WRITE

A. Why was New Orleans important to western farmers?

B. What events made it possible for Jefferson to buy Louisiana from France?

C. How did Lewis and Clark prepare for exploring the Louisiana Territory?

D. Why did the decision to let Sacajawea join the expedition turn out to be wise?

E. What were the achievements of the Lewis and Clark expedition?

SKILLS CHECK

MAP SKILL

Look at the map on page 332 and the Atlas map of the United States on page 620. Through which modern-day states did Lewis and Clark travel?

335

The War of 1812

THINK ABOUT WHAT YOU KNOW
Recall some of the words to the national anthem. What, do you think, is the song about? What are your feelings when you hear the national anthem?

STUDY THE VOCABULARY
neutral   **embargo**
impressment

FOCUS YOUR READING
What were the causes and results of the War of 1812?

A. America's Anger Rises over Britain's Actions

War in Europe In 1803, the same year of the Louisiana Purchase, France and Great Britain went to war again. The United States was **neutral**, that is, it did not take sides in the war. At first this paid off. For several years, American merchants enjoyed a growing trade with both Great Britain and France.

Soon, however, each warring country decided to keep the other from trading with neutral countries. Problems began when France said it would seize any ship that traded directly with Great Britain. Then Great Britain announced that it would seize any ship that traded with France. Before long the British and the French navies were taking turns capturing American ships.

As Great Britain had the larger navy, it seized the most ships. That was not all that Great Britain did. Because conditions in the British navy were terrible, many of its sailors deserted, or ran away. Thus the British navy was always short of sailors. Many of the British deserters took jobs on American merchant ships. So the British navy began stopping American ships to search for these deserters. Sometimes by accident and sometimes on purpose, the British carried off American as well as British sailors and forced them to serve in the British navy. This practice was called **impressment**.

Anger with Britain The impressment of seamen outraged Americans. Many demanded that their government do

The battle for Lake Erie between American and British navies is shown in progress here. The victory of the American forces under Oliver Hazard Perry was an important turning point in the War of 1812.
▶ Which ship, do you think, is Commodore Perry's?

something to stop these seizures, even if it meant war. But President Jefferson opposed war. Instead he asked Congress for an **embargo**, or a law to end all foreign trade until the warring countries stopped their illegal actions against American ships and sailors. Jefferson believed that Great Britain and France needed American trade so badly that they would agree to leave American ships and sailors alone.

Instead of solving the problem, the embargo hurt Americans more than it hurt Great Britain and France. Merchants could not sell their goods to other countries. Farmers could not sell their crops. Shipbuilders lost business, and sailors lost their jobs. After one year, Congress repealed the law. The British and French

continued seizing American ships, and the British impressed more American sailors.

Anger against Great Britain kept growing. Even conflicts with the Indians made Americans want to take action against the British. In the Northwest, Tecumseh kept his vow of revenge. Indians attacked settlements, killing some settlers and driving out others. Many Americans believed that the British in Canada were supplying Tecumseh with guns. They said the only way to stop these Indian attacks was to drive the British out of Canada.

B. War Breaks Out

In Congress, representatives from the western states wanted a war against Great Britain. These representatives became known as the War Hawks. In June 1812 the War Hawks had their way. President James Madison asked Congress to declare war on Great Britain.

Even though many Americans had demanded war, the country was not prepared for it. The United States Navy had only 16 ships, compared to 600 ships for Great Britain. The American army had fewer than 7,000 soldiers. America had had more troops at the beginning of the Revolutionary War.

In the early part of the War of 1812, most of the fighting took place in the West. There, things did not go well for the Americans. That autumn, United States troops tried to invade Canada. Not only were they driven back but they were also forced to surrender some American land.

The first American victory came on the water rather than on land. Commodore Oliver Perry was the commander of a small fleet of ships on Lake Erie. Perry was only 28 years old, but he had served in the navy since he was 14. In September 1813,

Perry's fleet defeated a British naval force on Lake Erie, forcing it to surrender. Perry then sent this message to General William Henry Harrison: "We have met the enemy and they are ours."

After this naval victory, General Harrison's troops were able to drive the British and their Indian allies from the American territory they had taken. In the fighting the great Indian leader Tecumseh was killed.

C. The British Attack Washington and Baltimore

Attacking Washington In the spring of 1814, Great Britain defeated its main enemy, France. Now the British could move some of the troops that had been fighting in Europe to the United States. In August 1814 a British fleet sailed into the Chesapeake Bay with several thousand troops.

As the British advanced to Washington, D.C., residents fled to the countryside. But Dolley Madison, the wife of the President, coolly remained at the White House, rescuing important government records. Guards gathered up a fine portrait of George Washington, saving it from destruction. Then the group fled, only hours before the redcoats arrived.

British soldiers who burst into the empty mansion found a dinner that had been prepared for the Madisons. British officers enjoyed the fine food, Then the troops went through the place, destroying everything in their path. The redcoats set fire to the White House, the Capitol, and many other government buildings. The next day a tornado hit Washington, adding to the damage. Luckily a heavy rainstorm put out most of the fires.

The Star-Spangled Banner From Washington the British troops marched north

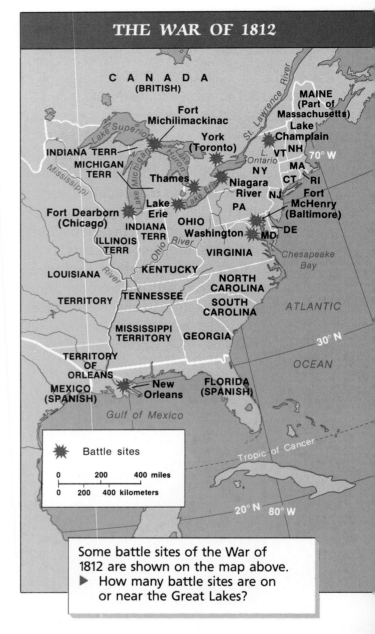

THE WAR OF 1812

Some battle sites of the War of 1812 are shown on the map above.
▶ How many battle sites are on or near the Great Lakes?

to attack the nearby city of Baltimore, Maryland. This time they were stopped by American troops. But the British fleet waiting offshore bombarded Fort McHenry, at the entrance to Baltimore's harbor. All day and into the night, the British ships fired on the fort.

Watching this attack from the deck of a British ship was an American named Francis Scott Key. A lawyer, Key had gone on board the ship to ask for the release of an American prisoner. All night long, as he heard the guns roaring, Key wondered whether the Americans at Fort McHenry could hold out.

The next morning, "by the dawn's early light," Key got his answer. There was the American flag, still flying over the fort. Francis Scott Key was so moved that he wrote a poem to express his feeling at that moment. Later the poem was put to music. You know the song and the words very well. In 1931 it became America's national anthem, "The Star-Spangled Banner."

D. The War Ends Without a Winner

Near the end of 1814, the British tried to capture New Orleans. A British fleet landed 7,500 soldiers near the city. Ready to meet them were General Andrew Jackson and a tough ragtag band of 5,000 militia and frontiersmen.

The British opened fire on January 8, 1815. Time after time the redcoats attacked the American defenses. Each wave of British troops was thrown back. After 10 days the British retreated to their ships. They left behind 2,000 dead and wounded, plus 500 prisoners. The American losses were just 8 dead and 13 wounded.

The battle of New Orleans was the final battle of the War of 1812. In fact the battle actually took place after the war officially ended. News traveled so slowly in those days that neither side knew that representatives of the United States and Great

(Left) Francis Scott Key discovers "by the dawn's early light" that the American flag is still flying over Fort McHenry. (Right) The actual flag is carefully preserved in a national museum in Washington, D.C.
▶ What might Key's feelings have been if he had not seen the flag at dawn?

On his great white horse, Andrew Jackson led his troops to victory over the British at the battle of New Orleans in 1815.
▶ How might Americans have felt about Jackson after the battle of New Orleans?

Britain had signed a peace treaty in Europe two weeks before the battle of New Orleans began.

The War of 1812 did not have a winner and a loser. Each side kept the same territory it had had before the war. But after the early defeats, the smashing victory at New Orleans gave Americans great pride and confidence. The Americans had shown themselves and the world that they could hold their own against a mighty nation like Great Britain.

One important effect of the war, however, was that Great Britain stopped aiding the Indians on the frontier. With Tecumseh dead, Indian resistance was much weaker. The West now truly belonged to the United States, and pioneers moved westward in ever-greater numbers. For a while a state entered the Union every year: Indiana, 1816; Mississippi, 1817; Illinois, 1818; Alabama, 1819; Maine, 1820; Missouri, 1821. In addition the United States bought Florida from Spain in 1819.

LESSON 3 REVIEW

THINK AND WRITE

A. What were the two main disagreements between the United States and Great Britain that led to war?

B. How successful were the United States Army and Navy in the first two years of the war?

C. What military actions took place at Washington and Baltimore in 1814?

D. Why can it be said that the war ended without a winner?

SKILLS CHECK

THINKING SKILL

List events in the lesson, with their dates, in order to make a time line. Include the peace treaty that ended the war. Explain how you know where to place the peace treaty on your time line.

Manufacturing Comes to America

THINK ABOUT WHAT YOU KNOW

How would your life be different without machines?

STUDY THE VOCABULARY

Industrial Revolution

textile

cotton gin

interchangeable parts

FOCUS YOUR READING

How did inventions change the way goods were made during the nation's early years?

A. The Industrial Revolution Begins in Great Britain

Inventions When George Washington became our first President, Americans were still making goods by hand, just as their grandparents had done. People nearly everywhere in the world were making goods at home. To make cotton cloth, for example, they first spun the raw cotton into thread on a spinning wheel. Then a person wove the thread into cloth, a yard or so a day, using a hand loom at home.

In Great Britain, however, important changes were taking place in cloth making. First, several inventors designed machines for spinning cotton into thread. Just one of these machines could do the work of 200 people at spinning wheels. Then machines that wove thread into cloth were invented. A single machine could produce hundreds of yards of cloth a day. Businesspeople began to build factories to house the new machines. And they brought workers together in factories to tend them.

Industry These inventions were the beginning of the **Industrial Revolution**. A revolution, you will remember, is a very

This woman is weaving thread into cloth on a hand loom.
► How did the Industrial Revolution change the way cloth was made?

The Granger Collection, New York

big change that takes place in a short span of time. Throughout history up until then, human or animal muscles supplied the power needed to do almost all work. The Industrial Revolution produced machines that could make large quantities of goods in a short time. Instead of human or animal energy, these machines ran on water power. Later they ran on steam power.

Using these new machines, the British could make cloth, or **textiles**, faster, cheaper, and better than anyone else. British manufacturers sold their textiles all over the world. To keep this advantage for British manufacturers, Parliament passed laws forbidding anyone to sell the new machines. No one was allowed to take plans for making them out of the country, either. A law was even passed preventing people who worked in cotton mills that used the new machines from leaving Great Britain.

B. The United States Gets Its First Factories

Samuel Slater American businesspeople became very interested in England's new machines. Some Americans placed advertisements in English newspapers. They offered a reward to anyone who could build a spinning machine for them.

Samuel Slater took advantage of this offer. At 14 years old, Samuel Slater went to work in a mill that made cloth. He was a bright, hard-working child. Before he was 21 years old, the owners put him in charge of the mill.

Samuel Slater's textile mill in Pawtucket, Rhode Island, was the first successful one in America.
▶ What, do you think, provided the power to run the mill?

A Cloth Label

What can you learn from a label? From this label a person interested in the history of the textile industry could learn that in the nineteenth century cloth that was color fast was being made. This cloth would not lose its color when it was wet. The label also gives the information that patterns were not woven into the cloth made in this factory but printed on it.

Study the label and decide whether each statement below is true (T) or false (F). Put a question mark next to the number of any statements for which you can't find an answer only by studying the label. Write your answers on a separate sheet of paper.

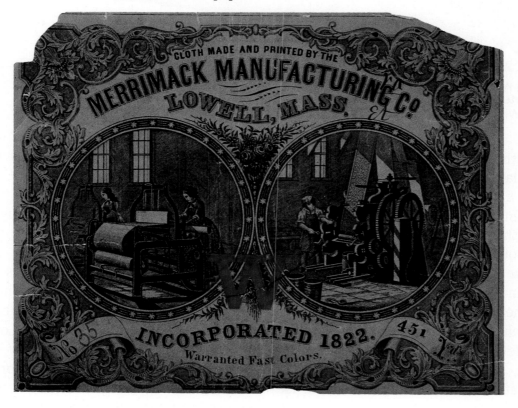

CLOTH MADE AND PRINTED BY THE
MERRIMACK MANUFACTURING Cº.
LOWELL, MASS.
INCORPORATED 1822.
Warranted Fast Colors.

Understanding Source Material

1. The Merrimack Manufacturing Co. was located in Lowell, Mass.
2. The company was founded in 1820.
3. Many people worked in this factory.
4. This factory employed both women and men.
5. The factory was not a healthy place in which to work.

This wooden spinning machine was built by Samuel Slater in 1790 for a Pawtucket, Rhode Island, mill owner named Moses Brown.
▶ Why, do you think, is this machine now in a national museum?

Although he had a good job in England, Slater decided to move to the United States. He knew that factories were just beginning to grow there. Slater could not leave England with any written information about the machines at the mill. But he did have a good memory and was skilled in mathematics. Slater memorized how the machines looked and how they worked. With all this information in his mind, Slater left England for the United States in 1789.

Slater first landed in New York. He eventually was able to get together with Moses Brown, the owner of a textile mill in Rhode Island. Brown supplied the money for Slater to build a cotton spinning machine.

Slater's work took many months to complete. He built the machine from memory and each wooden part had to be made by hand. In 1791 he finished his machine, and the first cotton mill in the United States opened. A few years later, Slater became a part-owner in the company that had hired him.

Lowell, Massachusetts Slater's mill made only cotton thread, not cloth. The next step was taken in 1814 by a wealthy Boston merchant named Francis Lowell. While visiting England, Lowell saw some factories where machines spun cotton into thread, and separate factories where machines wove thread into cloth.

Lowell believed he could do better. He persuaded several wealthy friends to join him in building a factory not far from Boston. In this factory, machines spun the cotton, dyed the thread, and wove it into cloth, all under a single roof. Soon Lowell and his friends built more factories in Lowell, Massachusetts. Others also started small factories along the rivers and streams of New England, using rushing water to power the new machines.

With these factories the first small beginnings of the Industrial Revolution took shape in America. As you will read later in this book, the Industrial Revolution would grow and spread in the coming years.

C. A New Invention Brings Change to the South

One result of the Industrial Revolution was to increase demand for cotton, which machines could make into cloth. Southern planters had been growing cotton since the mid-1700s. But the kind of cotton that grows best in the southern part of the United States is filled with green sticky seeds. These seeds had to be removed before the cotton could be used. It took a worker a whole day just to clean one pound of cotton. That made the South's cotton expensive. Because planters could not sell much of it at high prices, they grew small amounts.

All of that changed after 1793 as a result of another invention. Just two years after Samuel Slater built his mill, a young New Englander named Eli Whitney visited a Georgia plantation. The owner of the plantation learned that Eli liked to tinker with machines and solve problems. Showing him some cotton, she suggested that Eli try to invent a machine to remove the seeds. Eli did exactly that—in just ten

These spinning machines produced the thread that was later woven into lengths of cotton cloth. The machines were operated by men, women, and often young children.
▶ How can you tell that children worked in this factory?

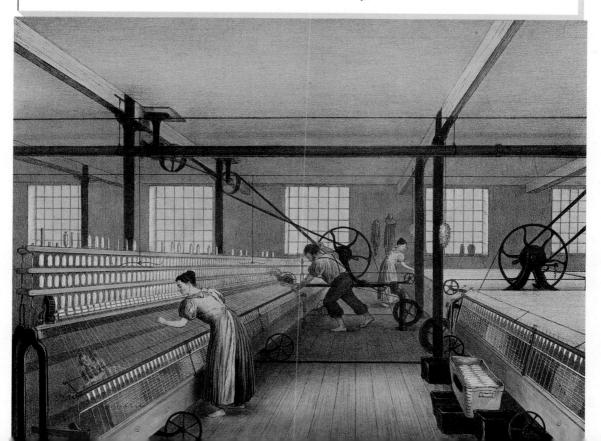

days! He called his little machine a cotton engine, or **cotton gin**. In a short time, Whitney built a larger cotton gin that cleaned 50 pounds of cotton a day.

Now southern cotton could be sold cheaply. As southerners learned how much money they could make by selling cotton to factories in the North and in Great Britain, they raised more and more of this crop. Many southerners moved west into the rich cotton-growing land in the Mississippi and Alabama territories. Cotton became the South's biggest crop. By 1820 the South was growing 100 times more cotton than it had raised before Eli Whitney invented the cotton gin. And, needing more and more workers, southern planters depended more than ever on the system of slavery.

D. Interchangeable Parts Are Introduced

Many people would be content to come up with just one really brilliant idea in a lifetime. Eli Whitney came up with two. His first one changed farming in the South and made possible a great American textile industry. His second invention changed the way goods were manufactured and led to the spread of the factory system in the North.

In the 1790s the United States government wanted to buy a large quantity of guns quickly. In those days, guns were made by craftsmen called gunsmiths. These skilled workers made one gun at a time, part by part. It took a long time to make each gun, with no two guns alike. If a

---

This diagram shows how the cotton gin worked. Hooks on the cylinder removed the seeds from the cotton.
▶ Did the cotton go through the brushes before or after the seeds were removed?

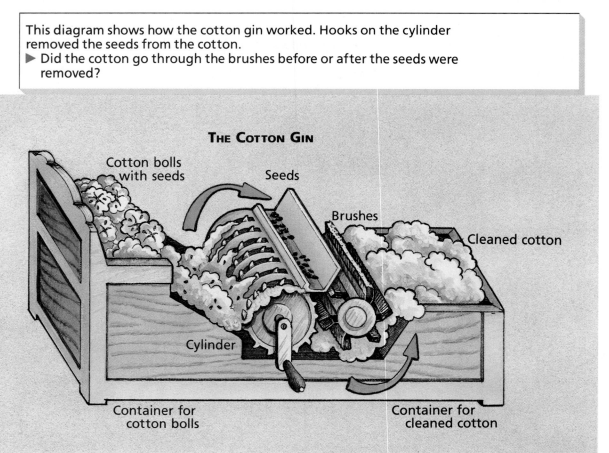

THE COTTON GIN

Cotton bolls with seeds

Seeds

Brushes

Cleaned cotton

Cylinder

Container for cotton bolls

Container for cleaned cotton

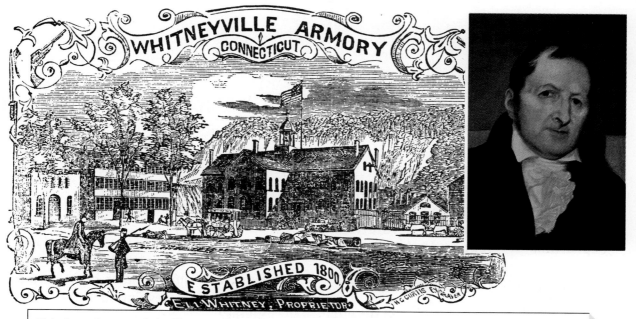

This is a picture of the factory Eli Whitney built in Connecticut. It produced guns with interchangeable parts for the United States government.
▶ How might this factory have affected the lives of people nearby?

part of a gun broke, a new part had to be handmade to fit that particular gun.

Whitney's idea was to build machines that would each make just one part of a gun and then make thousands of these parts—all exactly alike. Each trigger would be the same as every other trigger, and each gun barrel the same as every other gun barrel. An unskilled worker could then assemble the machine-made parts into a gun in far less time, and at much less cost, than it took a gunsmith to make a gun from start to finish. And, if a

part of a gun broke, it could easily be replaced with an identical part. Whitney's idea of assembly is known as the principle of **interchangeable parts.**

This time it took Eli Whitney two years to solve the problem. But in 1798 the United States government gave Whitney a contract to make 10,000 guns. He built a factory in Connecticut to do this work. Later, makers of other machines adopted Whitney's idea of interchangeable parts. In fact all modern factory production is based on Whitney's principle.

LESSON 4 REVIEW

THINK AND WRITE

A. Explain the term *Industrial Revolution*.
B. How did Samuel Slater and Francis Lowell change the way cotton thread and cloth were made in the United States?
C. Why did the invention of the cotton gin lead to a great increase in cotton production in the early 1800s?
D. How did the principle of interchangeable parts change the way many products were made?

SKILLS CHECK

THINKING SKILL

Shoemakers, who once had made shoes from start to finish, worked only on parts of shoes in factories. Do you think they had the same pride in their work as before? Why?

347

USING THE VOCABULARY

pioneer	embargo
flatboat	Industrial Revolution
expedition	textile
neutral	cotton gin
impressment	interchangeable parts

On a separate sheet of paper, write the number of the definition and the word from the list that matches the definition.

1. The forcing of American sailors to serve in the British navy.
2. Identical parts of an item
3. One of the first settlers in an area
4. Producing greater amounts of goods by machine
5. An exploring party
6. A law ending all foreign trade
7. Cloth
8. Not taking sides in a war
9. A machine that removes seed from cotton
10. A kind of raft used by the pioneers

REMEMBERING WHAT YOU READ

On a separate sheet of paper, write your answers in complete sentences.

1. Where did the Warriors' Path lead Daniel Boone and his men?
2. What was Tecumseh's plan to stop the loss of Indian lands to the settlers?
3. Why was New Orleans an important port to western farmers?
4. Why did President Jefferson send Lewis and Clark to explore the Louisiana Purchase Territory?
5. What were two causes of the War of 1812?
6. What were two important results of the War of 1812?
7. In what industry did the Industrial Revolution first take place?
8. How did Samuel Slater contribute to the Industrial Revolution in the United States?
9. What invention changed farming in the South?
10. Upon what idea is modern factory production based?

TYING LANGUAGE ARTS TO SOCIAL STUDIES

The word *pass* has many definitions. Look in a dictionary to find which meaning is used in each of the sentences below. Reword each sentence, using a synonym from the definition instead of the word pass. The first one has been done for you. Write your sentences on a separate sheet of paper.

1. Daniel Boone found a pass through the mountains.
   Daniel Boone found an **opening** through the mountains.
2. Tecumseh saw that the matters had come to a sad pass for the Indians.
3. The hours passed, and Francis Scott Key noticed that the American flag was still flying over the fort.
4. Parliament passed laws forbidding anyone to sell the new machines.
5. Samuel Slater passed the plans for a spinning machine to an American merchant who wanted to build a textile mill.

THINKING CRITICALLY

On a separate sheet of paper, write your answers in complete sentences.

1. Use statements from the text to prove why Daniel Boone is described as "one of those restless people."
2. What might have happened if all the Indian tribes had cooperated with Tecumseh after the battle of Fallen Timbers?
3. How did planning and good luck help make the Lewis and Clark expedition a success?
4. Use adjectives such as *brave*, *intelligent*, *stubborn*, *patriotic*, to describe each of the following people: Daniel Boone, William Henry Harrison, Sacajawea, Samuel Slater, Eli Whitney, and Dolley Madison.
5. Explain why the title of this chapter—"Moving West"—is appropriate.

SUMMARIZING THE CHAPTER

On a separate sheet of paper, draw a graphic organizer like the one shown here. Copy the information from this graphic organizer to the one you have drawn. Under each lesson theme, write three statements that support the main idea.

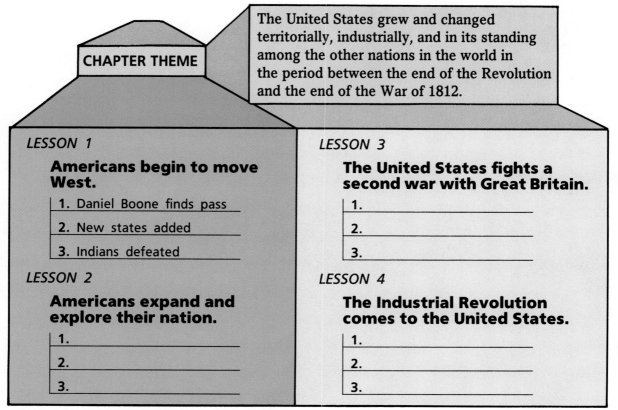

CHAPTER THEME

The United States grew and changed territorially, industrially, and in its standing among the other nations in the world in the period between the end of the Revolution and the end of the War of 1812.

LESSON 1

Americans begin to move West.

1. Daniel Boone finds pass
2. New states added
3. Indians defeated

LESSON 2

Americans expand and explore their nation.

1.
2.
3.

LESSON 3

The United States fights a second war with Great Britain.

1.
2.
3.

LESSON 4

The Industrial Revolution comes to the United States.

1.
2.
3.

15

AGE OF THE COMMON PEOPLE

Andrew Jackson was the first President elected by large numbers of the so-called common people. Many Americans however, were still denied their rights.

The People's President

THINK ABOUT WHAT YOU KNOW

Imagine that your class is going to elect a class president. Only some of the people in the class will be allowed to vote. How, do you think, might the rest of the class feel?

STUDY THE VOCABULARY

**democratic spirit   Trail of Tears
equality**

FOCUS YOUR READING

What group of Americans gained from the spread of democracy, and what groups did not?

A. Andrew Jackson Is Elected President

"I never saw anything like it before," wrote an amazed United States senator. Neither had anyone else. The senator was writing about the crowds in Washington, D.C., on March 4, 1829. Twenty thousand Americans—farmers, frontier people, ordinary people from towns and countryside —had flocked into the city to see Andrew Jackson sworn in as President of the United States.

They had come to celebrate the election of their hero. After Jackson took the oath of office at the Capitol, the crowds followed him to the White House. In they went, walking across the carpeted floors in muddy boots, standing on chairs and furniture to get a good look at their President. Dishes were broken and punch bowls were knocked over as people helped themselves to refreshments. A woman who was there wrote this account.

Ladies fainted, men were seen with bloody noses and such a scene of confusion took place as is impossible to describe—those who got in could not get out by the door again, but had to scramble out the windows.

President Jackson had to escape by a side door and spend his first night as President at a hotel. The crowd finally left the White House when someone got the idea of carrying the tubs of punch out to the lawn and the people followed.

B. More Americans Gain the Right to Vote

A New Spirit The scene at the White House was a result of an important change that had taken place in the United States. As you know, in a democracy the people do govern themselves. In the United States, voters choose representatives who make the rules and laws the people live under. In the earlier years of the country, however, only adult white males who owned property and paid taxes could vote. Now Americans began to feel that more and more people should have the right to vote and take part in government. In the early 1800s a **democratic spirit** had swept across the country. A democratic spirit is a feeling that people are able to, and should have the power to, govern themselves.

This new democratic spirit had deep roots in the West. The settlers who moved to the frontier were used to relying on themselves. They were used to making their own decisions. They expected to make decisions also about who would serve in their governments. At the same time, ordinary people in the older eastern states also were demanding more say in government. So, by the late 1820s, except in a handful of states, all adult white males

351

could vote, whether or not they owned property or paid taxes. This change has been called "the rise of the common man."

Today this change might not seem so great, for it left out many people. Women could not vote. Indians could not vote either. And free blacks could vote in only five states. Still, at that time, giving all white adult males the right to vote was a big step toward democracy. There was more democracy in the United States than in any other country in the world.

Andrew Jackson Along with the growth of democracy came a spirit of **equality**. Americans believed that every person was as good as the next. When voting for President, they wanted a person who had some things in common with themselves. They wanted someone who had started life as a common person and who had made good.

For many Americans, Andrew Jackson was just such a person. Earlier Presidents, such as John Adams and Thomas Jefferson, had all come from wealthy or well-known families. But Andrew Jackson had been born in a log cabin on the South Carolina frontier. Later he moved to Tennessee, before it became a state.

Andrew had made his own way in life. His father died two months before he was born. His mother died when he was 14. Like most people on the frontier, Andrew Jackson did not get much schooling. As an adult, however, he became a lawyer. In those days a person could become a lawyer by studying for a while with someone who was already a lawyer.

Later, at different times, Jackson was a judge, a member of Congress, and a soldier. He also bought land in Tennessee,

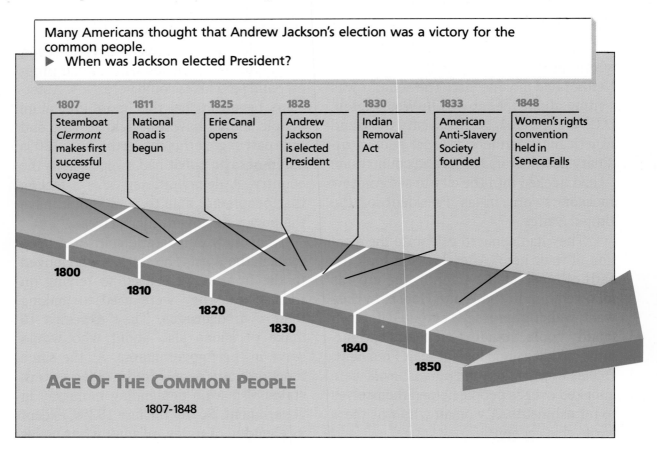

Many Americans thought that Andrew Jackson's election was a victory for the common people.
▶ When was Jackson elected President?

1807 — Steamboat *Clermont* makes first successful voyage

1811 — National Road is begun

1825 — Erie Canal opens

1828 — Andrew Jackson is elected President

1830 — Indian Removal Act

1833 — American Anti-Slavery Society founded

1848 — Women's rights convention held in Seneca Falls

1800 1810 1820 1830 1840 1850

AGE OF THE COMMON PEOPLE
1807-1848

Jackson Forever!
The Hero of Two Wars and of Orleans!
The Man of the People!
HE WHO COULD NOT BARTER NOR BARGAIN FOR THE
PRESIDENCY!

Who, although " *A Military Chieftain*," valued the purity of Elections and of the Electors, **MORE** than the Office of **PRESIDENT** itself! Although the greatest in the gift of his countrymen, and the highest in point of dignity of any in the world,

BECAUSE
It should be derived from the
PEOPLE!

(left) This is part of a poster used by the pro-Jackson party in the 1828 presidential campaign. (right) Andrew Jackson
▶ What fine qualities does the poster claim for Andrew Jackson?

where he raised tobacco and cotton and became well-to-do. You met him earlier at the battle of New Orleans at the end of the War of 1812.

Jackson was the first President from the West. Ordinary Americans felt close enough to him to call him Andy or refer to him by his nickname, Old Hickory. The hickory tree was the hardest and strongest tree in the woods of Tennessee. No one would have dreamed of calling Washington or Jefferson Georgie or Tommy or some other nickname. But the plain people thought Andy Jackson was one of them. They saw his election as a victory for the common man. Those thousands of people who filled Washington, D.C., to celebrate Andrew Jackson's victory were also celebrating their own victory.

C. Native Americans Are Driven from Their Land

Indian Removal As you have just read, some people were left out of the changes that followed President Jackson's victory party. Eastern Indians were among them. By the time Jackson became President, most Indians had been forced to move west of the Mississippi River. However, a number of Indian tribes still held large areas of land in the East. White settlers wanted this land for farming. They demanded that the government force the Indians to leave.

In 1830, the United States Congress responded by passing the Indian Removal Act. Under this law, the federal government forced nearly 100 Indian tribes to leave their lands. The Indians were to move west of the Mississippi River to a territory set aside for them in the present-day state of Oklahoma.

Black Hawk War A few Indian groups resisted, but they could not hold out against the United States Army. In Illinois, in 1832, the Sauk and the Fox Indians fought the government in the Black Hawk War. The Indians were defeated. Many of them were killed, and the rest were forced

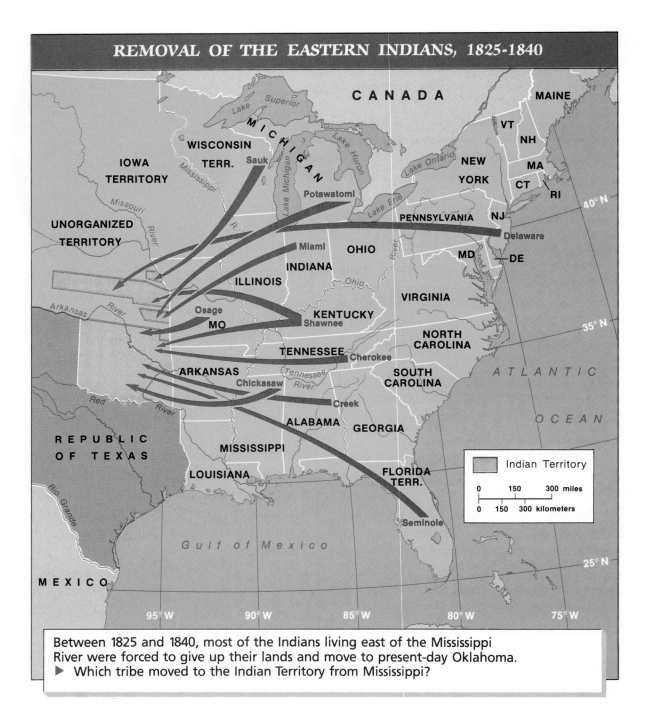

REMOVAL OF THE EASTERN INDIANS, 1825-1840

Indian Territory

| 0 | 150 | 300 miles |
| 0 | 150 | 300 kilometers |

Between 1825 and 1840, most of the Indians living east of the Mississippi River were forced to give up their lands and move to present-day Oklahoma.
▶ Which tribe moved to the Indian Territory from Mississippi?

to move. In the South, the Seminoles (SEM uh nohlz) fought bravely for several years to keep their lands. But they, too, were defeated, and most of them were forced to move to the West. However, several hundred escaped, and Seminoles still live in the state of Florida.

The Cherokee Nation Among the groups of Indians living east of the Mississippi River at that time were the Cherokees (CHER uh keez). About 15,000 Cherokees lived in parts of Georgia, North Carolina, Tennessee, and Alabama. In 1791 the federal government had made a treaty with the Cherokee nation. The United States agreed that the land the Cherokees were living on should be theirs and that they should be an independent nation.

Over the years the Cherokees adopted many of the ways of the farmers and other settlers who had moved near them. They dressed like the settlers, and many of them became Christians. Like their neighbors, the peaceful Cherokees grew corn and vegetables for food, and they raised tobacco and cotton to sell. Some of them even held slaves, just as other southern farmers did. They had a written language, and they put out a weekly newspaper. They built schools for their children. Cherokee leaders even wrote a constitution that was based on the United States Constitution.

None of this was enough to save the Cherokees. White settlers wanted their land, and that was all that mattered. To make matters worse, in 1828, gold was discovered on Cherokee land. Settlers rushed in. One after another, Cherokee families were driven off their land.

The Cherokees reminded the United States government of the 1791 treaty, and they asked the government for help. While some whites said the Cherokees should be allowed to stay on their land, President Jackson did not agree. Instead of supporting the treaty, he sent the army to help

Soldiers, like the one in the picture, escorted the Cherokees along the Trail of Tears.
▶ Why was an army escort necessary?

settlers remove the Cherokees. In the winter of 1838, 15,000 Cherokee Indians gave up their homes and began the long journey that other Indians had earlier been forced to make.

It was a sad and terrible journey. During the next few months, the Cherokees suffered from disease, hunger, and bitter cold. Four thousand of them died before what was left of the tribe reached Indian territory. Indians called this journey the **Trail of Tears**.

LESSON *1* REVIEW

THINK AND WRITE

A. How did Jackson's supporters celebrate his election as President?

B. What change had occurred in the United States by the 1820s that has been called "the rise of the common man"?

C. What was the Indian Removal Act?

SKILLS CHECK

WRITING SKILL

Imagine that you are a Cherokee boy or girl in 1838. Write a story about what happened to you and your family along the Trail of Tears.

A Transportation Revolution

THINK ABOUT WHAT YOU KNOW
List the kinds of transportation you might use to visit a friend who lives far away. Then tell how you might have made the same trip 150 years ago.

STUDY THE VOCABULARY
turnpike   **locomotive**

FOCUS YOUR READING
How did better roads, steamboats, canals, and railroads help Americans in the 1800s?

A. Turnpikes and Roads Improve Transportation

Poor Roads   During the early 1800s the United States was changing. More Americans could vote than before. The size of the country nearly doubled with the Louisiana Purchase. Restless settlers pushed into new areas. As they did, they demanded goods and services like the ones they had in other parts of the country.

The young nation's growth put strains on its transportation system. In the early years, people moving west had simply traveled on paths beaten down by buffalo herds or had followed Indian trails. Pioneers went mainly on foot, leading a horse or mule that carried their supplies. In the whole country there were few roads wide enough for wagons.

New Roads   In the 1790s some people saw a chance to make money by building good roads and charging the people who would use them. Every 10 miles (16 km) or so, road builders placed a pike, or pole, across the road. At each such place, travelers had to pay a toll, or fee, for using the road. Then the pike was turned so that the traveler could pass. These toll roads became known as **turnpikes**.

Turnpikes were a great improvement over earlier roads. However, you would not mistake a turnpike of the 1800s for one of today's wide, smooth highways. Only a few of the early turnpikes were paved with stone or gravel. The rest were just dirt. In heavy rain the dirt turned to mud. Tree stumps stuck up in the middle of many of the turnpikes. Road builders cut the stumps low enough to allow wagons to go over without scraping.

The National Road   Most turnpikes ran between eastern cities, where there were lots of users to pay tolls. No turnpike ran very far west. So in 1811 the United States

The first macadam road in the United States was built in 1823. We would call this kind of road a "black top."
► What is a big difference between how these men worked and how today's road builders work?

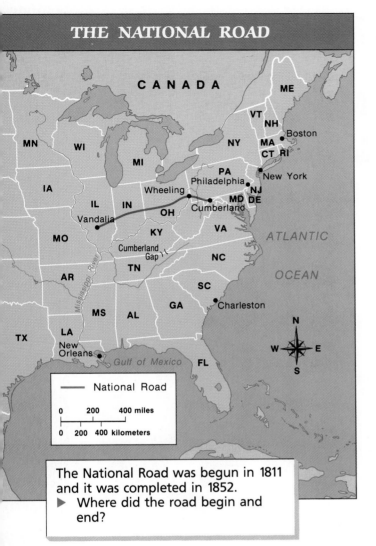

THE NATIONAL ROAD

The National Road was begun in 1811 and it was completed in 1852.
▶ Where did the road begin and end?

In 1852, the National Road was finally completed. It ran from Maryland to Vandalia, Illinois. The National Road soon became the main highway to the west.

B. Steamboats Improve River Transportation

New roads alone could not satisfy America's need for new ways to move things. As you know, western farmers used flatboats to float their crops downstream on the Ohio and Mississippi rivers. But flatboats could not return upstream against the current. After reaching New Orleans, farmers would break up these boats and sell them for lumber. Then they returned north by horseback or on foot.

An important invention that changed river travel came in 1807. An American inventor named Robert Fulton built a boat powered by a steam engine. Fulton named his boat the *Clermont*. But when people saw this odd-looking boat with its two huge paddle wheels on the sides and its smokestack in the middle, they laughed and gave it a different name. They called it Fulton's Folly. In August 1807, the *Clermont* successfully steamed up the Hudson River, against the current, from New York City to Albany — 150 miles (241 km) in only 32 hours. Within a few years, steamboats were regularly carrying people and goods up and down the Hudson River and on the Ohio and Mississippi rivers, too. You can read more about steamboats in the literature selection on page 358.

C. Canals Provide Cheap and Quick Transportation

Geography and Transportation Most of the great rivers in the eastern part of the United States run north and south. Steamboats made it easier to ship goods in those directions. But anyone who wanted to send goods east or west still had to send

government started a road to the West, called the National Road. The National Road was not a turnpike. Travelers could use the road without paying a toll. Look at the map on this page. You can see that the National Road began at Cumberland, Maryland. Then the road ran west across the Appalachian Mountains, toward Vandalia, Illinois.

By 1818, the road reached Wheeling, West Virginia. Each year the government put up money to add a few more miles to it.

FROM:

Life on the Mississippi

By: Mark Twain
Setting: Mississippi River

In the 1840s, Sam Clemens was growing up in Hannibal, Missouri, a town on the Mississippi River. The arrival of the steamboat was an exciting event. All the boys in Hannibal, including young Sam Clemens, dreamed about working on the steamboats. One boy did more than daydream. He left town and returned one day as a striker, an apprentice engineer on a steamboat.

H e would always manage to have a rusty bolt to scrub while his boat tarried [stayed on] at our town, and he would sit on the inside guard [rail] and scrub it, where we all could see him and envy him and loathe him. And whenever his boat was laid up he would come home and swell around the town in his blackest and greasiest clothes, so that nobody could help remembering that he was a steamboatman; and he used all sorts of steamboat technicalities in his talk, as if he were so used to them that he forgot common people could not understand them. . . . If ever a youth was cordially admired and hated by his comrades, this one was.

This creature's career could produce but one result, and it speedily followed. Boy after boy managed to get on the river. Pilot was the grandest position of all. The pilot, even in those days of trivial wages, had a princely salary — from a hundred and fifty to two hundred and fifty dollars a month, and no board to pay. Two months of his wages would pay a preacher's salary for a year. . . .

So, by and by I ran away. I said I would never come home again till I was a pilot and could come in glory. . . .

Sam Clemens did become a pilot. Later, using the name Mark Twain, he went on to write many books.

CANALS IN 1845

After the success of the Erie Canal, canal building spread to other states.
▶ Where were most canals built—in the northern or southern part of the country?

canal all the way across that northern part of New York. A canal is a waterway made by people to cut across land and connect two bodies of water. Clinton's idea was for a canal that would connect Lake Erie and the Hudson River. This would make it possible for farmers in the West to send their corn, wheat, and hogs all the way to New York City by water. The New York legislature agreed with Governor Clinton, and work on the Erie Canal started in 1817.

The Erie Canal The Erie Canal was the greatest construction project of its time. It was to be 363 miles (584 km) long—the longest canal ever built in all human history. In fact, the longest canal in the United States until then was only 27 miles (43 km) long. Remember, in those days there were no chain saws for cutting down trees and no steam shovels for digging dirt. Every bit of earth had to be dug up by workers, one shovelful at a time. No wonder Thomas Jefferson thought it would be another hundred years before such a canal could be built.

However, in 1825, eight years after the first shovelful of earth was dug, the Erie Canal was completed. To celebrate the event, Governor Clinton took two barrels of water from Lake Erie all the way to New York Harbor on a canalboat. There he dumped the fresh water of the Great Lakes into the salt water of the ocean. Meanwhile, New York City held its own celebration with a parade stretching through the city's long streets.

The Erie Canal was a success from the day it opened. The cost of shipping goods fell sharply. A ton of grain had cost $100 to ship by wagon from Buffalo to New York City. It now could be sent on the Erie Canal for just $5. And the goods arrived in less than half the time.

them overland. And as you have read, most roads were poor. An even bigger problem was that the Appalachian Mountains stood in the way. If you look at the physical map of the United States in the Atlas on page 621, you will see there are only a few low places that cut across the Appalachian Mountains.

One of these is in the northern part of New York. Governor DeWitt Clinton of New York proposed that the state build a

Importance of Canals Many more people now went to settle in the West. They knew they could get their crops to market cheaply and quickly. Other states copied New York and built canals connecting east and west. But none was as successful as the Erie Canal.

In good weather, people often rode the canalboats for pleasure. Sitting on the top deck, they enjoyed the scenery as mules on the towpath alongside the canal towed, or pulled, their boats slowly along. Passengers had to stay alert, however, to avoid injury. There were many low bridges across the canal. As the boat approached a bridge, the mule driver called out the warning, "Low bridge, everybody down!" A passenger who didn't duck wound up with some bad bruises and a big headache.

The job of the mule drivers was very boring. To pass the time, they often sang songs they made up. Some of these songs have become famous American folk songs. Here is one of the best known.

I've got a mule, her name is Sal,
Fifteen miles on the Erie Canal,
She's a good old worker and a good old
*   pal,*
Fifteen miles on the Erie Canal
We've hauled some barges in our day,
Filled with lumber, coal, and hay, and we
*   know every inch of the way*
From Albany to Buffalo.
Low bridge, everybody down
Low bridge, for we're coming to a town!
And you'll always know your neighbor,
You'll always know your pal,
If you've ever navigated on the Erie Canal.

This painting shows the Erie Canal locks at Lockport, New York. The locks helped equalize the level of the water, making it possible for boats to go up or down the steep slope of the hill.
► Where in the picture are the locks located?

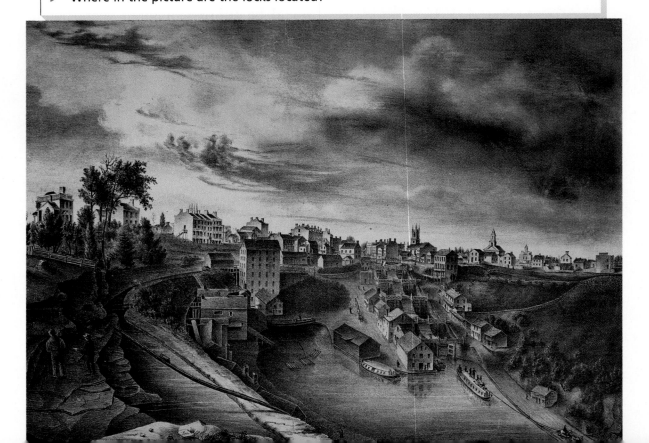

D. Railroads Take Over

Even while some states were building canals, a new form of transportation was making its appearance. This was the railroad. The world's first railroad had been built in England in 1825. Three years later, several citizens of Baltimore, Maryland, built the first railroad in the United States.

This early railroad didn't have much in common with railroads of today. It was only 13 miles (21 km) long. The railroad cars were made of wood, and a team of horses pulled these cars along wooden tracks that were covered by a strip of iron on top. In 1830, a young mechanic named Peter Cooper designed and built a steam engine to pull a train. Cooper called his steam engine, or **locomotive**, the *Tom Thumb*. Pulled by the *Tom Thumb*, the Baltimore train whizzed along the track at a speed of 18 miles (29 km) an hour.

Early railroads were not successful at first. Railroad cars often jumped off the tracks. Steam engines had a nasty habit of blowing up. Also, the smokestacks of the engines spit out sparks that set fires in nearby fields. Sometimes the engine broke down. Then the male passengers had to get out and push the train to the next town.

Despite their problems, railroads had several advantages over canals. A canal

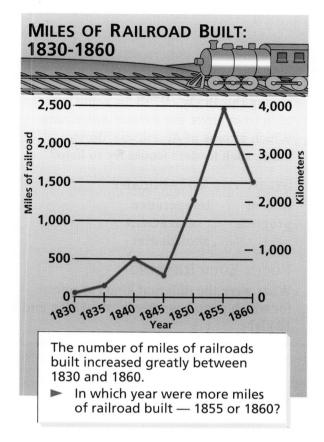

MILES OF RAILROAD BUILT: 1830-1860

The number of miles of railroads built increased greatly between 1830 and 1860.

► In which year were more miles of railroad built — 1855 or 1860?

needed fairly level ground, but a railroad could be built almost anywhere. Trains were much faster than canalboats, which traveled at only about 4 miles (6 km) an hour. Also, many canals froze in winter and could not be used. Soon the United States had more railroads than canals. Railroads became the most important form of transportation in America.

LESSON 2 REVIEW

THINK AND WRITE

A. What were the differences between turnpikes and the National Road?

B. How did steamboats change river travel?

C. How did the Erie Canal help western farmers?

D. What advantages did railroads have over canals?

SKILLS CHECK

MAP SKILL

Using the scale of miles on the map on page 357, find out the approximate length in miles (km) of the National Road.

Reform

THINK ABOUT WHAT YOU KNOW

During the 1830s and 1840s some leaders tried to improve the lives of Americans. Which groups of Americans, do you think, such leaders would try to help?

STUDY THE VOCABULARY

reform   temperance
progress   movement
             abolitionist

FOCUS YOUR READING

What were the different kinds of reform for which people worked in the 1830s and 1840s?

A. Many Americans Become Reformers

As you have read, the age of the common man brought improvements in government as well as in travel. Better means of travel made faraway places easier to get to. Democracy brought people and government closer. The growth of democracy was followed by many other **reforms**. A reform is an improvement, or a change for the better. The 1830s and 1840s were a time of reform. Thousands and thousands of Americans took part in reform movements. They wanted to help the less fortunate. They also wanted to help individuals to improve themselves and become better persons. They believed that if each person became a better person, the whole society would be improved.

Why did so many Americans gain interest in reform at that time? One reason was that they were a confident people. They believed that they could do anything

they set their minds to. They believed in **progress**. *Progress* means "a moving forward toward better ways of doing things and better ways of living." And Americans believed that if they wanted to make things better, they could. Another reason was that Americans were a strongly religious people. Religious beliefs led reformers to want to help people to live better lives.

B. The Temperance Movement Begins

One group of reformers tried to improve the lives of people by getting them to stop drinking alcoholic beverages. In the early 1800s, America had a serious drinking problem. Americans then drank three times as much alcohol as Americans do today. Most of the heavy drinkers were men, but a large number were teenagers. On the frontier, women also drank heavily.

One member of this "Cold Water Army" tries to get a drinker to sign a pledge to stop drinking.
► What does the skeleton mean?

Reformers believed that "Demon Drink" ruined many lives and that it was also a main cause of poverty, crime, and broken homes. This belief led reformers to begin the **temperance movement**. *Temperance* means "the drinking of very little alcohol or none at all." The reformers in the temperance movement tried to persuade drinkers to stop drinking or at least to cut down.

Reformers wrote songs, put on plays, handed out pamphlets, and delivered sermons in churches — all urging people not to drink. They also held large parades in which children carried banners begging grownups to give up drinking for the sake of their families. Reformers called these children's parades the Cold Water Army. They also got drinkers to sign a pledge, or promise, that they would cut down or cut out their drinking. More than a million people took the pledge.

C. Reformers Improve Education and the Care of the Mentally Ill

Education   Other reformers tried to improve education. They urged states to provide free public schools for children. In the early 1800s, few states had public schools. Only the well-to-do could afford to send their children to school.

One leader in the movement for public schools was Horace Mann. He said that democracy and education went together. Mann believed that if democracy were to succeed, all children needed to be educated to become good citizens and wise voters. Reformers also said that education would give people a chance to improve and would help them get better jobs.

Not everyone agreed with Mann and other education reformers. Some people said that if you "give away" education to the children of the poor, they will grow up lazy! Others grumbled that they would have to pay taxes to educate other people's children. But most Americans realized that educating children was good for the whole society. Most northern and western states started free public schools.

Caring for Others   Another remarkable reformer was Dorothea Dix. She led a movement to improve care for mentally ill people. In those days the mentally ill were often kept in jails, even though they had committed no crime. Dorothea Dix visited some of these prisons. She reported that mentally ill people were held "in cages, closets, cellars, stalls, pens! Chained naked, beaten with rods, and lashed [whipped] into obedience!" Dix spent the next 45 years of her life getting states to build hospitals for the mentally ill.

Dorothea Dix was a most highly respected reform leader.
► What kind of person does she look like in this picture?

Other reformers turned their attention to helping people in other ways. For example, a Boston doctor named Samuel Gridley Howe devoted his life to training the deaf and blind.

D. Antislavery Movement Grows

William Lloyd Garrison In the early 1800s many people in both the North and South believed slavery was wrong. In fact, a small number of southern slaveholders decided to free their slaves. However, most slaveholders were not willing to do that. Slavery was very important to the southern economy and to the southern way of life. Without slavery, the plantation owners would have had to find other sources of labor.

In the 1820s a small number of people began to speak out against slavery. They wanted to abolish, or end, slavery. These people were called **abolitionists**. A leading abolitionist was William Lloyd Garrison. Garrison was a deeply religious man. He believed slavery was a great sin in the eyes of God. In 1831, Garrison started a newspaper called *The Liberator* to carry his message. In his newspaper he described the cruelty of slavery. He said that slaveholders were sinful people, as were all others who did not want to end slavery immediately. In issue after issue of *The Liberator,* Garrison urged Americans to take steps to end slavery immediately.

Frederick Douglass Another well-known abolitionist was Frederick Douglass. Douglass had been a slave in Maryland. He escaped to the North when he was a young man. There he became friends with Garrison. Douglass gave talks on slavery, and he wrote a book telling the story of his life as a slave. He also started a newspaper like Garrison's paper in his

Frederick Douglass was an important black leader about 100 years ago. Here he is giving an antislavery speech before a white audience.
▶ Why were his speeches effective?

home city of Rochester, New York. In all these ways, Frederick Douglass helped make northerners aware of the evils of slavery.

At first, abolitionists were a small group. In the whole country, only a few thousand people bought *The Liberator* or heard Douglass's speeches. Abolitionists were not popular. Southerners were angered by William Lloyd Garrison's attacks on their way of life. Many northerners also were not ready to hear the antislavery message. They said the abolitionists were stirring up trouble. Often, angry mobs

There was a great deal of bad feeling toward abolitionists, even in the North, and they were subject to acts of violence. Here an angry mob sets fire to Elijah Lovejoy's printing plant in Illinois.

▶ Why would Lovejoy's printing plant be a target for destruction?

threatened abolitionist speakers and broke up abolitionist meetings. Things got so bad that one mob in the state of Illinois killed an abolitionist printer named Elijah Lovejoy.

The Grimkés In time, however, more people joined the cause. Most were religious people who believed that slavery was sinful. The Anti-Slavery Society, started by Garrison in 1833, grew into the largest such organization. More than half the members of the Anti-Slavery Society were women. Many of its leaders also were women. Among them were two sisters named Sarah and Angelina Grimké.

The Grimké sisters had grown up on a South Carolina plantation. They had lived with slavery, and they hated it. They felt so strongly about slavery that they left the South. In the 1830s they began giving talks against slavery in northern towns and cities. You will read more about the effort to abolish slavery in Chapter 18.

E. Reformers Fight for Women's Rights

Equal Rights Many people were shocked to hear the Grimkés lecture on the evils of slavery. They were not so shocked by what the sisters *said* about slavery. They were shocked by the fact that the sisters were speaking in public *at all*. At that time, women, like children, were supposed to be "seen and not heard." It was said that "a woman's place is in the home." Women were not expected to speak out in public meetings.

This was only one of the many ways in which women lacked equal rights. Women also had little opportunity to go to school beyond the first few grades. Women were not allowed to vote. When a woman married, everything she owned became the property of her husband. In a divorce, the husband usually kept the children.

Although women were important in the antislavery movement, they were expected to take a back seat to men. In 1840, for example, a number of women attended a world antislavery meeting in London, England. They were told they could watch from the balcony but could not take part in the meeting.

Seneca Falls   Among the many women who attended this meeting were two Americans, Lucretia Mott and Elizabeth Cady Stanton. The two women were angered by their treatment. They agreed to devote the rest of their lives to work for women's rights. Mott and Stanton called for a convention on women's rights to meet in Seneca Falls, New York, in 1848.

Several hundred women attended the Seneca Falls convention. The highlight of the convention came when Elizabeth Cady Stanton read aloud a Declaration of Sentiments. This declaration was modeled on the Declaration of Independence. In a firm voice, Stanton said, "We hold these truths to be self-evident: all men *and women* are created equal." The Declaration of Sentiments went on to demand that women be

In 1848 many women attended the women's rights convention in Seneca Falls, New York. Among those who attended this meeting were Lucretia Mott and Elizabeth Cady Stanton.
▶   What was the highlight of the Seneca Falls convention?

given the right to vote and "all the rights . . . which belong to them as citizens of the United States."

Lucy Stone In the years that followed, a brave group of leaders worked to win these rights for all women. In addition to Stanton and Mott, they included Lucy Stone and Susan B. Anthony. Lucy Stone was the best speaker of the group. She traveled all over the country to win support for women's rights. She insisted on these rights in her private life too. When Lucy Stone married Henry Blackwell, they made a contract protecting all her property and other rights in marriage. She also chose to keep her own name instead of becoming known as Mrs. Blackwell. Susan Anthony was the best organizer among these outstanding leaders. She headed a national organization for women and was the leader in the struggle to win the right to vote for women.

These outstanding leaders helped to advance the cause of women's rights during the rest of the 1800s. They had some success. However, it would be many years before women would win many of the rights they demanded.

Susan Anthony, champion of women's rights, was herself arrested and fined for voting in 1872.
▶ Why, do you think, did she refuse to pay her fine?

LESSON **3** *REVIEW*

THINK AND WRITE

A. Why did so many Americans become reformers in the 1830s and 1840s?

B. How did the reformers in the temperance movement try to keep people from drinking?

C. Name one important person in education reform, one in the movement to improve the life of mentally ill people, and one in the attempt to help the blind and deaf.

D. What did abolitionists believe?

E. What were the causes for and effects of the women's rights movement in the 1840s?

SKILLS CHECK

THINKING SKILL

List the reformers mentioned in this lesson. Next to the name of each, write the cause or causes the person supported.

USING THE VOCABULARY

democratic spirit   temperance
turnpike   abolitionist
progress

Choose the phrase that best completes the definition. Write your answers on a separate sheet of paper.

1. A turnpike is
   (a) a weapon.   **(b)** a gate.
   (c) a toll road.   **(d)** a wagon.

2. Abolitionists wanted to abolish
   (a) toll roads.   **(b)** slavery.
   (c) steamboats.   **(d)** railroads.

3. An example of the democratic spirit is
   (a) the Trail of Tears.
   (b) the National Road.
   (c) the election of Andrew Jackson.
   (d) the Erie Canal.

4. The temperance movement wanted people to stop
   (a) owning slaves.
   (b) voting.
   (c) using steamboats.
   (d) drinking alcohol.

5. An example of progress is
   (a) public education.
   (b) the Trail of Tears.
   (c) allowing only property owners to vote.
   (d) the Black Hawk War.

REMEMBERING WHAT YOU READ

On a separate sheet of paper, write your answers in complete sentences.

1. Why was the election of Andrew Jackson important to the common people?
2. Who could vote in most states by the late 1820s?
3. Where did the Indian Removal Act send the Indians?
4. Why is the Cherokee removal called the Trail of Tears?
5. Why was the National Road important?
6. What was the importance of the steamboat to river travel?
7. What other form of travel was based on steam?
8. What two bodies of water did the Erie Canal connect?
9. Why did Horace Mann think public education was important?
10. Who were the people that Dorothea Dix wanted to help?

TYING SCIENCE TO SOCIAL STUDIES

Steam power was very important to the development of transportation in the nineteenth century. Steam engines are a part of our history. Look in science books or encyclopedias to find out how a steam engine works. Make a poster or a model describing the process. Or you may make a report on the history of steam and its uses.

THINKING CRITICALLY

On a separate sheet of paper, write your answers in complete sentences.

1. Why did women feel they did not have equality with men?
2. Why could the removal of the Cherokee nation be considered as even worse than the removal of the other Indian groups?
3. What form of modern transportation might not have developed if bulky goods were still shipped on canals today?
4. In what ways has the temperance movement continued today?
5. Which reformer, do you think, did the most important work? Explain the reasons for your choice.

SUMMARIZING THE CHAPTER

On a large sheet of paper, copy the graphic organizer shown below. Fill in the spaces in the table, using information from the chapter. Some parts of the table have been begun for you.

CHAPTER THEME	As the western territories were settled, many changes began to take place in the nation. Voting rights were extended to more people, transportation improved, and a general reform movement developed.		
	The People's President	Transportation Revolution	Reform
People	Andrew Jackson		
Events		Tom Thumb	
Ideas	Democratic spirit		Public education

16

A GROWING NATION

The years from 1830 to 1850 saw thousands of pioneers pour west in search of new opportunities. It would take 20 years before the borders of the nation stretched from "sea to shining sea."

Texas

THINK ABOUT WHAT YOU KNOW

In this lesson, you will read about how Texas won its independence from Mexico. Remember that in the Revolutionary War, a small American army fought and won against a larger British army. Why, do you think, does an outnumbered or weaker army sometimes win?

STUDY THE VOCABULARY

border   Lone Star
            Republic

FOCUS YOUR READING

What events led to Texas's becoming a state?

A. Sam Houston Wins a Battle

For weeks General Sam Houston had waited for this moment. Time after time he and his small army of Texans had retreated from the larger Mexican army. Sam Houston had been avoiding a battle until his army grew larger and became better trained. He knew that he must be patient and choose the right place to fight and wait for the right time.

At last that time had come. It was 3:30 in the afternoon of April 21, 1836. The Mexican army was camped less than a mile away, near the bank of the San Jacinto (san juh SIHN toh) River. In those days, battles nearly always began in the morning and ended at nightfall. Since it was now afternoon, the Mexican commander, General Antonio López de Santa Anna, believed there would be no fighting until the next day. He allowed his men to put down their guns and rest.

General Sam Houston had only 783 men. The Mexicans outnumbered his army by nearly two to one, but Houston had surprise on his side. At four o'clock he lifted his sword—the signal for his army to move forward. The Texans moved out of the woods that had sheltered them and advanced quickly and silently through a meadow of tall grass. About 200 yards (183 m) from the Mexican camp, they were spotted by Mexican guards. Mexican guns fired. Two Texas cannons quickly answered the fire. The Texan soldiers continued moving forward, while General Sam Houston warned them, "Keep low, men! Hold your fire!"

Sam Houston leads his troops into the battle of San Jacinto.
► On the map on page 67, find a city named for this general.

Twenty yards (18 m) from the edge of the Mexican camp, Houston gave the order: "Kneel! Shoot low! Fire!" The Texans halted and opened fire. Then Houston, riding high on horseback, waved his hat—the signal to advance. The Texans rushed forward, guns firing and knives drawn, shouting, "Remember the Alamo! Remember the Alamo!"

In less than 20 minutes, the battle of San Jacinto was over. Half the Mexican army had been killed, and the rest had been captured. Nine Texans were killed and 23 wounded, including General Sam Houston, who took a bullet in the ankle.

B. Americans Settle in Texas

Rule by Mexico Why were Texans fighting the Mexican army? Why was the Texans' battle cry "Remember the Alamo"? The story begins some years earlier. Spain had ruled Mexico and all the lands of the present-day southwestern United States since the days of Cortes and Coronado in the 1500s. Then, in 1821, Mexico won its independence from Spain and took over all the Spanish lands in North America, including Texas.

At this time, few people lived in Texas. The Mexican government wanted to build up the area by having more people settle there. The government encouraged Mexicans to settle in Texas. Most Mexicans, however, lived far away from Texas and did not want to move. So Mexico gave an American named Stephen Austin a piece of land in Texas to start a colony of American settlers.

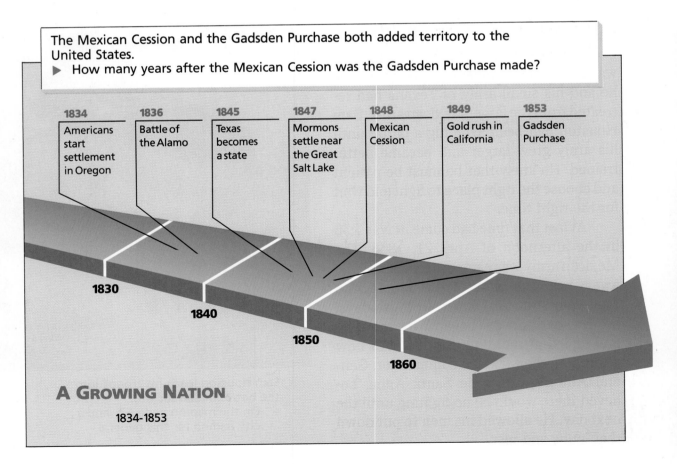

The Mexican Cession and the Gadsden Purchase both added territory to the United States.
▶ How many years after the Mexican Cession was the Gadsden Purchase made?

1834 Americans start settlement in Oregon

1836 Battle of the Alamo

1845 Texas becomes a state

1847 Mormons settle near the Great Salt Lake

1848 Mexican Cession

1849 Gold rush in California

1853 Gadsden Purchase

1830 1840 1850 1860

A GROWING NATION
1834–1853

These German settlers are still wearing their silk city dresses.
▶ Do you think these women knew how to milk cows when they first came to Texas?

American Settlers In the early 1820s, Austin brought 300 settlers to Texas from the United States. Later he brought several hundred more. Other Americans also received land from the Mexican government to start colonies in Texas.

Most of the American settlers were from southern states near Texas. Some raised livestock or started small family farms in Texas. Others brought their slaves and started cotton plantations.

Before long the Mexican government decided it had made a mistake to invite so many Americans into Texas. The settlers were not living up to the promises they had made to the Mexican government. They had promised to adopt the Catholic religion, which was the official religion of Mexico. Nearly all the settlers, however, remained Protestant. The settlers in Texas had also promised to give up slavery, which was not allowed in Mexico. They didn't do that, either.

The new settlers were also supposed to become Mexican citizens and be loyal to the Mexican government. But the new settlers remained Americans instead of becoming Mexicans. They grumbled about Mexican rule and talked about wanting more self-government. Some even said they wanted to be independent from Mexico. In addition, the English-speaking Americans hardly bothered to learn more than a few words of Spanish.

So, in the year 1830 the Mexican government announced that people from the United States would no longer be allowed to settle in Texas. The Mexican government had waited too long to make its decision. There were already 20,000 white Americans in Texas and another 2,000 black slaves. These Americans far outnumbered the 4,000 Spanish-speaking Texans. More Americans continued to come, for it was easy for them to cross the **border** into Texas. A border is a dividing line, or boundary, between two countries or states.

C. Texans Are Defeated at the Alamo

Texas Rebels In the 1830s the Mexican government tried to tighten its rule over Texas. This angered the Texans. In 1835, fighting broke out between Mexican soldiers and Texans in a number of places. Texans talked more and more of independence from Mexico.

General Santa Anna, the ruler of Mexico, decided it was time to put an end to such talk. Early in 1836 he led an army of 4,000 soldiers into Texas to crush the rebellion. You may remember that a rebellion is an armed resistance to the government. Santa Anna's army marched toward the settlement of San Antonio (san un TOH nee oh).

San Antonio was defended by a small group of Texans under the command of 27-year-old William Travis. Travis and his men could have safely retreated from San Antonio. Instead they decided to take shelter behind the thick walls of the Alamo, an abandoned Spanish mission. There they would make their stand. It was a decision that would cost them their lives.

Battle for the Alamo On February 23, 1836, the Mexican army began its attack. Day after day Mexican cannons pounded the Alamo. Travis and his soldiers returned the fire. After 12 days the Texans' ammunition was nearly gone, and the men were exhausted. At four o'clock in the morning on March 6, the thirteenth day of battle, Mexican troops stormed the walls of the Alamo. Twice they were beaten back, with heavy losses. Finally, however, the Mexican soldiers scaled the walls.

The hand-to-hand fighting that followed was furious. The Mexican army lost 1,500 men at the Alamo. All but seven of the defenders of the Alamo were killed. Among them were several famous American pioneers. They included Davy Crockett of Tennessee and Jim Bowie (BOO ee), who invented the bowie knife, a special American hunting knife. The Mexicans spared only the lives of a number of women, children, and servants who were in the Alamo. The battle gave the Texans a rallying cry: "Remember the Alamo!"

This famous painting shows Davy Crockett fighting bravely in the battle for the Alamo.
▶ How is Crockett using his rifle?

D. The Lone Star Republic Becomes a State

Texas Independence Four days before the Alamo fell, Texans had declared their independence from Mexico. They created their own flag with a single large star on it. So the new Republic of Texas came to be called the **Lone Star Republic**.

In 1836 the Texans' chances of defeating General Santa Anna and the Mexican army did not look good. In that year, Texas had only 35,000 people, but Mexico had a population of millions. As was the case at the Alamo, the Mexicans greatly outnumbered the Texans.

Santa Anna chased the small Texan army, forcing it to retreat again and again. It was this situation that brought the Mexican and Texan armies to the bank of the San Jacinto River on that fateful day of April 21, 1836. The future of the Lone Star Republic rested on the shoulders of Sam Houston and his 783 soldiers. As you read at the start of this chapter, they did not fail.

Victory At the end of the battle of San Jacinto, the Texans captured Santa Anna. As the price for his freedom, Santa Anna agreed to withdraw all Mexican troops

The flag of the Texas Lone Star Republic is still loved by Texans.
▶ Why was the single star a good symbol for the Republic of Texas?

from Texas. He also agreed that Texas would be independent.

Texans elected Sam Houston to be the first president of their new country. But Houston and most other Texans really wanted Texas to become a part of the United States. However, Texas allowed slavery, and many people in the United States objected to bringing another slave state into the Union. Not until 1845 did the United States Congress agree that Texas should become a state.

LESSON 1 REVIEW

THINK AND WRITE

A. Why was Sam Houston's small army able to win the battle of San Jacinto?

B. Why did the Mexican government regret its decision to allow Americans to settle in Texas?

C. Why, do you think, did "Remember the Alamo!" become a battle cry for the Texans?

D. What were the results of the battle of San Jacinto?

SKILLS CHECK

WRITING SKILL

Pretend you are an American settler in Texas during the 1830s. Write a letter to relatives still living in the United States telling how you feel about Mexican rule.

Settling the Oregon Country

THINK ABOUT WHAT YOU KNOW

Imagine that you are living in the East in the 1840s. You and your family are planning to settle in the West. List the things you will pack in your wagon. Remember, there are no stores or neighbors near your new home.

STUDY THE VOCABULARY

Oregon Country **Oregon Trail**
Mountain Men

FOCUS YOUR READING

What reasons did people have for going to the Oregon Country in the 1800s?

A. Traders and Mountain Men Go to the Oregon Country

Over the Rockies In the 1830s the United States reached only to the Rocky Mountains. Both Great Britain and the United States claimed the land between the Rockies and the Pacific Coast in the north. But almost no people from either country lived there. Farther south a vast area of North America belonged to Mexico.

Many Americans believed that the Stars and Stripes should fly from the Atlantic Ocean to the Pacific. In the 1830s and 1840s, this desire for land pushed Americans beyond the Rockies into the **Oregon Country**. The Oregon Country lay between the Rocky Mountains and the Pacific Ocean. It stretched from 42° north latitude, which is the northern boundary of California, to just below 55° north latitude, which is the southern boundary of Alaska. The Oregon Country included the present-day states of Oregon, Washington, Idaho,

and parts of Montana and Wyoming as well as a large piece of Canada. Find the Oregon Country on the map on page 377.

Fur Trade It was the beaver and the sea otter that first drew Americans to the Oregon Country. Even before 1800, New England traders were making the long and difficult voyage around Cape Horn at the tip of South America to trade for beaver and sea otter furs with Native Americans living in the Oregon Country. These furs brought a high price in the United States and Europe, where they were used in making hats and coats.

In the early 1800s, trappers and fur traders began to reach the Oregon Country by land. These trappers called themselves **Mountain Men**, because they lived in the Rocky Mountains. Once a year they came out of the mountains to meet a wagon train from St. Louis at an agreed-upon place.

Kit Carson, a Mountain Man at 20, became a famous Indian scout and guide in the Oregon Country.
▶ What are his clothes made of?

There they traded furs for coffee, sugar, gunpowder and bullets, and other supplies. Then back to the mountains they went.

Mountain Men Kit Carson, Jim Bridger, and Jim Beckwourth opened trails to the western side of the Rockies for others to follow. Beckwourth was once a slave and had lived with the Crow Indians for 11 years. He found a pass through the Sierra Nevada to California. Other Mountain Men also opened up trails across the Rockies to the Oregon Country.

B. Settlers in Oregon Country

Missionaries Mountain Men were wanderers, not settlers. Actual American settlement in Oregon began in 1834 when a new group of Americans went west. In that year the Methodist Missionary Society sent Reverend Jason Lee to the Oregon Country to carry Christianity to the Indians. Guided by fur traders and Mountain Men, Reverend Lee reached the Willamette (wih LAM iht) Valley in Oregon. Two years later, Marcus and Narcissa Whitman set up another mission in the Oregon Country near Fort Walla Walla, in present-day Washington. Other missionaries also went to the Oregon Country.

These missionaries did not succeed in converting many Indians to Christianity. However, they sent back glowing reports about Oregon. When they returned to the East to raise money for their missionary work, they gave public talks about the beauty and the mild climate of Oregon. They told about the rich farmland that was there for the taking. They encouraged their listeners to take up a new life in Oregon.

Farmers Soon a trickle of farm families began to flow along the trail to Oregon. Before long the trickle became a steady stream. In 1843 the first large group—

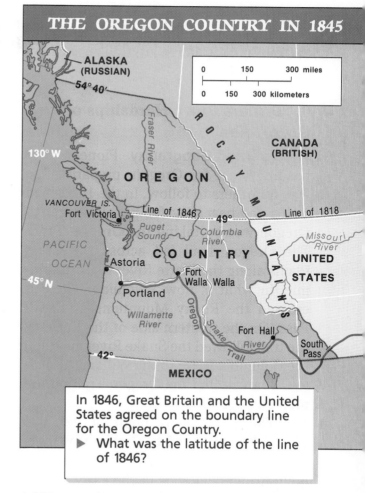

THE OREGON COUNTRY IN 1845

ALASKA (RUSSIAN)
54° 40'
130° W
CANADA (BRITISH)
ROCKY MOUNTAINS
Fraser River
OREGON
VANCOUVER IS.
Fort Victoria
Line of 1846
49°
Line of 1818
Puget Sound
Columbia River
Missouri River
PACIFIC OCEAN
COUNTRY
UNITED STATES
Astoria
Fort Walla Walla
45° N
Portland
Oregon Trail
Willamette River
Snake River
Fort Hall
South Pass
42°
MEXICO

In 1846, Great Britain and the United States agreed on the boundary line for the Oregon Country.
▶ What was the latitude of the line of 1846?

1,000 settlers—gathered at Independence, Missouri, for the long trip westward. Marcus Whitman, who was on his way back to Oregon from the East, served as a guide. In the next few years, thousands more went to Oregon. Americans had caught "Oregon fever." By 1846 there were more than 5,000 Americans living in Oregon.

Compromise Both the United States and Great Britain still claimed the Oregon Country, and for a short time it looked like the two countries might go to war over it. But in 1846 they compromised. The United States and Great Britain agreed to divide the Oregon Country at 49° north latitude. North of that latitude, the land would be-

377

long to Great Britain. South of that latitude, the land would belong to the United States. Find 49° north latitude on the map on page 377.

C. Settlers Brave Hardships on the Oregon Trail

The Trail and Geography Pioneers kept heading west for Oregon, preparing the way for others to follow. In the 1830s and 1840s the best way for people to get to Oregon was by taking the **Oregon Trail**. The Oregon Trail led across the Great Plains along the Platte River to Fort Laramie, in what is now Wyoming. There it crossed the Rocky Mountains at South Pass. On the western side of the Rockies, the trail followed the Snake River and then the Columbia River to the Willamette Valley. You can find the Oregon Trail on the map on page 379.

The "jumping off" point for the 2,000 (3,218 km) mile trip to Oregon was Independence, Missouri. Pioneer families gathered at Independence in the early spring.

They waited until late spring to set out so that there would be grass along the trail for their animals to graze on.

Starting Out When the time came for the wagon train to leave, the families chose leaders and hired a guide. Then they formed their wagons into two columns. In the first column were families that were taking along no livestock, or perhaps only a few animals. Behind them came the second column, which was called the cow column. This was made up of families that were taking a large number of cattle, horses, and oxen. Some wagon trains had as many as 200 wagons. They stretched a mile or more across the plains.

You can imagine the mixed feelings of the pioneers as they set out on the trail that first morning. There was sadness at leaving behind families and friends, but

This western-bound wagon train has stopped for the night. Almost everyone has a job to do.
▶ What work is being done here?

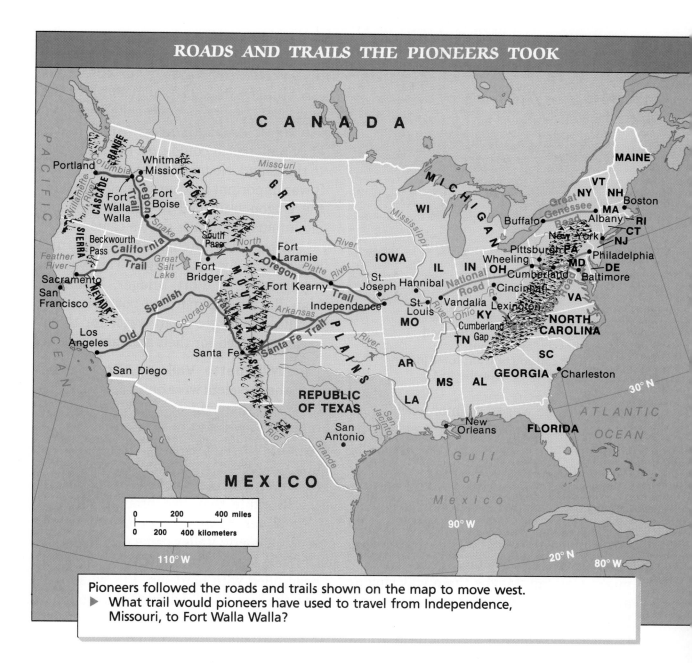

ROADS AND TRAILS THE PIONEERS TOOK

Pioneers followed the roads and trails shown on the map to move west.
▶ What trail would pioneers have used to travel from Independence, Missouri, to Fort Walla Walla?

there was also excitement about the adventure ahead. The first part of the journey took the wagon train across the Great Plains, where the grassland stretched as far as the eye could see. Each day the guide rode ahead to scout out camping places that were near water and to keep a lookout for Indians.

A Day on the Oregon Trail The day began at 4 A.M. for the people on the wagon train. After breakfast the children milked the cows and helped take down the tents. Tents, bedding, pots and pans—all had to be loaded in the wagons. The oxen were hitched up, and by 7 A.M. the wagon train was ready to roll and travel another 15 to 20 miles (24 to 32 km).

Only mothers, small children, and the sick or injured could ride in the wagons. Most of the men rode horseback, acting as

Military units as well as pioneer families found rest, water, and supplies at Fort Bridger.
► How can you tell that some Indians also camped near the fort?

guards for the wagon train or leaving it to hunt game for the evening meal. Older children walked. They had to keep the cattle moving along behind the wagons.

At sunset the drivers would pull the wagons into a circle. The animals were herded inside the circle so that they would not wander off. There was a little time to relax after the evening meal. Children might play tag. Maybe there was singing around the campfire. Bedtime came soon, however, because the next day would begin again at four o'clock in the morning.

Hardships and Problems   This was the least difficult part of the trip, but still things could go badly. Wagon wheels and axles broke. Animals drank bad water and died. The hot summer sun baked the trail, leaving it dry and dusty. Any sudden heavy rainstorm could turn the same trail to thick mud. No matter what the weather, it was important to keep moving along, for the wagon train had to get through the mountains before the snows came.

After going through South Pass, pioneers found a welcome sight. This was the supply post at Fort Bridger. Mountain Man Jim Bridger ran this post. Here the families could get clean water for themselves and feed for their animals.

The Willamette Valley   After a short stop the travelers were on their way again. Now came the hardest part of the trip. The trail on the western side of South Pass was rugged and hilly. The wagon train moved more slowly. In order to lighten the load in their wagons, many families threw away the furniture they had brought for their new homes. Finally the green meadows of the Willamette Valley came into view. The trip had taken 5 to 6 months, and it had been filled with hardship. But when they saw the beautiful land that was to be their new home, most pioneers must have felt it was worth all they had suffered.

LESSON 2 REVIEW

THINK AND WRITE
A. If there had not been Mountain Men, do you think that other people would have moved to the Oregon Country as early as they did?
B. Why, do you think, did so many people catch the "Oregon fever"?
C. What hardships did pioneers suffer along the Oregon Trail?

SKILLS CHECK
MAP SKILL
Look at the map on page 379. Use the scale to measure the shortest route settlers could take between Independence, Missouri, and Santa Fe, New Mexico.

Settlements in Utah and California

THINK ABOUT WHAT YOU KNOW

Imagine that you are the leader of a group of people who are very unpopular in your community. Would you stay in that community, or would you move to another place where your group could live as they wanted to?

STUDY THE VOCABULARY

ranch

FOCUS YOUR READING

Why did Americans settle in Utah and California?

A. Mormons Find a Home in Utah

Brigham Young Among the pioneers who headed west were members of a religious group known as the Mormons. Mormons belonged to the Church of Jesus Christ of Latter-day Saints. The Mormon Church had been started in western New York in 1830. However, many of the Mormons' neighbors disliked their religious teachings and forced them to move. The Mormons moved to Ohio, then to Missouri, and then to Illinois. In each place, trouble developed, and they were chased out. In Illinois a mob killed the founder of the Mormon religion, Joseph Smith.

The new leader, Brigham Young, decided that the Mormons should move someplace far from everyone else. They should find a place where they would be left alone to follow their religious beliefs. In 1846, Young and a group of Mormons left Illinois. Eventually they reached the Oregon Trail. At South Pass they left the trail and headed south. In July 1847 the group reached the top of a range of mountains near the Great Salt Lake, in present-day Utah. At that time this land belonged to the country of Mexico. Gazing at the valley spread out below, Brigham Young said, "This is the place."

Settling in the Desert The place Young chose for the Mormon settlement was a desert next to the Great Salt Lake. Here is how one of the Mormons described it:

These Mormons, like other pioneers, needed great strength and endurance to reach their goal.
▶ What hardships do you see here?

[It is] a broad and barren plain hemmed in by mountains, blistering in the burning rays of the midsummer sun. No waving fields [of grain], no swaying forests . . . but on all sides . . . a waste of sagebrush . . . the paradise of the lizard, the cricket, and the rattlesnake.

Under Brigham Young's leadership the Mormons were able to turn this desert into a paradise for themselves. Working together under the direction of church leaders, they dug irrigation canals between the mountain streams and the desert plains. Soon the Mormons were producing wheat, vegetables, and other crops in the rich desert soil.

Other Mormons began to arrive from the East. Before long the population numbered 15,000. Most of the Mormons lived in the City of the Saints, which later became known as Salt Lake City. Others spread out into the valleys of what later became Utah and Idaho. The Mormons

Franciscan monks lead a procession out of a mission in California.
▶ How can you tell which people in the painting are missionaries?

also prospered by selling supplies to pioneers who were heading west to settle in California.

B. The Spanish Settle California

Missions and Forts The Spanish were the first Europeans to settle in California. They started a settlement in San Diego in 1769. That was only a few years before the start of the American Revolution. This settlement was both a mission and a military fort. Soldiers at the fort protected Spain's claim to the land. In the mission a priest named Father Junípero Serra (hoo NEE peroh SER ah) taught Indians about Christianity. He also showed them how to grow rice, grapes, oranges, and other crops from Europe in the California sunshine.

Over the next 50 years, the Spanish built a string of forts and missions from San Diego to San Francisco. The missions became small trading centers. Soon other Spanish settlers moved into California from Mexico. Many brought cattle and started **ranches.** A ranch is a large farm that raises livestock.

Cowboys from Mexico brought their skills to California ranches.
► What is the cowboy on the left trying to do?

Rule By Mexico As you read earlier, Mexico became independent from Spain in 1821. All of Spain's land in North America, including California, was taken over by Mexico. The Mexican government gave large gifts of land in California to certain important Mexican families. Using this land, these families started more large ranches there.

Meanwhile a number of Americans began to arrive in California in the early 1800s. American merchant ships stopped in California ports to trade with Mexican ranchers. A number of sailors from these ships decided to remain in the pleasant California climate. Also, traders and fur trappers often crossed the Sierra Nevada, and some of them stayed in California.

By the 1840s the population of California looked like this. There were about 250,000 American Indians. There were 10,000 or so *Californios*, or Spanish-speaking people from Spain or Mexico. There were also about 1,000 Americans.

LESSON *3* REVIEW

THINK AND WRITE

A. How did people's reasons for settling in Utah differ from people's reasons for settling in the Oregon Country?

B. Why does California have a strong Spanish heritage?

SKILL CHECK

MAP SKILL

Use the Gazetteer to find the latitude and longitude of the Great Salt Lake, San Diego, and San Francisco. Which place is located the farthest north?

The United States Gains California

THINK ABOUT WHAT YOU KNOW

Have you ever had to give up something that was yours? How did you feel?

STUDY THE VOCABULARY

Bear Flag
  Republic
Mexican
  Cession

Gadsden
  Purchase
forty-niners

FOCUS YOUR READING

How did the United States gain its present-day Southwest?

A. The United States and Mexico Go to War

Conflict With Mexico By the 1840s many Americans were saying that all of Mexico's territory in the present-day southwestern United States should become a part of the United States. President James K. Polk agreed with those Americans. In 1846, President Polk offered to buy California and New Mexico from Mexico. The Mexican government, however, refused to sell this land.

In the end the United States gained both of these territories, and more, as a result of war. The war didn't start over California and New Mexico, however. It started over a quarrel about the border between Texas and Mexico. Mexico said the border was the Nueces (noo AY says) River. The United States said the border was farther south, at the Rio Grande (REE-oh grand). This meant that both the United States and Mexico claimed the land between these two rivers.

War In 1846, President Polk sent United States troops into the territory that both countries claimed. He knew that this move would lead to a fight, and it did. Both Mexican and American soldiers were killed in the clash. President Polk told Congress "American blood has been shed on Ameri-

The last important battle of the war with Mexico took place near the governor's palace, which guarded the western approaches to the Mexican capital. The American victory brought this war to an end.
▶ Do you think that a painting like this is as accurate as a photograph?

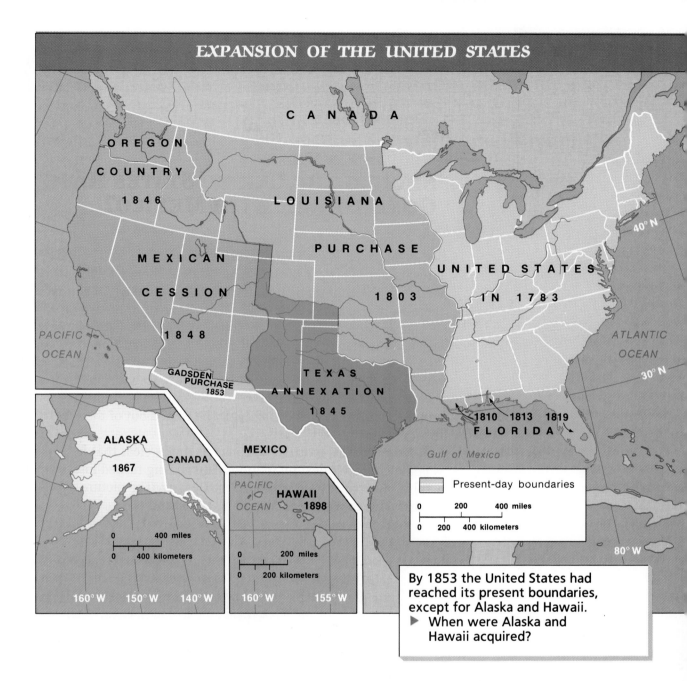

EXPANSION OF THE UNITED STATES

CANADA

OREGON
COUNTRY
1846

LOUISIANA

PURCHASE

MEXICAN

CESSION

1848

UNITED STATES

IN 1783

1803

PACIFIC
OCEAN

GADSDEN
PURCHASE
1853

TEXAS
ANNEXATION
1845

ATLANTIC
OCEAN

40° N

30° N

1810 1813 1819
FLORIDA

ALASKA
1867

CANADA

MEXICO

Gulf of Mexico

PACIFIC
OCEAN

HAWAII
1898

Present-day boundaries

0   200   400 miles

0   200   400 kilometers

80° W

0   400 miles

0   400 kilometers

0   200 miles

0   200 kilometers

160° W   150° W   140° W

160° W   155° W

By 1853 the United States had
reached its present boundaries,
except for Alaska and Hawaii.
▶ When were Alaska and
   Hawaii acquired?

can soil.'' He asked Congress to declare war on Mexico. Congress did so.

The United States armies quickly struck against the Mexicans in three different places. One American army marched from Texas into northern Mexico and defeated a Mexican army there. A second American army marched into New Mexico and captured the capital city of Santa Fe (SAN tuh fay) without a fight.

These troops then moved on to California. When they got there, they found that a handful of Americans in California had already overthrown Mexican rule and set up their own government. They called this government the **Bear Flag Republic**. This name was used because in the center of their flag was sewn a cutout of a brown grizzly bear.

YOU DECIDE:
SHOULD THE UNITED STATES HAVE GONE TO WAR WITH MEXICO?

The Mexican War (1846–1848) was one of the most unpopular wars in the history of the United States. There was strong feeling in the country against it from the beginning. Of course there were also many people who were in favor of the war.

Most people in the United States at that time felt that there was no reason why this country should not spread from the Atlantic Ocean to the Pacific Ocean and from Canada in the north to the Rio Grande in the south. The nation's growth would raise a very important question, however. Would the new territories and the states that would eventually be carved out of them be free or slave?

Nevertheless, most Americans felt it was clear that it was the country's destiny to grow. This feeling turned into a spirit of expansion called Manifest Destiny. The picture on this page expresses that spirit.

American Blood Shed on American Soil

President James Polk believed very strongly in Manifest Destiny. When Mexico refused his offer to buy the Mexican territory, Polk sent General Zachary Taylor south to the Rio Grande. United States troops were now stationed on land that the Mexicans felt was theirs. The Mexican army moved up to the Rio Grande. Eventually there was a small skirmish between two scouting parties.

President Polk asked Congress to declare war, stating that

> "We have tried every effort at reconciliation. Our cup of forbearance [patience] had been exhausted even before the recent information from the frontier. . . . But now, after reiterated [many] menaces, Mexico has passed the boundary of the United States, has invaded our territory and shed American blood upon the American soil. She has proclaimed that hostilities have commenced, and that the two nations are now at war.
>
> As war exists, and, notwithstanding all our efforts to avoid it, exists by the act of Mexico herself, we are called upon by every consideration of duty and patriotism to vindicate [defend] with decision the honor, the rights, and the interests of our country. . . .
>
> In further vindication of our rights and defence of our territory, I invoke the prompt action of Congress to recognize the existence of war. . . . "

A War Without Just or Adequate Cause

When the war bill came before Congress, Representative Joshua Giddings of Ohio voted against it with these words:

> "This war is waged against an unoffending people, without just or adequate cause, for the purpose of conquest; with the design to extend slavery; in violation of the Constitution, against the dictates [ideals] of justice and humanity, the sentiments of the age in which we live, and the precepts [rules] of the religion we profess. I will not bathe my hands in the blood of the people of Mexico, nor will I participate in the guilt of those murders which have been, and which will hereafter be, committed by our army there. For these reasons I shall vote against the bill under consideration, and all others calculated to support this war."

Thinking For Yourself

On a separate sheet of paper, write the answers to the questions below in complete sentences.

1. What was the idea of Manifest Destiny?
2. Why was slavery an issue?
3. Would you have been for or against the war with Mexico? Support your answer with statements from what you have just read.

Sutter's Mill, Valoy Eaton. Copyright The Church of Jesus Christ of Latter-Day Saints. Used by permission.

A third American army invaded Mexico by sea and fought its way to Mexico City. Although Mexican troops defended their capital, the Americans captured the city early in 1847.

Peace In 1848, Mexico and the United States signed a peace treaty ending the Mexican War. The United States received all the land that makes up California, Nevada, and Utah today. It also gained most of what is now the state of Arizona, and parts of Wyoming, New Mexico, and Colorado. In return for this land, the United States paid Mexico $15 million. This area of land is known as the **Mexican Cession**. Find the area of the Mexican Cession on the map on page 385.

In 1853 the United States bought another piece of land from Mexico. This strip of land makes up the southern parts of Arizona and New Mexico today. It is known as the **Gadsden Purchase**. This area is shown on the map on page 385. The Gadsden Purchase gave the United States the final piece of land it has on North America today, except for Alaska which was bought from Russia in 1867.

Miners pan for gold at Sutter's Mill in California.
▶ Why, do you think, did these miners come to Sutter's Mill to look for gold?

B. Gold Is Discovered in California

Sutter's Mill On a January morning in 1848, James Marshall was checking the sawmill he was building near the city of Sacramento, California. Marshall had been hired to build the mill by the owner of the land, a Swiss immigrant named John Sutter. You may recall that immigrants are people who leave their own country to settle in another country.

On this January day, as Marshall looked down at the shallow stream that would supply power for the mill, something shiny caught his eye. Marshall bent down and picked up a piece of yellow metal about the size of a tiny stone. Then he picked up another. He quickly realized that both pieces were pure gold.

Marshall rushed to Sutter's house to tell him the news. The two men agreed to keep their discovery a secret. But keeping a secret about finding gold is like trying to hold a rainbow in a bottle.

"Gold! Gold at Sutter's mill!" Within months these words had spread through California. In the port city of San Francisco, fortune-seekers dropped everything and rushed off to Sutter's land.

Gold Rush By the middle of 1848, the news had reached the eastern part of the United States and Europe. People from all over the United States and even from other countries hurried to California. The great gold rush was on!

There were three ways to get to California from the East in those days. One was to sail around Cape Horn and then north to San Francisco, a trip that took between six and eight months. A second method was to take a short cut across Panama. You sailed to the Atlantic coast of Panama and then crossed the 40 miles

(64 km) of steaming, mosquito-filled jungle by mule to the Pacific coast. From there, you took a ship to California. The third way to reach California was to travel overland by wagon. Each route had its advantages and its dangers. In their rush to get rich, gold seekers used all three routes.

In 1849 more than 80,000 people went to California. They became known as the **forty-niners.** Most of these people went to mine for gold. A few of them struck it rich. But most forty-niners barely managed to make a living by mining.

Other people went to California to sell things that the miners wanted. Merchants became rich by selling picks and shovels for 10 or 20 times what they sold for back east.

A woman from Boston made $11,000 in one year — a fortune in those days — by baking and selling pies to miners. A German immigrant named Levi Strauss made

The lone gold seeker, mounted on a mule and carrying his pick and shovel, was a colorful character.
▶ Why does this man carry a gun?

389

EXPANSION OF THE UNITED STATES: 1790-1853

Territory	Date	Area
United States	1790	888,811 sq mi (2,302,020 sq km)
Louisiana Purchase	1803	827,192 sq mi (2,142,427 sq km)
Florida	1819	72,003 sq mi (186,488 sq km)
Texas	1845	390,144 sq mi (1,010,473 sq km)
Oregon	1846	285,580 sq mi (739,652 sq km)
Mexican Cession	1848	529,017 sq mi (1,370,154 sq km)
Gadsden Purchase	1853	29,640 sq mi (76,768 sq km)

This table shows the areas that were added to the United States in the years between 1790 and 1853.
► Which territory almost doubled the size of the United States?

work pants for miners, who soon called them Levis. In fact, it has been said that more people became rich by "mining" miners than by mining gold!

By 1850 about 100,000 new people had arrived in California. California became a state in the Union in 1850. *The Union* is another way of saying all the states in the United States. The United States had grown from 23 states in 1820 to 31 in 1850. In the same years a vast amount of western land had been added to the country. But, as you will read in Chapter 17, by 1850 many people wondered how the United States could stay united for much longer.

LESSON 4 REVIEW

THINK AND WRITE

A. What was different about the way the United States acquired the Mexican Cession and the way it acquired the Gadsden Purchase?

B. How did the discovery of gold help in the settlement of California?

SKILLS CHECK

THINKING SKILL

Use the table above to make a list of the areas that were added to the United States from 1803 to 1853. Then rank each area according to size. The largest area should be number 1. The smallest area should be number 7.

USING THE VOCABULARY

border	ranch
Lone Star Republic	Bear Flag Republic
Oregon Country	Mexican Cession
Mountain Men	Gadsden Purchase
Oregon Trail	forty-niners

On a separate sheet of paper, complete these sentences, using the words listed above.

1. The _____ between the two states was crossed by many settlers.
2. A cattle _____ is one type of large farm.
3. _____ were fur trappers and traders who helped open many trails to the West.
4. The land added to the United States as a result of the _____ forms the southern parts of Arizona and New Mexico.
5. Because Texans created their flag with a single star on it, the Republic of Texas became known as the _____.
6. Many pioneers used the _____ as they headed west to the Willamette Valley.
7. The Californians who overthrew the Mexican government set up their own government, which was known as the _____.
8. Both Great Britain and the United States claimed the _____.
9. As a result of the war with Mexico, the United States gained the territory called the _____.
10. Very few _____ struck it rich during the California gold rush.

REMEMBERING WHAT YOU READ

On a separate sheet of paper, write your answers in complete sentences.

1. What did Stephen Austin have to do with the settlement of Texas?
2. Why did the relationship between the Mexican government and the American settlers change?
3. What battle did the Texans win to gain their independence from Mexico?
4. Why did Texas not become a part of the United States in 1836?
5. How did the Mountain Men contribute to the westward movement?
6. Why did settlers begin to move to Oregon?
7. Why did the Mormons settle in Utah?
8. What were the signs of Spanish influence in California?
9. What land did the United States gain as a result of the Mexican War?
10. Why did merchants become rich during the California gold rush?

TYING ART TO SOCIAL STUDIES

Create an advertisement encouraging settlers to come to Texas, California, Oregon, or Utah. It can be in the form of a poster, a magazine ad, or a newspaper ad.

THINKING CRITICALLY

On a separate sheet of paper, write your answers in complete sentences.

1. What do you think would have happened if the settlers of Texas had kept all the promises they made to the Mexican government?
2. What characteristics do you think were necessary to be a Mountain Man?
3. What would happen, do you think, if gold were discovered somewhere in the United States today?
4. Suppose you were joining a wagon train heading west on the Oregon Trail. What supplies do you think would be absolutely necessary to take along?
5. Do you think the Southwest would have become part of the United States if we had not gone to war with Mexico? Explain your answer.

SUMMARIZING THE CHAPTER

On a separate sheet of paper, draw a graphic organizer like the one shown here. Copy the information from this graphic organizer to the one you have drawn. Under the main idea for each lesson, write three items that support the main idea. The first one has been done for you.

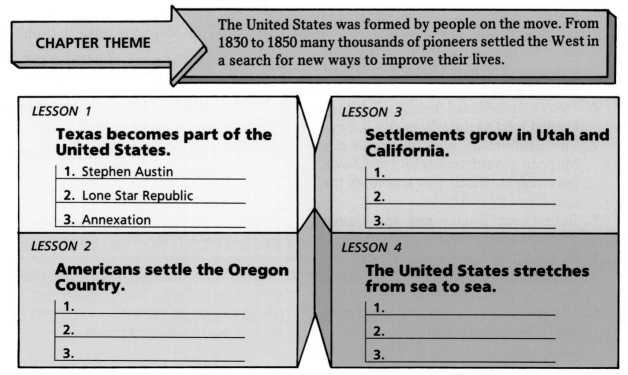

CHAPTER THEME

The United States was formed by people on the move. From 1830 to 1850 many thousands of pioneers settled the West in a search for new ways to improve their lives.

LESSON 1

Texas becomes part of the United States.

1. Stephen Austin
2. Lone Star Republic
3. Annexation

LESSON 2

Americans settle the Oregon Country.

1. _____
2. _____
3. _____

LESSON 3

Settlements grow in Utah and California.

1. _____
2. _____
3. _____

LESSON 4

The United States stretches from sea to sea.

1. _____
2. _____
3. _____

COOPERATIVE LEARNING

As new territories were added to the United States, Americans moved to settle the new lands. They traveled into unknown areas.

PROJECT

How helpful it would have been if the pioneers had had guidebooks. Your teacher will assign one of the territories mentioned in this unit to your group. Imagine that you are part of a family that will be leaving soon to settle in the territory. Discuss with your group what information you would like to see in a guidebook.

It is important that everyone in the group makes suggestions about what should be in the guidebook.

- Listen carefully to the suggestions.

- Choose someone to record the suggestions.

- Everyone should take part in deciding which suggestions will be part of the guidebook.

After the group has decided what kind of information should be included, select the following workers.

- A mapmaker to make and label a map of the territory

- An illustrator to draw pictures
- A book designer to make a cover and to put the book together
- Researchers to find the information, share it with other members, and write neat reports

The researchers can use this unit as well as Chapter 1 and the map on page 395 to find the information they need for the guidebook. They may also want to go to the school library to find more information.

Have a working meeting to submit all the parts and help the book designer to put the guidebook together.

PRESENTATION AND REVIEW

- Exchange guidebooks with another group.
- Ask the other group to read the guidebook as if they were a pioneer family moving into unknown territory.
- Ask the other group to evaluate how useful they would find the guidebook.
- Meet with your group again and discuss how successfully the group completed the project.

REMEMBER TO:
- Give your ideas.
- Listen to others' ideas.
- Plan your work with the group.
- Present your project.
- Discuss how your group worked.

Reading
SKILLBUILDER
Climate Maps

A. WHY DO I NEED THIS SKILL?

Climate is the kind of weather a region has over a period of years. There are several types of climate. We study climate to see how it affects people, plants, and animals. Reading a climate map helps us tell at a glance what type of climate an area has.

Climate	Description
Humid Continental	Cold winters and mild to hot summers
Mediterranean	Cool, wet winters and hot, dry summers
West Coast Marine	Cool winters and warm summers
Humid Subtropical	Mild winters and hot summers
Desert	Hot days, cool nights year-round Little precipitation
Semidesert	Almost desert climate, but with enough precipitation to allow grass to grow
Equatorial	Hot and wet year-round
Mountain	Cold winters and cool summers
Tundra	Cold winters and cool summers
Subarctic	Very cold winters and cool summers

B. LEARNING THE SKILL

The United States has just about every climate there is. The various types are described on the chart on this page.

There is a climate map of the United States on the next page. The various climates are shown in different colors. The map key shows what color represents each climate.

C. PRACTICING THE SKILL

Answer the following questions by referring to the chart and to the climate map. Write your answers on a separate sheet of paper.

1. What is the climate of the New England states?
2. What kind of climate do most of the states in the Midwest have?
3. What type of climate do the states in the Southeast have?
4. Which states have a West Coast marine climate?
5. Which states have a mountain climate?
6. Which state has a tundra climate region?
7. Which state is in an equatorial climate region?
8. Which state is most likely to have the coldest winters?
9. How many states have a Mediterranean climate?
10. What climate regions are in your state?

D. APPLYING THE SKILL

Suppose you lived in Ohio in the 1830s. You are like most American people of that time.

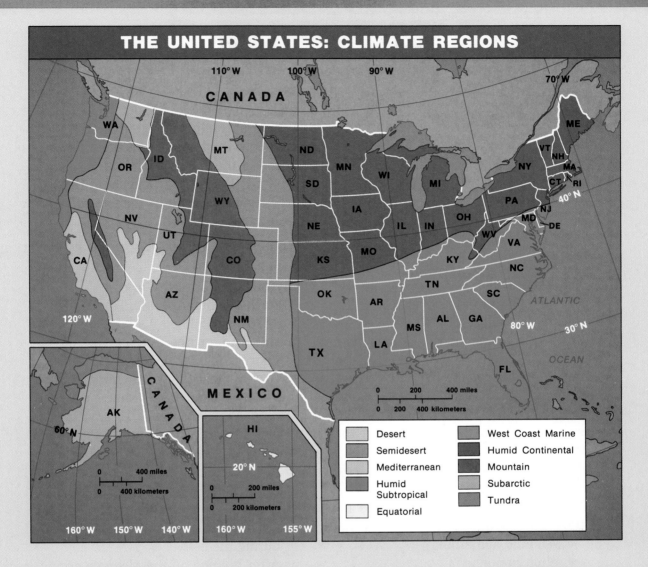

THE UNITED STATES: CLIMATE REGIONS

Legend:
- Desert
- Semidesert
- Mediterranean
- Humid Subtropical
- Equatorial
- West Coast Marine
- Humid Continental
- Mountain
- Subarctic
- Tundra

You have a dream to move westward. You want the United States to reach from the east coast to the west coast.

You decide in early spring to pack up, take your family and move west. You know that it will not be easy to do this. But you really don't have any real idea of what is ahead of you.

Study the map and answer the following questions. Write your answers on a separate sheet of paper.

1. What will the weather be like as you move from Ohio through Indiana, Illinois, and Missouri?

2. It will be late fall when you arrive in Colorado. What will the weather be like in the eastern part of the area? How will the weather change as you move west?

3. If you had the map shown here in your possession and you decided to move southwest from Colorado, what kind of weather difficulties would you have faced? What if you had decided to move northwest from Colorado?

Writing a SKILLBUILDER News Report

A. WHY DO I NEED THIS SKILL?

Newspaper articles tell people what is happening. People learn about events in their community, their state, their country, and countries around the world. Knowing how to write news articles will help you understand them when you read a newspaper.

B. LEARNING THE SKILL

There are five parts to a news article.

Headline — The title of the article.

Byline — The name of the person who wrote the article.

Dateline — The location of the news event and the date it happened.

Lead — A short paragraph of 2 or 3 sentences that tells the main idea of the news article.

Body — Additional paragraphs that give details about the news event.

The lead and body of a news article answer the following questions.

- Who did something?
- What happened?
- When did it happen?
- Where did it happen?
- How or why did it happen?

The writers of news articles try to answer as many of these questions as possible in the lead part of the article. The body includes details that tell more about the information in the lead. Think of an upside-down pyramid to see how the main ideas of a news article come first and the details follow. The details are usually presented in order of importance, with the least important coming at the end of the article.

Study the news article about the battle of the Alamo to see how the five parts of an article can be written.

Headline — AMERICANS DEFEATED AT ALAMO

Byline — By Jose DeCarlo

Dateline — San Antonio, Texas, March 6, 1836

Lead — Americans fighting for independence from Mexico were defeated today in a battle at the Alamo mission. Major William Travis and all but 7 of his soldiers were killed after 13 days of fighting. The Mexican army was led by General Antonio Lopez Santa Anna.

Body — Among those Americans killed were Davy Crockett, of Tennessee, and Jim Bowie, inventor of the bowie knife. Over 1,500 Mexican troops were killed during the battle.

After holding off the Mexican army for 12 days, the outnumbered and exhausted Americans were defeated in hand-to-hand fighting along the walls of the abandoned mission.

Americans in Texas say that in spite of their defeat at the Alamo, they will continue to fight for independence. One American said that their battle cry in the future will be "Remember the Alamo!"

C. PRACTICING THE SKILL

Write a news article reporting the battle of San Jacinto River. (See Chapter 16, pages 371–372.) Prepare to write your article by answering these five questions. Write your answers on a separate sheet of paper.

1. Who fought in the battle?
2. Who led the two opposing armies?
3. When did the battle occur?
4. Where did the battle take place?
5. How did the battle come out?

Now write an actual news article. Remember to include a title, your name in the byline, and a dateline in addition to the lead, and the body.

D. APPLYING THE SKILL

Listen to the news on the radio or on television. Select a news event that you find interesting. Take notes about the event so that you have the who, what, when, where, how or why information. Then write a news article describing the event.

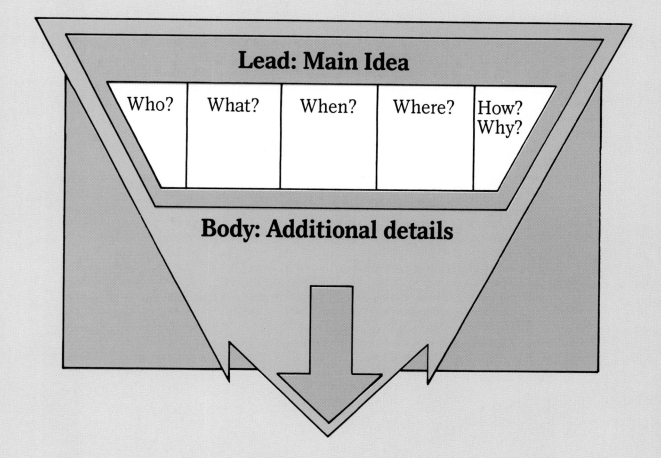

Lead: Main Idea

| Who? | What? | When? | Where? | How? Why? |

Body: Additional details

unit 5

THE NATION DIVIDES AND REUNITES

The United States was split by the Civil War when the North and the South could not settle their differences peaceably.

▶ *The Fifty-fourth Regiment, a unit of African American soldiers, gained fame for their bravery during the Civil War.*

In 1850 most Americans still lived in villages or on farms. Some people were moving to crowded cities or getting jobs in small factories.

Growth and Change

THINK ABOUT WHAT YOU KNOW

What new products can you think of that have changed the way people work or live in your lifetime?

STUDY THE VOCABULARY

invention   **telegraph**
reaper   **famine**

FOCUS YOUR READING

What were some important changes that took place in the United States between the 1790s and 1850?

A. The Face of America Changes

The Growth of Cities   If we could take a picture of America in 1850—if we could stop everything and everybody just as they were—what would we see? How different would the country look from the way it did 60 years earlier, when George Washington was our first President? What would our picture tell us about how Americans lived?

Our picture would show us that the face of America had changed in many ways since the 1790s. For one thing, there were now many more cities. In the 1790s, there were only five places in the whole country that could be called cities. Every other place was either a farm or a village. By 1850, there were nearly 100 cities in the United States.

Most of these cities were in the Northeast, although some cities had also sprung up in the West and the South. What large cities they were! When George Washington arrived in New York City to become the nation's first President, that city had barely 33,000 people. But in 1850, New York's population was more than a half million. Philadelphia was not far behind. When George Washington was President, Pittsburgh, Cincinnati, St. Louis, and Chicago didn't even exist. By 1850 they were fast-growing cities.

Railroads   Our picture of America in 1850 would also show railroads crisscrossing parts of the country. Like the cities, most of the railroads were in the Northeast. Some of the railroads tied cities in the East to those farther west. In just a few more years, it would be possible to travel between New York City and Chicago in only two days. In George Washington's time, remember, not only was there no railroad, there was no Chicago!

In the 1850s, coal brought by railroads provided power for this busy iron factory.
► How might coal transported by rail have helped cities to grow?

Factories The map below shows where cities were located in 1850. In these cities and towns there were thousands of factories. New factories were being added nearly every day. Most factories were in the Northeast, where swiftly flowing rivers provided power to run the machines. There were also a growing number of factories in the West.

These factories were not like the giant factories of today. Most of them employed only 10 or 20 workers. Still, hundreds of thousands of Americans made their living by working in these small factories. Many of the workers were women. This was especially true of textile, or cloth, factories. Many other factory workers were children under 12 years old.

THE UNITED STATES: CITIES IN 1850

By 1850 there were many cities in the United States that had not even existed in 1790.
▶ Where did most Americans live in 1850—in the East or in the West?

B. Americans Are a Restless, Busy People

What about the people? What were Americans of 1850 like? They were a restless people who moved from east to west, looking for good, cheap land to farm. They moved from one frontier to another when they felt that other people were settling too close by. They moved from farm to town and from town to city, seeking new opportunities.

It seemed that Americans were always moving, moving, moving. A visitor from South America guessed that if time were to stop suddenly, two thirds of the American people would be on a road at that very instant. This visitor was exaggerating, but probably not by very much.

Americans of 1850 were also a busy people. Whether on farms or in cities, they always seemed to be working hard to make a living and to improve their lives. They believed in their own futures and in the future of their country.

C. Strive for Improvement

"Yankee Know-how" In addition to being restless and busy, Americans of 1850 also had a knack for finding ways to do things better. Each year Americans came up with **inventions.** An invention is something that is made or produced for the first time. In President Washington's time in America, there were only about 20 inventions a year. In our year of 1850, there were nearly 900 inventions. Ten years later, Americans would produce nearly 4,800 inventions!

Europeans had a phrase for this American talent for invention. They called it "Yankee know-how." In 1850 many British factory owners visited the United

In the 1850s, this New York factory's 500 sewing machines turned out 3,000 to 4,000 skirts a day.
► Explain the words on the wall.

States to learn from the inventive Americans. How different that was from earlier days! Years before it was the Americans who went to Great Britain to learn about new ways of doing things.

New Machines Some American inventions started whole new industries. For example, in 1846, Elias Howe had invented the sewing machine. Until then, someone in your family made your clothes, or else you paid a tailor or a dressmaker to make them. With a sewing machine, however, one worker could produce many suits or dresses that would then be sold in stores. By 1850, you would be going to stores to buy clothes that had been already made up. The "ready-made" clothing industry had been born.

There were also some inventions that brought big changes to farming. In 1832 a

INVENTIONS: 1800-1860

Year	Number of inventions
1800	41
1810	223
1820	155
1830	544
1840	458
1850	883
1860	4,357

This table shows the number of inventions in the years between 1800 and 1860.

► What is the first year shown on the table in which there were more than 500 inventions?

radios or televisions or computers. So the telegraph was an exciting invention.

D. Newcomers Add to America's Population

The Land of Opportunity In 1850 there were many Americans who had not been born in the United States. They had started life in other lands, and then they came to the United States to seek a better life.

Immigrants often wrote letters to family and friends in their native lands. They told how they were now able to make a living in America. "Tell Miriam there is no sending children to bed without supper," wrote one immigrant. Another wrote with surprise, "Nearly all people eat three meals a day." A newcomer from Norway wrote, "It is possible for all to live in comfort and without want."

Some immigrants thought the most important thing about America was the feeling of equality here. One wrote, "This is a free country, and nobody has a great deal of power over another." Another immigrant wrote, "If I went to Sweden now and entered your office, I would have to hold my hat in hand and bow and scrape and [say] 'My lord'; while here in America a worker and a government official are regarded as equals." And a woman wrote, "One cannot see any difference between the shoemaker's wife and the wife of an important gentleman."

young man named Cyrus McCormick invented a machine to reap, or cut, wheat in the fields at harvest time. McCormick's **reaper** was pulled by horses and did the work of many people. By the year 1850, Cyrus McCormick had a large factory in Illinois that made thousands of reapers every year.

Communication Another important invention made during the nineteenth century was the **telegraph**. Samuel F. B. Morse had perfected this machine that sent messages electrically by wire. By 1850, thousands of workers were stringing telegraph wires between cities, and thousands of other workers were sending messages swiftly across America. To understand how important an invention the telegraph was, you have to recall that in 1850 people did not have telephones or

Growing Numbers A steady stream of immigrants like these had been coming to America for many years. By 1850, this stream had become a mighty river of people seeking freedom and a better life. In 1850, more than 300,000 immigrants entered the United States. That is more than the number of people who lived in any American city, except New York, in 1850.

A ship full of Irish immigrants has just arrived at a New York Harbor immigration center.

► Why have these people come here?

These immigrants came from many countries in Europe. The two largest groups at this time were the Irish and the Germans. In Ireland there was a terrible **famine**. A famine is a time when there is not enough food for everyone. Thousands of people starved during the Irish famine. A million Irish fled the famine and came to the United States. Almost all of the Irish immigrants were too poor to buy land.

Most of them settled in whatever city they landed in, and they took whatever jobs they could get.

Many German farmers also came to America to escape hard times. Other Germans came to seek more freedom than they had in their native land. Many Germans moved to the West and settled in Illinois, Missouri, and Wisconsin, where they started farms or businesses.

LESSON 1 REVIEW

THINK AND WRITE

A. What were three major changes that took place in America between the 1790s and 1850?

B. What reasons did the Americans of 1850 have for moving so often?

C. How did inventions help to create new kinds of jobs for people?

D. Why could many immigrants have a better life in America than in their native lands?

SKILLS CHECK

MAP SKILL

Find these cities in the Gazetteer: Chicago, Cincinnati, New York, Philadelphia, Pittsburgh, and St. Louis. List each city and the river or lake near which it is located.

405

Life in the Cities

THINK ABOUT WHAT YOU KNOW
Make a list of things that you like about big cities. Make another list of things that you do not like about big cities.

STUDY THE VOCABULARY
omnibus   division of labor
specialize

FOCUS YOUR READING
What were American cities like in 1850?

A. Getting Around in Cities Is Difficult

If you visited an American city in the year 1850, you would quickly notice how crowded the streets were. Soon after the sun rose, wagons, carriages, horses, and mules jammed the streets. Few cities had sidewalks, so people walked in the street or along the side of it with the rest of the traffic. There were no laws about which side of the street to ride on, so people traveled on both sides of the street in both directions! There were no traffic lights and no police to direct traffic. You can imagine the traffic jam where two busy roads crossed.

In the years before 1850, cities had grown so fast that they could not keep up with the need for new streets. Most city streets were still just unpaved dirt. If you walked on a city street when the weather was very dry, you could count on being covered with dust. If it rained for a few days, the city streets were turned into a sea of mud. Wagons sank in mudholes up to their axles. In many cities and towns, people repeated the tall story about a stranger who was up to his neck in a mud hole on a local street. When a citizen offered to help him, the stranger replied, "No need to worry, I have a horse underneath me."

In a number of American cities of 1850, there was a new way for people to get around. This was the **omnibus**. The omnibus was a boxlike wooden car with 12 seats. It was pulled along the main streets by horses. The omnibus saved you from the dirt and the mud of walking. It didn't save you much time, though, for it could go no faster than the rest of the traffic on the crowded streets.

B. Cities Were Not Healthy Places

Garbage   Another thing you would quickly realize if you visited an American city of 1850 was that the city was not very clean. For one thing, cities had no regular collection of garbage. In the countryside,

people buried their garbage or carried it to the edge of the farm. In cities, however, there was not enough land near a house for burying garbage. People simply threw their garbage out the front door into the street, even though they were not supposed to. In warm weather, the smell of rotting garbage was awful.

Cities did have unofficial, unpaid "garbage collectors." These were bands of pigs that roamed around eating garbage in the streets. In 1850 the regular collection of garbage and trash was still in the future.

Water Another problem facing American cities in 1850 was getting a supply of pure water. A few cities, like Philadelphia and New York, had good water supplies. But if you lived in one of America's other cities, your water was not very pure. Most people

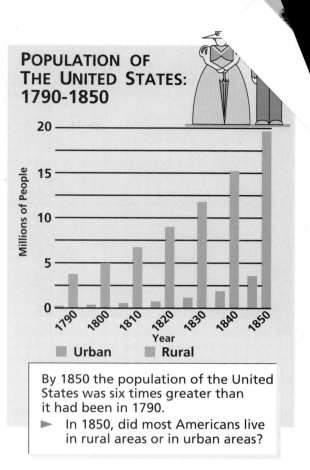

POPULATION OF THE UNITED STATES: 1790-1850

Millions of People / Year

■ Urban   ■ Rural

By 1850 the population of the United States was six times greater than it had been in 1790.

► In 1850, did most Americans live in rural areas or in urban areas?

got their water from a well in their yards. Unfortunately, however, this water was often polluted by *sewage*, or waste matter. That was because cities did not yet have systems to carry away sewage. This waste matter was simply buried in the yard.

Disease As a result of the lack of garbage collection and sewage systems, the cities of 1850 were not healthy places to live. There was always the danger of an epidemic — that is, a disease that spreads through a population rapidly. In 1849, just the year before we took our picture of America, we would see thousands of city people dying in an epidemic of a disease called *cholera*.

Housing Housing was also a big problem in the cities. Americans moving from farms and villages to cities and immigrants

This 1850s traffic jam is taking place in New York City.
► What special problem is making getting around even more difficult than usual?

407

In 1850, this strange parade lets New Yorkers know that a special show has come to town. It will be in a tent and feature clowns and animal acts.
▶ What kind of show do we have that is something like this one in 1850?

coming from other countries crowded into the cities. Cities were growing so fast that they could not keep up with the need for more housing. Immigrants and the poor lived in the worst housing. Sometimes entire families were crowded into attics and basements.

C. Cities Provide Opportunities and Excitement

Still, people continued to move into America's cities. Cities offered work and opportunity. Young men and women from the countryside could find a chance to get ahead through education in the city schools. Immigrants with no money to buy farms could find jobs in the cities.

The opportunity to get ahead wasn't the only reason people were moving to cities. Cities were also exciting places to live. There were things to do and to see for people of every age. Only in cities could one find theaters, restaurants, bookstores, and shops with all kinds of goods. Only in

the cities were there music halls where one could hear a band or orchestra.

Streets were busy even at night, for by 1850 most larger cities had gas street lamps. Cities also were starting to hire and train full-time police forces that worked both day and night. Before this time, cities hired a handful of police who worked only in the daytime.

D. Factories Change the Way People Work

You read earlier about the thousands of small factories that America had by 1850. The growing number of factories and workshops in America's cities changed the way Americans of 1850 worked. Take shoemaking as an example. In earlier days, most families made their own shoes at home, just as they made almost everything else. If you lived in a larger town or a city and could afford to buy shoes, you paid a skilled shoemaker to make them. The shoemaker measured the size and shape of your foot. Then this worker made the shoe from start to finish. Working in this way, a shoemaker could make only two or three pairs of shoes a day.

By 1850, however, most shoes were being made in large factories that employed hundreds of workers. In these factories the work of making shoes was divided into separate steps. Each worker **specialized** in one of these steps instead of making a pair of shoes from start to finish. So one worker cut the leather, another hammered it, still another stitched it, and so on. A system in which each worker specializes in a particular job or a step in a job is called a **division of labor**. Each group of 20 or 30 workers who worked this way could make hundreds of shoes a day.

Specializing greatly lowers the cost of making goods. Because of specialization and division of labor, factory-made shoes were cheap enough for almost everyone to afford. They cost far less than shoes made by the skilled shoemaker. The jobs of these skilled shoemakers began to disappear. Some skilled workers joined in protests against the new methods. But many of them took jobs in the shoe factories, where

they performed just one step in the making of shoes.

In 1850, factories in America made millions of shoes and shipped them to stores all over the country for sale. These shoes had no size numbers, and there were not different shoes for the left and right feet. You had to try on a lot of shoes before finding two that fit.

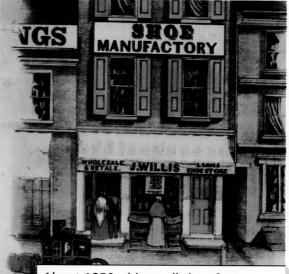

About 1850, this small shoe factory and shop was doing business in Philadelphia.
▶ For whom were these shoes intended?

LESSON *2* REVIEW

THINK AND WRITE

A. What are some ways in which city streets in 1850 were like city streets today and some ways in which they were different?
B. Why was it unhealthy to live in an American city in 1850?
C. Why were cities exciting places to live for many people?
D. How did specialization and division of labor change the way many people worked in 1850?

SKILLS CHECK

THINKING SKILL
Make a chart comparing cities of 1850 and today. To do this, review Lessons 1 and 2 of this chapter. Then fill in information for the following topics: location, traffic, jobs, problems.

Life on Farms and in Villages

THINK ABOUT WHAT YOU KNOW

Have you ever gone on vacation to a place that is very different from where you live? List ways in which people in that place live differently than you do.

STUDY THE VOCABULARY

credit   schedule
barter

FOCUS YOUR READING

What was life like for Americans who lived on farms and in small towns in 1850?

A. Most Americans Live in the Country

Farm Families In 1850 there were more cities in America than there had been in the 1790s. However, if you were like most Americans in 1850, you didn't live in a city. Four out of five Americans still lived on a farm, in a village, or in a small town.

In 1850 there were many differences between living in a city and living on a farm. However, living on a farm in 1850 was not very much different than it had been a hundred years earlier. The main jobs for a pioneer farm family were still the same — to clear the land, plant the crops, and put up a shelter.

A farm family's first shelter was small, even if the family was a large one. Usually the shelter was a one-room cabin. The doorway was just an open space in the side of the cabin with a bearskin hanging over it. The small window openings were covered with paper smeared with animal grease. The greased paper let in some light, but of course no one could see through these windows. The pioneer house had a dirt floor that had been packed down. The house had a few simple pieces of furniture — probably a table and a few chairs or stools that the father had made.

Neighbors In time, the area that a pioneer family lived in became more settled. There were more people around. Even though the nearest house might be a mile away, people began to think of one another as neighbors. When a frontier person said, "Howdy, neighbor!" it meant something special.

Neighbors helped one another in many ways, and they depended on each other. When the time came for a family to build a better log cabin, neighbors helped.

The hard work on this Vermont farm was often made pleasant by the help and company of friends and neighbors.
▶ What work are these farmers doing?

BUILDING A LOG CABIN

Raising a log

Chinking between logs

Notching a log

Framing the fireplace

Making shingles for the roof

Splitting a log

Pioneers in the back country worked together to build their log cabin homes.
▶ Why were the logs notched?

They helped chop down trees and saw them into logs. Working together, neighbors could put up a cabin in a single day.

However, neighbors did not get together often, and farm life was very lonely for all the members of the family. When you finished your daily tasks, you didn't go to a neighbor's house to play, because even the closest neighbor was too far away. You played with your own brothers and sisters.

Going to School Children of pioneer families did not spend much time in school. Frontier schools were open for only two or three months in the winter. The rest of the year children were needed at home to help their family with the work around the farm.

In the one-room frontier school, children of all ages sat on hard benches and learned how to read, write, and spell. Usually the teacher had the only book in the class. Each student had a notebook for copying important rules and information. Writing was done with a quill pen, which was made by sharpening the end of a long feather from a wild turkey or goose.

Teachers would read a lesson aloud to the students. The students would then recite the lesson back to the teacher. It was this method that gave the schools the name "blab schools." Everyone blabbed, or all said their lessons out loud, at the same time. Many Americans learned in blab schools. One of them was Abraham Lincoln, who later became President of the United States.

As for things to play with, pioneer children usually did not have store-bought toys. They "made do." If you wanted a jump rope, you made one by tying together grape vines. You made your own ball, too. You started with a small stone, wrapped yarn around it, and covered it with deerskin. Then you stitched the deerskin together tightly, and you had a ball. Look on page 413 to see some old and new toys.

B. Americans on Farms and in Villages Shop for Goods

General Stores If you lived in a village or small town, there were probably no more than a few hundred people living there with you. Many towns had fewer people than there are in your school today. Your family knew everyone in the town, and everyone knew you. A stranger would be noticed very quickly.

One of the most important places in a village or town was the general store. Every town had one or two of these stores. The general store was a meeting place for people who came from miles around. At the general store, people could buy almost everything they needed — farm tools, seed, hardware, cloth, pots and pans, coffee, and the like. Everyone in town shopped at the general store.

Some people paid for their purchases at the store in cash. More of them bought on **credit**. That is, the merchant agreed to let them pay for the goods later. Many customers paid by exchanging goods from their farms. This kind of trade is called **barter**. Many farmers would enter the general store carrying a few dozen eggs, a sack of vegetables, or a chunk of salt pork. They would leave with sugar, coffee, pins and needles, and a yard or two of cloth.

Peddlers People who lived far from town might get to the general store only once or twice a year. Some families lived too far away even for that. They had to wait for a peddler to show up at their door one day. A peddler was a person who traveled through the countryside with goods for sale. Some peddlers came with a horse carrying their packs of goods for sale. Others walked through the countryside with their packs on their back.

There was no special time when the peddler might show up. Farm families were glad to see him whenever he came. It meant they could finally buy some of the things they had been waiting for — a new pot, a knife, or maybe a piece of cloth for making a dress or shirt.

A visit from the peddler also meant a chance to talk with another person, and to hear news from other places. Often a peddler would be invited to share a drink or

Here a family in the New England countryside gathers to welcome a peddler and look at his wares.
▶ How does the peddler travel?

TOYS THEN AND NOW

1 This wooden doll was carved for a child in Pennsylvania sometime in the 1790s.

2 This fancy whistle still works, even though it was carved in the early 1800s.

3 These wooden acrobats, made around the 1880s, could be put together in many ways.

4 Model trains like this Lionel set from around 1930 are still fun today.

5 Today, computer games provide hours of adventure and fantasy.

Have toys changed very much over the last 200 years? Perhaps the biggest change is in the way toys are made. The doll and the whistle were probably crafted by a parent. Toys made in factories were popular by the 1850s. And today, the computer has become a toy box filled with many different kinds of games.

▶ What is, or was, your favorite toy?

have a meal. If he arrived near the end of a day and the weather was poor, the family might invite the peddler to sleep over.

C. Slavery Makes the South Different

A Farming Region In the South, too, most people lived in the country. But life in the South was different from life in other parts of the United States. Unlike the Northeast, the South had few big cities. And unlike midwestern farmers, farmers in the South grew just a few crops.

King Cotton The reason for these differences was the slave system. In the South "cotton was king." Farmers made good money from the fluffy white plant, which they sold to textile factories in England. Over the years they planted more and more cotton, hoping for bigger profits.

Growing cotton required large numbers of workers. As you have learned, many southern farmers bought slaves to do the hot, dusty work. A few planters owned great plantations on which a hundred or more slaves toiled. These planters became the leaders of the South. Their houses were large mansions. Their children went to fine schools. Family members enjoyed the free time and riches that great wealth bring.

But most southern whites were not rich. Many farmers had little land and few slaves. And most southern whites had no slaves at all. These southerners had small farms on which they grew corn and other crops instead of cotton. Most of these farmers barely made a living.

Life in Slavery For slaves, life was even harsher. They could be bought or sold at public sales. Often families were split up at sales. Whether they lived on a plantation

Above is a cotton plantation on the banks of the Mississippi River. Slaves make up the labor force here.
▶ What are the main activities going on in this picture?

or a small farm, slaves worked from dawn until dusk. Those who did not work hard or fast enough were whipped. Slaves were forbidden to leave the plantations on which they lived. Fearing that books might stir ideas of freedom, owners did not even allow slaves to learn reading and writing.

In these harsh conditions, slaves hoped for freedom. Most slaves managed to keep their families together. Storytelling kept African culture alive. Some slaves continued to hold African religious beliefs. Many others became Christians. You will learn more about what life was like for people in slavery in Chapter 18.

D. Americans Have Less Noise and More Time

The next time you are outdoors, close your eyes and listen for a moment to the many noises that are part of our lives today. People who lived on farms and in villages in 1850 heard very little noise. There were no cars or trucks, and no gas or electric motors of any kind. There were no radios or television sets or cassette players

to shatter the quiet. No airplanes thundered across the sky. Now and then the silence might be broken by the sound of people talking or the clattering hoofs of a passing horse or the hammer of the village blacksmith or perhaps the ringing of a church bell. But most Americans of 1850 lived their days and their nights in a silence that would amaze us.

Americans in the countryside thought about time in a different way than we do. Today we live our lives by the clock. Our school day starts and ends at a certain hour. We know that we have to be "on time" for a music lesson or a Little League baseball game. We check the **schedule** in the newspaper to find out what television programs will be on today and when they will start. A schedule is a printed list that tells us exactly when certain things will take place and in what order. Today, clocks are everywhere, reminding us of the exact time. In our world, knowing the time and keeping a schedule are important.

In 1850, however, time was not as important to a person living on a farm or in a village as it is to us. Back then a person would not say to a friend, "I'll meet you at the general store at half-past nine," or "Let's meet in front of the church at 3:45." Instead he or she would probably say, "Let's meet in the morning," or "I'll see you in the afternoon." Few people bothered with clocks, for not many things depended on knowing the exact time.

All in all, life was far quieter and simpler in 1850 than it is today. But people who lived then had their own kinds of problems to deal with. As you will read in the next chapter, the nation had to solve big problems, too. When it failed to solve one special problem, the result was tragic.

LESSON **3** REVIEW

THINK AND WRITE

A. Describe the shelter of a pioneer farm family in 1850.

B. Why were peddlers important to many farm families?

C. What made life in the South different from life in other parts of the United States?

D. What were two ways in which farm or village life in 1850 was different from life today?

SKILLS CHECK

WRITING SKILL

Write a short story. Tell what might happen during a day on which you had no way to know the exact time.

USING THE VOCABULARY

invention
reaper
telegraph
famine
omnibus
specialize
division of labor
credit
barter
schedule

On a separate sheet of paper, write the words that correctly fill the blanks in the following paragraphs.

As factories grew in size, workers began to (1) _____ in certain jobs. This (2) _____ made it possible to produce more goods in less time. Workers on farms also became more efficient at harvesting crops because they had the benefit of McCormick's (3) _____. Farmers who were short of cash would often buy goods on (4) _____. Another method of payment used by farmers was (5) _____. American farmers produced so much that (6) _____ was not a problem in this country as it sometimes was in Europe.

The (7) _____ of the sewing machine and the (8) _____ made a difference in the way people lived. Other ideas also made life easier. Traveling by (9) _____ made it possible to avoid the dirt of city streets. The streets were so crowded, however, that keeping to a (10) _____ was almost impossible to accomplish.

REMEMBERING WHAT YOU READ

On a separate sheet of paper, write your answers in complete sentences.

1. Why did people move to the West?

2. What was "Yankee know-how"?

3. Why was the invention of the sewing machine important?

4. What was the importance of the telegraph to the expanding nation?

5. What did new immigrants like about life in the United States?

6. Why did people leave Ireland to come to the United States around 1850?

7. Why was it hard to walk from one place to another in a city?

8. Why were cities dirty places?

9. How did the coming of factories change the way some products, such as shoes, for example, were made?

10. How did people who lived in the country usually tell time?

TYING LANGUAGE ARTS TO SOCIAL STUDIES

Are you wearing a watch? Is there a clock in your classroom? Imagine what it would have been like to live on a farm in 1850. Write a poem or descriptive paragraph comparing the different feelings about time and schedules then and now.

THINKING CRITICALLY

On a separate sheet of paper, write your answers in complete sentences.

1. If you were a person living in 1850, would you choose to live in a city or in the country? Explain your answer.
2. The text tells about the invention of the sewing machine, the telegraph, and the reaper. Which of these do you think made the biggest difference in the way people lived?
3. Why did many immigrants think the most important thing about America was the feeling of equality here?
4. Why was the peddler an important part of farm life?
5. Is it better to have shoes made just for you or to buy shoes made in a factory? Explain your answer.

SUMMARIZING THE CHAPTER

On a separate sheet of paper, draw a graphic organizer like the one shown here. Copy the information from this graphic organizer to the one you have drawn. Under the main idea for each lesson, write three items that support the main idea. The first has been done for you.

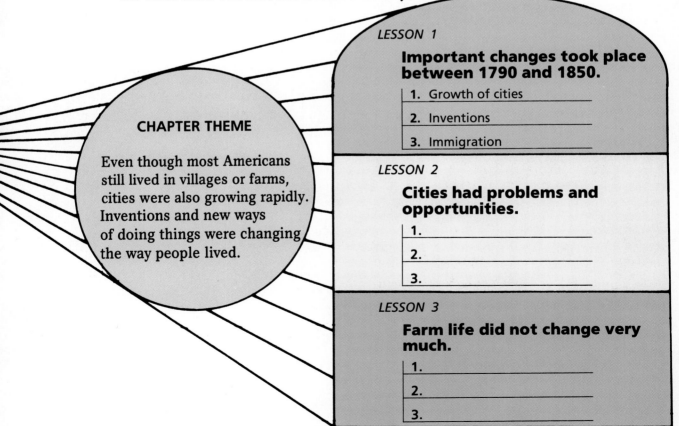

CHAPTER THEME

Even though most Americans still lived in villages or farms, cities were also growing rapidly. Inventions and new ways of doing things were changing the way people lived.

LESSON 1

Important changes took place between 1790 and 1850.

1. Growth of cities
2. Inventions
3. Immigration

LESSON 2

Cities had problems and opportunities.

1.
2.
3.

LESSON 3

Farm life did not change very much.

1.
2.
3.

The 1850s were troubled years. The North and the South were bitterly divided over slavery. Leaders tried to find solutions to the conflict. In the end, however, they failed.

Slaves Resist a Cruel System

THINK ABOUT WHAT YOU KNOW

Slaves had no weapons. Then how, do you think, might slaves resist, or fight against, slavery?

STUDY THE VOCABULARY

**Underground   free state
    Railroad   spiritual
slave state**

FOCUS YOUR READING

In what ways did slaves in the South resist the slave system?

A. Harriet Tubman Joins the Underground Railroad

For days, the slaves on the Bordas family's plantation in Maryland talked about nothing else. The rumor was that the slaves would be sold and sent farther south. Would their new owners be kind, or would they be cruel? Would their families be sold together to the same buyer, or would they be broken up? No one knew.

One slave, 29-year-old Harriet Tubman, did not wait to find out. Late one night Harriet Tubman went to the home of a white woman who had promised to help her escape. The woman sent Tubman to another white family a few miles away. This family let Tubman stay with them the next day. Then at night the husband drove Tubman in his wagon to the next town, where still another family took her in.

In this way, Tubman made her way to the North, hiding by day and traveling by night. At last she crossed the border of Pennsylvania, where slavery was prohibited. Harriet Tubman was free at last!

The people who helped Harriet Tubman to escape to freedom were members of the **Underground Railroad**. The Underground Railroad was not a real railroad at all. It was a system for helping runaway

(Left) Harriet Tubman helped many slaves escape to freedom in the North.
(Right) Escaping slaves hurry along through a driving rain to the next hiding place on the Underground Railroad.
▶ Why is *Underground Railroad* a good name for this escape route?

Portrait of Harriet Tubman, by Robert S. Pious. National Portrait Gallery, Washington. (NPG 67.41)

419

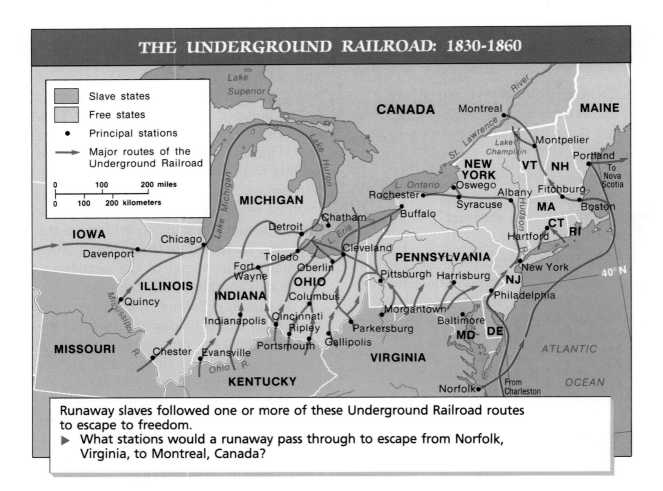

THE UNDERGROUND RAILROAD: 1830-1860

Slave states

Free states

• Principal stations

→ Major routes of the Underground Railroad

Runaway slaves followed one or more of these Underground Railroad routes to escape to freedom.

▶ What stations would a runaway pass through to escape from Norfolk, Virginia, to Montreal, Canada?

slaves escape to free states or to Canada. The people who were helping slaves to gain freedom used railroad words as a kind of secret code. Escaping slaves were called "passengers," and the homes, barns, and cellars where they were hidden were called "stations." Those who hid the fleeing slaves and guided them to freedom were called "conductors."

Harriet Tubman escaped in 1849. The next year she joined the Underground Railroad herself. Over the next ten years, she made 19 trips into the South to "conduct" slaves to freedom. During those years, she led about 300 slaves to the North. In the South, a reward of $12,000 was offered for her capture, but she was never caught. Many years later, when she looked back on her work in the Underground Railroad, Harriet Tubman said, "I never ran my train off the track, and I never lost a passenger."

B. The Slaves Resist

Rebellions Slaves resisted, or fought against, the system of slavery in a number of ways. A few slaves organized rebellions. One such person was Nat Turner. Turner was known to his master's family as a religious, peaceful man. And he was. But in 1831, Turner led a group of slaves in an uprising in the Virginia county he lived in. In a three-day period, Turner and his followers killed 60 men, women, and children. In the end, all the slaves who took part in Turner's Rebellion were caught, tried, and hanged. There were not many slave rebellions, for slaves knew they had almost no chance to succeed.

Runaways A good many slaves ran away at one time or another. But not many ever escaped. Slaves from Mississippi and Louisiana had to cross hundreds of miles of **slave states** to reach a **free state**. A slave state was a state in which slavery was permitted. A free state was a state in which slavery was not permitted.

Slave catchers hunted down most of the runaways long before they could reach freedom. Most runaways, in fact, returned on their own to rejoin their families and accept their punishment. Slaves were not put to death for running away, for they were much too valuable. But owners did punish runaways severely.

Most slaves did not rebel or run away. However, they resisted slavery in other ways. Sometimes they would work very slowly. They would "accidently" break tools, or set fire to the buildings where the tools were kept. They would pretend to be ill, or let themselves become ill on purpose. Some slaves even cut off a hand or a foot so they could not be forced to work in the fields. Were these just accidents, or were the slaves doing these things on purpose? The slaveowners never knew for sure.

C. Slave Songs Carry a Message of Freedom

Owners were fond of saying that their slaves loved them. They said that slaves

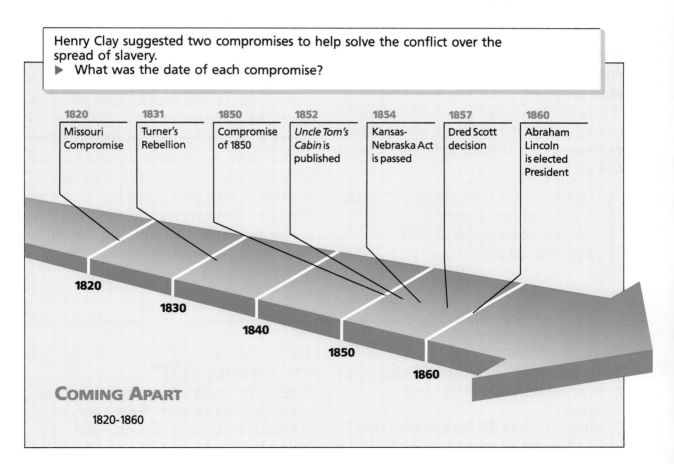

Henry Clay suggested two compromises to help solve the conflict over the spread of slavery.
▶ What was the date of each compromise?

1820	1831	1850	1852	1854	1857	1860
Missouri Compromise	Turner's Rebellion	Compromise of 1850	*Uncle Tom's Cabin* is published	Kansas-Nebraska Act is passed	Dred Scott decision	Abraham Lincoln is elected President

1820   1830   1840   1850   1860

COMING APART
1820-1860

These Louisiana slaves are cutting sugar cane as an overseer watches the backbreaking labor.
▶ Which person is the overseer?

were glad to have masters to take care of them. Owners who said such things could not have been listening very carefully to what their slaves were singing.

Slaves did not dare to speak openly of their misery. Instead, they spoke of freedom through their songs called **spirituals**. Most spirituals told of the weariness of the slaves and their hope for a better world to come. But in some spirituals, slaves clearly expressed their longing to be free. This is one such song.

> *Didn't my Lord deliver Daniel, deliver*
> *Daniel, deliver Daniel?*
> *Didn't my Lord deliver Daniel?*
> *Then why not a every man?*

> *He delivered Daniel from the lion's den,*
> *Jonah from the belly of the whale,*
> *And the Hebrew children from the fiery*
> *furnace,*
> *Then why not deliver a every man?*

Not all black people in the South were slaves. In fact, there were about 250,000 free blacks in the South. Most of these were the children or grandchildren of slaves who had been given their freedom earlier. Also, some slave owners allowed certain of their slaves who were skilled workers to earn money and buy their own freedom. However, even though these people were free, they still had almost no legal rights and were treated poorly.

LESSON 1 REVIEW

THINK AND WRITE

A. How did the Underground Railroad work?
B. How did slaves resist the slave system?
C. What messages did the spirituals carry?

SKILLS CHECK

WRITING SKILL

Imagine that you are a runaway slave trying to escape to a free state. Write a paragraph describing a day on the Underground Railroad.

Searching for a Compromise

THINK ABOUT WHAT YOU KNOW

Suppose you had a big argument with a friend. Would you try to work things out, or would you break up your friendship without trying to solve your differences? Why would you make the decision you did?

STUDY THE VOCABULARY

secede   **fugitive**

FOCUS YOUR READING

How did the Compromise of 1850 differ from the Missouri Compromise?

A. Congress Passes the Missouri Compromise

Slavery in Territories Many Southerners were angered by the help Northerners gave runaways. More and more, in the early 1800s, the North and South disagreed about slavery. One major conflict was whether slavery should be allowed in the territories of the United States. A territory, you'll remember, was an area that was not yet a state.

In 1820, Congress had to decide whether there would be slavery in lands acquired in the Louisiana Purchase. So in that year Congress passed a compromise law proposed by Senator Henry Clay of Kentucky. Congress drew an imaginary line at 36°30′ north latitude between Missouri and the Rocky Mountains. The compromise was that slavery would be prohibited in the area north of 36°30′. But in the area south of 36°30′, slavery would be permitted. Another part of the new law stated that the Missouri Territory would enter the Union as a slave state, and Maine would enter as a free state. The new law was called the Missouri Compromise, or the Compromise of 1820.

New Territories The Missouri Compromise covered all the land that belonged to the United States in 1820. But the war with Mexico gave the United States a great deal more land. The Missouri Compromise didn't cover this new territory. So Congress had to make a new law to deal with it.

But times had changed since 1820. Feelings about slavery had grown stronger. Northerners were more determined than ever that slavery should not spread into any more territories. Many, believing that the land of the West should be free, began calling themselves "free soilers."

Southerners were more determined than ever that the territories should be open to slavery. Slaves are property, they

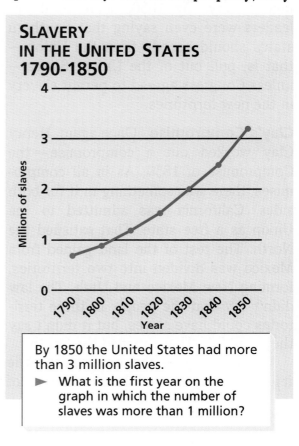

SLAVERY IN THE UNITED STATES 1790-1850

Millions of slaves

Year

By 1850 the United States had more than 3 million slaves.

► What is the first year on the graph in which the number of slaves was more than 1 million?

said. If Northerners could bring their property into the territories, why couldn't Southern slaveholders bring in theirs? Because, replied the free soilers, slavery is wrong. And if something is wrong, it should not be allowed to spread.

B. Henry Clay Helps the North and South to Compromise Again

North and South Disagree In 1850, there were 15 slave states and 15 free states. Both sides knew that sooner or later, a free territory would become a free state. And a slave territory would become a slave state. But Southerners feared that free states would someday greatly outnumber slave states. When that happened, they said, Northerners would change the Constitution and make all slavery illegal, even in the Southern states, where it already existed.

The South searched for ways to protect slavery. By 1850, some Southern leaders were even saying that Southern states should **secede** from the Union — that is, pull out of the United States — unless Congress agreed to permit slavery in the new territories.

Clay's Compromise Once again, Henry Clay worked out a compromise — the Compromise of 1850. As in all compromises, there was something in it for both sides. California was admitted to the Union as a free state. That satisfied the North. The rest of the land gained from Mexico was divided into two territories, forming New Mexico and Utah. The law didn't say that the people in these territories could have slaves, but it didn't say they couldn't. That satisfied the South.

Another part of the compromise made it illegal to buy and sell slaves in the city of Washington, D.C., the nation's capital. That satisfied the North. Still another part of the compromise was laws regarding **fugitive** slaves. A fugitive is someone who escapes and is being searched for. The Fugitive Slave Law made it easier for slave owners to get runaway slaves returned to them. That satisfied the South.

Trouble Continues Indeed, the Compromise of 1850 cooled down the argument between North and South for a short time. But many people were not happy with it. Some Southerners felt that the South gave up too much and got too little from the compromise. Senator John Calhoun of South Carolina opposed the compromise. He believed the South should insist on the right to take slaves into all the territories.

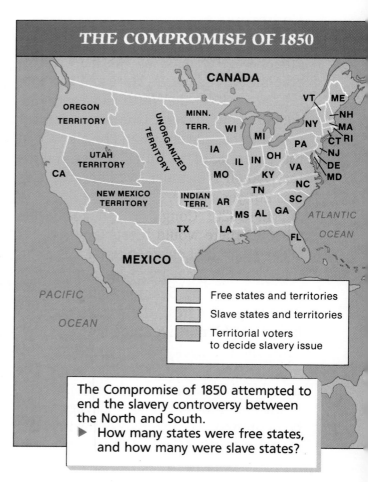

THE COMPROMISE OF 1850

Free states and territories

Slave states and territories

Territorial voters to decide slavery issue

The Compromise of 1850 attempted to end the slavery controversy between the North and South.
▶ How many states were free states, and how many were slave states?

A few Southern leaders wanted the South to secede right away.

And some Northerners also doubted the new laws could work. Some pledged not to obey the Fugitive Slave Law. No law, they said, could make them send a fellow human being back into slavery.

C. Harriet Beecher Stowe Writes a Book

One of the Northerners who opposed the Fugitive Slave Law was Harriet Beecher Stowe. Stowe came from a family of New England abolitionists. Angered by the Fugitive Slave Law, she decided to write a story that would show how cruel slavery was. "I will write something," she declared, "I will if I live." She called her book *Uncle Tom's Cabin.*

It appeared in 1852 and was an immediate sensation. More than 300,000 copies of *Uncle Tom's Cabin* were sold in the first year. The book was translated into 20 languages and was read by millions of people around the world. It was also turned into a play that was performed before large audiences. On page 426 you can learn more about *Uncle Tom's Cabin.*

The story and the characters of *Uncle Tom's Cabin* became familiar to millions of Americans.

Portrait of Harriet Beecher Stowe, by Alanson Fisher, 1853. National Portrait Gallery, Washington. (NPG 68.1)

Harriet Beecher Stowe was the first American writer to make an African American the hero of a book.

▶ Why did Harriet Beecher Stowe write *Uncle Tom's Cabin?*

Northerners who had been unmoved by abolitionists' lectures about the evils of slavery were deeply touched by Stowe's book. But Southerners said that the book gave a false picture of slavery. The two groups took yet another step apart.

LESSON **2** *REVIEW*

THINK AND WRITE

A. Why didn't the Missouri Compromise solve the problem of whether slavery would be permitted in the territories?

B. What did the North and the South each gain in the Compromise of 1850?

C. What was the impact of the book *Uncle Tom's Cabin?*

SKILLS CHECK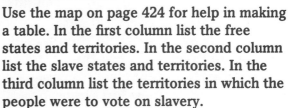

THINKING SKILL

Use the map on page 424 for help in making a table. In the first column list the free states and territories. In the second column list the slave states and territories. In the third column list the territories in which the people were to vote on slavery.

Uncle Tom's Cabin

By: Harriet Beecher Stowe
Setting: Southern United States, 1800s

Probably the most famous and most exciting part of *Uncle Tom's Cabin* is Eliza's escape from the slave state of Kentucky to the free state of Ohio. Eliza discovers that her baby son has been sold to a slave dealer and that the baby will be taken from her the next day. Eliza decides to take her son and make a dash for freedom. Eliza reaches the Ohio River, the border between the two states, when she sees the slave dealer catching up to her.

. . . **N** *erved with strength such as God gives only to the desperate, with one wild cry and flying leap, she vaulted sheer over the turbid [muddy] current by the shore, on to the raft of ice beyond. It was a desperate leap — impossible to anything but madness and despair. . . .*

The huge green fragment of ice on which she alighted [landed] pitched and creaked. . . . With wild cries and desperate energy she leaped to another and still another . . . stumbling — leaping — slipping. . . . Her shoes are gone — her stockings cut from her feet — while blood marked every step; but she saw nothing, felt nothing, till dimly . . . she saw the Ohio side, and a man helping her up the bank.

The man who pulled Eliza onto the Ohio shore pointed out a house to which she could go for safety. Eliza and the baby were on the road to freedom.

The Nation Divides

THINK ABOUT WHAT YOU KNOW

Suppose you live in a territory that has just voted on the slavery issue. The vote goes against what you believe in. What will you do?

STUDY THE VOCABULARY

**Confederate States   civil war
   of America
inaugural address**

FOCUS YOUR READING

How did the quarrel over slavery lead to the Civil War?

A. The Kansas-Nebraska Act Is Passed

Stephen Douglas's Idea   In 1854 there was still one large part of the Louisiana Purchase that Americans had not yet settled. Congress passed a law that opened this land for settlement. This law, the Kansas-Nebraska Act, divided the land into two territories—Kansas and Nebraska.

As you can see from the map on this page, both the Kansas and Nebraska territories were above the 36°30′ latitude line. According to the Missouri Compromise, slavery was not to be allowed in either territory. But the Kansas-Nebraska Act repealed, or cancelled, the Missouri Compromise. The new law left it up to the settlers in the Kansas and Nebraska territories to decide whether to allow slavery.

Repealing the Missouri Compromise was the idea of Senator Stephen A. Douglas of Illinois. Stephen Douglas, who was a short man, was known as the Little Giant because of his great ability as a senator.

Senator Douglas had no feelings about slavery one way or the other. He argued that the people of a territory should be allowed to vote whether to have slavery. It was all the same to him.

However, it wasn't all the same to people who believed it was wrong for one person to own another. To such people, even if a majority of settlers voted for slavery, that wouldn't make slavery right.

Bitter Disagreement   The Kansas-Nebraska Act opened up the argument between North and South all over again. Northerners were outraged that the new law repealed the Missouri Compromise. Southerners were pleased that it did. They realized that Nebraska was too far north for slavery to take root there. However,

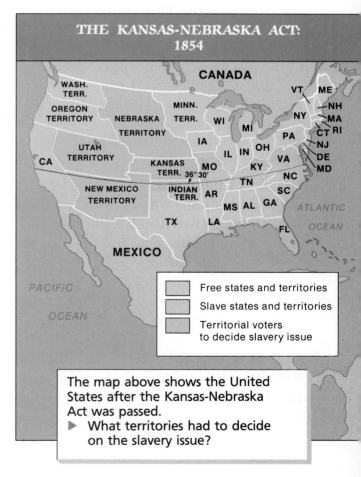

THE KANSAS-NEBRASKA ACT: 1854

Free states and territories

Slave states and territories

Territorial voters to decide slavery issue

The map above shows the United States after the Kansas-Nebraska Act was passed.
▶ What territories had to decide on the slavery issue?

Southerners were determined to make Kansas a slave territory and then a slave state. Antislavery Northerners were just as determined that Kansas should become a free state.

Both sides encouraged their people to move to Kansas. Soon groups of armed Northerners and armed Southerners were attacking each other in Kansas. So much blood was spilled that the territory became known as Bleeding Kansas. Two hundred settlers were killed before the United States Army moved in. Even then, armed settlers and raiders from nearby states kept up the fighting.

The troubles in Kansas and rising tensions over slavery made Northerners search for new solutions. Many who opposed slavery were attracted by a new political party—the Republican party. The new party appealed to the people from the North and the West who wanted to halt slavery. Those who joined hoped to elect antislavery leaders who would pass laws against slavery in the territories.

B. Abraham Lincoln Prepares for Public Office

Lincoln's Childhood One of the leaders of the Republicans was a lawyer from Illinois. His name was Abraham Lincoln. Lincoln started out in life with many disadvantages. He was born in a one-room log cabin in Kentucky. The Lincoln family was poor. Abraham's mother could not read or write, and his father could barely write his own name.

When Abraham was seven, the Lincoln family moved to Indiana. Like other children on the frontier, Abraham helped with farm chores. He and his older sister went to school when they were not needed to work at home, but that was not often.

Boyhood of Lincoln, by Eastman Johnson, 1868. The University of Michigan Museum of Art. Bequest of Henry C. Lewis (1895.90)

Although Lincoln as a boy had very little schooling, he learned a great deal through his reading.
▶ Why is Lincoln reading by the light of a fire?

Altogether, Abraham probably spent less than one year in school.

When Abraham was nine years old, his mother died. His father remarried the next year. Abraham was fortunate, for his stepmother was an educated person. She taught Abraham to read. The family had only a few books, but Abe read them over and over. He also traveled many miles to borrow books from others.

A strong, tall boy, Abraham Lincoln did more than his share of clearing and plowing the land. He also took on odd jobs to earn money. One of these jobs was splitting logs with an axe. One spring Abe and a cousin got a job splitting 5,000 logs into rails for fencing. That was a huge amount of work. People later gave Lincoln the nickname the Rail-Splitter.

A Young Adult At 21, Abe Lincoln set out on his own. He went to live in the small town of New Salem, Illinois. Soon after arriving there, he was challenged to a wrestling match by the strongest young man in town. Lincoln won, and he and his opponent became the best of friends.

For a time, Lincoln and a partner kept a small store in New Salem. The store lost money, and the two partners went out of business. Lincoln insisted on paying off all debts of the business. It took several years, but he paid back every penny that was owed. After that, Lincoln was known as "Honest Abe."

Meanwhile, Lincoln continued to read. He studied grammar and mathematics on his own. Later he studied law and became a lawyer. Lincoln then moved to nearby Springfield, Illinois. He soon became one of the most successful lawyers in town, but you would never have guessed it from the look of his office. The windows were never washed. Papers were scattered everywhere and piled high on desks and tables. On one large envelope Lincoln wrote, "When you can't find it anywhere else, look into this."

Lincoln was liked and trusted by his neighbors. They elected him to serve four terms in the Illinois State Legislature. Later he also served a term in Congress.

C. Lincoln Opposes Slavery

Opposing Slavery Abe Lincoln was firmly against slavery. For him, the question of whether slavery was right or wrong was simple. "As I would not be a *slave*, so I would not be a *master*," he said. Another time he told someone, "Whenever I hear anyone arguing [in favor of] slavery, I feel a strong impulse to see it tried on him personally."

However, Lincoln was not an abolitionist. Abolitionists wanted to immediately abolish slavery everywhere — not just in the territories but in the Southern states as well. Lincoln knew that, under

In this trial, Lincoln is defending the son of a couple who had once been kind to him. Their son is charged with murder. Lincoln won the case.
► In this picture, find the jury, the judge, and the onlookers.

the Constitution, the federal government did not have the right to interfere with slavery in the states. But he believed the government could, and should, stop the spread of slavery into the territories. He hoped that if slavery stopped spreading, it would die out gradually.

Running for Senator In 1858, Illinois Republicans chose Lincoln to run for the United States Senate against Senator Stephen A. Douglas. The two men held debates in seven Illinois cities before thousands of people. Lincoln explained to the crowds that the Union could not last half slave and half free. Douglas shot back that the issue should be left to the people of each new territory. Newspapers all over the country reported what they said. When the votes were counted, Douglas had won the election, but the campaign made Lincoln a well-known figure throughout America.

D. Tensions Rise

Dred Scott Lincoln was ready for bigger things. But the country was divided as never before. Two events showed this clearly. The first was a decision made in 1857 by the Supreme Court. The case involved Dred Scott, a black man who had been a slave. Scott's master had taken him from Missouri, a slave state, into free territory. There Scott had lived with his master for five years. So Scott had gone to court to be declared a free man.

The Supreme Court decided against Dred Scott. It ruled that he was a slave, even though he had lived where slavery was against the law. A slave was like any other property, the Supreme Court said. No law could take property away from its owner. Therefore, Congress could not outlaw slavery in any territory.

United States marines storm the building that John Brown had taken over at Harpers Ferry, Virginia.
► Why couldn't Brown have won?

Harpers Ferry People in the North reacted to the Dred Scott decision with bitterness. Southerners were delighted. But soon a second event worsened the tension. In October 1859 John Brown led a raid on an armory at Harpers Ferry, Virginia. Brown's raiders killed several people and seized the armory.

John Brown was an abolitionist who believed he had been chosen by God to end slavery. With support from wealthy Northerners, Brown had organized a small band of followers. They went to Virginia to lead a slave rebellion. But Brown's plan failed at once. Most of his followers were killed in fighting the day after their raid. Brown himself was caught and quickly tried. He was later put to death.

Brown's raid split Northerners. Some praised Brown as "God's angry man" and a hero. To others, violence was not the way to end slavery. But Southerners were outraged. How, they asked, can any Northerners praise the killing of innocent people? Many Southerners felt that the North was preparing stronger measures against the South.

E. The Country Divides

Electing a New President Both sides eagerly awaited the election of 1860. Many Northerners hoped for a Republican victory that would stop the spread of slavery into the territories. Many in the South decided to secede if a Republican won.

In 1860, the Republican party chose Lincoln as its candidate for President of the United States. Lincoln had often said that, if elected, he would leave slavery in the Southern states alone.

But promises no longer mattered. Southerners simply did not trust Lincoln. They felt that he and the Republicans planned to abolish slavery and end their way of life. Fearing the worst, Southerners were ready to secede.

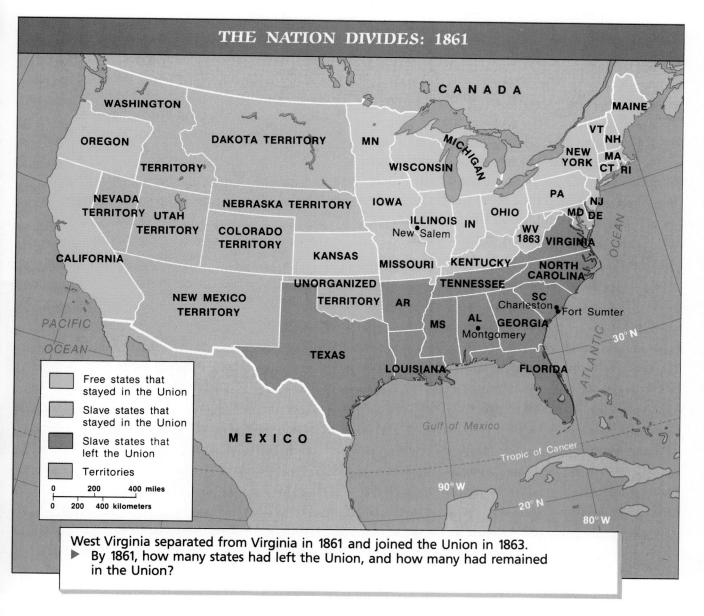

THE NATION DIVIDES: 1861

Legend:
- Free states that stayed in the Union
- Slave states that stayed in the Union
- Slave states that left the Union
- Territories

0 200 400 miles
0 200 400 kilometers

West Virginia separated from Virginia in 1861 and joined the Union in 1863.
▶ By 1861, how many states had left the Union, and how many had remained in the Union?

That is just what they did. Abraham Lincoln was elected President in November 1860. One month later, South Carolina seceded from the Union. Six more states later voted to leave the Union. They were Mississippi, Florida, Alabama, Georgia, Louisiana, and Texas.

The Confederacy Is Formed Representatives from these seven states met in Montgomery, Alabama on February 4, 1861. They formed a new nation, the **Confederate States of America**. The representatives then chose Jefferson Davis of Mississippi to be president of the Confederate States, or the Confederacy. Jefferson Davis was a cotton planter and a slave owner. He had fought in the Mexican War and had served as a United States senator.

Meanwhile, the states that had seceded began to take over forts and other government property located in their states. They said that these properties now belonged to them. Soon the United States had only two forts left in the South.

F. The Civil War Begins

Lincoln Takes Office This was the situation when Lincoln took over as President. In his **inaugural address**—the speech made at the start of his term of office—President Lincoln made a last appeal to the South. But he knew he had little hope of winning Southern support. "We are not enemies, but friends," said Lincoln. "We must not be enemies."

Abraham Lincoln was trying to find a way to prevent **civil war**. A civil war is a war in which people of the same country fight each other. As President, Lincoln had a duty to preserve the Union. He said that no state could just decide on its own to leave the Union. President Lincoln told the South that he would hold onto all property the United States government owned in the South.

Fort Sumter One Southern fort still in the hands of the United States government

A large crowd gathered in Washington, D.C., to hear the inaugural address of Abraham Lincoln (left).
▶ Can you find Lincoln in the painting below?

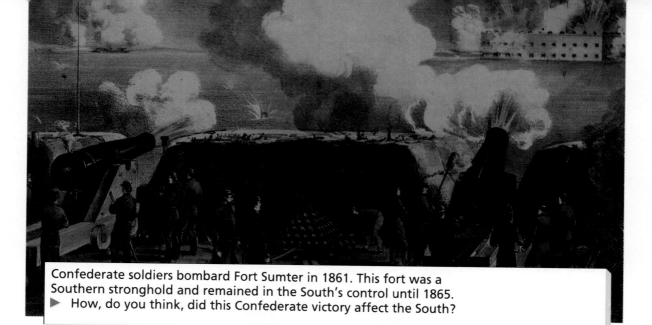

Confederate soldiers bombard Fort Sumter in 1861. This fort was a Southern stronghold and remained in the South's control until 1865.
► How, do you think, did this Confederate victory affect the South?

was Fort Sumter. This fort is located on an island in the harbor of Charleston, South Carolina. Major Anderson, the commander of the fort, had refused to hand it over to South Carolina.

As time went by, however, Fort Sumter began to run short of supplies. Major Anderson told the President that he would have to give up the fort unless food arrived soon.

In April of 1861, President Lincoln told South Carolina that he was sending supply ships to Fort Sumter. He said the ships would not carry guns or troops. By saying this, he hoped the Confederates would allow the ships to go through.

But the Confederates would not agree to let the fort hold out any longer. Before the ships arrived, they demanded that Anderson surrender the fort. When he refused, Confederate cannons on shore opened fire. The bombardment continued for 30 hours. Finally, Major Anderson surrendered the fort to the Confederates. The shooting had started.

Soon after, Lincoln called for Americans to join the army to put down the rebellion. Even so, four more Southern states — Arkansas, Virginia, North Carolina, and Tennessee — seceded from the Union and joined the Confederacy. The American Civil War had begun.

LESSON 3 REVIEW

THINK AND WRITE

A. What were the effects of the Kansas-Nebraska Act?
B. Describe Lincoln's boyhood.
C. How did Lincoln's ideas on ending slavery differ from those of the abolitionists?
D. What two events in the 1850s divided the North and South even further?
E. Why did the South secede?

F. What events at Fort Sumter led to the firing of the first shots of the Civil War?

SKILLS CHECK

MAP SKILL

Look at the map on page 431. List the free states that stayed in the Union, the slave states that stayed in the Union and the slave states that left the Union.

USING THE VOCABULARY

Underground Railroad
spiritual
secede
fugitive
civil war

On a separate sheet of paper, write the term that matches the definition from the list below.

1. A song sung by slaves, sometimes carrying a message
2. A system for helping runaway slaves
3. When one part of a nation fights another part
4. Someone who escapes and is being sought
5. To withdraw from a country

REMEMBERING WHAT YOU READ

On a separate sheet of paper, write your answers in complete sentences.

1. Why did Harriet Tubman speak so proudly of her work with the Underground Railroad?
2. For what kind of things were slaves punished?
3. Aside from a few who rebelled openly, how did other slaves show their resistance to the system of slavery?
4. How did slaves express their desire for freedom?
5. What were the terms of the Missouri Compromise?
6. Why did Harriet Beecher Stowe write *Uncle Tom's Cabin*?

7. What law caused the repeal of the Missouri Compromise?
8. What was the Dred Scott decision?
9. What happened after Abraham Lincoln was elected President?
10. How did the Civil War begin?

TYING LANGUAGE ARTS TO SOCIAL STUDIES

Read the literature selection on page 426. Pretend you are either the slave trader trying to catch Eliza or the man who helps her up from the river on the "free side." Write a journal entry describing your feelings as you watch Eliza cross the river. Or you can pretend to be Eliza and write a letter that will be smuggled back to your friends, telling them how you felt when you crossed the river.

THINKING CRITICALLY

On a separate sheet of paper, write your answers in complete sentences.

1. What method of resistance would you have chosen if you had been a slave? Explain your choice.
2. Why did the compromises of 1820 and 1850 fail to solve the problem of slavery in the United States?
3. What did Stephen A. Douglas do that deepened the division between North and South?
4. Why couldn't Abraham Lincoln be called an abolitionist?
5. Some historians say that John Brown was a madman. Others say that he was a hero. What do you think?

SUMMARIZING THE CHAPTER

On a separate sheet of paper, draw a graphic organizer like the one shown here. Copy the information from this graphic organizer to the one you have drawn. Fill in the chart by describing the Northern reaction and the Southern reaction to each of the items listed.

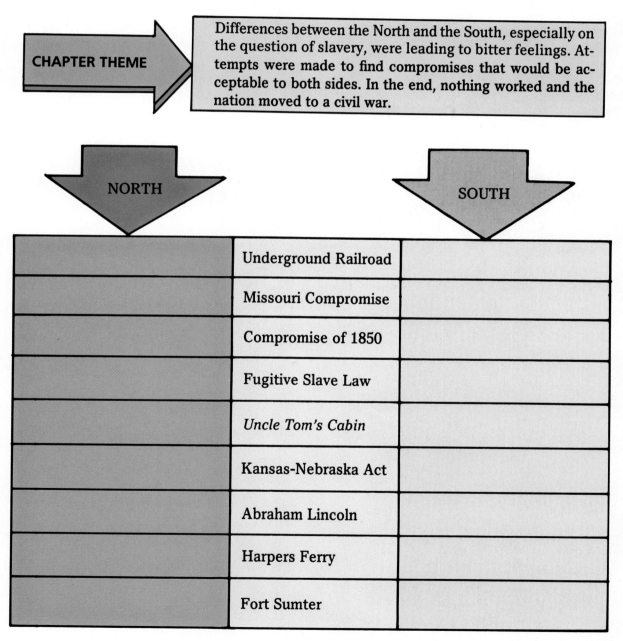

CHAPTER THEME

Differences between the North and the South, especially on the question of slavery, were leading to bitter feelings. Attempts were made to find compromises that would be acceptable to both sides. In the end, nothing worked and the nation moved to a civil war.

NORTH

SOUTH

NORTH		SOUTH
	Underground Railroad	
	Missouri Compromise	
	Compromise of 1850	
	Fugitive Slave Law	
	Uncle Tom's Cabin	
	Kansas-Nebraska Act	
	Abraham Lincoln	
	Harpers Ferry	
	Fort Sumter	

19 THE CIVIL WAR

The North took up arms to preserve the Union; the South, to preserve its way of life. After four long, bloody, and uncertain years, the South surrendered.

North and South Square Off

THINK ABOUT WHAT YOU KNOW

Suppose that you are watching your hometown basketball team. Your team is playing a game against a rival team on your school's home court. What advantages, do you think, would your team have?

STUDY THE VOCABULARY

defensive war

FOCUS YOUR READING

What advantages did each side have in the Civil War?

A. Union Troops Are Defeated at Bull Run

July 21, 1861, was another hot day in Washington, D.C. There was a holiday mood as people climbed into their carriages that morning for a ride into the Virginia countryside. They were heading for Manassas Junction, Virginia, about 30 miles (48 km) away. There they planned to enjoy their picnic lunches while watching the first battle of the Civil War.

Five days earlier, about 35,000 Union troops had marched out of the nation's capital, shouting, "Forward to Richmond!" Richmond, Virginia, was the capital of the new Confederate States of America, and the Union army wanted to capture it. After several days the Union soldiers had reached Manassas Junction, where they met a Confederate force of 25,000 men. Washington newspapers reported that a battle was expected to begin shortly. This was the battle that the people from Washington had come to watch.

At Manassas the sightseers from Washington spread their picnic lunches and opened brightly colored umbrellas to protect themselves from the hot sun. A few miles away, near a small stream called Bull Run, fighting had already started. Picnickers could hear the roar of cannons and the crackle of gunfire in the distance.

At Bull Run the Union and Confederate armies face each other in the first great battle of the Civil War.
▶ Was it a good idea for people to picnic near this battlefield?

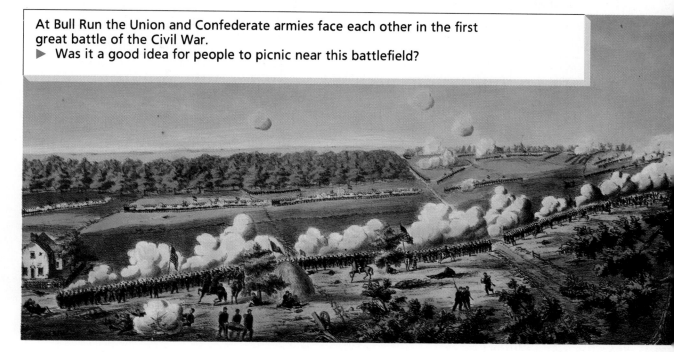

Most of the picnickers — in fact, most people in the North — thought that this first battle of the war would probably also be the last one. The Union army, they believed, would defeat the rebels and go on to capture Richmond. Then the Southern states would return to the Union, and the war would be over.

It didn't turn out that way. At first the Union forces at Bull Run seemed to be winning. Then fresh Confederate troops appeared, and the battle turned. The half-trained Union soldiers began to retreat — first a few, then more and more until finally thousands dropped their guns and ran in panic toward the picnickers.

Frightened sightseers scrambled back to their carriages, knocking each other over in their rush to get away. For hours the road to Washington was clogged with fleeing Union soldiers and sightseers.

Fortunately for the Union side, the Confederate generals decided that their own troops were too tired to pursue the enemy.

After the battle of Bull Run, the hard truth began to sink in. The war would not end quickly after all. It would probably be long, bitter, and bloody. And no one could say how it would end.

B. Each Side Has Advantages

Northern Advantages As the war began, the North could count on certain advantages. With a population of 22 million, the North had by far the larger population. The whole population of the South was only 9 million, and 3.5 million of those were slaves. This meant that the North had many more people to produce food, guns, and ships. The North also had more people who could serve in the army and the navy. As the war dragged on and more soldiers

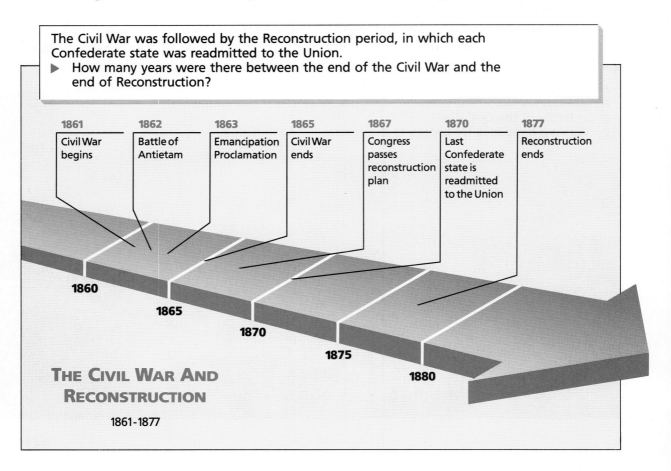

The Civil War was followed by the Reconstruction period, in which each Confederate state was readmitted to the Union.
▶ How many years were there between the end of the Civil War and the end of Reconstruction?

1861	1862	1863	1865	1867	1870	1877
Civil War begins	Battle of Antietam	Emancipation Proclamation	Civil War ends	Congress passes reconstruction plan	Last Confederate state is readmitted to the Union	Reconstruction ends

1860
1865
1870
1875
1880

THE CIVIL WAR AND RECONSTRUCTION

1861-1877

This iron foundry near West Point, New York, made war materials for the North. Here hot liquid metal is being poured into a cannon mold.

▶ Why was it dangerous to work in a foundry like this one?

were needed, the North's advantage in population became even more important.

Also the North had most of the nation's factories and mills. The North could produce 20 times as much iron as the South could and more than 30 times as many guns. Northern factories supplied all the clothing, blankets, tents, and medical supplies that Union armies needed. The South had to depend on getting many of these goods from European countries. The North also had more railroads to move troops and supplies than did the South.

Southern Advantages But the South also had some advantages. The biggest advantage was that the South was fighting a **defensive war**. This means that the South was fighting to defend its own territory,

not to take Northern territory. For the North to win the war, Northern armies would have to conquer the South. But the South could win without having to capture an inch of Northern soil. All that the Southern armies had to do was to defend their own territory.

Also, when Southern soldiers fought on Southern soil, they had an extra reason to fight hard. They were defending their land, their homes, and their way of life.

In addition the South had better generals than the North in the early years of the war. Many of these generals had been trained at the United States Military Academy at West Point, New York. They had gained fighting experience in the Mexican War. When the Southern states seceded,

This picture is part of a huge wall painting in the Virginia Historical Society's headquarters building in Richmond, Virginia. It is a purely imaginary scene showing General Robert E. Lee and his commanders.
▶ Why, do you think, was Richmond chosen to have this painting?

most of these experienced generals resigned from the United States Army and fought for the Confederacy.

The most brilliant Southern general was Robert E. Lee. President Abraham Lincoln knew that Lee loved the United States and disliked slavery. He asked Lee to take charge of all the Union armies. But Lee's home state of Virginia had joined the Confederacy. Lee refused President Lincoln's offer. He explained, "If I owned four million slaves, I would cheerfully give them up to save the Union. But to lift my hand against Virginia is impossible. . . . [I cannot] fight against my relatives, my children, my home."

Throughout the war, Lee was one of the South's greatest strengths. Although his armies were usually outnumbered, General Lee used daring surprise moves to win many victories.

C. Women Aid the War Effort

Running Farms   With thousands of men going off to war, women and children on both sides took on the work usually done by men. In the South, women had always run some farms and plantations. During the war, many more did. The same was true of farm women in the North and West. A traveler to western farm states in 1863 reported that "women were in the fields everywhere, driving the reapers . . . and loading grain." One woman explained:

Harvesting isn't any harder than cooking, washing, and ironing over a red-hot stove in July and August—only we have to do both now. My three brothers went into the army, all my cousins, most of the young men about here, and the men we used to hire. So there's no help to be got but women, and the crops must be got in all the same, you know.

440

The Granger Collection, New York

Women in a United States arsenal in Watertown, New York, are filling cartridges for Union guns.
▶ Why might the soldier be here?

Caring for the Wounded In addition, women on both sides made bandages, knitted socks, and sewed clothing to send to the soldiers. About 3,000 served as nurses. In those days, nursing was a man's job. But so many nurses were needed during the war that women were accepted.

One of the heroic nurses on the Union side was Clara Barton. Barton got permission from the army to drive her wagon of medical supplies and food right onto the battlefields. Time and again she risked her life to care for the wounded. Soldiers called her the Angel of the Battlefield. Many years after the war, Clara Barton founded the American Red Cross.

On the Confederate side, Sally Tompkins ran a private hospital in Richmond, Virginia. In this hospital she cared for both Confederate soldiers and Union prisoners. Sally Tompkins and her nurses saved hundreds of lives.

Helping in Fighting Women served on both sides in other ways, too. Some carried mail for the armies. Others worked as spies. One of the North's spies was Harriet Tubman, the famed "conductor" on the Underground Railroad. Several hundred other women managed to reach the battlefields disguised as men.

LESSON **1** *REVIEW*

THINK AND WRITE

A. How did the Confederate victory at Bull Run change the way people thought about the Civil War?

B. What do you think was the greatest advantage that each side had during the Civil War?

C. How did women help the war effort during the Civil War?

SKILLS CHECK

THINKING SKILL

Think about how a newspaper reporter from the North might write the story of the battle of Bull Run differently than a Southern reporter. Write one or two paragraphs describing how news stories on the battle by the two reporters might differ.

CLARA BARTON: A PERSON WHO CARED FOR OTHER PEOPLE

The Civil War was a terrible war. Many were killed and wounded on both sides. One soldier wrote home before a battle that he was not afraid of dying, but he prayed that he would not be wounded. For most of the war, there were very few hospitals, not many doctors, and no trained nurses to care for the wounded.

Clara Barton was a special person. She was nearly 40 years old and working in Washington, D.C., when the war started in 1861. She left her job as a clerk in the Patent Office and traveled to various battlefields to care for the wounded. She organized other women to help with the wounded. In time she was appointed superintendent of nurses for one of the Union armies. Following the war, she worked hard to locate missing soldiers.

In 1881, Clara Barton established the American branch of the Red Cross. She became its first president, a post she held for 22 years. Clara Barton's love for humanity inspired her to see beyond the need of people in war. When the constitution of the American Red Cross was written, she saw to it that the Red Cross would give help in other disasters as well as in war.

Clara Barton was an outstanding citizen. The Red Cross is still following the guidelines she established. Clara Barton has left us an important legacy. By her example, she calls on each one of us to recognize the suffering of other people and to do all that we can to help them.

Thinking for Yourself

Write your answers on a separate sheet of paper.

1. Is there a Red Cross chapter in your community? What do you know about the work it is doing?
2. Clara Barton became famous because of her work in helping others. Can you think of other people in history who also helped others? Are there people in your community whom you admire for being helpful to others?
3. What can you do to help other people?

CLARA BARTON
1821~1912

443

The North Looks for a Victory

THINK ABOUT WHAT YOU KNOW
Imagine that you are rooting for a sports team that fails to win game after game. How would you feel? What might change your feelings?

STUDY THE VOCABULARY
blockade	Emancipation
border	Proclamation
states	

FOCUS YOUR READING
During the first years of the Civil War, why could neither side claim complete victory?

A. The Union Develops a Plan for Victory

Blocking Southern Ports Soon after the Confederates took Fort Sumter at the beginning of the Civil War, President Lincoln ordered a naval **blockade** of the South. A blockade is a shutting off of enemy ports during a war. Union warships patrolled the ocean outside of Southern ports to keep ships from going in or out. The plan was to keep the South from selling its cotton to European countries and from receiving needed supplies from Europe.

However, during the first years of the Civil War, the Union did not have enough warships, so the blockade did not work well. Nine out of every ten ships that tried to get through the blockade succeeded.

Controlling the Mississippi Another part of the Union's plan to win the war was to gain control of the Mississippi River. Doing so would cut the Confederacy in two. Texas, Arkansas, and most of Louisiana would be split from the rest of the Confederate states. They would then be unable to contribute much to the South's war effort.

By the end of 1862, Union armies had made progress toward this second goal. After fierce fighting in western Kentucky and Tennessee, Union armies led by General Ulysses S. Grant won control of most of the Mississippi River. However, Confederate troops still held several important ports, including Vicksburg, Mississippi.

On their way to capture New Orleans, Farragut's ships fire on the two forts that were the city's main defense.
▶ Why was the capture of New Orleans important?

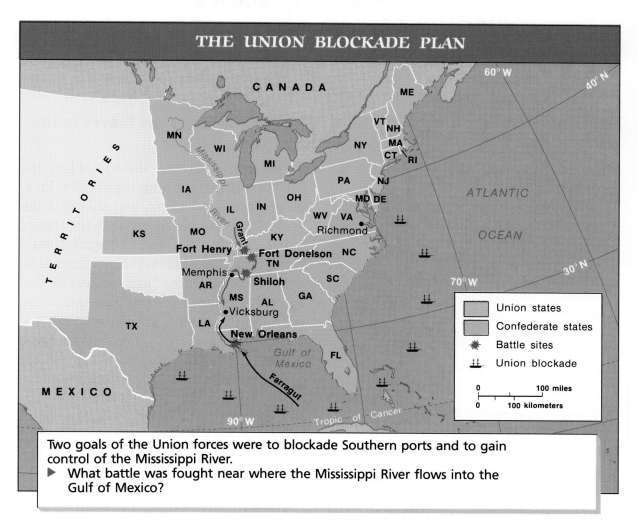

THE UNION BLOCKADE PLAN

Two goals of the Union forces were to blockade Southern ports and to gain control of the Mississippi River.

▶ What battle was fought near where the Mississippi River flows into the Gulf of Mexico?

Meanwhile, Union warships commanded by Captain David G. Farragut surprised the Confederates at New Orleans and captured that city. After that, Confederate ships could no longer use the Mississippi River to get to the open sea.

B. A Bloody War Rages in the East

The Battle for Richmond In the East, Union armies had almost no success. General George B. McClellan was in charge of the armies in the East. He spent nearly a year training his army. Whenever President Lincoln urged him to start fighting the Confederate army, McClellan said that his army needed more training.

Lincoln badly wanted a victory in the East. Finally, in June 1862, he got McClellan to move his troops south toward Richmond. But General Robert E. Lee and General Thomas "Stonewall" Jackson were ready for them. After seven days of fighting, the Union forces were no closer to capturing Richmond than they had been on the first day of the war.

Lee Turns North In the next months General Lee's forces handed Union armies a number of defeats in Virginia. In September 1862, Lee decided to carry the war into the North. He sent his troops into Maryland, one of the slave states that had remained in the Union. Lee thought that if

445

CIVIL WAR BATTLES: 1861-1862

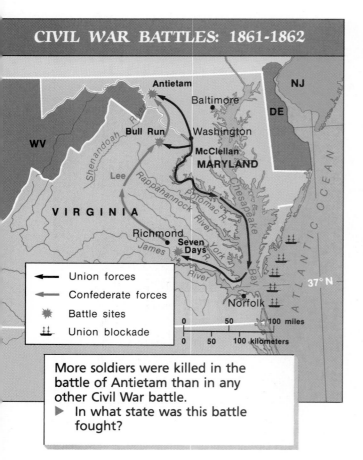

Union forces
Confederate forces
Battle sites
Union blockade

More soldiers were killed in the battle of Antietam than in any other Civil War battle.
▶ In what state was this battle fought?

he could defeat a Union army in Maryland, the state might decide to join the Confederacy. Also, such a victory might cause the Northern army to lose its spirit and decide to quit the war.

General Lee might have succeeded except for some bad luck. A Union soldier poking through an abandoned Confederate campsite found a few cigars with a piece of paper wrapped around them. The paper turned out to be a message from General Lee, telling of his battle plans. Armed with this information, General McClellan was able to stop Lee's army at Antietam Creek in Maryland.

Antietam The day of the battle of Antietam—September 17, 1862—was the bloodiest day of the entire Civil War. Altogether 24,000 Union and Confederate

soldiers were killed in that one awful day. Antietam was not really the victory Lincoln had been looking for, but Lee's advance into the North had been stopped.

C. Lincoln Frees the Slaves in the Confederate States

Slave States in the Union When the Civil War began in the spring of 1861, President Abraham Lincoln had said that the goal of the war was to preserve the Union. Many people said that the goal should have been to end slavery. Even though he hated slavery, Lincoln had reasons for disagreeing. Four slave states—Missouri, Kentucky, Maryland, and Delaware—had stayed in the Union. These states were called the **border states**, because they were located between the North and the South. Lincoln feared that if he said the Union's goal was to end slavery, these border states might join the Confederacy. That would be a serious blow to the Union's chances of winning the war.

Both sides fought equally bravely at Antietam, and the North's victory was hard won and bloody.
▶ What flag can you see here?

Lincoln Reading the Emancipation Proclamation to His Cabinet, By Alonzo Chappel. Oil on paper, Monochrome, 16⅛ x 22 inches. M. and M. Karolik Collection

In this painting Abraham Lincoln is shown reading the Emancipation Proclamation to the members of his Cabinet.
► How do you think Lincoln might have felt as he read this proclamation?

Emancipation As the war went on, however, more and more people in the North wanted to end slavery. In mid-1862, President Lincoln decided that the time was ripe to do so. He had kept the border states in the Union, and Lee had been stopped at Antietam. So in September, Lincoln announced that slaves in states still rebelling against the United States on January 1, 1863, would be "forever free." His order did not apply to slaves in the border states. On January 1, 1863 the **Emancipation Proclamation** was signed by Lincoln. To *emancipate* means "to make free." From then on, the war was fought to preserve the Union *and* to free the slaves.

LESSON 2 REVIEW

THINK AND WRITE

A. Why was the Union blockade of Southern ports unsuccessful at first?

B. Why can it be said that the battle of Antietam was not a victory for either side?

C. How did the Emancipation Proclamation affect slaves in the Confederate states and in the border states that did not secede from the Union?

SKILLS CHECK

MAP SKILL

Use the Gazetteer to find the latitudes and longitudes of Antietam, New Orleans, Richmond, and Vicksburg. Which battle was the farthest north?

447

The North Triumphs

THINK ABOUT WHAT YOU KNOW

You and your friends decide to organize a school campaign against littering. What qualities, do you think, a leader of this campaign should have? What qualities make a successful leader?

STUDY THE VOCABULARY

Gettysburg Address   Congressional Medal of Honor

FOCUS YOUR READING

What were the results of the Civil War?

A. The Battle of Gettysburg Is the Beginning of the End

The Battle In 1863, General Robert E. Lee once again decided to carry the war into the North. Lee led his troops out of Virginia, across a corner of Maryland, and into Pennsylvania. There, in the small town of Gettysburg, the Union and Confederate armies came face to face.

The battle of Gettysburg was a turning point in the war. For the first three days of July 1863, a furious battle raged. Again and again General Lee's forces attacked, only to be thrown back. In the end, Lee lost a third of his men, and the Confederate army had to retreat to Virginia. Never again would the Confederate army invade the North.

Gettysburg Address Four months after this battle, President Lincoln went to Gettysburg to dedicate a cemetery for the soldiers who died there. Abraham Lincoln's **Gettysburg Address** took less than five minutes to deliver. But in that five minutes, he tried to express the meaning of the horrible conflict for the whole world. He closed with these words:

. . . that we here highly resolve these dead shall not have died in vain [that is, for nothing], that this nation, under God, shall have a new birth of freedom, and that government of the people, by the people, and for the people, shall not perish from the earth.

These monuments were erected at Gettysburg by the states of (left) New Jersey, (center) North Carolina, and (right) Virginia.
▶ Why were these monuments erected?

THE GETTYSBURG ADDRESS

There are five copies of the Gettysburg Address in Abraham Lincoln's handwriting in existence today. And each is just a little different from the others. The words below come from the copy that historians at the Library of Congress say President Lincoln held in his hands when he delivered the address. That copy is also shown in the photograph on this page.

Four score and seven years ago our fathers brought forth, upon this continent, a new nation, conceived in liberty, and dedicated to the proposition that "all men are created equal"

Now we are engaged in a great civil war, testing whether that nation, or any nation so conceived, and so dedicated, can long endure. We are met on a great battle field of that war. We have come to dedicate a portion of it, as a final resting place for those who died here, that the nation might live. This we may, in all propriety [proper behavior] do. But, in a larger sense, we can not dedicate — we can not consecrate — we can not hallow, this ground — The brave men, living and dead, who struggled here, have hallowed it, far above our poor power to add or detract. The world will little note, nor long remember what we say here; while it can never forget what they *did* here.

It is rather for us, the living, here be dedicated to the great task remaining before us — that, from these honored dead we take increased devotion to that cause for which they here, gave the last full measure of devotion — that we here highly resolve these dead shall not have died in vain, that this nation, shall have a new birth of freedom, and that government of the people, by the people, for the people, shall not perish from the earth.

Understanding Source Material

1. President Lincoln gave this speech in 1863. The new nation he spoke of was "brought forth" in 1776. How much is four score and seven years?
2. Why did President Lincoln make this speech?

449

Vicksburg The course of the war had finally turned—in the North's favor. A day after the victory at Gettysburg, on July 4, 1863, President Lincoln had received more good news from the West. Union armies led by General Ulysses S. Grant had captured the Confederate stronghold of Vicksburg, Mississippi. The Union at last controlled the entire Mississippi River, and Arkansas, Texas, and Louisiana were cut off from the rest of the Confederacy. No longer could these states send troops and supplies across the Mississippi River to the main Confederate armies.

The Blockade Works Meanwhile, the North was building warships to strengthen its blockade of Southern ports. The new ships gave the North what was needed for an effective blockade. By 1864 half the ships that tried to get through to Southern ports were captured or sunk. Cotton piled up on Southern docks. Southern armies began to run short of the supplies they needed to fight the war.

B. Free Blacks Join the Union Army

At the start of the Civil War, many black Americans volunteered to fight for the Union. However, the army and the navy would not accept blacks as soldiers or sailors. They would only hire blacks to cook, drive wagons, and work with shovels and hammers.

As the war went on, however, the Union armies needed more soldiers. After the Emancipation Proclamation in 1863, blacks were finally allowed to join the army and the navy. Frederick Douglass, the black abolitionist, urged blacks to join the army and help to free 3.5 million

SOME CIVIL WAR BATTLES

Battle	Date	Results
Bull Run (Manassas Junction), Virginia	July 21, 1861	The North realizes the war will not be won easily after the Union army retreats.
New Orleans, Louisiana	April 25, 1862	Admiral David Farragut occupies New Orleans for the Union.
Seven Days Battle, Virginia	June 25 - July 1, 1862	Confederate army saves Richmond from capture and forces Union army to retreat.
Antietam Creek, Maryland	September 17, 1862	Union army stops Lee's advance into the North in the bloodiest battle of the war.
Fredericksburg, Virginia	December 13, 1862	Union army suffers severe defeat.
Vicksburg, Mississippi	May 19 - July 4, 1863	After a long siege the Union army gains control of the Mississippi River.
Gettysburg, Pennsylvania	July 1 - 3, 1863	Union victory is the turning point of the war.
Wilderness, Virginia	May 5 - 6, 1864	Union army continues to move southward, despite heavy losses.
Five Forks, Virginia	April 1, 1865	Union army wins the last important battle of the war.

slaves. Douglass believed that after black people helped fight to save the Union, no one would dare deny them their rights as citizens.

By war's end, 186,000 blacks were serving in the army and the navy. About 40,000 were free blacks from the North. The rest were men who had escaped from the slave states.

Black soldiers were not treated equally in the war. At first they received only half as much pay as white soldiers. But by the end of the war, white and black soldiers received the same pay. However, black soldiers were organized into separate, all-black units because most white soldiers would not fight alongside them.

The fighting record of black soldiers who served in the Civil War was outstanding. Twenty-one black soldiers received the **Congressional Medal of Honor** for acts of bravery. This is our country's highest award.

C. The Union Wins the War

General Grant You may recall that at the start of the Civil War, the South had better generals than the North. By 1863, however, the Union armies had a number of able generals. Chief among them was General Ulysses S. Grant. Grant had graduated from West Point and fought in the Mexican War. Later he left the army. When the Civil War started, Grant was working in a clothing store. He quickly rejoined the army and showed his skill in battle. He was one of the few successful Union commanders. So,

soon after Grant's victory at Vicksburg, President Lincoln put him in charge of all Union armies. In addition to this command, General Grant personally led the armies in northern Virginia.

Grant explained his ideas about warfare this way.

The art of war is simple enough. Find out where your enemy is. Get at him as soon as you can. Strike at him as hard as you can, and keep moving on.

Grant's plan in Virginia was to force the Confederate armies of General Lee to fight whenever he could. "When in doubt, fight," Grant liked to say. Both sides suffered heavy losses in the bloody battles in northern Virginia. But Grant did not flinch at these losses. He knew that the North, with its large population, could replace the soldiers that had been killed and wounded. He also knew that the South could not.

Sherman's March Meanwhile, General William Tecumseh Sherman marched his Union armies from Tennessee into Georgia and captured the city of Atlanta. From there, Sherman began what came to be called his "march to the sea." Sherman's

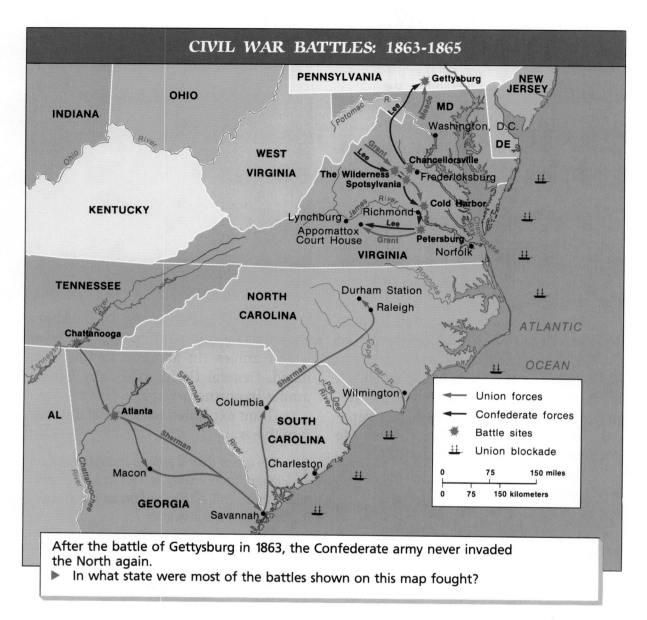

CIVIL WAR BATTLES: 1863-1865

After the battle of Gettysburg in 1863, the Confederate army never invaded the North again.
▶ In what state were most of the battles shown on this map fought?

armies destroyed everything that might help the South's war effort, including crops, railroad tracks, and bridges. Once he reached the Atlantic Ocean, Sherman turned north and took his armies into South Carolina and North Carolina.

The War Ends By this time it was spring 1865. Southern armies were running out of men and supplies. The pounding from Grant, Sherman's bloody march, and the blockade had taken their toll. Lee had only

25,000 tired, hungry troops left. Grant took the Confederate capital of Richmond and kept after Lee's army. Finally, Lee knew there was nowhere else to go. On April 9, 1865, he met Grant in a farmhouse at Appomattox Court House, Virginia. There, in a moving ceremony, the proud Southern general surrendered.

The Civil War had ended. The Union was saved, and slavery was abolished everywhere in the country. But the cost of the war had been terrible. More than

detail, Assassination of Lincoln, by H. Hill, © 1872. Collection of the Albany Institute of History and Art. Gift of the American Legion City Post No. 225

President Abraham Lincoln's assassination was one of the nation's most tragic events. Here he is shown after the shooting, as several men prepare to carry him out of Ford's Theatre.

▶ Describe how the people who are gathered around Lincoln are feeling.

625,000 Confederate and Union soldiers were killed. That is more than all the soldiers lost in all of America's other wars put together, up to the present time. Another 250,000 soldiers were disabled for life.

Lincoln's Death The man who guided the Union to victory did not live to help the nation heal its wounds. On April 14, 1865 President Lincoln went to Ford's Theater in Washington, D.C. As Lincoln watched a play, John Wilkes Booth, an actor made bitter by the defeat of the Confederacy, took his revenge. Booth stepped behind Lincoln's seat, drew a gun, and shot the President. John Wilkes Booth escaped but was later hunted down and shot while hiding in a barn.

Lincoln was still alive as he was carried to a house across the street from the theater. But there was no hope for the President. The next morning, the great leader lay dead.

LESSON **3** *REVIEW*

THINK AND WRITE

A. What was the main point Abraham Lincoln made in the Gettysburg Address?

B. How did the Union army and navy's treatment of black volunteers differ from the way white soldiers and sailors were treated?

C. How did the advantages of having a larger population and many factories contribute to the Union's winning of the Civil War in 1865?

SKILLS CHECK

MAP SKILL

Use the map on page 452 to make a list of the sites where battles were fought between Grant's Union forces and Lee's Confederate forces.

453

Reconstruction

THINK ABOUT WHAT YOU KNOW

Suppose you and your best friend had an argument and you did not speak to each other for a week. Then you talked about your argument and decided to be friends again. How would you feel? What, do you think, could you do to make up and become friends again?

STUDY THE VOCABULARY

sharecropper
Reconstruction
Black Codes
Radical
   Republican

impeach
scalawag
carpetbagger
segregation

FOCUS YOUR READING

How were the presidential reconstruction plan and the congressional reconstruction plan different?

These freed slaves are farming a piece of land belonging to their former owner. They must work very hard to make a poor living.
► What work is shown here?

A. The Freedmen's Bureau Helps Former Slaves

Conditions in the South The South had suffered great destruction in the Civil War. By the time the fighting ended, cities like Atlanta, Georgia; Columbia, South Carolina; and Richmond, Virginia, lay in ruins. Railroad lines and bridges in the South were torn up. Factories and cotton gins were destroyed. Fields that once produced fine harvests of cotton, tobacco, and grain were covered with weeds. Nearly half the South's farm animals were gone.

The Freedmen's Bureau To help people get back on their feet, Congress created the Freedmen's Bureau. Freedmen were former slaves. The Freedmen's Bureau was a government agency that was to help needy blacks and whites in the South.

These people desperately needed food, clothing, fuel, and medical supplies.

The Freedmen's Bureau had its greatest success in education. It set up more than 4,000 schools, where the former slaves could learn to read and write. Thousands of freed blacks, both children and adults, flocked to these schools. Many were deeply religious people who wanted to be able to read the Bible.

Changes on the Farm The Freedmen's Bureau was not able to make much of a difference in other ways. So Southerners created their own arrangements. In the first months of peace, many black people left their old plantations. They wanted to experience their new freedom. Many of them also wanted to find family members who had been separated from them when they were slaves.

Freed slaves gather around their school in South Carolina. School was a symbol of liberty to them.
► How does this school compare in size with your school?

The Granger Collection, New York

Most black people, though, stayed on to farm the lands that belonged to their former owners. The owners of the lands had no money to pay them wages, and the freedmen had no money to pay the owners rent. So the owners let the freedmen use some of the land and lent them plows, tools, mules, and seed. In return the owners got a share of the crops the freedmen raised. These new farmers were known as **sharecroppers**. Nine out of ten former slave families became sharecroppers. Many poor white families also became sharecroppers.

B. Congress and the President Disagree over Reconstruction

Lincoln's Plan Just as important as the ruins the war had created were the emotional scars. With the war over, America's leaders turned to the rebuilding of the Union. This period of rebuilding is known as **Reconstruction**. How, these leaders asked, could the country be brought back together after such a bitter war? President Lincoln had a plan for bringing the defeated Southern states back into the Union quickly. After Lincoln died, Vice President Andrew Johnson became President. Johnson took over Lincoln's plan, with a few changes. This plan came to be known as *presidential reconstruction*.

This is how presidential reconstruction would work. First, 10 percent of the voters in each Southern state would have to take an oath of loyalty to the Union. Then that state could write a new state constitution and elect a new government. Finally, the new state government would ratify the Thirteenth Amendment to the Constitution of the United States. The Thirteenth Amendment outlawed slavery. When those things were done, a state could be received back into the Union.

455

This photograph shows some of the destruction to Richmond.
▶ Which part of the photograph shows the most severe damage to Richmond?

Debate in Congress However, many Republican members of Congress refused to go along with presidential reconstruction. The Confederate states had caused the Civil War, they argued, so those states deserved a harsh punishment. Instead, some of those states had actually elected leaders of the Confederacy to represent them in Congress!

Republicans in the United States Congress were also angered by Southern laws that were aimed at keeping down the former slaves. One Southern state allowed blacks to work only on farms or as housekeepers. Another state said that blacks could not change jobs or travel from place to place. No Southern state allowed blacks to vote. Laws like these were known as **Black Codes**.

Many Republicans in Congress said that presidential reconstruction would hardly change the South at all. These members of Congress believed that a more extreme, or *radical*, plan for reconstruction was needed. Supporters of this plan became known as **Radical Republicans**.

All through 1866 the Radical Republicans and President Johnson argued angrily over Reconstruction. Finally in 1867, Radical Republicans put an end to presidential reconstruction. Then they passed their own plan, which became known as *congressional reconstruction*.

C. Congress Takes Over Reconstruction

Congress's Plan Under congressional reconstruction the United States Army would be in charge of the South until the Southern states were back in the Union. Southern states would have to meet new conditions before being let back in. Congress said that black people as well as white people must take part in writing each new state constitution. Also, black people would have the vote, could hold office, and would enjoy the same rights that white people had.

However, Southerners who had supported the rebellion against the United States would not be allowed to have a say in writing their state's constitution. Even more important, these people could not vote or hold office. This included the hundreds of thousands who had served in the Confederate army.

After a state adopted its new constitution and elected a new government, it had to ratify the Fourteenth Amendment to the United States Constitution. This amendment made African Americans citizens. It also guaranteed that all citizens would receive "equal protection of the law." When a state did all these things, it would be received back into the Union. Only then would the United States troops leave that state.

The President on Trial Congress no longer trusted President Johnson. So laws to limit his power were passed. When Johnson ignored those laws, the House of Representatives voted to **impeach** him. To *impeach* means "to charge an officeholder with wrongdoing." Under our Constitution the members of the House of Representatives have the job of impeaching a President. Once impeached, the President is tried in the Senate. If two thirds of the senators find the President guilty of the charges brought against him, the President is removed from office.

When Johnson was President, 36 senators would have had to vote "guilty" in order to remove him from office. When the votes were counted, it was found that only 35 senators had voted "guilty." So by one vote, President Johnson stayed in office until the end of his term.

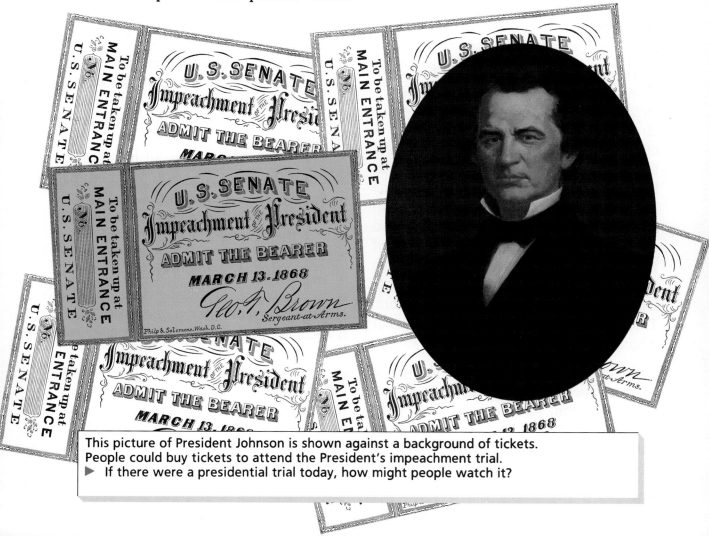

This picture of President Johnson is shown against a background of tickets. People could buy tickets to attend the President's impeachment trial.
► If there were a presidential trial today, how might people watch it?

Robert Elliot of South Carolina delivers a great civil rights speech to Congress in 1874.
▶ Explain the words on the banner.

D. Reconstruction Brings Changes to the South

Black Officeholders By 1870 all the former states of the Confederacy had rejoined the Union. Congressional reconstruction led to big changes in the South. A number of blacks held office for the first time. Many blacks were elected to serve in the state legislatures. Blacks served as lieutenant governors in Mississippi, Louisiana, and South Carolina. Several also were elected to the United States House of Representatives and the United States Senate. About half of these black officials had been slaves only a few years before. The other half were free blacks, some of whom had moved from the North.

Other Officeholders Even though a good number of blacks held office during Reconstruction, most officeholders were still white. Some were business leaders. Others were poor whites who were getting their first chance in government. All of

them thought the South would be better off if it changed some of its old ways. Many Southern whites opposed these ideas, and they called the leaders who suggested them **scalawags.** That was the name Southerners gave to small, worthless farm animals.

Some whites who served in the new Southern governments were Northerners who had gone south after the war. Some started farms or businesses. Others went to help the freedmen as teachers and ministers. Still others went in hopes of making money from the South's troubles. Most white Southerners hated these Northerners. They called them **carpetbaggers.** A carpetbag is a cheap suitcase made of pieces of carpet. Southerners said these people came to the South with all their belongings in a carpetbag that they hoped to fill with riches.

Results of Reconstruction The Reconstruction governments of the South did many things to improve their states. They rebuilt roads, railroads, and buildings destroyed in the war. They started the first public school system in the South. They built hospitals and orphanages. The Reconstruction governments also ratified the Fifteenth Amendment. This amendment says that no state can keep a person from voting because of his race or color. (The Fifteenth Amendment did not, however, give black women the right to vote. At this time no women in the United States, black or white, were allowed to vote.)

E. Reconstruction Ends

Anger in the South Most Southern whites hated the Reconstruction governments. Seeing their former slaves take part in government outraged them. They opposed paying taxes to send black children to school. They refused to accept equal rights for black people. These whites were determined to win back control of their states and end such changes.

A number of these whites formed secret societies, such as the *Ku Klux Klan*. Their aim was to frighten the freed slaves and their white supporters. Wearing white sheets and hoods, Ku Klux Klan members threatened and beat blacks to keep them from voting. They also whipped whites who were friendly with blacks. Klansmen sometimes burned schools and churches, and they killed a number of people.

The federal government finally sent troops to put a stop to the Klan. But whites formed other groups to keep blacks from voting. They warned that blacks who voted would lose their jobs. They also threatened violence.

Reconstruction Is Over Those people who wanted to get rid of the Reconstruction governments in the South finally

Two armed and robed members of the Ku Klux Klan are shown in 1868.
▶ Why, do you think, did Klan members often hide their faces?

succeeded. The North was growing weary of the trouble in the South. After a few years the United States government gave back the vote to those who had served in the Confederate army. At the same time, blacks were kept away from the voting places by threats and violence.

In one Southern state after another, scalawags, carpetbaggers, and blacks were voted out of office. In 1877 the last United States troops were removed from the South. Whites who wanted to return to the old ways now controlled all the Southern states. Reconstruction was over.

Changes in the South Over the next 20 years, blacks in the South lost nearly every right they had won during Reconstruction. They were separated from whites in restaurants, hotels, streetcars, theaters, and other public places. State laws that required such **segregation** were known as

This 1874 cartoon shows how African Americans were harassed and kept from voting at the polling places.
► Why is one man holding a gun?

Jim Crow laws. Segregation is the separation of black and white people from each other. Segregation was practiced in much of the North, too, even though few Northern states had Jim Crow laws.

Southern states also passed a number of laws that made it nearly impossible for blacks to vote. One such law required that all voters pay a poll tax of two dollars. This was a tax that people had to pay to be allowed to vote. For many poor blacks and poor whites, too, a two-dollar tax was nearly a week's wages.

Another law said that people had to pass a test to prove that they were able to read and understand the state constitution in order to vote. Blacks were almost never allowed to pass the test, no matter how well they could read. But when a white man couldn't read, a way was usually found to allow him to vote anyway.

Before long there were once again few black voters and no black officeholders in the South. Black Americans would have to wait for many more years before they would enjoy equal rights.

LESSON 4 REVIEW

THINK AND WRITE

A. How did the Freedmen's Bureau help former slaves and needy whites in the South?

B. Why did the Radical Republicans oppose the presidential Reconstruction plan?

C. What were the main points of the congressional Reconstruction plan?

D. What were three things the Reconstruction governments did to improve conditions in the Southern states after the Civil War?

E. How were black Southerners kept from achieving equal rights after Reconstruction ended?

SKILLS CHECK

WRITING SKILL

Suppose that you are a Southern child who is learning to read and write at a school set up by the Freedmen's Bureau. Write a letter to a friend, describing how you feel about going to school for the first time.

USING THE VOCABULARY

defensive war   Black Codes
blockade   impeach
border state   scalawag
Emancipation   carpetbagger
   Proclamation   segregation
Reconstruction

On a separate sheet of paper, complete these sentences, using the words listed above.

1. The _____ declared that slaves in rebelling states would be "forever free."

2. The period of rebuilding the Union is known as _____.

3. After the war, Southern states passed _____, which denied the newly freed slaves their rights.

4. Laws requiring _____ were known as Jim Crow laws.

5. The Northern _____ tried to keep Confederate ships from sailing to Europe.

6. The Radical Republicans wanted to _____ President Johnson.

7. A white Southerner who joined a Reconstruction government was called a _____.

8. One advantage that the South had during the war was that it was fighting a _____.

9. A Northerner in a Southern government during Reconstruction was called a _____.

10. Maryland was a _____.

REMEMBERING WHAT YOU READ

On a separate sheet of paper, write your answers in complete sentences.

1. Why was population a Northern advantage during the war?

2. What roles did women fill during the war?

3. What were two parts of the Union plan for victory?

4. What was the bloodiest battle of the war?

5. Why didn't Lincoln include the slaves in the border states in the Emancipation Proclamation?

6. Why did Frederick Douglass urge black men to join the Union forces?

7. What happened at Appomattox Court House?

8. For what purposes was the Freedmen's Bureau created?

9. What did the Thirteenth, Fourteenth, and Fifteenth amendments to the Constitution say?

10. Which two laws kept poor blacks and poor whites in the South from voting?

TYING READING TO SOCIAL STUDIES

Read a biography of one of the following people: Robert E. Lee, Clara Barton, Harriet Tubman, Ulysses S. Grant, or Thomas "Stonewall" Jackson. Pay attention to the kind of person he or she was. What choices did this person make? How was he or she affected by events? What effect did he or she have on events? Write a paragraph expressing your opinion of this person. Discuss your opinion with your classmates.

461

THINKING CRITICALLY

On a separate sheet of paper, write your answers in complete sentences.

1. Was Robert E. Lee right, do you think, in choosing loyalty to Virginia over loyalty to the Union? Explain your answer.
2. The North had greater advantages than the South when the war started. Why did it take four years for the North to win?
3. What is your opinion of General Grant's ideas about warfare?
4. Do you think education is as important today as it was at the end of the Civil War? Explain your answer.
5. If you had been alive at that time, which plan of reconstruction—that of the President or that of Congress—would you have supported? Explain your answer.

SUMMARIZING THE CHAPTER

On a separate sheet of paper, draw a graphic organizer like the one shown here. Copy the information from this graphic organizer to the one you have drawn. Under the main idea for each lesson, write three statements that support the main idea.

CHAPTER THEME

The Civil War was a long and bloody war. Reconstruction did little to bring the nation back together. State laws tried to deny black Americans the rights they gained under the Constitution.

LESSON 1

Each side had advantages at the start of the war.

1. The North had more people.
2. The South was fighting a defensive war.
3. Women aided the war effort

LESSON 3

The North gained as the war continued.

1. _____
2. _____
3. _____

LESSON 2

Several important battles and events occurred in the early years of the war.

1. _____
2. _____
3. _____

LESSON 4

Reconstruction punished the South and attempted to help the freed slaves.

1. _____
2. _____
3. _____

COOPERATIVE LEARNING

The period around the Civil War was a very difficult time for the United States. People felt very strongly about the events that were taking place.

PROJECT

Your group will choose an event from this unit and create a newspaper that describes and discusses that event. After your group has chosen the event, but before it begins to work on the newspaper, pick one member to be the group representative. This person will meet with representatives from the other groups in the class. The purpose of this meeting is to see that each group works on a different event. After this meeting, each group can begin to work on its newspaper.

Your newspaper should have headlines, articles, editorials, and pictures. If your group is ambitious, you could include advertisements, social notes, and local news. These are items that are not connected with the event but reflect the time during which the event took place.

Your newspaper will need the following workers.

- An editor to plan the articles and help the other group members
- Reporters to write the articles

- A headline writer
- An artist or someone to trace pictures from books

PRESENTATION AND REVIEW

The newspaper can be presented in a number of ways. Articles could be neatly printed in columns on notebook paper, cut out, and pasted on large sheets of butcher paper under headlines and around pictures. Or the material could be written directly on large sheets of poster paper. If your group has the use of a word processor, the articles could be printed out and pasted up. The results of this last method can look very much like an actual newspaper.

When your group has completed this project, each member should write an evaluation. Everyone should consider the following questions.

- How successful was the project?
- What did I contribute to this project?
- How well did I do my work?

- What improvements could be made in my work and in the way the group worked together?

Meet again as a group and discuss what everyone learned from working together.

REMEMBER TO:
- Give your ideas.
- Listen to others' ideas.
- Plan your work with the group.
- Present your project.
- Discuss how your group worked.

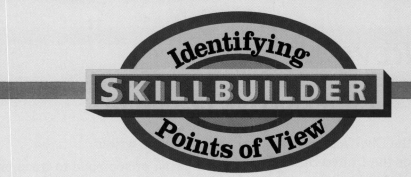

A. WHY DO I NEED THIS SKILL?

History books contain facts — many, many facts. In this unit you have learned about the great Civil War that divided the United States. You learned about sectionalism and slavery, about the industrial North and the agricultural South, and about compromises that worked for a while. History books, however, are more than collections of facts. They are also collections of people's points of view.

It is worthwhile to develop the skill of identifying points of view. When Harriet Beecher Stowe wrote *Uncle Tom's Cabin*, she was expressing the viewpoint that slavery was a horrible institution. Someone who favored slavery would have written an entirely different book.

B. LEARNING THE SKILL

People's viewpoints are usually revealed by what they say or do. However, quite often people will not come right out and tell you what they feel. Sometimes they will even try to hide their views. During the American Revolution an officer named Benedict Arnold was a trusted American general until he sold secret plans to the British. On the other hand, Robert E. Lee made his viewpoint very clear. He turned down President Lincoln's offer to lead the Union army. His loyalty to Virginia was stronger than his loyalty to the United States. So he took command of the army of the Confederacy.

Turn to page 108 and read the story of the capture of the Kingdom of Chimor. Who is the hero of that story? Who, in the author's viewpoint, is the better leader? Was your answer to both questions the Topa Inca? Why did you make that choice?

Did Henry Wadsworth Longfellow think that Paul Revere was a hero? Look at the poem on page 266. List the words that Longfellow uses to show his point of view.

How does Elizabeth Yates use facts to tell you how she feels about the slave trade? Read the selection on page 201. Make a list of some of the facts. Now write a short para-

The Granger Collection, New York.

graph telling how you feel about the slave trade based on what you read.

C. PRACTICING THE SKILL

Alexis de Tocqueville (ah lek SEE duh TOHK vihl) was a French historian who traveled in the United States from 1835 to 1840. He wrote *Democracy in America* about what he saw during that time. He wrote about how people lived and worked. He compared the free state of Ohio with the slave state of Kentucky.

> *It is true that in Kentucky the planters are not obliged to pay the slaves whom they employ, but they derive [get] small profits from their labor, while the wages paid to free workmen would be returned with interest in the value of their services. . . . The white sells his services, but they are purchased only when they may be useful; the black can claim no re-muneration [pay] for his toil, but the expense of his maintenance [care] is perpetual [endless]. . . . Payment must equally be made in order to obtain [get] the services of either class of men; the free workman receives his wages in money; the slave in education, in food, in care, and in clothing. The money the master spends in the maintenance of his slaves goes gradually . . . so that it is scarcely perceived [hardly noticed] . . . but in the end the slave has cost more than the free servant, and his labor is less productive.*

Which of the following is the most accurate statement of de Tocqueville's point of view?
1. Slaves, because they are taken care of, are better off than free workmen.
2. Hired workmen will always do better work than slave labor.
3. Slavery is probably not a very profitable institution.

Do you think de Tocqueville approved of slavery? Explain your answer.

D. APPLYING THE SKILL

A newspaper expresses its point of view on the editorial page. Analyze an editorial from a recent issue of your local paper. In a paragraph, tell what you think the editorial writer's point of view is.

SKILLBUILDER

Drawing Conclusions

A. WHY DO I NEED THIS SKILL?

Writers cannot put every fact and idea about a subject in the books they write. The books would be much too heavy to carry. A writer must depend on readers to fill in some of the information. When readers do this, they are drawing conclusions. Knowing how to draw conclusions will help you to understand the events, characters, and reasons why things happen in this and other history books.

B. LEARNING THE SKILL

It is not difficult to draw conclusions. The first thing you do is read a selection to learn the information the writer is giving you. We will call this *selection information*. Then you add to that the facts and ideas that you already know. This can be called *known information*. To draw a conclusion, you add one kind of information to the other.

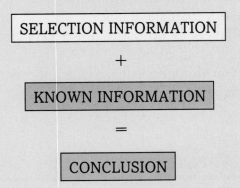

SELECTION INFORMATION

+

KNOWN INFORMATION

=

CONCLUSION

Read the following paragraph and think about a conclusion you might draw. Use the facts in the selection and add to them information that you already know.

At the time of the Civil War, the population of the North was 22 million. The population of the South was only 9 million, of which 3 1/2 million were slaves. Most of the nation's factories were in the North. Northern factories could produce 20 times as much iron as factories in the South and more than 30 times as many guns. The Union army was supplied with all the clothing, blankets, tents, and medical supplies it needed.

Was the conclusion you drew something like this: The North had several advantages during the Civil War? The diagram on the next page shows how this conclusion could be reached by using selection information and known information.

C. PRACTICING THE SKILL

Read the paragraph on the South. On a sheet of paper, draw a diagram like the one used for the paragraph on the North. Fill in the boxes to show your conclusion and the ideas you used to reach it.

All the South had to do to win the war was to successfully defend its own territory. It would not be necessary to invade the North. Therefore, the Confederate soldiers fought in their homeland. Also, the South had well-trained generals. Most of them had attended the United States Military Academy at West Point, New York. They had gained valuable fighting experience in the Mexican War 12 years earlier.

D. Applying the Skill

The lessons in this social studies book have been designed to help you use this skill. Each lesson begins with the section Think About What You Know. Sometimes you are asked to remember something you learned in an earlier chapter or lesson. Other times you are asked to think of a personal experience or to imagine yourself in some other time or place. In doing this activity, you are using your known information. The Focus Your Reading question will help you look for information as you read the lesson or selection. This question can also serve as a hint of the conclusion you can draw.

Make a special effort to use this skill as you read Chapter 20. You will find it easier in the beginning if you make a how-to-draw-a-conclusion diagram for each lesson.

HOW TO DRAW CONCLUSIONS

SELECTION INFORMATION

- The North had more people.
- The North had more factories to produce guns, clothing, and medical supplies.

+

KNOWN INFORMATION

- Armies need soldiers, guns, and supplies in order to win a war.

=

CONCLUSION

- The North had some definite advantages during the Civil War.

NO
MORE
WAR

THE UNITED STATES EXPANDS

In less than 100 years, the United States changed from a nation expanding on a continent to an expanding world power. At home, there was a growth of cities, industries, immigration, and reform movements.

▶ *This montage reflects how the role of women has changed in the twentieth century.*

Between 1865 and 1890 the last frontier of the West changed. Miners scoured the mountains looking for gold and other precious metals. Railroads steamed across the land from east to west.

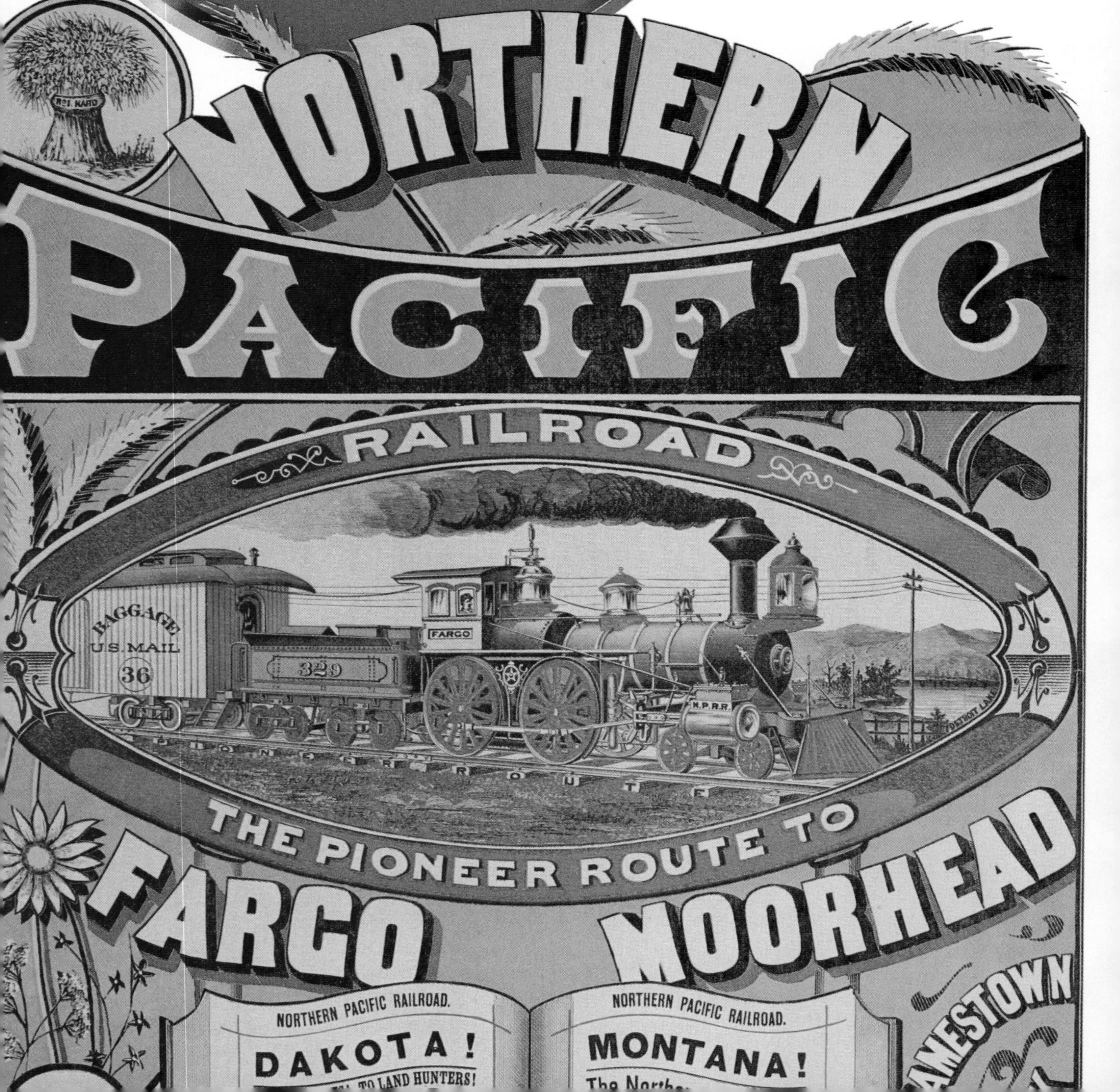

NORTHERN PACIFIC

RAILROAD

BAGGAGE
U.S. MAIL
36

FARGO

329

N.P.R.R.

THE PIONEER ROUTE TO

FARGO   MOORHEAD

JAMESTOWN

NORTHERN PACIFIC RAILROAD.
DAKOTA!

NORTHERN PACIFIC RAILROAD.
MONTANA!

The Mining Frontier

THINK ABOUT WHAT YOU KNOW

Imagine that you are going to search for gold and silver in the West during the 1860s. What are some things you might want to know about before starting your journey?

STUDY THE VOCABULARY

lode

ghost town

transcontinental railroad

FOCUS YOUR READING

How did miners and railroad builders help the United States grow?

A. Two Miners Stumble upon a Rich Find

In 1859 the North and the South were moving closer and closer to war. But Pete O'Reilly and Pat McLaughlin had other things on their minds. O'Reilly and McLaughlin were Irish immigrants who had gone west to hunt for gold. When they heard that a prospector had struck gold near Pikes Peak, in Colorado, O'Reilly and McLaughlin hurried there. Like most others who rushed to Colorado, O'Reilly and McLaughlin found no gold.

Soon after, the two fortune hunters moved on to a place called Six Mile Canyon in the Sierra Nevada, located in what is now Nevada. There a man named Henry Comstock talked the two immigrants into letting him become their partner.

One day, O'Reilly and McLaughlin dug up some heavy, blue-colored rock. Not knowing what the rock was, they showed it to a couple of rich Californians. The Californians realized that the rock was filled with silver. However, they did not tell that

to O'Reilly, McLaughlin, and Comstock. Instead the Californians offered several thousand dollars to buy the land that the ore came from. The three partners agreed to sell. Later, Comstock bragged about the terrific deal he had made.

In the next 20 years, the piece of land that the prospectors had sold for a few thousand dollars and the area around it produced *$300 million* worth of silver! It became known as the *Comstock Lode*. A **lode** is a rich deposit of ore.

News of the rich find traveled quickly. Soon thousands of miners rushed to the region. About a dozen of these miners became rich. The others soon found that most of the silver ore in Six Mile Canyon was too deep in the ground for them to dig it out with their simple pickaxes and shovels. Only large mining companies with expensive machinery could do that. In time most of the miners who had come to Six Mile Canyon to seek their fortunes went to work for these mining companies.

B. Miners Help to Open the West

Gold Rushes The rush to find gold and silver in the West lasted only about 25 years. In that time it gave us one of the most colorful periods in our history. Farmers and city people, poor workers and the sons of rich families, Southern whites and Northern blacks, native-born Americans and immigrants all took part in the search for riches. In just one mining camp, for example, a visitor found 73 white Americans, 18 black Americans, 37 Chinese, 29 Mexicans, 35 British people, and 24 people from other European countries.

Life in these mining camps was rough, for there were neither laws nor police. Miners had to guard their possessions against thieves. Murders were common.

Mining Towns News of a big gold or silver discovery could turn a mining camp into a good-sized town in just a few days. Hundreds of miners and other workers rushed to the area. In a few weeks a string of wooden stores stretched along the town's main street. There, miners lined up to buy tents, tools, clothes, and food.

A mining town might last for five or ten years—only as long as gold or silver remained in the ground nearby. When the gold and silver were gone, the miners moved on. Without miners to buy their goods, merchants left the town, too. Soon little remained but the deserted wooden buildings, and the mining town became a **ghost town**.

Not all mining towns became ghost towns, though. Each new gold rush brought men and women to run the stores, farm the land, and start schools, churches, and newspapers. When the gold and silver ran out, many of these people stayed on to raise families and build up the country. In this way, mining helped to settle present-day Colorado, Nevada, Montana, Idaho, Washington, and South Dakota.

C. Tying the Nation Together

From the time that California became a state in 1850, Americans had dreamed of a **transcontinental railroad**. Such a railroad would run across the entire continent. In 1862, Congress gave two companies the right to build such a railroad. To help those companies, Congress lent them money and gave them land.

The next year, with the Civil War raging, the railroad builders began their work. One company, the Central Pacific, started in Sacramento, California, and built tracks toward the East. The other company, the Union Pacific, began in Omaha, Nebraska, and built tracks toward the West. The transcontinental railroad would be complete when the two tracks met.

Each company hired thousands of workers. Most of the workers on the Central Pacific were Chinese immigrants. The Union Pacific workers were mostly Irish immigrants. Mexican Americans, blacks, and Indians also labored on this huge project. After the Civil War, Union and Confederate army veterans joined the work crews.

Building the tracks was difficult and dangerous. Workers on the Central Pacific

A busy mining town (left) could quickly become a ghost town (right) if the mines stopped operating.
▶ List the businesses shown below.

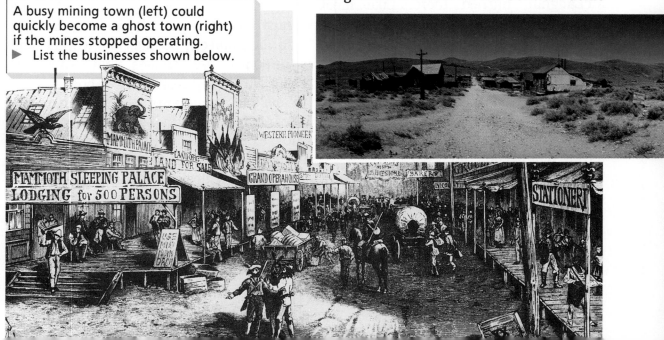

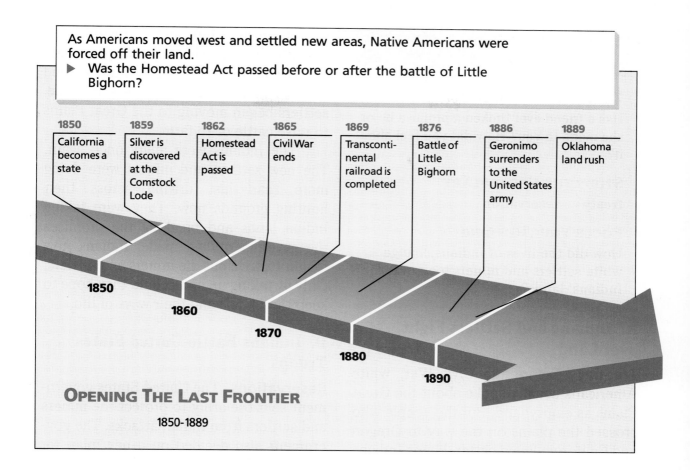

As Americans moved west and settled new areas, Native Americans were forced off their land.

▶ Was the Homestead Act passed before or after the battle of Little Bighorn?

1850	1859	1862	1865	1869	1876	1886	1889
California becomes a state	Silver is discovered at the Comstock Lode	Homestead Act is passed	Civil War ends	Transcontinental railroad is completed	Battle of Little Bighorn	Geronimo surrenders to the United States army	Oklahoma land rush

OPENING THE LAST FRONTIER

1850-1889

had to build around mountains, and sometimes right through them. Their only tools were pickaxes and shovels, for dynamite had not yet been invented. The Union Pacific's workers often faced attacks by Indians as they built westward across the Great Plains.

On May 10, 1869, the two railroad lines met at a place called Promontory (PRAHM un tor ee) Point, Utah. There, at exactly 12:47 P.M., a golden spike was driven into the last railroad tie, linking the two lines. Telegraph wires flashed the news to a cheering nation. Over the next 15 years, other companies built three more transcontinental railroads. From one coast to another, gleaming ribbons of steel track tied the nation together.

LESSON *1* REVIEW

THINK AND WRITE

A. Why did so few miners become rich from the Comstock Lode?

B. Describe a western mining community of the late 1800s.

C. Why, do you think, did the railroad builders use a golden spike to link the two tracks at Promontory Point in 1869?

SKILLS CHECK

THINKING SKILL

Explain why you would or would not like to have lived in a mining town.

473

The Indians' Last Stand

THINK ABOUT WHAT YOU KNOW

Has a friend ever broken a promise he or she made to you? How did you feel about it?

STUDY THE VOCABULARY

treaty   **reservation**

FOCUS YOUR READING

How did the lives of Indians change as white settlers and miners took over the Indians' lands?

A. Indians and Settlers Fight over Land

Treaties   Before the Civil War, white Americans usually spoke about the Great Plains as empty land. But the people who crossed the plains on the way to Oregon and California knew better. Plains Indians lived on this land, as they had for centuries. These Indians depended on the buffalo for food, clothing, and shelter. They were not happy to see the wagons full of settlers rolling across their hunting grounds. Sometimes, bands of angry Indians attacked the wagon trains and killed the settlers.

To keep the peace, the United States government signed treaties with the Indians. A **treaty** is an agreement between groups of people or nations. In these treaties the government promised that settlers would not take over the Indians' hunting grounds. The government promised that the hunting grounds would belong to the Indians forever. In exchange the Indians agreed not to attack the settlers.

The Lure of Riches   The United States did not obey the agreements for long,

though. In the 1860s and 1870s, prospectors discovered gold and silver in many parts of the West. Fortune hunters rushed to claim land for mining. At the same time, settlers began moving to the Great Plains to raise cattle or to farm.

The Indians were angry once again. The new settlers and miners were doing more than just driving across their hunting grounds now. They were taking Indian lands and breaking the promises the government had made. Indians now fought to drive out the miners and settlers. Only by taking up arms could they hope to keep their lands and their ways of life.

B. Indians Battle United States Troops

Reservations   The United States government sent the army to protect the miners and settlers from Indian attacks. The government also decided on a new plan for

This 1870 painting shows Plains Indians hunting buffaloes for food, clothing, and shelter.
► What weapon is being used?

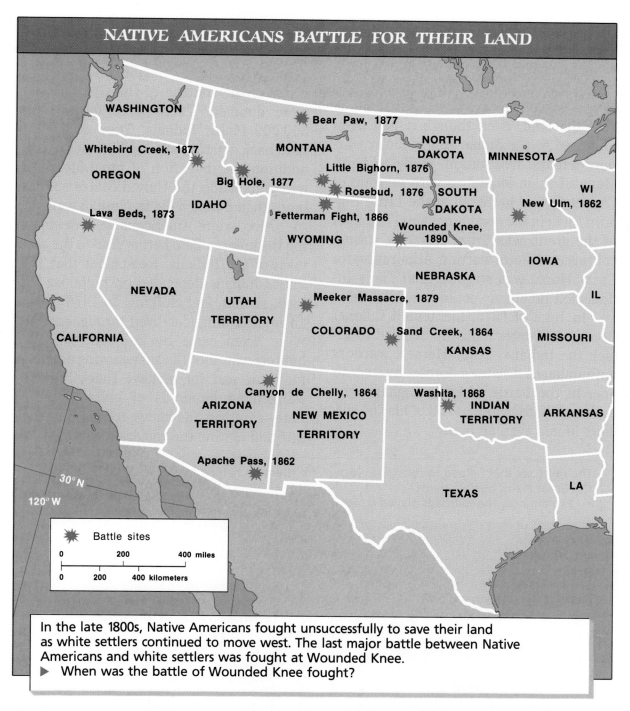

NATIVE AMERICANS BATTLE FOR THEIR LAND

WASHINGTON

Bear Paw, 1877

Whitebird Creek, 1877

MONTANA

NORTH DAKOTA

MINNESOTA

OREGON

Big Hole, 1877

Little Bighorn, 1876

Rosebud, 1876 SOUTH

WI

New Ulm, 1862

IDAHO

DAKOTA

Lava Beds, 1873

Fetterman Fight, 1866

Wounded Knee, 1890

WYOMING

IOWA

NEVADA

NEBRASKA

IL

UTAH

Meeker Massacre, 1879

TERRITORY

CALIFORNIA

COLORADO

Sand Creek, 1864

MISSOURI

KANSAS

Canyon de Chelly, 1864

Washita, 1868

ARIZONA

NEW MEXICO

INDIAN

ARKANSAS

TERRITORY

TERRITORY

TERRITORY

Apache Pass, 1862

30° N

LA

120° W

TEXAS

✹ Battle sites

0   200   400 miles

0   200   400 kilometers

In the late 1800s, Native Americans fought unsuccessfully to save their land as white settlers continued to move west. The last major battle between Native Americans and white settlers was fought at Wounded Knee.

▶ When was the battle of Wounded Knee fought?

dealing with the Indians. The Indians would have to give up their lands and move onto **reservations**. A reservation was land that the government reserved, or put aside, for the Indians. Most reservations were on poor land that white settlers did not want.

Indians did not want to leave their homelands. But some tribes agreed to move onto the reservations. Others refused. Fierce fighting broke out between these Indians and the army along the frontier. Between 1868 and 1875, Indians and the army fought over 200 battles.

Little Bighorn One great battle began after Sioux Indians moved to a reservation in the Black Hills of South Dakota. In 1874, miners discovered gold on this reservation. Thousands of miners rushed in to take the land, even though it had been promised to the Sioux. Angry Sioux warriors left the reservation, ready to fight. Many of them joined up with a group of Cheyenne and gathered at the Little Bighorn River in the northern plains. The chief of the group was Crazy Horse, a strong, courageous Sioux warrior. Admiration for Crazy Horse was so great that many Indians felt no enemy could ever kill him.

In June of 1876, Lieutenant Colonel George A. Custer foolishly decided to attack the Indians. Crazy Horse's warriors outnumbered Custer's forces by ten to one. In the battle of Little Bighorn, the Indians killed Custer and all of his 264 soldiers in less than an hour.

C. The United States Forces All Indian Groups onto Reservations

A Losing Struggle Despite their skill and bravery, the Indians of the Great Plains were doomed. There were fewer than 300,000 Plains Indians. They could not hold back a nation of 40 million people. In addition the invention of rapid-fire rifles and guns made the United States soldier more than a match for the Indian warrior.

Also, white Americans were destroying the great buffalo herds, vital to the survival of the Indians. Remember that the Plains Indians depended on buffaloes for food, shelter, and clothing. In 1870 about 13 million buffaloes lived throughout the West. Then came the railroad, bringing hunters who shot the slow-moving animals for sport and for money. These hunters slaughtered hundreds of buffaloes at a time, shipping the hides to the East for sale and leaving the carcasses to rot.

The railroads that helped to open the western frontier also helped to wipe out the Great Plains buffalo herds.
▶ Explain how the railroads played a part in destroying the buffaloes.

The Thomas Gilcrease Institute of American History and Art, Tulsa, Oklahoma

This Indian family had to move to a small wood cabin on the Tonkawa Reservation, in Oklahoma, on land allotted by the government.
▶ Are these Indians dressed in traditional Native American clothes?

By 1880 only a few hundred buffaloes remained on the western plains. The main source of the Indians' livelihood had disappeared. Many Indians no longer had enough to eat. One after another the weakened and defeated tribes agreed to live on the reservations.

The Apaches' Last Stand The Apaches were the last Indian group to hold out. Apaches lived in the southwestern part of the United States. Led by their chief, Geronimo (juh RAHN un moh), they attacked white settlements from their camps in the Sierra Madre. For ten years they managed to escape from the pursuing army. Finally in 1886, United States troops trapped Geronimo and forced him to surrender. Then, like the other Plains Indians, the Apaches moved onto a reservation.

The Plains Indians found it hard to keep their former way of life on the reservations. No longer could they hunt for food. They now had to learn to be farmers or to raise sheep and cattle. No longer did land belong to the whole tribe together. Now each individual family owned a small patch of ground. Indians could not freely roam the western plains under the open sky. Now they had to live within the boundaries of the reservations. The wide-open lands that had once been theirs now belonged to others.

LESSON *2* REVIEW
_____

THINK AND WRITE

A. How did the United States break its promises to the Plains Indians?
B. Why did fighting break out between Indians and United States troops during the late 1860s and 1870s?
C. List three important reasons explaining why the United States government was finally able to force all Indian groups onto reservations.

SKILLS CHECK

MAP SKILL

Use the map on page 475 to find the site of the battle of Little Bighorn. Name the present-day state in which that battle took place.

The Cattle Frontier

THINK ABOUT WHAT YOU KNOW

The cowboy of the Old West is one of the most popular American characters. How do you picture the cowboy?

STUDY THE VOCABULARY

long drive   **open range**
vaquero

FOCUS YOUR READING

How and why did cattle ranching spread to the Great Plains?

A. Texans Start Cattle Ranches

When the Spanish came to the New World in the 1500s, they brought a few cattle. Over the next 300 years, the cattle multiplied in northern Mexico and Texas. By 1845, when Texas became part of the United States, the young state had about 5 million cattle. These cattle did not belong to anyone. They were there for anyone to take. So a few Texans gathered large numbers of cattle and started huge ranches.

After the Civil War, ranchers sold these cattle in Texas for three or four dollars each. The ranchers knew that they could get at least ten times as much from buyers in the East, but they needed a railroad to move the cattle there. At the time the railroad closest to Texas was in Missouri.

A number of ranchers decided that if they could not bring the railroad to the cattle, they would take the cattle to the railroad. Starting in 1866, ranchers began bringing their herds together every spring for the **long drive** to the railroad in Missouri. For two or three months, they moved thousands of cattle from Texas to the railroad. These long drives were hard and dangerous. Many cattle were lost or stolen, or they died along the way. But enough of them got to the railroad to make their owners rich. The long drives opened

A cowboy's life was not easy. Here, trying to rope a range cow, is a cowboy about to fall with his pony. His partner rides to help him.
► Why, do you think, was being a cowboy sometimes a dangerous job?

The Thomas Gilcrease Institute of American History and Art, Tulsa, Oklahoma

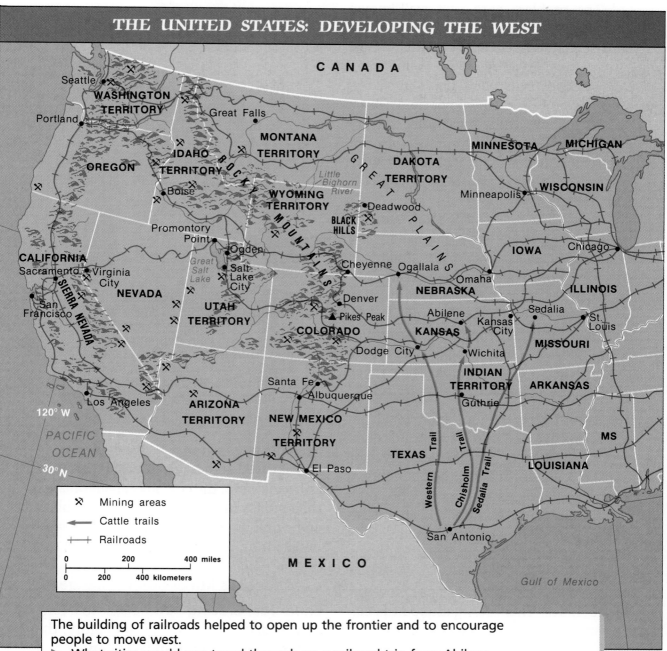

THE UNITED STATES: DEVELOPING THE WEST

The building of railroads helped to open up the frontier and to encourage people to move west.

▶ What cities would you travel through on a railroad trip from Abilene, Kansas, to Salt Lake City?

the cattle frontier in the West. They also helped to create a new character in American history—the cowboy.

B. The Cowboy Lives a Rough Life

The Cowboy Everyone knows about the American cowboy. Books, movies, and television have made the cowboy a familiar figure around the world. You can probably picture him galloping along on his horse, living a life of adventure, and fighting outlaws with his blazing guns. The cowboy has been a great hero to generations of American children.

The problem with that well-known picture of the western cowboy is that it is not true. The real-life cowboy was a wage earner. Most cowboys were young men. Many were even in their teens. Quite a few of them were black cowboys from Texas. These cowboys came west after slavery ended. An even greater number of cowboys were Mexicans. In fact the Mexican cowboy, or **vaquero** (vah KER oh), was the first American cowboy.

Western cowboys took on many of the vaquero's ways, including his style of dress and many Spanish words. American cowboys wore wide-brimmed *sombreros*, or hats, on their heads for protection against the strong sun. To protect their legs from the brush, they wore *chaparajos* (chap uh RAY hohz). Cowboys shortened that Spanish word to *chaps*. They roped horses and cattle with a *lasso* or *lariat*.

The Long Drive As for the life of adventure, cowboys had little of that. For eight or nine months of the year, the cowboy rode back and forth along the boundary of his boss's land. As no fences were built yet, the cowboy's job was to keep the cattle from wandering off or being stolen. In the spring he joined the cattle roundup. Cowboys lassoed the calves. Next they burned a special brand, or mark, into the calves' hides. Then they gathered the cattle that were ready for market and set out on the long drive.

The drive lasted two to three months, with no days off. The only break in the day was at mealtime. Then the cowboys would eat, sitting cross-legged on the ground. Each day the food was the same — beef, bacon, beans, and biscuits.

For all their work, cowboys usually earned about one dollar a day. That was half as much as many other workers in the

A statue and a photograph give two views of the American cowboy.
► Which makes the cowboy's life look more exciting — the statue or the photograph?

United States earned. And when they finally arrived at the "cow towns" where the railroads were, the cowboys spent most of their money in a few wild days of gambling and drinking. Cowboys called these wild breaks from boredom "big times."

C. Ranchers Make Some Changes

Land for Grazing Although the long drives made many ranchers wealthy, the drives were costly. Ranchers saw that if they grazed their cattle nearer to the railroads, they would not need the long drives. They began to eye the miles of grassy lands on the central and northern Great Plains in Kansas and present-day Nebraska, Colorado, Wyoming, and Montana. For hundreds of years, buffaloes had grazed on these grasslands. But by the mid-1870s, most of the buffaloes had been

Troubled Times   For several years on the open range, cattle ranchers prospered, so they kept increasing the size of their herds. But by the mid-1880s there were more cattle than the buyers wanted. Prices for cattle began to fall. Meanwhile, the grazing herds ate parts of the grassland bare.

Then nature delivered the cattle business a series of heavy blows. First a bitterly cold winter in 1885–1886 killed many cattle. Next a hot, dry summer killed much of the grass and dried up the streams. Cattle became thin and weak from lack of food and water. Then came a second terrible winter. Blizzards and strong winds piled the snow high. This time the cattle could not reach the grass under the snow. When spring came, dead cattle lay all over the open range. Ranchers lost more than half their cattle, and many ranchers went broke.

After this terrible experience, cattle ranchers realized they had to make some changes. They could no longer depend on open-range grazing year-round. Ranchers fenced in their cattle and raised enough feed to take the cattle through the winter. As a result the cowboy's job changed. Now he spent more time digging holes for fence posts than riding on horseback and rounding up cattle. The cowboy became a hired ranch hand.

killed, and most Indians were living on reservations. The way was clear for cattle ranchers to move into this fertile region.

The United States government owned this vast area of grassland. The land was known as **open range** because no fences broke it up. The government allowed cattle ranchers to graze their herds for free on the open range. Before long, millions of cattle were feeding on the open range year-round. Even in winter the animals could push aside the cool snow and nibble on the dried grass underneath. From time to time, cowboys would round up some of the cattle and herd them to the nearby railroads so that they could be sold in the East.

LESSON **3** REVIEW

THINK AND WRITE

A. What problem did the long drive help cattle ranchers solve?

B. How were the lives of real cowboys different from the lives of cowboys shown in movies and on television?

C. Why did ranchers on the open range have to fence in their lands and begin to raise feed for their cattle?

SKILLS CHECK

MAP SKILL

Use the map on page 479 to find the Western Trail, the Chisholm Trail, and the Sedalia Trail. Where did each of these cattle trails begin and end?

The Farming Frontier

THINK ABOUT WHAT YOU KNOW

How does the climate of the area that you live in affect your life? What special measures do you take to deal with your area's climate?

STUDY THE VOCABULARY

homesteader **dry farming**
barbed wire

FOCUS YOUR READING

What were some of the rewards and problems of farming in the great American West?

A. Farmers Move to the Great Plains

Farmers began streaming onto the Great Plains in the 1860s. By the 1880s several million people owned farms on the Great Plains. Congress encouraged farm settlement by passing the Homestead Act in 1862. This act promised 160 acres (65 ha) free to anyone who would live on the land and farm it for five years.

Many Civil War veterans took advantage of this offer to start new lives in the West. Thousands of other Americans were also given free land. So were immigrants from Germany, Norway, Sweden, and other countries in Europe. People who received land under the Homestead Act were called **homesteaders.**

Railroad companies also encouraged farmers to settle on the Great Plains. The United States government had given land to these railroad companies as a reward for building tracks in the unsettled West. Now the companies began to sell some of this land to farmers.

B. Settlers Learn to Farm in a New Environment

The Plains Climate The many farmers who settled on the Great Plains found an environment different from anything they had known in the East or in Europe. Summer heat reached 110°F (43°C). In the winter, icy winds howled across the open plains. The sunbaked sod, or top layer of soil and roots, was so tough that ordinary

This painting is called *The Homesteader*. It shows the artist's idea of a farming family crossing the plains to build a new life.
▶ Find a food source in the picture.

Courtesy of the Buffalo Bill Historical Center, Cody, Wyoming

This Great Plains farmer used an ox-drawn plow to turn the top layer of soil on his broad fields.

► How would a farmer on the Great Plains plow his fields today?

iron plows broke when trying to dig into it. Rainfall was low. Few trees grew to supply wood for houses and fences. And without fences, cattle trampled the crops.

Inventions Help Settlers had to learn new ways of farming in this harsh region. Two inventions helped them. One was a plow made of extra-strong iron that could cut through the tough sod. The other invention was **barbed wire**, a type of wire that has barbs, or sharp points, every few inches. With barbed wire, farmers could build fences with less wood. Cattle soon learned to stay away from barbed wire fences. Demand for this product became so great that the barbed wire factory soon made 600 miles (965 km) of wire a day!

Dry Farming Plains farmers also had to find a way to farm where there was little water. To deal with the dry climate, they adopted a method known as **dry farming**. In dry farming the farmer digs furrows, or small ditches, about a foot deep on each side of the crop. These furrows collect rain. After a rainfall the farmer quickly turns over the soil. This moves the wet soil closer to the roots of the plants. Turning the wet soil also keeps it from drying out. In addition to dry farming, farmers switched to certain kinds of wheat and other crops that needed less water.

Pests One problem that farmers could do nothing about was grasshoppers. These troublesome insects appeared on the plains every few years. Sometimes there were so many of them that they actually blocked out the sun and darkened the sky. These pests ate everything in sight. A farmer might have acres of golden grain one day and a broad empty field the next. One settler explained the problem.

> *So thick were the grasshoppers in the cornfield . . . that not a spot of green could be seen. And within two hours of the time they had come, not a leaf was left in all that field.*

C. Farmers Get Used to Plains Life

The plains were a region of beauty and opportunity. With high hopes, pioneers moved there to begin new lives. Willa Cather, who grew up in Nebraska, wrote books about the pioneers who settled the Great Plains. In one book, Cather describes a woman settler's love for the land. "It seemed beautiful to her, rich, and strong and glorious." The woman felt as many settlers did when they arrived on the plains to start new lives. One homesteader in Nebraska wrote to her sister in Chicago, telling of her fine new house and 100 acres of land. "I wouldn't trade with anyone," the homesteader declared.

Soon after they arrived, however, homesteaders and other settlers learned that life on the plains could be very hard. Most farm families did not get a fine house for many years. With so few trees on the plains to supply lumber, settlers had to build houses with blocks of sod. A thick-walled sod house could be cozy. It stayed warm in winter and cool in summer. But dirt was always crumbling from the walls and spilling onto everything. Insects, snakes, and small animals slithered through the walls into the room. And while farmers were happy when it rained, they knew their walls and floors would stay soaked and muddy for days.

Yet the greatest hardship of life on the Great Plains was probably loneliness. The nearest family might be a mile away. Except for mealtimes, when the family sat together, farmers in the field could go for days without seeing another person.

The members of this frontier family pose for a photograph outside their sod home on the almost treeless Great Plains.
► What, do you think, might have been the advantages of having large families on the Great Plains?

The land rush begins. Hopeful settlers dash headlong into Oklahoma to claim their free homesteads.
► Is offering free land a good way to distribute land among possible owners?

Frontier families found ways to break up the loneliness, though. One way was to make a weekly trip to a nearby town to get supplies and talk with people. And there were the bees, social get-togethers where people also performed some needed task. Farm families gathered at quilting bees, sewing bees, sod–house-building bees, and any other kind of bee that offered an excuse to get together.

D. Settlers Head for Oklahoma

For many years, settlers left one area of the plains to the Indians. That land, present-day Oklahoma, was known as the Indian Territory. The United States government had promised this territory to the Indians. It was here that the Trail of Tears of the 1830s had ended. The Cherokees and other Indians removed from the East had lived in Oklahoma peacefully since that time.

But more and more settlers wanted land in the Indian Territory. So the government forced the Indian tribes to sell back 2 million acres (810,000 ha). The government then divided this rich land into homesteads of 160 acres. That was still not enough to satisfy the land-hungry settlers. So the government announced that it would give away a long strip of land in western Oklahoma, starting at noon, April 22, 1889 — first come, first served!

At the Oklahoma border on the morning of April 22, about 100,000 people lined up. They seemed ready for a race. At noon the crack of the starter's gun sent these people rushing across the border. Noisy wagons raised dust as settlers rushed to get the best land. Bicycles bumped over

MAIL ORDER CATALOGS

Folding cameras are favorites with the amateur photographer, as by the style of their construction much greater compactness is secured than it is possible to obtain with the regular style boxes. They are extremely simple to open, ready for use. Merely lower the front of camera, which forms a bed, and draw the front with lens forward until the pinion engages in the rack, and the final adjustment is made with the apparatus placed at the front for that purpose. The appearance of these folding cameras are especially handsome, as the entire front and bed are made of polished mahogany or cherry, which contrasts perfectly with the black leather covering.

24357 THE BO PEEP FOLDING CAMERA. The "Bo-Peep" will be found by those desiring a light and compact hand camera to be just the thing, being a high grade, 4x5 folding camera, fitted with all the latest improvements to date, at a low price. The size of the Bo-Peep is 7¼x5½x4¾ inches, and it weighs but 2¾ pounds; has a rising and falling front board, swing back, and is fitted with a new time and instantaneous shutter with bulb attachment and patent anastigmat lense. Price includes one plate holder.

Price, 4x5...............................$13.75
Price, 5x7............................... 22.50
Extra, 4x5, double plate holders, each...... .90
"   5x7.............................. 1.12

24358 THE FOLDING PREMO CAMERA is a most complete and practical little instrument, possessing all the latest improvements. Has rising and falling front, swing back, reversible view finder and two tripod plates, so that either vertical or horizontal pictures can be taken.

The shutter is of special construction, and the lens is a rapid rectilinear of great power, made specially for this camera. A roll holder can be used in this style Premo when desired.

	4x5	5x7	6½x8½
With one dry plate holder. Prices	$27.00	$34.00	$45.00
Extra plate holders............	1.13	1.35	1.60
Film holders..................	1.28	1.45	1.70
Roll holders..................	7.25	9.00	14.60

24359 THE FOLDING PREMO CAMERA—Style "B." Almost identical with No. 24362, except that it is fitted with single view lens and roll holder cannot be used in it. 4x5 5x7
Premo B, with one plate-holder. Prices. .$18.00 $24.25

24360 THE FOLDING PREMO CAMERA-Style"D" Cheaper in construction than Nos. 24358, 24359 but a thoroughly practical camera. Fitted with single view lens with rigid diaphrams, and new noiseless shutter. Either glass plates or cut films can be used in this style. Size, when closed 5½x5⅜x6¼ inches; weighs 2 pounds and holds three plate holders.
Price, 4x5.................................$10.75

24361 THE ROCHESTER FOLDING CAMERA for 4x5 pictures. This is one of the strongest and most compact of its kind. It measures, when closed, but 4⅜x5¼x7 inches. Glass plates only can be used in this camera. Fitted with high grade symmetrical lens, with rotating diaphrams Price........$22.50
Extra plate holders. Each....................$0.90

24362 THE ROCHESTER FOLDING CAMERA, fitted with rapid symmetrical lens, and silent shutter for time and instantaneous exposures.
Price with one plate holder................$35.00
Extra plate holders, 5x7. Each............ 1.13

During much of the 1800s farm families shopped at small country stores. By the late 1800s, they had a new way of making purchases. They could order from a mail order catalog.

You can study old catalogs to get a good idea of how people lived in those days. Catalogs are good sources of information for a particular type of history—social history. Study this small part of the 1895 Montgomery Ward & Co. catalog index, and answer the questions that follow on a separate sheet of paper.

Book, Blanks, etc......... 40	Buckskin Gloves 289,290	Camel's Hair Brushes.....220
Book-keeping Blanks.. 40,112	Buckle Shields ,........328	Cameras, Photo.......217-219
Book Cases and Stands 607,608	Buffalo Robes...........321	Camp Bed.............. .617
Book Holders............ 41	Buggy Aprons...........591	Camp Blankets..........299
Books, Letter........... 40	Buggy Bodies...........591	Camp Chair............617
Books, Memorandum... 38,39	Buggies,Carriages,etc....	Camp Stools............617
Books, Scale.............. 40	579,580,598	Camping Outfits..430,503 504
Book Markers...........187	Buggy Cushions........591	Camphor..............260,261
Books, Music 250,252	Buggy Gears, etc.......593	Camphor Ice. See Drug List.
Book Sets..............121	Buggy Paints...........623	Cans, Milk..............570
Book Straps............567	Buggy Poles 593	Can Openers............396
Book Slates............119	Buggy Seats............592	Cans, Oil..............438
Bootees, Infants'........303	Buggy Spokes...........592	Candies—See Grocery List.
Boot and Shoe Dept....508-526	Buggy Tops.............590	Candles—See Grocery List.
Boots, Horse...........323	Buggy Wrenches.........405	Candlesticks..187, 437, 535, 545
Boots, Hunting and Wading.........520-524	Buggy Whips............ 319	Candle Wicking..........558
Bootjacks 396	Buggy Wheels..........592	Candy Scales...........390
Borax................260	Bugles...........230,249	Cane Mills.............590
Boring Machines, etc....362	Building Papers........386	Canes..............187, 298
Borer, Tap............396	and Grocery List.	Canisters, Tea and Coffee
Bosom Linen............ 29	Building Blocks........231	 437
Bottle Brushes..........107	Bull Snaps and Rings......394	Canned Goods, All Kinds—
Bottles, Nursing........107	Bullets...............470	See Grocery List.
Bottoms, Chair..........622	Bullet Molds...........478	Cannons, Toy,..........230
Bouquet Holders........547	Bundle Carriers........558	Cantanas, Leather.....336,337
Bows, Violin, etc....243,245	Bunion Medicine........261	Canteens, Pocket, etc....425
Bow Hair, Violin........248	Buntings...........7,15	Canvas, Artists'........253
Bows and Ties, Men's..94-96	Bureaus...............604	Canvas Boats...........503
Bows and Ties, Ladies'.... 79	Burlap Patterns........124	
	Burlap Sacking 17	

Understanding Source Material

1. How many items having to do with buggies are listed in the index? Would you expect to see them in a modern mail order catalog? Explain your answer.
2. Make a list of three items that are unfamiliar to you. What, do you think, would they have been used for? See if you can find the items listed in a dictionary. Were your guesses close to their actual use?
3. Find an ad for cameras in a recent newspaper. Compare the prices. Were cameras more of a luxury in 1895 than they are today? Explain your answer.

Five days after the opening of the Oklahoma Indian territory to white settlers, this crowded tent city called Guthrie had sprung up.

▶ Why were tents practical shelters at this time?

the rough land. Some settlers walked, others ran. In fact, settlers raced toward their new homes in every imaginable way.

After just two hours, settlers had claimed nearly every homestead. At noon on April 22, the town of Guthrie, Oklahoma, did not even exist. Before sundown that same day, Guthrie had a population of 15,000! And America's settlers had taken another giant leap west.

LESSON 4 REVIEW

THINK AND WRITE

A. Imagine that you are a farmer planning to move to the West around 1867. Make a list of the advantages of such a move.

B. How did plains farmers solve the problems of tough soil and the lack of wood?

C. How did frontier farmers deal with loneliness?

D. How did Guthrie, Oklahoma, spring up as a town of 15,000 people in less than one day?

SKILLS CHECK
WRITING SKILL

Imagine that you have just moved to the Great Plains in the late 1800s. Write a short description of your new home, including your hopes and fears about your new life there.

487

USING THE VOCABULARY

lode	vaquero
ghost town	open range
treaty	homesteader
reservations	barbed wire
long drive	dry farming

On a separate sheet of paper, complete each sentence correctly.

1. Fences made with _____ helped keep cattle from the plowed fields.
2. The government made the Indians live on _____.
3. The _____ moved herds of cattle to market.
4. A cowboy in Mexico is called a _____.
5. Miners search for a _____ of gold or silver.
6. Crops can be raised in dry climates by _____.
7. An abandoned town is called a _____.
8. The _____ was important to cattle ranchers.
9. An agreement between countries or groups is a _____.
10. The government offered free land to the _____ who would farm it.

REMEMBERING WHAT YOU READ

On a separate sheet of paper, write your answers in complete sentences.

1. What effect did the discovery of the Comstock Lode have on the region where it was found?
2. What was life like in a mining town?
3. Why was building a transcontinental railroad difficult?
4. What happened at Promontory Point?
5. Who were Crazy Horse and Geronimo?
6. Why did Texas ranchers drive their cattle to Missouri?
7. What was the life of the cowboy really like?
8. What did a homesteader have to do in order to keep the land the government provided?
9. What two inventions helped farmers on the Great Plains?
10. Why were most of the first houses on the Great Plains built of sod?

TYING MUSIC TO SOCIAL STUDIES

The building of the railroads stirred the imagination of many Americans. "The Wabash Cannon Ball" is a traditional folk song that appeared around that time.

From the coast of the Atlantic to the wide Pacific shore,
From the warm and sunny Southland to the isle of Labrador,
There's a Western Combination called the Wabash Cannon Ball.
There are cities of importance that are reached along the way,
Chicago and Saint Louis and Rock Island, Santa Fe,
And Springfield and Decatur and Peoria, Montreal,
On the Western Combination called the Wabash Cannon Ball.

Do you know where the places mentioned in the song are? The maps in the Atlas of this textbook may help you locate them.

THINKING CRITICALLY

On a separate sheet of paper, write your answers in complete sentences.

1. What long-lasting effects did the discovery of gold and silver lodes have on the growth of the West?
2. Why was it so important to build a transcontinental railroad?
3. Do you think the government should have kept its treaties with the Indians? Explain your answer.
4. How did the real-life cowboy differ from the picture given by movies and books?
5. What would your life have been like if your parents had been homesteaders on the Great Plains?

SUMMARIZING THE CHAPTER

On a separate sheet of paper, draw a graphic organizer like the one shown here. Copy the information from this graphic organizer to the one you have drawn. Use information from the chapter to complete each section of the map. Add at least three subsections to each heading. You may add more if you wish. The first one has been done for you.

CHAPTER THEME → Miners, ranchers, farmers, and the transcontinental railroad all helped settle the West in spite of the Indians who had been told by the government that it was their land.

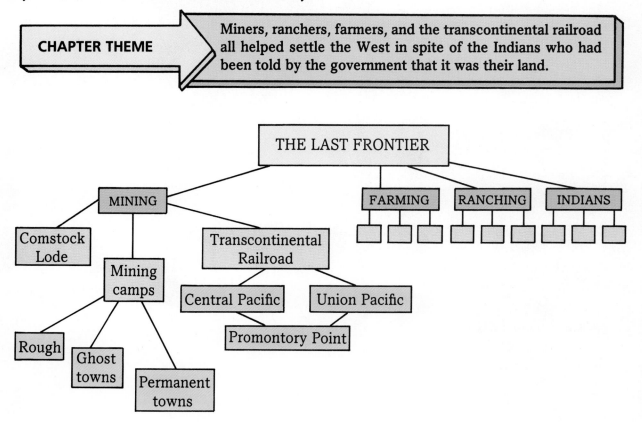

THE LAST FRONTIER

MINING — FARMING — RANCHING — INDIANS

Comstock Lode
Mining camps
Transcontinental Railroad
Central Pacific
Union Pacific
Promontory Point
Rough
Ghost towns
Permanent towns

21 THE NATION INDUSTRIALIZES

Industry was changing American life. Newcomers from Europe and Asia were crowding into the cities. All this growth and change created new problems and challenges.

The Age of Industry

THINK ABOUT WHAT YOU KNOW

List three inventions that are important to your life. Explain why each is important.

STUDY THE VOCABULARY

Centennial Exposition   **generator**

FOCUS YOUR READING

How did the United States become a powerful industrial country by the late 1800s?

A. Inventions Help the Nation Grow

The Nation Celebrates Have you ever heard of a birthday party that lasted six months? In 1876 there was one party that lasted just that long. It was the 100th birthday party of the United States of America. The party took place in a large park in Philadelphia, the nation's birthplace.

This grand festival was called the **Centennial Exposition.** The word *centennial* (sen TEN ee ul) means "the 100th anniversary," and an exposition is a show. And what a show it was! Countries from around the world joined the celebration by sending special exhibits, or displays. Philadelphia had to build 1,678 buildings to hold all the exhibits.

The Centennial Exposition displayed many of the latest inventions. These included the sewing machine, the typewriter, a printing press that printed newspapers with amazing speed, and the telephone. The telephone was one of the newest inventions. It had been created that very year by a Scottish immigrant named Alexander Graham Bell. When the visiting emperor of Brazil put the instrument to his ear, his eyes widened in amazement. "It talks!" exclaimed the emperor.

Thomas Edison Meanwhile in Menlo Park, New Jersey, about 80 miles (129 km) from the Centennial Exposition, an inventor named Thomas Edison opened a building of his own. Tom Edison had already invented the mimeograph machine and had made important improvements on the telegraph. In his new building, Edison planned to make more inventions. He told newspaper reporters that he and his 15 assistants expected "to turn out a minor invention every 10 days and a big thing every six months or so."

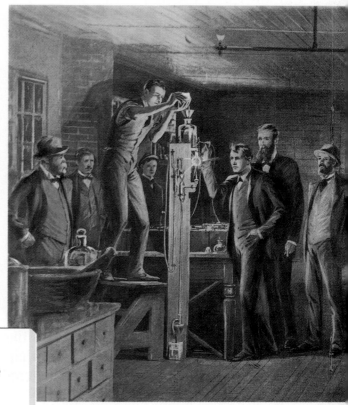

In Menlo Park, New Jersey, Thomas Edison successfully tests his incandescent lamp.
▶ What, do you think, were the reactions of the people who were with Edison?

The Granger Collection, New York

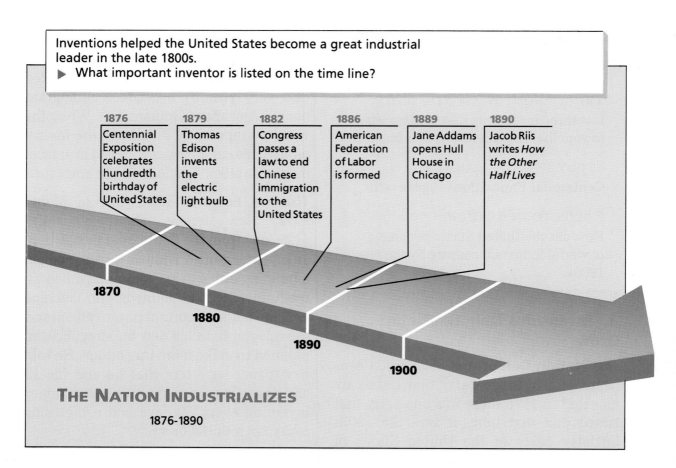

Inventions helped the United States become a great industrial leader in the late 1800s.
▶ What important inventor is listed on the time line?

1876 Centennial Exposition celebrates hundredth birthday of United States

1879 Thomas Edison invents the electric light bulb

1882 Congress passes a law to end Chinese immigration to the United States

1886 American Federation of Labor is formed

1889 Jane Addams opens Hull House in Chicago

1890 Jacob Riis writes *How the Other Half Lives*

1870

1880

1890

1900

THE NATION INDUSTRIALIZES
1876-1890

Edison was true to his word. One year later, in 1877, he invented the phonograph, which recorded and played back sound. And just two years after that, Edison produced an invention so important that it would change life throughout the entire world. This invention was the electric light bulb. Also, in his laboratory Edison invented the first moving-picture machine, the storage battery, and many other useful products.

The Centennial Exposition and Thomas Edison showed how inventions were helping America grow and change. In the late 1800s the number of inventions made by Americans climbed upward every year. In the centennial year of 1876, the number of inventions reached more than 14,000. In the year 1900, Americans created 24,000 inventions!

B. The United States Becomes an Industrial Giant

Telephones In Chapter 14 you read about the beginnings of the Industrial Revolution. Inventions helped the Industrial Revolution spread quickly. These inventions helped the United States become a truly industrial country.

Some inventions led to the creation of entirely new industries. After Bell invented the telephone, factories were started to make these new instruments. Thousands of people worked in the new factories. In addition, thousands of men got jobs putting up telephone poles and stringing telephone wire. Thousands of women found work as telephone operators.

Electric Lights Think of the jobs created by Edison's light bulb. When Edison made his first light bulb, there was no such thing as a company that produced electric power. But now such companies were needed. Edison built a **generator** for New York City in 1882. A generator is a machine that makes electric power. Soon electric companies were started in city after city. Other companies made the wire needed to send the electricity to homes, stores, and offices. In no time at all, the small electric power industry grew into a giant one.

America's Resources The stream of inventions was not the only reason the United States grew into a great industrial nation. America was rich in resources needed for industry. These included minerals such as iron ore and coal. Also the United States had a rapidly growing population. There were enough people to work in the factories, mines, and offices. There were also enough people to buy the goods.

Railroads Railroads also helped the country grow. The last half of the 1800s saw an age of great railroad building in the United States. The map on this page shows the major railways that crisscrossed the nation by 1895. Railroad builders laid thousands of miles of steel tracks during

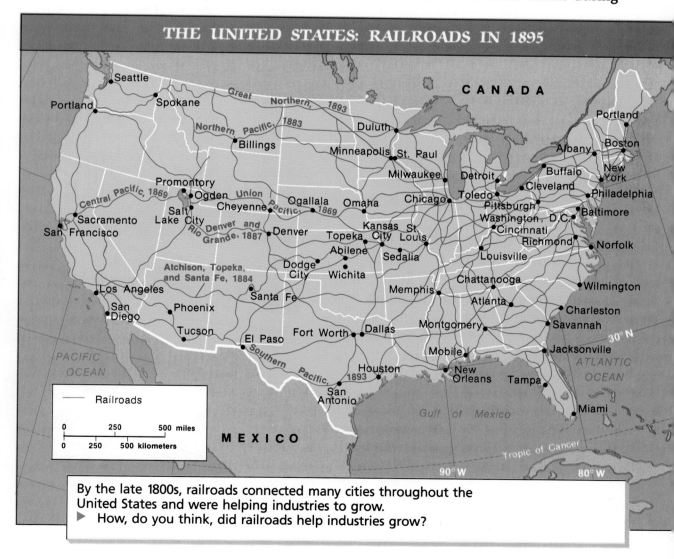

THE UNITED STATES: RAILROADS IN 1895

By the late 1800s, railroads connected many cities throughout the United States and were helping industries to grow.
▶ How, do you think, did railroads help industries grow?

those years. This new rail system gave a big boost to the steel industry. Still other companies made locomotives and railroad cars. Just one such company, the Pullman Palace Car Company, employed thousands of workers.

Railroads helped other industries grow by carrying goods quickly and cheaply to every part of America. In 1885 it cost less than a penny to ship a ton of steel one mile by railroad. As one amazed person said, you would pay more than that to a youngster for carrying a small envelope across the street!

C. Andrew Carnegie: Captain of the Steel Industry

Ambitious Leaders The new industries were unlike anything Americans had seen before. To build these industries, new kinds of business leaders were needed. These leaders had to have a great ability to organize. When they saw opportunities, they would have to be willing to take risks to succeed. For if they succeeded, huge fortunes would be theirs.

One such captain, or leader, of industry was Andrew Carnegie (KAHR nuh gee). Andrew came to the United States from Scotland when he was 13. His family was poor, and soon after arriving in America, young Andrew went to work in a textile factory. There, working from sunup to sundown, he earned 20 cents a day. Later, Andrew learned to be a telegraph operator. Meanwhile, he went to school in the evenings to learn bookkeeping, and he did a lot of reading on his own.

Andrew was always on the lookout for ways to get ahead. When he was 18, he got a job as a telegraph operator and private secretary to a man named Tom Scott. Scott was a top official of the Pennsylvania Railroad Company. The young Carnegie's starting pay was $35 a week. In later years Carnegie wrote, "I couldn't imagine what I could ever do with so much money." Tom Scott showed him. Scott taught Carnegie to invest his savings. That is, Carnegie

Soon after arriving in America from Scotland, young Andrew Carnegie started to work in a textile mill.
▶ Does this look like an interesting job?

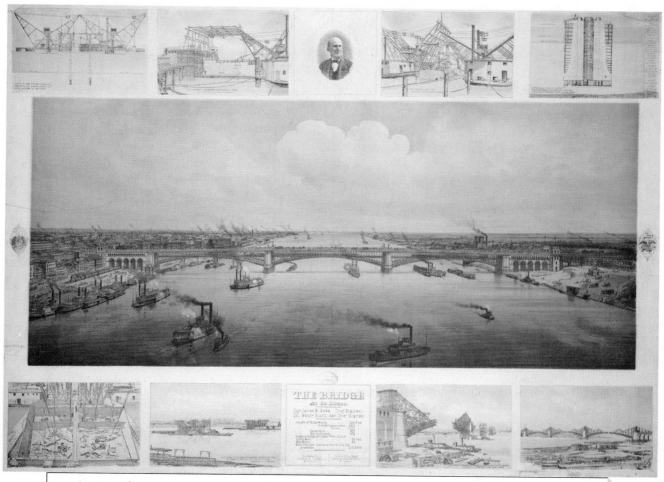

In 1874, Andrew Carnegie's company provided the steel and iron to build the Eads Bridge, in St. Louis, Missouri. This was the first bridge to be made of steel.

▶ Can you tell why this bridge was called an arched bridge?

bought a share of each of several growing companies. When the companies did well, Carnegie shared in the earnings. As Carnegie's pay increased, he invested more.

Going into Business In his 30s, Carnegie left his job with the Pennsylvania Railroad Company to go into business on his own. With the money he had made by investing, he bought a company that made iron bridges. Carnegie had realized that old wooden bridges would not do for carrying railroad trains across rivers. He was right. His company became very successful.

Steel Some years later, Carnegie sold his bridge company and everything else he owned. He used the money he made to build a steel company. Why steel? Steel is stronger than iron and easier to work with. People had known that about steel for hundreds of years. However, steel was very expensive to make, so not much of it was made. Then in the 1850s, two men, working separately, discovered a way to make steel quickly and cheaply. One was an Englishman named Henry Bessemer. The other was a kettle maker from Kentucky named William Kelly.

Making steel was hard work. In the painting shown above, Pennsylvania steel workers strain to pour molten metal into molds. The inset shows a portrait of Andrew Carnegie.

▶ Do you think that the men's safety concerned the company?

Carnegie saw that steel was much better than iron for railroad tracks. He knew that as railroads grew there would be a great demand for steel. So Carnegie risked everything to get into the steel business early. Later, hundreds of others followed Carnegie into the steel business. However, Carnegie kept ahead of them all by using the latest methods of steelmaking and by hiring the best managers. By the 1890s, Carnegie's steel mills made nearly as much steel as all the other companies put together.

In the late 1800s, other men like Carnegie also built great businesses. Among them were John D. Rockefeller in the oil business, Gustavus Swift in meatpacking, and James B. Duke in tobacco processing. These people grew fabulously wealthy. And as they did, they helped the United States become the greatest industrial country in the world.

LESSON *1* REVIEW

THINK AND WRITE

A. What did the Centennial Exposition show about the United States in 1876?

B. How did the railroads help other industries grow in the United States during the late 1800s?

C. Why were people like Andrew Carnegie important to the United States during the late 1800s?

SKILLS CHECK

MAP SKILL

Use the map on page 493 to list the cities you would travel through on a train trip from Chicago to San Francisco.

THINK ABOUT WHAT YOU KNOW

Briefly describe a large city that you are familiar with. Would you prefer to live in such a city or in a farming area?

STUDY THE VOCABULARY

slum   **shantytown**

FOCUS YOUR READING

What were the advantages and disadvantages of living in a rapidly growing city during the late 1800s?

A. Cities Grow into Centers of Industry

Kansas City   In the late 1800s, American places were growing very fast. Small towns grew into large cities, and large cities grew into huge ones. Many cities doubled or even tripled in population in just ten years. The biggest cities were far larger than any of the country's cities before the Civil War.

A number of these cities grew rapidly because of railroads. The growth of Kansas City, Missouri, shows how this happened. In 1860, Kansas City was a small town of about 4,000 people. Then several railroad companies built their main lines through the town. These new railroads connected Kansas City to the farming and cattle country farther west.

Before long, business was booming in Kansas City. Businesspeople built flour mills there. Farmers throughout Kansas and Nebraska began to ship their wheat by railroad to these mills. Other businesspeople in Kansas City built meatpacking plants. Ranchers on the Great Plains shipped cattle to these plants. The flour and beef were then loaded on trains in the rail yards of Kansas City. There they began the long haul to eastern cities.

As a result of all the business made possible by the railroads, Kansas City grew from a sleepy little town of 4,000 to a busy city of 50,000 in just 20 years. Twenty years after that, its population reached 160,000.

Industrial Centers   Because of their large population and because railroads came through them, cities were ideal places for industry. Captains of industry built factories in many cities. Some cities even became known for certain products. Pittsburgh, Pennsylvania, and Birmingham, Alabama, became known as steel cities. Milwaukee, Wisconsin, was famous for its beer. St. Paul and Minneapolis, in

The Pillsbury flour mill was in Minneapolis, Minnesota.
► Why, do you think, does the railroad run past the mill?

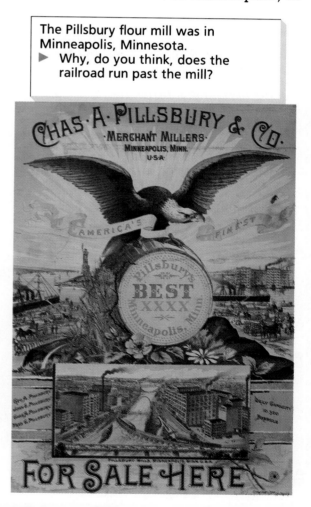

FROM:

"Chicago"

By: Carl Sandburg
Setting: Chicago

Cities have always been exciting places in which to live. In the 1800s, when the United States was changing from a farming nation to an industrial nation, small villages and towns grew rapidly into big cities. In 1916, Carl Sandburg wrote a poem about an important American city that grew that way. Look for the words that describe the kind of city it was.

Hog Butcher for the World,
Tool Maker, Stacker of Wheat,
Player with Railroads and the Nation's
Freight Handler;
Stormy, husky, brawling,
City of the Big Shoulders:

. . . .
Come and show me another city with
lifted head singing so proud to be

. . . .
Bareheaded,

Shoveling,
Wrecking
Planning
Building, breaking, rebuilding,
Under the smoke, dust all over his
mouth, laughing with white teeth,
Under the terrible burden of destiny
laughing as a young man laughs,
Laughing even as an ignorant fighter
laughs who has never lost a battle,
Bragging and laughing that under his
wrist is the pulse, and under his ribs
the heart of the people,
Laughing!
Laughing the stormy, husky, brawling,
laughter of Youth, half-naked,
sweating, proud to be Hog Butcher,
Tool Maker, Stacker of Wheat,
Player with Railroads and Freight
Handler to the Nation.

Minnesota, were the leading cities for flour milling. After 1900, Detroit, Michigan, became the center of the automobile industry. Very large cities like New York, Chicago, and Philadelphia were home to many kinds of factories. You can read a description of Chicago on page 498.

B. Cities Offer New Opportunities

Farmers and Immigrants Where did all the people in America's cities come from and why did they move there? Many came from America's farms. During the late 1800s, farmers found it hard to make a living. Some gave up farming and moved to the cities to find jobs. Some farm people went to the city to escape the long hours, hard work, and loneliness of farm life.

A second large group of newcomers to America's cities came from other countries. These immigrants hoped for good jobs and a better life. You will read more about immigrants later in this chapter.

Inventions such as the telephone created more jobs for people.
▶ What job are the women below working at?

City Life People could find a great variety of jobs in cities. There were jobs in the new factories that were springing up everywhere. People could also work in stores and in offices. There were jobs for skilled workers like tailors. There were jobs for unskilled workers, too. Cities especially offered opportunities to women. One invention, the typewriter, created thousands of jobs for women as secretaries in offices. As you have read, another invention, the telephone, created more new jobs for women, as operators. In cities, women also worked as schoolteachers and as store clerks.

The city also offered opportunities for an exciting life. Cities had museums, theaters, sports arenas, and concert halls. Where else but in a city could you regularly watch great sporting events in the days before television? Where else could you listen to good music or hear talks by some famous people? Cities also had shops and department stores with goods from around the world. Even if you didn't buy these goods, you could have fun walking down the streets and window-shopping. And unlike farms or villages, cities were alive with activity after dark, thanks to gas and electric street lights.

In addition, cities also offered opportunities for education. In a city a young person could attend high school. Most colleges and libraries were also found in these rapidly growing cities.

C. Rapid Growth Creates New Problems

Unpaved Streets Cities grew so fast in the late 1800s that they could not keep up with the need for services. Take paved streets, for example. Minneapolis, one of the fastest-growing cities, had 200 miles of

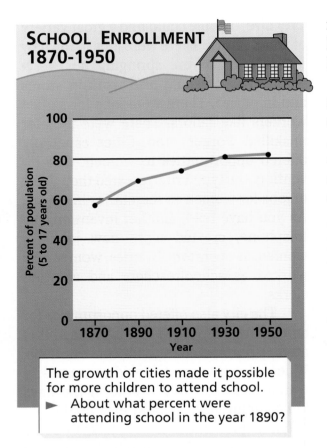

SCHOOL ENROLLMENT 1870-1950

The growth of cities made it possible for more children to attend school.

► About what percent were attending school in the year 1890?

mainly on dead animals. Charleston even had a law to protect these birds from hunters.

Disposal of human wastes was also a major problem. In the late 1800s most cities were only beginning to build sewers. As a result, disease spread quickly through cities. In one poor neighborhood in Chicago, more than half the babies died of diseases before their first birthday.

Housing Housing was yet another problem of growing cities. Builders could not put up houses fast enough for the thousands of new people who poured in. Most poor people lived in **slums**, or areas filled with old, run-down buildings. Sometimes six or seven people lived in a single room in one of these buildings. Some of the poor lived in shelters made from scraps of wood and cardboard. These shelters were called shanties. Nearly every American city had at least one **shantytown**.

Reforms By 1900, cities were starting to face their problems. Most cities provided a clean water supply and sewage systems. City governments had begun to provide regular garbage pickups. Cities also hired full-time police and firefighters. Roads were finally paved. Housing, however, remained a big problem in every city.

streets in 1890. Not one of them was paved. Most cities had a similar problem.

Health Also, cities were often dirty, unhealthy places to live. Many had no garbage collectors. Instead it was hoped hogs and dogs would eat all the garbage. Charleston, South Carolina, depended on vultures, which are large birds that feed

---

LESSON **2** REVIEW

THINK AND WRITE

A. How did Kansas City, Missouri, grow from a town to a busy city in just 20 years?

B. List some benefits that a farm family of the late 1800s might have found if they moved to the city.

C. What were the major problems of the growing cities during the late 1800s?

SKILLS CHECK

THINKING SKILL

Make a list of the ways in which cities of the late 1800s might have attracted newcomers.

500

A Nation of Immigrants

THINK ABOUT WHAT YOU KNOW

Imagine that you and your family must move to a new country where you do not know the language or the ways of life. What problems might you have in your new home?

STUDY THE VOCABULARY

ghetto   prejudice
settlement house

FOCUS YOUR READING

What problems did European and Asian immigrants to the United States experience during the late 1800s?

A. Many Immigrants Arrive from Europe

Crossing the Atlantic From the start of America's history, immigrants had been coming here in search of a better life. In the late 1800s they came in larger numbers than ever before. Crossing the Atlantic Ocean by then was much faster, safer, and cheaper than in the earlier days of sailing ships. Steamships made the crossing from England in just five or six days. The journey from countries like Italy and Greece took less than two weeks and cost only $10 or $15. So in the 1880s and 1890s, hardly a day went by without at least one shipload of immigrants arriving in America from somewhere in Europe.

The Statue of Liberty Most of these immigrants entered the United States through New York. Those who arrived after 1886 saw a wonderful sight in the harbor. It was a beautiful statue of a woman, 15 stories high. In one hand the woman held high a great torch. In the other

was a tablet bearing the date of the Declaration of Independence.

The people of France had presented this statue as a gift to the United States. The sculptor, or artist who made the statue, gave it the name *Liberty Enlightening the World*. Americans, however, soon gave it a shorter name, the *Statue of Liberty*. The statue was built to celebrate the friendship of the French and Americans during the American Revolution. But over the years the statue has come to mean something else, too. It stands for the promise of freedom and opportunity that drew so many people to America.

On October 28, 1886, more than 1 million people watched the unveiling of the Statue of Liberty.
► Why was this a special event?

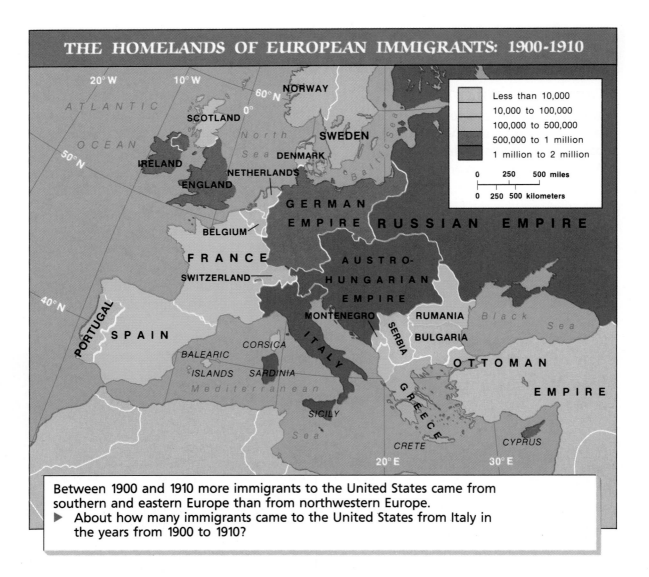

THE HOMELANDS OF EUROPEAN IMMIGRANTS: 1900-1910

Less than 10,000
10,000 to 100,000
100,000 to 500,000
500,000 to 1 million
1 million to 2 million

0   250   500 miles
0   250 500 kilometers

Between 1900 and 1910 more immigrants to the United States came from southern and eastern Europe than from northwestern Europe.
► About how many immigrants came to the United States from Italy in the years from 1900 to 1910?

B. Most Immigrants Live in the Cities

Big Cities Some of the immigrants who arrived in New York continued on to the West, where they became farmers. But most immigrants lived in such cities as New York, Chicago, Philadelphia, Cleveland, and Boston.

Immigrants and their children made up more than half the population of America's big cities in 1900. That year more Italians lived in New York City than in any city in Italy except Rome. And more Irish lived in New York City than in any city in Ireland except Dublin. And more Germans lived there than in any German city except Berlin. And more Greeks lived there than in any city in Greece except Athens. And more Jews lived in New York City than in any city anywhere in the world. Just imagine — all those different peoples living in New York City at the very same time!

Immigrant Neighborhoods Members of the same immigrant group usually lived near each other in American cities. They wanted to live with people who spoke their language and who shared their ways. So in most cities there were Italian neighborhoods, Jewish neighborhoods, and Polish neighborhoods as well as German, Irish, and Greek neighborhoods.

These neighborhoods were in the poorer parts of town because the immigrants were poor. Often the immigrants lived in slum housing. In time some earned enough money to afford better housing. However, they often found they were not welcome in other parts of the city. So they stayed where they were. These neighborhoods where immigrants were forced to stay were sometimes called **ghettos**.

Finding Work Most of the immigrants in the cities were unskilled workers. Many spoke no English. They had to take whatever jobs they could get. Usually they wound up with the hardest work for the lowest pay. Often everyone in the family — including young children — had to work to earn enough to live on.

In spite of all the problems, though, most immigrants still felt happy to be in America. They knew that their children would have a chance to learn skills, get an education, and get ahead in life.

C. Settlement Houses Help Immigrants

Some Americans tried to help poor immigrants. In 1889 a young woman named Jane Addams started Hull House, a **settlement house** in an immigrant neighborhood in Chicago. A settlement house was a place where immigrants and poor people came for help.

At Hull House, Addams and her helpers taught young mothers about good child care. They provided day care for the children of working women. They helped the unemployed find jobs and offered classes to people who wanted to learn English. Hull House was also a place where the poor could meet together for concerts and other activities.

Over the next 20 years, people like Addams started about 400 settlement houses in many American cities. But settlement houses could reach only a small portion of the millions of poor in the cities.

At Hull House, young men could learn the skills they needed to get jobs.
▶ What kind of class are the young men in this photograph taking?

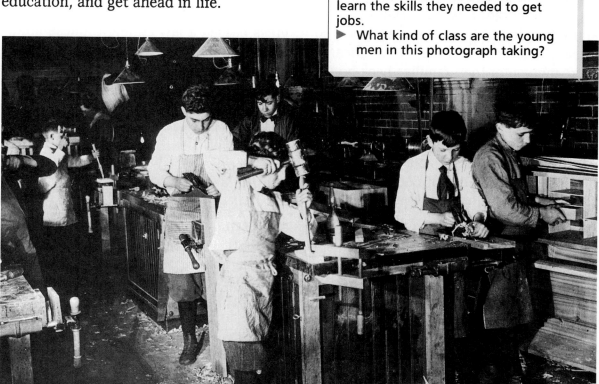

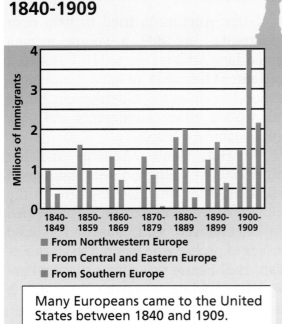

IMMIGRANTS FROM EUROPE: 1840-1909

Millions of Immigrants

4
3
2
1
0

1840-1849 | 1850-1859 | 1860-1869 | 1870-1879 | 1880-1889 | 1890-1899 | 1900-1909

■ From Northwestern Europe
■ From Central and Eastern Europe
■ From Southern Europe

Many Europeans came to the United States between 1840 and 1909.
► When did the greatest number of immigrants come from Central and Eastern Europe?

D. Immigrants Come from Asia

Immigrants also arrived in the United States from Asia in the 1800s. Most of these immigrants were Chinese men. Many people in China were very poor, so some Chinese men came to America to make money for their families back home.

These Chinese men took on a number of different jobs. The first group came at the time of the gold rush in California, and most of them worked in the mines. Some Chinese moved to the cities, where they opened small shops or restaurants. In addition, Chinese workers found jobs building railroads in the West. Many also became farm workers in California. By the late 1800s, Chinese communities could be found in many cities and towns of the West. Chinese workers helped to build the great towns and cities of the West.

But to get jobs, the Chinese had to accept work for low wages. Some white workers felt that when Chinese workers accepted low wages, wages for everyone were pulled down. Also many whites had a **prejudice** against the Chinese. Prejudice is a feeling, without reason, that one group is better than another group.

All immigrants faced some prejudice at one time or another. But in the 1880s, prejudice was strongest against the Chinese. In some western towns, white workers rioted against the Chinese, killing some in their attacks. Finally in 1882, Congress passed a law ending Chinese immigration to the United States. That law was not changed until 60 years later.

LESSON **3** *REVIEW*

THINK AND WRITE

A. Why did the number of European immigrants to America greatly increase in the late 1800s?

B. What was life like for a European immigrant family in an American city about 1900?

C. Why might an immigrant to Chicago have gone to Hull House during the 1890s?

D. How did most Chinese immigrants make a living during the late 1800s?

SKILLS CHECK

MAP SKILL

Use the map on page 502 to find the number of immigrants that came to the United States between 1900 and 1910 from the following places: Greece, the Russian empire, and Ireland.

Challenges of a New Age

THINK ABOUT WHAT YOU KNOW

How might your life change if the police, bus drivers, and mail carriers stopped working?

STUDY THE VOCABULARY

labor union   depression
strike

FOCUS YOUR READING

In what ways did many workers and farmers seek to solve their problems during the late 1800s?

A. The Industrial Revolution Changes Workers' Lives

Factory Work The Industrial Revolution brought more goods and a better way of life to many people. As you have read, the Industrial Revolution created many jobs. People with new skills were needed—skills to make and repair machines, manage offices, and run large companies.

But the Industrial Revolution put many other skilled workers out of work. These workers included shoemakers and weavers who made goods in their own homes or in small workshops. By the end of the 1800s, shoes and cloth were being made by machines in factories.

In earlier times it took years for a skilled worker to learn how to make shoes or cloth well. But in just a few days, a newly arrived immigrant or a boy or girl fresh from the farm could learn to run a machine that made shoes or cloth. The factory owner had to pay very little for the labor of these unskilled machine operators. Skilled shoemakers and weavers could not compete with the machines.

They had to find other ways to make a living. Many of them became low-paid factory workers themselves.

Working Conditions The Industrial Revolution also changed the way people worked. A factory worker usually put in 10 or 12 hours a day, 6 days a week. Such long hours were not unusual for most Americans in the 1800s. Farmers, for example, had always worked long hours. Many skilled workers who worked in their own homes or shops did also.

Also, working conditions in factories and mines were unsafe. Factories were poorly lighted and had little fresh air. Often factory workers were not protected from dangerous machinery. Thousands of miners died young as a result of coal dust they breathed into their lungs. Coal mines sometimes caved in, killing hundreds of mine workers.

Young children are working in a textile mill in North Carolina.
► Can you name one unsafe working condition in this picture?

B. Workers Organize

Unions How could workers in the large factories and mines of America improve their working conditions and their pay? A worker had no chance of doing it alone. Some workers thought they could make their employer listen to their demands by uniting and forming **labor unions**. A labor union is an organization of workers that tries to help its members get higher wages and better working conditions.

Union members elected leaders to speak for them. If the employer refused to make improvements, the union members might **strike**. That meant they might stop working until the employer gave them better wages or working conditions. Workers did not earn any pay during a strike. However, if enough workers went on strike, the owner didn't make money either.

The first Labor Day parade took place on September 5, 1882.
▶ How is Labor Day honored in your community?

The Granger Collection, New York

Starting a labor union in the late 1800s was not easy. Owners of businesses were strongly against unions. Some owners of mines and factories would not hire workers unless they promised never to join a union. Often when workers managed to get a union started, employers refused to sit down and talk with union leaders. Also, many workers were not interested in joining a union.

The AF of L Skilled workers organized the strongest unions. For example, carpenters had their own union, cigar makers had a union, and railroad engineers also had a union. When skilled workers went on strike, employers could not easily replace them. Thus a strike by skilled workers had a better chance of success.

In 1886 the leaders of several unions of skilled workers decided to bring their unions together into the American Federation of Labor (AF of L). The AF of L was a kind of union of unions. Members helped each other by supporting each other's strikes. For example, the hat makers' union might go on strike against a company. Then members of the other unions in the AF of L might boycott, or refuse to buy, hats made by that company. The president of the AF of L for nearly 40 years was a cigar maker named Samuel Gompers.

Some strikes in the late 1880s were successful, and the striking unions got at least part of what they wanted. When that happened, more workers would join unions. But more often the strikes failed. Union members had to go back to work without gaining anything. Sometimes they even lost their jobs. When that happened, many workers dropped out of their unions. Other workers decided not to join unions. As a result, unions grew very slowly in the late 1800s.

C. The Industrial Revolution Changes Farming

Hard Times for Farmers The Industrial Revolution also changed farming. Machines allowed farmers to produce larger crops than their grandparents had. Railroads and steamships made it possible to sell these crops in markets thousands of miles away.

You might think that as a result of these changes, farmers in the late 1800s would be well-off. But many were not. Railroads sometimes charged farmers very high prices to ship the crops. Also, since farmers produced so much, the supply of farm goods became greater than the demand for them. In other words there were more farm goods than buyers needed. And when supply is greater than demand, prices go down.

In the 1890s the United States fell into a **depression**. A depression is a time when business slows and many people are out of work. Farmers were hit especially hard during this depression. Prices fell lower than ever. More and more farmers were in danger of losing their farms.

The Populist Party Many farmers in the South and the West formed a new political party to seek help from the government. The party was called the Populist party, or the people's party. Populists wanted the government to make it easier for farmers to

This is how wheat was harvested in the early 1900s.
▶ How do you think wheat harvesting is different today?

borrow money. They also wanted the government to see that railroads did not charge unfair rates. And they wanted help in getting higher prices for crops.

The Populists helped to elect many people to state legislatures and to Congress. However, the party never came close to winning the presidency. After a number of years, the depression ended. As times got better, fewer people supported the Populists, and the party disappeared soon after 1900.

LESSON 4 REVIEW

THINK AND WRITE

A. What problems did the Industrial Revolution create for workers?

B. Why did workers form unions during the late 1800s?

C. What were the goals of the Populist party?

SKILLS CHECK

WRITING SKILL

Review Section A of this lesson, including the pictures of factory work. Then write an imaginary diary entry of a person working in a factory in the late 1800s.

USING THE VOCABULARY

Centennial
  Exposition
generator
slum
shantytown
ghettos

settlement house
prejudice
labor unions
strike
depression

On a separate sheet of paper, complete each sentence, using one of the terms listed above.

1. Many Americans showed _____ against immigrants.
2. A _____ made enough electric power to light up a small city.
3. The shelters in the _____ were made with scraps of wood and cardboard.
4. The _____ took place in Philadelphia, in 1876.
5. Workers went on _____ for higher wages and better working conditions.
6. During the _____ many people were out of work.
7. Many poor families lived in old, run-down buildings in a _____.
8. The _____ helped immigrants learn English and find jobs.
9. Immigrants who came from the same country often lived near each other in a neighborhood that came to be called _____.
10. Workers organized _____ to get better working conditions and wages.

REMEMBERING WHAT YOU READ

On a separate sheet of paper, write your answers in complete sentences.

1. What helped the United States become an industrialized nation?
2. Name four captains of industry and tell what industry each person controlled.
3. What opportunities did life in the city offer?
4. How did Chinese immigrants suffer because of prejudice?
5. How did the Industrial Revolution change farming in the United States?

TYING LANGUAGE ARTS TO SOCIAL STUDIES

Emma Lazarus wrote a poem for the dedication of the Statue of Liberty. It appears on a plaque at the base of the statue. Lazarus calls the statue Mother of Exiles and in the poem has the statue saying, ". . . Give me your tired, your poor, Your huddled masses yearning to breathe free, . . ."

Write a poem that an immigrant coming to the United States might have written. Tell about the hopes and dreams this person might have had. Or, if you wish, find a copy of Emma Lazarus's poem, memorize it, and recite it for your classmates.

THINKING CRITICALLY

On a separate sheet of paper, write the answers in complete sentences.

1. What qualities do you think Thomas Edison had that made him a great inventor?
2. Is it possible for people today to become captains of industry as Andrew Carnegie did? Explain your answer.
3. Do you think that immigrants coming to the United States today go through the same hardships that immigrants in the past did?
4. Jane Addams helped the poor and needy who went to Hull House. What ways can you think of to help poor and needy people today?
5. Why do people organize in groups to solve their problems?

SUMMARIZING THE CHAPTER

On a separate sheet of paper, draw a graphic organizer like the one shown here. Copy the information from this graphic organizer to the one you have drawn. Under the main idea for each lesson, write three statements that support the main idea. The first one has been done for you.

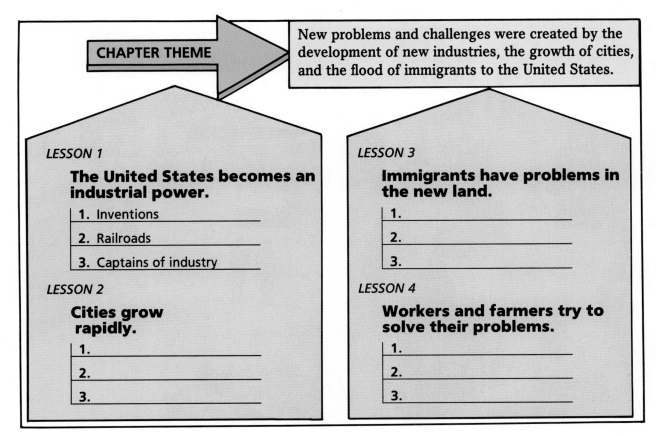

CHAPTER THEME → New problems and challenges were created by the development of new industries, the growth of cities, and the flood of immigrants to the United States.

LESSON 1

The United States becomes an industrial power.

1. Inventions
2. Railroads
3. Captains of industry

LESSON 2

Cities grow rapidly.

1. _____
2. _____
3. _____

LESSON 3

Immigrants have problems in the new land.

1. _____
2. _____
3. _____

LESSON 4

Workers and farmers try to solve their problems.

1. _____
2. _____
3. _____

CHAPTER 22 INTO A NEW CENTURY

The United States had become a modern country. The nation was expanding overseas. The United States emerged from World War I as a winner and a world power.

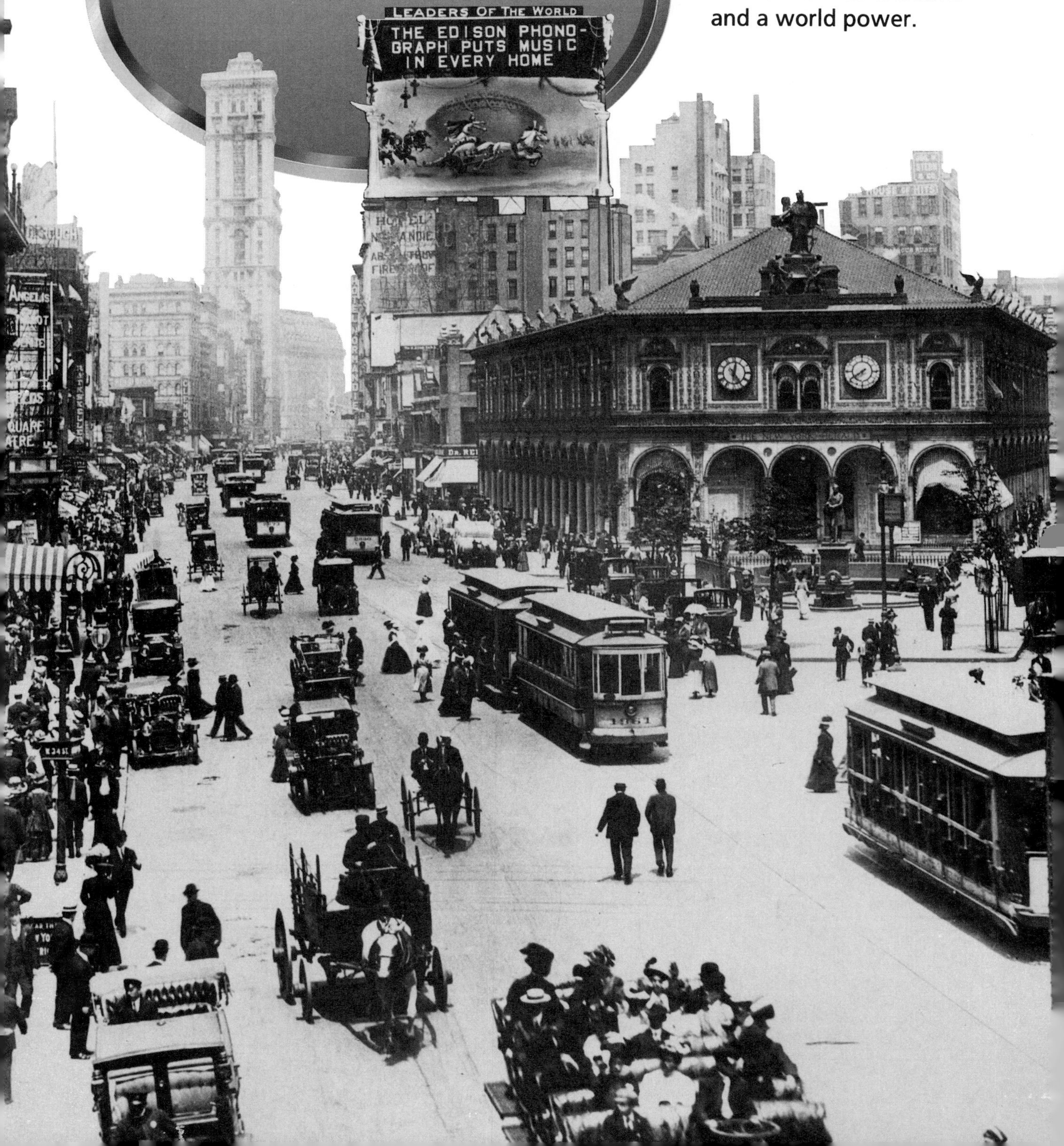
LEADERS OF THE WORLD
THE EDISON PHONOGRAPH PUTS MUSIC IN EVERY HOME

Reforming a Nation

Have you ever noticed a problem that no one else seemed able to solve? How might you try to get people to recognize the problem and find ways to solve it?

progressive   **monopoly**
conservation   **suffrage**

Why did some Americans change their ideas about what government should do around 1900?

A. Theodore Roosevelt Changes His Thinking

Sometimes a single experience can change a person's thinking forever. That's what happened to Theodore Roosevelt. In 1883, young Theodore Roosevelt was serving as a member of the New York state legislature. At that time, streetcar conductors in New York City often worked 14 or 15 hours a day. The conductors wanted a law that limited their working day to 12 hours.

Like many other Americans of that time, Roosevelt believed that government had no business making laws about working conditions. So he voted against the law the conductors wanted.

But the next year something happened that led Theodore Roosevelt to change his mind. In those days, cigar makers worked at home, in their apartments. Living and working in a tiny room with so much tobacco was unhealthy for the cigar makers. The New York legislature was considering a law to stop cigar making in the workers' homes. Roosevelt planned to vote against this law too.

Then Samuel Gompers, the labor union leader, offered to take Theodore Roosevelt to a cigar maker's home to see the conditions for himself. Roosevelt agreed to go. Here is his description of the visit.

I have always remembered one room in which two families were living. . . . There were several children, three men, and two women in this room. The tobacco was . . . [stored] everywhere, alongside the foul [smelly] bedding, and in a corner where there were scraps of food. The men, women, and children in this room worked by day and far on into the evening.

This family earned a living by making cigars in a tenement building in New York City.
▶ Does this scene seem to agree or disagree with Roosevelt's description above?

Roosevelt realized that new ideas were needed to improve things. Without them, working conditions would not get better. Roosevelt now believed that, in the modern industrial world, governments had to make laws that would protect workers. So this time he voted to outlaw cigar making in the workers' apartments.

The living conditions Theodore Roosevelt saw that day stayed with him. In later years, as a governor and then as President, Roosevelt fought for laws to protect workers from unhealthy, unsafe working conditions. He also favored laws to limit the number of hours a person had to work each week. In addition, Roosevelt supported laws to end child labor.

Young boys were often made to work long hours at dangerous jobs.
▶ What kind of work do you think the boys in this photograph did?

B. Working in 1900

Most children your age spent weekdays in school in 1900, but not all did. Many children were working. Their families needed whatever money the children could earn. Children worked ten or more hours a day, six days a week, and were paid as little as 50 cents a day for doing very hard work.

What kind of work did children do? Some of them worked in slaughterhouses, the places where cattle and hogs are slaughtered for meat. The smells of the slaughterhouse were sickening, but after several months the young workers got used to the smells.

Other children worked in factories that made cotton thread and cloth. Many girls worked at the spinning machines and looms. Their fingers were thought to be more nimble than those of boys. Work often went on there day and night. Accidents were common in the dim light. To keep workers from falling asleep at their machines and getting injured, the person in charge would splash the workers with cold water.

Breaker boys worked at coal mines. As the large chunks of coal were brought from the mine, steel rollers called breakers crushed them into lumps of coal and rock. For ten hours a day, breaker boys sat at a long table picking out pieces of rock from the coal. They were often injured by the machinery, the sharp rocks, or the coal dust. You can see how young these breaker boys were in the photograph at the left.

As you learned earlier, some children worked at home with their families, making cigars or artificial flowers, sewing shirts, or doing some other work. For this sort of work, families were paid by the number of items they made, so everyone

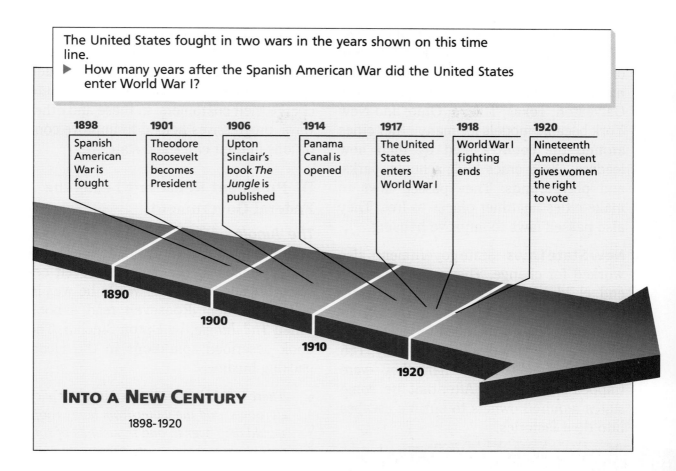

The United States fought in two wars in the years shown on this time line.

▶ How many years after the Spanish American War did the United States enter World War I?

1898 Spanish American War is fought

1901 Theodore Roosevelt becomes President

1906 Upton Sinclair's book *The Jungle* is published

1914 Panama Canal is opened

1917 The United States enters World War I

1918 World War I fighting ends

1920 Nineteenth Amendment gives women the right to vote

1890   1900   1910   1920

INTO A NEW CENTURY

1898–1920

had to work very fast. Other children added to family incomes by becoming shoeshine boys or by selling newspapers on the city streets.

C. Americans Want Better Government

A Time of Reform As Americans thought about their country in the early 1900s, they knew that much was good. But they also saw problems like the ones young Theodore Roosevelt saw. As a result, many Americans began to accept new ideas like those of Roosevelt. These Americans became a new group of reformers. You read about an earlier group of reformers in Chapter 15. Reformers want to take action to change things for the better.

In the early 1900s, reformers were called **progressives**. Like Theodore Roosevelt, progressives wanted to use the city, state, and federal governments to bring about much needed reforms. However, many city and state governments around 1900 were corrupt, or dishonest. These governments had officeholders who broke many laws. They used their power to make themselves and their friends rich.

Electing Honest Leaders Reformers knew that change could only occur when corrupt leaders were no longer in power. So they took steps to replace corrupt officeholders with honest people. Once honest people were in office, city and state governments could then work for laws that would benefit the people.

513

Reformers swung into action in cities all across the country. By 1900, they had driven corrupt leaders out of office in a number of cities. Reform governments in Galveston, Texas; Toledo, Ohio; and New York became models for many other cities around the country. Led by their new leaders, these cities built schools, parks, and playgrounds. They passed laws to make cities healthier places to live. They also passed laws to improve housing.

New State Laws State governments also worked for change. They passed laws to end child labor and to protect workers against unsafe conditions. A tragedy in New York showed the need for such laws. In 1911, in a New York shirt factory, 146 women workers died when they were trapped in a flash fire. After that fire, some states required owners to put fire escapes into their factories.

Theodore Roosevelt's dynamic speeches excited crowds.
► What do you think makes a dynamic speaker?

In addition, states began to make large companies pay their fair share of taxes. States also put limits on how much the electric and gas companies could charge their customers. In these and other ways, progressives helped to improve conditions in their cities and states.

D. President Roosevelt Leads the Federal Government

The Jungle After 1900, Americans also used the federal government to make important changes. Theodore Roosevelt became President in 1901. While he was in office, President Roosevelt read a book called *The Jungle*, by Upton Sinclair. The book described conditions in the meat-packing business.

There would be meat stored in great piles in rooms; and the water from leaky roofs would drip over it, and thousands of rats would race about on it. These rats were nuisances [annoyances], and the packers would put poisoned bread out for them, they would die, and then the rats, bread, and meat would go into the hoppers [meat grinders] together.

Sinclair's book shocked the President. He sent investigators to find out if its descriptions were true. When he learned that they were, the President called on the nation to act. He got Congress to pass a law ending such unhealthy conditions. Congress also passed laws to make sure that canned foods and medicines were safe to use.

Conservation President Roosevelt put the government to work for people in other ways, also. For example, he got the government to help with **conservation,** or the wise use of natural resources. Under his leadership, nearly 200 million acres were added to the national forests — lands that are protected by the federal government. President Roosevelt and Congress also created five new national parks.

E. Progressives Challenge Big Business

Giant Businesses Under President Roosevelt's leadership the government also tried to control businesses that had become too powerful. During the 1890s, you'll remember, giant companies had been formed in many industries.

In 1901, a banker named J.P. Morgan put together the biggest company of all. To do so, he bought Andrew Carnegie's steel business and combined it with other, smaller companies to form the United States Steel Corporation. This company was the first to be worth over a billion dollars.

People hoped that big business would benefit all Americans. Because of their size, big companies could produce goods at a lower cost. But the giant companies did not often pass along their savings to buyers.

Instead, they tried to drive small companies out of business. When a few companies got control of an industry, they would agree to keep prices high. A business that controls an entire industry in this way is a **monopoly**. Monopolies were formed in the oil, steel, rubber, and other industries.

Limits on Big Business Many Americans were upset by the power and wealth of the monopolies. So they turned to the government for help. New laws were passed to limit the power of big business and to protect small businesses. President Theodore Roosevelt even went to court to break up the most powerful monopolies into smaller companies.

F. Women Win the Vote

Women's Rights In Chapter 15 you read about women's struggle to win equal rights in the late 1800s. By 1900, women had made some gains. Each year, more young women finished high school and went on to college. More women also took jobs outside the home. In most states, lawmakers finally allowed wives to own property and to keep their earnings. In earlier days the wife's property and earnings belonged to her husband.

But women continued to face unequal treatment. For one thing, jobs were divided into "men's work" and "women's work." Women's work included such jobs

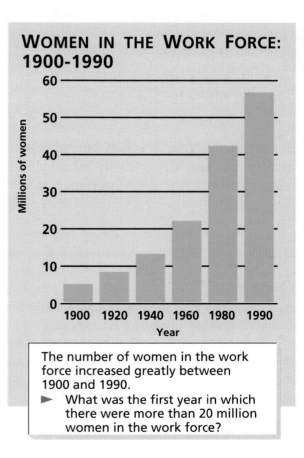

WOMEN IN THE WORK FORCE: 1900-1990

The number of women in the work force increased greatly between 1900 and 1990.
► What was the first year in which there were more than 20 million women in the work force?

In the early 1900s, teaching school was considered "women's work."
► How have attitudes about "women's work" changed?

lawyers, doctors, trolley car conductors, police officers, bankers, mail carriers, or scientists.

Voting In addition, most women in the United States still did not have the right to vote. By 1900 only the western states of Wyoming, Colorado, Idaho, and Utah had granted women **suffrage**, or the right to vote.

For the next twenty years, women worked hard to win the right to vote. Their leaders included Carrie Chapman Catt, Anna Howard Shaw, and Alice Paul. Women held marches to demand the right to vote. They made speeches, wrote letters, and visited representatives in Congress. They called on the new President, Woodrow Wilson, for help. Some women even chained themselves to the fence of the White House to protest unequal treatment of women.

Little by little, women made gains. By 1913, women could vote in 12 states. Finally in 1920 they achieved one of their major goals. The Nineteenth Amendment was added to the Constitution. This amendment gave adult women in the United States the right to vote.

as secretary, nurse, teacher, housekeeper, factory worker, department store clerk, telephone operator, and librarian. But few people in 1900 expected women to become

---

LESSON 1 REVIEW

THINK AND WRITE

A. How did a visit to a cigar maker's apartment change Theodore Roosevelt's thinking about the role of government?

B. What kinds of work did children do in 1900?

C. Why did reformers work to elect new city and state governments around 1900?

D. Describe two progressive actions taken by Theodore Roosevelt while he was President.

E. Why did Americans want the national government to take action to control business?

F. Why was the Nineteenth Amendment important?

SKILLS CHECK

THINKING SKILL

Reread the section on reform on pages 362–367. Then make a chart comparing the causes of reformers in the 1830s and 1840s with the causes of reformers in the early 1900s.

A World Power

THINK ABOUT WHAT YOU KNOW

As you know, the United States was formed when thirteen colonies decided to become independent of the British Empire. How, do you think, have Americans since felt about acquiring colonies of their own?

STUDY THE VOCABULARY

Rough Riders

FOCUS YOUR READING

What new lands did the United States acquire during the late 1800s and the early 1900s?

A. The United States Buys Alaska

By the 1850s, Americans held land across the North American continent, between the Atlantic and Pacific oceans, south of Canada and north of Mexico. For the country to grow more, Americans would have to look elsewhere. In the year 1867 the United States gained land to the north — the large territory of Alaska. You can find Alaska on the map on page 620. Russia sold this land to the United States for $7.2 million.

It was William Seward, the United States' secretary of state, who wanted Alaska for its plentiful fish and animal furs. Many Americans at the time thought it was foolish for the United States to buy Alaska. They believed the land was worthless and that no one would want to live there. They called this vast, cold land Seward's Ice Box and Seward's Folly. A *folly* is "a foolish action."

For thirty years, Americans paid little attention to Seward's Ice Box. Then in 1897, prospectors discovered gold there. In no time, 100,000 people rushed to Alaska, seeking their fortunes. Many of these people stayed on to live there after the gold ran out.

Since those early days, oil and other minerals have also been found in Alaska. With all of Alaska's wealth, "Seward's Folly" has turned out to be "Seward's Bargain." Alaska became the 49th state of the Union in 1959.

B. Hawaii Becomes Part of the United States

American Influence The United States acquired Hawaii in a different way. As you can see on the map on page 518, Hawaii is a group of islands about 2,000 miles (3,218 km) from the Pacific Coast of the United States. In the early 1800s, American ships began to stop at Hawaii for fresh supplies on their way to and from Asia.

Prospectors in Alaska had to deal with harsh conditions.
▶ What difficulties are the prospectors in this photograph facing?

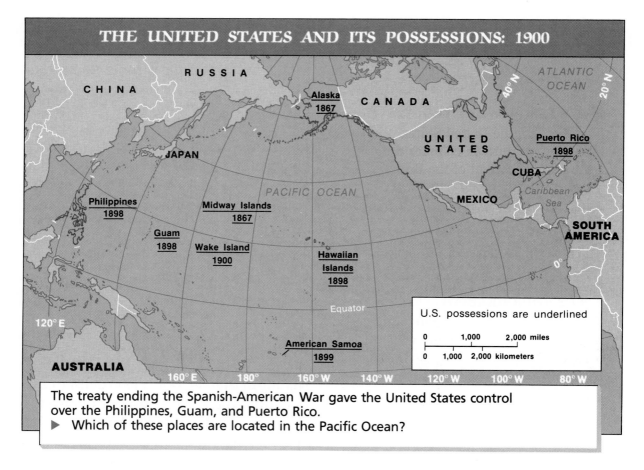

THE UNITED STATES AND ITS POSSESSIONS: 1900

RUSSIA

CHINA

Alaska
1867

CANADA

ATLANTIC
OCEAN

JAPAN

UNITED
STATES

Puerto Rico
1898

CUBA

MEXICO

Caribbean
Sea

PACIFIC OCEAN

Philippines
1898

Midway Islands
1867

Guam
1898

Wake Island
1900

Hawaiian
Islands
1898

SOUTH
AMERICA

Equator

U.S. possessions are underlined

0   1,000   2,000 miles

0   1,000   2,000 kilometers

120° E

American Samoa
1899

AUSTRALIA

160° E   180°   160° W   140° W   120° W   100° W   80° W

The treaty ending the Spanish-American War gave the United States control
over the Philippines, Guam, and Puerto Rico.
▶ Which of these places are located in the Pacific Ocean?

Soon Protestant missionaries from the United States arrived in Hawaii. Missionaries are religious teachers. They try to win new followers for their religion. After the missionaries came businesspeople who bought land and started large sugar plantations. By the mid-1800s, Americans owned most of Hawaii. Even though Hawaiians had their own kings and queens, American planters ran the islands.

Hawaii Joins the United States In 1891 a new queen named Liliuokalani (lih LEE oo-oh kah LAH nee) came to power in Hawaii. She decided that foreigners would not rule Hawaii. The American sugar planters became quite worried. So in 1893 they overthrew Queen Liliuokalani and set up a republic. Immediately, they asked the United States government to take over Hawaii.

At first, the United States said no. President Grover Cleveland thought the planters had been wrong to overthrow the queen. He would not allow the United States to take over another country.

But by 1898 the United States had a new President, William McKinley. President McKinley and the Congress agreed to make Hawaii a territory of the United States. Years later, in 1959, Hawaii became the nation's fiftieth state.

C. United States Goes to War Against Spain

A Revolt Against Spain You'll remember that Spain was the first European country to build a great empire in the Americas. In later years, this empire rebelled against Spanish rule. By the end of the 1800s, all that Spain still held of its former American empire were the islands of Cuba and Puerto Rico.

The people of Cuba had also rebelled against Spain several times. However, each time the Spaniards had crushed the revolt. In 1895, however, Cuba rebelled again. Most Americans hoped the Cuban rebels would win. Some secretly sent guns and money to the Cubans.

Newspapers in the United States printed stories about the exciting events in Cuba. American newspaper owners found that they could increase sales by printing shocking stories. So to sell more papers, some American newspaper publishers began to make the Spaniards sound like terrible beasts. Americans did not know that many of the reports they were reading were untrue. Soon, many Americans were saying that their government should help Cuba win its independence.

"Remember the _Maine!_" At first the United States stayed clear of the fight. Then in February 1898, a United States Navy ship, the _Maine_, arrived at Havana, Cuba. The ship was there to take home Americans who felt they were in danger. On the night of February 15, the _Maine_ lay at anchor in the harbor. Suddenly, an explosion ripped the ship apart, sinking it and killing 260 American sailors.

"Remember the _Maine!_" went the cry. Newspaper headlines all across the country said that the Spanish were to blame for the sinking of the _Maine_. They demanded revenge. But to this day, we do not know the cause of the explosion. Still, on April 25, 1898, the United States declared war on Spain.

D. The United States Wins an Empire

War Begins The first battle of the war took place in the Philippine (FIHL uh peen) Islands, halfway around the world from Cuba. You can find the Philippine Islands on the map on page 518. Spain ruled the Philippines. Part of Spain's navy was based at Manila, the Philippines largest city. On May 1, 1898, an American fleet commanded by Commodore George Dewey opened fire on the Spanish ships in Manila, destroying them.

A few weeks later a man named Emilio Aguinaldo (ahg ee NAHL doh) led some Filipinos in an uprising against Spanish rule. American troops arrived two months later and joined the Filipino rebels. Together, they forced the Spaniards in the Philippines to surrender.

The sinking of the _Maine_ was one of the causes of the Spanish-American War.
► What year did the war start?

Teddy Roosevelt Meanwhile, thousands of Americans volunteered to fight in Cuba. One of them was Theodore Roosevelt. Roosevelt at that time was an official in the Navy Department. He quit his office job and assembled a group of volunteers he called the **Rough Riders**. Roosevelt's Rough Riders were an odd collection of cowboys, college athletes, western sheriffs, American Indians, ranchers, and miners.

The first American troops landed in Cuba in June 1898. Never was an American army less prepared for battle. Many of the soldiers were scarcely trained. They had to drill under the hot summer sun in woolen winter uniforms, because summer uniforms did not arrive. Soldiers who were supposed to fight on horseback went on foot because their horses never got to Cuba. Some soldiers did not even have rifles. To make matters worse, food supplies often spoiled in the heat.

The bravery of the Americans made up for their lack of training and supplies. In July, for example, Roosevelt led the Rough Riders in a charge up San Juan Hill. They were supported by two nearby regiments of black soldiers who fired at the Spanish troops on the hill. Despite their heavy losses, the Rough Riders were finally able to capture the hill.

Other American troops also won battles in Cuba. Meanwhile, the United States Navy sank what was left of the Spanish navy off the coast of Cuba. At the same time, United States troops landed in Puerto Rico and defeated the Spanish there.

Peace Less than four months after the war began, it was over. In the peace treaty that ended the war, Spain freed Cuba and gave Puerto Rico to the United States. Spain also gave the United States the Philippines and a Pacific Ocean island, Guam, for $20 million.

The 24th and 25th Colored Infantry provided supporting fire for the Rough Riders when they captured San Juan Hill, in Cuba.
► What types of weapons can you see in this painting?

The United States had gone to war to help Cuba gain independence. By war's end, it had destroyed what was left of the Spanish empire. And, almost without warning, the United States had won an empire of its own.

Most Americans felt pleased with the peace treaty. But many Americans were not happy to see their country building an empire. And almost all Filipinos were unhappy with the way things had turned out. They had fought against Spain to win their independence. But now they were ruled by the United States.

Events in the Philippines Led once again by Emilio Aguinaldo, Filipinos fought a guerrilla war against the American troops. In a guerrilla war, small groups of soldiers make surprise attacks on their enemy. After three years of fighting, Aguinaldo was captured. With his capture the Filipinos' war for independence came to an end.

Still, Filipinos longed to be independent. Over the years, the United States gave them more say in their own government. Finally, on July 4, 1946, the United States granted the Philippine Islands full independence.

E. The United States Builds the Panama Canal

The Need for a Canal The Spanish-American War made Theodore Roosevelt a national hero. The people of New York elected Roosevelt their governor. Then, in 1900 he became vice-president of the United States. When a crazed gunman killed President William McKinley in 1901, Roosevelt became President.

At about this time the United States decided to build a canal connecting the

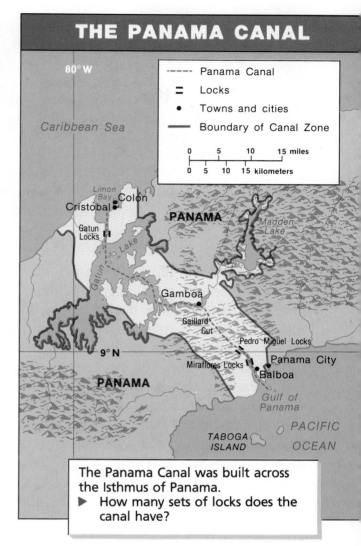

THE PANAMA CANAL

- - - - - Panama Canal
= Locks
• Towns and cities
—— Boundary of Canal Zone

The Panama Canal was built across the Isthmus of Panama.
▶ How many sets of locks does the canal have?

Atlantic and Pacific Oceans. Such a canal would make trade and travel between the two oceans much faster and easier. A French company had already tried to build a canal across the country of Panama, in Central America, 20 years earlier. But the French had failed.

Panama Until 1903 Panama was a part of the Republic of Colombia, the South American country just to its south. Roosevelt offered to pay Colombia for a strip of land in Panama on which to build a canal. However, the Colombian government wanted more money and rejected the offer.

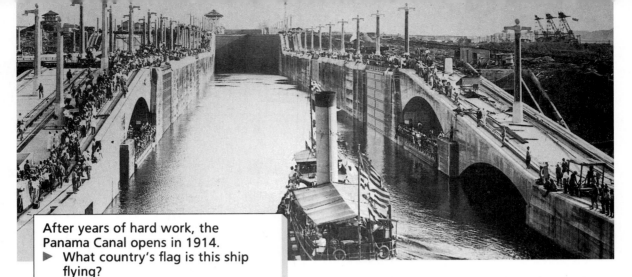

After years of hard work, the Panama Canal opens in 1914.
▶ What country's flag is this ship flying?

Blocked in his effort to get land for the canal, Roosevelt grew angry. When a group of Panamanians decided to overthrow Colombia's rule, Roosevelt saw a way to get his wish. He decided to help the rebels. In November 1903, the rebels declared Panama's independence. Colombia sent a shipload of troops to quash the rebellion, but United States ships kept the troops from landing. So Panama won its independence almost without a fight. Two weeks later, the new government of Panama agreed to sell the United States the right to build a canal across its territory.

Building the Canal Great difficulties still stood in the way of building a canal, however. Workers had to clear thick jungles, move millions of tons of earth, and cut through mountains. The greatest problem, though, was much smaller than a jungle or a mountain. In fact it was barely a half inch long. It was the mosquito.

Mosquitoes in that region carried two deadly diseases, yellow fever and malaria. They had caused the death of thousands of French canal workers 20 years earlier. Now, however, an army doctor named Colonel William Gorgas figured out how to get rid of the mosquitoes. "We can destroy the mosquitoes' breeding places," Colonel Gorgas said. The army did, and within two years, the mosquitoes were gone.

After that, the great work of building the canal could go forward. In August 1914, the first ship sailed through the Panama Canal.

LESSON *2* REVIEW

THINK AND WRITE

A. How did "Seward's Folly" turn out to be "Seward's Bargain"?

B. Why did American planters overthrow Hawaii's Queen Liliuokalani?

C. How did some American newspapers help bring the United States into war with Spain in 1898?

D. What were the results of the war with Spain?

E. What problems did the United States have to overcome to build a canal across Panama?

SKILLS CHECK

MAP SKILL

Use the scale of miles on the map on page 521 to find the distance from the Pedro Miguel Locks to the Gatun Locks.

The First World War

In today's world, terrorists sometimes threaten to kill airplane passengers. How have you felt when you heard about such events?

STUDY THE VOCABULARY

Allied Powers   **communism**
Central Powers   **armistice**
submarine

FOCUS YOUR READING

How was World War I started, fought, and brought to an end?

A. The Great War Begins

In 1914, war broke out on the continent of Europe. On one side were Great Britain, France, and Russia. They were known as the **Allied Powers**, or the Allies. On the other side were Germany, Turkey, and Austria-Hungary, which were known as the **Central Powers**. Soon, the colonies of these nations in Asia, Africa, the Middle East, and the Pacific were drawn into the war. Europe's war thus became the First World War.

The First World War was different from all earlier wars. Not only was the war truly worldwide, but it was also a war fought with deadly new weapons. Never before did armies have tanks and airplanes. Never before did they have machine guns. Using a machine gun, a single soldier could mow down hundreds of the enemy in seconds.

In earlier wars, if a thousand men died in a battle, that was thought to be a very big battle. In the First World War, however, losses were much bigger than ever

Above, United States marines fight in the Battle of Ypres. It was during World War I that the machine gun was first used.
► Why was the machine gun such a deadly weapon?

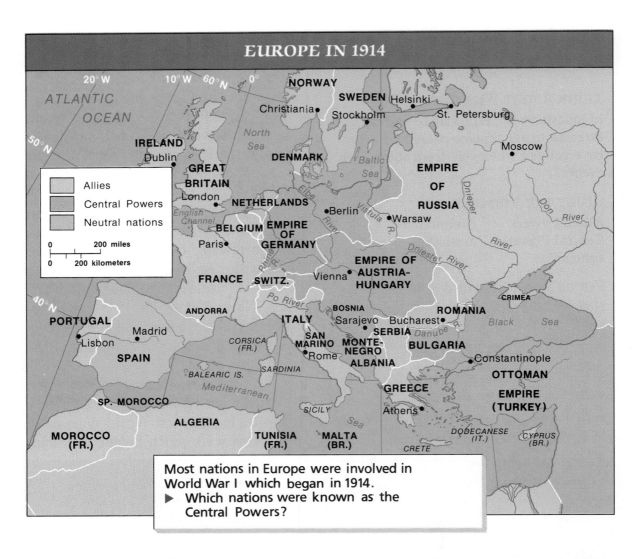

EUROPE IN 1914

Allies

Central Powers

Neutral nations

0   200 miles

0   200 kilometers

ATLANTIC OCEAN

NORWAY
Christiania•
SWEDEN
Stockholm•
Helsinki•
St. Petersburg•
Moscow•

North Sea

IRELAND
Dublin•

GREAT BRITAIN
London•

DENMARK

Baltic Sea

EMPIRE OF RUSSIA

NETHERLANDS
Berlin•
Warsaw•

BELGIUM
EMPIRE OF GERMANY
Paris•

FRANCE
SWITZ.

Vienna•
EMPIRE OF AUSTRIA-HUNGARY

PORTUGAL
Lisbon•
Madrid•
SPAIN

ANDORRA

ITALY
San Marino
Rome•

BOSNIA
Sarajevo•
Bucharest•
ROMANIA

CRIMEA

SERBIA

MONTE-NEGRO

BULGARIA

ALBANIA

Constantinople•

GREECE
Athens•

OTTOMAN EMPIRE (TURKEY)

Black Sea

CORSICA (FR.)

SARDINIA

BALEARIC IS.

Mediterranean Sea

SICILY

CRETE

DODECANESE (IT.)

CYPRUS (BR.)

SP. MOROCCO

MOROCCO (FR.)

ALGERIA

TUNISIA (FR.)

MALTA (BR.)

Most nations in Europe were involved in World War I which began in 1914.
▶ Which nations were known as the Central Powers?

before. A million men died in machine gun fire in just the first few months of the world war. To protect against the machine gun, soldiers dug long, deep trenches, or ditches in the ground, and lived in them for weeks at a time.

B. The United States Is Drawn into War

Staying Out of War Soon after World War I started, President Woodrow Wilson declared that the United States would remain neutral. You'll remember that a neutral country is one that stays out of a war. Most Americans agreed with President Wilson. As one newspaper said, "Luckily we have the Atlantic between us and Europe. It is their war, not ours."

In the early years of the war, the United States even found ways to profit. American businesses sold badly needed goods like cotton to European countries, mainly the Allies. There were dangers in this, for each side tried to stop ships from carrying goods to the other. But profits were big, so Americans kept selling.

Underwater Warfare The longer the war lasted, however, the harder it was for the United States to remain neutral. One main reason was yet another new weapon, the **submarine**. A submarine is a small boat that travels underwater. It was called the U-boat, for "undersea boat." A submarine could sink a large ship with a single torpedo, or large shell, fired from under the water. Germany hoped to weaken the Allies by using its submarines to sink their ships. But if a submarine attacked a passenger ship without warning, many innocent people could be killed.

The Lusitania That's just what happened on May 7, 1915. That day a German U-boat sank the British passenger ship *Lusitania* without warning off the coast of Ireland. The attack killed nearly 1,200 people, including 128 Americans.

Even though the ship had been carrying arms as well as passengers, Americans were outraged. President Wilson demanded that Germany stop torpedoing ships without warning. If the submarine at least gave a warning, passengers would be able to get into lifeboats and get off the ship. After several months, Germany agreed to warn passenger ships before sinking them. Later, Germany also promised to warn Allied merchant ships before sinking them. Merchant ships carry goods rather than passengers.

Entering the War In early 1917, however, the German government decided to make an all-out effort to win the war. The Germans declared that their submarines would no longer give any warnings. They also said that U-boats would sink not only Allied ships but also ships of neutral countries, like the United States. Within days, the Germans attacked three American ships. In April 1917, a solemn President Wilson asked Congress to declare war against Germany. Congress agreed, and the United States entered World War I.

During the early years of World War I, German U-boats sank many ships. On May 7, 1915, a German U-boat sank a British passenger ship, the *Lusitania,* with 1,200 passengers aboard.
▶ Why did this incident outrage the American people?

During World War I many women helped the war effort by joining the Nurse Corps of the army and the navy. These doctors and nurses are working in a field hospital in Europe.
► What kinds of services are these nurses providing?

C. The United States Helps Win the War

American Help Americans pitched in to help win the war in many ways. Nearly 5 million entered the armed services, including thousands of women who joined the Nurse Corps of the army and the navy. Farmers produced extra-large harvests, and Americans observed "meatless Mondays" and "wheatless Tuesdays" so that more food could be sent to the fighting forces. Factories ran day and night to produce guns and supplies. In many factories, women workers took over for the men who went off to war.

Communism in Russia In 1917, however, events in Russia weakened the Allies. The Russians overthrew their *czar* (zahr), or emperor, and set up a representative government. It looked like Russia was taking the first steps on the road to democracy. But six months later, Communists overthrew Russia's new government. **Communism** is a system in which the government owns all the land and businesses.

Soon after the Communists took over, Russia decided to stop fighting Germany. Thus Germany could move its troops out of Russia and send them into action against the Allies in France.

The Tide Turns Slowly, however, the advantage shifted to the Allies. The United States Navy began sinking German submarines. American troops arrived in Europe to take part in the fighting. Along with the troops came needed food and supplies for the Allies.

By the summer of 1918, American troops were truly making a difference in the war. First they helped to stop a major

Woodrow Wilson

detail, Signing of the Treaty of Versailles, by John Christen Johansen, 1919. 248.9x224.8 cm. National Portrait Gallery, Smithsonian Institution. (NPG 65.82). Transfer from the National Museum of American Art; Gift of the City of New York through the National Committee, 1923

The treaty ending World War I was signed at Versailles, France.
▶ Who represented the United States at this meeting?

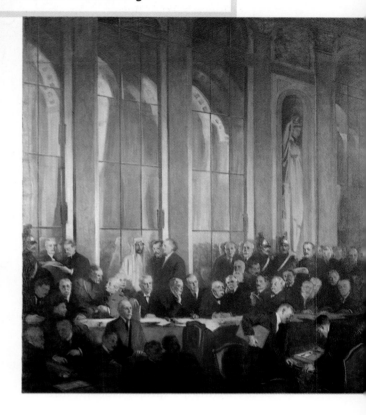

German attack in France. Then United States troops joined other Allied armies in driving back the Germans.

D. The War Comes to an End

In the fall of 1918, the weakened Central Powers saw they had no chance to win the war. Germany asked for an **armistice** (AHR muh stihs), or a cease-fire. On November 11, 1918, at 11:00 A.M., the guns fell silent. The First World War had ended.

Early in 1919, leaders of the victorious Allied nations gathered at the Palace of Versailles outside of Paris, France, to write a peace treaty. President Woodrow Wilson was among these leaders. The leaders hoped the treaty would bring about lasting peace. They agreed to make Germany pay for war damages and give up its colonies and some land.

The treaty also included Wilson's plan for a League of Nations, an organization for all nations. It was hoped that nations would use this organization to settle their differences peacefully. Most countries soon joined the League. However, the Senate of the United States voted against joining the League of Nations. Many senators did not believe the United States should be involved in an organization with other nations. Without the support of the United States, the League of Nations was never truly effective.

LESSON *3* REVIEW

THINK AND WRITE

A. In what ways was the First World War different from all earlier wars?

B. What happened in early 1917 to bring the United States into World War I?

C. How did the United States make a difference in World War I?

D. What was President Wilson's goal for the League of Nations?

SKILLS CHECK

WRITING SKILL

In a few sentences, tell how you think an American soldier might have felt as he left home to fight in World War I.

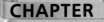
USING THE VOCABULARY

>   **progressive**
>   **conservation**
>   **monopoly**
>   **suffrage**
>   **Rough Riders**
>   **Allied Powers**
>   **Central Powers**
>   **submarine**
>   **communism**
>   **armistice**

On a separate sheet of paper, write the terms from the list that match each of the following definitions.

1. The right to vote

2. Great Britain, France, Russia, and the United States in World War I

3. The government owns all land and business

4. A cease-fire

5. The wise use of natural resources

6. One business controls an entire industry

7. An undersea boat

8. A group of volunteers who fought in the Spanish-American War

9. A reformer

10. Germany, Austria-Hungary, and Turkey in World War I

REMEMBERING WHAT YOU READ

On a separate sheet of paper, write your answers in complete sentences.

1. What were the goals of the progressives?
2. What reform laws were passed while Theodore Roosevelt was President?
3. What did women do to gain the right to vote?
4. How did Alaska and Hawaii become part of the United States?
5. How did the United States get involved in the Spanish-American War?
6. What territories did the United States gain as a result of the Spanish-American War?
7. Why was building the Panama Canal such a difficult undertaking?
8. Why did the United States wait until 1917 to enter World War I?
9. What did people at home do to help the United States and its allies win the war?
10. What happened in Russia in 1917?

TYING HEALTH TO SOCIAL STUDIES

Create menus for a family of five for a meatless Monday and a wheatless Tuesday. Use a standard list of food values and nutritional needs. Be sure that the menus give the family their required proteins and carbohydrates for each day. Find other sources for protein on Monday and for carbohydrates on Tuesday.

THINKING CRITICALLY

On a separate sheet of paper, write your answers in complete sentences.

1. What suggestions would you make to correct situations that exist today that you feel are in need of reform?
2. Are all business monopolies bad? Explain your answer.
3. Hawaii and Alaska became the 49th and 50th states in 1959. Do you think that Puerto Rico will become the 51st state?
4. Was it right, do you think, for newspapers to print shocking stories just to increase the amount of papers they could sell?
5. Explain why it became very difficult for the United States to stay neutral in world conflicts after it became a world power.

SUMMARIZING THE CHAPTER

On a separate sheet of paper, draw a graphic organizer like the one shown here. Copy the information from this graphic organizer to the one you have drawn. Under each main idea, write three statements that support it.

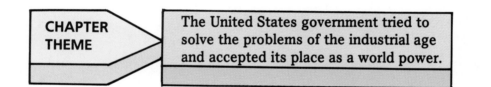

CHAPTER THEME

The United States government tried to solve the problems of the industrial age and accepted its place as a world power.

LESSON 1

Rapid industrial growth caused problems that progressives tried to solve.

1. Unsafe working conditions
2. Monopolies
3. Corrupt government

LESSON 2

The United States gained overseas territories.

1. _____
2. _____
3. _____

LESSON 3

The United States became involved in a world war.

1. _____
2. _____
3. _____

23 HARD TIMES AND WAR

★ ★ ★ ★ ★

The 1920s brought good times, but the 1930s were the years of the Great Depression. The economy only improved after the United States joined the fight in World War II.

Good Years

THINK ABOUT WHAT YOU KNOW
How, do you think, might your life be different if there were no automobiles, trucks, or buses in your community?

STUDY THE VOCABULARY
assembly line   Prohibition
prosperity   discrimination

FOCUS YOUR READING
How did America change during the 1920s?

A. Americans Enter the Automobile Age

Henry Ford When "horseless carriages," or automobiles, first appeared on American streets in the years before 1900, few people thought cars had much of a future. "Too noisy," said some. "Dangerous," said others. "Just a rich man's toy," said still others.

The person who did the most to make Americans change their ideas about cars was a young man from Michigan named Henry Ford. Ford was one of the early automobile makers. It was his idea to make automobiles cheap enough for ordinary farmers and workers, not just rich people, to buy one.

Ford did this by changing the way cars were made. Before then, one or two skilled mechanics would put together each car from start to finish, adding every part and tightening every nut and bolt. Ford's improvement was to divide the building of automobiles into a number of simple steps. Each step was assigned to a different worker. One worker, for example, did nothing but attach hoses to the radiators.

Another specialized in putting on fenders or headlights. Working this way, workers produced many more cars in far less time than before. That meant that each car cost less to make, so each could be sold at a lower price.

Ford's Factories A few years later, Ford introduced the moving **assembly line.** The assembly line was a large moving belt that carried the unfinished automobile to one worker after another. At each station, the worker would perform his step in the building of the automobile. The assembly line saved Ford even more time and money this way. Before long, other car makers adopted his method of manufacturing. In fact, the assembly line was soon being used by makers of hundreds of other products, too.

The moving assembly line made the automobile more affordable.
▶ What part of the automobile are these workers assembling?

From the collections of the Henry Ford Museum and Greenfield Village

© Keith Ferris

As the 1920s began, the increase in the number of automobiles on the road meant new jobs, such as gas station attendant and automobile mechanics.
► How are gas stations today different from the station pictured above?

By the mid-1920s, factories were turning out thousands of cars. Automobiles rolled through the streets of every American city and town. About half the families in America owned a car. Truly, America had entered the Automobile Age.

B. Automobiles Mean New Jobs

The automobile created millions of new jobs. First, there were jobs in the car factories. Also, people got jobs producing the steel, glass, rubber, paint, and other materials used in cars. Thousands of people also found work building roads and putting up signs and traffic lights. Gas stations needed people to sell gasoline and repair tires. Roadside restaurants and motels sprang up to serve the people who now traveled by car.

In addition, cars created a huge demand for gasoline, a motor fuel made from oil. That meant work for thousands in the oil fields of Pennsylvania and Ohio. Then in 1901 came a great new oil discovery at Spindletop, Texas. This new find started an oil boom in the West and Southwest.

The millions of people who held all these new jobs spent their earnings on goods and services. That helped still more businesses to grow and made still more jobs. As a result, the 1920s were a time of **prosperity** when business was good and unemployment was low.

C. Ways of Living Change in the 1920s

New Products The automobile gave people a new feeling of freedom. With a car, people could drive to distant places. Or they could just leave home for a spin through the city or into the countryside. And they could go whenever they felt like it. Those who could afford to could live in the countryside and drive to work in the city.

Other new products of the 1920s also changed the way Americans lived. Washing machines, refrigerators, and vacuum cleaners allowed women to spend less time on housework. More women were free to take jobs outside the home and to take part in other activities, such as politics and education.

Entertainment New developments also changed the ways Americans had fun. In earlier years, Americans usually provided their own entertainment with games and family get-togethers. By the 1920s, however, entertainment was mainly provided by others. Americans listened to the radio and went to the movies. The movies, in fact, were the most popular form of entertainment, with many Americans seeing two or three films a week.

Organized sports provided another favorite form of entertainment. Saturday afternoons in autumn, fans cheered on their favorite high school and college football teams. Baseball captured the attention of Americans in spring and summer. Millions either went to baseball games or listened to them on the radio.

Sports were so popular that the 1920s became an age of sports heroes. What American of that day had not heard of the famed baseball slugger Babe Ruth? Nearly everyone knew about the heroes of other sports — boxing champion Jack Dempsey or Gertrude Ederle, the first woman to swim the English Channel.

Lindbergh's Flight The greatest hero of the 1920s was not an athlete, however. He was a 25-year-old flyer named Charles Lindbergh. On May 20, 1927, Lindbergh headed out over the Atlantic Ocean in his one-seater airplane, the *Spirit of St. Louis*. Lindbergh was trying to become the first person to fly across the ocean to Europe alone. For the next $33\frac{1}{2}$ hours, millions followed Lindbergh's flight through special radio news bulletins. Then, at 10:21 P.M., May 21, Lindbergh landed in Paris, France. The report came over the radio: "He made it!" The nation went wild over "Lucky Lindy."

The Eighteenth Amendment The 1920s were a time of other great changes, too. One change came when Congress added the Eighteenth Amendment to the Constitution in 1920. This amendment

In the 1920s new products made people's lives easier.
▶ How, do you think, did the vacuum make life easier?

ONE perfected feature — the MOTOR DRIVEN BRUSH — is alone worth to you the entire price of the Electric SWEEPER-VAC. This efficient, soft brush (motor driven) revolves 1350 times per minute. It gets ALL lint, threads, hairs and embedded dirt, and, with Powerful Suction, draws them into the dust bag. Ask your dealer for the "Electric SWEEPER-VAC" (don't accept a substitute.) Give it a thorough test on your own rugs.

Pneuvac Company — 166 Fremont Street — Worcester, Mass.

Electric
SWEEPER-VAC
With Motor Driven Brush

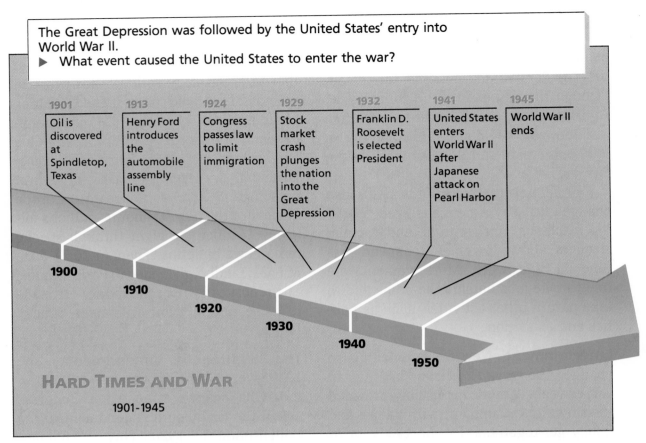

The Great Depression was followed by the United States' entry into World War II.

▶ What event caused the United States to enter the war?

| 1901 | 1913 | 1924 | 1929 | 1932 | 1941 | 1945 |

Oil is discovered at Spindletop, Texas

Henry Ford introduces the automobile assembly line

Congress passes law to limit immigration

Stock market crash plunges the nation into the Great Depression

Franklin D. Roosevelt is elected President

United States enters World War II after Japanese attack on Pearl Harbor

World War II ends

1900 · 1910 · 1920 · 1930 · 1940 · 1950

HARD TIMES AND WAR
1901–1945

prohibited, or made illegal, the sale of alcoholic beverages. **Prohibition** reduced the amount of drinking in the nation. But many Americans ignored the law and went right on drinking. Some gangsters became rich by supplying people with illegal liquor. When it became clear that Prohibition was not working, Congress and the states repealed the Eighteenth Amendment.

D. Immigrants and Minorities Face Discrimination

Immigration Limits Many Americans welcomed the changes taking place in American life. For some, however, America was changing too much. Some people, for example, were troubled by the millions of immigrants who had recently entered the United States. They believed that these newcomers brought with them dangerous ideas. Some Americans also did not like

the fact that so many of the immigrants were Catholics and Jews. In 1924, Congress passed a law to greatly limit the number of immigrants who could enter the country.

Fighting Prejudice African Americans, too, still faced **discrimination** (dih-skrihm ih NAY shun). Discrimination is the unequal and unfair treatment of a person or group. In the 1920s, as before, most blacks lived in the South. There few of them could vote, and life was still segregated. But African Americans were ready to claim equal rights.

Many African Americans had fought bravely for their country in World War I. Black soldiers came home from the war with a new feeling of pride. They had shown that they deserved to be treated the same as other Americans.

Also, during World War I and after, new industries were like magnets drawing

Langston Hughes was a twentieth-century African-American poet.
► What did many of Hughes's poems talk about?

People who are cruel
And afraid . . .
Who are scared of me
And me of them.

I pick up my life
And take it away
On a one-way ticket—
Gone up North,
Gone out West,
Gone!

Blacks found, however, that prejudice was alive in the North as well as in the South. In some cities, believing that blacks were taking their jobs, whites rioted against African Americans. In one city, when blacks tried to use a segregated beach, a terrible riot broke out. In time, Langston Hughes and other blacks were left wondering about what had become of their dreams.

What happens to a dream deferred
[delayed]?
Does it dry up
Like a raisin in the sun? . . .
Does it stink like rotten meat?
Or crust and sugar over—
Like a syrupy sweet?

Maybe it just sags
Like a heavy load.
Or does it explode?

people to the cities of the North and Midwest. Thousands of blacks left the South in search of better jobs and better treatment. Langston Hughes, an African American poet, wrote about the feeling of hope many blacks had after World War I.

I am fed up
With Jim Crow laws,

LESSON 1 REVIEW

THINK AND WRITE

A. How did Henry Ford make cars inexpensive enough for farmers and workers to buy?

B. How did the automobile help make the 1920s a time of prosperity?

C. What were some important changes in Americans' ways of life in the 1920s?

D. What were some of the problems that African Americans faced during the 1920s?

SKILLS CHECK

THINKING SKILL

Make a chart listing each of these new products: automobile, washing machine, radio, movies, refrigerators. Next to each item list at least one way it changed people's lives.

The Great Depression

THINK ABOUT WHAT YOU KNOW

How might getting a new leader affect the way people feel about what will happen in the future?

STUDY THE VOCABULARY

Great Depression	**New Deal**
stock market	**Social Security**
Dust Bowl	

FOCUS YOUR READING

How did Americans deal with the Great Depression?

A. The Depression Begins

October, 1929 Many Americans believed that the prosperity of the 1920s would last forever. But in 1929 the nation slipped into a long period of hard times known as the **Great Depression**. It was a terrible time for our country.

The Great Depression had many causes. One of the major causes was events in the **stock market.** Stocks, or shares in businesses, are bought and sold in the stock market. When you buy shares in a business, you become a part owner of that business, along with thousands of others who own shares.

In the late 1920s, businesses were doing well. Many people wanted to own stock in these prosperous companies. The prices of stock shares went up. Seeing this, some people thought, "Why not make some easy money by buying stocks and selling them later at a higher price?" That's just what they did. Prices climbed still higher. It all looked so easy that people began borrowing money to buy more and more stocks.

In early autumn of 1929, however, stock prices stopped rising. In fact, they began to fall. People rushed to sell their stocks before they lost too much money. In October, with so many people wanting to sell stocks and so few interested in buying them, stock prices took a sudden plunge. Instead of making easy money, many people lost everything they owned.

Unsold Goods Another cause of the Depression was that Americans could not buy all the goods that the nation's factories were turning out. Farmers, for example, did not do well in the 1920s. So after paying expenses, they had little left over. As the years went by, they could afford to buy fewer cars and less furniture. Most city workers earned more than farmers, but they, too, did not receive enough pay to buy all the goods being produced.

During the Great Depression people often stood in line for free bread.
► How, do you think, might the people in this line feel?

As unsold goods piled up, some companies decided to produce less. They needed fewer workers, so they let some of their employees go. Without pay, these people had to cut down on the things they bought. As a result, fewer and fewer goods were sold in the nation. Many companies went out of business, and that put even more people out of work.

Bank Failures Unwise banking practices also helped cause the Depression. A number of banks used their customers' savings to buy stocks. When the stock market crashed, the banks lost this money. Also, once the Depression began, many people who had borrowed money couldn't repay the banks. For these reasons, hundreds of banks went broke. And when a bank went out of business, people could not get back their savings.

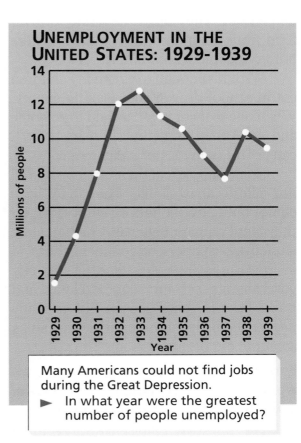

UNEMPLOYMENT IN THE UNITED STATES: 1929-1939

Many Americans could not find jobs during the Great Depression.

► In what year were the greatest number of people unemployed?

B. Life Becomes Grim During the Great Depression

Workers Without Jobs By 1932, one out of every four Americans was out of work. Day after day, year after year, millions looked for jobs but could find none. Families could not pay for things they needed —like car or house repairs or visits to the doctor or dentist. At the market, shoppers bought stale bread instead of fresh vegetables and meat.

Many people went hungry. One writer described how some people managed without food.

You learned to pay for a nickel cup of coffee, to ask for another cup of hot water free, and by mixing the hot water with the ketchup on the counter, to make a kind of tomato soup.

Kitchen workers in restaurants sometimes

Chicago Historical Society

537

helped out. They might separate leftover food from trash and put it outside where hungry people would find it.

Without enough to eat, many children sat in school drowsy and lacking energy. When one teacher urged a child to go home and eat something, the child replied, "I can't. This is my sister's day to eat."

Some people lost their homes or could not afford apartments. They had little choice but to live in huts on empty lots. Or they slept on park benches. The homeless stuffed newspapers under their shirts to keep warm in the cold. Charities and city governments set up soup kitchens and bread lines for poor people. But so many needed help that the charities and cities soon ran out of money.

Farmers Go Broke Conditions grew worse each year. As farm prices fell lower and lower, more and more farmers could not pay off their loans. They lost their farms. Soon many farmers were moving to cities in search of jobs.

Farmers on the southern Great Plains had an additional problem. A drought began in 1932. The drought lasted for three years. During that time, the land became so dry that topsoil turned to dust. Tons of the region's best soil blew away in strong winds. Sometimes, the cloud of dirt and dust in the air grew thick enough to block out the sun. This region thus became known as the **Dust Bowl.** The map on this page will show you which states were part of the Dust Bowl. With their farms ruined, thousands of Dust Bowl farmers left the Great Plains to look for work elsewhere.

Minorities Times became especially hard for minority groups, such as African Americans, Mexican Americans, and American Indians. Even in good times, minorities

THE DUST BOWL

The Dust Bowl

0   50   100 miles

0   50 100 kilometers

During the 1930s a severe drought turned the southern Great Plains into the Dust Bowl.
► What states were part of the Dust Bowl?

were the last people hired for jobs. In bad times, they were the first to be fired. Unemployment and suffering among these groups was especially great.

C. The New Deal Battles the Depression

A New President In 1932, Americans elected a new President, Franklin Delano Roosevelt. They hoped a new leader could do something to relieve the nation's hardship. Roosevelt knew about fighting back when life got rough. He was 39 when a disease called polio left him without the use of his legs. His struggle with polio had given Roosevelt an understanding of suffering. "If you had spent two years in bed trying to wiggle your big toe," he liked to say, "after that, anything else would seem easy."

When Franklin Delano Roosevelt took office in March 1933, it looked like the country had hit bottom. Fifteen million people were out of work. Yet FDR had boldly promised "a new deal for the American people." As a result, his presidency became known as the **New Deal**.

In his first speech as President, Roosevelt gave hope to millions of Americans. He declared, "The only thing we have to fear is fear itself." The federal government would take action, he promised, to bring the Depression to an end.

New Ideas In the next few months, President Roosevelt and his advisors tried many new ideas for getting the country going again. Congress made many of these ideas into law. Before long, many New Deal programs were at work. One such job program was the Civilian Conservation Corps (CCC). The CCC hired several hundred thousand young people to do conservation work. They planted trees, put fish in streams, built wildlife shelters, and fought forest fires. One of their most successful efforts was planting a line of trees 1,000 miles (1,609 km) long on the Great Plains. These trees today shelter farmland from the strong winds that could blow away topsoil.

What was the idea behind such job programs? President Roosevelt and Congress believed that once people were getting paid again, they could buy goods. That would mean factories could reopen and hire more people to make even more goods. Thus the Depression, they hoped, would end.

President Franklin Roosevelt gained the support of the American people by promising a "new deal."
► What do you think President Roosevelt meant when he promised Americans a "new deal"?

Another New Deal program aimed to help farmers. Under this program the federal government paid farmers *not* to plant on some of their land. The goal was to cut down the amount of wheat, corn, and other crops farmers grew. If there were fewer crops for sale, farmers might then get better prices for them.

Another important New Deal law set up the Tennessee Valley Authority (TVA). The TVA built dams on the Tennessee River and its branches in seven southeastern states. These dams controlled the flooding that had caused great damage in the past. They also harnessed the river's water to produce electricity for the region. In this way, most of the people in the Tennessee Valley got electricity for the first time. The project worked so well that the government later built dams on several rivers in the West.

Meanwhile, the New Deal also made laws to reform the way the stock market and the banks did business. You'll remember that unwise practices on the stock market and in banking had helped bring on the Great Depression.

One of the most important New Deal laws was called the Social Security Act. **Social Security** is a kind of insurance for

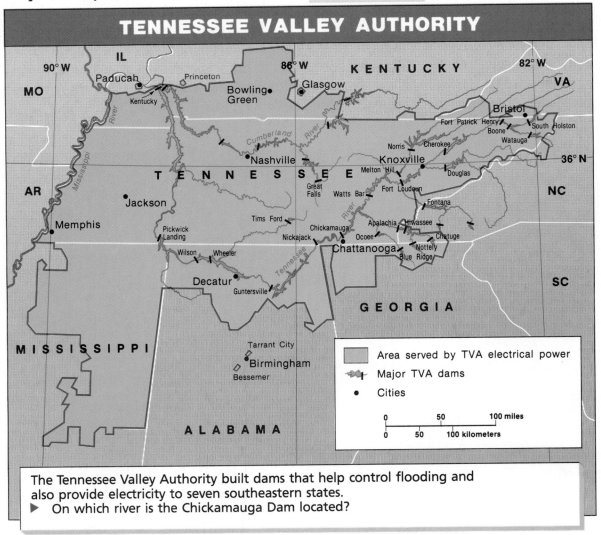

TENNESSEE VALLEY AUTHORITY

The Tennessee Valley Authority built dams that help control flooding and also provide electricity to seven southeastern states.
▶ On which river is the Chickamauga Dam located?

The photograph above shows the construction of a dam built by the Tennessee Valley Authority (TVA). To the left is a completed dam in operation.
► How did the TVA dams improve the lives of the people in the southeastern states?

workers who retire. During their years on the job, workers and their employers both pay a tax into a special Social Security fund. When workers retire, they receive monthly payments from the Social Security fund for as long as they live. This same law also helps states pay people who become unemployed for a short time.

Despite the efforts of the New Deal, the Depression continued throughout the 1930s. By 1939, millions of people were still without regular work. But the New Deal did help in important ways. Because of its programs, some people did find jobs. Farm prices rose a bit. And new laws reformed banking practices and the stock market and protected needy Americans. Most important, the New Deal gave people hope and a renewed faith in their government and in their country.

LESSON 2 REVIEW

THINK AND WRITE

A. What were three causes of the Great Depression?

B. What are three examples of the grim life in the United States during the Great Depression?

C. Why do you think the New Deal gave Americans renewed hope?

SKILLS CHECK

WRITING SKILL

Imagine that you are a newspaper reporter in 1933. Write a brief article about President Roosevelt's New Deal. In your article describe how Americans feel about the New Deal.

A Troubled World

THINK ABOUT WHAT YOU KNOW
During the 1930s, some leaders told the people of their countries that war was glorious. They insisted that war was good for a nation. Remembering the story of World War I, how would you answer such leaders?

STUDY THE VOCABULARY
dictator   concentration camp
Nazi   Axis Powers

FOCUS YOUR READING
What events led to the Second World War?

A. Dictators Come to Power in Europe

Germany The Depression of the 1930s hit Europe as well as the United States. In some European countries, people turned to strong leaders who had no use for democracy. These leaders were **dictators**. A dictator is an all-powerful ruler. Some of these dictators said that war would solve the problems of hard times and would bring glory to their countries. Unfortunately, many people listened to them.

In Germany, conditions were especially harsh. In addition to facing economic hardship, Germany was still dealing with problems from the First World War. The peace treaty that ended the war had forced Germany to accept blame for starting the fighting. It also made Germany pay for damage done during the war and took away some of Germany's land.

Germans felt angry about the peace treaty and the economic hardship. Adolf Hitler, a former soldier, rode Germans' feelings of bitterness to power. Hitler was the head of the **Nazi** (NAHT see) political party, which used violence to scare its opponents. The Nazis told Germans that their country had lost the war because it had been "stabbed in the back" by some of its own people. In the Nazis' thinking, the Jews were one of the groups to blame for Germany's defeat in the First World War. Hitler claimed that the German people were a "master race" that should conquer and rule all of Europe.

In 1933, Hitler and his Nazis gained control of Germany's government. Shortly afterward, he ended democracy in Germany and became the country's dictator. Hitler then began building up Germany's armed forces and preparing for war.

Adolf Hitler and his Nazi party quickly gained the support of the German people as he rose to power in that country.
▶ Which person, do you think, is Adolf Hitler?

During World War II, Hitler and the Nazis put many Europeans in concentration camps. The photograph above shows Polish Jews being taken from their homes to concentration camps.

▶ What do the expressions on the people's faces say about their feelings?

The Nazis ruled with an iron fist. The government rounded up people whom the Nazis didn't like and sent them to special prisons called **concentration camps**. In these camps, prisoners were made to work like slaves. In the late 1930s many of the Nazis' prisoners were Jews, who suffered the harshest treatment. Many of them, as well as other Europeans, died from overwork and brutal treatment in Hitler's camps.

Dictators in Italy and Japan Hitler was not the only war-hungry dictator who came to power around this time. In Italy, another dictator, Benito Mussolini, took power and rallied his followers with speeches about the glories of war. Meanwhile, on the other side of the world, military leaders began to gain power in Japan.

The Japanese army seized Manchuria, a large area in the north of China. In 1936, Italy, Germany, and Japan agreed to cooperate with each other. The three countries called themselves the **Axis Powers**.

Seeds of War Hitler began to threaten his European neighbors. In 1938 he took over Austria. In 1939 his forces rolled into Czechoslovakia and took over that country. Next he demanded that Poland give Germany some of its land.

Britain and France warned Hitler that they would defend Poland if he attacked. In September 1939, Hitler sent his armies crashing into Poland anyway. Britain and France immediately declared war on Germany. Hardly 20 years after the end of World War I, Europe was in flames again. The Second World War had begun.

B. Hitler Conquers Much of Europe

Hammered by German armies, Poland fell in less than three weeks. Europe stayed quiet through the fall and winter that followed. Then in the spring of 1940, German troops swept swiftly across Western Europe. Germany captured Norway, Denmark, the Netherlands, Luxembourg, and France. Now only Great Britain and the United States stood between Hitler and total victory.

Americans had expected to remain neutral in this war. They knew that Hitler was evil and dangerous, but they thought that Britain and France could stop him. With Germany's swift advance, however, the United States was shocked into taking steps to defend itself. The army and navy were expanded, and factories began to produce planes, tanks, and guns. Some of these supplies were shipped to Britain.

In the summer of 1941, Hitler made a costly mistake. He attacked the Soviet Union, as Russia was then called. At first, German armies drove deep into Soviet territory. There, special units murdered many civilians, especially hundreds of thousands of Jews. Finally, however, Soviet troops, with the help of the bitterly cold Russian winter, stopped the Germans. With so many of his troops, tanks, and planes tied down in the Soviet Union, Hitler was unable to knock Britain out of the war.

C. Japan Attacks Pearl Harbor

At the same time, the island country of Japan, in Asia, attacked and conquered much of China's huge land. Japan also had its eye on some other parts of Asia. These lands had oil, aluminum, rubber, and other raw materials that Japan needed.

Soviet troops cut through barbed wire fences as they advance on German troops that had attacked the Soviet Union.
► How, do you think, did the climate affect both armies?

On the morning of December 7, 1941, American forces based at Pearl Harbor, Hawaii, were awakened by a surprise attack of Japanese bombers.
▶ Why, do you think, did Japan destroy American warships in this attack?

The United States complained to Japan about the war against China. President Roosevelt also opposed Japan's taking of more territory. When the Japanese threatened to seize more lands in Asia, the United States and Britain stopped selling Japan the goods it needed.

Japan now had a big decision to make. It could give up its goal of conquest and keep on trading with the United States. Or it could continue taking over lands in Asia with its military forces and go to war with the United States.

Japan chose war. On Sunday, December 7, 1941, Japanese warplanes made a surprise attack on the United States naval base at Pearl Harbor, in the Hawaiian Islands. They killed more than 2,400 Americans and destroyed many of our warships.

LESSON 3 REVIEW

THINK AND WRITE

A. In what ways were Hitler and Mussolini alike?
B. What was Hitler's great mistake in 1941?
C. Why did the Japanese attack the United States naval base at Pearl Harbor?

SKILLS CHECK

THINKING SKILL

List the dates mentioned in this lesson. Then write the event or events that happened on those dates. Make a time line, using the information that you have gathered.

Winning the Second World War

THINK ABOUT WHAT YOU KNOW

What might people's feelings about a war be if the battles took place on their country's land? Would their feelings be different if the fighting occurred far from where they lived?

STUDY THE VOCABULARY

Allies   **Holocaust**
ration   **radiation**

FOCUS YOUR READING

What important decisions did the leaders of different nations make during World War II?

A. Americans Pitch in for Victory

American Aid   The day after the attack on Pearl Harbor, the United States declared war on Japan. Three days later, Japan's friends—Germany and Italy—declared war on the United States. The United States had thus entered World War II on the side of Britain and the Soviet Union. These nations and others that helped them became known as the **Allies**.

For the second time in 25 years, Americans geared up to help win a world war. More than 15 million men served in the armed forces. About 200,000 women took on nonfighting jobs in the army, navy, and air force.

At home, factories ran day and night, turning out tanks, guns, and planes. What a change from the Great Depression! In those days, workers could not find jobs. Now, there were not enough workers for all the jobs. Six million women left their homes and took jobs to help the war effort.

Goods Are Scarce   As the war continued, some goods became scarce. These included meat, butter, shoes, tires, and gasoline. To make sure everyone, including the fighting forces, got a fair share of these goods, the government **rationed** them. To *ration* means "to limit the amount each person can get." Few people complained about this rationing, for they knew that rationing was necessary in order for America to win the war.

With everyone pitching in this way, the United States was able to produce enough weapons, food, clothing, and supplies not only for our own armed forces but also for our allies. The production of all these goods helped to win the war. It was an accomplishment that all Americans could be proud of.

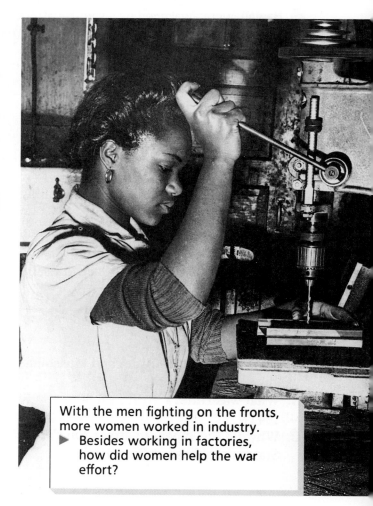

With the men fighting on the fronts, more women worked in industry.
▶ Besides working in factories, how did women help the war effort?

WORLD WAR II: EUROPE AND NORTH AFRICA

Axis Powers

Allied nations or nations liberated by Allies

Neutral nations

By 1940 the Axis Powers had occupied many of the countries of Europe.
▶ Which countries remained neutral during World War II?

B. The United States Helps Bring Victory to the Allies

Germany is Defeated When the United States entered the war at the end of 1941, Germany controlled nearly all of Europe and North Africa. But by the next year, British and American troops were pushing the Germans back. First they drove the Germans out of North Africa. Then in 1943 they invaded Sicily and Italy.

On June 6, 1944, Allied troops sailed from England across the narrow but choppy waters of the English Channel and landed on the beaches of Normandy in France. The famous General Dwight D. Eisenhower of the United States Army planned and led this historic invasion. By the end of the summer of that year, the Allies had pushed the Germans out of France. By spring 1945, the Allies had conquered a large part of Germany.

Meanwhile, Soviet troops had driven the Germans out of the Soviet Union and Poland. The Soviets then entered Germany from the east. Hitler finally realized that Germany was defeated. Early in May 1945, the Nazi leader killed himself. A few days later, Germany surrendered, and the war in Europe was over.

Nazi Death Camps Long before the war ended, though, it had become clear that the Germans were shipping Jews from all over Europe to specially built death camps in conquered Poland. In these camps, thousands of Jews were killed every day, along with other people whom the Nazis hated. As Allied soldiers advanced, they came upon the grim evidence of Nazi madness. They found these death camps filled with weakened, starving survivors and with countless bodies of victims. Alto-

gether, the Nazis killed about 6 million Jews and several million others. This great destruction of European Jews is known as the **Holocaust**.

C. The Allies Defeat Japan

Japan Holds Out As the Allies defeated the Nazis in Europe, American forces made steady progress in the war against Japan. In hard fighting, Americans took back islands in the Pacific Ocean that Japan had won. By early 1945, American forces had destroyed most of the Japanese navy and air force. American planes rained bombs on Japan almost daily.

Still, Japan refused to surrender. To end the war, Allied leaders thought it

In addition to fighting in Europe, American troops fought many battles on islands in the Pacific Ocean.
► Whom were the Americans fighting against in these island battles?

would be necessary to invade Japan. Generals figured that a million soldiers would be killed or wounded in such an invasion. **A New Weapon** By the summer of 1945, however, there was another way to end the war. For years, scientists had worked in secret to develop a powerful new weapon, the atomic bomb. In July 1945, they successfully tested this bomb. The President would have to decide whether to use this terrible new weapon. Since President Roosevelt had died in the spring, the new President, Harry Truman, now faced the difficult decision. Truman got advice from scientists and government officials. Scientists who developed the bomb told him

WORLD WAR II: EAST ASIA AND THE PACIFIC

The United States entered World War II after Japan made a surprise attack on a United States naval base at Pearl Harbor.
▶ In what group of islands is Pearl Harbor located?

RIGHTING A WRONG: JAPANESE AMERICANS IN WORLD WAR II

Americans are proud of what they accomplished during World War II. There is one part of America's wartime record that does not make Americans proud, however. Japanese Americans were very badly treated during the war. Most of them lived on the West Coast of the United States. When the war began, after the surprise Japanese attack on Pearl Harbor, some military officials believed that Japan might attack the West Coast, too. They feared that Japanese Americans would be more loyal to Japan than to the United States. They were afraid, too, that Japanese Americans could be spies.

The government made many Japanese Americans give up their jobs, their businesses, and their homes. They were moved inland, to camps away from the coast. These camps consisted of shacks surrounded by barbed wire and were guarded by soldiers. Whole families were forced to live in single rooms. There were no schools, and there was very little medical care.

Despite this treatment, several thousand Japanese Americans volunteered to serve in the American army. They fought in France and Italy and won many medals for bravery. And no Japanese American was ever found guilty of spying for Japan or any other country against the United States.

In later years, Americans realized that what had been done to these fellow citizens was wrong. In 1988, Congress passed a law apologizing for the mistreatment and humiliation of Japanese Americans. The government also promised to pay $20,000 to each person still living who had been forced to live in the camps. The government has been contacting those people who are eligible for this restitution, or payment for past losses. The restitution began in 1990 with a ceremony in Washington, D.C., when ten recipients received their payments. The oldest recipient at that presentation was 108 years old. The process will continue for several years until approximately 75,000 eligible Japanese Americans, or their heirs, receive restitution.

Thinking for Yourself

On a separate sheet of paper, write your answers in complete sentences.

1. Why did many Americans and the government become suspicious of Japanese Americans?
2. Was there any evidence that Japanese Americans were disloyal to the United States?
3. World War II ended in 1945. Why, do you think, did Japanese Americans have to wait over 40 years for the American government to formally apologize for its wartime actions?
4. Should there be laws, do you think, to keep such a thing from happening again?

Atomic bombs destroyed the cities of Hiroshima and Nagasaki. This is what the city of Nagasaki, Japan, looked like after the bomb was dropped.
► What one adjective describes the Nagasaki that is shown above?

that it would kill many people and would release a long-lasting kind of poison called **radiation**. For this reason, some of President Truman's advisors opposed use of the bomb. Other advisors believed using the bomb would end the war and save the lives of many Allied troops.

At last, President Truman made the decision. The United States would use the deadly bomb. On August 6, 1945, a bomber dropped a single atomic bomb on the Japanese city of Hiroshima (hihr uh-SHEE muh). When the bomb exploded, an enormous light flashed as bright as the sun. The brilliant flash gave off more heat than the hottest oven imaginable. Over 60,000 people died instantly. At least 40,000 more died in the days that followed. Radiation caused 100,000 more deaths in the next several years.

Three days later the United States dropped a second atomic bomb on the city of Nagasaki (nah guh SAH kee). The destruction was just too much for the Japanese. On August 14, 1945, Japan surrendered. World War II was over.

LESSON 4 REVIEW

THINK AND WRITE
A. How did Americans pitch in to help in the war effort?
B. What did the Allies discover about how the Nazis treated the Jews?
C. How did the Allies finally defeat Japan?

SKILLS CHECK
MAP SKILL

Use the Gazetteer to find the latitudes and longitudes of the following places: London, Nagasaki, Pearl Harbor, Rome, and Tokyo. List each place from farthest north to farthest south.

USING THE VOCABULARY

assembly line	New Deal
Prohibition	Social Security
discrimination	dictator
Great Depression	Allies
Dust Bowl	radiation

On a separate sheet of paper, write the appropriate term that completes each sentence.

1. Adolf Hitler was the _____ responsible for the Holocaust.
2. The _____ Act made it possible for retired people and people not able to work to receive monthly income.
3. The stock market crash of 1929 marked the beginning of the _____.
4. Each person on the _____ had a special job to do.
5. The drought caused a _____ in the Great Plains.
6. In World War II, Great Britain, the United States, and the Soviet Union were the _____.
7. The unequal and unfair treatment of a person or group is _____.
8. President Roosevelt promised the American people a _____.
9. The period in the 1920s when no liquor could be sold in the United States was called _____.
10. People became sick because of the _____ from the atom bomb.

REMEMBERING WHAT YOU READ

On a separate sheet of paper, write your answers in complete sentences.

1. Who created the moving assembly line?
2. What were some of the new products available in 1920?
3. Who was the first person to fly across the Atlantic Ocean alone?
4. What were some of the causes of the Great Depression?
5. What effect did the drought of the 1930s have on farmers on the Great Plains?
6. Which countries became dictatorships in the 1930s?
7. How did Hitler use concentration camps?
8. Who were the Axis Powers?
9. What was the result of the Japanese attack on Pearl Harbor?
10. What made the Japanese government decide to surrender?

TYING MATH TO SOCIAL STUDIES

Suppose you have been given $500 to invest in a stock. Look in a newspaper that lists the stocks traded on the New York Stock Exchange and choose a stock to buy. For $500 you should be able to buy more than one share of stock. Make a graph that shows the days of the week along the bottom and the amounts of money on the left side. Your first entry on the graph will be the price you paid for your stock on the day you bought it. For the next four days, check the price at which your stock is selling. Plot those figures on your graph. Did the price go up or down? If you sold your stock at the end of the week, would you have made a profit or taken a loss?

THINKING CRITICALLY

On a separate sheet of paper, write your answers in complete sentences.

1. How did the growth of the automobile industry lead to growth in other industries?
2. Our history shows that many people came to the new world to escape discrimination in their homelands. Why, do you think, has discrimination developed in the United States in spite of our beginnings?
3. What happens to the economy of a country when there is a depression?
4. How was Adolf Hitler able to become so powerful?
5. How would you have ended the war in the Pacific?

SUMMARIZING THE CHAPTER

On a separate sheet of paper, draw a graphic organizer like the one shown here. Copy the information from this organizer to the one you have drawn. List at least six items under each major heading. The first ones under each heading have been done for you.

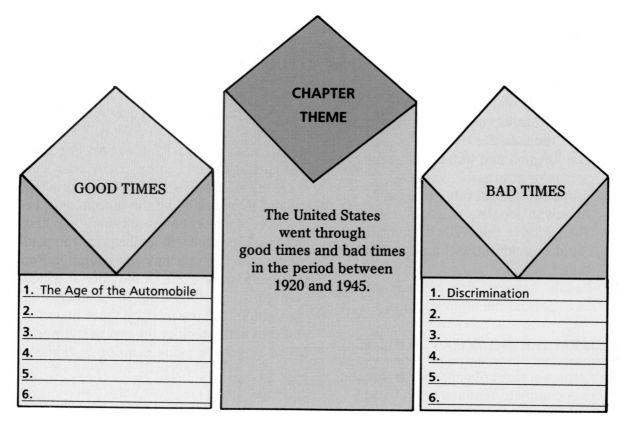

CHAPTER THEME

The United States went through good times and bad times in the period between 1920 and 1945.

GOOD TIMES

1. The Age of the Automobile
2.
3.
4.
5.
6.

BAD TIMES

1. Discrimination
2.
3.
4.
5.
6.

COOPERATIVE LEARNING

In this unit you learned how inventions have changed the way people lived. Every day there are more inventions. Some inventions are the work of just one person. But many inventions are the result of shared ideas and teamwork.

PROJECT

Your group is going to think of an invention. Possibly you will decide that it will be used to solve a problem that people are facing today. Or it might be an invention that will make people's lives easier.

First the group will brainstorm. Brainstorming means mentioning *any* idea you think of without stopping to think whether it will work or not. One person should write down all the ideas. The group should try to come up with at least ten. When the brainstorming is finished, ask the recorder to write the list on the chalkboard or on a piece of poster paper. Discuss the ideas and vote on the best one. This will be the group's invention.

Brainstorm again. Discuss how your invention will change the way people live.

● One member should take notes of the discussion.

● One member should use these notes to write a description of the group's invention.

● One member should write an explanation of how the invention would affect people's lives.

PRESENTATION AND REVIEW

The group's invention could be presented to the class in one of two ways. All the group members, however, should be prepared to answer any questions.

● Choose a member to explain the invention. He or she would read aloud the description and explanation of the group's invention.

● Prepare a bulletin-board display. Neatly print the information about the invention on a large sheet of poster paper. A drawing of the invention would be a helpful addition to the display.

When all the groups have presented their inventions, discuss how each invention would improve people's lives.

REMEMBER TO:
● **Give your ideas.**
● **Listen to others' ideas.**
● **Plan your work with the group.**
● **Present your project.**
● **Discuss how your group worked.**

A. WHY DO I NEED THIS SKILL?

In 1863, President Abraham Lincoln accepted an invitation to speak at the dedication of a cemetery in Gettysburg, Pennsylvania. You have already studied the speech he gave that day. See page 449. You learned that there are five handwritten copies of that speech. The Gettysburg Address is one of the most important documents in our history.

Analyzing the speech tells us how President Lincoln felt about the war. It tells us how he felt about the United States. What he said and how he said it tells us a great deal about Abraham Lincoln.

B. LEARNING THE SKILL

Documents take many forms. They can be speeches or letters. They can be legal documents like laws or treaties. The Constitution of the United States is a document. So, too, are letters written by ordinary people. They can provide a first-hand account of an event. Letters written long ago help us understand what life was like at that time.

The following questions will help in analyzing a document.

1.	What is the topic of the document? What is it about?
2.	What are the main parts of the document?
3.	What are the main ideas in each part?
4.	How well are the main ideas related to the topic?
5.	How well do the various parts of the document relate to each other?
6.	How does the content of the document compare with other types of information about the same topic?

Chief Joseph

National Portrait Gallery, Smithsonian Institution, Washington.

C. PRACTICING THE SKILL

As you learned in this unit, Chief Joseph was the leader of the Nez Percé Indians. The Nez Percé lived in the Northwest, at the point where today the states of Idaho, Washington, and Oregon come together. Chief Joseph was a proud man. He believed the land on which his people lived belonged to them.

The United States government, giving in to pressure, opened the land to settlers. The Nez Percé tried to convince the settlers and the United States Army to leave them alone. They failed and decided they had to fight. They were not successful. At last the tribe decided as a last resort to escape to Canada. The whole tribe of men, women, and children moved north with the army in pursuit. The army caught up with the Nez Percé just before the border and forced them to surrender. This is Chief Joseph's surrender speech.

Tell General Howard I know his heart. What he told me before, I have it in my heart. I am tired of fighting. Our Chiefs are killed. Looking Glass is dead. Too-hoo-hool-zote is dead. It is the young men who say "Yes" or "No." He who led the young men is dead. It is cold and we have no blankets. The little children are freezing to death. My people, some of them, have run away to the hills, and have no blankets, no food. No one knows where they are, perhaps freezing to death. I want to have time to look for my children and see how many of them I can find. Maybe I shall find them among the dead. Hear me, my chiefs! I am tired. My heart is sick and sad. From where the sun now stands, I will fight no more forever.

Chief Joseph's speech is a document. The following questions will help you analyze it.
1. What key phrase tells the main idea of Chief Joseph's speech?
2. One reason given by Chief Joseph for not wanting to fight anymore was the death of elders of the tribe—"the old men." What other reasons did he give?
3. Is it appropriate, do you think, to call this a surrender speech?

D. APPLYING THE SKILL

We analyze documents so that we can better understand what happened at a particular time or in a special place. Answer the following questions about Chief Joseph's speech.
1. How would you describe Chief Joseph's condition during the surrender?
2. What was most important to Chief Joseph after the surrender?
3. Did Chief Joseph think he could get more help from the young men of his tribe? Explain your answer.
4. Why, do you think, did Chief Joseph say that he would "fight no more forever"?

SKILLBUILDER
Evaluating Fact and Opinion

A. WHY DO I NEED THIS SKILL?

Not every statement you read in a book, magazine, or newspaper is a fact. A fact is information that can be checked to see if it is correct. If the information is not correct, it is a false statement, as in a true-or-false test.

Sometimes what you read is not a fact, but it is not a false statement either. It is the writer's *opinion*. An opinion tells what the writer thinks or believes. Understanding the difference between facts and opinions will help you to become a critical reader. You can also use this skill to become a critical listener.

B. LEARNING THE SKILL

Each of the following statements can be checked by information in Chapter 23, "Hard Times and War."

- In 1932, one out of every four Americans was out of work. (fact, page 537)
- The three Axis Powers did not cooperate with one another. (false, page 543)

An opinion is often based on facts, but it is the writer's or speaker's interpretation of the facts. It is what the person feels, thinks, or believes.

- The United States should not have dropped atomic bombs on Japanese cities because many thousands of innocent people were killed.

- It was all right for the United States to drop atomic bombs on Japanese cities because it helped to end World War II.

These two opinions are different, but they both are based upon fact. The United States did drop atomic bombs on Japanese cities. It is up to you to decide if you agree with either opinion.

Some opinions, however, might be based on incorrect information, or they might include illogical arguments.

- It was all right to drop the atomic bombs because we know there are no long-lasting effects from them.

This opinion includes an inaccurate statement. Radiation from the atomic bombs continued to harm people long after the bombs were dropped. So, this might be an opinion you would choose not to agree with.

C. PRACTICING THE SKILL

Evaluate the ten statements that follow. All the statements are based on material in Chapter 23. Number a sheet of paper from **1** to **10**. If the statement is a fact, write **F** after the number on your paper. If the statement is an opinion based on a fact, write **OF**. If the statement is an opinion that is not based on fact, write **O**. If the opinion is based on inaccurate information, write **OI**.

1. Henry Ford was a great man.

Copyright 1930 *The Detroit News*

2. An unfinished product moves along an assembly line from one worker to another.
3. The prosperity of the 1920s was based on the automobile, a product most Americans could not afford.
4. Movies were so important in the 1920s that family life suffered.
5. The passage of the Eighteenth Amendment, the Prohibition Amendment, was the best thing that ever happened.
6. Langston Hughes was an African-American poet.
7. The most important cause of the Great Depression was poor banking practices.
8. The New Deal gave people hope.
9. One of the first things Hitler did after he came to power in Germany was to end democracy.
10. The Japanese government made a big mistake when it ordered the bombing of Pearl Harbor.

D. APPLYING THE SKILL

On page 142 there is a selection on the death of Atahualpa that was written by one of Francisco Pizarro's captains. Read the selection again. As you read, evaluate the statements as to whether they are facts or opinions. List two examples of fact and two examples of opinion from the selection. Write a statement explaining how you think the writer of this selection felt about the way Atahualpa faced his death.

STUDENTS

PLEASE...

Unit **7**

THE UNITED STATES IN A CHANGING WORLD

In the late twentieth century, many social, political, and technological changes took place in the United States and in the world.

▶ *Computer skills are important in a world in which technology is growing rapidly.*

24 A PORTRAIT OF AMERICA IN 1950

★ ★ ★

Most Americans enjoyed the prosperity of the 1950s. Automobiles and new highway systems made it easy to work in the city and live in the suburbs. There was a new American way of life.

A Changing America

THINK ABOUT WHAT YOU KNOW

What are some advantages of living in cities? What are some disadvantages?

STUDY THE VOCABULARY

baby boom   **skyscraper**

FOCUS YOUR READING

How did American life change in the years just after World War II?

A. The Nation's Population Is Young

The Baby Boom   Every hundred years in this study of our country's history, we have paused to take a look at America. We have now reached 1950, and it is time to look at an imaginary "photograph" of America, just as we did for the year 1850. In 1950 your grandparents were probably young adults. In this portrait of our country, you will see that much about their lives is familiar to you. But you will also see ways in which life in 1950 was different from your life today.

The first thing to notice about the America of 1950 is the great number of young children. The Second World War had ended just five years before. You'll recall from Chapter 23 that the war had disrupted life for almost every American. One big change was that young people put off getting married. After the war, Americans were eager to get back to normal living. With renewed hope for the future, millions of young men and women married and started families. These families had so many children that the increase in birthrate from the mid-1940s through the 1950s is called the **baby boom.**

An Economic Boom   The baby boom affected the United States in many ways. Almost immediately it helped bring an economic boom, as new houses and other buildings were built for the new families. Young parents needed such goods as food, clothing, and even toys for their children. As children of the baby boom grew older, companies began to make products to sell to young buyers themselves—bikes, records, and fashions. And communities had to build more schools and hire more teachers for the swelling numbers of students.

B. Cities Grow in All Parts of the Nation

Population Shifts   By 1950, more than two of every three Americans lived in or near a city. Cities had grown into immense places. There were five cities with over 1 million people. You'll remember that no city in the nation had even close to a million people in 1850. You can read more about American cities on page 564.

And by 1950, big cities were found in every part of the country. The fastest-growing cities were in the South and the Southwest. As you learned earlier, this area is known as the Sunbelt because the climate is mostly warm and sunny. The big move to the Sunbelt started during World War II. People moved there to take jobs in aircraft factories and shipyards.

After the war many of the newcomers stayed on. The climate and job opportunities attracted still others to the Sunbelt. By 1950, millions were moving to this area and increasing the size of its cities. The city of Houston, Texas, for example, doubled in population in just ten years. Other cities, such as San Diego, California, and Baton Rouge, Louisiana, also grew rapidly.

The invention of air conditioning helped the Sunbelt grow. In the summertime much of the Sunbelt is uncomfortably hot. By 1950, though, many office buildings and homes in the Sunbelt were kept cool with air conditioning.

Building Up Whether in the Sunbelt or to the north, cities of 1950 looked different from those of a hundred years earlier. For one thing, cities had grown upward by 1950. In 1850 the tallest buildings had been five or six stories high. But by 1950, the downtown areas of many cities were crowded with buildings whose tops seemed to scrape the sky. In fact we call these tall buildings **skyscrapers**.

Most skyscrapers were office buildings. In the cities of 1950, more and more men and women worked in offices instead

By early in the 1950s, skyscrapers dotted many city skylines. Below is Lever House, in New York City.
▶ How does Lever House compare with the building on its right?

of in factories and workshops. They might work for large insurance companies and banks. They might work in the offices of the companies that made furniture and cars and a thousand other products.

These office workers used business machines — typewriters and telephones — that had not existed a century before. In 1950, however, you would not find office workers using business machines such as computers. Computers had been invented by 1950, but they were not yet commonly used.

C. Suburbs Grow Up Around the Cities

Suburbs Another important change was that American cities grew outward as well as upward. In 1850 no city had spread much more than three or four miles (five or six km) from its center. That was because the main way of getting around was walking. The cities of 1950, however, sprawled miles from their downtown areas. New methods of transportation enabled people to move out from the city center. With buses, subways, and — increasingly — cars, people could live far from where they worked or shopped.

More and more people used their new-found freedom to move outside of cities. On the outskirts of a city of 1950, you might see several new homes in a cluster. Each home might have a neat green lawn around it. Close by would lie another cluster of new homes, and then another. Some of the clusters would be so close that they would run into one another. These clusters of houses ringing a city were the suburbs, or communities that surround cities. Suburbs together with a nearby city made up a giant metropolitan area.

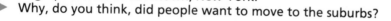

By 1950, suburbs were growing outside of major cities throughout the United States. New homes in the suburbs were built in clusters as shown in the photograph below of Levittown, New York.
▶ Why, do you think, did people want to move to the suburbs?

The automobile changed the way people lived in the 1950s. Above is the busy Hollywood Freeway in Hollywood, California.
► How do you think a photograph of that area would look today?

After World War II, suburbs grew even more rapidly than cities. By the 1950s about a million people were moving to the suburbs each year. In the suburbs, young families could buy inexpensive homes that had yards. Builders bought up orchards and large amounts of farmland to make room for all the people who wanted to live in the suburbs. The new communities built roads, schools, and play areas. Stores, banks, and other services soon opened along suburban roads. Even office buildings began to move out of the cities and into the suburbs.

The Auto Age The move to the suburbs was helped by the growing use of cars. In 1950 most families owned cars. Miles and miles of new roads were under construction. But as they took to their cars, Americans were giving up on the great railroads they had once depended on.

In 1950 the nation had ten times as many miles of railroad track as it had had a hundred years earlier. But few trains used the track. In fact, cars, buses, and trucks were passing trains by. For daily travel and even for long trips, Americans used cars. Those who could afford the higher cost of flying often took airplanes for longer trips. And although trains still carried many tons of goods, even more goods were shipped by truck over the country's new highways.

LESSON *1* REVIEW

THINK AND WRITE
A. What effect did the baby boom have on life around 1950?
B. Where were the most rapidly growing American cities in the 1950s?
C. What attracted young American families to the suburbs around 1950?

SKILLS CHECK
THINKING SKILL
Make a list of reasons why people moved to the Sunbelt during and after World War II. Do you think the Sunbelt will continue to grow? Give reasons for your answer.

Life in 1950

THINK ABOUT WHAT YOU KNOW
How do you and your family like to spend your free time?

STUDY THE VOCABULARY
supermarket   **leisure**

FOCUS YOUR READING
What were some improvements in American life by 1950?

A. Americans' Diets Improve

Foods of 1850   Between 1850 and 1950 the American diet changed greatly. If you had lived in 1850, you would have eaten meals that were neither tasty nor balanced. The daily diet of most Americans included potatoes, bread, milk, and salt beef or salt pork. (Salt beef and salt pork are meats preserved in salt.)

During most of the year, there was no way to keep dairy products fresh. So you got used to drinking sour milk and eating spoiled butter. Foods that spoiled could not be shipped far, so you could only eat fruits and vegetables that were grown near where you lived. Even then you might not have eaten many fruits and vegetables, because many people considered these foods dangerous to the health of children!

An Improving Diet   In the years after 1850, Americans began to eat a more balanced diet. Trains carried fresh foods to the cities in refrigerator cars. Food companies preserved and sold many other foods in cans and jars. Americans soon enjoyed a much more varied and tasty diet.

In the late 1800s, Americans bought their foods in small grocery stores. In the early 1900s, the first **supermarket**, or large self-service food store, opened. Supermarkets did not catch on at first, but they became popular in the 1930s and 1940s. By 1950 most Americans did their food shopping in supermarkets.

And what a variety of foods the supermarkets of 1950 offered! Shoppers could choose from hundreds of canned and packaged foods. They could also buy fresh fruits and vegetables nearly all year-round. And if shoppers couldn't find a certain fresh vegetable or fruit they wanted, they could probably buy it frozen.

The great variety of foods improved the American diet. As a result, Americans of 1950 enjoyed longer and healthier lives than had Americans a hundred years before. Still, in 1950, Americans ate more sugar and starches than doctors today consider healthy.

In the 1950s, more and more frozen foods became available.
► What frozen foods are being advertised?

B. Americans Have More Leisure Time

Less Working Time In 1850, Americans spent nearly the whole day working. They worked about 66 hours every week. Sunday was a day off, but there were no vacations. The only holidays were Christmas, New Year's Day, and the Fourth of July. Even in 1900, Americans still worked about 60 hours a week. That means they worked 10 hours a day, 6 days a week. There wasn't much time for people to enjoy themselves.

But by 1950, Americans had far more **leisure**, or free time. Most workers had a 40-hour workweek. The workday ended at about five or six o'clock, and workers usually had Saturdays and Sundays off. In addition, workers also got time off for several holidays. Most workers were allowed two weeks of vacation each year. Americans in the early 1900s could not have imagined having so much time for themselves!

Entertainment in 1950 Americans of 1950 spent this leisure time in many different ways. Movies entertained millions of people every week. Until the end of the 1930s, movies had been in black and white. But by 1950 most movies were being made in color. The movie remained the king of entertainment.

Americans even found a way to combine two of their favorite things — the movies and the automobile. They did this at drive-in theaters. On the outskirts of most towns were open fields that were turned into large parking lots. At the front of each lot was a large white screen. At night, crowds of people drove in and parked in neat rows. Then, from the comfort of their cars, they watched a movie or two on the big screen.

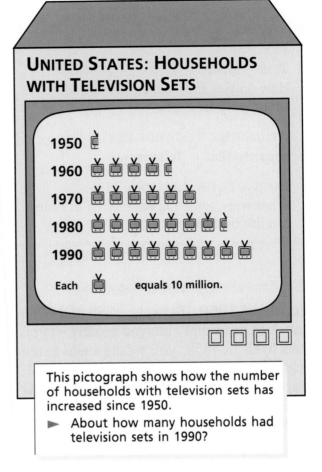

UNITED STATES: HOUSEHOLDS WITH TELEVISION SETS

1950
1960
1970
1980
1990

Each ▯ equals 10 million.

This pictograph shows how the number of households with television sets has increased since 1950.

► About how many households had television sets in 1990?

New kinds of home entertainment also became available. A growing number of Americans spent their evenings watching television. To them the TV was an amazing little box that brought pictures into their living rooms. People could scarcely believe the convenience.

Television was still fairly new in 1950, but it became popular almost overnight. Just five years earlier, you might not have known a single person who had ever seen a television set. By 1950, though, someone on your block almost surely owned one. Families all across the country tuned into the same shows and watched commercials for the same products. The broadcasts of 1950 were in black and white, because color TV was still in the future.

C. Americans Enjoy Shopping, Playing, and Traveling

Shopping By 1950, prosperity had returned. With extra money in their pockets, millions of Americans could enjoy another leisure activity—shopping. Not far from their homes in the suburbs were new shopping centers. There, parking lots overflowed with shoppers' cars, as people came looking for household appliances, clothing, and other items.

Americans of 1950 loved to shop. They shopped in the daytime, and they shopped in the evening. They shopped for goods they needed and for goods they thought they might need. They even shopped for goods they really didn't need at all. Some people joked that shopping had become America's great indoor sport. They said that shopping, not baseball, was America's pastime.

Sports Americans also spent much of their leisure time at play. Many of the favorite sports and games of the time are still popular. For example, bowling became a favorite of both men and women. People formed bowling teams and bowling leagues. Millions of Americans also fished and hunted. And they enjoyed boating—much as people do today.

Travel To many Americans of 1950, vacations were a time to relax at home. Yet to more than half of all Americans, a vacation meant an automobile trip. Parents and children piled into family cars and headed out for state or national parks. Some people visited exciting cities like New York, New Orleans, or Los Angeles. Still others visited relatives. How times had changed!

In the 1950s, Americans had much more leisure time to spend on family vacations.
▶ What items is this family taking on vacation?

LESSON **2** *REVIEW*

THINK AND WRITE

A. In what ways was the American diet of 1950 different from the diet of 1850?

B. Why, do you think, did television become popular so quickly?

C. What changes in American life were making Americans in all parts of the country more alike?

SKILLS CHECK

MAP SKILL

In 1950, like today, many Americans enjoyed taking trips to our neighboring nations of Canada and Mexico. Use the Atlas map of the United States to list the states that border on Canadian land. Then list the states that border on Mexico.

The Other Americans

THINK ABOUT WHAT YOU KNOW
Imagine that your school suddenly had the following new rule: Students from your classroom can no longer use the drinking fountains in your school. The new rule does not apply to students from other classrooms. How would you feel about such a rule?

STUDY THE VOCABULARY
migrant worker   **literacy test**

FOCUS YOUR READING
Which Americans were left out of the nation's good times?

A. Many Americans Did Not Prosper

Not all Americans of 1950 shared in the country's good times. Some Americans could afford neither new cars nor new homes. They rarely went shopping for television sets or other new appliances. They had too little money to afford any vacations. Many could not even enjoy the improved diet that most Americans had in 1950.

These were the "Other Americans," the Americans who lived in poverty. Many of these Americans were older people who had retired. Millions of retired people in 1950 were not yet included in the Social Security system. They did not receive monthly Social Security payments. Even those on Social Security often found it hard to pay all their bills, since the payments they got in 1950 were still quite small.

Many divorced and widowed women with children also were among the poor in 1950. These women found they could not hold jobs and take care of their families at the same time. And when they did get jobs, they received lower pay than men.

Prosperity also passed over some parts of the country. People in coal mining areas of West Virginia, for example, did not share in the nation's good times. Some western and southern farmers also had rough times around 1950.

Minority groups did not share in the prosperity, either. American Indians had long lived in poverty in the United States. There was no sign of improving conditions for them in 1950. Mexican Americans who worked as **migrant workers** made barely

This miner and his son did not share in the prosperity of the1950s.
► How do you think their lives differed from that of the family shown on page 569?

enough to survive. Migrant workers travel from one farm to another to harvest crops. Thousands of migrant workers came from Mexico to the United States with the dream of a better life. But once here they often faced dreadful working and living conditions. Their children had little chance for schooling. Also many African Americans struggled to make a living on southern farms and in northern cities.

B. Segregation Is Widespread in 1950

Segregation Continues In 1950 much of America was still segregated. In the South, laws kept blacks and whites apart from birth to death. Blacks had to attend separate churches and schools. They had to live in segregated housing and eat in segregated restaurants. At the movies, on buses, and on trains, they had to sit apart from whites.

In the South, African Americans had to use separate entrances into many places like movie theaters.
▶ Why were laws like this wrong?

In public places there were two drinking fountains — one for whites and one for blacks. African American children could not use playgrounds reserved for whites. They could swim only in pools marked For Colored. White hospitals would not take black patients, even for emergencies. The segregation of whites and blacks continued even after death, for blacks had to be buried in separate cemeteries.

Southern states also continued to use the **literacy test** to keep African Americans from voting. To become a voter, a person had to read and explain the state's constitution. White officials made it almost impossible for black voters to pass this test.

Discrimination There were few segregation laws outside the South. But conditions were not much better. In the America of 1950, African Americans in all parts of the country faced prejudice and discrimination.

Discrimination was worst in jobs, housing, and schools. In most places of work, the good jobs went to whites. Blacks got the poorest jobs, when they got jobs at all. They earned the lowest pay and had fewer chances to work their way up to better paying jobs.

Blacks found it hard to rent or buy homes in white neighborhoods. In the nation's big cities, most black people lived in ghettos. Because children went to neighborhood schools, most black children attended schools that were as segregated as the communities they grew up in. Few African Americans went on to college, and many colleges refused to accept any black students.

Change Comes Slowly You'll remember that African Americans began to press for

ONCE UPON A TIME WHEN WE WERE COLORED

By: Clifton L. Taulbert
Setting: Mississippi, 1950s

Clifton Taulbert grew up in Mississippi in the 1950s. During those years many African Americans, who were then often called "colored," moved from the South to the North. They hoped to escape segregation, enjoy civil rights fully, and find opportunities to make a better living.

Clifton Taulbert remembers how he used to go to the nearby train station to see off relatives and friends who were moving North.

. . . We'd get there with plenty of time to spare, and the Union station would be packed on both the colored and the white sides. I never really knew what happened on the white side of the station, but I will always remember the side which was a part of my life. Colored men and women in their Sunday best lined the walls to the ticket cage, buying one-way tickets north. Their worn suitcases were held together with leather belts and neckties, and they were weighted down with brown paper bag lunches. Their eyes would be as bright as light bulbs, while their relatives would be crying as if the train were taking the loved ones to those eternal green pastures. Some who were departing would cry too. I don't know if the tears were for joy, because now they had a chance to go north and be somebody, or for fear that once they boarded the old Illinois Central, they might never return again. I have found that fear to be justified. Many of the colored passengers never returned home again.

On page 571 of this book you can learn whether these hopeful passengers realized their dreams of a better life in the North.

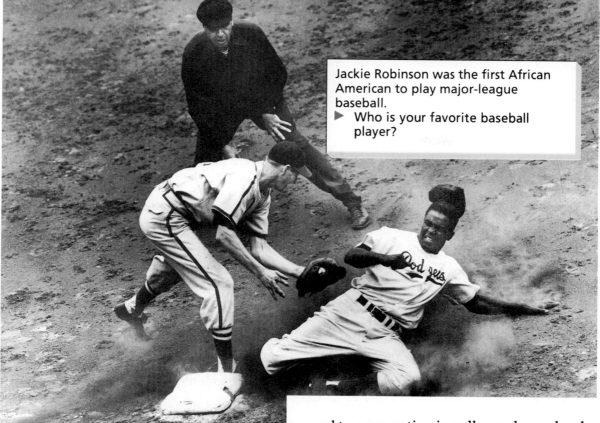

Jackie Robinson was the first African American to play major-league baseball.
► Who is your favorite baseball player?

change after World War I. A similar wave of hope and pride stirred African Americans after World War II. By 1950 the walls of segregation had begun to fall in a number of areas of American life. Major-league baseball at last had its first black player in 1947, when Jackie Robinson took the field for the Brooklyn Dodgers. In 1948, President Truman ordered an end to segregation in the United States Army. Lawyers working for the National Association for the Advancement of Colored People (NAACP) went to court to try to put an end to segregation in colleges, law schools, and other places.

Even so, African Americans found that change was slow. In 1950 there were few black clerks behind the counters in shopping centers. There were few black families in the suburbs. Few black police officers directed traffic, few black professors taught college, and few black doctors practiced in hospitals. In 1950 many blacks—and some whites—were wondering how they might begin to change all this. In Chapter 25 you will read about the steps they took and what these Americans achieved.

LESSON **3** *REVIEW*

THINK AND WRITE

A. Who were the "other Americans?"

B. What important problems did black Americans face as the 1950s began?

SKILLS CHECK

WRITING SKILL

Review the part of the lesson that describes segregation and discrimination in 1950. Then write a paragraph telling what you think the actions of black leaders will be. You will read about them in Chapter 25.

USING THE VOCABULARY

baby boom
skyscrapers
leisure
migrant worker
literacy test

On a separate sheet of paper, write the terms from the list to complete the sentences below.

1. A person who follows the cycle of harvesting to pick fresh fruits and vegetables is a _____.

2. Because the workweek shrank from 66 hours to 40 hours or less, workers today have time for _____ activities.

3. By the 1950s, many of our nation's cities had tall buildings called _____.

4. The great number of babies born after World War II is called the _____.

5. A _____ was used to keep some people from voting.

REMEMBERING WHAT YOU READ

On a separate sheet of paper, write your answers in complete sentences.

1. What were some of the effects of the baby boom?

2. Where were the fastest-growing cities in 1950?

3. Why were the southern and southwestern parts of the United States called the Sunbelt?

4. How had cities changed between 1850 and 1950?

5. How did American diets change and improve between 1850 and 1950?

6. What kinds of vacations did American families enjoy?

7. How did supermarkets, drive-in theaters, and television affect the way Americans lived?

8. How did Americans use their leisure time?

9. What groups of Americans did not share the good times of the 1950s?

10. How did segregation affect the lives of black Americans and white Americans?

TYING ART TO SOCIAL STUDIES

Many comparisons were made in this chapter between life in the United States in 1850 and in 1950. Make a collage or a montage entitled "Portrait of America in the 1990s." Compare life at the present with American life in 1950. A collage is a picture that is at least partly three-dimensional. A montage is a group of pictures about the same subject.

THINKING CRITICALLY

On a separate sheet of paper, write your answers in complete sentences.

1. Why was the baby boom good for the United States?
2. Would Houston, Texas; San Diego, California; and other Sunbelt cities have grown so large if air conditioning had not been invented?
3. How can the growth of suburbs lead to the decline of cities?
4. How would you have used your leisure time if you had lived in 1950?
5. What problems were developing in the 1950s that would have to be solved in the decades to come?

SUMMARIZING THE CHAPTER

On a separate sheet of paper, draw a graphic organizer like the one shown here. Copy the information from this graphic organizer to the one you have drawn. Under the main idea for each lesson, write three statements that support the main idea. The first one has been done for you.

CHAPTER THEME

The 1950s was a good time for many Americans, but not for all. The country enjoyed a period of prosperity, and Sunbelt cities grew larger.

LESSON 1

Young families and growing cities are signs of change in America.

1. Baby boom
2. Sunbelt cities
3. Suburbs

LESSON 2

Americans enjoy life in the 1950s.

1.
2.
3.

LESSON 3

Not all Americans enjoy the good life.

1.
2.
3.

CHAPTER 25

THE SEARCH FOR PEACE AND JUSTICE

*T*he years following World War II were not without their problems. Relations with the Soviet Union worsened. Many Americans felt they were being denied their rights —in voting booths, in workplaces, and in schools.

WE MARCH FOR HIGHER MINIMUM WAGES COVERAGE FOR ALL WORKERS NOW!

WE MARCH TOGETHER CATHOLIC JEWS PROTESTANT FOR DIGNITY

WE MARCH FOR FIRST CLASS CITIZENSHIP NOW!

WE MARCH FOR HIGHER MINIMUM WAGES COVERAGE FOR ALL WORKERS NOW!

WE DEMAND AN END TO BIAS NOW!

WE DEMAND DECENT HOUSING NOW!

JOBS AND FREEDOM

JOBS FOR ALL A DECENT PAY NOW!

The Search for a Lasting Peace

Why do people sometimes become enemies? Do you think the same kinds of problems might sometimes make countries become enemies?

Communist   **free enterprise**
capitalist   **cold war**

What caused the United States and the Soviet Union to become enemies after World War II?

A. The Victorious Nations Form the United Nations

Aftermath of War   World War II was the most destructive war ever fought. More than 50 million people were killed. These included not only the soldiers killed in combat but also ordinary people—men, women, and children who died in bomb attacks on cities, in the Holocaust, or from disease or starvation.

After World War II, millions of people on the continents of Europe, Asia, and Africa were hungry and homeless. The fighting had destroyed countless homes, farms, cities, factories, and roads. Of the major countries involved in the war, only the continental United States escaped bombing. And the United States alone came out of the war stronger than it had been when the war started.

The United Nations   Even before the war was over, President Franklin Roosevelt proposed an idea that he hoped would prevent wars from happening in the future. President Roosevelt wanted the nations of the world to establish a new organization to keep peace.

THE UNITED NATIONS AND ITS AGENCIES

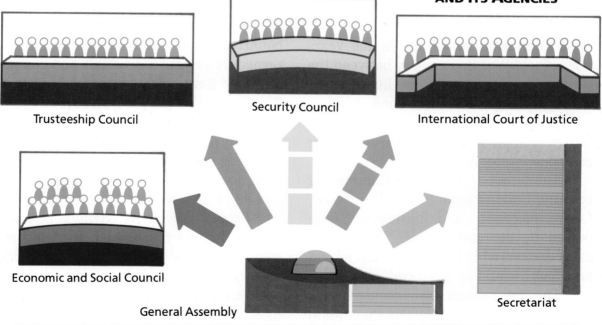

Trusteeship Council

Security Council

International Court of Justice

Economic and Social Council

General Assembly

Secretariat

Solid arrows indicate agencies that the General Assembly controls directly. Broken arrows indicate agencies that the Assembly has less control over.
▶ What agencies does the General Assembly control directly?

In April 1945, representatives from 50 nations met in San Francisco, California, to write a charter, or constitution, for this new organization. The organization was called the United Nations, or the UN. It was hoped that the United Nations would be a place where countries could talk over their disagreements and settle them peacefully. The founders also hoped that the United Nations would protect human rights around the world.

The United Nations is now nearly 50 years old. It has not been as successful as its founders had hoped. Although there has not been another world war, many smaller wars have been fought since the UN was founded. And human rights are still ignored in many parts of the world.

The UN has helped to end some wars, however. It has also helped countries work together to fight such problems as disease and hunger.

B. The United States and the Soviet Union Had Important Differences

Two Economic Systems In the years after World War II, a conflict between the United States and the Soviet Union threatened world peace. This conflict arose partly from the fact that the American and Soviet peoples lived under very different economic systems.

The Soviet Union was a **Communist** country. Under communism, all the land, farms, factories, and businesses were owned by the government. The government decided what would be produced and how much would be produced.

The government also decided what jobs people would have, where they would live, who could go to college, and many other things. The Communist government

This is a Soviet television factory in 1956. Not many Soviet factories made luxury goods, or goods purely for pleasure.
▶ Name some luxury goods you enjoy.

was supposed to take care of each citizen's basic needs, such as food, housing, health care, and education. However, in practice, the government did this poorly.

The United States is a **capitalist** country. Most land and businesses are owned by private individuals and companies. We have a **free enterprise** system. This means that people are free to start any business, or enterprise, they wish. If the business does not satisfy the buyers of its goods or services, it will fail. If the business does satisfy buyers, it will succeed, and its owners will make money.

People risk their savings in businesses, hoping to succeed. In doing so, they create new products. They also find better and cheaper ways to make products. As a result the free enterprise system is the most productive system the world has known. In our system, people are also free to live where they want, study any subject they want, and work at any job for which they are qualified. People make these decisions for themselves.

Two Forms of Government Another important difference between the United States and the Soviet Union was in the governments of the two countries. The United States is a democratic republic. We choose our government officials in free elections. There are two main political parties — the Republicans and the Democrats — each of which helps candidates run for office. People are free to form other parties if they wish. Also, like people in other democratic countries, Americans enjoy many political freedoms. They have freedom of speech and may criticize their government.

By contrast, what the Soviet Union called "elections" were not real elections at all. Only the Communist party was allowed to run candidates, and only one candidate ran for each office. Naturally, that person always won.

Furthermore, the Soviet people enjoyed few freedoms. In fact, under the cruel dictator Joseph Stalin, they did not dare to oppose his decisions or to speak freely. Stalin ruled from the 1920s to the early 1950s. During these years he executed many of his opponents and sent millions of his own people to prison camps. At least 10 million Soviet citizens were killed under Stalin's rule.

C. The Cold War Begins

From Allies to Rivals During World War II the United States and the Soviet Union had a common enemy, Nazi Germany. The two countries set aside their differences in order to defeat Hitler.

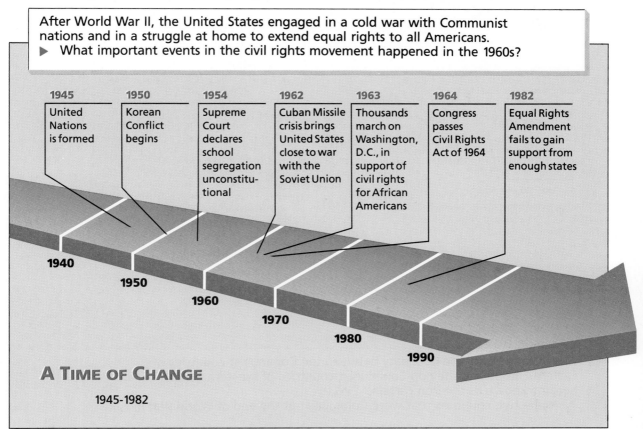

After World War II, the United States engaged in a cold war with Communist nations and in a struggle at home to extend equal rights to all Americans.
▶ What important events in the civil rights movement happened in the 1960s?

1945	1950	1954	1962	1963	1964	1982
United Nations is formed	Korean Conflict begins	Supreme Court declares school segregation unconstitutional	Cuban Missile crisis brings United States close to war with the Soviet Union	Thousands march on Washington, D.C., in support of civil rights for African Americans	Congress passes Civil Rights Act of 1964	Equal Rights Amendment fails to gain support from enough states

1940   1950   1960   1970   1980   1990

A TIME OF CHANGE

1945-1982

At the end of the war, the United States and the Soviet Union were the two greatest military powers in the world. Each wanted to see its own system of government spread to other countries.

Serious disagreements between the two soon arose in Eastern Europe. During the war, Allied leaders had agreed to hold elections in each country they freed from Nazi rule. The United States did hold elections in the countries our armies freed.

However, Stalin refused to hold elections in the Eastern European countries freed by Soviet armies. Instead the Soviets used force to set up Communist governments in such countries as Poland, Hungary, and Bulgaria.

To keep a tight grip on their power, these new governments made it a crime to criticize the government. Secret police watched and listened everywhere. The Communist governments closed their countries' borders because they knew that many people would try to flee. Few people were allowed either into or out of their countries. It was said that the Communists had lowered an "iron curtain" between Eastern and Western Europe.

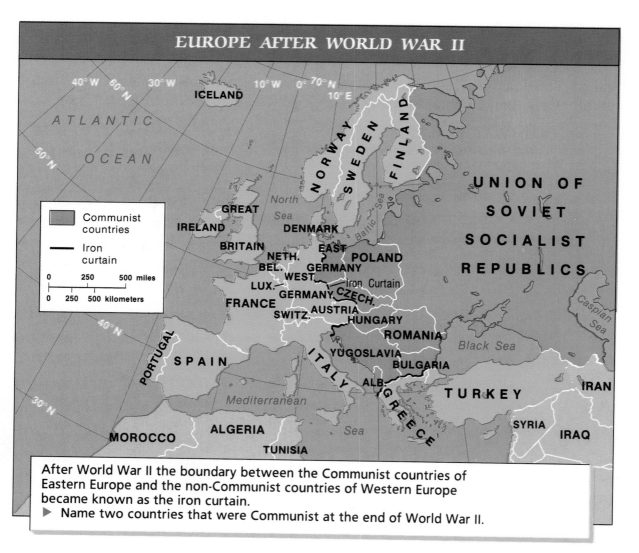

EUROPE AFTER WORLD WAR II

After World War II the boundary between the Communist countries of Eastern Europe and the non-Communist countries of Western Europe became known as the iron curtain.
▶ Name two countries that were Communist at the end of World War II.

These workers are building a road in Italy. The money for this road came from the United States.
▶ In what ways might this project have helped Italy?

The Cold War President Harry S. Truman and his advisors were angry. They were determined to stop the spread of communism. The United States and the Soviet Union soon became bitter enemies.

The struggle between the two countries is known as the **cold war**. The cold war was not a shooting war. Armies did not fight, and planes did not drop bombs. Instead the cold war was fought with angry words, threats, and money. Each side accused the other of breaking agreements and of planning a war. Each tried to win over other countries to its side.

The main battleground of the cold war was Europe. As you have read, European countries were in terrible shape at the end of the war. Communists tried to convince the many hungry and unemployed people there that communism was the answer to their problems.

President Truman and Congress wanted to help Europe recover quickly from the damage of the war. Therefore the United States offered these countries billions of dollars to help them rebuild their factories, farms, and railroads.

The Soviets forced the countries under their thumb to refuse any aid from the United States. Democratic countries, such as Great Britain, Greece, France, and Italy, however, accepted the offer of American aid. As a result of this aid, the democratic countries quickly recovered.

Germany Is Divided It might surprise you to learn that the country that American aid helped most was our former enemy, Germany — or rather, part of Germany. Here is what happened. At the end of the war, the victorious Allies had temporarily divided Germany between them.

581

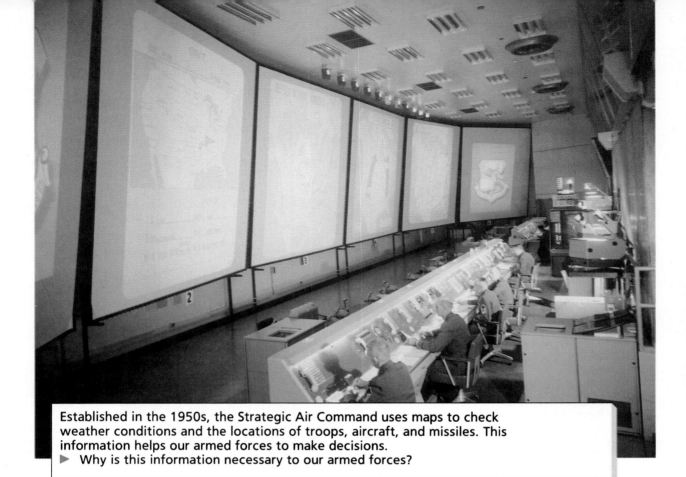

Established in the 1950s, the Strategic Air Command uses maps to check weather conditions and the locations of troops, aircraft, and missiles. This information helps our armed forces to make decisions.

▶ Why is this information necessary to our armed forces?

As the cold war grew colder, this division became permanent. In the western part of Germany, the United States encouraged a democratic government to grow. In the eastern part, the Soviet Union set up a Communist government. West Germany accepted American aid. East Germany did not. American aid helped West Germany get back on its feet and become one of the most prosperous countries in Europe.

Meanwhile, the Soviet Union developed its own atomic bomb. Soon both the Soviet Union and the United States had nuclear weapons a thousand times more powerful than the bomb that destroyed Hiroshima. Each of the great powers had enough bombs to destroy the entire world. The rivalry between the United States and the Soviet Union had reached a dangerous point.

LESSON *1* REVIEW

THINK AND WRITE

A. What was the purpose of the United Nations?
B. What are two important differences between capitalism and communism?
C. What happened in Eastern Europe that started the cold war?

SKILLS CHECK

MAP SKILL

Look at the map on page 580. List the countries that the Soviet Union controlled after World War II.

The Cold War Continues

What steps might people who have a disagreement take to prevent their disagreement from becoming bitter? How might the leaders of countries try to prevent conflict when they disagree?

STUDY THE VOCABULARY

satellite   **hot line**
space race

FOCUS YOUR READING

Into what areas did the cold war spread during the 1950s and 1960s?

A. War Breaks Out in Korea

In 1950 a war broke out in Korea, a country in Asia. Japan had ruled Korea since the early 1900s. At the end of World War II, however, the Allies forced Japan to give up Korea.

As the war ended, Soviet armies had control of the northern half of Korea, and the United States gained control of the southern half. As in Germany, this wartime division was to last for years. The two halves of Korea became enemies.

In 1950, Communist North Korea attacked South Korea. The United Nations sent troops to help South Korea defend itself. Most of the UN troops and weapons were American.

UN armies drove the North Koreans out of South Korea and pursued them into North Korea. For a time it looked as though the North Koreans were defeated. Then China sent a huge army to help the North Koreans. China had become a Communist country in 1949. The Chinese troops drove back the UN armies.

In 1953 the two sides finally agreed to end the bitter fighting. The boundary between North and South Korea was set at just about where it was at the start of the war. Today, North and South Korea are still two separate countries.

B. The Cold War Spreads Around the World and into Space

Asia and Africa During the 1950s the cold war spread to many corners of the earth. In Asia and Africa the old colonial empires of European countries were breaking up. New nations were being formed. The United States and the Soviet

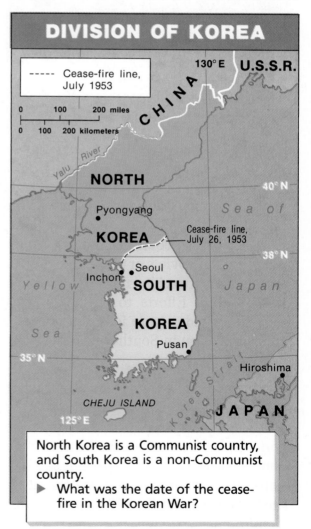

DIVISION OF KOREA

- - - - - Cease-fire line, July 1953

0   100   200 miles
0   100   200 kilometers

CHINA
U.S.S.R.
130° E

Yalu River

NORTH
40° N
Pyongyang
KOREA
Cease-fire line, July 26, 1953
38° N

Seoul
Inchon
SOUTH
Yellow
Sea of
Japan

Sea
KOREA
Pusan
35° N

Hiroshima

CHEJU ISLAND
125° E
Korea Strait
JAPAN

North Korea is a Communist country, and South Korea is a non-Communist country.
► What was the date of the cease-fire in the Korean War?

In 1958, these Soviet students were learning about their country's successful satellite Sputnik.
▶ How were these students feeling?

Union each tried to win over these new countries. They sent money, supplies, and experts to help build up these countries. They also supplied the new countries with weapons.

Some of the countries did line up on the side of the Soviets or the United States. However, most decided not to take sides in the cold war. Efforts to keep countries from taking sides were led by Indonesia, an island nation in Southeast Asia.

The Space Race The competition between the United States and the Soviet Union spread to space as well. In October 1957 a new chapter in the history of the world was opened when the Soviet Union launched a **satellite** into space. A satellite is an object that orbits, or circles, the earth. The Soviets named the 178 pound (81 kg) satellite *Sputnik*.

The United States was stunned by this Soviet achievement. In the area of science and technology, the United States had always been in the lead. Now the Soviets had suddenly zoomed ahead!

President Dwight Eisenhower speeded up the United States space program. Congress also provided money to universities to improve the teaching of mathematics and science.

The United States soon launched its own small satellite. By then, however, Soviet rockets were boosting much heavier objects into space. The United States hurried to catch up with the Soviets. The **space race** was on.

In 1961 the United States launched its first space flight with a person aboard.
▶ Is this space vehicle larger or smaller than today's space vehicles?

C. The Cuban Missile Crisis Nearly Leads to War

In 1962 the United States and the Soviet Union came dangerously close to war. Three years earlier the island nation of Cuba had become a Communist country. Cuba is just 90 miles (145 km) from the coast of Florida.

The leader of Cuba, Fidel Castro, secretly asked the Soviet Union to build military bases in Cuba. From these bases the Soviet Union could launch nuclear missiles that could reach targets in the United States within minutes.

When President John F. Kennedy learned about these bases, he demanded that the Soviets remove them. He also ordered the United States Navy to stop Soviet ships that were steaming toward Cuban ports with missiles for the bases.

For a week it seemed that war between the superpowers might break out at any minute. However, with tension at a peak, the Soviet government ordered its ships to stop and turn back. And a few days later, the Soviets agreed to remove their missile bases in Cuba.

After this crisis was over, the United States and the Soviet Union both realized how close they had come to war. They decided that even though the two countries were not friends, they must find a way to get along better with each other. If they did not, the entire world could be destroyed.

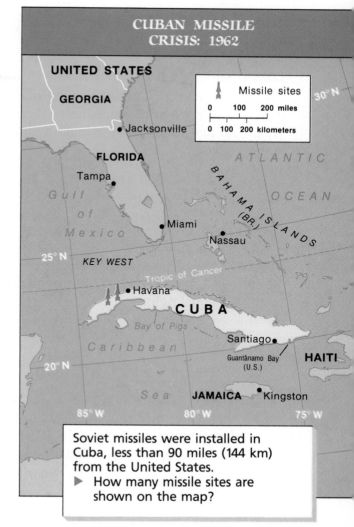

Soviet missiles were installed in Cuba, less than 90 miles (144 km) from the United States.
▶ How many missile sites are shown on the map?

One thing they agreed to do was to install a **hot line,** a direct telephone line between the President of the United States and the Soviet leader (later, the Russian leader). The hot line would allow these leaders to talk directly to each other if a crisis arose.

LESSON 2 REVIEW

THINK AND WRITE
A. How did the Korean War end?
B. What event started the space race?
C. What was the Cuban missile crisis?

SKILLS CHECK

THINKING SKILL
Review Lessons 1 and 2 of this chapter. Then make a list of the events that caused conflict between the United States and the Soviet Union.

585

The Struggle for Equal Rights

THINK ABOUT WHAT YOU KNOW

Think about what one person can do to improve life in his or her community. What qualities do people who make a difference have?

STUDY THE VOCABULARY

civil rights   Hispanic
nonviolent   feminist

FOCUS YOUR READING

How did African Americans, Hispanic Americans, American Indians, and women try to gain equal rights?

A. The Supreme Court Orders an End to School Segregation

As you read in Chapter 24, many states still had segregation laws in 1950. And even in states without such segregation laws, African Americans faced many kinds of discrimination.

In the 1950s and 1960s, African Americans made important progress in their struggle to win their **civil rights**.

Civil rights are the rights guaranteed to all citizens by the Constitution.

The first big step towards civil rights began in September 1950 in Topeka, Kansas. A black railroad worker named Oliver Brown took his seven-year-old daughter, Linda, to register at the grade school a few blocks from their house.

When the Browns arrived, the principal refused to register Linda. "This is a whites only school," he said. Linda would have to attend the school for black students, which was a mile away.

Linda's father decided to fight back. He went to the National Association for the Advancement of Colored People (NAACP). The NAACP is an organization that tries to help African Americans gain their civil rights. With the NAACP's help, the Browns took their case to court.

In 1954 the Supreme Court said that the Constitution does not allow states to set up separate schools for black children and for white children. The court ordered that segregated schools be ended.

For a number of years, some southern states tried to find a way around the Supreme Court's decision. In the end they had to accept the fact that the Constitution

Thurgood Marshall (middle) and fellow lawyers argued Linda Brown's (inset) case in the Supreme Court.
▶ Why is this case important?

DECLARATION OF THE RIGHTS OF THE CHILD

From the very beginning the United Nations has been concerned with the health and welfare of the world's children. In 1959 the General Assembly of the United Nations passed a ten-part Declaration of the Rights of the Child. Here is part of the declaration.

2. The child shall enjoy special protection, and shall be given opportunities . . . by law and by other means, to enable [the child] to develop physically, mentally, morally, spiritually and socially in a healthy and normal manner and in conditions of freedom and dignity.

7. The child is entitled to receive education, which shall be free and compulsory, at least in the elementary stages. [The child] shall be given an education which will . . . enable [the child] to become a useful member of society. . . . The child shall have full opportunity for play and recreation . . . society and the public authorities shall endeavour [try] to promote the enjoyment of this right.

9. The child shall be protected against all forms of neglect, cruelty, and exploitation [misuse] . . . [the child] shall in no case be caused or permitted to engage in any occupation or employment which would . . . interfere with [the child's] physical, mental or moral development.

Understanding Source Material

1. Which statement says that children should be able to grow up in freedom and dignity? Explain what you think this means.
2. Why, according to the declaration, should a child receive a free and compulsory education?
3. Why, do you think, did the United Nations feel that a Declaration of the Rights of the Child was necessary?

is the law of the land. Gradually, they began to obey the Supreme Court's order.

Some cities in the North also tried to find ways to keep their segregated schools. But in the 1970s the Supreme Court ordered that, if necessary, students be bused from one neighborhood to another to end segregated schools.

B. A Boycott Brings a Victory over Segregation

The next important step toward ending segregation came with a bus ride in Montgomery, Alabama. One day in December 1955, Rosa Parks got on a city bus to return home after a hard day's work. At each stop the bus took on more passengers. Soon some passengers had to stand.

The segregation laws of Montgomery said that if white passengers were standing, blacks had to give up their seats. Rosa Parks had given up her seat a hundred times in the past. But on this day she refused. The driver stopped the bus and called for the police. Rosa Parks was arrested and fined.

Black citizens of Montgomery protested. They decided to boycott, or stop using, city buses until the bus law was changed. The man who led this bus boycott was a young Baptist minister, Martin Luther King, Jr.

For over a year the African Americans living in Montgomery walked to work or rode in car pools. When one grandmother was offered a ride by someone, she refused. "I'm not walking for myself," she explained. "I'm walking for my children and grandchildren."

Meanwhile, the NAACP took Rosa Parks's case to court. In 1956 the Supreme Court ruled that Montgomery's segregation law went against the Constitution. The court said that blacks and whites must be treated the same on city buses.

C. Dr. King Becomes a National Leader

King's Leadership As a result of his success in Montgomery, Dr. Martin Luther King, Jr., became a national leader in the

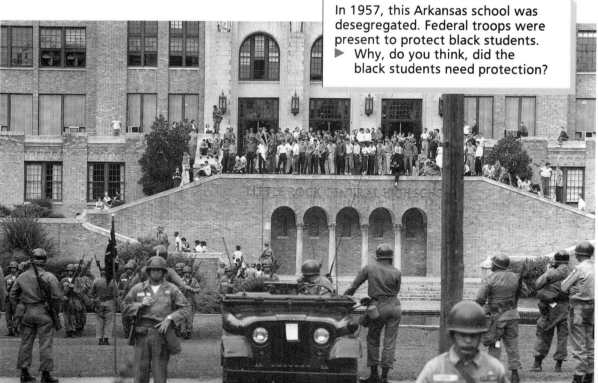

In 1957, this Arkansas school was desegregated. Federal troops were present to protect black students.
▶ Why, do you think, did the black students need protection?

African Americans peacefully protest being asked to leave this restaurant's dining room.
▶ Was this an effective means of demonstration?

struggle for equal rights. Reverend King believed that African Americans had to protest against segregation laws and refuse to obey them if they wanted to improve their condition. However, he insisted that the protests be **nonviolent**, that is, peaceful.

King urged his followers to be nonviolent even when opponents insulted and threw rocks at them. Instead of fighting back, he said, they must show their foes Christian love. "Don't let anyone pull you so low as to hate them," Dr. King told his followers. "We must use the weapon of love."

With King leading the way, thousands of black Americans and white Americans worked side by side nonviolently for the cause of equal rights. They sang the song of the civil rights movement:

We shall overcome,
we shall overcome,
we shall overcome someday.
Oh, deep in my heart,
I do believe,
we shall overcome someday.

Through their actions, these brave people helped to end segregation. They sat in at segregated lunch counters, bought tickets at whites only windows in bus stations, swam at segregated pools, and went to countless other public places reserved for whites.

The March on Washington In 1963, Dr. King led a march of over 200,000 people in Washington, D.C., the nation's capital. The purpose of the march was to urge Congress to pass a national civil rights law. At this gathering, King made one of the most famous speeches in American history. Millions watched on television as King told of his dream for America.

I have a dream that one day on the red hills of Georgia the sons of former slaves and the sons of former slave-owners will be able to sit down together at the table of brotherhood. . . .
I have a dream that my four little children will one day live in a nation where they will not be judged by the color of their skin but by the content of their character.

589

New Laws In 1964, Congress passed an important civil rights law. This law ended segregation against African Americans in hotels, restaurants, and other public places.

Congress passed another important civil rights law the next year. This was the Voting Rights Act. This law said that southern states could no longer keep blacks from voting. As a result several million black citizens in the South soon voted for the first time.

Today, African Americans vote freely everywhere in the United States. Many of our nation's largest cities have elected African Americans as their mayors. A growing number of African Americans serve in Congress, in state legislatures, and as judges. In 1984 and 1988, as you will read in the next chapter, one of the main candidates seeking to be President of the United States was an African American, Jesse Jackson. In the 1950s and 1960s, Jackson worked with Martin Luther King, Jr., in the civil rights movement.

In 1968, Reverend King's work for justice and equality was cut short. While in Memphis, Tennessee, to lead another march, King was shot and killed. He was only 39 years old.

In his short lifetime, Reverend King had done more than any other American to advance the goal of civil rights. His dedication to the idea that courage and nonviolence are the best weapons against hatred and injustice continues to inspire people all over the world. Today Americans celebrate Dr. King's birthday, January 15, as a national holiday.

D. Other Minorities Also Struggle for Equal Rights

Hispanic Americans Others who struggled for equal rights and better opportunities after World War II included **Hispanic**,

MAJOR EVENTS IN THE CIVIL RIGHTS MOVEMENT

Date	Event
1954	In Brown v. Board of Education of Topeka, the Supreme Court rules that segregation in public schools is unconstitutional.
1955	The Supreme Court orders public schools to be desegregated "with all deliberate speed."
1955	Black citizens begin a bus boycott in Montgomery, Alabama, after Rosa Parks refuses to give her seat on a bus to a white passanger.
1957	The Civil Rights Act of 1957 sets up the Commission on Civil Rights.
1963	Dr. Martin Luther King, Jr., gives his "I have a dream" speech during the march on Washington, D.C.
1964	Congress passes civil rights laws to end segregation in hotels, restaurants, theaters, and other public places.
1965	The Voting Rights Act of 1965 prohibits southern states from barring black citizens from voting.
1968	The Civil Rights Act of 1968 prohibits discrimination in the sale or rental of housing.
1969	The Supreme Court orders school systems to be desegregated "at once."
1970	Literacy tests are made illegal in all the states.

Dr. Antonia Novello was the first woman and the first Hispanic American to be Surgeon General.
▶ What, do you think, does the Surgeon General do?

Douglas Wilder is the first African American governor of the state of Virginia.
▶ On what occasion do you think this photograph was taken?

or Spanish-speaking, Americans. Hispanic Americans include people from Mexico, Central America, South America, and the Caribbean islands.

Mexican Americans make up the largest group of Hispanics in the United States. Most Mexican Americans live in the Southwest. A great many came from Mexico to work as migrant farm laborers in California and Texas.

Puerto Ricans make up a second large group of Hispanics. Puerto Ricans live mostly in cities in the Northeast. A majority live in New York City. In fact more Puerto Ricans live in New York City than in San Juan, the capital of Puerto Rico.

A third large Hispanic group is made up of Cuban Americans. Many Cubans fled to America after 1959 to escape Communist rule in their homeland. Most settled in and around Miami, Florida.

For many years, Hispanic Americans faced the same kind of discrimination that black Americans faced in such areas as schooling, jobs, and housing. By making all kinds of discrimination illegal, the Civil Rights Act of 1964 helped Hispanics as well as African Americans.

In recent years, Hispanics have taken a larger part in elections. This has given them more say in governing their own communities. Hispanic voters have helped to elect Hispanic governors in New Mexico and Florida, Hispanic mayors, and a number of Hispanic congresspersons.

American Indians Native Americans have also made some gains in the struggle for equality. In our country's early years, the United States government made many treaties with the Indians. Often, however, the government did not keep its promises in these treaties.

In the 1960s and 1970s, Indian groups protested and went to court to make the United States government live up to its agreements. Sometimes the courts have ordered the government to give back land to the Indians. Other times the courts have ordered the government to pay the Indians money for the promises it did not keep.

These Navaho Indians and friends protest a 1974 law ordering the Indians off their land in return for large sums of money.
▶ What does the sign mean?

This land and money have made it possible for a few Indian tribes to have more independence and a better chance to make economic gains.

However, most American Indians are still discriminated against. They have few opportunities to improve their condition. Indians are still the poorest of all of America's minorities.

E. Women Seek Equal Rights

The Women's Rights Movement One group that worked to gain equal rights was not a minority. It was a majority. This group was American women.

Even though women had gained the right to vote in 1920, they still faced discrimination in the 1960s. Women were still shut out of many jobs. Often they got paid less than men who held the same jobs. Few women got promoted to top positions. There were few women governors, congresspersons, judges, and other government officials.

In the 1960s some women organized to work for equal rights. A growing number of Americans listened to them. Congress responded by passing a law stating that women could not be denied jobs just because they were women. Congress also said that women must receive equal pay for equal work.

Today more women than ever before work outside their homes. It is no longer unusual to see women police officers, bus drivers, TV reporters, and lawyers. Women still do not often get promoted to top positions, though. And while there are more women in government than ever before, they still hold only a minority of government jobs.

A Continuing Debate The debate over equal rights for women continues today. Women and men who work for such rights are called **feminists**. Feminist leaders, such as Betty Friedan and Gloria Steinem, say that men and women should be treated the same in all areas of life. Both should be able to work in any job they are qualified for. Both should share the housework and care of children. Many people have come to share these views of feminists.

Others, however, do not agree with feminist views. Leaders such as Phyllis Schlafly say that men and women are naturally different and should be treated differently. These leaders say that women should have the main responsibility for taking care of their families and homes. They argue that when women have careers outside the home, family life is often harmed.

In the 1970s and 1980s, feminists worked to get an equal rights amendment added to the Constitution. This amendment would guarantee equal treatment for both women and men. Debate over the proposed amendment was angry on both sides. Many leaders in favor of this amendment were women. However, some of the leaders against the amendment were also women. In the end the amendment did not win enough votes in the state legislatures to become a part of the Constitution.

In 1978, these people were parading in Washington, D.C., trying to persuade people to favor an equal rights amendment.
▶ Explain the words on the banner.

LESSON 3 REVIEW

THINK AND WRITE

A. What important decision did the Supreme Court make about segregation in schools?

B. How did a brave act by Rosa Parks lead to the end of segregated buses?

C. How did Martin Luther King, Jr., teach his followers to challenge segregation laws?

D. What other minorities tried to gain their civil rights in the 1960s?

E. What did Congress do to end discrimination against women who worked outside the home?

SKILLS CHECK

WRITING SKILL

Pretend you are a newspaper reporter. Write an article telling about Rosa Parks and the Montgomery bus boycott. Be sure to explain the role of Martin Luther King, Jr.

USING THE VOCABULARY

Communist	space race
capitalist	civil rights
free enterprise	nonviolent
cold war	Hispanic
satellite	feminist

On a separate sheet of paper, number from 1 to 10 and write the words from the list that would correctly complete the sentences in the paragraphs below.

In the decades that followed World War II, the United States had to face many problems. The (1) _____ with the Soviet Union and other (2) _____ countries was one problem. The Soviet Union was not a (3) _____ country like the United States. An economy based on (4) _____ was not a part of the way of life under communism. Neither were free elections. Competition between the Soviet Union and the United States grew, especially in the (5) _____. The Soviets put a (6) _____ into orbit before the United States did.

The (7) _____ movement presented another problem that the United States had to deal with. African Americans, (8) _____ Americans, and Native Americans felt they were not being treated fairly. Many women, too, joined a (9) _____ movement to claim equal rights with men. Dr. Martin Luther King, Jr. reached many Americans with his plan for (10) _____ protest.

REMEMBERING WHAT YOU READ

On a separate sheet of paper, write your answers in complete sentences.

1. For what two reasons was the United Nations founded?
2. Who was Joseph Stalin?
3. How did the United States help many European nations after World War II?
4. What went on in Europe during the cold war?
5. What were the results of the Korean War?
6. What group of nations was led by Indonesia?
7. What was the purpose of the hot line?
8. What two important Supreme Court decisions affected the civil rights movement?
9. In what parts of the United States do many Hispanic Americans live?
10. Identify the following people and explain their connection to the struggle for equal rights: Linda Brown, Rosa Parks, Jesse Jackson, Betty Friedan, and Phyllis Schlafly.

TYING ART TO SOCIAL STUDIES

Choose some event in the cold war, the space race, or the civil rights movement and make a poster about it. Remember that a poster usually presents its message through a combination of art and words rather than words alone.

THINKING CRITICALLY

On a separate sheet of paper, write your answers in complete sentences.

1. Are there ways, do you think, in which the United Nations has been successful? Explain your answer.
2. How would you describe life on the eastern side of the iron curtain in the years after World War II?
3. What do you think is the value of the hot line?
4. How would you go about protesting a situation that you felt was wrong?
5. Do you think women need a constitutional amendment to get equal rights with men? Explain your answer.

SUMMARIZING THE CHAPTER

On a separate sheet of paper, draw a graphic organizer like the one shown here. Copy the information from this graphic organizer to the one you have drawn. Fill in the blank boxes with important events from the chapter that support the chapter theme. The first has been done for you. Be prepared to explain why you chose the events you did.

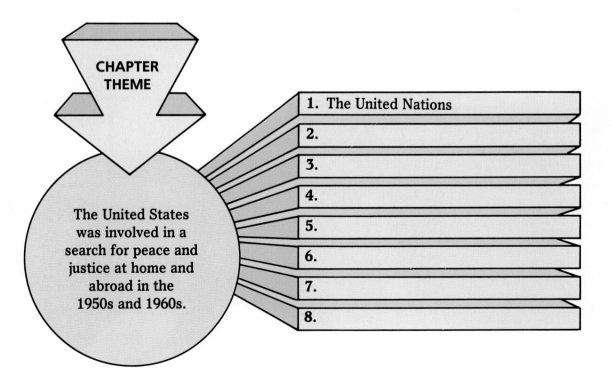

CHAPTER THEME

The United States was involved in a search for peace and justice at home and abroad in the 1950s and 1960s.

1. The United Nations
2.
3.
4.
5.
6.
7.
8.

CHAPTER 26 NEW CHALLENGES, NEW SOLUTIONS

In the last few decades, Americans have seen very dramatic changes in world affairs. We continue to search for solutions to problems at home and abroad.

The Changing Federal Government

THINK ABOUT WHAT YOU KNOW

How might the sudden death of a leader affect a country and its citizens?

STUDY THE VOCABULARY

Interstate Highway System   Peace Corps

FOCUS YOUR READING

What new actions did the federal government take in the 1950s and 1960s?

A. President Eisenhower Steers a Middle Course

During the Great Depression and World War II, the American people had called on their government to take on many new tasks. You'll remember that the federal government started the Social Security program, helped farmers and workers, and set rules for many businesses. By the 1950s the mood of the country was changing. Dwight Eisenhower, a famed World War II general, was elected President in 1952. While he was President, the country was prosperous.

With the Depression and the war over, many Americans felt they needed less help from the government than before. Many people wanted the government to return to a smaller, less active role. But not all Americans agreed. Many wanted the federal government to continue the activities it had begun in the 1930s and 1940s and even to take on new duties.

President Eisenhower steered a middle course between these two directions. He turned some of the federal government's activities over to state and local governments. On the other hand he and Congress continued and expanded such federal programs as Social Security.

President Eisenhower and Congress also started two great construction projects. One of these projects was the building of the **Interstate Highway System**. This highway system cost billions of dollars and took more than 20 years to complete. Today many of the great superhighways that crisscross our country are part of it. These modern roads have made travel by car and truck faster, safer, and cheaper.

The second great project was the St. Lawrence Seaway. You read about the St. Lawrence Seaway in the first chapter of this book. The seaway was opened in 1959, while President Eisenhower was still in office. Using the seaway, ocean ships can sail directly to such midwestern cities as Chicago, Illinois, and Detroit, Michigan.

In 1954, Eisenhower signed a bill to allow the United States to join with Canada to build the seaway.
▶ Why was this seaway a good idea?

During Eisenhower's presidency, the United States Congress added two new states to the Union. In 1959, Alaska became the forty-ninth state, and Hawaii became the fiftieth state.

B. The Presidency of John F. Kennedy

John F. Kennedy was elected President in 1960. Kennedy had been a war hero in World War II. He was the first Roman Catholic to be elected President of the United States. He was also the youngest person to be elected President.

President Kennedy brought new ideas to the presidency. He proposed a different way to help the poorer nations of the world. This was the **Peace Corps**. The Peace Corps sent volunteers to many poor countries that needed their skills. A volunteer is a person who takes a job or does a task with little or no pay. Peace Corps volunteers usually served for a few years. Thousands of Peace Corps doctors, carpenters, teachers, farmers, nurses, and others went to 46 countries that asked for their help.

President Kennedy was also a strong supporter of the space program. Soon after he took office, the Soviet Union again surged ahead in the space race when it put the first man into orbit around the earth. Kennedy responded with a bold plan. He said the United States should land a man on the moon before 1970. (His plan was brought to success in 1969, when astronaut Neil Armstrong became the first person to set foot on the moon's surface.)

President Kennedy believed the country should have a strong and active

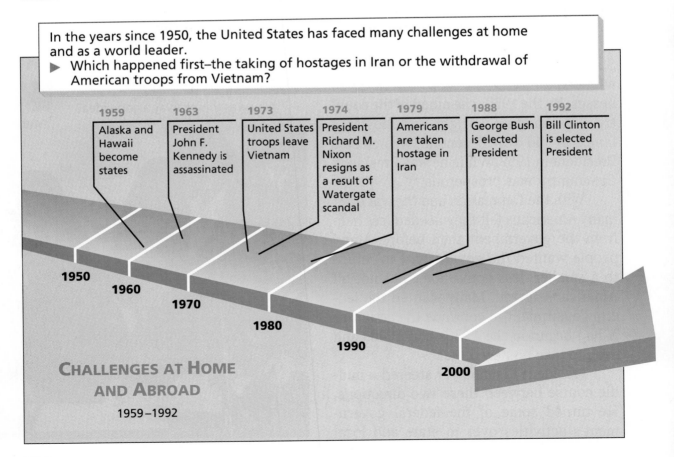

In the years since 1950, the United States has faced many challenges at home and as a world leader.

▶ Which happened first—the taking of hostages in Iran or the withdrawal of American troops from Vietnam?

1959 Alaska and Hawaii become states

1963 President John F. Kennedy is assassinated

1973 United States troops leave Vietnam

1974 President Richard M. Nixon resigns as a result of Watergate scandal

1979 Americans are taken hostage in Iran

1988 George Bush is elected President

1992 Bill Clinton is elected President

1950 · 1960 · 1970 · 1980 · 1990 · 2000

CHALLENGES AT HOME AND ABROAD
1959–1992

This woman is a Peace Corps volunteer. Here, she is in the South American country of Ecuador. She is fitting in the last pipe length of a system that will carry fresh spring water to a village.

▶ Find Ecuador on the map on page 618.

national government. He extended the activities of the federal government into a number of new areas. He proposed laws to provide more money to the nation's schools. He also asked Congress for funds to help cities deal with such problems as transportation and housing.

President Kennedy also was strongly in favor of civil rights for all Americans. He asked Congress to pass a civil rights law that would forbid racial discrimination in all public places.

President Kennedy did not live to see most of his proposals become law. In November 1963 the President took a trip to Dallas, Texas. While riding in an open car, he was shot and killed by an assassin. His sudden death saddened all Americans.

C. Lyndon Johnson and the Great Society

When John F. Kennedy died, Vice President Lyndon Johnson took over as President. Lyndon Johnson was the first Texan ever to serve as President. As a leader in the United States Senate, he had been known for his skill in getting other senators to vote for laws that he favored. As President he used this same skill to get Congress to pass many laws.

Like Kennedy, President Johnson favored an active government. His plan for making life better for all Americans was called the Great Society. It promised assistance especially for those who were poor or disadvantaged.

This man is teaching a 1966 Head Start class in Mississippi.
▶ How might this class have helped these children in elementary school?

Led by the President, Congress created a program to teach job skills to unemployed youths. Congress gave money to local communities to provide relief and jobs for the poor. Congress also approved a new program called Head Start. In Head Start preschools disadvantaged children were taught skills that would help them when they started elementary school. Congress provided more money for public schools and higher education. It also started the Medicare program. Medicare helps older people pay medical bills.

Like Kennedy, Johnson worked with Congress for stronger civil rights laws. You read earlier about the Civil Rights Act of 1964 and the Voting Rights Act of 1965. President Johnson's leadership made the passage of these laws possible.

In 1965, Congress made important changes in our country's immigration law. For the first time, immigrants from Europe were no longer favored over other groups. As a result, today most immigrants come from Latin America and from the Philippines, Korea, and Vietnam.

In 1965, these young men were part of a job skills program. They were learning to run a bulldozer.
▶ Why was this training helpful?

LESSON *1* REVIEW

THINK AND WRITE

A. What two great construction projects were started when Dwight Eisenhower was President?
B. What new idea did President Kennedy propose for helping poor nations?
C. Name three programs that were part of President Johnson's Great Society.

SKILLS CHECK

WRITING SKILL

Write a sentence telling why some Americans hoped the government would do less in the 1950s. Write a sentence telling why some Americans hoped the government would take on new responsibilities.

Troubled Years

THINK ABOUT WHAT YOU KNOW

Why is it important in a democracy that everyone, including the highest government official, obey the law?

STUDY THE VOCABULARY

escalation   resign
Vietnamization   hostage
Watergate

FOCUS YOUR READING

What were some of the problems that our country faced in the 1960s and 1970s?

A. The Vietnam War

Vietnam: A Divided Country After World War II, many Asian and African colonies of European countries won independence. One of the new nations was Vietnam, a French colony in Southeast Asia.

Vietnam is over 10,000 miles (16,090 km) away from the United States. Before the 1950s the United States had had little contact with this small and distant land. Few Americans in the 1950s, therefore, would have guessed that American soldiers would soon be fighting and dying in a war there. But that is what happened.

In 1954, the nation of Vietnam became a divided country. North Vietnam was Communist, and South Vietnam, was non-Communist. These two parts fought each other. Each part wanted to gain control of the entire country.

American Involvement Presidents Eisenhower and Kennedy felt the United States should take action to stop communism from spreading in Asia. Both Presidents thought that sending weapons and

supplies to South Vietnam would be one way to help do this. The United States also sent military advisors to train South Vietnam's soldiers and to help them plan and prepare for battles. The American advisors, however, were not supposed to take part in the fighting.

VIETNAM AND ITS NEIGHBORS

In 1975, North Vietnam and South Vietnam were united under a Communist government.
▶ What countries border on Vietnam?

Despite this help the South Vietnamese government was losing the war against North Vietnam. President Johnson decided to use American armed forces to prevent South Vietnam's defeat. Johnson's plan for a bigger war effort was known as **escalation** (es kuh LAY shun). Eventually more than 500,000 American soldiers were serving in Vietnam.

Debate over the War Americans were sharply divided over the decision to send American troops to Vietnam. Some believed Johnson was right to increase American involvement. They agreed it was necessary to stop the spread of communism.

Other Americans believed it was wrong to send American troops to fight in Vietnam. They said that the war was between the people of Vietnam and that the United States should not get involved in it. Opponents of the war held great protest marches in many cities.

The Fighting Continues Meanwhile the war dragged on. In 1969 Richard Nixon became President. Nixon knew the American people were tiring of this war. He announced a plan for getting the United States out of the war. The United States would train South Vietnamese troops to take over more of the fighting. Nixon's plan for turning over the fighting to the South Vietnamese was called **Vietnamization**.

President Nixon's plan was only partly successful. In 1973, the last American troops came home from South Vietnam. However, fighting between North Vietnam and South Vietnam soon started again. Without American support the South Vietnamese army quickly crumbled. In 1975 the Communist government of North Vietnam united both parts of the country under its rule.

The Vietnam Veterans Memorial honors all dead or missing American service people from the Vietnam War. A Chinese-American woman named Maya Ying Lin designed the memorial.
▶ Why, do you think, is this memorial important to Americans?

B. The Nixon Years

Foreign Relations Soon after President Nixon took office in 1969, he began to search for ways to improve America's relations with China. China and the United States had once been very friendly. However, in 1949, Communists won control of China. After that, China and the United States were enemies for more than 20 years.

In about 1970 the Communist government of China began hinting that it would like to have better relations with the United States. President Nixon seized this opportunity. In 1971 he startled the world by announcing he would visit China. The two countries agreed to trade with one another and took steps toward establishing friendly relations again.

President Nixon also tried to improve relations with the Soviet Union. He became the first President to visit that country. As a result of his efforts, the United States and the Soviet Union made a treaty to limit the number of new weapons each country would build. They also made agreements to increase trade and to encourage artists, teachers, musicians, and students to exchange visits.

The President Resigns President Nixon's presidency was wrecked by a scandal known as **Watergate**. In 1972, President Nixon was running for reelection. Four men working for his reelection committee broke into the headquarters of the Democratic party—Nixon's opponents in the election. These headquarters were in the Watergate building. The burglars tried to find information they could use to help the President get reelected.

When these men were caught, President Nixon tried to cover up their connection with his campaign. He said he knew

Above, President and Mrs. Nixon are shown in China. They are with the Chinese leader Chou En-Lai.
▶ Why was this visit a good idea?

nothing about their break-in, and he tried to block investigations of the break-in.

After two years of investigation by newspapers and by Congress, the truth came out. Nixon was faced with the possibility that Congress might remove him from office. He decided to **resign**, or give up, the presidency instead.

C. The Presidencies of Gerald Ford and Jimmy Carter

Gerald Ford When President Nixon resigned, Vice President Gerald Ford became President. He served the last two years of Nixon's term of office.

President Ford continued the efforts to limit the arms race with the Soviet Union. In 1975 he made another agreement with the Soviets to limit the number of new weapons each side would make. The United States Senate later approved this treaty.

603

Carter Takes Office   In 1976 the voters elected a new President. He was Jimmy Carter, former governor of the state of Georgia. President Carter worked hard to win back trust in government after the Watergate scandal. He was also a strong believer in equal opportunity for minorities and women. He appointed more blacks, Hispanics, and women to office than any other American President.

President Carter's greatest accomplishment was to help the Middle Eastern countries of Israel and Egypt agree to a peace treaty. The country of Israel had been created in 1948. Its Arab neighbors, however, did not accept this new nation. Over the next 30 years, the two sides fought four wars. Even in between the wars, small-scale fighting continued.

President Carter invited the leaders of the two countries to the United States. For two weeks he worked with them day and night to find a way to settle their differences. As a result of President Carter's efforts, Israel and Egypt signed a peace treaty.

The Iran Crisis   Things did not go so well for the United States and President Carter in Iran, another Middle Eastern country. In 1979 a revolution overthrew the ruler of Iran. A new leader took control of Iran and blamed the United States for his country's problems. He became an outspoken enemy of the United States.

Late in 1979 a group of Iranians broke into the United States Embassy in Teheran, the capital city of Iran, and took 52 Americans as **hostages**. A hostage is a person who is held prisoner until the demands of the hostage-takers are met.

President Carter refused to meet the demands of the Iranians, and the hostages were held for more than a year. The United States was unable to do anything to get them out. The Americans were not released until President Carter's last day in office, January 20, 1981.

President Carter met with the leaders of Israel and Egypt in 1979. They agreed to a peace treaty.
▶ Where did the meeting take place?

LESSON 2 REVIEW

THINK AND WRITE

A. Summarize the United States' involvement in the Vietnam War.
B. Why did President Nixon resign?
C. How did President Carter help Israel and Egypt?

SKILLS CHECK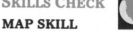

MAP SKILL

Look at the map of Vietnam on page 601. What two countries bordered South Vietnam?

3

Toward a New Century

THINK ABOUT WHAT YOU KNOW
What are the most important challenges for our country today?

STUDY THE VOCABULARY
nomination

FOCUS YOUR READING
What important changes took place in the 1980s?

A. The Reagan Revolution

Reagan Takes Over In 1980, Americans elected Ronald Reagan President. Ronald Reagan had once been a movie actor. He had also served as governor of California.

President Reagan became a very popular President. People liked his warm smile and the way he expressed his ideas in his speeches. As a result of his popularity, President Reagan was able to get Congress to go along with many of his ideas.

President Reagan made some important changes in the federal government.

The changes were so big that some people spoke of a Reagan Revolution. The new President believed that, except for defense, the federal government should have far fewer responsibilities than it had taken on in the years after Roosevelt's New Deal.

President Reagan wanted the government to make fewer rules and regulations for business. He also favored lowering taxes and having the government spend less on many programs. On the other hand, he favored more spending to build up America's military power. Congress passed the President's proposals into law.

The United States was prosperous during most of the 1980s. More people had jobs than ever before. But the prosperity was not shared by all. The number of poor people remained very high, and the number of homeless increased greatly.

Also, under President Reagan the United States government spent far more money than it received in taxes. The government had to borrow billions of dollars to make up the difference. As a result, the nation's debt grew to more than twice what it had been in 1980.

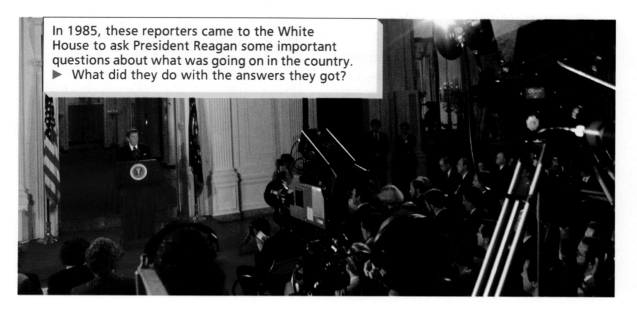

In 1985, these reporters came to the White House to ask President Reagan some important questions about what was going on in the country.
▶ What did they do with the answers they got?

Mikhail Gorbachev and Ronald Reagan exchange copies of the treaty they signed agreeing to destroy certain weapons.
► How might these men be feeling?

Changes in the Soviet Union When Ronald Reagan became President of the United States, he felt that the Soviet Union was a great threat to world peace. During his presidency, however, relations with the Soviet Union improved greatly. Much of the improvement had to do with changes made by the new leader of the Soviet Union, Mikhail Gorbachev (mee-kah EEL gor buh CHAWF).

Gorbachev saw that the Communist system was failing to meet his people's needs. People in the Soviet Union faced shortages of food, housing, and many basic services. So Gorbachev began to make changes in the system. The Soviet government adopted some ideas from capitalism in an effort to produce more and better goods.

Under Gorbachev, Soviet people had more freedom to criticize the government. Soviet citizens were even allowed some choice in electing candidates for office. Still, the Soviet Union was not a real democracy, for only members of the Communist party could hold office. However, things were changing rapidly. Some Soviet leaders and many ordinary citizens were speaking out in favor of allowing other parties to compete in free elections.

Gorbachev also wanted to end the cold war. He agreed with the United States that limiting the number of new weapons each side could build was not enough. He and President Reagan signed a treaty agreeing that each side would actually destroy some of the weapons it already had. This had never been done before.

B. The Bush Presidency

The 1988 Election In 1988 many candidates campaigned for their political party's **nomination** for President. A nomination is the naming of a person to be a candidate for office. Jesse Jackson, a longtime Civil Rights leader, was a major candidate for the Democratic party's nomination. Jack-

Jesse Jackson was a candidate for President in 1988.
► Why should young people take advantage of opportunities to talk to political leaders?

son did not win the nomination, but his candidacy encouraged African Americans and members of other minorities to take a greater part in our political system.

The man who was elected President in 1988 was George Bush, the Republican party's candidate. Bush had held many government jobs before, including that of Vice President under Ronald Reagan.

The War on Drugs As President, George Bush continued the war on drugs begun by President Reagan. Most illegal drugs are smuggled into the United States from other countries. President Bush worked with the leaders of many of those countries to help them stop the production of drugs in their countries. These efforts were partly successful. However, drugs continued to enter the United States, and the drug problem remained a serious one.

The Economy During George Bush's presidency, the nation's economy slowed down. Consumers bought fewer houses, cars, clothes, and other goods and services. At the same time, American manufacturers faced stiff competition both at home and overseas as they tried to sell their products. As a result, several million workers lost jobs.

When the economy slows down, state, local, and federal governments all collect less money from taxes. As a result they find it harder and harder to pay their bills. To reduce spending, nearly all cities and states had to cut out useful programs. To meet the expenses of the national government, the government borrowed larger amounts of money than ever before. Many Americans worried as the government's debt soared to new heights.

In January 1992, President George Bush delivered his annual State of the Union speech to Congress.
▶ What topics might a President discuss in such a speech?

The United States in a Changing World

Many dramatic changes occurred throughout the world while George Bush was President of the United States. The most important of these was the collapse of communism in Europe and the breakup of the Soviet empire.

The collapse of communism came with startling suddenness. It began in the countries of Eastern Europe. For more than 40 years, the Soviet Union had controlled these lands by making sure they had Communist governments friendly to the Soviet Union. In 1989, however, the peoples of Poland, Czechoslovakia, Hungary, and Romania held free elections and got rid of their Communist governments. The next year the people of East Germany did the same, and East and West Germany were reunited into one free country.

In earlier years the Soviet Union had used force to prevent such changes. But now Soviet President Gorbachev accepted them, saying that each country should be free to choose its own government. This new attitude of the Soviet Union marked the end of the Cold War.

Even more startling was the overthrow of communism in the Soviet Union itself. As you read earlier, the Communist system had failed to provide a better life for the people of the Soviet Union. Citizens had to stand in line for hours just to buy bread and milk. Many other foods, goods, and services were not available at all. Soviet citizens began to use their new right of free speech to criticize the government and communism. They then used their new right to vote in real elections to get rid of Communist rule.

Not only was the Communist party thrown out, but the Soviet Union itself was broken up. The Soviet Union had been made up of many different nationality groups. Many of these groups had always wanted their own independent country. In 1991, one after another of the republics that made up the Soviet Union declared its independence. By the end of the year, there was nothing left of the old Soviet Union. Instead, there were 15 independent nations. Russia is the largest of these nations. Ukraine (yoo KRAYN) is another. Although these nations agreed to cooperate with each other on certain things, mainly they have gone their separate ways.

Favorable developments also occurred in Central and South America. All through the 1980s, civil wars had taken thousands of lives in the Central American nations of Nicaragua and El Salvador. By 1991 both these wars were ended, and the people

In 1991, democratic elections were held in El Salvador.
▶ What, do you think, is the job of the woman at the front of the photograph?

chose new governments through democratic elections. In Panama, President Bush sent American troops to help the people get rid of a military dictator and allow leaders chosen by the people to take office. By the early 1990s every country in the Western Hemisphere except Cuba had a democratically elected government.

The Persian Gulf War The Middle East continued to be one of the world's great trouble spots during President Bush's presidency. In 1990 the country of Iraq suddenly attacked and took over its oil-rich neighbor, Kuwait. Find Iraq and Kuwait on the map on this page.

Both the United States and the United Nations Security Council demanded that Iraqi troops withdraw from Kuwait. However, Iraq's ruler, a cruel dictator named Saddam Hussein (sah DAHM hou SAYN), declared that Kuwait was now a part of Iraq.

Under President Bush's leadership, international army, navy, and air forces were sent to the Persian Gulf region. The United States provided most of the troops and weapons. When Saddam Hussein continued to refuse to leave Kuwait, these forces drove him out in Operation Desert Storm. First, American planes pounded the Iraqi army and Iraqi territory for six weeks. Then, American troops, along with soldiers from 20 nations, attacked by land. In just four days, these forces freed Kuwait and destroyed much of Iraq's army and air force. A great majority of the American people supported this war.

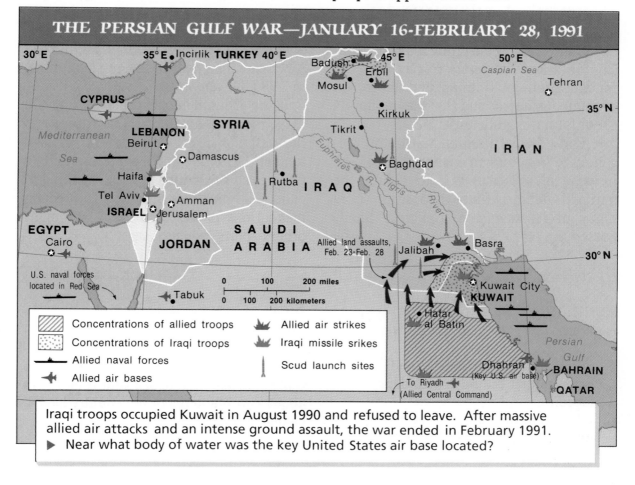

THE PERSIAN GULF WAR—JANUARY 16-FEBRUARY 28, 1991

Iraqi troops occupied Kuwait in August 1990 and refused to leave. After massive allied air attacks and an intense ground assault, the war ended in February 1991.
▶ Near what body of water was the key United States air base located?

C. Clinton Becomes President

Bill Clinton was elected President in 1992. He became the third youngest President, after Theodore Roosevelt and John F. Kennedy. Clinton had served as governor of Arkansas for twelve years.

In choosing Bill Clinton for the presidency, many voters hoped a new leader would focus more attention on issues at home than on foreign affairs. The unemployment rate in the United States had reached its highest level since 1984. The problems of the economy, poverty, homelessness, crime, drugs, and a huge national debt troubled the nation.

When Bill Clinton took office in 1993, he promised to support the interests of the American people. He and his advisors looked for ways to solve the country's economic and social problems. President Clinton asked that more money be spent for education, job training, and the growth of small businesses and that less money be spent for national defense.

Early in his presidency, Clinton presented to Congress an economic plan. The purpose of the plan was to reduce the national debt. Despite opposition from many of its members, Congress finally passed the plan.

President and Mrs. Clinton listen as a nurse describes health care for children.
▶ Why is caring for the health of America's children important?

One of President Clinton's major campaign promises had been to include all Americans in a health-care program. Early in 1993 he appointed First Lady Hillary Rodham Clinton to head a task force to make recommendations on how to reform the nation's health-care system. In September 1993 the President presented to Congress his plan for a national health program. The plan was based on the recommendations of the task force and many other experts in health care.

LESSON **3** REVIEW

THINK AND WRITE

A. What were President Reagan's main accomplishments?

B. Summarize the challenges and changes that the Bush presidency faced.

C. What were the main concerns of Americans when Bill Clinton became President?

SKILLS CHECK
THINKING SKILL

Imagine that you have a pen pal in the former Soviet Union. Write a list of questions that you would like to ask your friend about how life in his or her country has changed in recent years.

USING THE VOCABULARY

On a separate sheet of paper, write the letter of the phrase that most appropriately completes the statement.

1. The Interstate Highway System
   (a) was started by President Truman.
   (b) has made travel faster and safer.
   (c) is a series of old turnpikes.
   (d) was built quickly and cheaply.

2. The Peace Corps
   (a) is an international organization that tries to stop wars.
   (b) was started during the Great Depression to help people find work.
   (c) sends volunteers with skills to poor countries to teach.
   (d) was started by President Eisenhower.

3. Vietnamization was
   (a) a plan to train South Vietnamese troops to take over the fighting.
   (b) an escalation of the war.
   (c) President Johnson's plan to send American troops to South Vietnam.
   (d) the plan to hold free elections.

4. Watergate caused the resignation of
   (a) President Ford.
   (b) President Carter.
   (c) President Johnson.
   (d) President Nixon.

5. A candidate who has his or her party's nomination
   (a) is the party's choice for office.
   (b) is going to win the election.
   (c) can run only for the office of President of the United States.
   (d) must be able to make good speeches.

REMEMBERING WHAT YOU READ

On a separate sheet of paper, write your answers in complete sentences.

1. Why was the St. Lawrence Seaway an important project?
2. What was the purpose of the Peace Corps?
3. What were some of the programs in the Great Society plan?
4. How did Vietnam become divided?
5. What happened in Vietnam after the American troops left?
6. With what countries did President Nixon try to establish better relations?
7. What was unusual about the way Gerald Ford became President?
8. How did President Carter try to bring peace to the Middle East?
9. What was the Reagan Revolution?
10 What are some of the major world events that occurred during the presidency of George Bush?

TYING LANGUAGE ARTS TO SOCIAL STUDIES

Choose one of the problems that is facing the United States today. Read about it in newspapers and magazines. Talk to your parents about it. Think about how it might be solved. Write a letter to the President, explaining why you think the problem is important and how you think it might be solved. Or if the President has done something that you think was especially good, write and tell him so.

THINKING CRITICALLY

On a separate sheet of paper, write your answers in complete sentences.

1. Which of the programs supported by President Kennedy do you think was the most important? Explain your answer.
2. President Johnson believed that the federal government should actively help to solve problems. Which problems did he think were important?
3. Make a list that shows the development of United States involvement in Vietnam.
4. How have changes in the Soviet Union and in Eastern Europe affected the United States?
5. How successful, do you think, has the war on drugs been?

SUMMARIZING THE CHAPTER

On a separate sheet of paper, draw a graphic organizer like the one shown here. Fill in the table with the names of the Presidents mentioned in this chapter. Be sure they are in the correct sequence. Then write in the major events that occured during each Presidency. The first one has been started for you.

CHAPTER THEME

Americans have found solutions to many of the challenges of the last few decades. Some problems have yet to be solved and are the challenges of the future.

PRESIDENT	MAJOR EVENTS
Eisenhower	Interstate Highway System

COOPERATIVE LEARNING

Sometimes historical events can be the basis for works of fiction. Paul Revere's ride, for example, was the basis for a poem. You read part of that poem earlier in the school year when you studied the American Revolution.

PROJECT

Your group is going to write a play about some of the people or events you learned about in this unit.

- You must plan and perform your play together.
- Look through Chapters 24–26 for ideas.
- Choose characters and a setting for the play.
- Try to include at least one real historical character.

Your choice of character will help you decide on the plot for your play. For example, a play could be written about President John F. Kennedy. The characters could be the President and representatives from countries seeking our country's help. The setting would be the White House. The plot would be about the founding of the Peace Corps. It would focus on how President Kennedy got the idea to send volunteers from our country to help people in other countries.

There are many events in Unit 7 that could be turned into a play. Choose one person to record your group's ideas.

- Allow everyone to express an opinion.
- Work together.
- Keep to the task.

Once the group has decided on the characters and plot, it is ready to begin writing the play. Decide what lines each character will say.

When the play has been written, decide what roles people will play.

- The group should have a director. The director tells the performers how to act and how to say their lines.
- Perhaps a narrator is needed to introduce the play.
- Be sure everyone takes part in putting on the play.

PRESENTATION AND REVIEW

- After the group has rehearsed the play, present it to the class.
- Meet again with your group after all the plays have been presented. Discuss how plays can make history come to life.
- Evaluate how well your group accomplished this purpose.

REMEMBER TO:
- **Give your ideas.**
- **Listen to others' ideas.**
- **Plan your work with the group.**
- **Present your project.**
- **Discuss how your group worked.**

A. WHY DO I NEED THIS SKILL?

Political cartoons appear in newspapers and magazines just about every day. Cartoons are never objective. That is, cartoons always take sides. They are a quick and clever way of presenting a point of view. Understanding cartoons is an important reading skill that everyone should develop.

B. DEVELOPING THE SKILL

A political cartoon is a drawing that makes a statement about a subject of public interest. It can be about a person, an event, or an important problem. The cartoonist, the person who draws the cartoon, tries to get people to see things in a certain way.

In order to understand the cartoon, the reader must first recognize the subject. What is the subject of a cartoon showing a lake with soda cans and plastic bottles floating in dirty water and one duck saying to another, "It wasn't this bad last year"? If you correctly answered pollution, you had enough knowledge of the background of the problem to understand the subject. You knew that cans and bottles are part of the problem with polluted waterways. They are also easily recognizable symbols of the problem. You probably also know that wildlife cannot live for very long in polluted areas. The caption to the cartoon tells you that the cartoonist thinks that the problem of pollution is getting worse.

C. PRACTICING THE SKILL

As you learned in Chapter 25, the United States was involved for many years in a war in Vietnam. The cartoon on page 615 shows how one cartoonist felt abut the war. Herblock draws cartoons for the editorial page of a newspaper, *The Washington Post*.

What are the various parts of the cartoon? The people moving along the road represent South Vietnamese civilians. Civilians are the citizens of a country who are not in the military and are not actively fighting in the war. The civilians include women, children, the elderly, and sick people. Some people in the cartoon are carrying children and bundles. They are ragged, barefoot, and, in one case at least, injured. The impression given is that they are homeless.

The stars and stripes emblem on the planes is the symbol used on United States military aircraft. So the airplanes overhead are United States Air Force bombers. The house in the background has just been hit by a bomb. American military leaders felt that it was necessary to bomb South Vietnamese villages. Soldiers from North Vietnam would often hide in them.

Study the cartoon carefully and answer the following questions.

1. How can you tell these are South Vietnamese civilians?
2. How do you know that the house has been bombed?
3. What would lead you to think that these people are homeless?

4. Who, according to the caption, is losing the war?

5. Do you think the cartoonist is in favor of Americans continuing to fight in the Vietnam War?

D. APPLYING THE SKILL

Look in a newspaper or magazine for a cartoon about some current problem. Tape it on a sheet of paper. On another sheet of paper, make a list identifying the various parts of the cartoon and telling what each means. Then in a short paragraph, explain the point the cartoonist is trying to make.

You may, instead, wish to draw a cartoon of your own. Pick a topic from current events or take a school situation or problem as your topic. Decide what symbols you can use to state your point of view quickly and clearly. Remember: A good cartoon makes its point without any extra explanation.

"I DON'T KNOW IF EITHER SIDE IS WINNING, BUT I KNOW WHO'S LOSING."

"I don't know if either side is winning, but I know who's losing." — from THE HERBLOCK GALLERY (Simon & Schuster, 1968)

Making SKILLBUILDER Predictions

A. WHY DO I NEED THIS SKILL?

When you read a mystery story, do you try to guess what the outcome will be? If so, you are making a prediction. You find out if your prediction is correct when you get to the end of the story.

You can make predictions when reading other types of books as well. Learning how to make predictions will help you understand and remember information in your social studies book.

B. LEARNING THE SKILL

There are four steps you can use to make predictions. Let's see how these steps can be used with some of the material from Chapter 24, "A Portrait of America in 1950."

1. First **read** a part of the chapter, such as the paragraph below. As you read, think about what is happening and how that will affect what will happen next.

Another important change was that American cities grew outward as well as upward. In 1850 no city had spread much more than three to four miles (five or six km) from its center. That was because the main way of getting around was walking. The cities of 1950, however, sprawled miles from their downtown areas. New methods of transportation enabled people to move out from the city center. With buses, subways, and—increasingly—cars, people could live far from where they worked or shopped.

2. Now **predict** what will happen next. You can help yourself predict in these ways:

- Use what you know already about the information in the chapter.
- Think about an event that might cause something else to happen.
- Think about the sequence of events and what might happen next.
- Think about the people involved in the events and what they might do.

3. Next, **verify** your predictions. This means that you read on to see if your predictions were correct.

More and more people used their new-found freedom to move outside of cities altogether. On the outskirts of a city in 1950, you might see several new homes in a cluster. Each home might have a neat green lawn around it. Close by would lie another cluster of new homes, and then another. Some of the clusters would be so close that they would run into one another. These clusters of houses ringing a city were the suburbs, or communities that surround cities. Suburbs together with the nearby city made up giant metropolitan areas.

4. Finally, **change** your predictions if necessary or **make new predictions.** Then read on to verify them.

These four steps should be repeated as you go on with your reading.

HOW TO PREDICT AND VERIFY:

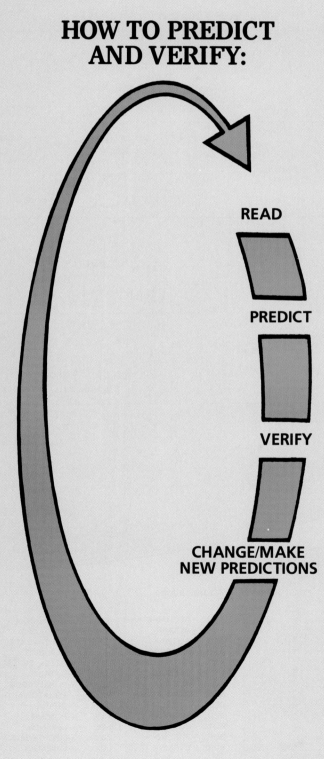

READ

PREDICT

VERIFY

CHANGE/MAKE NEW PREDICTIONS

C. PRACTICING THE SKILL

Try out the four steps, using parts of Chapter 26, "New Challenges, New Solutions," on pages 596–610.

1. Read the section "Changes in the Soviet Union," in Lesson 3.
2. Predict what will happen next. How will the changes that have taken place in the Soviet Union affect that country's relations with the United States?
3. Verify your predictions. Look in the newspapers or in newsmagazines. Watch the news programs on television. Were your predictions correct?
4. Change your predictions or make new predictions. Predict what will happen next.

D. APPLYING THE SKILL

You can make predictions for short parts of a lesson, or you can make predictions that cover an entire lesson, chapter, or even a unit. In Chapter 24 you learned what the United States was like in 1950. In Chapters 25 and 26 you read about events in the United States from after World War II to the early 1990s. Think about what you have learned about the many changes that have taken place during this time.

Make some predictions about what you think the United States will be like by the year 2000. How will people live? What kind of work will they do? What will people be doing with their leisure time? What will school be like? Make a list of predictions and discuss them with your classmates.

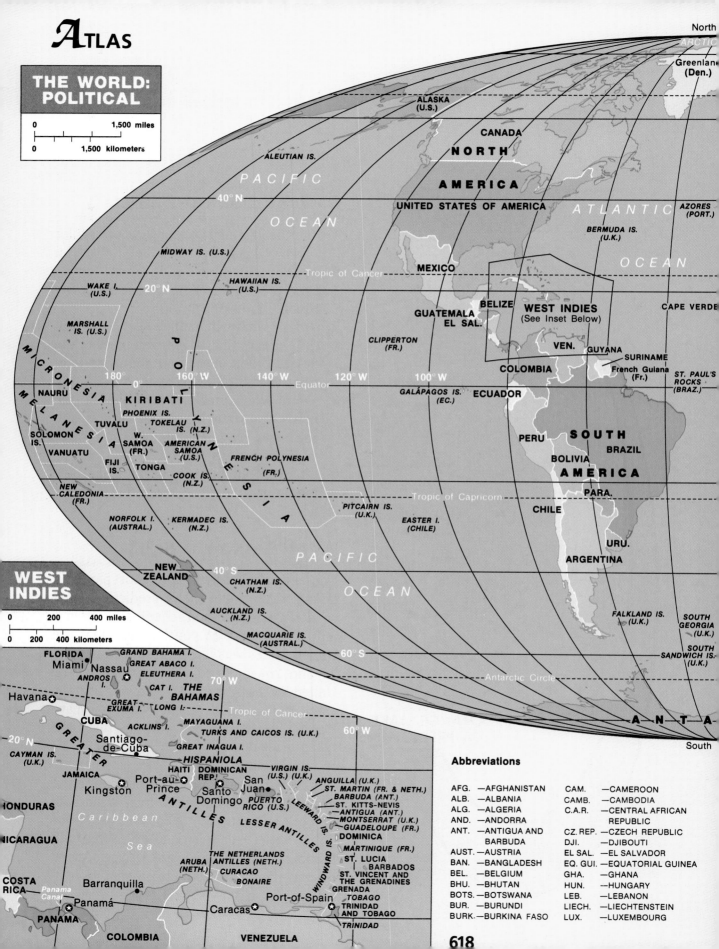

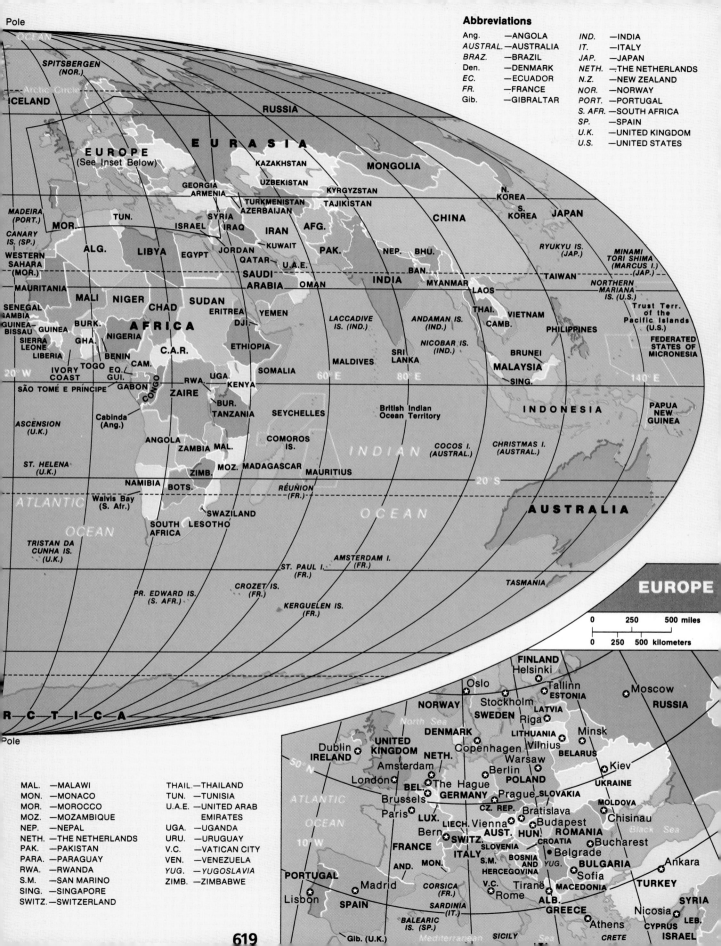

THE UNITED STATES: POLITICAL

Atlantic Time Zone 10 A.M.

Eastern Time Zone 9 A.M.

Central Time Zone 8 A.M.

Mountain Time Zone 7 A.M.

Pacific Time Zone 6 A.M.

Alaska Time Zone 5 A.M.

Hawaii-Aleutian Time Zone 4 A.M.

⊕ National capital
✳ State capitals
• Other cities

0   100   200 miles
0   100   200 kilometers

620

Legend / Labels

CANADA

St. Lawrence River

MAINE — Augusta, Portland, Lewiston
VT — Burlington, Montpelier, Rutland
NH — Concord, Manchester, Nashua
MA — Boston, Worcester, Springfield, Pawtucket
RI — Providence, Warwick
CT — Hartford, Bridgeport, New Haven
NY — Albany, Buffalo, New York
NJ — Newark, Trenton, Jersey City
PA — Harrisburg, Philadelphia, Pittsburgh
DE — Dover, Wilmington
MD — Baltimore, Annapolis
WV — Charleston, Wheeling, Huntington
Washington, D.C., Rockville, Richmond, Norfolk, Virginia Beach

VIRGINIA — Lexington
NC — Raleigh, Greensboro, Charlotte
SC — Columbia, North Charleston, Charleston
GEORGIA — Atlanta, Columbus, Savannah, Tallahassee
FLORIDA — Jacksonville, Miami

Lake Ontario, Lake Erie, Lake Huron, Lake Superior, Lake Michigan

MICHIGAN — Lansing, Detroit, Grand Rapids
OHIO — Columbus, Cleveland, Cincinnati
IN — Indianapolis, Fort Wayne, Gary
KENTUCKY — Frankfort, Louisville, Lexington
TENNESSEE — Nashville, Knoxville, Memphis
ALABAMA — Montgomery, Birmingham, Mobile
MS — Jackson, Meridian, Biloxi
LA — Baton Rouge, Shreveport, New Orleans

WISCONSIN — Madison, Green Bay, Milwaukee
IL — Springfield, Chicago, Rockford
MINNESOTA — St. Paul, Minneapolis, Duluth
IOWA — Des Moines, Cedar Rapids, Davenport
MISSOURI — Jefferson City, Kansas City, St. Louis
ARKANSAS — Little Rock, North Little Rock, Fort Smith

NORTH DAKOTA — Bismarck, Fargo, Grand Forks
SOUTH DAKOTA — Pierre, Sioux Falls, Rapid City
NEBRASKA — Lincoln, Omaha, Grand Island
KANSAS — Topeka, Wichita
OKLAHOMA — Oklahoma City, Tulsa, Lawton
TEXAS — Austin, Dallas, Houston

MONTANA — Helena, Billings, Great Falls
WYOMING — Cheyenne, Casper, Laramie
COLORADO — Denver, Aurora, Colorado Springs
NEW MEXICO — Santa Fe, Albuquerque, Las Cruces
IDAHO — Boise, Idaho Falls, Pocatello
UTAH — Salt Lake City, West Valley, Provo
ARIZONA — Phoenix, Mesa, Tucson

WASHINGTON — Olympia, Seattle, Spokane
OREGON — Salem, Portland, Eugene
NEVADA — Carson City, Reno, Las Vegas
CALIFORNIA — Sacramento, San Diego, Los Angeles

Missouri River, Columbia R., Rio Grande, Great Salt Lake

PACIFIC OCEAN, ATLANTIC OCEAN, Gulf of Mexico

MEXICO, CUBA, BAHAMAS, Tropic of Cancer

ALASKA — Juneau, Fairbanks, Anchorage
Arctic Circle, Yukon R., Bering Strait, Bering Sea, Gulf of Alaska
Alaska Time Zone 5 A.M.
CANADA

HAWAII — Honolulu, Pearl City, Kailua
Hawaii-Aleutian Time Zone 4 A.M.

25°N, 20°N, 35°N, 40°N, 30°N, 50°N
75°W, 80°W, 120°W, 140°W, 150°W, 160°W, 180°W, 60°N

0   100   200 miles
0   100   200 kilometers

THE UNITED STATES: PHYSICAL

Abbreviations
Mt. —MOUNT
MTS. —MOUNTAINS
I. —ISLAND

Elevations
Feet	Meters
12,000	3,658
9,000	2,743
5,000	1,524
2,000	610
1,000	305
500	152
0	0

0   100   200 miles
0   100   200 kilometers

CANADA

ATLANTIC OCEAN

PACIFIC OCEAN

Gulf of Mexico

MEXICO

CUBA

RUSSIA

ARCTIC OCEAN

Bering Sea

Gulf of Alaska

ROCKY MOUNTAINS

APPALACHIAN MTS.

ADIRONDACK MTS.

BLUE RIDGE

ALLEGHENY MTS.

GREAT PLAINS

COLUMBIA PLATEAU

COLORADO PLATEAU

GREAT BASIN

SIERRA NEVADA

CASCADE RANGE

COAST RANGES

CENTRAL VALLEY

MOJAVE DESERT

DEATH VALLEY

OZARK PLATEAU

LLANO ESTACADO

CONTINENTAL DIVIDE

ATLANTIC COASTAL PLAIN

GULF COASTAL PLAIN

BLACK HILLS

BROOKS RANGE

ALASKA RANGE

FLORIDA KEYS

Straits of Florida

Tropic of Cancer

Cape Cod
LONG ISLAND
Cape May
Cape Charles
Cape Hatteras
Cape Fear
Cape Canaveral
Cape Sable
Cape San Blas
Mississippi Delta
Cape Flattery
Cape Blanco
Cape Mendocino
Point Conception

Boston
New York
Philadelphia
Baltimore
Washington, D.C.
Atlanta
Jacksonville
New Orleans
Houston
Oklahoma City
Albuquerque
Phoenix
Los Angeles
Seattle
Portland
Denver
Kansas City
St. Louis
Chicago
Milwaukee
Detroit
Columbus
Indianapolis
Nashville
Memphis
Barrow
Anchorage

Seaside

Chesapeake Bay

St. Lawrence River
Hudson R.
L. Ontario
Lake Erie
Lake Huron
Lake Michigan
Lake Superior
Ohio River
Cumberland River
Tennessee River
Alabama River
Mississippi River
Wabash River
Illinois R.
Missouri River
Platte River
North Platte River
South Platte R.
Arkansas River
Red River
Canadian River
Brazos River
Rio Grande
Pecos R.
Colorado R.
Green River
Snake River
Humboldt River
Sacramento River
San Joaquin River
Yellowstone River
Columbia River
Yukon River

Mt. Mitchell
6,684 ft.
(2,037 m)

Longs Peak
14,256 ft.
(4,345 m)

Pikes Peak
14,110 ft.
(4,301 m)

Mt. Elbert
14,433 ft.
(4,399 m)

Blanca Peak
14,317 ft.
(4,364 m)

Grand Teton
13,766 ft.
(4,196 m)

Mt. Rainier
14,410 ft.
(4,392 m)

Mt. Whitney
14,495 ft.
(4,418 m)

Mt. McKinley
20,320 ft.
(6,194 m)

KODIAK I.

HAWAII
KAUAI
OAHU
MOLOKAI
MAUI
Honolulu

0   100   200 miles
0   100   200 kilometers

0   100   200 miles
0   100   200 kilometers

621

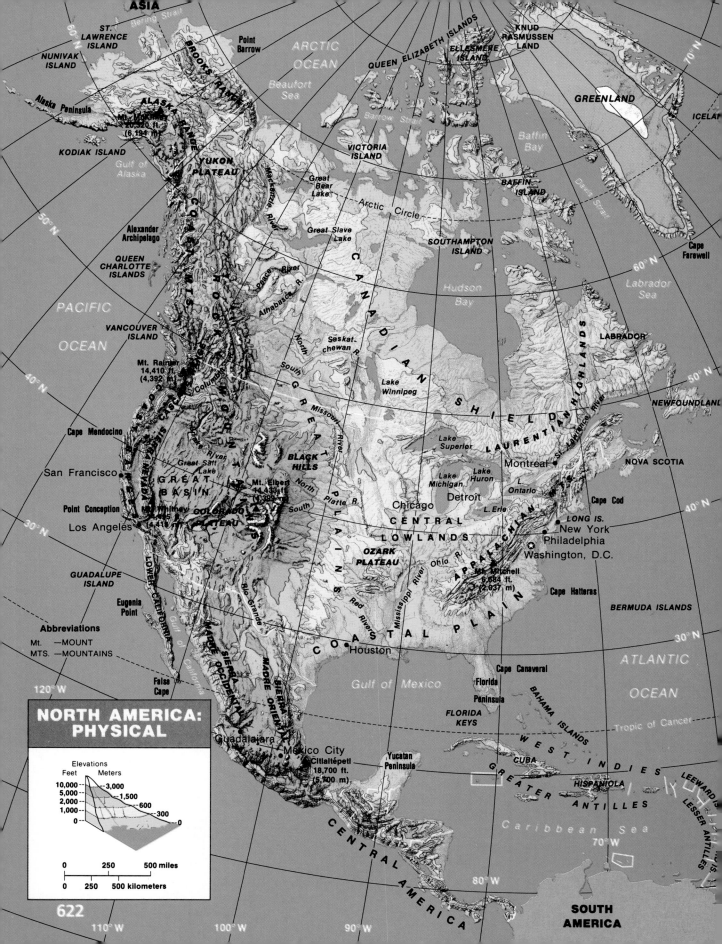

NORTH AMERICA: PHYSICAL

Elevations

Feet	Meters
10,000	3,000
5,000	1,500
2,000	600
1,000	300
0	0

0   250   500 miles

0   250   500 kilometers

Abbreviations

Mt. —MOUNT
MTS. —MOUNTAINS

622

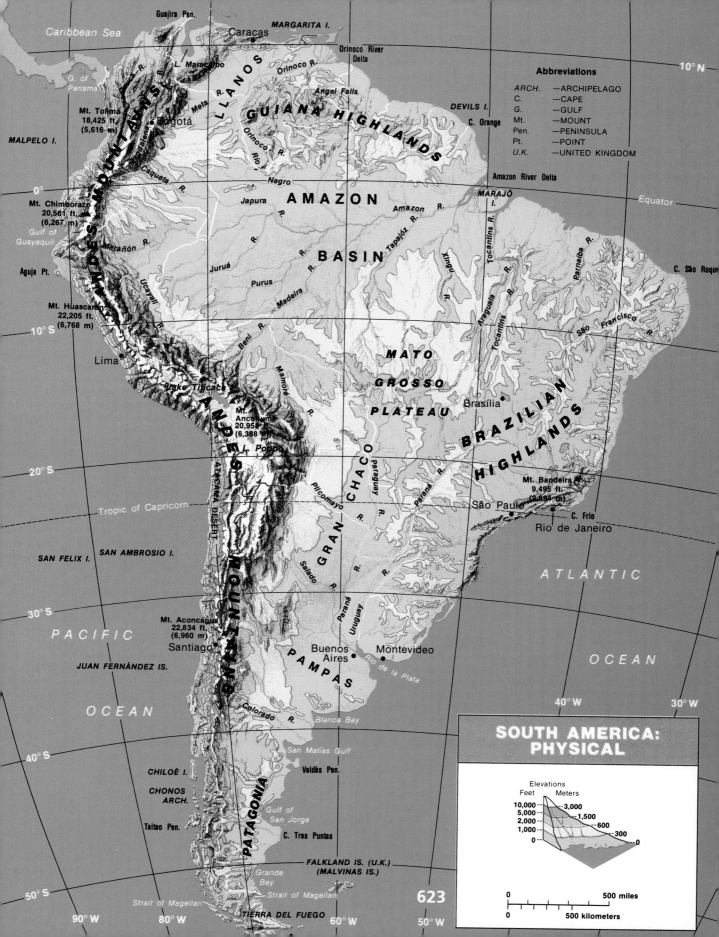

Caribbean Sea

Guajira Pen.

MARGARITA I.

Caracas

Orinoco River Delta

L. Maracaibo

Orinoco R.

Angel Falls

DEVILS I.

C. Orange

G. of Panama

LLANOS

GUIANA HIGHLANDS

MALPELO I.

Mt. Toñma
18,425 ft.
(5,616 m)

Bogotá

Meta

Orinoco R.

Rio

Negro

Amazon River Delta

MARAJÓ I.

Equator

0°

10° N

Mt. Chimborazo
20,561 ft.
(6,267 m)

Japura

AMAZON

Amazon R.

Caqueta R.

Gulf of Guayaquil

Marañón R.

Juruá

BASIN

Tapajós R.

Xingu R.

Tocantins R.

Parnaiba R.

C. São Roque

Aguja Pt.

Ucayali R.

Purus

Madeira R.

Araguaia R.

Tocantins R.

São Francisco R.

Mt. Huascarán
22,205 ft.
(6,768 m)

10° S

Beni R.

Mamoré R.

MATO

Lima

Lake Titicaca

ANDES

Mt. Ancohuma
20,958 ft.
(6,388 m)

L. Poopó

GROSSO

PLATEAU

Brasília

BRAZILIAN

HIGHLANDS

MOUNTAINS

Paraguay R.

GRAN CHACO

Paraná R.

Mt. Bandeira
9,495 ft.
(2,894 m)

20° S

Pilcomayo R.

São Paulo

C. Frio

Rio de Janeiro

Tropic of Capricorn

ATACAMA DESERT

SAN FELIX I.

SAN AMBROSIO I.

Salado R.

R.

Paraná R.

ATLANTIC

Mt. Aconcagua
22,834 ft.
(6,960 m)

Santiago

Paraná R.

Uruguay R.

30° S

PACIFIC

JUAN FERNÁNDEZ IS.

Buenos Aires

Montevideo

Rio de la Plata

OCEAN

OCEAN

PAMPAS

Colorado R.

40° W

30° W

Blanca Bay

40° S

CHILOÉ I.

San Matías Gulf

CHONOS ARCH.

Valdés Pen.

PATAGONIA

Taitao Pen.

Gulf of San Jorge

C. Tres Puntas

FALKLAND IS. (U.K.)
(MALVINAS IS.)

Grande Bay

50° S

Strait of Magellan

Strait of Magellan

TIERRA DEL FUEGO

623

90° W

80° W

70° W

60° W

50° W

SOUTH AMERICA:
PHYSICAL

Elevations
Feet   Meters
10,000 ---   --- 3,000
5,000 ---
2,000 ---   --- 1,500
1,000 ---   --- 600
0 ---   --- 300
               --- 0

0   500 miles

0   500 kilometers

ATLANTIC
OCEAN

MADEIRA
ISLANDS

BRITISH ISLES

North
Sea

•London

SCANDINAVIA

LAPLAND

SPITSBERGEN

ARCTIC OCEAN

NORTH
LAND

NOVAYA ZEMLYA

Kola
Peninsula

Barents
Sea

Kara Sea

Taymyr

Arctic

Circle

Yamal
Peninsula

Yenisei
River

Loire R.

•Paris

Hamburg

Stockholm

Rhine R.

•Berlin

Elbe River

Madrid•

PYRENEES

Iberian
Peninsula

Tagus R.

ALPS

BALEARIC
IS.

Milan•

CORSICA

Po R.

Danube River

SARDINIA

Rome•

Tyrrhenian
Sea

Adriatic Sea

SICILY

Ionian
Sea

MALTESE
ISLANDS

Balkan
Peninsula

•Bucharest

CARPATHIAN

Vistula River

Baltic
Sea

BALTIC PLAINS

•St. Petersburg

NORTH EUROPEAN PLAIN

Dnieper River

Moscow•

N.
Dvina R.

Volga
River

Kama
River

URAL MOUNTAINS

Ob River

WEST

SIBERIAN

PLAIN

Ob
River

Irtysh
River

Danube River

Don R.

Volga River

Ural River

Istanbul•

Black
Sea

CAUCASUS

Aegean Sea

CRETE

ASIA MINOR

CYPRUS

Mediterranean Sea

Strait of Gibraltar

Abbreviations

Mt. —MOUNT
MTS. —MOUNTAINS

SYRIAN
DESERT

Euphrates River

Tigris R.

Baghdad•

ELBURZ MTS.

Tehran•

ZAGROS MOUNTAINS

PLATEAU
OF
IRAN

Caspian
Sea

KIRGIZ
STEPPE

Aral
Sea

TURAN LOWLAND

Syr Darya

Amu
Darya

KAZAKH

UPLANDS

Lake
Balkhash

Ishim
River

ALTAI

TARIM
BASIN

KUNLUN

PLATEAU
OF
TIB

HINDU KUSH

AFRICA

MESOPOTAMIA

HEJAZ

Red
Sea

ASIR

Arabian

Peninsula

Persian Gulf

Gulf of Oman

Karachi•

INDIAN
DESERT

Indus River

Sutlej River

Mt. Everest
29,028 ft.)
(8,848 m)

Ganges River

Delhi•

HIMALAYA

GANGES

PLAIN

HADHRAMAUT

Gulf of Aden

Arabian Sea

Bombay•

WESTERN GHATS

Godavari R.

DECCAN

PLATEAU

Ganges River

10° N

LACCADIVE
ISLANDS

Madras•

SRI
LANKA

MALDIVES

0°

Equator

INDIAN

OCEAN

50° E

60° E

70° E

80° E

624

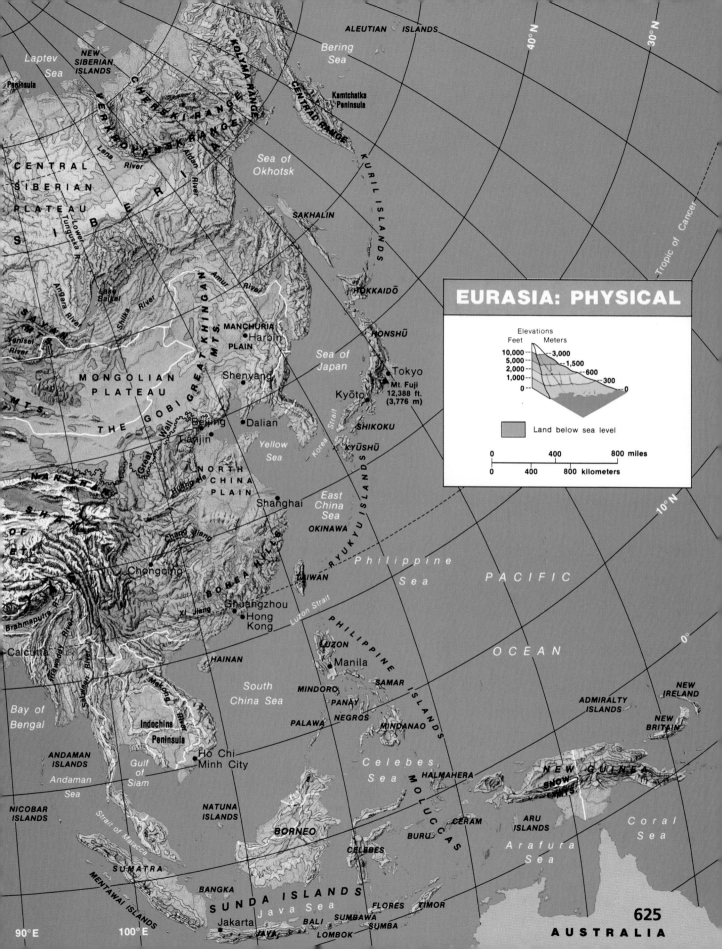

Laptev Sea
Peninsula
NEW SIBERIAN ISLANDS
ALEUTIAN ISLANDS
Bering Sea
40° N
30° N

CHERSKI RANGE
VERKHOYANSK RANGE
KOLYMA RANGE
CENTRAL RANGE
Kamchatka Peninsula

CENTRAL SIBERIAN PLATEAU
Lena River
Aldan River
Sea of Okhotsk

S I B E R I A

Lower Tunguska R.
Angara River
Lake Baikal
Shilka River
Amur River
SAKHALIN
KURIL ISLANDS
Tropic of Cancer

SAYAN MTS.
Yenisei River
MANCHURIA
Harbin
PLAIN
HOKKAIDŌ
HONSHŪ
Sea of Japan

MONGOLIAN PLATEAU
THE GOBI
GREAT KHINGAN MTS.
Shenyang
Tokyo
Mt. Fuji 12,388 ft. (3,776 m)
Kyōto
SHIKOKU
Korea Strait
KYŪSHŪ

Great Wall
Beijing
Dalian
Tianjin
Yellow Sea
NORTH CHINA PLAIN

NAN
SHAN
OF
TI
Huang He
SHANTUNG
Chang Jiang
Shanghai
East China Sea
OKINAWA
RYUKYU ISLANDS

Chongqing
SHOREA HILLS
TAIWAN
Philippine Sea
PACIFIC

Brahmaputra R.
Xi Jiang
Guangzhou
Hong Kong
Luzon Strait
10° N

Calcutta
HAINAN
LUZON
Manila
OCEAN

Irrawaddy River
Salween River
Mekong River
South China Sea
MINDORO
SAMAR
PHILIPPINE ISLANDS
NEW IRELAND
ADMIRALTY ISLANDS

Bay of Bengal
Indochina Peninsula
PANAY
NEGROS
PALAWAN
MINDANAO
NEW BRITAIN

ANDAMAN ISLANDS
Gulf of Siam
Ho Chi Minh City
Celebes Sea
HALMAHERA
NEW GUINEA
SNOW MTS.

Andaman Sea
NATUNA ISLANDS
MOLUCCAS
ARU ISLANDS
Coral Sea

NICOBAR ISLANDS
BORNEO
CERAM
BURU
Arafura Sea

Strait of Malacca
CELEBES

SUMATRA
MENTAWAI ISLANDS
SUNDA ISLANDS
BANGKA
Java Sea
FLORES
TIMOR
SUMBAWA
SUMBA
625

Jakarta
JAVA
BALI
LOMBOK
AUSTRALIA

90° E
100° E

EURASIA: PHYSICAL

Elevations
Feet   Meters
10,000 -- --3,000
5,000 -- --1,500
2,000 -- --600
1,000 -- --300
0 -- --0

Land below sea level

0   400   800 miles
0   400   800 kilometers

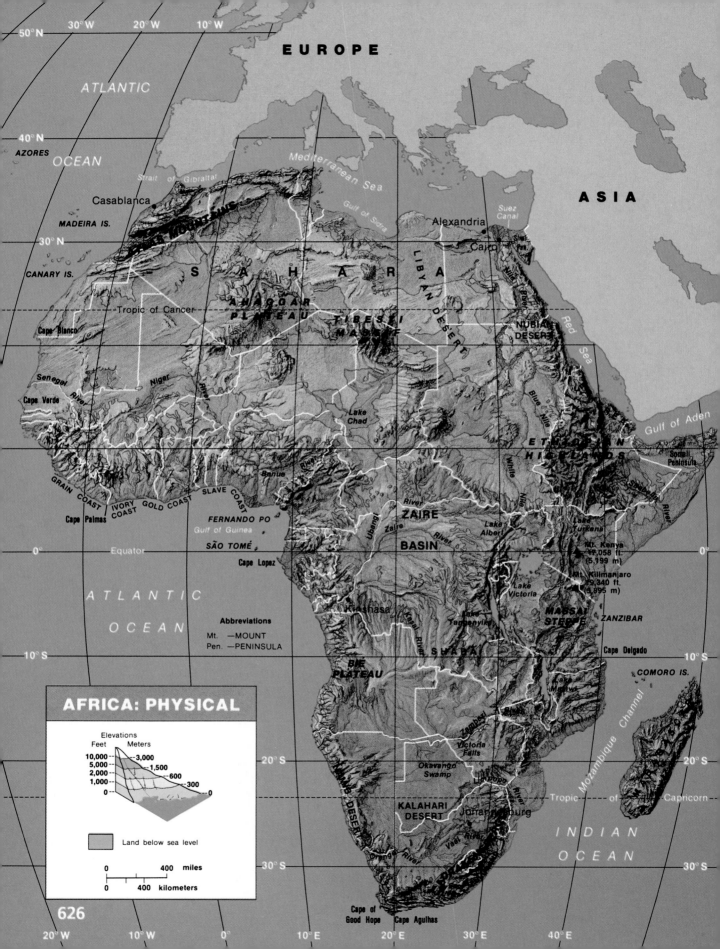

EUROPE

ATLANTIC

AZORES

OCEAN

40° N

MADEIRA IS.

Casablanca

ASIA

Strait of Gibraltar

Mediterranean Sea

Gulf of Sidra

Alexandria

Suez
Canal

30° N

Cairo

Sinai
Pen.

CANARY IS.

ATLAS MOUNTAINS

S   A   H   A   R   A

LIBYAN DESERT

Cape Blanco

Tropic of Cancer

AHAGGAR
PLATEAU

TIBESTI
MASSIF

NUBIAN
DESERT

Red Sea

*Senegal
River*

Niger

River

Cape Verde

Lake
Chad

Cape Palmas

GRAIN COAST
IVORY GOLD COAST SLAVE COAST
COAST

Benue

River

Gulf of Aden

ETHIOPIAN
HIGHLANDS

*Somali
Peninsula*

White

Nile

Shebell

River

FERNANDO PO

Gulf of Guinea

SÃO TOMÉ

Ubangi

River

ZAIRE

Zaire

River

Lake
Albert

Lake
Turkana

Mt. Kenya
17,058 ft.
(5,199 m)

Equator

BASIN

Cape Lopez

Blue Nile

Nile

Kinshasa

Abbreviations

Mt. —MOUNT
Pen. —PENINSULA

*Kasai
River*

Lake
Victoria

Mt. Kilimanjaro
19,340 ft.
(5,895 m)

MASSAI
STEPPE

ZANZIBAR

Lake
Tanganyika

SHABA

Cape Delgado

10° S

ATLANTIC

OCEAN

BIÉ
PLATEAU

Lake
Malawi

COMORO IS.

AFRICA: PHYSICAL

Elevations

Feet   Meters

10,000   —3,000
5,000   —1,500
2,000   —600
1,000   —300
0   —0

Zambezi

Victoria
Falls

Mozambique Channel

Okavango
Swamp

20° S

Land below sea level

KALAHARI
DESERT

Limpopo

River

Tropic of Capricorn

Johannesburg

0   400 miles

0   400 kilometers

NAMIB DESERT

*Orange
River*

Vaal River

DRAKENSBERG

INDIAN

OCEAN

30° S

626

Cape of
Good Hope   Cape Agulhas

20° W   10° W   0°   10° E   20° E   30° E   40° E

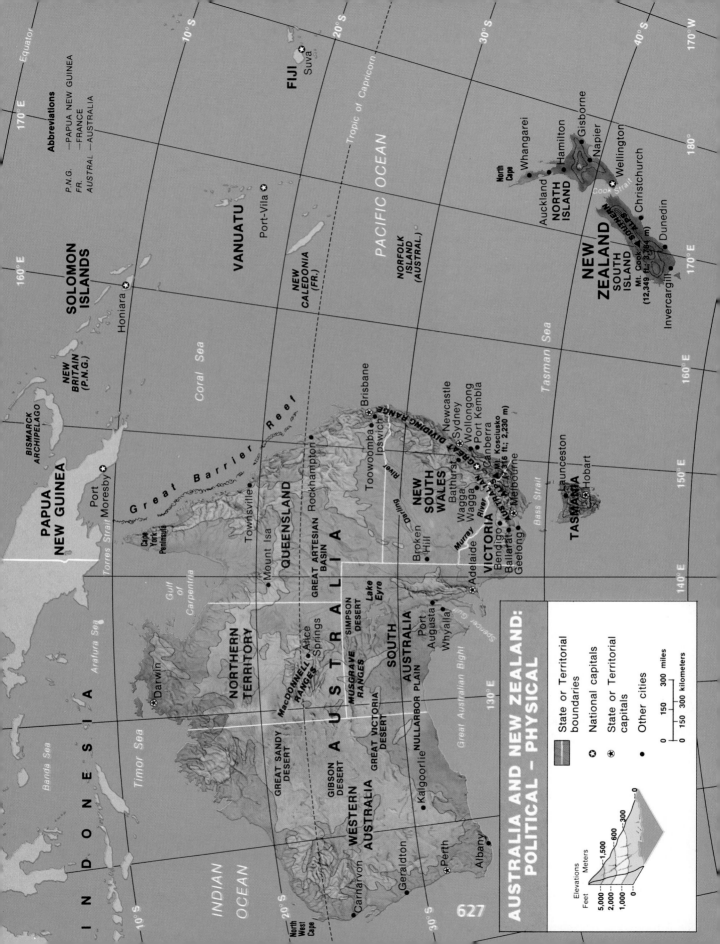

INDONESIA

Banda Sea

Timor Sea

Arafura Sea

BISMARCK
ARCHIPELAGO

NEW
BRITAIN
(P.N.G.)

PAPUA
NEW GUINEA

Port
Moresby

Torres Strait

Gulf
of
Carpentaria

Cape
York
Peninsula

Coral Sea

Great Barrier Reef

SOLOMON
ISLANDS

Honiara

VANUATU

Port-Vila

PACIFIC OCEAN

FIJI
Suva

Tropic of Capricorn

NEW
CALEDONIA
(FR.)

NORFOLK
ISLAND
(AUSTRAL.)

INDIAN OCEAN

North
West
Cape

Carnarvon

Geraldton

Perth

Albany

GREAT SANDY DESERT

GIBSON
DESERT

GREAT VICTORIA
DESERT

WESTERN
AUSTRALIA

Kalgoorlie

NULLARBOR PLAIN

Great Australian Bight

Darwin

NORTHERN
TERRITORY

MacDONNELL
RANGES

Alice
Springs

MUSGRAVE
RANGES

SIMPSON
DESERT

SOUTH
AUSTRALIA

Lake
Eyre

AUSTRALIA

Townsville

Mount Isa

QUEENSLAND

GREAT ARTESIAN
BASIN

Rockhampton

Brisbane

Toowoomba

Ipswich

GREAT DIVIDING RANGE

River

Darling

Broken
Hill

Murray

River

Murrumbidgee

NEW
SOUTH
WALES

Newcastle

Sydney

Wollongong

Port Kembla

Bathurst

Wagga
Wagga

Canberra

Mt. Kosciusko
(7,316 ft; 2,230 m)

VICTORIA

Bendigo

Ballarat

Melbourne

Geelong

Adelaide

Port
Augusta

Whyalla

Spencer Gulf

Bass Strait

Launceston

Hobart

TASMANIA

Tasman Sea

NEW
ZEALAND

NORTH
ISLAND

North
Cape

Whangarei

Auckland

Hamilton

Gisborne

Napier

Wellington

Cook Strait

Christchurch

SOUTHERN ALPS

SOUTH
ISLAND

Mt. Cook
(12,349 ft; 3,764 m)

Dunedin

Invercargill

627

AUSTRALIA AND NEW ZEALAND:
POLITICAL – PHYSICAL

State or Territorial
boundaries

✪ National capitals

✪ State or Territorial
    capitals

•   Other cities

0   150   300 miles

0   150 300 kilometers

Elevations
Feet   Meters
5,000   1,500
2,000   600
1,000   300
0   0

GAZETTEER

Some words in this book may be new to you or difficult to pronounce. Those words have been spelled phonetically in parentheses. The syllable that receives stress in a word is shown in small capital letters.

For example: **Chicago** (shuh KAH goh)

Most phonetic spellings are easy to read. In the following Pronunciation Key, you can see how letters are used to show different sounds.

```
┌─ PRONUNCIATION KEY ──────────────────────────────────────────────────────────┐
│ a     after    (AF tur)        ye   lie    (lye)        ch   chicken  (CHIHK un)   │
│ ah    father   (FAH thur)      oh   flow   (floh)       g    game     (gaym)       │
│ ai    care     (kair)          oi   boy    (boi)        ing  coming   (KUM ing)    │
│ aw    dog      (dawg)          oo   rule   (rool)       j    job      (jahb)       │
│ ay    paper    (PAY pur)       or   horse  (hors)       k    came     (kaym)       │
│                                                          ng   long     (lawng)      │
│ e     letter   (LET ur)        ou   cow    (kou)        s    city     (SIH tee)    │
│ ee    eat      (eet)           yoo  few    (fyoo)       sh   ship     (shihp)      │
│                                u    taken  (TAY kun)    th   thin     (thihn)      │
│                                     matter (MAT ur)     thh  feather  (FETHH ur)   │
│ ih    trip     (trihp)         uh   ago    (uh GOH)     y    yard     (yahrd)      │
│ eye   idea     (eye DEE uh)                             z    size     (syz)        │
│ y     hide     (hyd)                                    zh   division (duh VIHZH un)│
└──────────────────────────────────────────────────────────────────────────────┘
```

A

Adirondack Mountains (ad uh RAHN dak MOUNT-unz). Mountains in northeastern corner of New York. Highest peak is Mount Marcy, with an elevation of 5,344 ft (1,629 m). p. 621.

Africa (AF rih kuh). The earth's second largest continent. p. 626.

Albany (AWL buh nee). Capital of New York. Located on the Hudson River. (43°N/74°W) p. 51.

Albuquerque (AL buh kur kee). Most populated city in New Mexico. Located on the Rio Grande. (35°N/107°W) p. 620.

Allegheny Mountains (al uh GAY nee MOUNT-unz). Part of Appalachian Mountain system in Pennsylvania, Maryland, Virginia, and West Virginia. p. 216.

Annapolis (uh NAP uh lihs). Capital of Maryland. Located on Chesapeake Bay. Site of the United States Naval Academy. (39°N/77°W) p. 192.

Antarctica (ant AHRK tih kuh). The earth's third smallest continent. pp. 618–619.

Antietam (an TEET um). Site of a Maryland battle fought as a result of General Lee's first invasion of the North. His army retreated south following this battle. (39°N/78°W) p. 446.

Appalachian Mountains (ap uh LAY chun MOUNT unz). Chain of mountains stretching from Canada to Alabama. Highest peak is Mount Mitchell, at 6,684 ft (2,037 m). p. 41.

Appomattox (ap uh MAT uks). Site in Virginia where General Lee surrendered his army to General Grant. (37°N/79°W) p. 452.

Arkansas River (AHR kun saw RIHV ur). Rises in central Colorado and flows into the Mississippi River in southeastern Arkansas. p. 40.

Asia (AY zhuh).   The earth's largest continent. p. 119.

Athens (ATH unz).   City-state in ancient Greece. Today the capital of and largest city in modern Greece. (38°N/24°E)   p. 524.

Atlanta (at LAN tuh).   Capital of and most populated city in Georgia. (34°N/84°W)   p. 67.

Atlantic Coastal Plain (at LAN tihk KOHS tul playn).   Large plain located along the Atlantic coast from Maine to Florida.   p. 41.

Atlantic Ocean (at LAN tihk OH shun).   Large body of water separating North America and South America from Europe and Africa.   p. 41.

Augusta (aw GUS tuh).   Capital of Maine. Located on the Kennebec River. (44°N/70°W) p. 620.

Austin (AWS tun).   Capital of Texas. Located near the western edge of the Gulf Coastal Plain. (30°N/98°W)   p. 620.

B

Baltimore (BAWL tuh mor).   The most populated city in Maryland. Located on Chesapeake Bay. One of the nation's busiest seaports. (39°N/77°W)   p. 620.

Baton Rouge (BAT un roozh).   Capital of Louisiana. Located on the Mississippi River. (30°N/91°W)   p. 620.

Beijing (BAY jing).   Capital of the country of China. (40°N/116°E)   p. 116.

Bering Sea (BER ing see).   Part of the North Pacific Ocean, bounded on the east by the mainland of Alaska and on the south and southeast by the Aleutian Islands.   p. 95.

Bering Strait (BER ing strayt).   Narrow body of water connecting the Arctic Ocean and the Bering Sea. Separates Asia from North America. p. 95.

Berkshires (BURK shihrz).   Low mountains or hills in Massachusetts. They are part of the Appalachian Mountain system. Highest peak is Mount Greylock, with an elevation of 3,491 ft (1,064 m).   p. 177.

Birmingham (BUR ming ham).   Most populated city in Alabama. One of the nation's leading iron- and steel-producing centers. (34°N/87°W)   p. 620.

Bismarck (BIHZ mahrk).   The capital of North Dakota. Located on the Mississippi River. (47°N/101°W) p. 620.

Black Hills (blak hihlz).   Mountainous area with steep canyons. Located in South Dakota and Wyoming. Harney Peak, South Dakota, the highest peak in the North Central region, is in the Black Hills. Its elevation is 7,242 ft (2,207 m).   p. 621.

Blue Ridge Mountains (bloo rihj MOUNT unz). Eastern part of the Appalachians. They stretch from Pennsylvania to Georgia.   p. 196.

Boise (BOI see).   Capital of and most populated city in Idaho. (44°N/116°W)   p. 620.

Boston (BAWS tun).   Capital of and most populated city in Massachusetts. Located on Massachusetts Bay. (42°N/71°W)   p. 177.

Buffalo (BUF uh loh).   City in New York. Located on Lake Erie and the Niagara River. (43°N/79°W)   p. 67.

Bull Run (bool run).   The first big battle of the Civil War, fought in Manassas, Virginia, and won by the South. (39°N/77°W)   p. 446.

Bunker Hill (BUNG kur hihl).   Hill in Boston where a battle of the American Revolution took place in 1775. (39°N/117°W)   p. 272.

C

Canada (KAN uh duh).   A country in the northern part of North America.   p. 19.

Cape Canaveral (kayp kuh NAV ur ul). National Space Center. Site of launching for space flights. Located on Florida's eastern coast. (28°N/81°W) p. 621.

Caribbean Sea (kar uh BEE un see). Part of the Atlantic Ocean bounded by South America on the south, Central America on the west, and Cuba, Puerto Rico, and other islands on the north and east. p. 129.

Carson City (KAHR sun SIHT ee). Capital of Nevada. Located near Lake Tahoe. (39°N/120°W) p. 620.

Cascade Range (kas KAYD raynj). Mountains that extend from northern California through Oregon and Washington and into Canada. The highest peak is Mount Rainier, at 14,408 ft (4,392 m) p. 40.

Catskill Mountains (KATS kihl MOUNT unz). Part of the Appalachian Mountain system in New York. Highest peak is Slide Mountain, with an elevation of 4,294 ft (1,309). p. 216.

Central America (SEN trul uh MER ih kuh). Made up of Guatemala, El Salvador, Honduras, Nicaragua, Costa Rica, Panama, and Belize. p. 146.

Central Plains (SEN trul playnz). Large plains area in the middle of the United States, between the Appalachian and Rocky mountains. pp. 40–41.

Charleston (CHAHRLS tun). Port city in South Carolina. Founded in 1670. (33°N/80°W) p. 192.

Charleston (CHAHRLS tun). Capital of West Virginia. Located at the point where the Elk and Kanawha rivers join. (38°N/82°W) p. 620.

Charlotte (SHAHR lut). Largest city in North Carolina. (35°N/81°W) p. 67.

Chesapeake Bay (CHES uh peek bay). Inlet of the Atlantic Ocean in Virginia and Maryland. It is about 190 miles (306 km) long. p. 196.

Cheyenne (shye AN). Capital of Wyoming. (41°N/105°W) p. 620.

Chicago (shuh KAH goh). One of eight cities in the United States with a population of more than 1,000,000. Located in Illinois, on the southern tip of Lake Michigan. (42°N/88°W) p. 67.

China (CHYE nuh). Country of Asia. Officially named People's Republic of China. (33°N/105°E) p. 619.

Cincinnati (sihn suh NAT ee). Large city in Ohio. Located on the Ohio River. (39°N/84°W) p. 67.

Cleveland (KLEEV lund). Second most populated city in Ohio. Located on Lake Erie, at the mouth of the Cuyahoga River. (42°N/82°W) p. 67.

Colorado River (kal uh RAD oh RIHV ur). Rises at the Continental Divide in Rocky Mountain National Park in northern Colorado and flows into the Gulf of California in Mexico. A very important source of irrigation water in the southwestern United States. p. 40.

Columbia (kuh LUM bee uh). Capital of South Carolina. Located on the Congaree River. (34°N/81°W) p. 620.

Columbia River (kuh LUM bee uh RIHV ur). Rises in the Rocky Mountains in Canada and flows into the Pacific Ocean along the Washington-Oregon boundary. p. 40.

Columbus (kuh LUM bus). Capital of and most populated city in Ohio. Located on the Scioto River. (40°N/83°W) p. 620.

Concord (KAHN kord). Massachusetts town where the American Patriots met the British Redcoats in a skirmish at the beginning of the American Revolution. (42°N/71°W) p. 272.

Concord (KAHN kord). Capital of New Hampshire. Located on the Merrimack River. (43°N/72°W) p. 620.

Connecticut River (kuh NET uh kut RIHV ur). Longest river in New England. Rises in northern New Hampshire and flows into Long Island Sound at Old Saybrook, Connecticut. p. 177.

Continental Divide (kahn tuh NENT ul duh-VYD). The very high ridges of the Rocky Mountains. The divide separates the rivers that flow east from the rivers that flow west. p. 40.

Cuba (KYOO buh). Island in the West Indies. Discovered by Columbus on his first voyage. (21°N/80°W) p. 123.

Cumberland Gap (KUM bur lund gap). Pass through the Cumberland Plateau in Tennessee. Used by Daniel Boone in his pioneer trips. (36°N/83°W) p. 357.

Cuzco (KOOS koh). City in Peru. Once the capital of the Inca Empire. (14°S/72°W) p. 141.

D

Dallas (DAL us). The second most populated city in Texas. Located on the Trinity River. (33°N/97°W) p. 67.

Death Valley (deth VAL ee). Very low valley located at the northern edge of the Mojave Desert. It is 282 ft (86 m) below sea level. p. 40.

Delaware Bay (DEL uh wer bay). Arm of the Atlantic Ocean between New Jersey and Delaware. p. 156.

Delaware River (DEL uh wer RIHV ur). Rises in the Catskill Mountains in New York. Flows into the Atlantic Ocean at Delaware Bay. p. 216.

Denver (DEN vur). Capital of and most populated city in Colorado. Located at the base of the Rocky Mountains where they join the Great Plains. Has an elevation of 5,280 ft (1,609 m). (40°N/105°W) p. 40.

Des Moines (duh MOIN). Capital of Iowa. Located on the Des Moines River. (42°N/94°W) p. 620.

Detroit (dih TROIT). One of eight cities in the United States with a population of more than 1,000,000. Located on the Detroit River in Michigan, near Lake Erie. (42°N/83°W) p. 67.

Dover (DOH vur). Capital of Delaware. (39°N/75°W) p. 620.

Duluth (duh LOOTH). Port city in Minnesota. Located at the western end of Lake Superior. (47°N/92°W) p. 41.

E

English Channel (ING glihsh CHAN ul). Arm of the Atlantic Ocean, between southern England and northwestern France. It is about 350 mi (560 km) long. p. 524.

Europe (YOOR up). The earth's second smallest continent. p. 580.

F

Fort Bridger (fort BRIHJ ur). Village in southwestern Wyoming. Near the site of the supply post on the Oregon Trail. (41°N/110°W) p. 379.

Fort McHenry (fort muk HEN ree). Fort in Baltimore. It was attacked by British warships during the war of 1812. During the attack, Francis Scott Key wrote the lyrics for "The Star-Spangled Banner." (39°N/77°W) p. 338.

Fort Sumter (fort SUM tur). Fort on the south side of the entrance to the harbor at Charleston, South Carolina. The first shots of the Civil War were fired here in 1861. (33°N/80°W) p. 431.

Frankfort (FRANGK furt). Capital of Kentucky. Located on the Kentucky River. (38°N/85°W) p. 620.

G

Gary (GER ee).   Large industrial city in Indiana. Located on the southern end of Lake Michigan. One of the most important steelmaking centers in the United States. (42°N/87°W)   p. 620.

Genoa (JEN uh wuh).   City in Italy. One of the most important Italian seaports. (44°N/9°E) p. 116.

Gettysburg (GET ihz burg).   Town in Pennsylvania. Site of a battle fought as a result of General Lee's second and last invasion of the North. His invasion was turned back. (40°N/77°W) p. 452.

Grand Banks (grand bangks).   Rich fishing area in the Atlantic Ocean, south of Newfoundland. p. 129.

Grand Canyon (grand KAN yun).   Famous canyon in Arizona formed by the Colorado River. (36°N/113°W)   p. 146.

Great Lakes (grayt layks).   A chain of five large lakes in central North America. Except for Lake Michigan, which is entirely in the United States, the lakes are on the Canada-United States boundary. p. 102.

Great Plains (grayt playnz).   Large plain area located in the western part of the Central Plains. p. 40.

Great Salt Lake (grayt sowlt layk).   Located in the Great Basin. An inland lake with no streams flowing out of it. (41°N/112°W) p. 21.

Greenland (GREEN lund).   Large island off the coast of northeastern North America, belonging to Denmark. Excluding the continent of Australia, it is the largest island in the world. p. 17.

Green Mountains (green MOUNT unz).   Located in Vermont. Part of the Appalachians. Highest point is Mount Mansfield, with an elevation of 4,393 ft (1,339 m). p. 177.

Guam (gwahm).   An island in the western Pacific, belonging to the United States. (13°N/ 145°E) p. 518.

Gulf Coastal Plain (gulf   KOHS tul playn).   Large plain located along the Gulf of Mexico from Florida to Texas. pp. 40–41.

Gulf of Mexico (gulf uv MEKS ih koh).   Body of water surrounded by the United States, Mexico, and Cuba. p. 17.

Gulf of St. Lawrence (gulf uv saynt LAHR-uns).   Deep gulf of the Atlantic Ocean, off the eastern coast of Canada. Receives the St. Lawrence River in the northwest. p. 51.

Guthrie (GUTH ree).   City in central Oklahoma. Capital of the Oklahoma territory and the state 1890–1910. (36°N/97°W)   p. 479.

H

Hanoi (hah NOI).   Capital of the country of Vietnam. (21°N/106°E) p. 601.

Harrisburg (HAR ihs burg).   Capital of Pennsylvania. Located on the Susquehanna River. (40°N/77°W) p. 620.

Hartford (HAHRT furd).   Capital of Connecticut. Located on the Connecticut River (42°N/ 73°W) p. 620.

Havana (huh VAN uh).   Capital of Cuba and the most populated city in the West Indies. (23°N/82°W) p. 585.

Hawaii (huh WAH ee).   A state of the United States, consisting of a group of islands (Hawaiian Islands) in the North Pacific. p. 41.

Helena (HEL ih nuh).   Capital of Montana. (47°N/112°W) p. 620.

Hiroshima (hihr uh SHEE muh).   Industrial city in Japan. On August 6, 1945, the city was destroyed by an atomic bomb. This was the first time an atomic bomb was ever used in warfare. (34°N/132°E) p. 549.

Hispaniola (hihs pun YOH luh). Second largest island in the West Indies, between Cuba and Puerto Rico. p. 123.

Honolulu (hahn uh LOO loo). Capital of and most populated city in Hawaii. Located on the island of Oahu. (21°N/158°W) p. 41.

Houston (HYOOS tun). City near Galveston Bay in Texas. One of the eight cities in the United States that has a population of more than 1,000,000. (30°N/95°W) p. 67.

Hudson River (HUD sun RIHV ur). Rises in the Adirondack Mountains and flows into New York Harbor at New York City. p. 216.

I

Iceland (EYE slund). Island between the North Atlantic and Arctic oceans. A quarter of the land is lowland and is only partly habitable. (65°N/18°W) p. 119.

Imperial Valley (im PIHR ee ul VAL ee). Located in the Sonoran Desert in southeastern California. One of the most productive farm areas in the world. Most of the land is below sea level. p. 40.

India (IHN dee uh). Subcontinent in South Asia. (20°N/80°E). p. 619.

Indianapolis (ihn dee uh NAP uh lihs). Capital of and most populated city in Indiana. (40°N/86°W) p. 620.

Isthmus of Panama (IHS mus uv PAN uh-mah). The link between North America and South America that separates the Atlantic and Pacific oceans. p. 136.

J

Jackson (JAK sun). Capital of Mississippi. Located on the Pearl River. (39°N/90°W) p. 620.

James River (jaymz RIHV ur). River in Virginia that flows into the Chesapeake Bay. p. 156.

Jamestown (JAYMZ toun). First permanent English settlement in America. Founded in 1607 (37°N/77°W) p. 156.

Jefferson City (JEF ur sun SIHT ee). Capital of Missouri. Located on the Missouri River. (39°N/92°W) p. 620.

Juneau (JOO noh). Capital of Alaska. Located on the Alaskan panhandle. (58°N/134°W) p. 620.

K

Kansas City (KAN zus SIHT ee). City in Kansas. Located where the Kansas and Missouri rivers meet. Separated from Kansas City, Missouri, by the state line. (39°N/95°W) p. 67.

Klamath Mountains (KLAM uth MOUNT unz). Mountain range of the Coast Ranges in northwestern California. p. 40.

Knoxville (NAHKS vihl). City in Tennessee. Located on the Tennessee River. (36°N/84°W) p. 620.

L

Lake Erie (layk IHR ee). Located along the border between Canada and the United States. Second smallest of the five Great Lakes. Has coastline in Michigan, Ohio, Pennsylvania, and New York. p. 15.

Lake Huron (layk HYOOR ahn). Located along the boundary between Canada and the United States. Second largest of the five Great Lakes. The United States' portion of the lake is in Michigan. p. 15.

Lansing (LAN sing). Capital of Michigan. Located on the Grand River. (43°N/85°W) p. 620.

Lexington (LEKS ing tun). Massachusetts town where, in April 1775, a group of Minutemen (militia) resisted British troops in the first battle of the American Revolution. (43°N/71°W) p. 272.

Lima (LEE muh). Capital and most populated city in Peru. (12°S/91°W) p. 141.

Lincoln (LING kun). Capital of Nebraska. Located on a tributary of the Platte River. (41°N/97°W) p. 620.

Little Rock (LIHT ul rahk). Capital of Arkansas. Located on the Arkansas River. (35°N/92°W) p. 620.

London (LUN dun). Capital and most populated city in the United Kingdom. Located along the Thames River. (52°N/0°long) p. 524.

Long Island Sound (lawng EYE lund sound). Body of water between the south shore of Connecticut and the north shore of Long Island. p. 177.

Los Angeles (laws AN juh lus). City in southern California, on the Pacific Ocean. One of eight cities in the United States with a population of more than 1,000,000. (34°N/118°W) p. 67.

Louisiana Purchase (loo ee zee AN uh PUR-chus). Area of land west of the Mississippi River to the Rocky Mountains, purchased by the United States from France in 1803. p. 385.

M

Madison (MAD ih sun). Capital of Wisconsin. Located on an isthmus between Lake Monona and Lake Mendota. (43°N/89°W) p. 620.

Manila (muh NIHL uh). Capital of the Philippines. (14°N/121°E) p. 549.

Massachusetts Bay (mas uh CHOO sihts bay). Inlet of the Atlantic Ocean, extending from Cape Ann to Cape Cod. p. 177.

Mediterranean Sea (med ih tuh RAY nee un see). Inland sea enclosed by Europe, Asia, and Africa. p. 524.

Memphis (MEM fihs). Most populated city in Tennessee. One of the 20 most populated cities in the United States. Located along the Mississippi River. (35°N/90°W) p. 620.

Mexico (MEKS ih koh). A country in North America, south of the United States. p. 3.

Mexico City (MEKS ih koh SIHT ee). Capital of Mexico. The most populated city in North America. (19°N/99°W) p. 622.

Milwaukee (mihl WAW kee). Most populated city in Wisconsin. Located on Lake Michigan. (43°N/88°W) p. 68.

Minneapolis (mihn ee AP ul ihs). Most populated city in Minnesota. Located on the Mississippi River. (45°N/93°W) p. 620.

Mississippi River (mihs uh SIHP ee RIHV-ur). Second longest river in the United States. Rises in northern Minnesota and flows into the Gulf of Mexico near New Orleans, Louisiana. p. 41.

Missouri River (mih ZOOR ee RIHV ur). Longest river in the United States. Rises in western Montana and flows into the Mississippi River near St. Louis, Missouri. p. 40.

Mojave Desert (moh HAH vee DEZ urt). A desert in southern California. p. 40.

Montgomery (munt GUM ur ee). Capital of Alabama. Located on the Alabama River. (32°N/86°W) p. 620.

Montpelier (mahnt PEEL yur). Capital of Vermont. Located on the Winooski River. (44°N/73°W) p. 620.

Montreal (mahn tree AWL). Most populated city in Canada. (46°N/74°W) p. 280.

Mount Elbert (mount EL burt). Highest peak in the Rocky Mountains in the United States. Located in Colorado, it has an elevation of 14,433 ft (4,399 m). (39°N/106°W) p. 40.

Mount Mitchell (mount MIHCH ul). Has an elevation of 6,684 ft (2,037 m). Located in North Carolina. Highest peak in the Appalachians. (36°N/82°W) p. 41.

Mount St. Helens (mount saynt HEL unz). Volcanic peak in Washington State. (46°N/122°W) p. 40.

Mount Whitney (mount HWIHT nee). Located in the Sierra Nevada mountain range. Highest peak in the United States outside of Alaska. It has an elevation of 14,495 ft (4,418 m). p. 40.

N

Nagasaki (nah guh SAH kee). Industrial city and seaport in Japan. Located on the island of Kyushu. Was destroyed by an atomic bomb near the end of World War II. (33°N/130°E) p. 549.

Nashville (NASH vihl). Capital of Tennessee. Located on the Cumberland River. (36°N/87°W) p. 620.

New Orleans (noo OR lee unz). Most populated city in Louisiana. Located on the Mississippi River. One of the busiest ports in the United States. (30°N/90°W) p. 41.

New York Bay (noo york bay). Inlet of the Atlantic Ocean at the mouth of the Hudson River. p. 216.

New York (noo york). Most populated city in the United States. Located at the mouth of the Hudson River, in the state of New York. (41°N/74°W) p. 41.

Newark (NOO urk). Most populated city in New Jersey. Located on the Passaic River and Newark Bay. (41°N/74°W) p. 620.

Newfoundland (NOO fund lund). Island in the Atlantic Ocean, off the coast of Canada. (48° N/56°W) p. 119.

Newport (NOO port). City in southeastern Rhode Island, on Narragansett Bay. (41°N/71°W) p. 177.

North America (north uh MER ih kuh). The earth's third largest continent. p. 622.

Northwest Territory (north WEST TER uh toree). Region around the Great Lakes and between the Ohio and Mississippi rivers. p. 296.

O

Oakland (OHK lund). A city in western California, on the eastern side of San Francisco Bay. (37°N/122°W) p. 620.

Ohio River (oh HYE oh RIHV ur). Formed at Pittsburgh, Pennsylvania, by the joining of the Allegheny and Monongahela rivers. Flows into the Mississippi River at Cairo, Illinois. Forms part of the boundaries of five states. p. 41.

Oklahoma City (oh kluh HOH muh SIHT-ee). Capital of Oklahoma. (35°N/98°W) p. 620.

Olympia (oh LIHM pee uh). Capital of Washington. Located on Puget Sound. (47°N/123°W) p. 620.

Omaha (OH muh haw). City in eastern Nebraska, on the Missouri River. (41°N/96°W) p. 620.

P

Pacific Ocean (puh SIHF ihk OH shun). Large body of water stretching from the Arctic Circle to Antarctica and from the western coast of North America to the eastern coast of Asia. pp. 618–619.

Palos (PAH lohs).   The town in southwestern Spain where Columbus started his first voyage to the Americas. (37°N/7°W) p. 123.

Paris (PAR ihs).   Capital and river port of France. (49°N/2°E) p. 524.

Pearl Harbor (purl HAHR bur).   Inlet on the island of Oahu in Hawaii. Site of United States naval base attacked by the Japanese on December 7, 1941. The next day the United States declared war on Japan. (21°N/158°W) p. 549.

Petersburg (PEET urz burg).   A city in southeastern Virginia. (37°N/77°W) p. 452.

Philadelphia (fihl uh DEL fee uh).   City at the point where the Delaware and Schuylkill rivers join. One of eight cities in the United States with a population of more than 1,000,000. (40°N/75°W) p. 67.

Philippine Islands (FIHL uh peen EYE lundz).   A country in the Pacific, north of Indonesia, made up of more than 7,000 islands. p. 549.

Phoenix (FEE nihks).   Capital of and most populated city in Arizona. Located on the Salt River. (33°N/112°W) p. 620.

Piedmont Region (PEED mohnt REE jun).   A stretch of high, hilly land along the western edge of the Atlantic Coastal Plain. p. 41.

Pierre (pihr).   Capital of South Dakota. Located on the Missouri River. (44°N/100°W) p. 620.

Pikes Peak (pyks peek).   Mountain peak in the Rocky Mountains. Has an elevation of 14,110 ft (4,301). (39°N/105°W) p. 332.

Pittsburgh (PIHTS burg).   Second most populated city in Pennsylvania. Located at the point where the Allegheny and Monongahela rivers join. (40°N/80°W) p. 620.

Platte River (plat RIHV ur).   Located in Nebraska. Flows into the Missouri River. p. 621.

Plymouth (PLIHM uth).   Town in Massachusetts. Site of the first permanent European settlement in New England. (42°N/71°W) p. 156.

Portland (PORT lund).   Most populated city in Oregon. Located on the Willamette River. (46°N/123°W) p. 620.

Princeton (PRIHNS tun).   City located in central New Jersey near Trenton. (40°N/75°W) p. 280.

Promontory Point (PRAHM un tor ee point).   Place near Ogden, Utah, where tracks for the Central Pacific Railroad and Union Pacific Railroad were joined in 1869. (41°N/112°W) p. 479.

Providence (PRAHV uh duns).   Capital of Rhode Island. Located at the head of the Providence River. (42°N/71°W) p. 67.

Puerto Rico (PWER tuh REE koh).   Self-governing commonwealth in union with the United States. An island of the West Indies. (18°N/67°W) p. 17.

Q

Quebec (kwee BEK).   City in Canada on the north side of the St. Lawrence River. It was founded in 1608 by Samuel de Champlain. Today it is the capital of the province of Quebec. (47°N/71°W) p. 166.

R

Raleigh (RAWL ee).   Capital of North Carolina. (36°N/79°W) p. 620.

Red River (red RIHV ur).   Rises in New Mexico. Flows across the Texas Panhandle and then forms part of the boundary between Texas and Oklahoma. p. 40.

Reno (REE noh).   Second most populated city in Nevada. Located on Truckee River near Lake Tahoe. (40°N/120°W)   p. 620.

Richmond (RIHCH mund).   Capital of Virginia. Located on the James River. (38°N/77°W) p. 359.

Rio Grande (REE oh grand).   Rises in the Rocky Mountains in Colorado. It empties into the Gulf of Mexico near Brownsville, Texas. It forms the boundary between Texas and Mexico.   p. 40.

Roanoke Island (ROH uh nohk EYE lund).   Island off North Carolina. Site of first English settlement in North America. (36°N/76°W) p. 156.

Rocky Mountains (RAHK ee   MOUNT unz).   In North America, stretches from Alaska to Mexico. Longest mountain chain in the United States. Highest peak is Mount Elbert, with an elevation of 14,433 ft (4,399 m).   p. 621.

Rome (rohm).   Capital of and most populated city in Italy. Located on the Tiber River. (42°N/13°E)   p. 524

S

Sacramento (sak ruh MEN toh).   Capital of California. Located on the Sacramento River. (38°N/121°W)   p. 70.

St. Augustine (saynt   AW gus teen).   City in Florida. Founded in 1565 by explorers from Spain. Oldest city in the United States. (30°N/81°W)   p. 146.

St. Lawrence River (saynt   LAHR uns RIHV-ur).   Forms part of the boundary between Canada and the United States. Flows northeast from Lake Ontario to the Atlantic Ocean at the Gulf of St. Lawrence. p. 51.

St. Louis (saynt   LOO ihs).   Most populated city in Missouri. Located on the Mississippi River near the point where it is joined by the Missouri River. (39°N/90°W) p. 41.

St. Paul (saynt pawl).   Capital of Minnesota. Located on the Mississippi River. (45°N/93°W) p. 620.

Salem (SAY lum).   Capital of Oregon. Located on the Willamette River. (45°N/123°W) p. 620.

Salt Lake City (sawlt layk SIHT ee).   Capital of and most populated city in Utah. Located near the Great Salt Lake. (41°N/112°W) p. 620.

San Antonio (san un TOH nee oh).   Large city in Texas. Located on the San Antonio River. Site of the Alamo. (30°N/98°W) p. 68.

San Diego (san dee AY goh).   First of 21 Spanish missions was built here. Today it is a large city located in southern California along the Pacific Ocean. (33°N/117°W) p. 67.

San Francisco (san frun SIHS koh). Fourth most populated city in California. (38°N/122°W) p. 67.

San Jacinto River (san juh SIHN toh RIHV-ur).   River in southeastern Texas, flowing into Galveston Bay. p. 379.

San Jose (san hoh ZAY).   California city. One of the nation's 20 largest cities. (37°N/122°W) p. 70.

San Juan (san wahn).   Capital of and most populated city in Puerto Rico. (18°N/66°W) p. 618.

San Salvador (san SAL vuh dor).   One of a group of islands called the Bahamas. Columbus landed on this island in 1492. (24°N/74°W) p. 141.

Santa Fe (SAN tuh fay).   Spanish settlement started in 1609. Today the capital of New Mexico. (36°N/106°W) p. 620.

Saratoga (sar uh TOH guh).   Revolutionary War battle site. Located in the present-day city of Schuylerville, New York. (43°N/74°W) p. 280.

Savannah (suh VAN uh).   City in Georgia. Georgia colony was founded here in 1733 by a group led by James Oglethorpe. (32°N/81°W) p. 192.

Savannah River (suh VAN uh RIHV ur).   Navigable river in eastern Georgia that is formed by the flowing together of the Tugallo and Seneca rivers. p. 196.

Seattle (see AT al).   Most populated city in Washington. Located on the eastern shore of Puget Sound. (48°N/122°W)   p. 40.

Seoul (sohl).   Capital of South Korea. Located on the Han River. One of the world's most populated cities. (37°N/127°E)   p. 583.

Sicily (SIHS ul ee).   Largest island in the Mediterranean Sea. Part of Italy. p. 502.

Sierra Nevada (see ER uh nuh VAD uh).   High mountain range located mostly in eastern California. Mount Whitney is located in this range. p. 40.

Snake River (snayk RIHV ur).   Rises in Yellowstone National Park in Wyoming. Flows into the Columbia River in Washington. p. 40.

South America (south uh MER ih kuh).   The earth's fourth largest continent. p. 623.

Soviet Union (SOH vee et YOON yun).   A country that was made up of 15 republics in eastern Europe and northern Asia, including Russia. A shorter name for the Union of Soviet Socialist Republics. p. 619.

Springfield (SPRIHNG feeld).   Capital of Illinois. Located on the Sangamon River. (40°N/90°W)   p. 620.

Strait of Magellan (strayt uv muh JEL un).   The winding strait near the southern end of South America, between the mainland and Tierra del Fuego. It connects the Atlantic and Pacific oceans. p. 129.

T

Tallahassee (tal uh HAS ee).   Capital of Florida. Located in northern Florida. (30°N/84°W) p. 620.

Tampa (TAM puh).   City in west central Florida on the northeast end of Tampa Bay. (28°N/82°W) p. 146.

Tenochtitlán (te nawch tee TLAHN).   Ancient name of Mexico City. Once the capital of the Aztec Empire. p. 106.

Tidewater Region (TYD wawt ur REE jun).   The lowest, flattest part of the Atlantic Coastal Plain. It is the land around Chesapeake Bay in Virginia. p. 196.

Tokyo (TOH kee oh).   Capital city of Japan. (36°N/140°E). p. 549.

Topeka (tuh PEE kuh).   Capital of Kansas. Located on the Kansas River. (39°N/96°W) p. 620.

Trenton (TRENT un).   Capital of New Jersey. Located on the Delaware River. (40°N/75°W) p. 620.

V

Valley Forge (VAL ee forj).   Village in southeastern Pennsylvania. Winter headquarters of Washington and his army from 1777 to 1778. (40°N/75°W) p. 280.

Vandalia (van DAYL yuh).   A city in south central Illinois. (39°N/89°W) p. 357.

Vicksburg (VIHKS burg).   Civil War battle site on the Mississippi River. Grant's victory here split the South in two. (32°N/91°W) p. 445.

Vietnam (vee et NAHM).   Country in southeastern Asia. North Vietnam and South Vietnam were united under one government in 1975. p. 601.

Vincennes (vihn SENZ).   City in southwestern Indiana on Wabash River. (38°N/88°W)   p. 286.

Vinland (VYN lund).   A portion of the North American coast visited by voyagers around A.D. 1000. (43°N/79°W)   p. 119.

W

Washington, D.C. (WAWSH ing tun dee see).   Capital of the United States. Located on the Potomac River. (39°N/77°W)   p. 10.

West Indies (west IHN deez).   Group of islands stretching about 2,500 mi (4,023 km) from near Florida to near Venezuela.   p. 17.

West Point (west point).   Military post in New York State on the Hudson River. (41°N/ 74°W)   p. 280.

Wheeling (HWEEL ing).   City in northwestern West Virginia. (40°N/81°W)   p. 357.

White Mountains (hwyt MOUNT unz).   Part of the Appalachian Mountain system. Located in New Hampshire. Highest peak is Mount Washington, with an elevation of 6,288 ft (1,917 m)   p. 177.

Y

Yorktown (YORK toun). The Americans won a decisive victory over the British here during the American Revolution. Following this loss the British were ready to make peace. (37°N/ 77°W)   p. 286.

The page references tell where each
entry first appears in the text.

A

abolitionist (ab uh LIHSH un ihst). A person opposed to slavery and in favor of ending it before the Civil War. p. 364.

Allied Powers (AL eyed POU urz). The name given to Great Britain, France, and Russia during World War I. p. 523.

Allies (AL eyez). The name given to those countries supported by and later joined by the United States in World War I and World War II. *See* Allied Powers. p. 546.

ally (AL ly). A person or state united with another for a special purpose. p. 252.

amendment (uh MEND munt). A formal correction or change. p. 301.

ancestor (AN ses tur). A family member who lived long ago. p. 141.

apprentice (uh PREN tihs). A person learning a trade or craft from a master craftsperson. p. 222.

archaeologist (ahr kee AHL uh jihst). A scientist who studies objects, ruins, and other evidence of human life in the past. p. 97.

armistice (AHR muh stihs). A halt to fighting by agreement between the warring nations. p. 527.

artifact (AHRT uh fakt). An object left by people who lived long ago. p. 97.

assembly (uh SEM blee). A law-making body. p. 159.

assembly line (uh SEM blee lyn). A process in which each worker in a factory performs a different step or job in putting together the work as it is passed along, often on a slowly moving belt. p. 531.

Axis Powers (AK sihs POU urz). The name given to the countries that fought against the Allies in World War II. p. 543.

B

baby boom (BAY bee boom). A name that refers to the period after the Second World War from 1946 to 1957 when many young people got married and started families. p. 563.

back country (bak KUN tree). The area above the Fall Line, in the Piedmont Region. p. 206.

barbed wire (bahrbd wyr). A type of wire that has barbs, or sharp points, every few inches. p. 483.

barter (BAHRT ur). The trading of goods. p. 412.

bay (bay). A part of a lake or ocean, indenting the land. p. 156.

Bear Flag Republic (bair flag rih PUB lihk). The name given to the government of California after the Americans living in California overthrew Mexican rule. p. 385.

Bill of Rights (bihl uv ryts). The first ten amendments to the Constitution. p. 310.

Black Codes (blak kohdz). Southern laws passed after the Civil War, aimed at limiting the rights and opportunities of African Americans. Such laws restricted African Americans from voting, holding political office, having a good job, and getting a good education. p. 456.

blockade (blah KAYD). To block, or stop, a particular group from moving goods or people. During the Civil War, the North used its navy to *blockade* ports in the South. p. 444.

blubber (BLUB ur). The fat of whales, from which an oil is obtained. p. 180.

border (BOR dur). A dividing line, or boundary. p. 373.

border states (BOR dur stayts). The states located between the North and the South that stayed in the Union during the Civil War. These states were Missouri, Kentucky, Maryland, and Delaware. p. 446.

Boston Massacre (BAWS tun MAS uh kur). An outbreak of fighting between the colonists and British soldiers in 1770, in which five colonists died. p. 259.

Boston Tea Party (BAWS tun tee PAHR tee). Colonists boarded British ships in 1773 and threw chests of tea into the water to protest the Tea Act. p. 260.

boycott (BOI kaht). An organized campaign in which people refuse to have any dealings with a particular group or business. p. 256.

C

Cabinet (KAB uh niht). A group of advisers to the President of the United States. p. 311.

canal (kuh NAL). A waterway made by people. *Canals* are dug to connect bodies of water and to drain swampy lands. p. 50.

canyon (KAN yun). A very deep valley with steep sides. p. 55.

capitalist (KAP ut ul ihst). Describes an economic system that supports the ownership of industries and land by private individuals or businesses. p. 578.

cardinal direction (KAHRD un ul duh REK shun). One of the four main directions known as north, south, east, and west. p. 8.

carpetbagger (KAHR put bag ur). The name given to a Northern white who moved to the South after the Civil War. p. 458.

cartogram (KAHR tuh gram). A map that changes the size of states or countries so that they represent something other than the true land area. p. 70.

cartographer (kahr TAHG ruh fur). A person who makes maps. p. 4.

cash crop (kash krahp). A crop that is sold for money. p. 199.

causeway (KAWZ way). A bridge made by building up earth in narrow strips until it is above water. p. 107.

census (SEN sus). A government count of the number of people in a country. p. 73.

Centennial Exposition (sen TEN ee ul eks puh ZISH un). A show of many exhibits held in Philadelphia, in 1876, that celebrated the 100th birthday of the United States. p. 491.

Central Powers (SEN trul POU urz). The name given to Germany, Austria-Hungary, and the Ottoman Empire (Turkey) during World War I. p. 523.

civil rights (SIHV ul ryts). Personal freedoms of citizens. p. 586.

civil war (SIHV ul wor). Armed fighting between two groups within the same country. p. 432.

climate (KLYE mut). The pattern of weather that a place has over a period of years. Temperature and precipitation are two important parts of *climate*. p. 20.

coastal plain (KOHS tul playn). A wide area of flat or gently rolling land that is bordered by a large area of water. p. 42.

cold war (kohld wor). A struggle fought with words, money, and political power. p. 581.

colony (KAHL uh nee). A place that is settled at a distance from the country that governs it. p. 148.

commerce (KAHM urs). Trade carried on between cities, states, or countries. p. 299.

Committee of Correspondence (kuh MIHT ee uv kor uh SPAHN duns). A colonial group that maintained contact with and sent news to other towns through letters. p. 259.

common (KAHM un). The name given to the land in the center of most colonial New England towns. p. 184.

communication (kuh myoo nih KAY shun). The exchanging of information or messages. p. 240.

communism (KAHM yoo nihz um). The common ownership of land and industries by people as a group. p. 526.

Communist (KAHM yoo nihst). Describes an economic system that supports the common ownership of industries and land by people as a group. p. 578.

compass rose (KUM pus rohz). A small drawing on a map, used to show directions. p. 9.

compromise (KAHM pruh myz). A settling of a dispute in which each side gives up part of what it wants so that an agreement can be reached. p. 300.

concentration camp (kahn sun TRAY shun kamp). A prison camp for holding people who are thought to be dangerous to the ruling group. p. 543.

Confederate States of America (kun FED ur iht stayts uv uh MER ih kuh). The nation formed by the states that seceded from the Union. p. 432.

Congress (KAHNG grus). The branch of government that makes laws; also known as the legislature. p. 295.

Congressional Medal of Honor (kun GRESH uh nul MED ul uv AHN ur). The highest award for acts of bravery given by the United States. p. 451.

conquistador (kahn KWIHS tuh dor). A Spanish conqueror. p. 135.

conservation (kahn sur VAY shun). The management of natural resources in such a way as to prevent their waste or complete destruction. p. 514.

conserve (kun SURV). To use wisely; to keep from being wasted. p. 81.

constitution (kahn stuh TOO shun). A set of laws by which a country is governed. p. 294.

Continental Divide (kahn tuh NENT ul duh VYD). High ridges dividing rivers or streams that flow to opposite sides of a continent. In the United States the *Continental Divide* is in the Rockies. p. 55.

contour line (KAHN toor lyn). Any of the lines that are used to show elevation on a physical map. p. 18.

convention (kun VEN shun). A meeting. p. 298.

cotton gin (KAHT un jihn). A machine used to separate cotton from its seeds. p. 346.

county seat (KOUNT ee seet). The seat of government of a county, or the main town of a county. p. 203.

credit (KRED iht). An agreement to pay back a debt in a certain amount of time. p. 412.

culture (KUL chur). The way of life of a group of people, including their customs, traditions, and values. p. 164.

custom (KUS tum). A long-established way of doing things. p. 243.

D

debtor (DET ur). A person who owes money. p. 194.

Declaration of Independence (dek luh RAY shun uv ihn dee PEN duns). The document that stated the reasons for the desire of the American colonies to be independent of British control. p. 275.

defensive war (dee FEN sihv wor). A war in which an army fights to defend its own territory. During the Civil War, the South fought to defend its own territory, not to take Northern territory. p. 439.

delegate (DEL uh gut). A representative. p. 256.

democratic spirit (dem uh KRAT ihk SPIHR iht). A feeling that people are able to, and should have the power to, govern themselves. p. 351.

depression (dee PRESH un). An economic condition in which business is very bad and large numbers of people are unemployed. p. 507.

desert (DEZ urt). A very dry place, with little rainfall and few plants. p. 103.

dictator (DIHK tayt ur). One who has absolute power of rule in a country. p. 542.

discrimination (dih skrihm ih NAY shun). The unequal and unfair treatment of a person or a group. p. 534.

division of labor (duh VIHZH un uv LAY bur). A system in which each worker specializes in a particular job or a step in a job. p. 409.

drought (drout). A long period of extremely dry weather. p. 53.

dry farming (drye FAHRM ing). Farming techniques, used in areas of little rainfall and no irrigation, that are designed to keep moisture in the soil. p. 483.

Dust Bowl (dust bohl). The area in the Great Plains in which soil erosion, caused by poor farming methods and a long period of little rainfall, resulted in severe dust storms. p. 538.

E

earthquake (URTH kwayk). A shaking or trembling of the earth, often leaving cracks in the earth's surface, that is caused by the shifting of layers of the earth far beneath the surface. p. 57.

elevation (el uh VAY shun). The height of something. The *elevation* of land is its distance above or below sea level, usually measured in feet or meters. p. 18.

Emancipation Proclamation (ee man suh PAY shun prahk luh MAY shun). An order that freed the slaves in all the states that had left the Union. p. 447.

embargo (em BAHR goh). Any government order that stops or hinders trade. p. 337.

empire (EM pyr). The territories and peoples under the control of a powerful leader or group. p. 106.

environment (en VYE run munt). The land, air, water, plants, animals — everything that affects the way people live. p. 100.

epidemic (ep uh DEM ihk). The spread of disease to a large number of people in a short period of time. p. 143.

equality (ee KWAHL uh tee). The condition of being equal, especially of having the same political, social, and economic rights and duties. p. 352.

Equator (ee KWAYT ur). An imaginary line of latitude that circles the earth, exactly halfway between the North Pole and the South Pole. p. 13.

escalation (es kuh LAY shun). The act of expanding or increasing in intensity. p. 602.

executive branch (eg ZEK yoo tihv branch). The part of the government responsible for carrying out the laws that Congress passes. The President is its head. p. 299.

expedition (eks puh DIHSH un). A journey undertaken for a specific purpose, such as exploration. p. 333.

explore (ek SPLOR). To search for new things or places. p. 113.

F

fall line (fawl lyn). An imaginary line that marks the point where waterfalls on the rivers flow to the coast. p. 45.

famine (FAM ihn). A time when there is not enough food for everyone. p. 405.

federal system (FED ur ul SIHS tum). A form of government in which the powers are divided between a national government and the state governments. p. 299.

feminist (FEM uh nihst). A man or a woman who works for equal rights for women. p. 592.

fertile (FURT ul). Able to produce a large amount of crops. p. 58.

First Continental Congress (furst kahn tuh-NENT ul KAHNG grus). The first meeting of a group of representatives from the colonies. p. 262.

flatboat (FLAT boht). A boat with a flat bottom; it can travel through shallow places in a river. p. 329.

forty-niner (FORT ee NYN ur). A person who went to California in 1849 to get rich. Most went to mine for gold. p. 389.

free enterprise (free ENT ur pryz). A system in which people are free to start any enterprise, or business, they wish. p. 578.

Free State (free stayt). A state, before the Civil War, in which slavery was not permitted. p. 421.

frontier (frun TIHR). The newly settled area that separates the older, more populated, and more "civilized" settlements from the wilderness. p. 235.

fugitive (FYOO jih tihv). Someone who has escaped and is being searched for. p. 424.

Fundamental Orders of Connecticut (fun duh-MENT ul OR durz uv kuh NET uh kut). A set of rules for government drawn up by several groups of colonists who left Massachusetts Bay to settle along the Connecticut River. p. 175.

G

Gadsden Purchase (GADZ dun PUR chus). A piece of land bought by the United States in 1853 from Mexico. The land makes up the southern parts of Arizona and New Mexico today. p. 388.

gasohol (GAS uh hawl). A fuel that is a mixture of gasoline and alcohol. Gasohol is cheaper and less polluting than gasoline. The alcohol in gasohol is made from corn. p. 81.

generator (JEN ur ayt ur). A machine that makes electric power. p. 493.

Gettysburg Address (GET ihz burg uh DRES). A memorial speech made by President Lincoln to honor the soldiers who had died in the battle of Gettysburg. p. 448.

ghetto (GET oh). A neighborhood where people of similar ethnic, racial, or religious backgrounds live. p. 503.

ghost town (gohst toun). A deserted town. p. 472.

goods (goodz). Things that are made or owned that can be sold. p. 82.

grammar school (GRAM ur skool). Name given to secondary school in colonial New England. p. 186.

Great Depression (grayt dee PRESH un). A long period of hard times in the United States, beginning in 1929, during which there was less business activity and many people lost their jobs. p. 536.

grid system (grihd SIHS tum). A network of lines that form a crisscross pattern. p. 9.

growing season (GROH ing SEE zun). The time of year when a crop can be grown. p. 217.

guerrilla warfare (guh RIHL uh WOR fair). A kind of hit-and-run fighting. p. 285.

gulf (gulf). A part of an ocean or a sea that pushes inland. p. 131.

H

harbor (HAHR bur). A protected body of water that is safe for ships and other vessels. p. 42.

hemisphere (HEM ih sfihr). Half of a sphere, or ball. Half of the earth. p. 13.

Hessian (HESH un). A German soldier hired to fight for the British in the Revolutionary War. p. 281.

Hispanic (hih SPAN ihk). A Spanish-speaking person. p. 590.

Holocaust (HAHL uh kawst). The destruction of millions of Jews by the Nazis. p. 548.

homesteader (HOHM sted ur). A person who received land under the Homestead Act of 1862. p. 482.

hostage (HAHS tihj). A person held against his or her will by an individual or group in an attempt to have certain demands met. p. 604.

hot line • *leisure*

hot line (haht lyn). A direct telephone line to be used in times of crisis. It connects the President of the United States and the leader of Russia (originally, the Soviet leader). p. 585.

House of Burgesses (hous uv BUR jihs ez). The representative assembly in colonial Virginia. p. 159.

Huguenot (HYOO guh naht). A French Protestant. p. 193.

I

immigrant (IHM uh grunt). A person from one country who comes into another country to live there. p. 235.

impeach (ihm PEECH). To charge a public official with having done something illegal while in office. p. 457.

impressment (ihm PRES munt). The practice of seizing and forcing people to serve in a navy or an army. p. 336.

inaugural address (ihn AW gyoo rul uh DRES). The speech made at the start of a term of office. p. 432.

inauguration (ihn aw gyoo RAY shun). A ceremony to put someone in office. p. 310.

indentured servant (ihn DEN churd SUR vunt). A person who sold his or her services for a certain period of time in exchange for free passage to a foreign land. p. 200.

indigo (IHN dih goh). A plant from which blue dye is made. p. 199.

Industrial Revolution (ihn DUS tree ul rev uh-LOO shun). The period of great change in the way people worked and lived, brought about by the invention of power-driven machines. p. 341.

interchangeable parts (ihn tur CHAYN juh bul pahrts). Identical parts that can be used in place of each other in making a product. p. 347.

intermontane (ihn tur MAHN tayn). Having to do with a land or region that lies between mountain ranges. p. 55.

Interstate Highway System (IHN tur stayt HYE-way SIHS tum). A system of superhighways that crisscross our country. p. 597.

Intolerable Acts (ihn TAHL ur uh bul akts). The name given by colonists to the laws passed by the Parliament to punish the people of Boston and the whole Massachusetts colony. p. 261.

invention (ihn VEN shun). Something made through study and experiment. p. 403.

irrigate (IHR uh gayt). To bring water to land from rivers, streams, and wells by the use of canals, ditches, pipes, or sprinklers. p. 59.

isthmus (IHS mus). A narrow strip of land joining two larger bodies of land and having water on both sides. p. 128

J

joint-stock company (JOINT stahk KUM puh-nee.) A company in which the people give money to share costs. Each person who gives money becomes a part owner of the company. p. 155.

judicial branch (joo DIHSH ul branch). The part of the government that is in charge of deciding the meaning of laws. It is made up of the Supreme Court and other federal courts. p. 299.

jury (JOOR ee). A group of people who decide whether a person is guilty or innocent after they have heard the facts of the case. p. 247.

K

key (kee). A device on a map used to tell what real things or places the symbols on the map stand for. p. 4.

L

labor union (LAY bur YOON yun). An organization of workers that tries to help its members get higher wages and better working conditions. p. 506.

landform (LAND form). A feature of the earth's surface created by nature. p. 17.

landlocked (LAND lahkt). Not having a seacoast; surrounded by land. p. 50.

latitude (LAT uh tood). Distance north and south, measured in degrees, from the Equator to the earth's poles. Lines of *latitude* are imaginary lines used to locate places on the earth. p. 12.

legislative branch (LEJ ihs layt ihv branch). The part or branch of the central government that makes the laws. p. 299.

legislature (LEJ ihs lay chur). Congress, or the branch of the central government that makes laws. p. 294.

leisure (LEE zhur). Free time, not taken up with work or duty, that a person may use for rest or play. p. 568.

literacy test (LIHT ur uh see test). A reading test used in the past in many southern states in an attempt to keep African Americans from voting. p. 571.

locomotive (loh kuh MOHT ihv). A steam, electric, or diesel engine on wheels that pulls or pushes railroad trains. p. 361.

lode (lohd). A rich deposit of ore. p. 471.

Lone Star Republic (lohn stahr rih PUB lihk). Another name for the Republic of Texas, symbolized by a flag with a single large star. p. 375.

long drive (lawng dryv). The movement of cattle for a long distance. p. 478.

long house (lawng hous). A large house built by Indians in which eight or ten families lived. p. 100.

longitude (LAHN juh tood). Distance, measured in degrees, east and west of the Prime Meridian. Lines of *longitude* are used to locate places on the earth. p. 12.

Loyalist (LOI ul ihst). A colonist who was a supporter of Great Britain and King George III. p. 276.

M

mammoth (MAM uth). A large, hairy elephant that lived a long time ago. p. 96.

Mayflower Compact (MAY flou ur KAHM pakt). A document signed by the Pilgrims by which they agreed to make laws as needed for the colony's good and to obey those laws. p. 162

meetinghouse (MEET ing hous). The most important building in a New England village: the place of worship. Meetinghouses were also used for public meetings. p. 184.

megalopolis (meg uh LAHP uh lihs). A group of cities so close to one another that they seem to form a continuous urban area. p. 67.

mercenary (MUR suh ner ee). A person hired to be a soldier. p. 276.

merchant (MUR chunt). A person who buys and sells goods. p. 116.

metropolitan area (me troh PAHL ih tun ER ee uh). An area made up of a large city or several large cities and the surrounding towns, cities, and other communities. p. 67.

Mexican Cession (MEKS ih kun SESH un). The area of land gained by the United States as a result of the Mexican War. p. 388.

migrant worker (MYE grunt WURK ur). A worker who travels from one place to another to harvest crops. p. 570.

migration (mye GRAY shun). Movement from one place to another. p. 96.

militia (muh LIHSH uh). Citizens who volunteer to be part-time soldiers. p. 263.

mill (mihl). A building with machinery for grinding grain into flour. p. 219.

Minutemen (MIHN iht men). An army of citizens, at the time of the Revolutionary War, who claimed to be ready to fight the British at "a minute's notice." p. 264.

mission (MIHSH un). A settlement of religious teachers. It consists of a church and other buildings. p. 149.

missionary (MIHSH un er ee). A person sent to teach a religion to people of a different faith and to provide them with any help they might need. p. 149.

monopoly (muh NAHP uh lee). Sole control of an entire industry. p. 515.

Mountain Men (MOUNT un men). Fur trappers who played an important part in the expansion of the United States in the 1800s. p. 376.

mountain range (MOUNT un raynj). A row or series of mountains closely related in direction or position. p. 176.

N

natural resources (NACH ur ul REE sor sez). Things that are provided by nature and are useful to people. p. 22.

naval stores (NAY vul storz). Supplies made from pine trees, such as ships' masts, tar, and turpentine. p. 180.

navigation (nav uh GAY shun). The science of getting ships from place to place. p. 117.

Nazi (NAHT see). A member of a political party that rose to power in Germany under Adolph Hitler in the 1930s. p. 542.

neutral (NOO trul). Standing apart in an argument or fight and not taking sides. p. 336.

New Deal (noo deel). A term used to describe policies put forward by President Franklin Roosevelt to fight the Great Depression. In the *New Deal*, the government created jobs and granted other types of aid to people. p. 539.

nomination (nahm uh NAY shun). The naming of a person to be a candidate for office. p. 606.

nonviolent (nahn VYE uh lunt). Peaceful. p. 589.

North Pole (north pohl). The most northern place on the earth. The *North Pole* is located in the Arctic Ocean. p. 8.

Northwest Ordinance (north WEST ORD un uns). A plan for forming new states from the Northwest Territory. It was later used for turning other territories into states. p. 296.

Northwest Passage (north WEST PAS ihj). An all-water route sought by early explorers that would provide a shortcut from Europe to Asia and the East Indies via North America. p. 130.

O

occupation (ahk yoo PAY shun). A job, or kind of work. p. 82.

omnibus (AHM nih bus). A boxlike wooden car with seats that was pulled by horses and used to carry people from place to place in the city, during the 1850s. p. 406.

open range (OH pun raynj). A vast area of grassland with no fences. p. 481.

Oregon Country (OR ih gun KUN tree). A term that was used during the 1830s and 1840s to refer to the area between the Rocky Mountains and the Pacific Ocean. It included the present-day states of Oregon, Washington, Idaho, and parts of Montana and Wyoming, as well as a large piece of western Canada. p. 376.

Oregon Trail (OR ih gun trayl). The route from Missouri to Oregon used by settlers moving to the northwest in the 1800s. p. 378.

P

Parliament (PAHR luh munt). The lawmaking body of England. Also, the lawmaking body of Canada. p. 245.

pass (pas). A narrow valley between mountains. p. 328.

Patriot (PAY tree ut). In the struggle against the British, a person who fought for the independence of the American colonies. p. 256.

Peace Corps (pees kor). A program started by President John F. Kennedy to help people in the developing world. p. 598.

peninsula (puh NIHN suh luh). A piece of land extending into the water from a larger body of land. p. 135.

petroleum (puh TROH lee um). A natural resource that is in the form of an oily liquid and that is found in the earth in certain layers of rock. p. 43.

physical map (FIHZ ih kul map). A map that shows the kinds of landforms on the earth by showing differences in elevation. p. 17.

Piedmont (PEED mahnt). The name given to the stretch of foothills, or high, hilly land between the Atlantic Coastal Plain and the Appalachian Mountains. The word *piedmont* means "foot of the mountain." p. 45.

Pilgrim (PIHL grum). A person who travels for religious reasons. p. 162.

pioneer (pye uh NIHR). A person who does something first, preparing the way for others. The first settlers were *pioneers*. p. 328.

pirate (PYE rut). A person who attacks and robs ships at sea. p. 153.

plain (playn). A wide area of flat or gently rolling land. p. 17.

plantation (plan TAY shun). A large farm on which one main crop is grown. p. 199.

plateau (pla TOH). A large, high, rather level area that is raised above the surrounding land. p. 55.

political map (puh LIHT ih kul map). A map that shows such things as national and state boundaries and the names and locations of towns and cities. p. 17.

political party (puh LIHT ih kul PAHR tee). A group of people who have the same ideas about how a government should be run and what it should do. p. 311.

population density (pahp yoo LAY shun DEN suh-tee). The average number of people per given unit of area (such as a square mile or square kilometer) in a state, country, or other area. p. 68.

port (port). A place where ships can safely unload and load supplies. p. 120.

precipitation (pree sihp uh TAY shun). Moisture that falls on the earth's surface in the form of rain, snow, sleet, hail, fog, or mist. p. 21.

prehistoric (pree hihs TOR ihk). Describes the time before written accounts of the past. p. 95.

prejudice (PREJ oo dihs). A feeling, without reason, that one group of people is better than another group of people. p. 504.

Prime Meridian (prym muh RIHD ee un). A line of longitude that passes through the city of

Greenwich, England. It is the 0° line of longitude, from which distances east and west are measured in degrees of longitude.   p. 14.

privateer (prye vuh TIHR). A privately owned, armed ship having a government's permission to attack enemy ships. In the Revolutionary War, *privateers* joined the United States in fighting the British. p. 286.

proclamation (prahk luh MAY shun). An official announcement. p. 254.

progress (PRAHG res). A moving forward toward better ways of doing things and better ways of living. p. 362.

Progressive (proh GRES ihv). The name used to refer to a reformer during the early 1900s. A progressive wanted to use the city, state, and federal governments to bring about reforms. p. 513.

Prohibition (proh ih BIHSH un). The period from 1920 to 1933 when there was a federal law that prohibited, or made illegal, the making or selling of alcoholic beverages.   p. 534.

proprietor (proh PRYE uh tur). An owner. p. 191.

prosperity (prah SPER uh tee). A time of economic well-being. p. 532.

proverb (PRAHV urb). A wise old saying. p. 223.

Puritan (PYOOR ih tun). A member of certain Protestant groups in sixteenth- and seventeenth-century England or New England. A person who wanted to worship in his or her own way without separating from the Church of England. p. 171.

Q

Quaker (KWAYK ur). A member of a religious group. *Quakers* also call themselves Friends. p. 212.

R

radiation (ray dee AY shun). The energy or rays released by a bomb that act as a long-lasting kind of poison to people. p. 552.

Radical Republican (RAD ih kul rih PUB lih kun). A member of the Republican party who wanted to punish the South. p. 456.

ranch (ranch). A large farm that raises livestock. p. 382.

rapid (RAP ihd). A place where shallow water races quickly across a rocky river bottom. p. 131.

ratify (RAT uh fye). To give formal approval to. p. 301.

ration (RASH un). To limit the amount each person can get. p. 546.

reaper (REE pur). A machine that reaps, or cuts, grain. p. 404

rebellion (rih BEL yun). An act of opposition to one's government. p. 297.

Reconstruction (ree kun STRUK shun). The name given to the period (1865–1877) following the Civil War. p. 455.

reform (rih FORM). An improvement, or a change for the better. p. 362.

region (REE jun). A part of the earth's surface that has common characteristics. p. 39.

renewable resource (rih NOO uh bul REE sors). A resource that can be replaced by nature or by people. p. 81.

repeal (rih PEEL). To cancel. p. 256.

represent (rep rih ZENT). To act and speak for people in an assembly or a lawmaking body. p. 159.

republic (rih PUB lihk). The political system in which the people elect representatives to manage their country. p. 273.

reservation (rez ur VAY shun). A piece of public land reserved, or set aside, by the government for the use of a particular group of people. p. 475.

resign (rih ZYN). To give up one's office, position, or membership. p. 603.

revolution (rev uh LOO shun). A sudden, complete change. p. 275.

Ring of Fire (ring uv fyr).The area that encircles most of the Pacific Ocean and has earthquake and volcanic activity.   p. 58.

river mouth (RIHV ur mouth). The end of a river or the place where a river flows into another body of water. p. 52.

river source (RIHV ur sors).The beginning, or start, of a river.   p. 52.

Rough Riders (ruf RYD urz). A group of volunteer soldiers in the Spanish American War led by Theodore Roosevelt. p. 520.

rural (ROOR ul). Having to do with the countryside; nonurban. p. 65.

S

saga (SAH guh). A folk tale that tells about the adventures of the Norse people. p. 115.

satellite • symbol

satellite (SAT uh lyt). An object made to go around the earth. p. 584.

scalawag (SKAL uh wag). A term used in the South, after the Civil War, to describe a white Southerner who sided with the new state governments. p. 458.

scale (skayl). 1. The relationship between real distance and distance used on a map or model. 2. The line, drawn on maps, that shows this relationship. p. 6.

schedule (SKE jool). 1. A printed timetable, such as for exact times of trains, buses, and planes. 2. A timetable giving the days and times of events. p. 415.

secede (sih SEED). To withdraw from an organization or nation. p. 424.

Second Continental Congress (SEK und kahn-tuh NENT ul KAHNG grus). The meeting of the representatives from the 13 colonies in 1775. p. 271.

segregation (seg ruh GAY shun). The separation of black and white people from each other. p. 459.

self-government (self GUV urn munt). A type of government that allows people the right to have a say in making their own laws and choosing their own leaders. p. 245.

separation of powers (sep uh RAY shun uv POU-urz). The division of governmental power into three parts: legislative, executive, and judicial. p. 299.

Separatist (SEP ur uh tihst). A person wishing to separate from the Church of England. p. 160.

service (SUR vihs). Some kind of useful work that a person or business does for another person or business. p. 82.

settlement house (SET ul munt hous). A place where immigrants and poor people went for help. p. 503.

shantytown (SHAN tee toun). The area of a city in which people live in shanties, or small, shabby shacks. p. 500.

sharecropper (SHER krahp ur). A person who farms land owned by another and gets part of the crop in return for the work done. p. 455.

shipwright (SHIHP ryt). A carpenter who is skilled in shipbuilding. p. 180.

skyscraper (SKYE skray pur). A very tall building. p. 564.

slash and burn (slash un BURN). A method of clearing land by cutting down trees and burning the stumps. p. 100.

slave (slayv). A person who is owned by another person. p. 144.

slave quarter (slayv KWORT ur). The area at the back of a plantation where the slaves lived, often in small cabins. p. 204.

slave state (slayv stayt). A Southern state that allowed slavery. p. 421.

slum (slum). A heavily populated, run-down part of a city where poor people live. p. 500.

smuggle (SMUG ul). To bring into or take out of a country in a way that is secret and against the law. p. 246.

Social Security (SOH shul sih KYOOR uh tee). A kind of insurance program for workers who retire. p. 540.

South Pole (south pohl). The most southern place on earth. The *South Pole* is located on the continent of Antarctica. p. 8.

space race (spays rays). A competition between the United States and the Soviet Union in which each nation tries to have the most advanced space program. p. 584.

specialize (SPESH ul eyz). To work only on a particular part of a job or to make a special study of something. p. 409.

spiritual (SPIHR ih choo ul). A religious folk song of the kind created by black Americans. p. 422.

Stamp Act Congress (stamp akt KAHNG grus). A meeting of delegates from the colonies who agreed on a number of statements about the rights of colonists. The delegates also asked the British Parliament to repeal the Stamp Act. p. 257.

stock market (stahk MAHR kiht). A place where stocks and bonds are bought and sold. p. 536.

strait (strayt). A narrow body of water connecting two larger bodies of water. p. 95.

strike (stryk). To stop work. p. 506.

submarine (sub muh REEN). A boat that travels underwater. p. 525.

suburb (SUB urb). A small community on the outskirts of a large city. p. 67.

suffrage (SUF rihj). The right to vote. p. 516.

Sunbelt (SUN belt). A name that refers to the part of the United States made up of most of the states in the South and Southwest. It has a warm, sunny climate. p. 71.

supermarket (SOO pur mahr kiht). A large self-service food store. p. 567.

symbol (SIHM bul). Something that stands for or suggests something else. p. 4.

T

tax (taks). Money that must be paid to a government. p. 107.

telegraph (TEL uh graf). A machine that sent messages electrically by wire. p. 404.

temperance movement (TEM pur uns MOOV-munt). The working together of reformers during the early 1800s to get people to stop drinking alcoholic beverages. p. 363.

tepee (TEE pee). The tentlike shelter used by certain tribes of Native Americans. The *tepee* was made of buffalo skins stitched together, draped over poles, and secured to the ground. p. 103.

terrace (TER us). A wide ledge cut into the side of a hill or mountain to make a place where crops can be grown. p. 109.

territory (TER uh tor ee). 1. In the United States, an area of land not yet a state. 2. In Canada, an area that has less self-government than a province. p. 296.

textile (TEKS tyl). Having to do with cloth. Also, woven fabric. p. 44.

Tidewater (TYD wawt ur). The lowest, flattest part of eastern Virginia around Chesapeake Bay. Many rivers flow across this low plain and into the ocean. p. 196.

totem (TOHT um). A particular animal used as a symbol by important families of an Indian tribe. p. 105.

town meeting (toun MEET ing). In colonial times, a gathering of men who made important decisions about the villages where they lived. p. 184.

trading post (TRAYD ing pohst). A place where people trade goods with the people who live in the area. p. 148.

Trail of Tears (trayl uv tihrz). The name given by the Cherokees to their journey from Georgia to Oklahoma after they had been forced off their land by the United States government. p. 355.

traitor (TRAYT ur). A person who tries to overthrow his or her government. p. 272.

transcontinental railroad (trans kahn tuh NENT-ul RAYL rohd). Train tracks going across a continent. p. 472.

transportation (trans pur TAY shun). The moving of people and goods from one place to another. p. 239.

treaty (TREET ee). A written agreement between two countries. p. 252.

triangular trade (trye ANG gyoo lur trayd). Trade with colonies that made up three routes and formed a triangle. p. 181.

tributary (TRIHB yoo ter ee). A stream or river that flows into a large river. p. 52.

turnpike (TURN pyk). In early America, a hard-surfaced tool road built by a private company. Today, any high-speed highway. p. 356.

U

Underground Railroad (UN dur ground RAYL-rohd). The secret routes by which abolitionists helped runaway slaves escape to free states or to Canada. p. 419.

urban (UR bun). Having to do with a town or city. p. 65.

V

valley (VAL ee). A long, low area, usually between hills or mountains, or along a river. p. 58.

vaquero (vah KER oh). Mexican cattle herder. p. 480.

veto (VEE toh). The power of the President to reject a bill, or keep it from becoming a law, by refusing to sign it. p. 299.

Vietnamization (vee et nuh muh ZAY shun). The name given to President Nixon's plan for turning over the fighting during the Vietnam War to the South Vietnamese. p. 602.

Viking (VYE king). A bold and brave sailing person that was from northern Europe. p. 113.

volunteer (vahl un TIHR). A person who offers to do something of his or her own free will. p. 224.

W

Watergate (WAWT ur gayt). A scandal that involved officials violating public trust through bribery, burglary, and other abuses of power in order to maintain their positions of authority. The name comes from *Watergate*, a building complex in Washington, D.C., that was burglarized under orders from officials during the Nixon administration. p. 603.

wigwam (WIHG wahm). A small, single-family house built by Indians out of branches and bark. p. 100.

The Declaration of Independence

☆ ☆ ☆ ☆ ☆ ☆ ☆ ☆ ☆ ☆ ☆ ☆ ☆

Why the Declaration of Independence Was Issued
This paragraph states that it has become necessary for the American colonists to break their political ties with Great Britain, and that it is only proper to explain why they are taking this step. (One reason was that the colonists hoped to get help from other nations.)

The Purposes of Government
This paragraph is the very heart of the Declaration of Independence. It states that all men are born with equal claims to "life, liberty, and the pursuit of happiness." These rights, given by the Creator, are "unalienable," that is, they cannot be given away, nor can a government take them away.

In Congress, July 4, 1776

When, in the course of human events, it becomes necessary for one people to dissolve the political bands which have connected them with another, and to assume, among the powers of the earth, the separate and equal station to which the laws of nature and nature's God entitle them, a decent respect to the opinions of mankind requires that they should declare the causes which impel them to the separation.

We hold these truths to be self-evident; that all men are created equal, that they are endowed by their Creator with certain unalienable rights, that among these are life, liberty, and the pursuit of happiness. That to secure these rights, governments are instituted among men, deriving their just powers from the consent of the governed; that whenever any form of government becomes destructive of these ends, it is the right of the people to alter or to abolish it, and to institute new govern-

ment, laying its foundation on such principles, and organizing its powers in such form, as to them shall seem most likely to effect their safety and happiness. Prudence, indeed, will dictate that governments long established should not be changed for light and transient causes; and accordingly all experience hath shown that mankind are more disposed to suffer, while evils are sufferable, than to right themselves by abolishing the forms to which they are accustomed. But when a long train of abuses and usurpations, pursuing invariably the same object, evinces a design to reduce them under absolute despotism, it is their right, it is their duty, to throw off such government, and to provide new guards for their future security.

The paragraph goes on to state that governments were created to protect these human rights. Whenever a government interferes with them, its citizens have the right as well as the duty to change or do away with the government. A government must be based on the consent of the governed. Changing or doing away with a government will be carried out, however, only after events have proved that the government has abused its powers.

*S*uch has been the patient sufferance of these colonies; and such is now the necessity which constrains them to alter their former systems of government. The history of the present king of Great Britain is a history of repeated injuries and usurpations, all having in direct object the establishment of an absolute tyranny over these states. To prove this, let facts be submitted to a candid world.

He has refused his assent to laws the most wholesome and necessary for the public good.

He has forbidden his governors to pass laws of immediate and pressing importance, unless suspended in their operation till his assent should be obtained; and when so suspended, he has utterly neglected to attend to them.

He has refused to pass other laws for the accommodation of large districts of people, unless those people would relinquish the right of representation in the legislature, a right inestimable to them, and formidable to tyrants only.

He has called together legislative bodies at places unusual, uncomfortable, and distant from the depository of their public records, for the sole purpose of fatiguing them into compliance with his measures.

He has dissolved representative houses repeatedly, for opposing, with manly firmness, his invasions on the rights of the people.

He has refused, for a long time after such dissolutions, to cause others to be elected; whereby the legislative powers, incapable of annihilation, have returned to the people at large for their exercise; the state remaining, in the meantime, exposed to all the dangers of invasion from without and convulsions within.

The Charges Against the British King

Here the Declaration of Independence reviews the years between 1763 and 1776, stating that the colonists believed the king's government had many times denied their basic human rights. King George III and his government are charged with committing a long list of misdeeds. Because of these acts, the declaration states that the king is no longer entitled to rule the American colonies. He no longer has the consent of the governed.

He has endeavored to prevent the population of these states; for that purpose obstructing the laws for the naturalization of foreigners, refusing to pass others to encourage their migrations hither, and raising the conditions of new appropriations of lands.

He has obstructed the administration of justice, by refusing his assent to laws for establishing judiciary powers.

He has made judges dependent on his will alone for the tenure of their offices, and the amount and payment of their salaries.

He has erected a multitude of new offices, and sent hither swarms of officers to harass our people and eat out their substance.

He has kept among us, in times of peace, standing armies, without the consent of our legislatures.

He has affected to render the military independent of, and superior to, the civil power.

He has combined with others to subject us to a jurisdiction foreign to our constitution and unacknowledged by our laws, giving his assent to their acts of pretended legislation:

For quartering large bodies of armed troops among us;

For protecting them, by a mock trial, from punishment for any murders which they should commit on the inhabitants of these states;

For cutting off our trade with all parts of the world;

For imposing taxes on us without our consent;

For depriving us, in many cases, of the benefits of trial by jury;

For transporting us beyond seas, to be tried for pretended offenses;

For abolishing the free system of English laws in a neighboring province, establishing therein an arbitrary government, and enlarging its boundaries, so as to render it at once an example and fit instrument for introducing the same absolute rule into these colonies;

For taking away our charters, abolishing our most valuable laws, and altering fundamentally the forms of our governments;

For suspending our own legislatures, and declaring themselves invested with power to legislate for us in all cases whatsoever.

He has abdicated government here, by declaring us out of his protection and waging war against us.

He has plundered our seas, ravaged our coasts, burned our towns, and destroyed the lives of our people.

He is at this time transporting large armies of foreign mercenaries to complete the works of death, desolation, and tyranny already begun with circumstances of cruelty and perfidy scarcely paralleled in the most barbarous ages, and totally unworthy the head of a civilized nation.

He has constrained our fellow-citizens, taken captive on the high seas, to bear arms against their country, to become the executioners of their friends and brethren, or to fall themselves by their hands.

He has excited domestic insurrection among us, and has endeavored to bring on the inhabitants of our frontiers, the merciless Indian savages, whose known rule of warfare is an undistinguished destruction of all ages, sexes, and conditions.

In every stage of these oppressions we have petitioned for redress in the most humble terms; our repeated petitions have been answered only by repeated injury. A prince whose character is thus marked by every act which may define a tyrant is unfit to be the ruler of a free people.

Nor have we been wanting in attentions to our British brethren. We have warned them, from time to time, of attempts by their legislature to extend an unwarrantable jurisdiction over us. We have reminded them of the circumstances of our emigration and settlement here. We have appealed to their native justice and magnanimity; and we have conjured them, by the ties of our common kindred, to disavow these usurpations, which would inevitably interrupt our connections and correspondence. They, too, have been deaf to the voice of justice and consanguinity. We must, therefore, acquiesce in the necessity which denounces our separation, and hold them, as we hold the rest of mankind, enemies in war; in peace, friends.

The Attempts to Obtain Justice
These two paragraphs state that the American colonists have asked the British king for justice. They have also appealed to the British people. Yet neither the king nor the British people have responded to the colonists' pleas.

We, therefore, the representatives of the United States of America, in General Congress assembled, appealing to the Supreme Judge of the world for the rectitude of our intentions, do, in the name and by the authority of the good people of these colonies, solemnly publish and declare that these United Colonies are, and of right ought to be, free and independent states; that they are absolved from all allegiance to the British crown, and that all

The Colonies Declare Their Independence
This final paragraph actually proclaims independence. It also lists those things that the new United States of America may do as an independent country.

In the last sentence the signers pledge their lives and all they own to support the cause of independence. This was a serious matter, for as Benjamin Franklin said, "Now we must all hang together, or we will all hang separately." Still, they took the risk and signed the document that proclaimed to the world the independence of the United States of America.

political connection between them and the state of Great Britain is, and ought to be, totally dissolved; and that, as free and independent states, they have full power to levy war, conclude peace, contract alliances, establish commerce, and do all other acts and things which independent states may of right do. And, for the support of this declaration, with a firm reliance on the protection of Divine Providence, we mutually pledge to each other our lives, our fortunes, and our sacred honor.

John Hancock, President

(MASSACHUSETTS)

NEW HAMPSHIRE
Josiah Bartlett
William Whipple
Matthew Thornton

MASSACHUSETTS
John Adams
Samuel Adams
Robert Treat Paine
Elbridge Gerry

NEW YORK
William Floyd
Philip Livingston
Francis Lewis
Lewis Morris

RHODE ISLAND
Stephen Hopkins
William Ellery

NEW JERSEY
Richard Stockton
John Witherspoon
Francis Hopkinson
John Hart
Abraham Clark

PENNSYLVANIA
Robert Morris
Benjamin Rush
Benjamin Franklin
John Morton
George Clymer
James Smith
George Taylor
James Wilson
George Ross

DELAWARE
Caesar Rodney
George Read
Thomas McKean

MARYLAND
Samuel Chase
William Paca
Thomas Stone
Charles Carroll of
    Carrollton

VIRGINIA
George Wythe
Richard Henry Lee
Thomas Jefferson
Benjamin Harrison
Thomas Nelson, Jr.
Francis Lightfoot Lee
Carter Braxton

NORTH CAROLINA
William Hooper
Joseph Hewes
John Penn

SOUTH CAROLINA
Edward Rutledge
Thomas Heyward, Jr.
Thomas Lynch, Jr.
Arthur Middleton

CONNECTICUT
Roger Sherman
Samuel Huntington
William Williams
Oliver Wolcott

GEORGIA
Button Gwinnett
Lyman Hall
George Walton

PRESIDENTS AND VICE PRESIDENTS OF THE UNITED STATES

President	Birth-death	State*	Term	Party	Vice President
George Washington	1732–1799	VA	1789–1797	None	John Adams
John Adams	1735–1826	MA	1797–1801	Federalist	Thomas Jefferson
Thomas Jefferson	1743–1826	VA	1801–1805	Democratic-Republican	Aaron Burr
			1805–1809		George Clinton
James Madison	1751–1836	VA	1809–1813	Democratic-Republican	George Clinton
			1813–1817		Elbridge Gerry
James Monroe	1758–1831	VA	1817–1825	Democratic-Republican	Daniel D. Tompkins
John Quincy Adams	1767–1848	MA	1825–1829	National Republican	John C. Calhoun
Andrew Jackson	1767–1845	TN	1829–1833	Democratic	John C. Calhoun
			1833–1837		Martin Van Buren
Martin Van Buren	1782–1862	NY	1837–1841	Democratic	Richard M. Johnson
William H. Harrison	1773–1841	OH	1841	Whig	John Tyler
John Tyler	1790–1862	VA	1841–1845	Whig	....
James K. Polk	1795–1849	TN	1845–1849	Democratic	George M. Dallas
Zachary Taylor	1784–1850	LA	1849–1850	Whig	Millard Fillmore
Millard Fillmore	1800–1874	NY	1850–1853	Whig	....
Franklin Pierce	1804–1869	NH	1853–1857	Democratic	William R. King
James Buchanan	1791–1868	PA	1857–1861	Democratic	John C. Breckinridge
Abraham Lincoln	1809–1865	IL	1861–1865	Republican	Hannibal Hamlin
			1865		Andrew Johnson
Andrew Johnson	1808–1875	TN	1865–1869	Democratic	....
Ulysses S. Grant	1822–1885	IL	1869–1873	Republican	Schuyler Colfax
			1873–1877		Henry Wilson
Rutherford B. Hayes	1822–1893	OH	1877–1881	Republican	William A. Wheeler
James A. Garfield	1831–1881	OH	1881	Republican	Chester A. Arthur
Chester A. Arthur	1830–1886	NY	1881–1885	Republican	....
Grover Cleveland	1837–1908	NY	1885–1889	Democratic	Thomas A. Hendricks
Benjamin Harrison	1833–1901	IN	1889–1893	Republican	Levi P. Morton
Grover Cleveland	1837–1908	NY	1893–1897	Democratic	Adlai E. Stevenson
William McKinley	1843–1901	OH	1897–1901	Republican	Garret A. Hobart
			1901		Theodore Roosevelt
Theodore Roosevelt	1858–1919	NY	1901–1905	Republican	....
			1905–1909		Charles W. Fairbanks
William H. Taft	1857–1930	OH	1909–1913	Republican	James S. Sherman
Woodrow Wilson	1856–1924	NJ	1913–1917	Democratic	Thomas R. Marshall
			1917–1921		Thomas R. Marshall
Warren G. Harding	1865–1923	OH	1921–1923	Republican	Calvin Coolidge
Calvin Coolidge	1872–1933	MA	1923–1925	Republican	....
			1925–1929		Charles G. Dawes
Herbert C. Hoover	1874–1964	CA	1929–1933	Republican	Charles Curtis
Franklin D. Roosevelt	1882–1945	NY	1933–1937	Democratic	John N. Garner
			1937–1941		John N. Garner
			1941–1945		Henry A. Wallace
			1945		Harry S. Truman
Harry S. Truman	1884–1972	MO	1945–1949	Democratic	....
			1949–1953		Alben W. Barkley
Dwight D. Eisenhower	1890–1969	NY	1953–1957	Republican	Richard M. Nixon
			1957–1961		Richard M. Nixon
John F. Kennedy	1917–1963	MA	1961–1963	Democratic	Lyndon B. Johnson
Lyndon B. Johnson	1908–1973	TX	1963–1965	Democratic	....
			1965–1969		Hubert H. Humphrey
Richard M. Nixon	1913–	NY	1969–1973	Republican	Spiro T. Agnew
			1973–1974		Agnew/Ford
Gerald R. Ford	1913–	MI	1974–1977	Republican	Nelson R. Rockefeller
James Earl Carter	1924–	GA	1977–1981	Democratic	Walter Mondale
Ronald Reagan	1911–	CA	1981–1985	Republican	George Bush
			1985–1989		George Bush
George Bush	1924–	TX	1989–1993	Republican	J. Danforth Quayle
William J. Clinton	1946–	AR	1993–	Democratic	Albert A. Gore, Jr.

*State of residence at election

The Constitution of the United States of America

The Preamble
This Constitution has been written and put into practice for the following reasons:
- To have a better government than that under the Articles of Confederation
- To see that everyone is treated fairly
- To keep peace within the country
- To defend the country from enemies
- To see that people live comfortably and well
- To keep people free both now and in the future.

Article I
The Legislative Branch
Section 1
All legislative, or law making, powers are given to the Congress. It has two parts, or houses: the Senate and the House of Representatives.

Section 2
Members of the House of Representatives serve a 2-year term. A term is a length of time. A representative must have been a citizen of the United States for at least 7 years, must be at least 25 years old, and must live in the state he or she will represent when elected.

The number of representatives from each state depends on that state's population. Each state has at least one representative. The total membership of the House of Representatives is limited to 435 voting members.

*W*e the people of the United States, in order to form a more perfect union, establish justice, insure domestic tranquility, provide for the common defense, promote the general welfare, and secure the blessings of liberty to ourselves and our posterity, do ordain and establish this Constitution for the United States of America.

ARTICLE I

SECTION 1.

All legislative powers herein granted shall be vested in a Congress of the United States, which shall consist of a Senate and House of Representatives.

SECTION 2.

The House of Representatives shall be composed of members chosen every second year by the people of the several States, and the electors in each State shall have the qualifications requisite for electors of the most numerous branch of the State legislature.

No person shall be a representative who shall not have attained to the age of twenty-five years, and been seven years a citizen of the United States, and who shall not, when elected, be an inhabitant of that State in which he shall be chosen.

Representatives and direct taxes shall be apportioned among the several States which may be included within this Union, according to their respective numbers, which shall be determined by adding to the whole number of free persons, including those bound to service for a term of years, and excluding Indians not taxed, three fifths of all other persons.* The actual enumeration shall be made within three years after the first meeting of the Congress of the United States, and within every subsequent term of ten years, in such manner as they shall by law direct. The number of representatives shall not exceed one for every thirty thousand, but each State shall have at least one representative; and until such enumeration shall be made, the State of New Hampshire shall be entitled to choose three, Massa-

NOTE: Items that have been changed or replaced are underlined.
* Changed by the Fourteenth Amendment

chusetts eight, Rhode Island and Providence Plantations one, Connecticut five, New York six, New Jersey four, Pennsylvania eight, Delaware one, Maryland six, Virginia ten, North Carolina five, South Carolina five, and Georgia three.

When vacancies happen in the representation from any State, the executive authority thereof shall issue writs of election to fill such vacancies.

The House of Representatives shall choose their speaker and other officers, and shall have the sole power of impeachment.

SECTION 3.

The Senate of the United States shall be composed of two senators from each State, <u>chosen by the legislature thereof,</u>* for six years; and each senator shall have one vote.

Immediately after they shall be assembled in consequence of the first election, they shall be divided as equally as may be into three classes. The seats of the senators of the first class shall be vacated at the expiration of the second year, of the second class at the expiration of the fourth year, and of the third class at the expiration of the sixth year, so that one third may be chosen every second year; <u>and if vacancies happen by resignation, or otherwise, during the recess of the legislature of any State, the executive thereof may make temporary appointments until the next meeting of the legislature, which shall then fill such vacancies.</u>*

No person shall be a senator who shall not have attained to the age of thirty years, and been nine years a citizen of the United States, and who shall not, when elected, be an inhabitant of that State for which he shall be chosen.

To decide the number of representatives from each state, the national government must count the number of people every 10 years. This count of population is called a census.

Section 3
The Senate is made up of two senators from each state. A senator serves a 6-year term. One third of the total membership of the Senate is elected every two years.

A senator must have been a citizen of the United States for at least 9 years, must be at least 30 years old, and must live in the state he or she will represent.

* Changed by the Seventeenth Amendment

The Vice President of the United States is in charge of the Senate but may vote only to break a tie vote.

Both the House and the Senate have roles in the process known as impeachment. It is the House of Representatives that charges a government official with misconduct. The Senate then acts as a court to decide if the official is guilty. If two thirds of the senators agree that the official is guilty, he or she is removed from office. If the official is the President, then the Chief Justice of the United States acts as the judge.

The Vice President of the United States shall be president of the Senate, but shall have no vote, unless they be equally divided.

The Senate shall choose their other officers, and also a president pro tempore, in the absence of the Vice President, or when he shall exercise the office of President of the United States.

The Senate shall have the sole power to try all impeachments. When sitting for that purpose, they shall be on oath or affirmation. When the President of the United States is tried, the Chief Justice shall preside: and no person shall be convicted without the concurrence of two thirds of the members present.

Judgment in cases of impeachment shall not extend further than to removal from office, and disqualification to hold any office of honor, trust or profit under the United States: but the party convicted shall nevertheless be liable and subject to indictment, trial, judgment and punishment, according to law.

SECTION 4.

The times, places, and manner of holding elections for senators and representatives shall be prescribed in each State by the legislature thereof; but the Congress may at any time by law make or alter such regulations, except as to the places of choosing senators.

The Congress shall assemble at least once in every year, and such meeting <u>shall be on the first Monday in December,</u>* unless they shall by law appoint a different day.

* Changed by the Twentieth Amendment

SECTION 5.

Each house shall be the judge of the elections, returns and qualifications of its own members, and a majority of each shall constitute a quorum to do business; but a smaller number may adjourn from day to day, and may be authorized to compel the attendance of absent members, in such manner, and under such penalties as each house may provide.

Each house may determine the rules of its proceedings, punish its members for disorderly behavior, and, with the concurrence of two thirds, expel a member.

Each house shall keep a journal of its proceedings, and from time to time publish the same, excepting such parts as may in their judgment require secrecy; and the yeas and nays of the members of either house on any question shall, at the desire of one fifth of those present, be entered on the journal.

Neither house, during the session of Congress, shall, without the consent of the other, adjourn for more than three days, nor to any other place than that in which the two houses shall be sitting.

SECTION 6.

The senators and representatives shall receive a compensation for their services, to be ascertained by law, and paid out of the Treasury of the United States. They shall in all cases, except treason, felony and breach of the peace, be privileged from arrest during their attendance at the session of their respective houses, and in going to and returning from the same; and for any speech or debate in either house, they shall not be questioned in any other place.

No senator or representative shall, during the time for which he was elected, be appointed to any civil office under the authority of the United States, which shall have been created, or the emoluments thereof shall have been increased during such time; and no person holding any office under the United States shall be a member of either house during his continuance in office.

SECTION 7.

All bills for raising revenue shall originate in the House of Representatives; but the Senate may propose or concur with amendments as on other bills.

Every bill which shall have passed the House of Representatives and the Senate, shall, before it become a law, be presented to the President of the United States; if he approve he shall sign it, but if not he shall return it, with his objections to that house in which it shall have originated, who shall enter the objections at

Sections 4–7
Rules for running the House and the Senate are described here. Each house must keep a daily record of its actions. This is published so that people can find out how their representatives voted on bills. Members of Congress are paid by the government.

large on their journal, and proceed to reconsider it. If after such reconsideration two thirds of that house shall agree to pass the bill, it shall be sent, together with the objections, to the other house, by which it shall likewise be reconsidered, and if approved by two thirds of that house, it shall become a law. But in all such cases the votes of both houses shall be determined by yeas and nays, and the names of the persons voting for and against the bill shall be entered on the journal of each house respectively. If any bill shall not be returned by the President within ten days (Sundays excepted) after it shall have been presented to him, the same shall be a law, in like manner as if he had signed it, unless the Congress by their adjournment prevent its return, in which case it shall not be a law.

Every order, resolution, or vote to which the concurrence of the Senate and House of Representatives may be necessary (except on a question of adjournment) shall be presented to the President of the United States; and before the same shall take effect, shall be approved by him, or being disapproved by him, shall be repassed by two thirds of the Senate and House of Representatives, according to the rules and limitations prescribed in the case of a bill.

Section 8
The powers and duties of Congress are listed here. Congress makes all laws concerning money and trade. Congress decides how people become citizens of the United States. It has the power to declare war.

SECTION 8.

The Congress shall have power to lay and collect taxes, duties, imposts and excises, to pay the debts and provide for the common defense and general welfare of the United States; but all duties, imposts and excises shall be uniform throughout the United States;

To borrow money on the credit of the United States;

To regulate commerce with foreign nations, and among the several States, and with the Indian tribes;

To establish a uniform rule of naturalization, and uniform laws on the subject of bankruptcies through the United States;

To coin money, regulate the value thereof, and of foreign coin, and fix the standard of weights and measures;

To provide for the punishment of conterfeiting the securities and current coin of the United States;

To establish post offices and post roads;

To promote the progress of science and useful arts by securing for limited times to authors and inventors the exclusive right to their respective writings and discoveries;

To constitute tribunals inferior to the Supreme Court;

To define and punish piracies and felonies committed on the high seas, and offenses against the law of nations;

To declare war, grant letters of marque and reprisal, and make rules concerning captures on land and water;

To raise and support armies, but no appropriation of money to that use shall be for a longer term than two years;

To provide and maintain a navy;

To make rules for the government and regulations of the land and naval forces;

To provide for calling forth the militia to execute the laws of the Union, suppress insurrections and repel invasions;

To provide for organizing, arming, and disciplining the militia, and for governing such part of them as may be employed in the service of the United States, reserving to the States respectively the appointment of the officers, and the authority of training the militia according to the discipline prescribed by Congress;

To exercise exclusive legislation in all cases whatsoever, over such district (not exceeding ten miles square) as may, by cession of particular States and the acceptance of Congress, become the seat of the government of the United States, and to exercise like authority over all places purchased by the consent of the legislature of the State in which the same shall be, for the erection of forts, magazines, arsenals, dockyards, and other needful buildings; and

To make all laws which shall be necessary and proper for carrying into execution the foregoing powers, and all other powers vested by this Constitution in the government of the United States, or in any department or officer thereof.

The last paragraph of Section 8 is the "elastic clause," which was discussed on page 307. It gives Congress the power to make whatever laws it thinks necessary to carry out the powers listed in Section 8.

Section 9
There are actions that Congress may not take. This section protects the people of the United States against injustice.

SECTION 9.

The migration or importation of such persons as any of the States now existing shall think proper to admit, shall not be prohibited by the Congress prior to the year one thousand eight hundred and eight, but a tax or duty may be imposed on such importation, not exceeding ten dollars for each person.

The privilege of the writ of habeas corpus shall not be suspended, unless when in cases of rebellion or invasion the public safety may require it.

No bill of attainder or ex post facto law shall be passed.

No capitation, _or other direct,_* tax shall be laid, unless in proportion to the census or enumeration herein before directed to be taken.

No tax or duty shall be laid on articles exported from any State.

No preference shall be given by any regulation of commerce or revenue to the ports of one State over those of another; nor shall vessels bound to, or from, one State be obliged to enter, clear, or pay duties in another.

No money shall be drawn from the Treasury, but in consequence of appropriations made by law; and a regular statement and account of the receipts and expenditures of all public money shall be published from time to time.

No title of nobility shall be granted by the United States: and no person holding any office of profit or trust under them, shall, without the consent of the Congress, accept of any present, emolument, office, or title of any kind whatever, from any king, prince, or foreign State.

Section 10
The states may not assume any of the powers that are specifically given to Congress. The states also may not do certain things that the national government cannot do.

SECTION 10.

No State shall enter into any treaty, alliance, or confederation; grant letters of marque and reprisal; coin money; emit bills of credit; make anything but gold and silver coin a tender in payment of debts, pass any bill of attainder, ex post facto law, or law impairing the obligation of contracts, or grant any title of nobility.

No State shall, without the consent of the Congress, lay any imposts or duties on imports or exports, except what may be absolutely necessary for executing its inspection laws: and the net produce of all duties and imposts laid by any State on imports or exports, shall be for the use of the Treasury of the United States; and all such laws shall be subject to the revision and control of the Congress.

No State shall, without the consent of Congress, lay any duty of tonnage, keep troops, or ships of war in time of peace, enter into any agreement or compact with another State, or with a

* Changed by the Sixteenth Amendment

foreign power, or engage in war, unless actually invaded, or in such imminent danger as will not admit of delay.

ARTICLE II

SECTION 1.

The executive power shall be vested in a President of the United States of America. He shall hold his office during the term of four years, and, together with the Vice President chosen for the same term, be elected as follows:

Each State shall appoint, in such manner as the legislature thereof may direct, a number of electors, equal to the whole number of senators and representatives to which the State may be entitled in the Congress: but no senator or representative, or person holding an office of trust or profit under the United States, shall be appointed an elector.

The electors shall meet in their respective States, and vote by ballot for two persons, of whom one at least shall not be an inhabitant of the same State with themselves. And they shall make a list of all the persons voted for, and of the number of votes for each; which they shall sign and certify, and transmit sealed to the seat of the government of the United States, directed to the president of the Senate. The president of the Senate shall, in the presence of the Senate and House of Representatives, open all the certificates, and the votes shall then be counted. The person having the greatest number of votes shall be the President, if such number be a majority of the whole number of electors appointed;

Article II
The Executive Branch
Section 1
The executive branch is the President, Vice President, and those who help carry out the laws passed by Congress. The President manages the government. The President and Vice President are elected to a 4-year term. The Vice President takes office if the President dies or resigns.

A President must have been born in the United States, must be at least 35 years old, and must have lived in the United States for at least 14 years.

and if there be more than one who have such majority, and have an equal number of votes, then the House of Representatives shall immediately choose by ballot one of them for President; and if no person have a majority, then from the five highest on the list the said house shall in like manner choose the President. But in choosing the President, the votes shall be taken by States, the representation from each State having one vote; a quorum for this purpose shall consist of a member or members from two thirds of the States, and a majority of all the States shall be necessary to a choice. In every case, after the choice of the President, the person having the greatest number of votes of the electors shall be the Vice President. But if there should remain two or more who have equal votes, the Senate shall choose from them by ballot the Vice President.*

The Congress may determine the time of choosing the electors, and the day on which they shall give their votes; which day shall be the same throughout the United States.

No person except a natural-born citizen, or a citizen of the United States, at the time of the adoption of this Constitution, shall be eligible to the office of President; neither shall any person be eligible to that office who shall not have attained to the age of thirty-five years, and been fourteen years a resident within the United States.

In case of the removal of the President from office, or of his death, resignation, or inability to discharge the powers and duties of the said office, the same shall devolve on the Vice President, and the Congress may by law provide for the case of removal, death, resignation, or inability, both of the President and Vice President, declaring what officer shall then act as President, and such offer shall act accordingly, until the disability be removed, or a President shall be elected.

The President shall, at stated times, receive for his services a compensation, which shall neither be increased nor diminished during the period for which he shall have been elected, and he shall not receive within that period any other emolument from the United States, or any of them.

Before he enter on the execution of his office, he shall take the following oath or affirmation: —"I do solemnly swear (or affirm) that I will faithfully execute the office of President of the United States, and will to the best of my ability, preserve, protect and defend the Constitution of the United States."

Sections 2–4
Some of the President's duties include carrying out the laws made by Congress, commanding all the armed forces, pardoning crimes, and reporting to Congress at least once a year on the overall condition of the nation. The President makes treaties and appoints government leaders with the approval of the Senate.

SECTION 2.

The President shall be commander in chief of the army and navy of the United States, and of the militia of the several States,

* Changed by the Twelfth Amendment

when called into the actual service of the United States; he may require the opinion, in writing, of the principal officer in each of the executive departments, upon any subject relating to the duties of their respective offices, and he shall huve power to grant reprieves and pardons for offenses against the United States, except in cases of impeachment.

He shall have power, by and with the advice and consent of the Senate, to make treaties, provided two thirds of the senators present concur; and he shall nominate, and by and with the advice and consent of the Senate, shall appoint ambassadors, other public ministers and consuls, judges of the Supreme Court, and all other officers of the United States, whose appointments are not herein otherwise provided for, and which shall be established by law: but the Congress may by law vest the appointment of such inferior officers, as they think proper, in the President alone, in the courts of law, or in the heads of departments.

The President shall have power to fill up all vacancies that may happen during the recess of the Senate, by granting commissions which shall expire at the end of their next session.

SECTION 3.

He shall from time to time give to the Congress information of the state of the Union, and recommend to their consideration such measures as he shall judge necessary and expedient; he may, on extraordinary occasions, convene both houses, or either of them, and in case of disagreement between them with respect to the time of adjournment, he may adjourn them to such time as he shall think proper; he shall receive ambassadors and other public ministers; he shall take care that the laws be faithfully executed, and shall commission all the officers of the United States.

SECTION 4.

The President, Vice President, and all civil officers of the United States, shall be removed from office on impeachment for, and conviction of, treason, bribery, or other high crimes and misdemeanors.

ARTICLE III

SECTION 1.

The judicial power of the United States shall be vested in one Supreme Court, and in such inferior courts as the Congress may from time to time ordain and establish. The judges, both of the Supreme and inferior courts, shall hold their offices during good behavior, and shall, at stated times, receive for their services, a compensation which shall not be diminished during their continuance in office.

SECTION 2.

The judicial power shall extend to all cases, in law and equity, arising under this Constitution, the laws of the United States, and treaties made, or which shall be made, under their authority;—to all cases affecting ambassadors, other public ministers and consuls;—to all cases of admiralty and maritime jurisdiction;—to controversies to which the United States shall be a party;—to controversies between two or more States;— between a State and citizens of another State;—between citizens of different States;—between citizens of the same State claiming

Article III
The Judicial Branch
Section 1
The federal court system is the judicial branch of government. The Supreme Court is the nation's highest court. It makes the final decisions in all matters of law. Federal judges are not elected. They are the only officials of the national government who may hold office for life.

lands under grants of different States, and between a State, or the citizens thereof, and foreign States, citizens or subjects.

In all cases affecting ambassadors, other public ministers and consuls, and those in which a State shall be party, the Supreme Court shall have original jurisdiction. In all the other cases before mentioned, the Supreme Court shall have appellate jurisdiction, both as to law and fact, with such exceptions, and under such regulations as the Congress shall make.

The trial of all crimes, except in cases of impeachment, shall be by jury; and such trial shall be held in the State where the said crimes shall have been committed; but when not committed within any State, the trial shall be at such place or places as the Congress may by law have directed.

SECTION 3.

Treason against the United States shall consist only in levying war against them, or in adhering to their enemies, giving them aid and comfort. No person shall be convicted of treason unless on the testimony of two witnesses to the same overt act, or on confession in open court.

The Congress shall have power to declare the punishment of treason, but no attainder of treason shall work corruption of blood, or forfeiture except during the life of the person attainted.

ARTICLE IV

SECTION 1.

Full faith and credit shall be given in each State to the public acts, records, and judicial proceedings of every other State. And the Congress may by general laws prescribe the manner in which such acts, records, and proceedings shall be proved, and the effect thereof.

SECTION 2.

The citizens of each State shall be entitled to all privileges and immunities of citizens in the several States.

A person charged in any State with treason, felony, or other crime, who shall flee from justice, and be found in another State, shall on demand of the executive authority of the State from which he fled, be delivered up to be removed to the State having jurisdiction of the crime.

No person held to service or labor in the State, under the laws thereof, escaping into another, shall, in consequence of any law or regulation therein, be discharged from such service or labor, but shall be delivered up on claim of the party to whom such service or labor may be due.*

Section 2
Federal courts handle certain kinds of cases. Only a few are handled directly by the Supreme Court. The judgment of the Supreme Court is final.

One of the great powers of our federal courts is their right to declare an act of Congress or a state legislature unconstitutional. This right is not mentioned specifically in any part of the Constitution.

Section 3
The crime of treason — that is, of trying to overthrow the government — is explained.

Article IV
The States
Sections 1–2
All states must accept acts, records, and laws of other states. A citizen of one state must be given the same rights as a citizen of another state when visiting that other state. The governor of one state has the power to send someone accused of a crime in another state back to that state for trial.

* Changed by the Thirteenth Amendment

Sections 3–4
New states may be added to the United States. The United States government will protect all states from enemies.

SECTION 3.

New States may be admitted by the Congress into this Union; but no new State shall be formed or erected within the jurisdiction of any other State; nor any State be formed by the junction of two or more States, or parts of States, without the consent of the legislatures of the States concerned as well as of the Congress.

The Congress shall have power to dispose of and make all needful rules and regulations respecting the territory or other property belonging to the United States; and nothing in this Constitution shall be so construed as to prejudice any claims of the United States, or of any particular State.

SECTION 4.

The United States shall guarantee to every State in this Union a republican form of government, and shall protect each of them against invasion; and on application of the legislature, or of the executive (when the legislature cannot be convened) against domestic violence.

Article V
Making Changes
The Constitution may be amended, or changed. The ways of amending the Constitution are explained. Only 26 amendments have been made since the Constitution was adopted.

ARTICLE V

The Congress, whenever two thirds of both houses shall deem it necessary, shall propose amendments to this Constitution, or, on the application of the legislatures of two thirds of the several States, shall call a convention for proposing amendments, which, in either case, shall be valid to all intents and purposes, as part of this Constitution, when ratified by the legislatures of three fourths of the several States, or by conventions in three fourths thereof, as the one or the other mode of ratification may be proposed by the Congress; provided [that no amendment which may be made prior to the year one thousand eight hundred and eight shall in any manner affect the first and fourth clauses in the ninth section of the first article, and] that no State, without its consent, shall be deprived of its equal suffrage in the Senate.

Article VI
The Highest Law
The Constitution of the United States is the highest law of the land. State laws must be in agreement with the laws of the Constitution. All national and state lawmakers must support the Constitution.

ARTICLE VI

All debts contracted and engagements entered into, before the adoption of this Constitution, shall be as valid against the United States under this Constitution, as under the Confederation.

This Constitution, and the laws of the United States which shall be made in pursuance thereof; and all treaties made, or which shall be made, under the authority of the United States, *shall be the supreme law of the land; and the judges in every State shall be bound thereby, anything in the Constitution or laws of any State to the contrary notwithstanding.*

The senators and representatives before mentioned, and the members of the several State legislatures, and all executive and judicial officers, both of the United States, and of the several States, shall be bound by oath or affirmation to support this Constitution; but no religious test shall ever be required as a qualification to any office or public trust under the United States.

ARTICLE VII

The ratification of the conventions of nine States shall be sufficient for the establishment of this Constitution between the States so ratifying the same.

Done in Convention by the unanimous consent of the States present the seventeenth day of September in the year of our Lord one thousand seven hundred and eighty-seven, and of the independence of the United States of America the twelfth. In witness whereof we have hereunto subscribed our names.

George Washington, President
(VIRGINIA)

**Article VII
Approving the Constitution**
The last article says that the Constitution was to become law when 9 of 13 states ratified, or approved, it. The members of the Constitutional Convention present on September 17, 1787, witnessed and signed the Constitution.

MASSACHUSETTS
Nathaniel Gorham
Rufus King

NEW YORK
Alexander Hamilton

GEORGIA
William Few
Abraham Baldwin

DELAWARE
George Read
Gunning Bedford
John Dickinson
Richard Bassett
Jacob Broom

VIRGINIA
John Blair
James Madison

PENNSYLVANIA
Benjamin Franklin
Thomas Mifflin
Robert Morris
George Clymer
Thomas FitzSimons
Jared Ingersoll
James Wilson
Gouvernor Morris

NEW HAMPSHIRE
John Langdon
Nicholas Gilman

NEW JERSEY
William Livingston
David Brearley
William Paterson
Jonathan Dayton

CONNECTICUT
William Samuel Johnson
Roger Sherman

NORTH CAROLINA
William Blount
Richard Dobbs Spaight
Hugh Williamson

SOUTH CAROLINA
John Rutledge
Charles Cotesworth Pinckney
Charles Pinckney
Pierce Butler

MARYLAND
James McHenry
Daniel of St. Thomas Jenifer
Daniel Carroll

The Bill of Rights
The first ten amendments are known as the Bill of Rights. They protect the basic freedoms of the American people.

First Amendment (1791)
Congress may not make rules to take away freedom of religion, freedom of speech, freedom of the press, or the right of people to come together in a peaceful way or to send petitions to their government.

FIRST AMENDMENT—1791

Congress shall make no law respecting an establishment of religion, or prohibiting the free exercise thereof; or abridging the freedom of speech, or of the press; or the right of the people peaceably to assemble, and to petition the government for a redress of grievances.

SECOND AMENDMENT—1791

A well-regulated militia, being necessary to the security of a free State, the right of the people to keep and bear arms, shall not be infringed.

Second Amendment (1791)
In order to have a prepared military, the people have the right to keep and bear arms.

Third Amendment (1791)
During peacetime the government cannot make citizens feed and house soldiers in their homes.

THIRD AMENDMENT—1791

No soldier shall, in time of peace, be quartered in any house, without the consent of the owner, nor in time of war, but in a manner to be prescribed by law.

FOURTH AMENDMENT—1791

The right of the people to be secure in their persons, houses, papers, and effects, against unreasonable searches and seizures, shall not be violated, and no warrants shall issue, but upon probable cause, supported by oath or affirmation, and particularly describing the place to be searched, and the persons or things to be seized.

Fourth Amendment (1791)
People or their homes may not be searched without a good reason.

FIFTH AMENDMENT—1791

No person shall be held to answer for a capital or otherwise infamous crime, unless on a presentment or indictment of a grand jury, except in cases arising in the land or naval forces, or in the militia, when in actual service in time of war or public danger; nor shall any person be subject for the same offense to be twice put in jeopardy of life or limb; nor shall be compelled in any criminal case to be a witness against himself, nor be deprived of life, liberty, or property, without due process of law; nor shall private property be taken for public use without just compensation.

SIXTH AMENDMENT—1791

In all criminal prosecutions, the accused shall enjoy the right to a speedy and public trial, by an impartial jury of the State and district wherein the crime shall have been committed, which district shall have been previously ascertained by law, and to be informed of the nature and cause of the accusation; to be confronted with the witnesses against him; to have compulsory process for obtaining witnesses in his favor, and to have the assistance of counsel for his defense.

SEVENTH AMENDMENT—1791

In suits at common law, where the value in controversy shall exceed twenty dollars, the right of trial by jury shall be preserved, and no fact tried by a jury shall be otherwise reexamined in any court of the United States, than according to the rules of the common law.

Fifth Amendment (1791)
Only a grand jury can accuse people of serious crimes. People cannot be forced to give evidence against themselves. If one is found not guilty of a crime, he or she cannot be tried again for the same crime. Peoples' lives, freedom, and property may not be taken from them unfairly. The government must pay the owner for any property taken for public use.

Sixth Amendment (1791)
Persons accused of serious crimes have the right to a speedy and public trial. They must be told what they are accused of. They have the right to have a lawyer and to see and question those who accuse them.

Seventh Amendment (1791)
In most cases, people have the right to a jury trial.

Eighth Amendment (1791)
Punishment may not be cruel or unusual.

Ninth Amendment (1791)
The people may have rights that have not been listed in the Constitution.

Tenth Amendment (1791)
If the Constitution does not give a certain right to the United States government and also does not forbid a state government to have that right, then the states and the people have that right.

Eleventh Amendment (1795)
The power of the judicial branch is limited to certain kinds of cases.

Twelfth Amendment (1804)
Electors vote for President and Vice President separately. An elector is a person chosen by the state legislature to elect the President.

EIGHTH AMENDMENT—1791

Excessive bail shall not be required, nor excessive fines imposed, nor cruel and unusual punishments inflicted.

NINTH AMENDMENT—1791

The enumeration in the Constitution of certain rights shall not be construed to deny or disparage others retained by the people.

TENTH AMENDMENT—1791

The powers not delegated to the United States by the Constitution, nor prohibited by it to the States are reserved to the States respectively, or to the people.

ELEVENTH AMENDMENT—1795

The judicial power of the United States shall not be construed to extend to any suit in law or equity, commenced or prosecuted against one of the United States, by citizens of another State, or by citizens or subjects of any foreign State.

TWELFTH AMENDMENT—1804

The electors shall meet in their respective States, and vote by ballot for President and Vice President, one of whom, at least, shall not be an inhabitant of the same State with themselves; they shall name in their ballots the person voted for as Vice President, and they shall make distinct lists of all persons voted for as President and of all persons voted for as Vice President, and of the number of votes for each, which lists they shall sign and certify, and transmit sealed to the seat of government of the United States, directed to the president of the Senate;—The president of the Senate shall, in the presence of the Senate and House of Representatives, open all the certificates and the votes shall then be counted;—The person having the greatest number of votes for President shall be the President, if such number be a majority of the whole number of electors appointed; and if no person have such majority, then from the persons having the highest numbers not exceeding three on the list of those voted for as President, the House of Representatives shall choose immediately, by ballot, the President. But in choosing the President, the votes shall be taken by States, the representation from each State having one vote; a *quorum for this purpose shall consist of a member or members from two thirds of the States, and a majority of all the States shall be necessary to a choice. And if the House of Representatives shall not choose a President whenever the right of choice shall devolve upon them, <u>before the fourth day of March next following,</u>* then the Vice President shall act as President, as in the case of the death or other constitutional disability of the President. The person having the greatest number of votes as Vice President shall be the Vice President, if such number be a majority of the whole number of electors appointed, and if no person have a majority, then from the two highest numbers on the list, the Senate shall choose the Vice President; a quorum for the purpose shall consist of two thirds of the whole number of senators and a majority of the whole number shall be necessary to a choice. But no person constitutionally ineligible to the office of President shall be eligible to that of Vice President of the United States.*

THIRTEENTH AMENDMENT—1865

SECTION 1.

Neither slavery nor involuntary servitude, except as a punishment for crime whereof the party shall have been duly convicted, shall exist within the United States, or any place subject to their jurisdiction.

SECTION 2.

Congress shall have power to enforce this article by appropriate legislation.

*Changed by the Twentieth Amendment

Thirteenth Amendment (1865)
Slavery is forbidden in the United States. Congress has the power to make laws to do away with slavery.

FOURTEENTH AMENDMENT —1868

**Fourteenth Amendment
(1868)**
People who are born in the United States or who are granted citizenship are United States citizens. They are also citizens of the states they live in.

States may not make laws that limit the rights of citizens of the United States. They may not take away a person's life, freedom, or property unfairly. They must treat all people equally under the law.

SECTION 1.

All persons born or naturalized in the United States, and subject to the jurisdiction thereof, are citizens of the United States and of the State wherein they reside. No State shall make or enforce any law which shall abridge the privileges or immunities of citizens of the United States; nor shall any State deprive any person of life, liberty, or property, without due process of law; nor deny to any person within its jurisdiction the equal protection of the laws.

SECTION 2.

Representatives shall be apportioned among the several States according to their respective numbers, counting the whole number of persons in each State, excluding Indians not taxed. But when the right to vote at any election for the choice of electors for President and Vice President of the United States, representatives in Congress, the executive and judicial officers of a State, or the members of the legislature thereof, is denied to any of the male inhabitants of such State, being twenty-one years of age, and citizens of the United States, or in any way abridged, except for participation in rebellion, or other crime, the basis of representation therein shall be reduced in the proportion which the number of such male citizens shall bear to the whole number of male citizens twenty-one years of age in such State.

SECTION 3.

No person shall be a senator or representative in Congress, or elector of President and Vice President, or hold any office, civil or military, under the United States, or under any State, who, having previously taken an oath, as a member of Congress, or as an officer of the United States, or as a member of any State legislature, or as an executive or judicial officer of any State, to support the Constitution of the United States, shall have engaged in insurrection or rebellion against the same, or given aid or comfort to the enemies thereof. But Congress may by a vote of two thirds of each house, remove such disability.

SECTION 4.

The validity of the public debt of the United States, authorized by law, including debts incurred for payment of pensions and bounties for services in suppressing insurrection or rebellion, shall not be questioned. But neither the United States nor any State shall assume or pay any debt or obligation incurred in aid of insurrection or rebellion against the United States, or any claim for the loss or emancipation of any slave; but all such debts, obligations and claims shall be held illegal and void.

SECTION 5.

The Congress shall have power to enforce, by appropriate legislation, the provisions of this article.

FIFTEENTH AMENDMENT—1870

SECTION 1.

The right of citizens of the United States to vote shall not be denied or abridged by the United States or by any State on account of race, color, or previous condition of servitude.

Fifteenth Amendment (1870)
No citizen may be denied the right to vote because of race or color.

SECTION 2.

The Congress shall have power to enforce this article by appropriate legislation.

SIXTEENTH AMENDMENT—1913

The Congress shall have power to lay and collect taxes on incomes, from whatever source derived, without apportionment among the several States, and without regard to any census or enumeration.

Sixteenth Amendment (1913)
Congress is allowed to pass a tax on income.

SEVENTEENTH AMENDMENT—1913

The Senate of the United States shall be composed of two senators from each State, elected by the people thereof, for six years; and each senator shall have one vote. The electors in each State shall have the qualifications requisite for electors of the most numerous branch of the State legislatures.

Seventeenth Amendment (1913)
United States senators are to be elected directly by the people.

When vacancies happen in the representation of any State in the Senate, the executive authority of such State shall issue writs of election to fill such vacancies: Provided, that the legislature of any State may empower the executive thereof to make temporary appointments until the people fill the vacancies by election as the legislature may direct.

Eighteenth Amendment (1919)
Liquor cannot be manufactured or sold in the United States.

EIGHTEENTH AMENDMENT*—1919

SECTION 1.

After one year from the ratification of this article the manufacture, sale, or transportation of intoxicating liquors within, the importation thereof into, or the exportation thereof from the United States and all territory subject to the jurisdiction thereof for beverage purposes is hereby prohibited.

SECTION 2.

The Congress and the several States shall have concurrent power to enforce this article by appropriate legislation.

SECTION 3.

This article shall be inoperative unless it shall have been ratified as an amendment to the Constitution by the legislatures of the several States, as provided in the Constitution, within seven years from the date of the submission hereof to the States by the Congress.

* Repealed by the Twenty-first Amendment

NINETEENTH AMENDMENT—1920

SECTION 1.

The right of citizens of the United States to vote shall not be denied or abridged by the United States or by any State on Account of sex.

SECTION 2.

Congress shall have power, by appropriate legislation, to enforce the provisions of this article.

Nineteenth Amendment (1920)
No citizen may be denied the right to vote because of sex.

TWENTIETH AMENDMENT—1933

SECTION 1.

The terms of the President and Vice President shall end at noon on the 20th day of January, and the terms of senators and representatives at noon on the 3d day of January, of the years in which such terms would have ended if this article had not been ratified; and the terms of their successors shall then begin.

SECTION 2.

The Congress shall assemble at least once in every year, and such meeting shall begin at noon on the 3d day in January, unless they shall by law appoint a different day.

SECTION 3.

If, at the time fixed for the beginning of the term of the President, the President-elect shall have died, the Vice President-elect shall become President. If a President shall not have been chosen before the time fixed for the beginning of his term, or if the

Twentieth Amendment (1933)
Presidents start their new terms on January 20. Congress starts its new term on January 3.

President-elect shall have failed to qualify, then the Vice President-elect shall act as President until a President shall have qualified; and the Congress may by law provide for the case wherein neither a President-elect nor a Vice President-elect shall have qualified, declaring who shall then act as President, or the manner in which one who is to act shall be selected, and such persons shall act accordingly until a President or Vice President shall have qualified.

SECTION 4.

The Congress may by law provide for the case of the death of any of the persons from whom the House of Representatives may choose a President whenever the right of choice shall have devolved upon them, and for the case of the death of any of the persons from whom the Senate may choose a Vice President whenever the right of choice shall have devolved upon them.

SECTION 5.

Sections 1 and 2 shall take effect on the 15th day of October following the ratification of this article.

SECTION 6.

This article shall be inoperative unless it shall have been ratified as an amendment to the Constitution by the legislatures of three fourths of the several States within seven years from the date of its submission.

TWENTY-FIRST AMENDMENT—1933

Twenty-First Amendment (1933)
This repeals, or cancels, the Eighteenth Amendment to the Constitution.

SECTION 1.

The eighteenth article of amendment to the Constitution of the United States is hereby repealed.

SECTION 2.

The transportation or importation into any State, territory, or possession of the United States for delivery or use therein of intoxicating liquors, in violation of the laws thereof, is hereby prohibited.

SECTION 3.

This article shall be inoperative unless it shall have been ratified as an amendment to the Constitution by conventions in the several States, as provided in the Constitution, within seven years from the date of submission hereof to the States by the Congress.

TWENTY-SECOND AMENDMENT—1951

No person shall be elected to the office of the President more than twice, and no person who has held the office of President, or acted as President, for more than two years of a term to which some other person was elected President shall be elected to the office of the President more than once.

But this Article shall not apply to any person holding the office of President when this Article was proposed by the Congress, and shall not prevent any person who may be holding the office of President, or acting as President, during the term within which this Article becomes operative from holding the office of President or acting as President during the remainder of such term.

Twenty-Second Amendment (1951)
A President is limited to two terms in office.

TWENTY-THIRD AMENDMENT—1961

SECTION 1.

The District constituting the seat of government of the United States shall appoint in such manner as the Congress may direct:

A number of electors of President and Vice President equal to the whole number of senators and representatives in Congress to which the District would be entitled if it were a State, but in no event more than the least populous State; they shall be in addition to those appointed by the States, but they shall be considered, for the purposes of the election of President and Vice President, to be electors appointed by a State; and they shall meet in the District and perform such duties as provided by the twelfth article of amendment.

SECTION 2.

The Congress shall have power to enforce this article by appropriate legislation.

Twenty-Third Amendment (1961)
Residents of Washington, D.C., have the right to vote for President.

TWENTY-FOURTH AMENDMENT—1964

SECTION 1.

The right of citizens of the United States to vote in any primary or other election for President or Vice President, for electors for President or Vice President, or for senator or representative in Congress, shall not be denied or abridged by the United States or any state by reason of failure to pay any poll tax or other tax.

SECTION 2.

The Congress shall have power to enforce this article by appropriate legislation.

TWENTY-FIFTH AMENDMENT—1967

SECTION 1.

In case of the removal of the President from office or his death or resignation, the Vice President shall become President.

SECTION 2.

Whenever there is a vacancy in the office of the Vice President, the President shall nominate a Vice President who shall take the office upon confirmation by a majority vote of both houses of Congress.

SECTION 3.

Whenever the President transmits to the president pro tempore of the Senate and the speaker of the House of Representatives his written declaration that he is unable to discharge the powers and duties of his office, and until he transmits to them a written declaration to the contrary, such powers and duties shall be discharged by the Vice President as Acting President.

SECTION 4.

Whenever the Vice President and a majority of either the principal officers of the executive departments or of such other body as Congress may by law provide, transmit to the president pro tempore of the Senate and the speaker of the House of Representatives their written declaration that the President is unable to discharge the powers and duties of his office, the Vice President shall immediately assume the powers and duties of the office as Acting President.

Thereafter, when the President transmits to the president pro tempore of the Senate and the speaker of the House of Repre-

Twenty-Fourth Amendment (1964)
Citizens cannot be asked to pay a tax in order to vote in national elections.

Twenty-Fifth Amendment (1967)
If the President becomes too ill to carry on the job, the Vice-President will take over as Acting President until the President is better.

sentatives his written declaration that no inability exists, he shall resume the powers and duties of his office unless the Vice President and a majority of either the principal officers of the executive department or of such other body as Congress may by law provide, transmit within four days to the president pro tempore of the Senate and the speaker of the House of Representatives their written declaration that the President is unable to discharge the powers and duties of his office. Thereupon Congress shall decide the issue, assembling within 48 hours for that purpose if not in session. If the Congress, within 21 days after receipt of the latter written declaration, or, if Congress is not in session, within 21 days after Congress is required to assemble, determines by two-thirds vote of both houses that the President is unable to discharge the powers and duties of his office, the Vice President shall continue to discharge the same as Acting President; otherwise, the President shall resume the powers and duties of his office.

TWENTY-SIXTH AMENDMENT—1971

SECTION 1.

The right of citizens of the United States, who are eighteen years of age or older, to vote shall not be denied or abridged by the United States or by any State on account of age.

SECTION 2.

The Congress shall have power to enforce this article by appropriate legislation.

Twenty-Sixth Amendment (1971)
No citizen 18 years of age or older may be denied the right to vote because of age.

CREDITS

Cover: Delta Queen Replication provided courtesy of The Delta Queen Steamboat Co., New Orleans, Louisiana

Graphs and Charts: Richard Puder Design/JAK Graphics, Ltd.

State Charts: Scott Wilson

Maps: Maryland Cartographics, Inc./General Drafting

Logo Artists: Denman Hampson

Unit openers: Forest C. Brown, SuperStock 36–37. Photo R. P. Sheridan, American Museum of Natural History 92. Photo D. Finnin, American Museum of Natural History 93. Culver Pictures, Inc. 232–233. National Museum of American Art, Smithsonian Institution/Art Resource 324–325. Anne S. K. Brown Military Collection, Brown University Library 398–399. Rick Wheeler 468–469. Will & Deni McIntyre/Photo Researchers, Inc. 560–561.

Contributing artists: Ernest Albanese: 51, 308. John Cymerman: 498; Ray Dallasta: 204. Ric Del Rossi: 577: Danilo Ducak: 302–303. Bob Jackson: 55. John Killgrew: 155. Peter Krempasky: 68. Richard Loehle: 201. Tom Miller: 81, 181, 219, 306. Kathy Mitchell: 346. Taylor Oughton: 207, 411. Den Schofield: 239. Brad Strode: 366. Arthur Thompson: 671.

Map Handbook 7: Everett C. Johnson/Folio Inc.; *inset:* © Robert Thayer. 11: Silver Burdett Ginn. 16: *l.* Pitkin Pictorials Ltd; *r.* © Paolo Koch/Photo Researchers, Inc. 18: D. DiLaura/After Image. 23: Bruce Thomas/The Stock Market.

Chapter 1 38: William Bachmann/Third Coast Stock Source. 42: Craig Aurness/West Light. 45: Robert Llewellyn. 46: Craig Blouin/f/Stop. 47: Jim Rudnick/The Stock Market. 48: Andy Sacks/TSW-Click/Chicago. 50: J. I. Case Company. 52: Peter Christopher/Masterfile. 53: Dave Darnell, The Commercial Appeal/The Picture Group. 56: Richard J. Quataert/Folio Inc. 58: Chamussy/Sipa Press. 59: Michael Baytoff/Black Star. 60: Peter Menzel/Stock, Boston.

Chapter 2 64: Kunio Owaki/The Stock Market. 65: Mark Gibson/The Stock Market. 73: Bob Daemmerich. 77: Larry Lefever/Grant Heilman Photography. 82: Michal Heron. 84: Keith Gunnar/Bruce Coleman. 91: Grant Heilman/Grant Heilman Photography.

Chapter 3 96: Field Museum of Natural History. 97: Robert W. Parvin Texas Photography; *inset* Richard Howard Collection/Photography by Jerry Jacka. 98: Reproduced from *Mysteries of the Ancient Americas,* © 1986 The Reader's Digest Association, Inc. Used by permission. 99: *l.* Courtesy of the Mound City Group National Monument. Photograph by Dirk Bakker. 101: Reproduced from *The Planting of Civilization in Western Pennsylvania,* by Solon J. and Elizabeth Hawthorn Buck. By permission of the University of Pittsburgh Press. © 1967 by Elizabeth H. Buck. 105: © 1991 Alon Reininger/Woodfin Camp & Associates 107: Robert Frerck/Odyssey Productions. 109: Sagara/Allstock.

Chapter 4 113: The Bridgeman Art Library. 114: Reproduced from *Mysteries of the Ancient Americas,* © 1986 The Reader's Digest Association, Inc. Used by permission. 117: The Bodleian Library, Oxford/The Bridgeman Art Library. 118: British Museum/Photo © Aldus Archives. 120: Historical Pictures Service. From *New Geography, Book One,* by Alexis Everett Frye, Copyright 1917 by Alexis Everett Frye, published by Ginn & Company. 121: North Wind Picture Archives. 122: *l.* Oronoz, Madrid. 124: Musee Bargoin, Clermont-Ferrand/The Bridgeman Art Library. 125: Robert Harding Picture Library. 130–131: Peter Newark's Western Americana.

Chapter 5 134: The Bettmann Archive. 135: The National Cowboy Hall of Fame. 137: Museo de America, Madrid. Photo Oronoz, Madrid. 139: Collection Miss Strickland, on loan to the Government Art Collection for the British Embassy, Mexico. Photograph by Derek Bayes. 140: From 16th century manuscript by Fray Martin de Murua titled *Historia General Del Peru, Origen y Descendencia de Los Incas.* Photograph courtesy of American Heritage. 141: Michael Holford. 142: Culver Pictures. 143: Museo de America, Madrid. Photo Oronoz, Madrid. 144: Artifacts courtesy of Waldo Studio Multi-Cultural Music and Art Productions, Northridge, California. Exhibited at EPCOT Center, Walt Disney World Resort. © The Walt Disney Company. 145: Syndication International LTD. 147: *t.* Culver Pictures; *b.* Jefferson National Expansion Memorial/National Park Service. 148: Courtesy of the Hispanic Society of America. New York. 149: Russ Finley/Holiday.

Chapter 6 152: Jamestown Festival Park. Photography by Positive Image/Chuck Thompson. 153: The Bettmann Archive. 157, 158: Colonial National Historical Park. 159: Private Collection. Photograph by Katherine Wetzel. 160, 163: Pilgrim Society, Plymouth, Massachusetts. 162: © J. L. G. Ferris, Archives of 76. Bay Village, Ohio, (Detail) 167: Clarence Davies Collection, Museum of the City of New York.

Chapter 7 170: New Haven Colony Historical Society (Detail). 174: Historical Pictures Service. 176: Bob Grant/Comstock. 177: David Madison/Bruce Coleman. 178: Clyde Smith/f/Stop. 179: Connecticut State Library. 180: Peabody Museum of Salem. 183: Courtesy Gateway Press, Inc. 184: Paul Rocheleau. 185: The Bettmann Archive. 186: North Wind Picture Archives. 187: Courtesy of National Life of Vermont, Montpelier.

Chapter 8 190: Berkeley Plantation and Hundred. Photograph courtesy Winston Spurgeon. 191: Janet W. Connor/Historic St. Mary's City. 193: Darby Erd. 194: Methodist Collection, Drew University. Photo courtesy of American Heritage. 195: Bob Burch/Bruce Coleman. 196: Robert Llewellyn. 197: Phil Degginger. 198: Michael F. O'Brien/Picturesque. 200: Colonial National Historical Park. 203: Boston Public Library. 205: Arents Collection, New York Public Library.

Chapter 9 210: Print Collection, Miriam & Ira D. Wallach Division of Art, Prints and Photographs, The New York Public Library, Astor, Lenox and Tilden Foundations. 211: North Wind Picture Archives. 213: *Quaker Meeting.* Courtesy Museum of Fine Arts, Boston; Bequest of Maxim Karolik. British, fourth quarter 18th century of first quarter 19th century. Oil on canvas. 64 × 76.2 cm. (Variant of a painting entitled *Gracechurch Street Meeting,* Society of Friends, London). 214: Colonial Williamsburg Foundation. Abby Aldrich Rockefeller Folk Art Collection. 215: E.R. Degginger. 216: Bruno Zehnder/Peter Arnold, Inc. 217: Steve Strickland/Woodfin Camp, Inc. 220: Reproduced from *The Planting of Civilization in Western Pennsylvania,* by Solon J. and Elizabeth Hawthorn Buck, by permission of the University of Pittsburgh Press. © 1939 by the University of Pittsburgh Press. © 1967 by Elizabeth Buck. 223: © J.L.G. Ferris, Archives of 76. Bay Village, Ohio (Detail).

Chapter 10 234: Courtesy of The New York Historical Society (Detail). 235: Historical Society of Pennsylvania. 237: Courtesy of the New York State Historical Association, Cooperstown (Detail). 238: Colonial Williamsburg Foundation. 240, 241: U.S. Department of Transportation, Federal Highway Administration. 243: Reproduced from *The Planting of Civilization in Western Pennsylvania,* by Solon J. and Elizabeth Hawthorn Buck, by permission of the University of Pittsburgh Press. © 1939 by the University of Pittsburgh Press. © 1967 by Elizabeth H. Buck. 244: Bob Daemmrich. 245: National Portrait Gallery, London. Photo courtesy Macdonald/Aldus Archive. 247: The Bettmann Archive.

Chapter 11 250: National Army Museum, London. 251: Courtesy of Alden Deming. 256: *l.* Historical Pictures Service; *r.* Massachusetts Historical Society. 257: North Wind Picture Archives. 258–259: Architect of the U.S. Capitol. 260: Historical Pictures Service. 261: North Wind Picture Archives. 262: Historical Society of Pennsylvania. 263: *l.* American Antiquarian Society; *r.* Historical Pictures Service. 264: North Wind Picture Archives. 265: National Army Museum, London. 266: The Bettmann Archive. 267: Copyrighted by the Paul Revere Life Insurance Company.

Chapter 12 270: Architect of the U.S Capitol. 271: Library of Congress. 275: Capitol Preservation Committee; Harrisburg, Pennsylvania. Photograph copyright © Hunt Commercial Photo. 276–277: Courtesy of the Cincinnati Historical Society. 278: Georgia Department of Archives and History. Photograph by Michael McKelvey. 281: Private Collection. 282: Historical Society of Pennsylvania. 283: Courtesy of the Valley Forge Historical Society. 284: Capitol Preservation Committee, Harrisburg, Pennsylvania. Photography copyright © Hunt Commercial Photo. 285: University of South Carolina. 287: © J.L.G. Ferris. Archives of 76. Bay Village, Ohio. 288: Yale University Art Gallery. 289: SuperStock.

Chapter 13 293: British Museum. Photo courtesy Weidenfeld & Nicolson Archives. 294: Massachusetts Art Commission. 297: The Bettmann Archive. 298: Culver Pictures; all portraits courtesy of Independence National Historical Park Collection. 305: *t.* Steve Elmore/The Stock Market; *b.l.* Rick Buettner/Folio Inc.; *b.r.* Steve Elmore/West Stock. 309: Trippet/Sipa press. 312: North Wind Picture Archives. 313: *l.* Architect of the U.S. Capitol; *r.* Historical Pictures Service. 316: *l.* Courtesy of the Historical Society of Washington, D.C.

Chapter 14 326: Burlington Northern Railroad. 327: The Filson Club, Louisville, Kentucky. From *The Old West: The Frontiersmen.* Photograph by Henry Beville. © 1977 Time-Life Books, Inc. 328: Washington University Gallery of Art, St. Louis. 333: From the Collection of the Louisiana State Museum. 335: National Cowboy Hall of Fame. 336–337: Metropolitan Toronto Library; *inset* portrait courtesy of The New York Historical Society. 339: *l.* The Peale Museum/Baltimore City Life Museums; *r.* National Museum of American History, Smithsonian Institution (73.2623). 343: Museum of American Textile History. 344: National Museum of American History, Smithsonian Institution (86.9625). 345: Mabel Brady Garvan Collection, Yale University Art Gallery. 347: New Haven Colony Historical Society.

Chapter 15 350: White House Historical Association. 353: *l.* Courtesy of The New York Historical Society (Detail). 355: Cherokee Historical Society. Photograph by Rod Jones. 356: U.S. Department of Transportation, Federal Highway Administration. 362: Courtesy of The New York Historical Society (Detail). 363: Colorado Publishers, Ltd. Ray Novak. 364: The Bettmann Archive. 365: Historical Picture Services. 367: Brown Brothers.

Chapter 16 371: San Jacinto Museum of History. 373: Courtesy of Mr. Russel Fish, III. Photograph courtesy of the Texan Memorial Museum. 374: Courtesy Continental Insurance. 375: Courtesy of the Star of the Republic Museum, Washington-on-the-Brazos State Historical Park, Washington, Texas. Photograph © by Herbert K. Barnett. 378: *The Emigrant Train Bedding Down for the Night,* by Benjamin Franklin Reinhart. In the collection of the Corcoran Gallery of Art, Gift of Mr. and Mrs. Lansdell K. Christie. 380: Utah State Historical Society. 381: Church of Jesus Christ of Latter-Day Saints. 382: *Mission San Carlos de Rio Carmelo,* by Oriana Day, late 19th century. Oil on canvas. 20 × 30". Fine Arts Museums of San Francisco. Gift of Eleanor Martin. 383: The Bancroft Library, University of California, Berkeley. 384: Anne S.K. Brown Military Collection, Brown University Library. 388: Church of Jesus Christ of Latter-Day Saints. 389: Picture courtesy National Cowboy Hall of Fame.

Chapter 17 401: The Mabel Brady Garvan Collection, Yale University Art Gallery (Detail). 403: Library of Congress. 405: Museum of the City of New York. 406–407, 408: Courtesy of The New York Historical Society. 409: The Library Company of Philadelphia. 410: Private Collection. 412: Collection of the Newark Museum. Gift of William F. LaPort, 1925. 413: *t.l.* Collection of the New York Historical Society; *m.* Museum of the City of New York; *t.r.* Museum of London; *b.l. Classic Toy Trains* Magazine, photograph by George Hall; *b.r.* Electronic Arts. 414–415: Museum of the City of New York.

Chapter 18 418: Missouri Historical Society (Detail). 419: *r.* Prints and Photographs Department, Moorland-Spingarn Research Center, Howard Univeristy, Mary O'H. Williamson Collection. 422: Glenbow Museum, Calgary. 426: New York Public Library Picture Collection. 429: Library of Congress. 432: *l.* Library of Congress; *r.* National Museum of American History, Smithsonian Institution (80.18524). 433: Anne S.K. Brown Military Collection, Brown University Library.

Chapter 19 436: Courtesy of Mr. Craig Caba (Detail). Photograph from *The Civil War Gettysburg,* photograph by Larry Sherer. © 1985 Time-Life Books, Inc. 437: Anne S.K. Brown Military Collection, Brown University Library. 439: *The Gun Foundry,* by John Ferguson Weir. Putnam County Historical Society, Cold Spring, New York. From *The Civil War: Twenty Million Yankees,* photograph by Henry Groskinsky. © 1985 Time-Life Books, Inc. 440: Collections of the Virginia Historical Society. 443: Courtesy of the Universalist National Memorial Church, Washington. Photograph by Charles Phillips. 444: Knox College Library, Galesburg, IL. 446: Anne S.K. Brown Military Collection, Brown University Library. 448: *l.* E.R. Degginger/Bruce Coleman; *m.* Mark Gibson/The Stock Market; *r.* Doris De Witt/TSW-Click/Chicago. 449: Library of Congress. 451: Courtesy of the West Point Museum Collections, U.S. Military Academy, West Point, New York. 455: U.S. Army Military Institute, Carlisle, Pennsylvania. Photograph by Jim Enos. 456: The Valentine Museum, Richmond. 457: *l.* Library of Congress; *r.* Copyrighted by the White House Historical Association; Photograph by the National Geographic Society.

Chapter 20 472: Historical Pictures Service; *inset* Peter Front/TSW-Click/Chicago. 474: The Nelson Atkins Museum of Art, Kansas City, Missouri (Nelson Fund). 477: Western History Collections, University of Oklahoma Library. 481: The Kansas State Historical Society. 484: Nebraska State Historical Society. 485, 487: Western History Collections. University of Oklahoma Library.

Chapter 21 494: Permission of Avis Maher. 495: Library of Congress. 496: Bethlehem Steel; *inset* Historical Pictures Service. 497: Minnesota Historical Society. 499: AT&T Archive Group. 501: Museum of the City of New York. 503: Copyrighted Chicago Tribune Company, all rights reserved. Used with permission. Photograph courtesy American Heritage. 505: Library of Congress. 507: National Museum of American History, Smithsonian Institution (67319).

Chapter 22 510, 511: Museum of the City of New York. 512: Library of Congress. 514: Architect of the U.S. Capitol. 516: Brown Brothers. 517: Library of Congress. 522: National Archives. 523: U.S. Marine Corps Art Collection. 525: Mary Evans Picture Library. 526: National Library of Medicine. 527: *l.* Copyrighted by the White House Historical Association; Photograph by the National Geographic Society.

Chapter 23 532: Brown Brothers. 533: Historical Pictures Service. 539: International News Photo/FDR Library. 541: Historical Pictures Service; *inset* Tennessee Valley Authority. 542: Hugo Jaeger/*Life* Magazine. © Time, Inc. 543: UPI/Bettmann. 544: Sovfoto. 545: National Maritime Museum, London. 546: Schomburg Center for Research in Black Culture, New York Public Library. 548: U.S. Marine Corps Art Collection. 551: National Archives. 552: U.S. Air Force Photograph/National Air and Space Museum, Washington; *inset* Los Alamos National Laboratory.

Chapter 24 562: H. Armstrong Roberts. 565: The Bettmann Archive. 566: Ben Martin/TIME Magazine. 567: The Bettmann Archive. 568: General Foods. 570: H. Armstrong Roberts. 571: Earl Palmer/Monkmeyer Press Photo Service. 572: Bern Keating/Black Star. 573: Hy Peskin/*Life* Magazine. © 1949 Time, Inc.

Chapter 25 576: Fred Ward/Black Star. 578: Sovfoto. 579: Courtesy DeGolyer Library, Southern Methodist University. 581: Harry S. Truman Library. 582: Department of Defense. 584: *l.* Pictorial Parade; *r.* NASA. 586: AP/Wide World Photos. 588: UPI/Bettmann. 589, 591: *l.* Reuters/The Bettmann Archive; *r.* Chip Mitchell/Picture Group. 592: Monty Russell/Black Star. 593: Ricardo Wilson/Pictorial Parade.

Chapter 26 596: NASA. 597: Dwight D. Eisenhower Library. 599: Pedro Meyer/Black Star. 600: AP/Wide World Photos. 602: Richard Pasley/Stock, Boston; *inset* Richard Howard/Black Star. 603: John Dominis/*Life* Magazine. © Time, Inc. 604: Dirk Halstead/Gamma/Liaison. 605: Dennis Brack/Black Star. 606: *t.* © 1987 Pool/Black Star; *b.* © 1988 Dennis Brack/Black Star. 607: © 1992 Dennis Brack/Black Star. 608: © Jeremy Bigwood/Gamma Liaison. 610: Pool/SABA. 657: © 1991 Peter Souza/Woodfin Camp & Associates, Inc. 658: Maass/Photo-reporters. 661: © 1991 George Hall/Woodfin Camp & Associates, Inc. 663: Official White House Photograph. 665: Mark Reinstein. © National Geographic Society. 670: Bob Smith/Third Coast Stock Source. 673: Henley and Savage/The Stock Market. 675: Cecile Brunswick/Peter Arnold, Inc. 676: U.S. Capitol Historical Society. 677: Brown Brothers. 679: Mark Segal/Folio Inc. 681: AP/Wide World Photos.